WITCH BUSTER

3-4

JUNG-MAN CHO

WITCH BUSTER

VOLUME 3-4

story & art by Jung-man Cho

STAFF CREDITS

translation	ChanHee Grace Sung
adaptation	Rebecca Scoble
lettering	Wacky Eloriaga-Dunglao
layout	Bambi Eloriaga-Amago
cover design	Nicky Lim
copy editor	Shanti Whitesides
editor	Adam Arnold
publisher	Jason DeAngelis
	Seven Seas Entertainment

WITCH BUSTER VOL. 3-4
©2006, 2007 by CHO Jung-man, Daewon C.I. Inc. All rights reserved.
First published in Korea under the title WITCH HUNTER in 2006 & 2007 by
Daewon C.I. Inc. English translation rights arranged by Daewon C.I. Inc.
through Topaz Agency Inc.

ISBN: 978-1-626920-23-1

Printed in Canada

First Printing: July 2013

10 9 8 7 6 5 4 3 2 1

Seven Seas

FOLLOW US ONLINE: www.gomanga.com

PREVIOUSLY...

Witches and humans lived together in peace, until the witches declared war. In the blink of an eye, the witches conquered two-thirds of the world, leaving unparalleled destruction in their wake. To survive, the remaining free countries gathered exceptional humans with special powers in an international agency—the Witch Hunters.

Tasha Godspell, aka "The Marksman," is an A-Class Witch Hunter. He and his pumpkin-headed supporter Halloween fight witches to protect humans. But he carries a dark secret—the witch who destroyed his hometown was none other than his sister, Aria. Tasha fought the shadow-controlling witch Varete for a chance to take his sister back, but Varete and Aria escaped.

Later, Tasha and his comrades Xing and Tarras came across a village under the thrall of a mind-controlling witch. Xing and Tarras quickly fell under the witch's control, but everyone was in for a surprise when Monica, who'd seemed like an ordinary girl, awakened as a witch right in front of them!

No.1!
SMART!

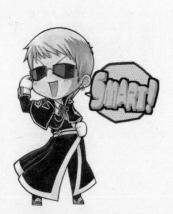

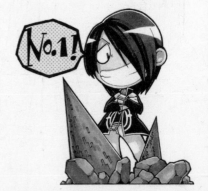

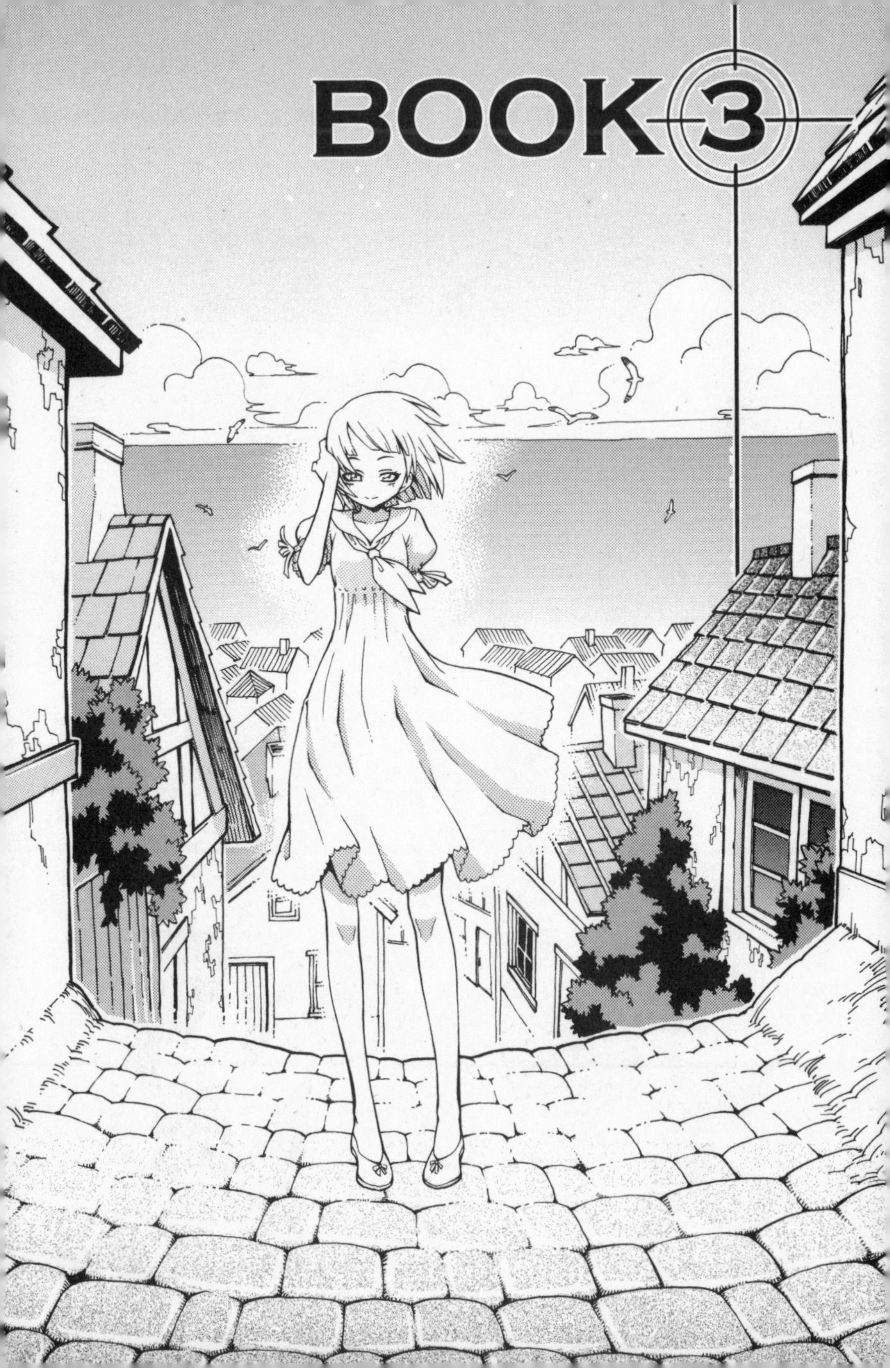
BOOK 3

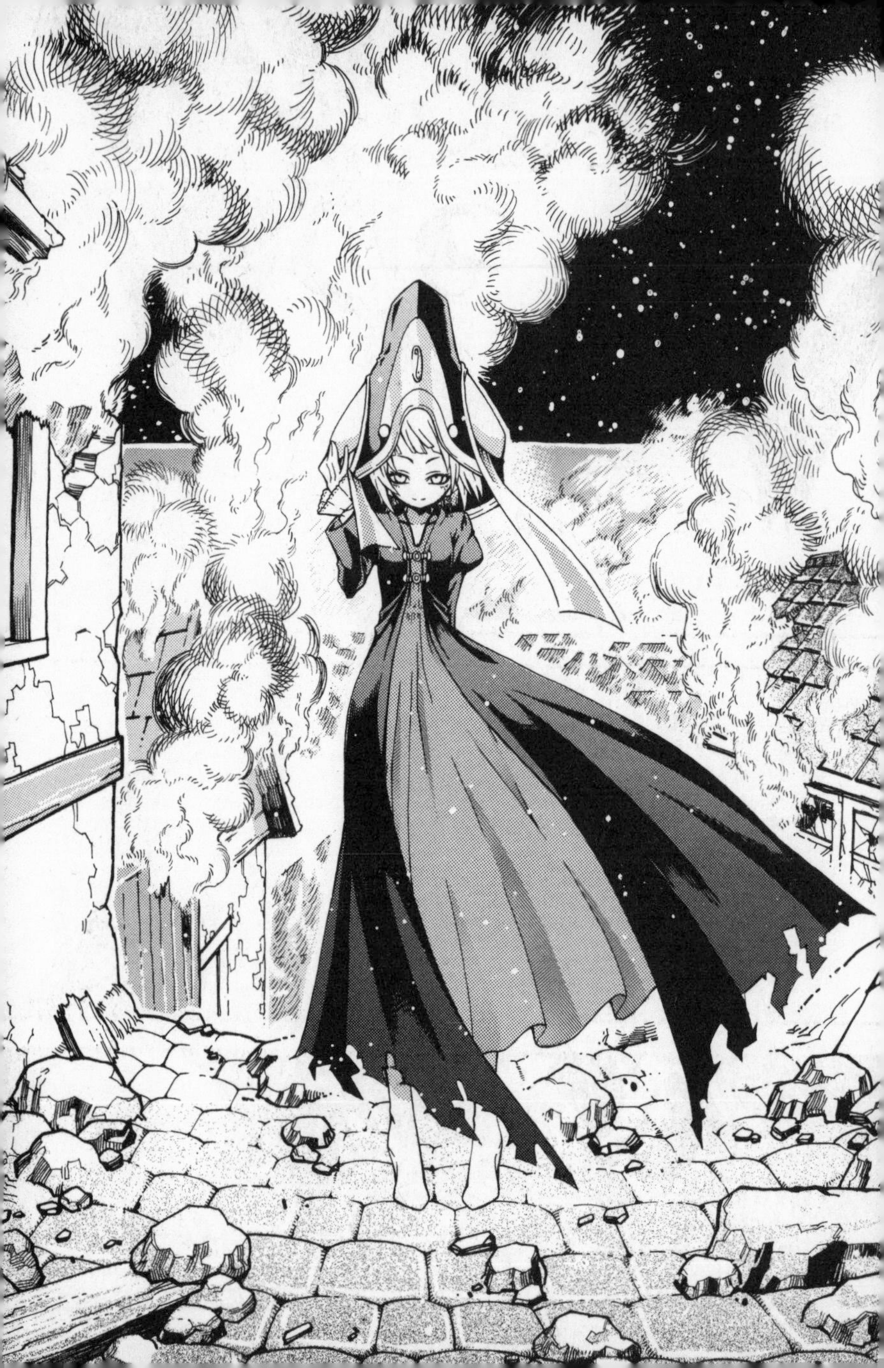

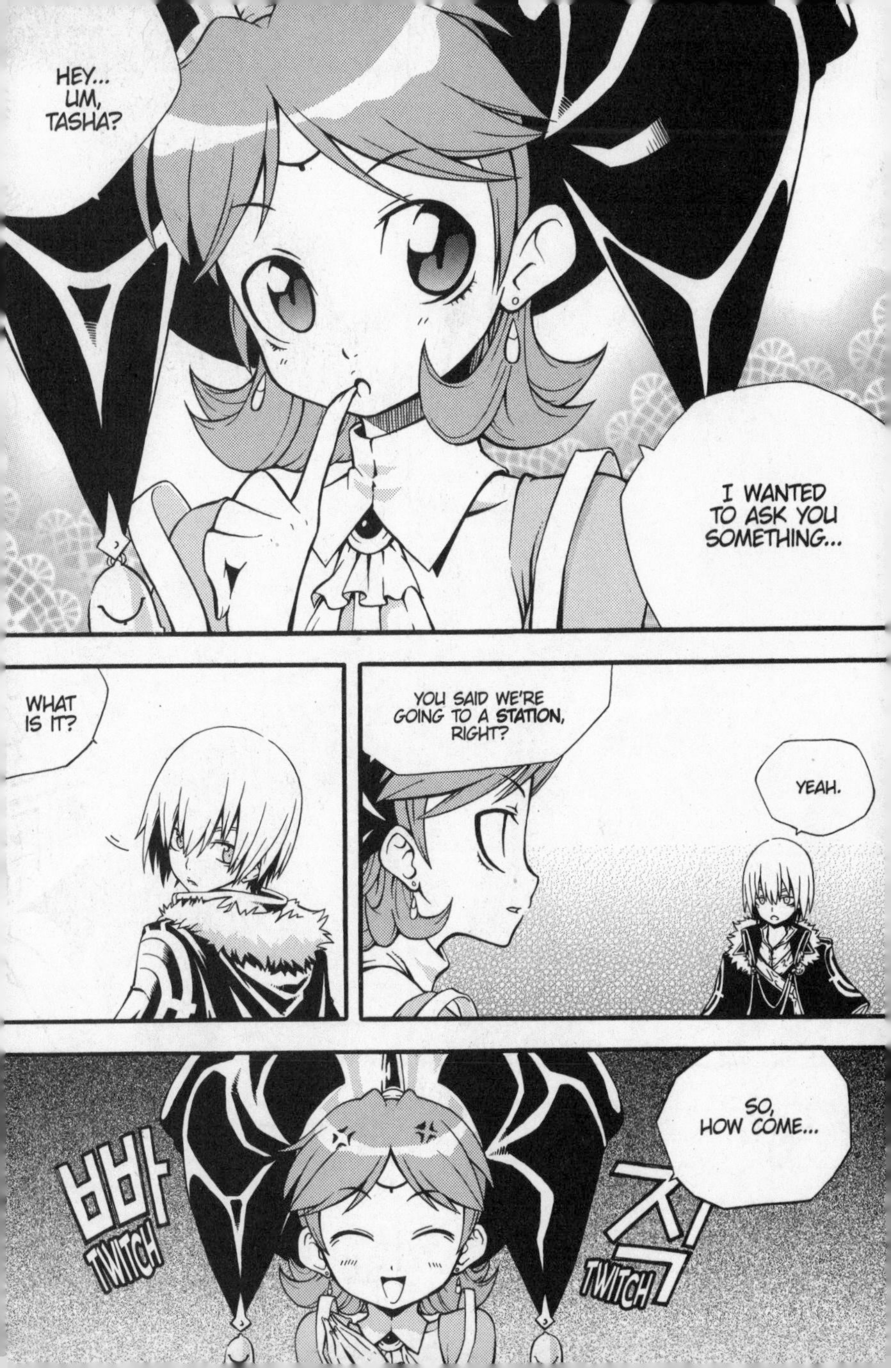
HEY... UM, TASHA?
I WANTED TO ASK YOU SOMETHING...
WHAT IS IT?
YOU SAID WE'RE GOING TO A STATION, RIGHT?
YEAH.
SO, HOW COME...
빠
TWITCH
직
TWITCH

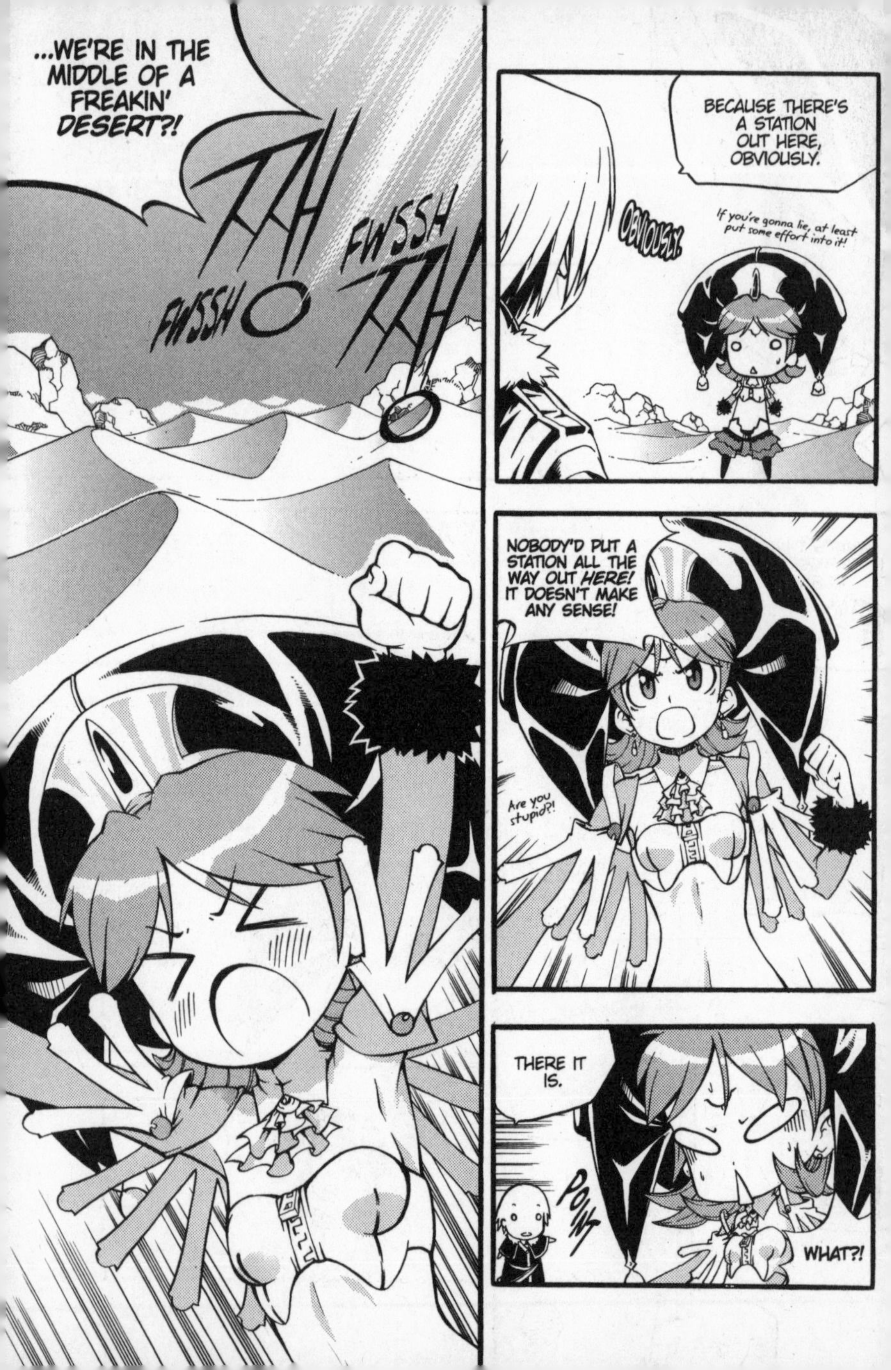
BECAUSE THERE'S A STATION OUT HERE, OBVIOUSLY.
OBVIOUSLY.
If you're gonna lie, at least put some effort into it!
NOBODY'D PUT A STATION ALL THE WAY OUT HERE! IT DOESN'T MAKE ANY SENSE!
Are you stupid?!
THERE IT IS.
POM
WHAT?!
...WE'RE IN THE MIDDLE OF A FREAKIN' DESERT?!
ZAH
FWSSH
FWSSH
ZAH

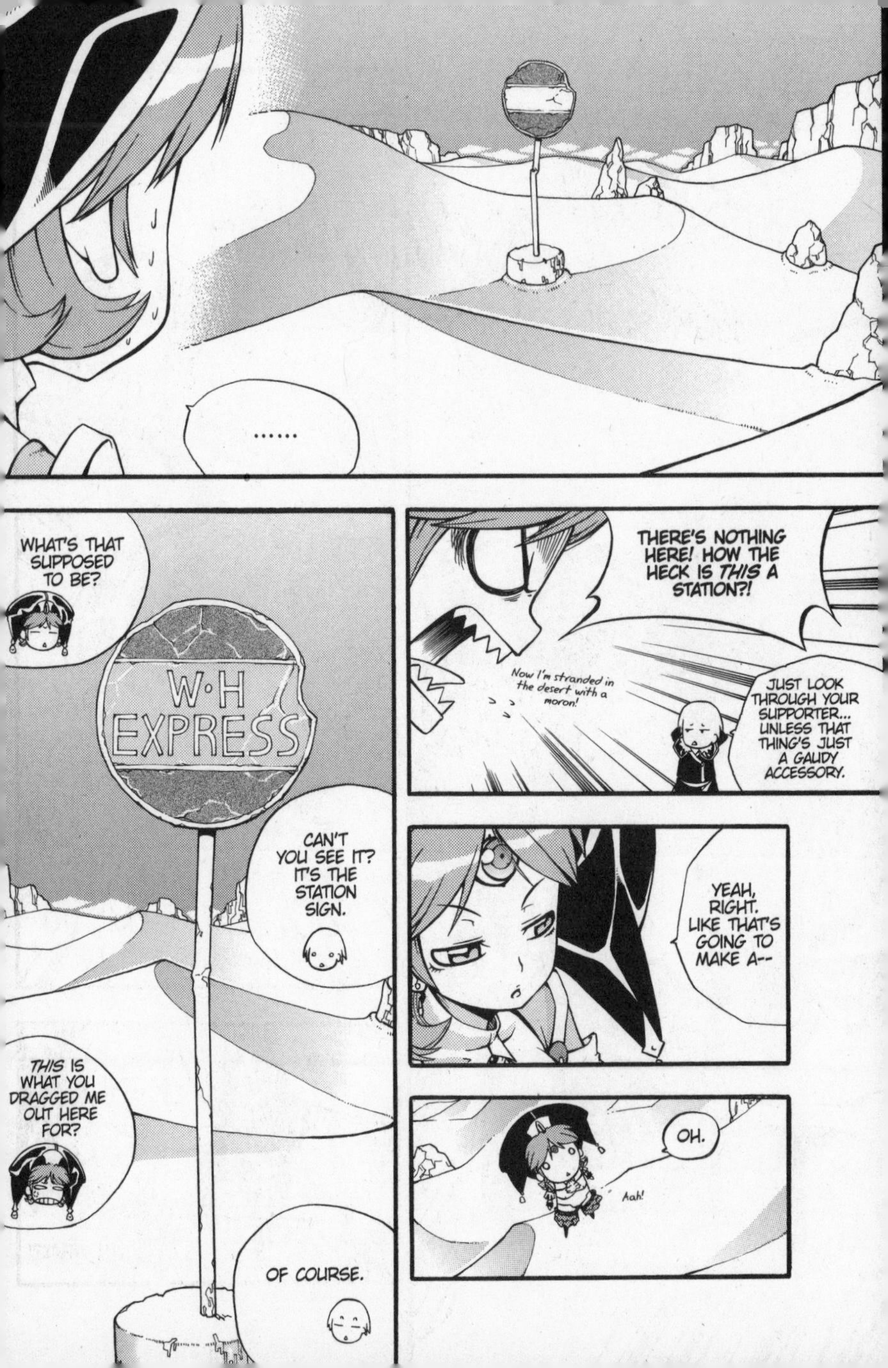

......
WHAT'S THAT SUPPOSED TO BE?
W·H EXPRESS
CAN'T YOU SEE IT? IT'S THE STATION SIGN.
THIS IS WHAT YOU DRAGGED ME OUT HERE FOR?
OF COURSE.
THERE'S NOTHING HERE! HOW THE HECK IS THIS A STATION?!
Now I'm stranded in the desert with a moron!
JUST LOOK THROUGH YOUR SUPPORTER... UNLESS THAT THING'S JUST A GAUDY ACCESSORY.
YEAH, RIGHT. LIKE THAT'S GOING TO MAKE A--
OH.
Aah!

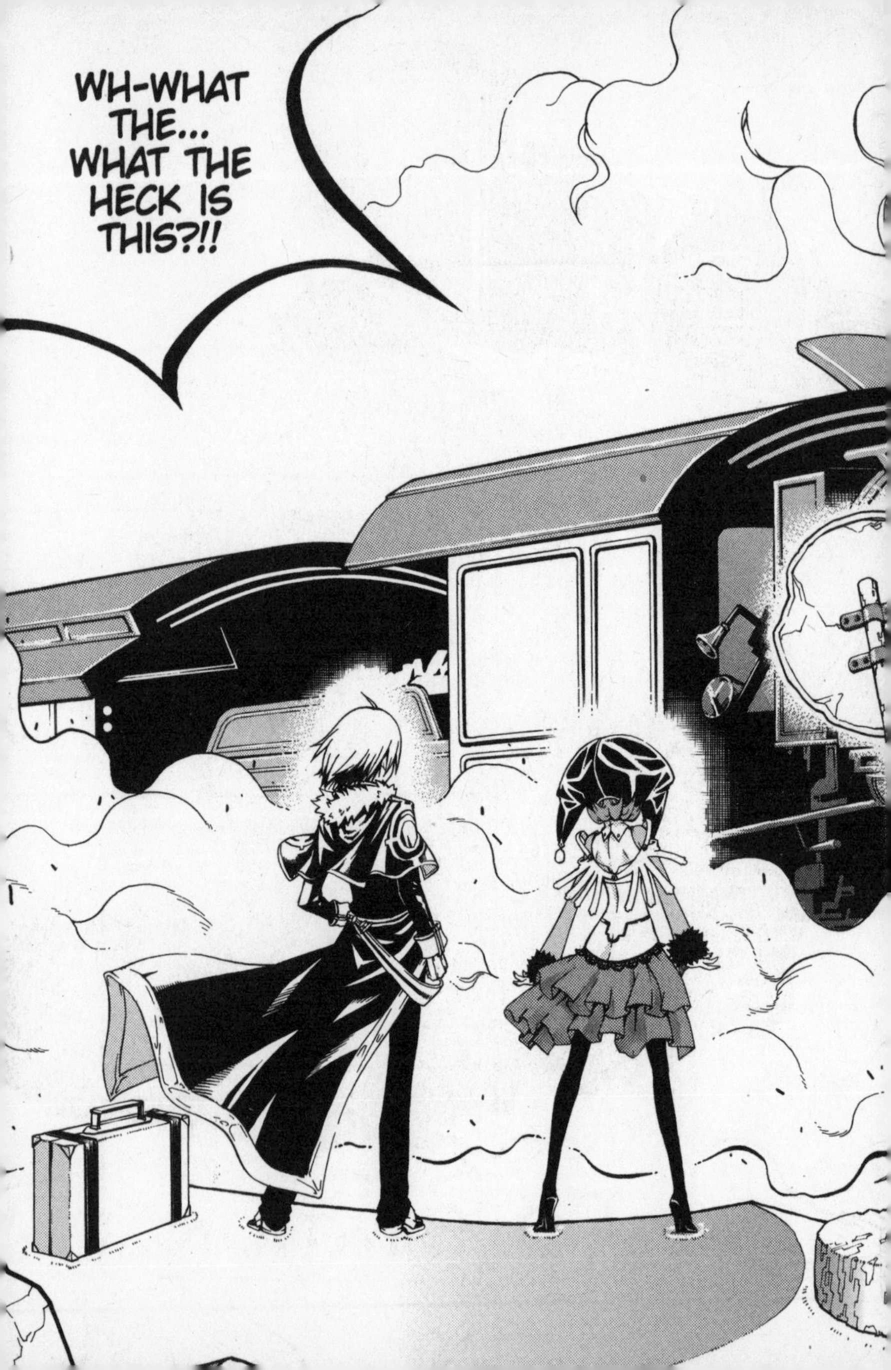
WH-WHAT THE... WHAT THE HECK IS THIS?!!

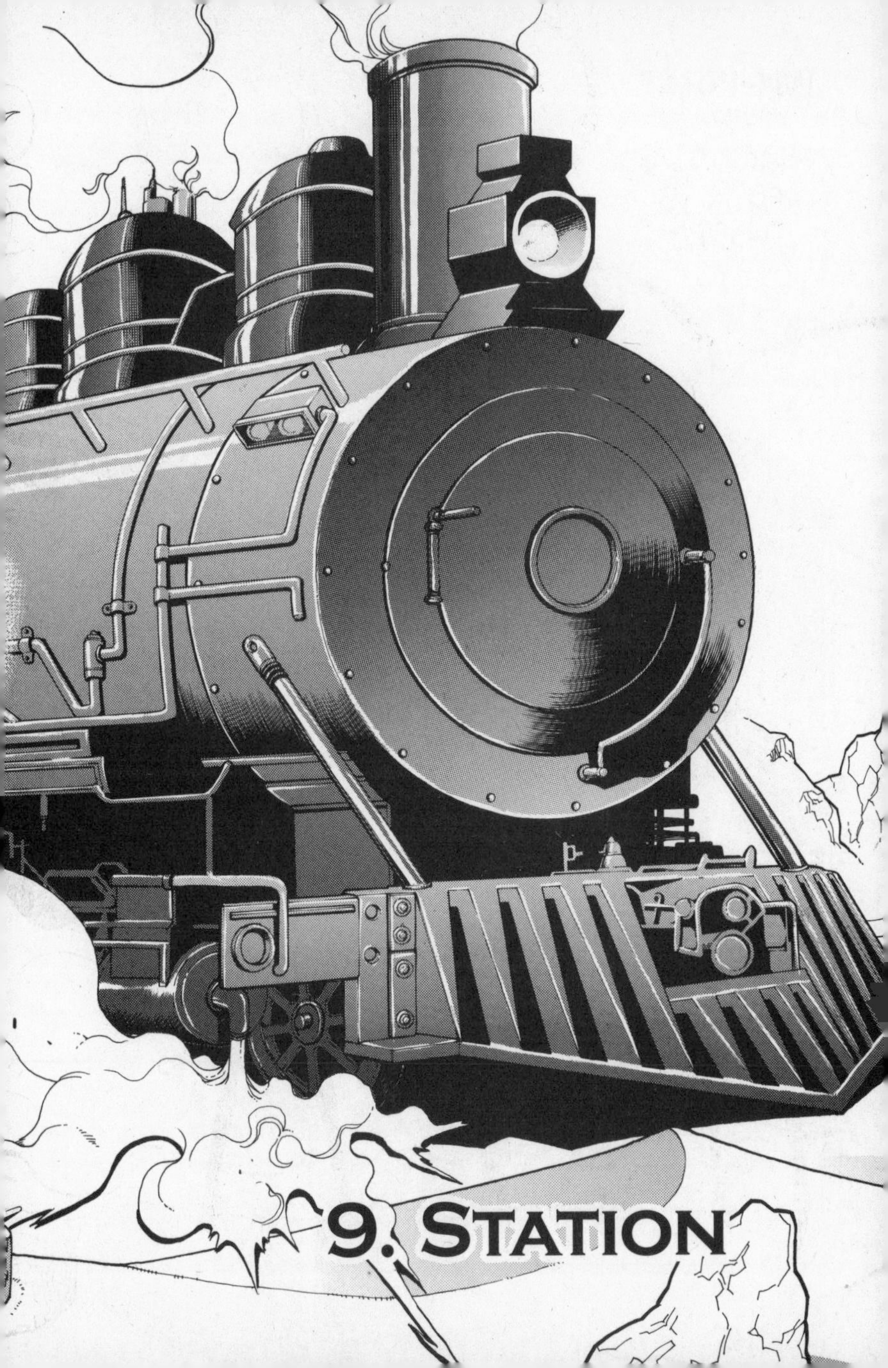
9. STATION

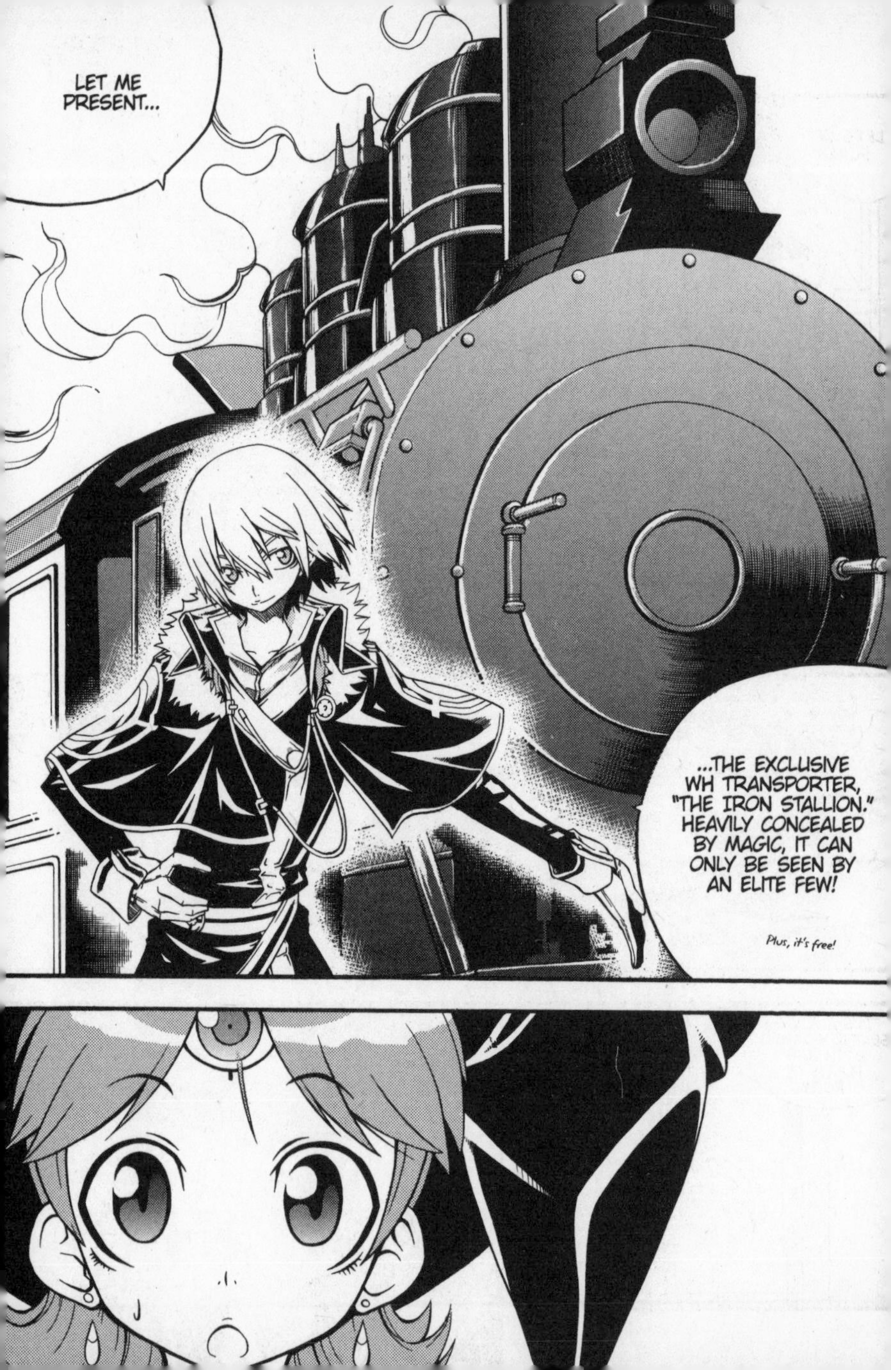
LET ME PRESENT...
...THE EXCLUSIVE WH TRANSPORTER, "THE IRON STALLION." HEAVILY CONCEALED BY MAGIC, IT CAN ONLY BE SEEN BY AN ELITE FEW!
Plus, it's free!

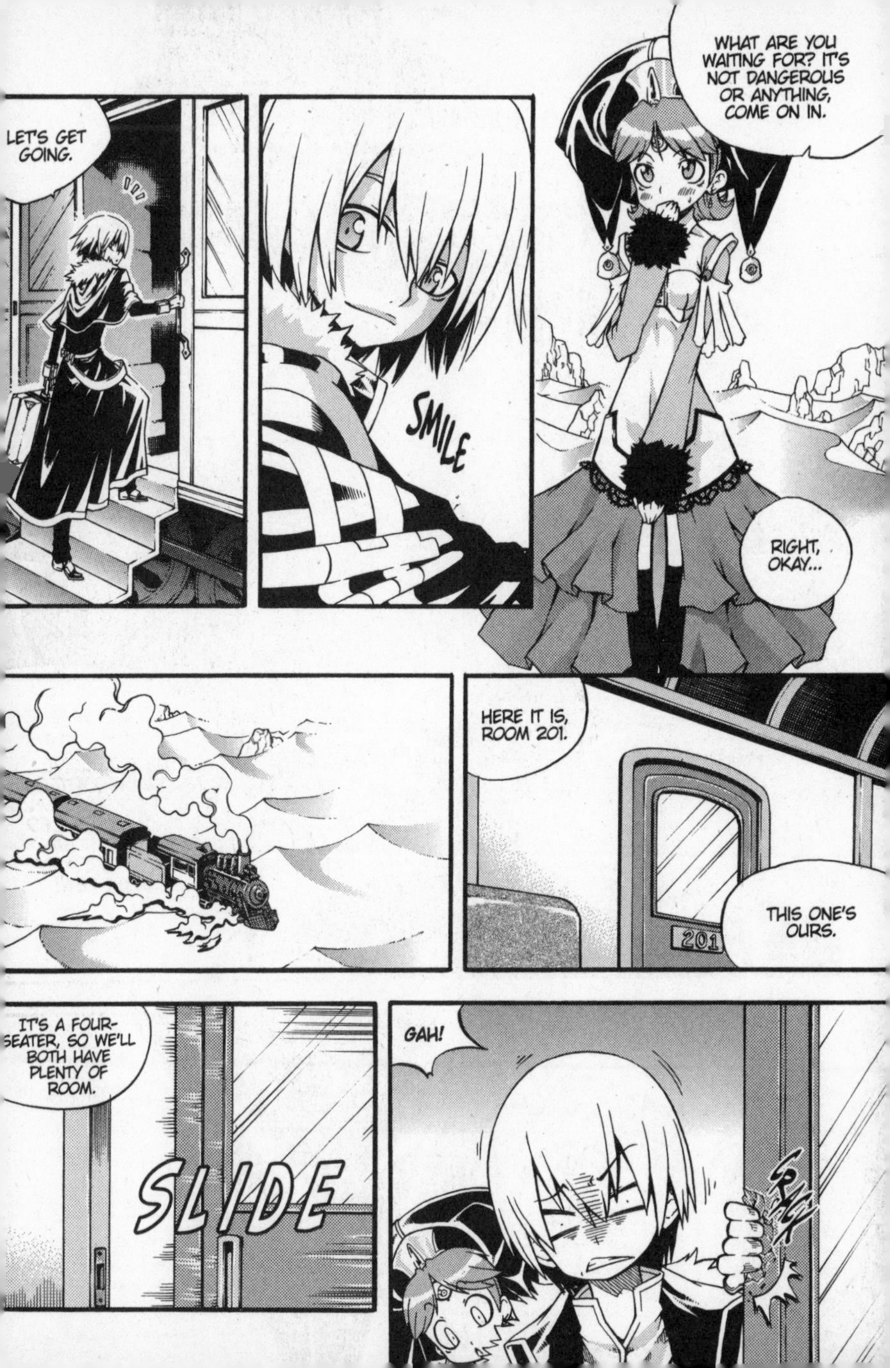
WHAT ARE YOU WAITING FOR? IT'S NOT DANGEROUS OR ANYTHING, COME ON IN.
LET'S GET GOING.
!!!
SMILE
RIGHT, OKAY...
HERE IT IS, ROOM 201.
THIS ONE'S OURS.
201
IT'S A FOUR-SEATER, SO WE'LL BOTH HAVE PLENTY OF ROOM.
SLIDE
GAH!

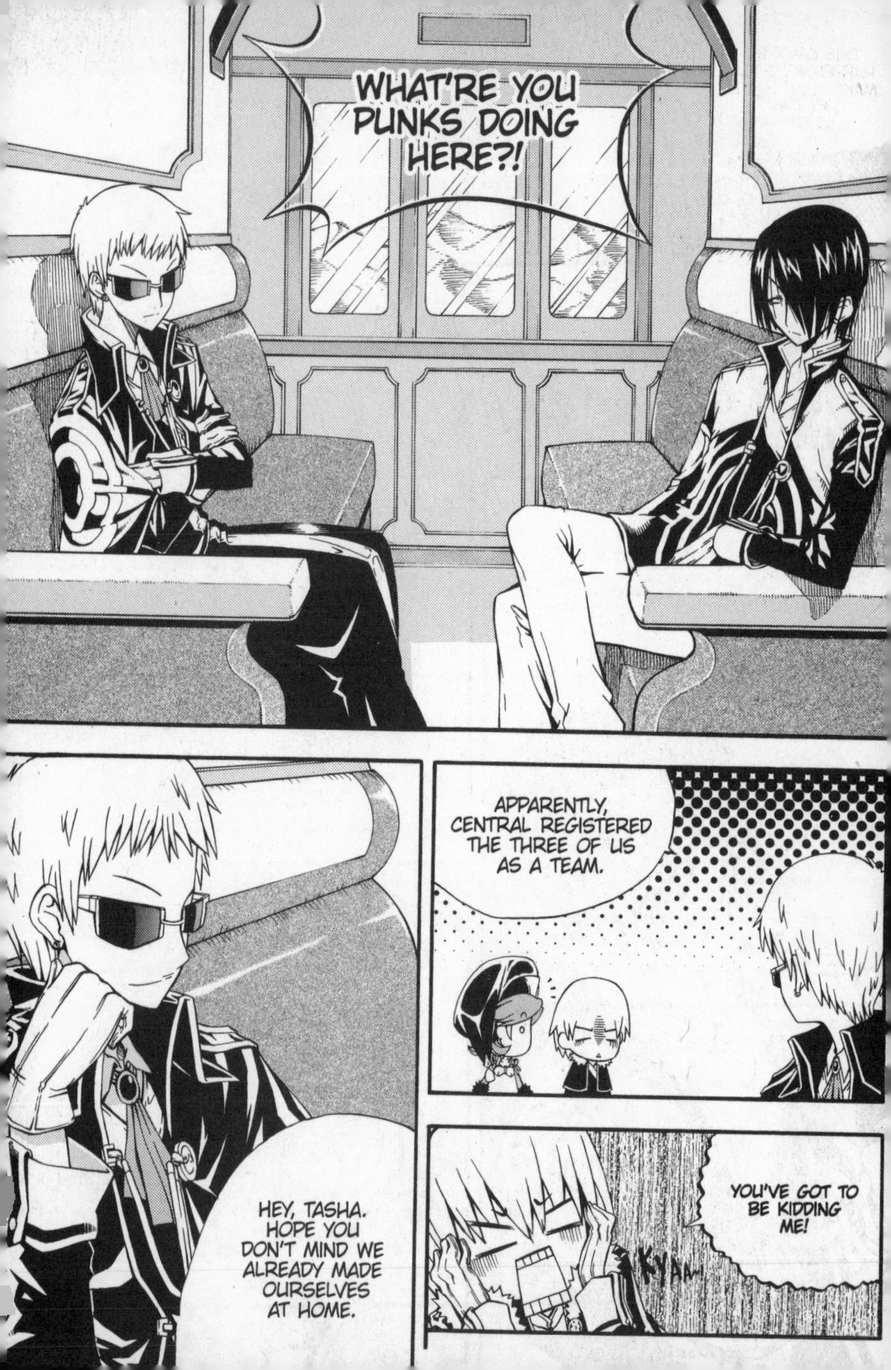
WHAT'RE YOU PUNKS DOING HERE?!
HEY, TASHA. HOPE YOU DON'T MIND WE ALREADY MADE OURSELVES AT HOME.
APPARENTLY, CENTRAL REGISTERED THE THREE OF US AS A TEAM.
YOU'VE GOT TO BE KIDDING ME!
KYAA

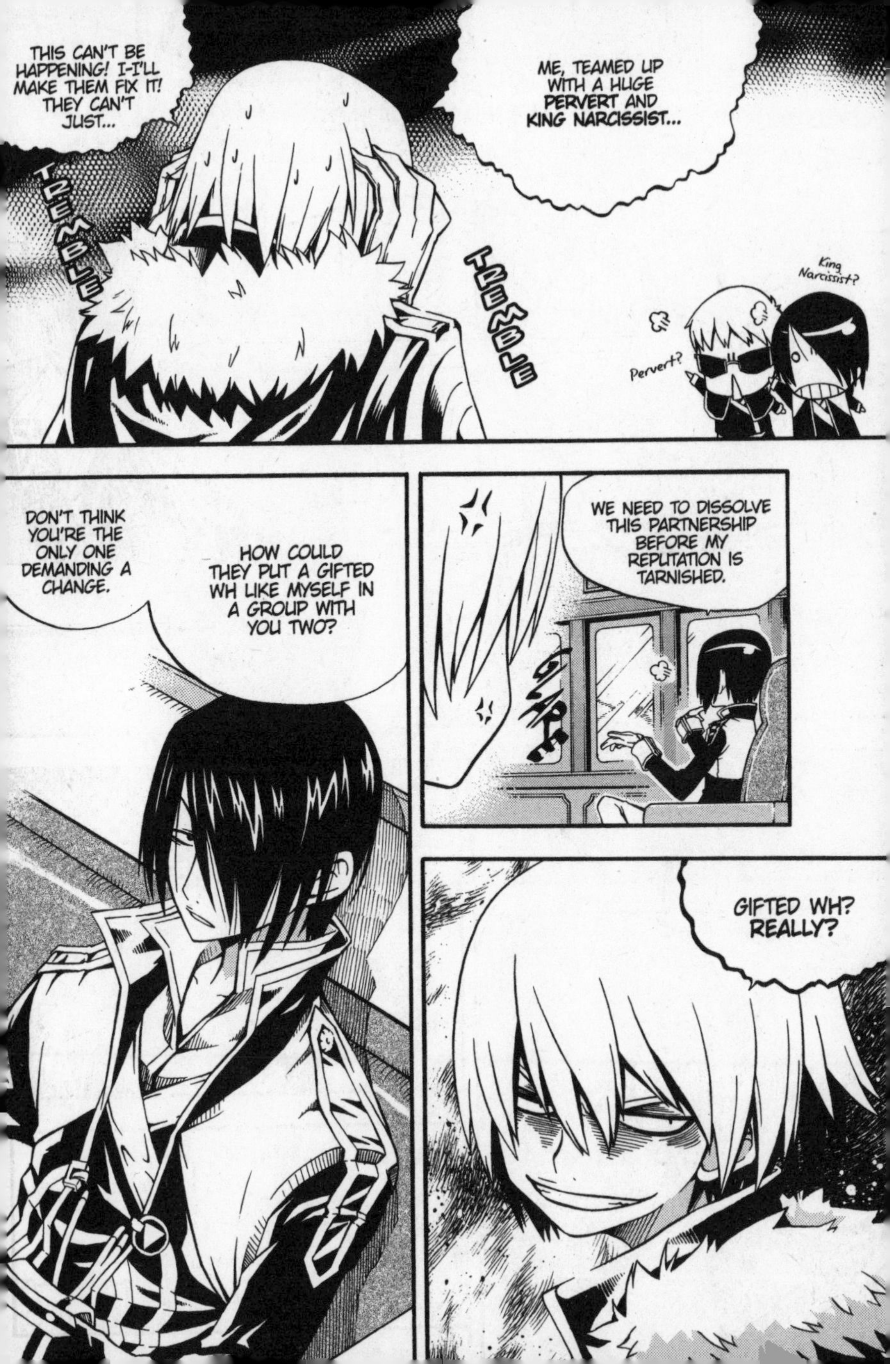
ME, TEAMED UP WITH A HUGE PERVERT AND KING NARCISSIST...
THIS CAN'T BE HAPPENING! I-I'LL MAKE THEM FIX IT! THEY CAN'T JUST...
TREMBLE
TREMBLE
King Narcissist?
Pervert?
WE NEED TO DISSOLVE THIS PARTNERSHIP BEFORE MY REPUTATION IS TARNISHED.
HOW COULD THEY PUT A GIFTED WH LIKE MYSELF IN A GROUP WITH YOU TWO?
DON'T THINK YOU'RE THE ONLY ONE DEMANDING A CHANGE.
GIFTED WH? REALLY?

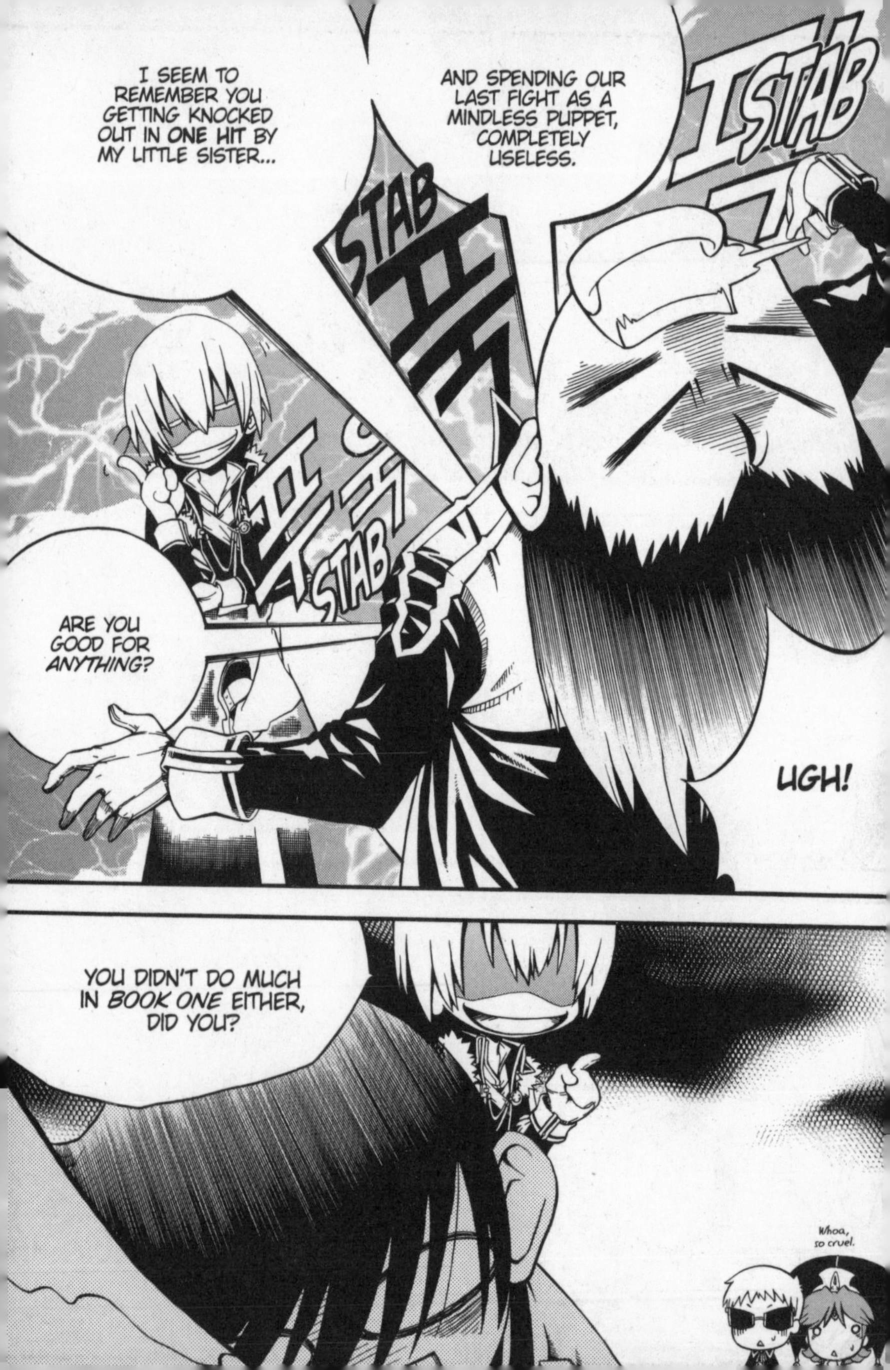
AND SPENDING OUR LAST FIGHT AS A MINDLESS PUPPET, COMPLETELY USELESS.
I SEEM TO REMEMBER YOU GETTING KNOCKED OUT IN ONE HIT BY MY LITTLE SISTER...
STAB
STAB
STAB
UGH!
ARE YOU GOOD FOR *ANYTHING?*
YOU DIDN'T DO MUCH IN *BOOK ONE* EITHER, DID YOU?
Whoa, so cruel.

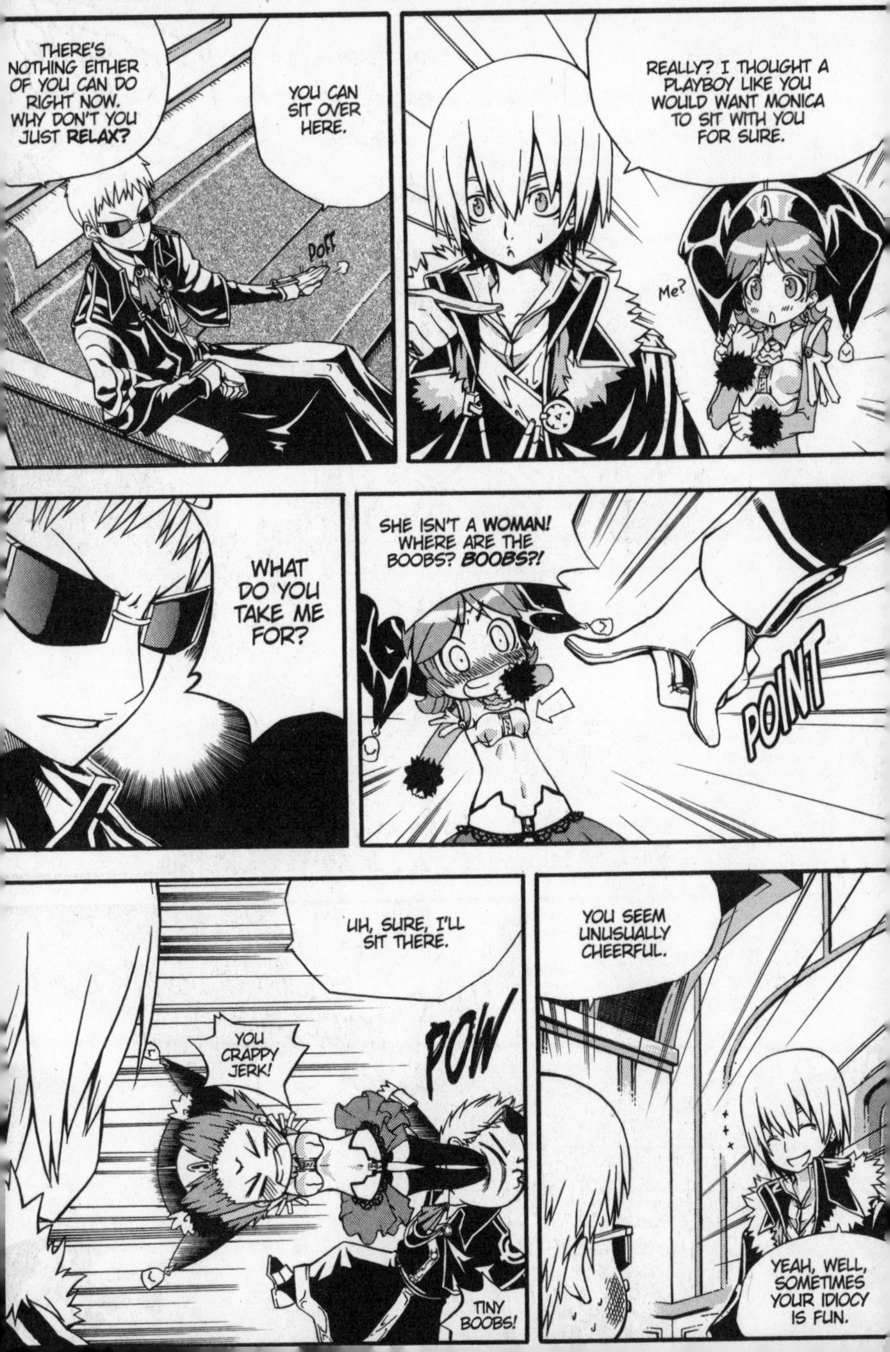
THERE'S NOTHING EITHER OF YOU CAN DO RIGHT NOW. WHY DON'T YOU JUST RELAX?
YOU CAN SIT OVER HERE.
POFF
REALLY? I THOUGHT A PLAYBOY LIKE YOU WOULD WANT MONICA TO SIT WITH YOU FOR SURE.
Me?
WHAT DO YOU TAKE ME FOR?
SHE ISN'T A WOMAN! WHERE ARE THE BOOBS? BOOBS?!
POINT
UH, SURE, I'LL SIT THERE.
YOU CRAPPY JERK!
POW
TINY BOOBS!
YOU SEEM UNUSUALLY CHEERFUL.
YEAH, WELL, SOMETIMES YOUR IDIOCY IS FUN.

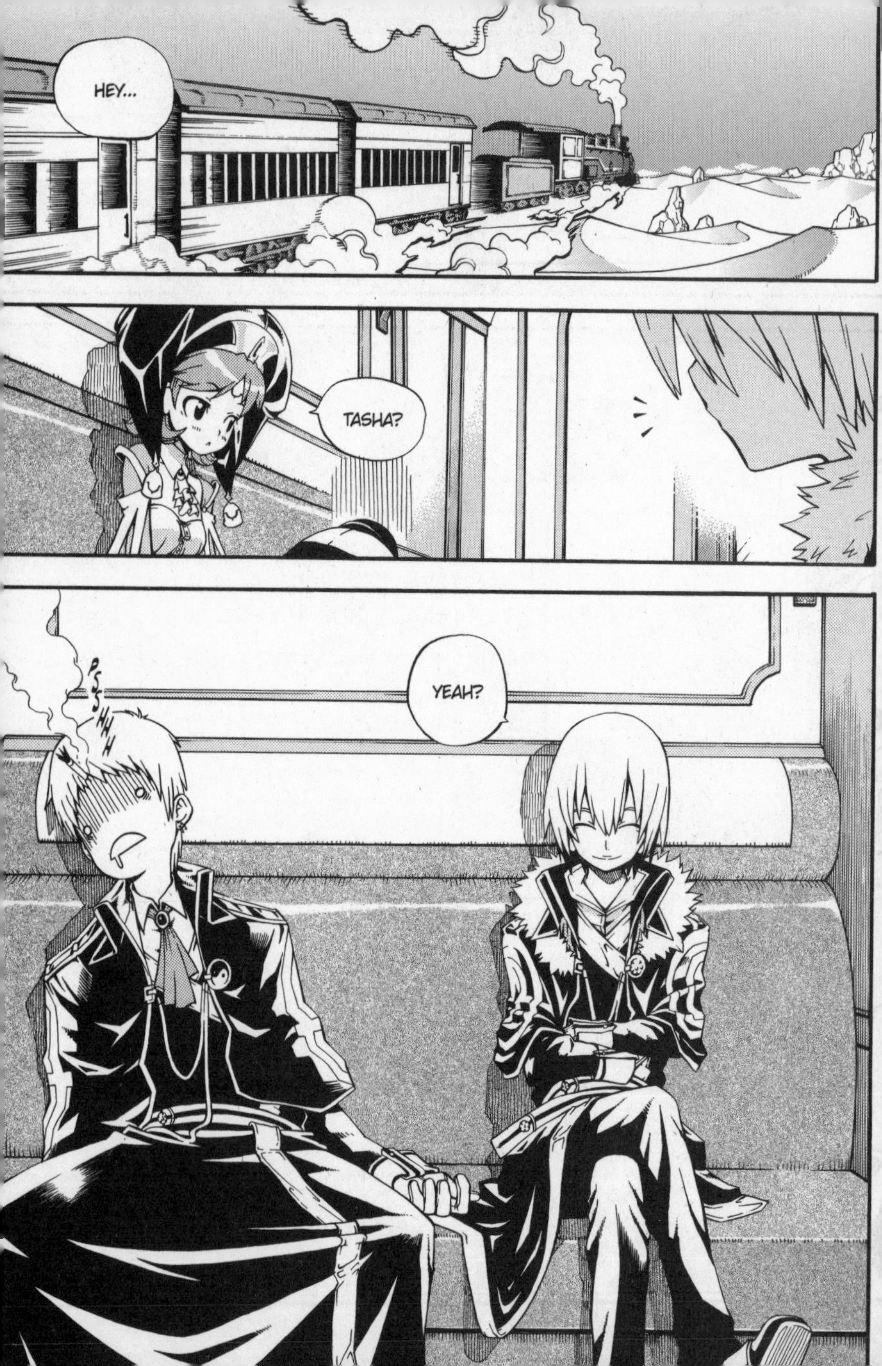
HEY...
TASHA?
YEAH?
PSSHHH

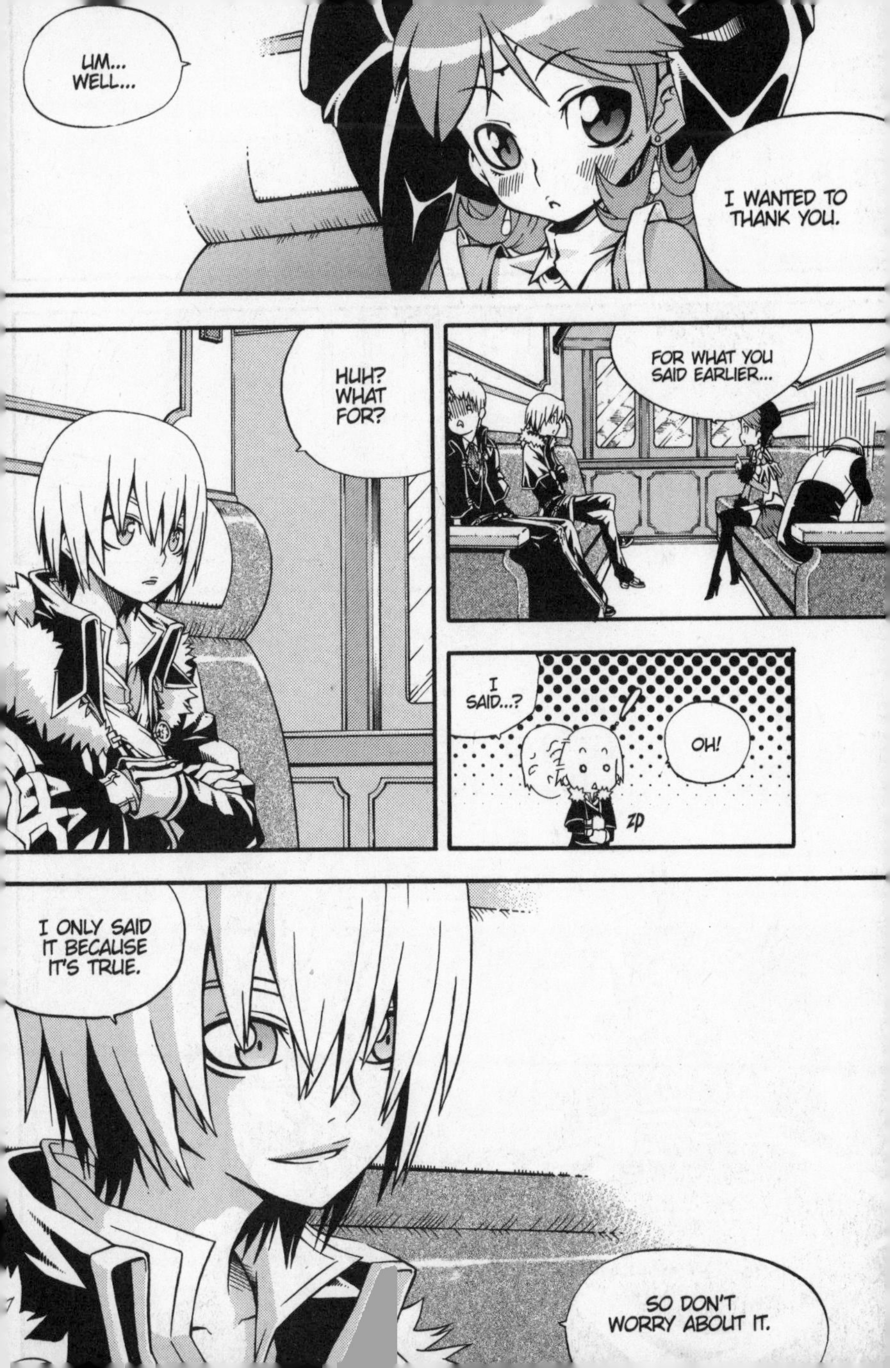
UM... WELL...
I WANTED TO THANK YOU.
HUH? WHAT FOR?
FOR WHAT YOU SAID EARLIER...
I SAID...?
OH!
ZP
I ONLY SAID IT BECAUSE IT'S TRUE.
SO DON'T WORRY ABOUT IT.

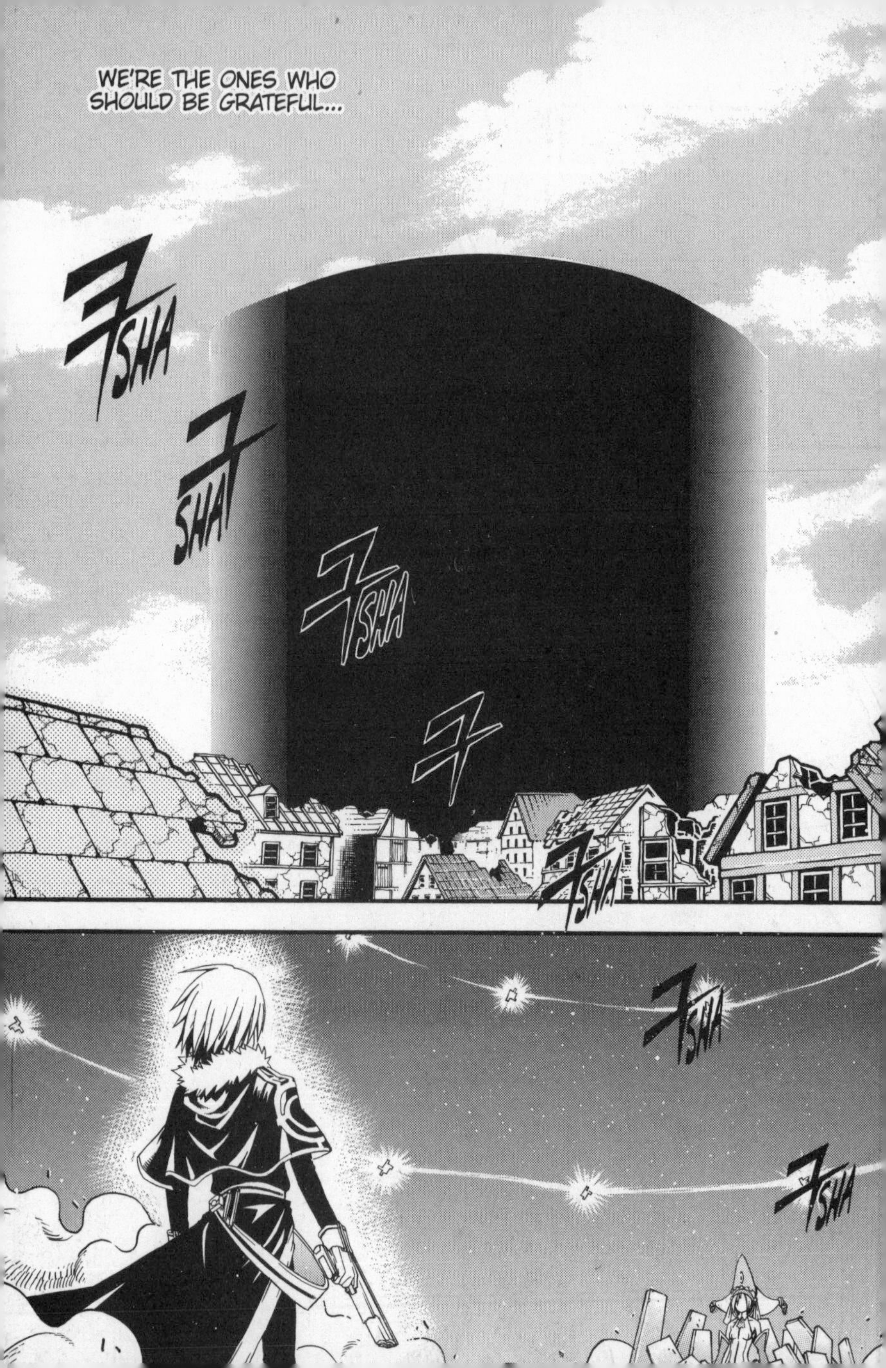

WE'RE THE ONES WHO SHOULD BE GRATEFUL...
SHA
SHA
SHA
SHA
SHA
SHA

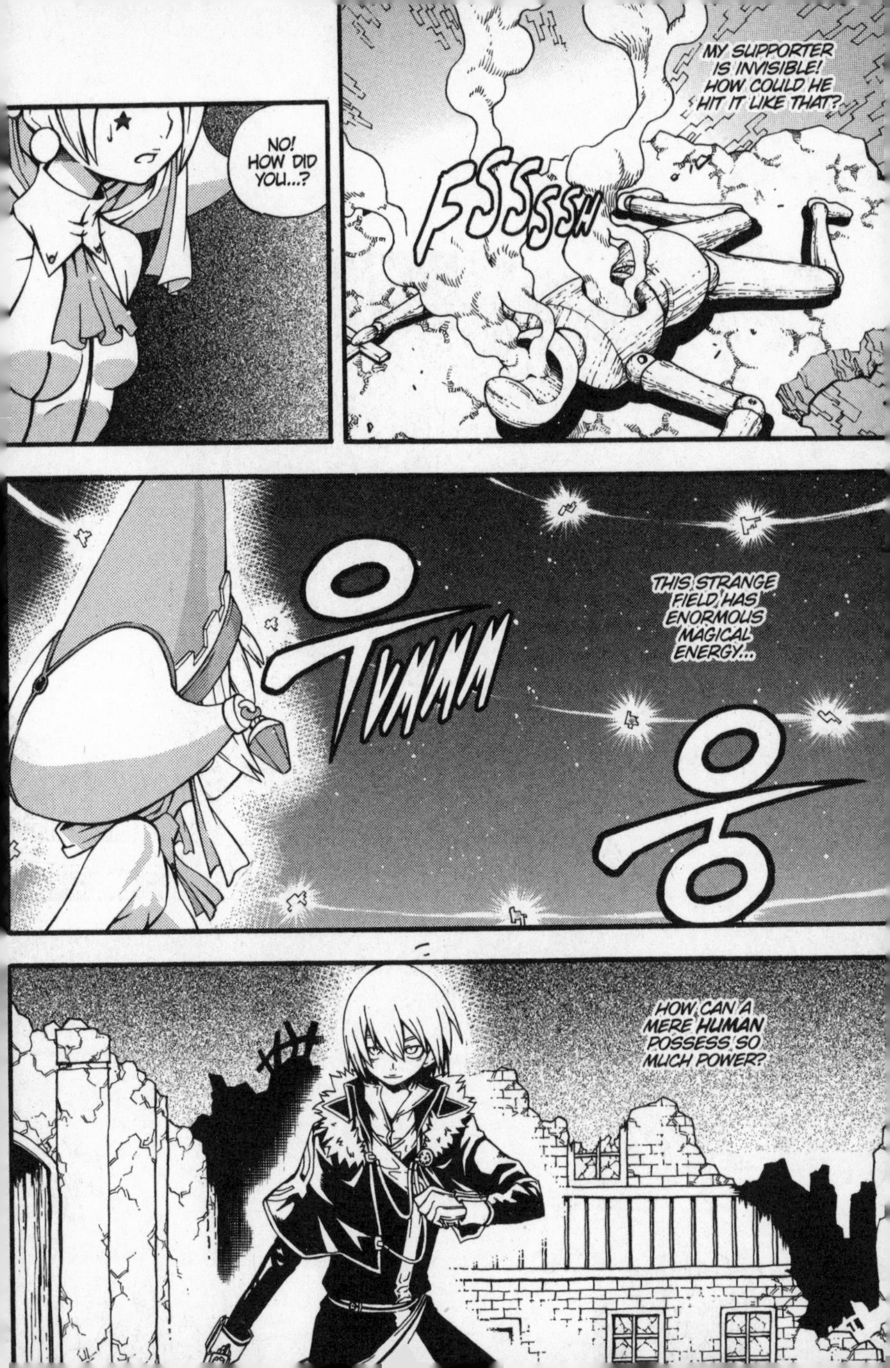
MY SUPPORTER IS INVISIBLE! HOW COULD HE HIT IT LIKE THAT?
FSSSSH
NO! HOW DID YOU...?
THIS STRANGE FIELD HAS ENORMOUS MAGICAL ENERGY...
우
웅
HOW CAN A MERE HUMAN POSSESS SO MUCH POWER?

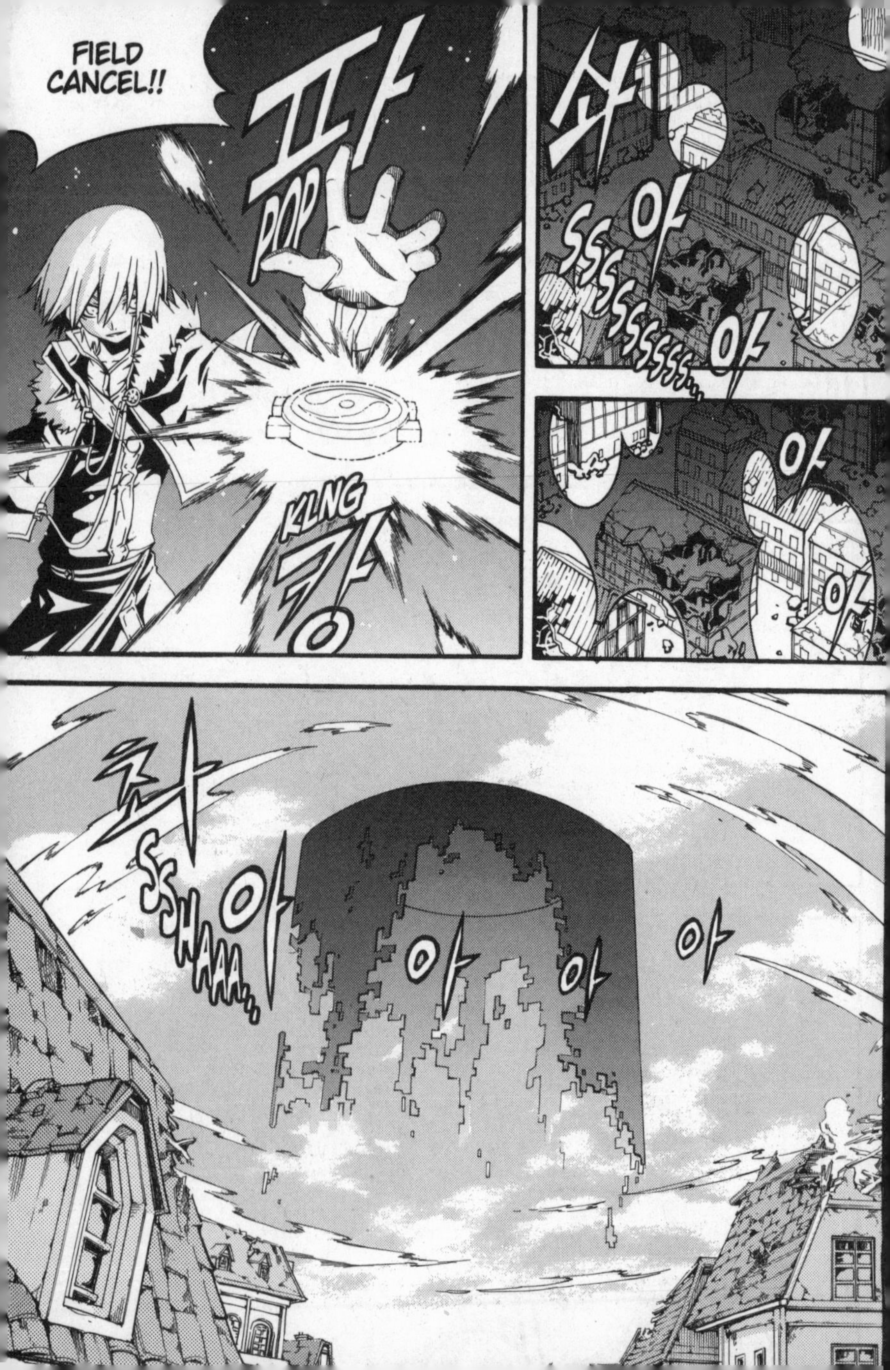
FIELD CANCEL!!
POP
SSSSSSSSS...
KLING
SSHAAA...

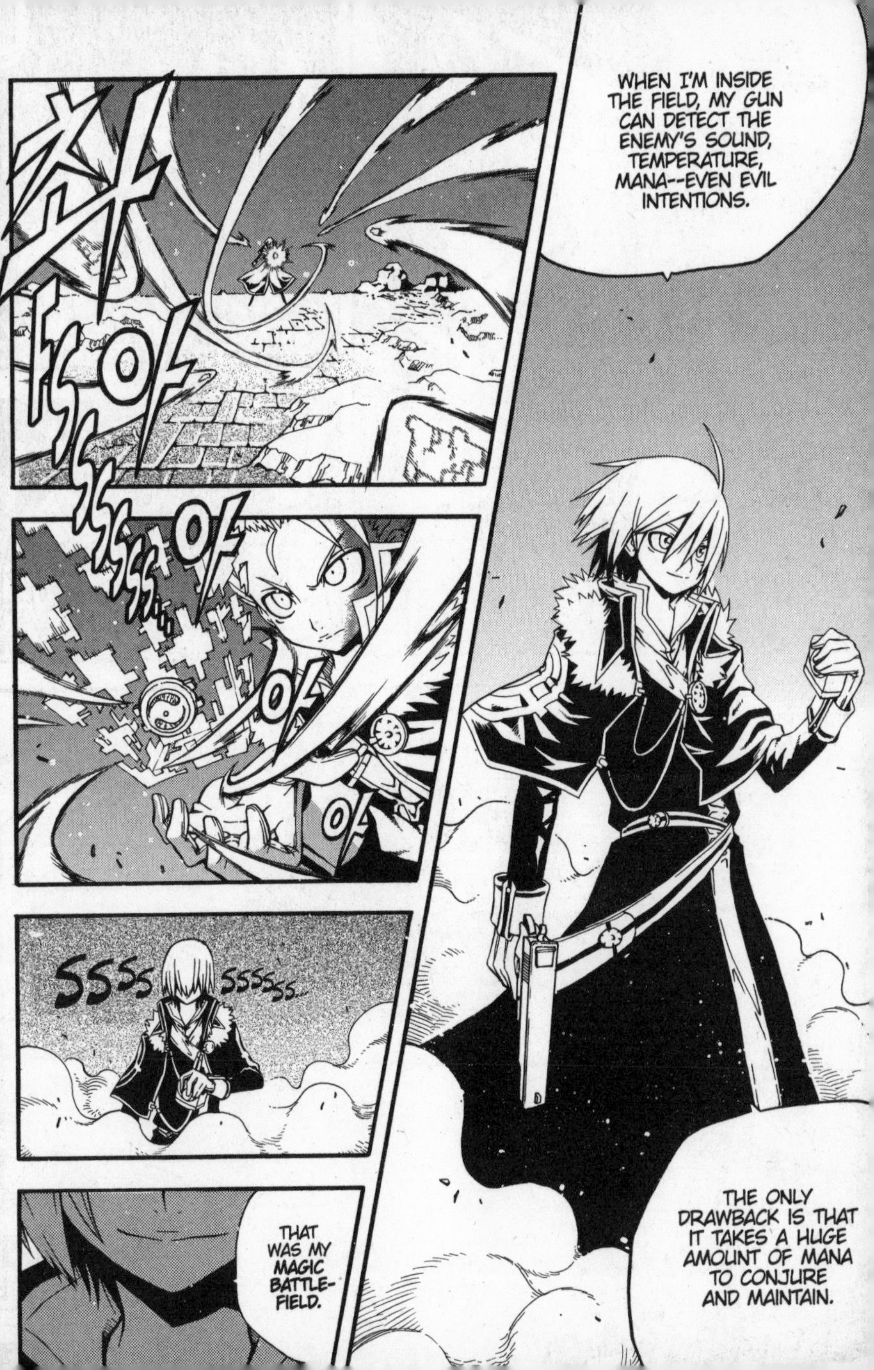
WHEN I'M INSIDE THE FIELD, MY GUN CAN DETECT THE ENEMY'S SOUND, TEMPERATURE, MANA--EVEN EVIL INTENTIONS.
SSSSS SSSSSS...
THE ONLY DRAWBACK IS THAT IT TAKES A HUGE AMOUNT OF MANA TO CONJURE AND MAINTAIN.
THAT WAS MY MAGIC BATTLE-FIELD.

THAT'S THE DUMBEST THING I'VE EVER **HEARD!** YOU PATHETIC HUMANS CAN'T USE MAGIC!

YOU DON'T EVEN HAVE A WITCH'S HAT!

YOU'RE RIGHT. HUMANS CAN'T USE MAGIC.

HUH?

THAT'S WHERE THIS COMES IN-- MY DIMENSIONAL GALLERY POUCH.

TA-DA

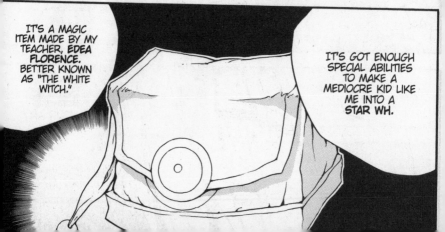

IT'S A MAGIC ITEM MADE BY MY TEACHER, EDEA FLORENCE. BETTER KNOWN AS "THE WHITE WITCH."

IT'S GOT ENOUGH SPECIAL ABILITIES TO MAKE A MEDIOCRE KID LIKE ME INTO A STAR WH.

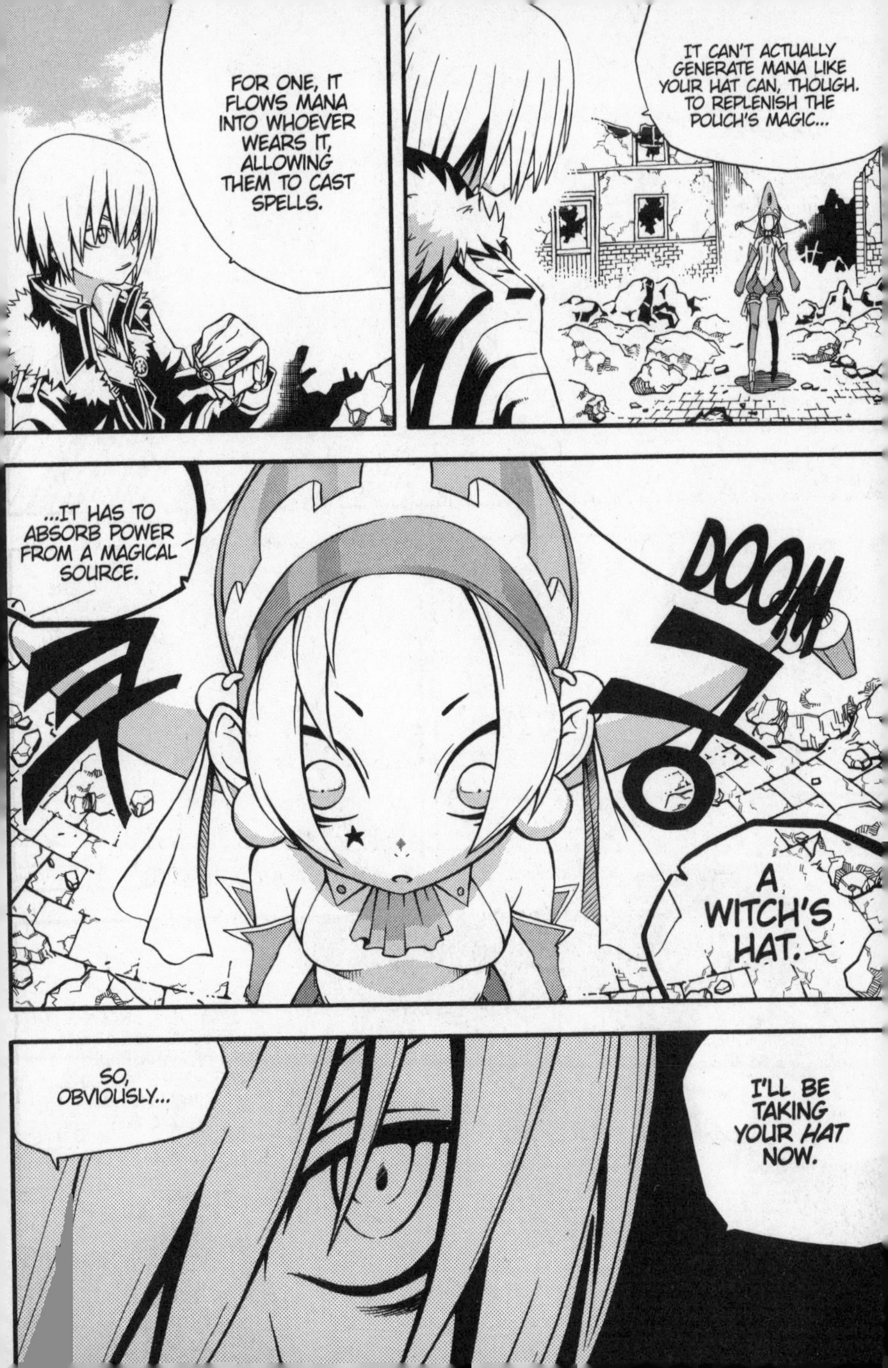
IT CAN'T ACTUALLY GENERATE MANA LIKE YOUR HAT CAN, THOUGH. TO REPLENISH THE POUCH'S MAGIC...
FOR ONE, IT FLOWS MANA INTO WHOEVER WEARS IT, ALLOWING THEM TO CAST SPELLS.
DOOM
...IT HAS TO ABSORB POWER FROM A MAGICAL SOURCE.
A WITCH'S HAT.
I'LL BE TAKING YOUR HAT NOW.
SO, OBVIOUSLY...

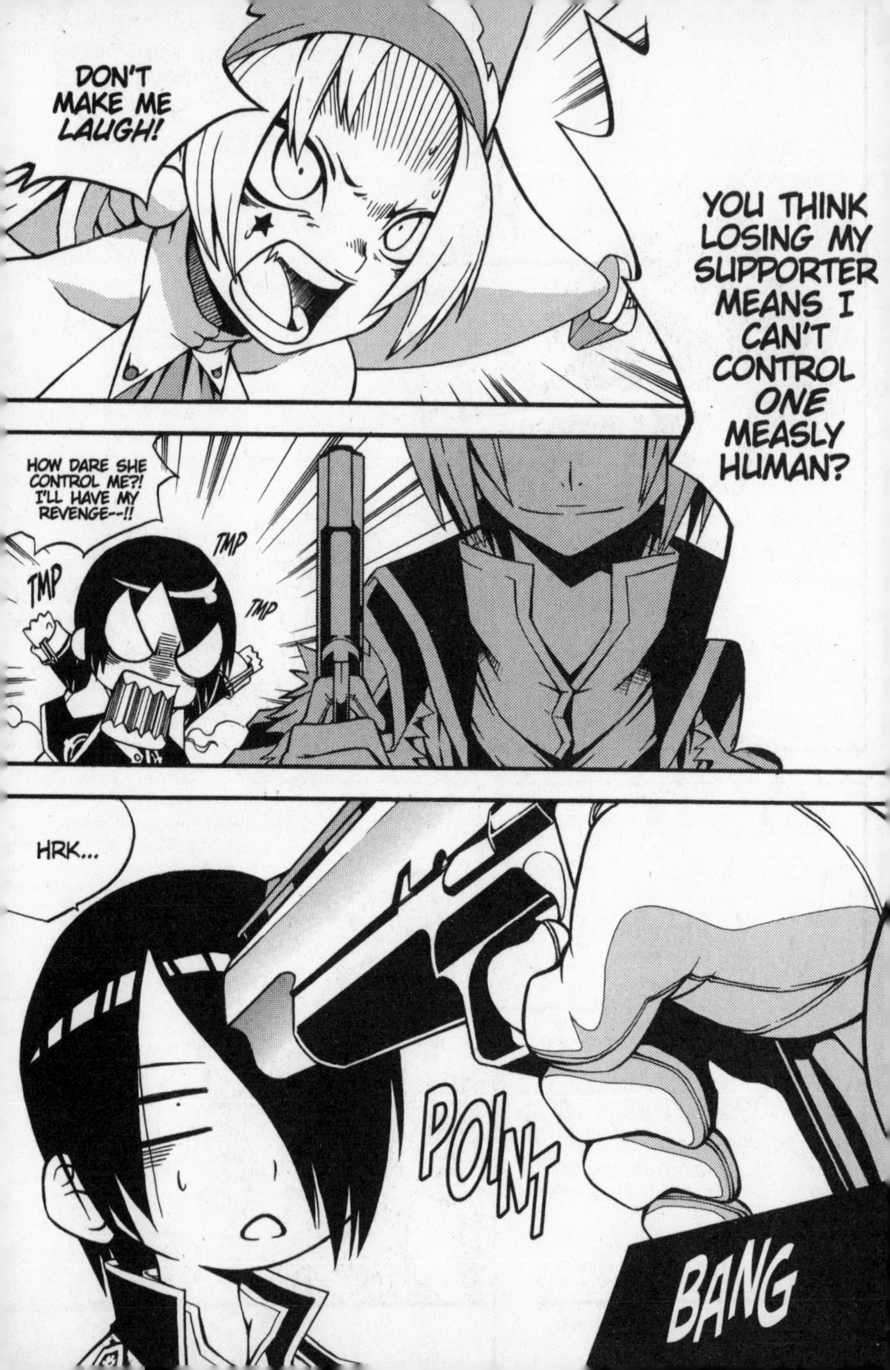
DON'T MAKE ME LAUGH!
YOU THINK LOSING MY SUPPORTER MEANS I CAN'T CONTROL ONE MEASLY HUMAN?
HOW DARE SHE CONTROL ME?! I'LL HAVE MY REVENGE--!!
TMP
TMP
TMP
HRK...
POINT
BANG

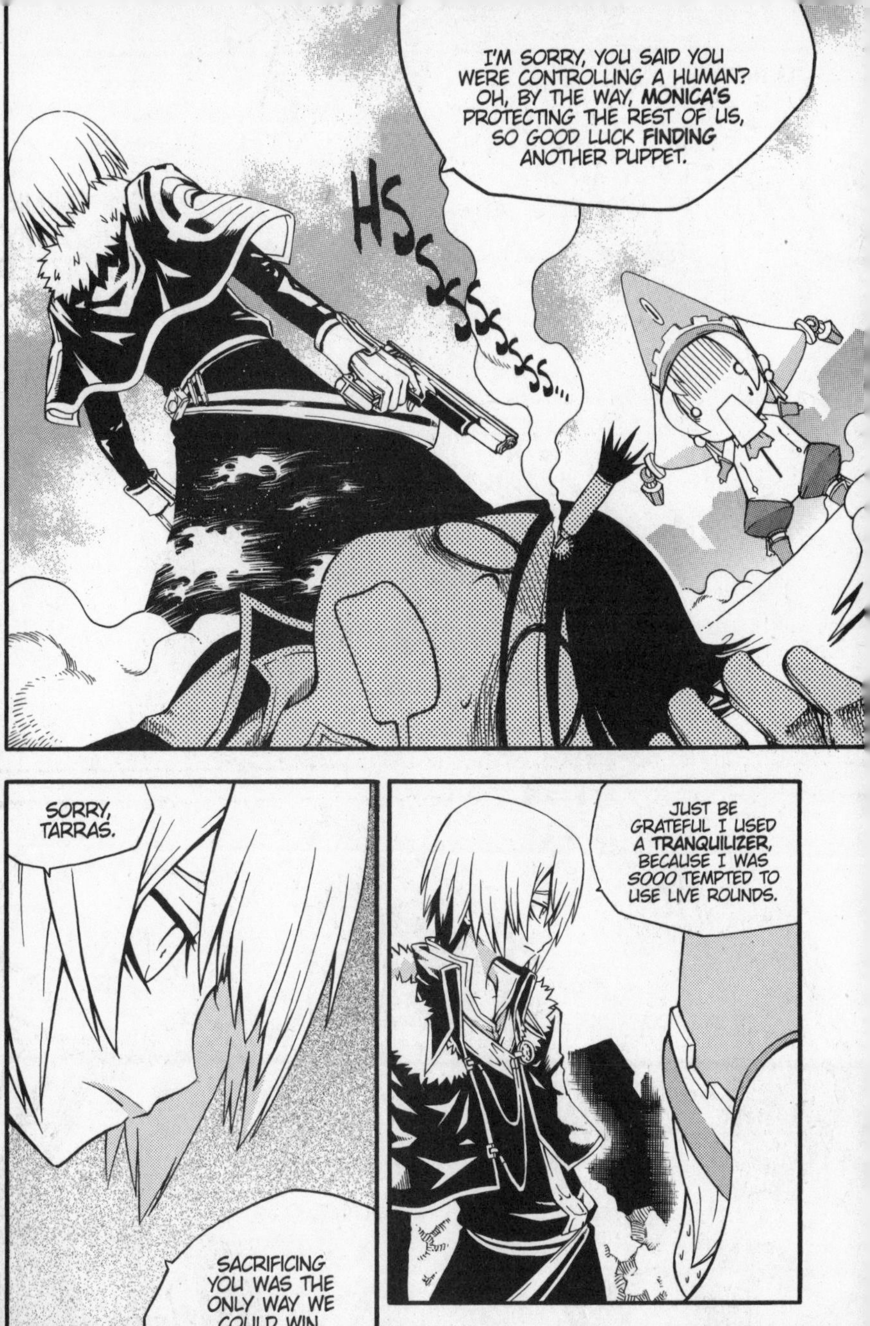
I'M SORRY, YOU SAID YOU WERE CONTROLLING A HUMAN? OH, BY THE WAY, **MONICA'S** PROTECTING THE REST OF US, SO GOOD LUCK **FINDING** ANOTHER PUPPET.
HSSSSSSSSSS...
JUST BE GRATEFUL I USED A **TRANQUILIZER**, BECAUSE I WAS SOOO TEMPTED TO USE LIVE ROUNDS.
SORRY, TARRAS.
SACRIFICING YOU WAS THE ONLY WAY WE COULD WIN.

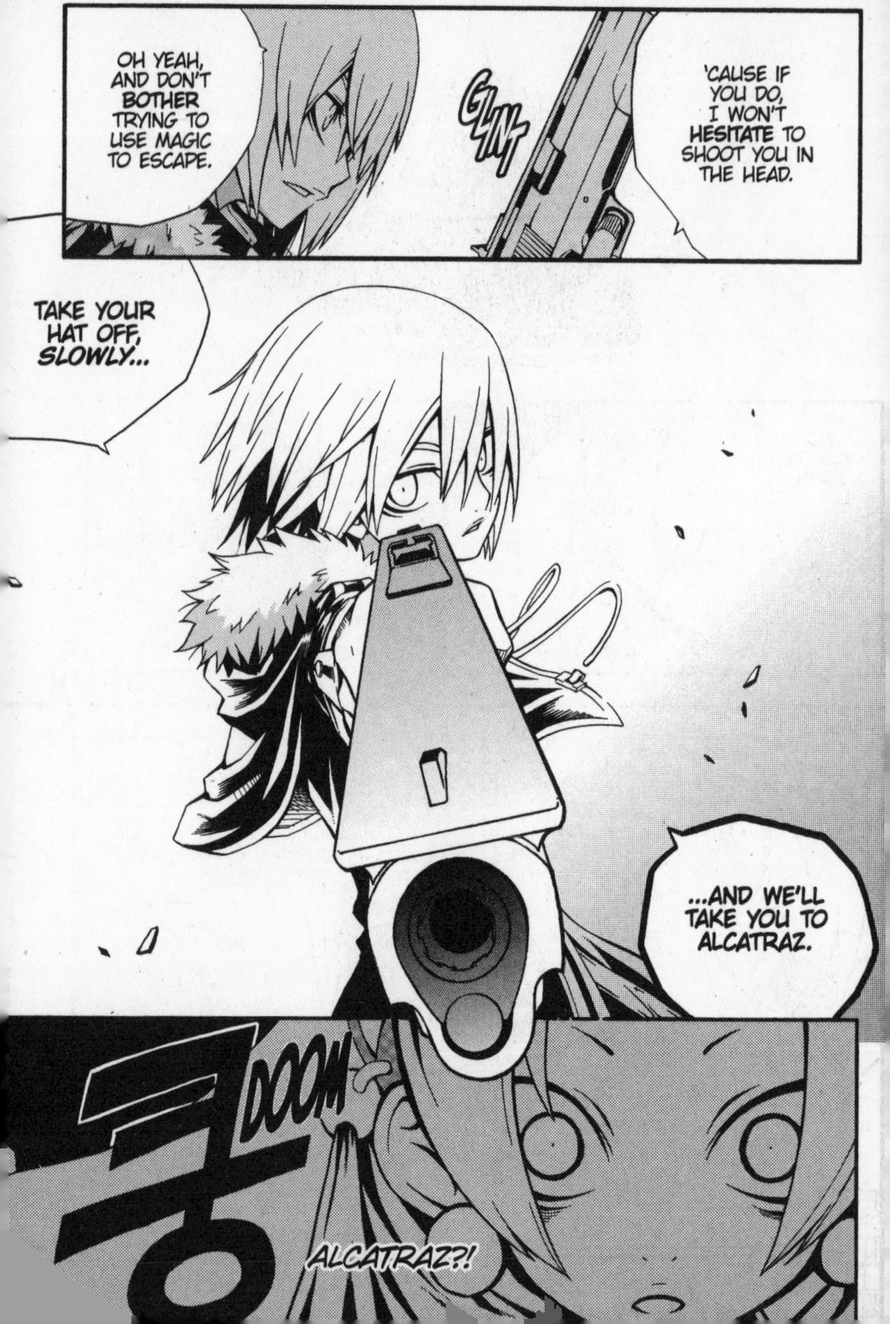
OH YEAH, AND DON'T BOTHER TRYING TO USE MAGIC TO ESCAPE.
GLINT
'CAUSE IF YOU DO, I WON'T HESITATE TO SHOOT YOU IN THE HEAD.
TAKE YOUR HAT OFF, SLOWLY...
...AND WE'LL TAKE YOU TO ALCATRAZ.
DOOM
ALCATRAZ?!

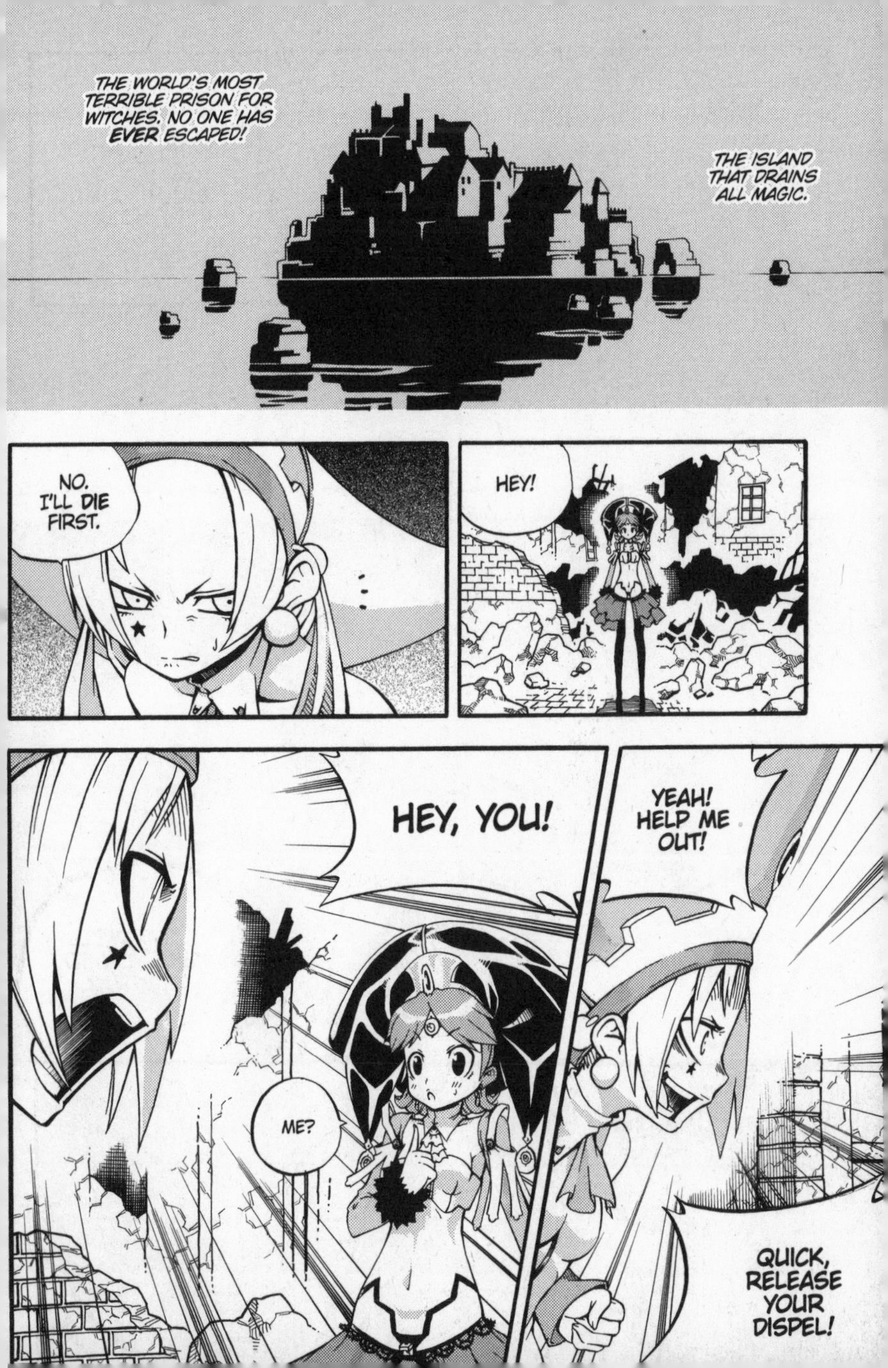
THE ISLAND THAT DRAINS ALL MAGIC.
THE WORLD'S MOST TERRIBLE PRISON FOR WITCHES. NO ONE HAS EVER ESCAPED!
HEY!
NO. I'LL DIE FIRST.
HEY, YOU!
ME?
YEAH! HELP ME OUT!
QUICK, RELEASE YOUR DISPEL!

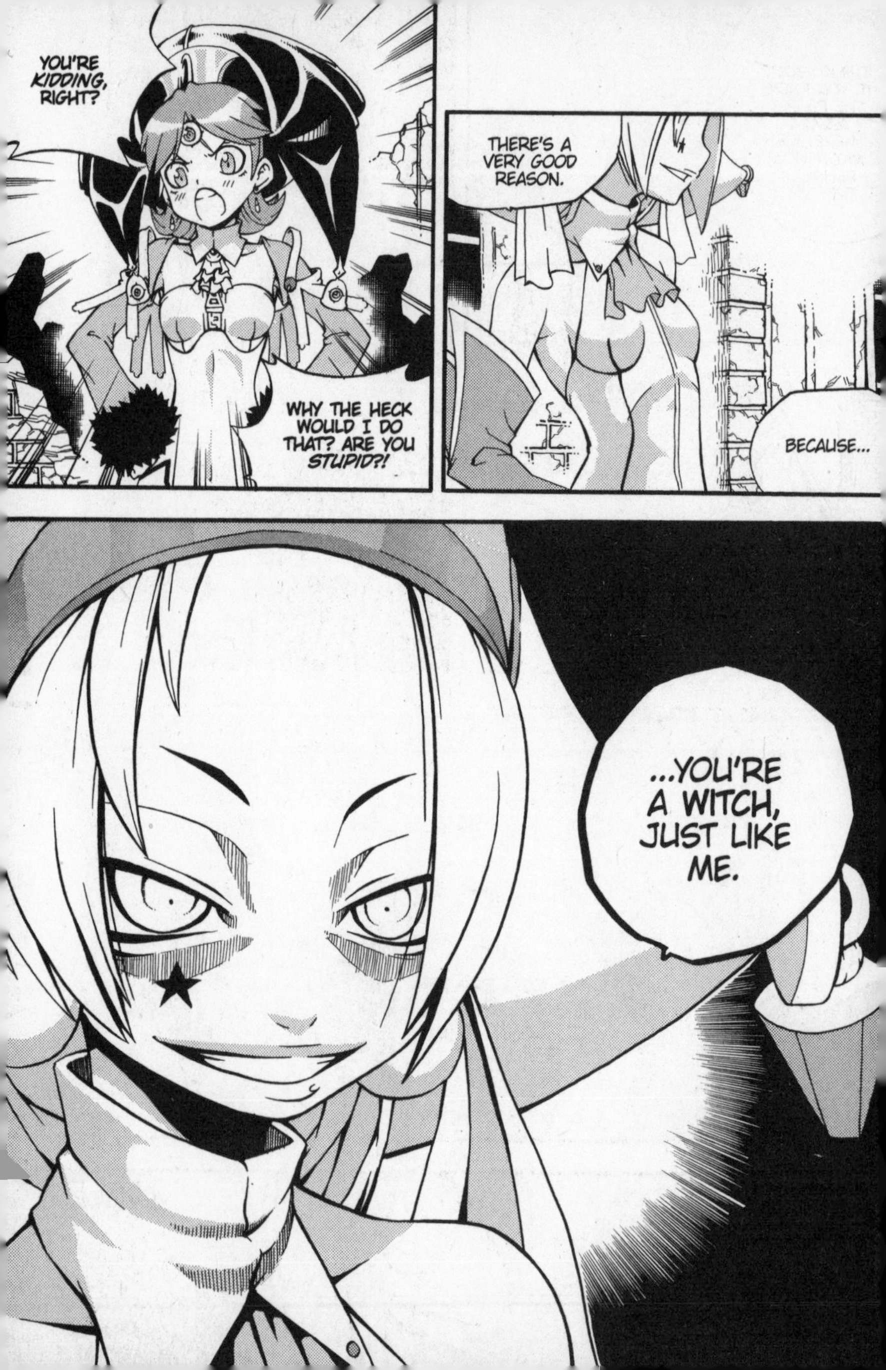
YOU'RE KIDDING, RIGHT?
WHY THE HECK WOULD I DO THAT? ARE YOU STUPID?!
THERE'S A VERY GOOD REASON.
BECAUSE...
...YOU'RE A WITCH, JUST LIKE ME.

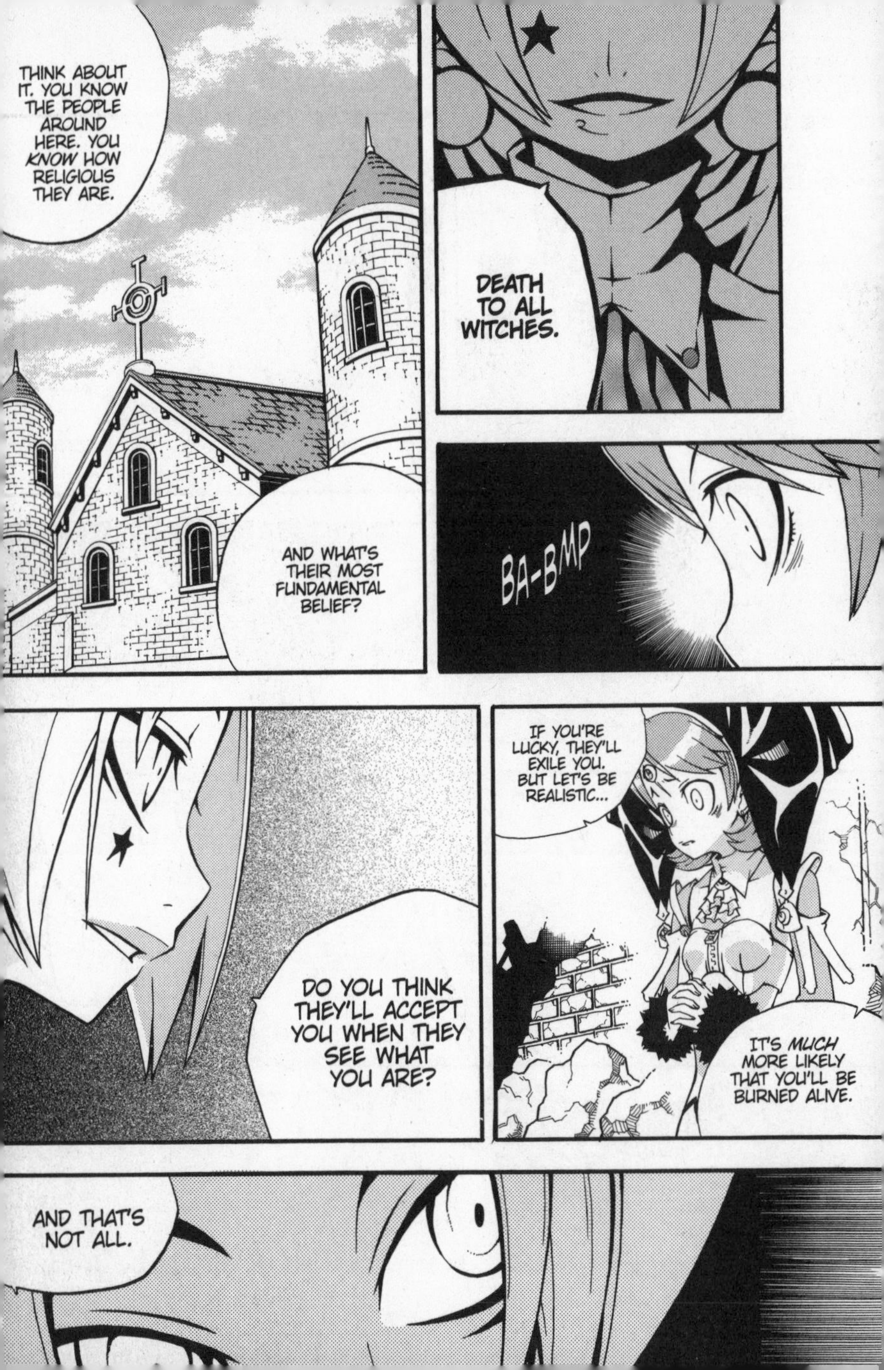

THINK ABOUT IT. YOU KNOW THE PEOPLE AROUND HERE. YOU *KNOW* HOW RELIGIOUS THEY ARE.
AND WHAT'S THEIR MOST FUNDAMENTAL BELIEF?
DEATH TO ALL WITCHES.
BA-BMP
IF YOU'RE LUCKY, THEY'LL EXILE YOU. BUT LET'S BE REALISTIC...
IT'S *MUCH* MORE LIKELY THAT YOU'LL BE BURNED ALIVE.
DO YOU THINK THEY'LL ACCEPT YOU WHEN THEY SEE WHAT YOU ARE?
AND THAT'S NOT ALL.

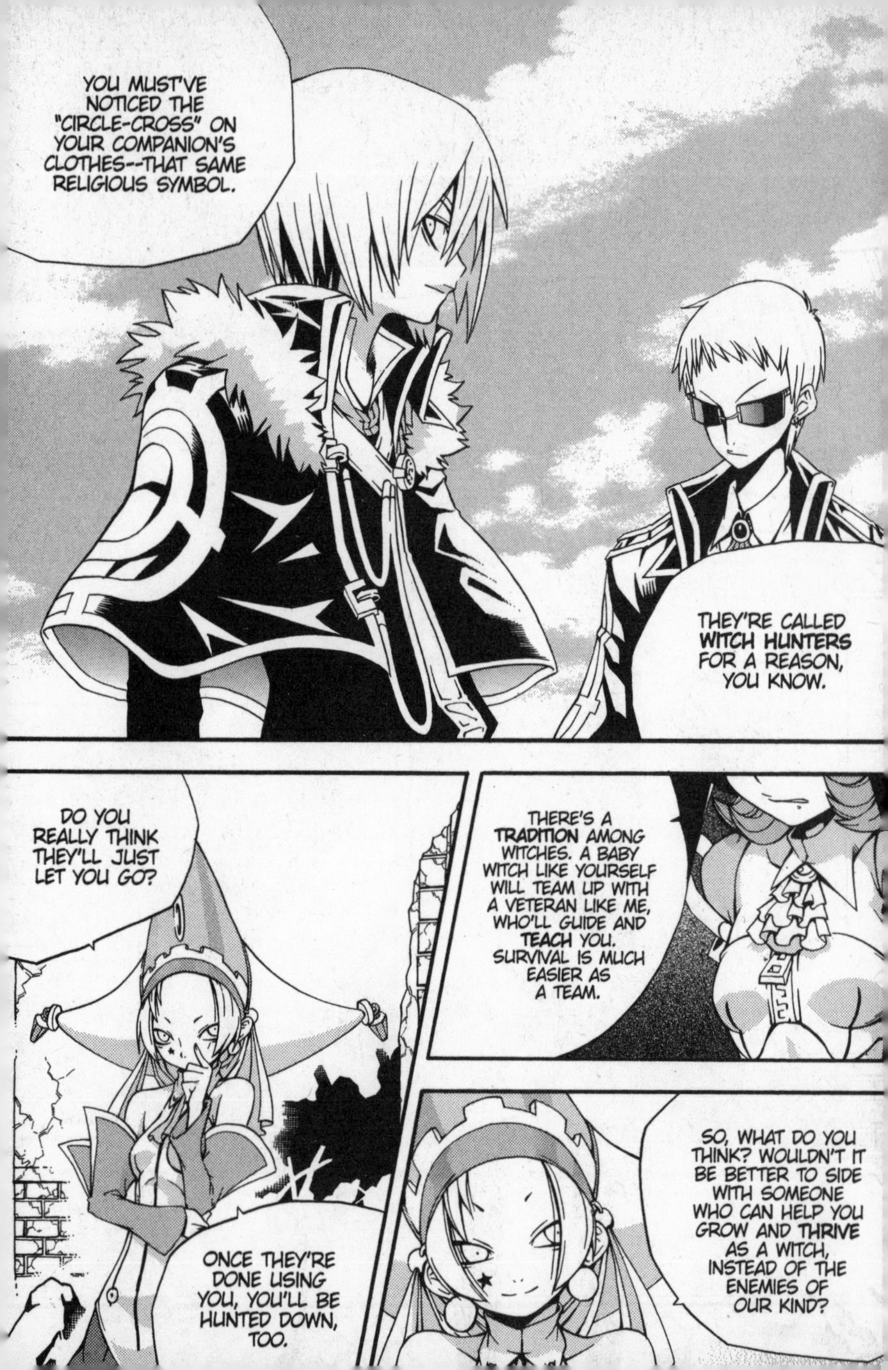
YOU MUST'VE NOTICED THE "CIRCLE-CROSS" ON YOUR COMPANION'S CLOTHES--THAT SAME RELIGIOUS SYMBOL.
THEY'RE CALLED **WITCH HUNTERS** FOR A REASON, YOU KNOW.
DO YOU REALLY THINK THEY'LL JUST LET YOU GO?
THERE'S A **TRADITION** AMONG WITCHES. A BABY WITCH LIKE YOURSELF WILL TEAM UP WITH A VETERAN LIKE ME, WHO'LL GUIDE AND **TEACH** YOU. SURVIVAL IS MUCH EASIER AS A TEAM.
ONCE THEY'RE DONE USING YOU, YOU'LL BE HUNTED DOWN, TOO.
SO, WHAT DO YOU THINK? WOULDN'T IT BE BETTER TO SIDE WITH SOMEONE WHO CAN HELP YOU GROW AND **THRIVE** AS A WITCH, INSTEAD OF THE ENEMIES OF OUR KIND?

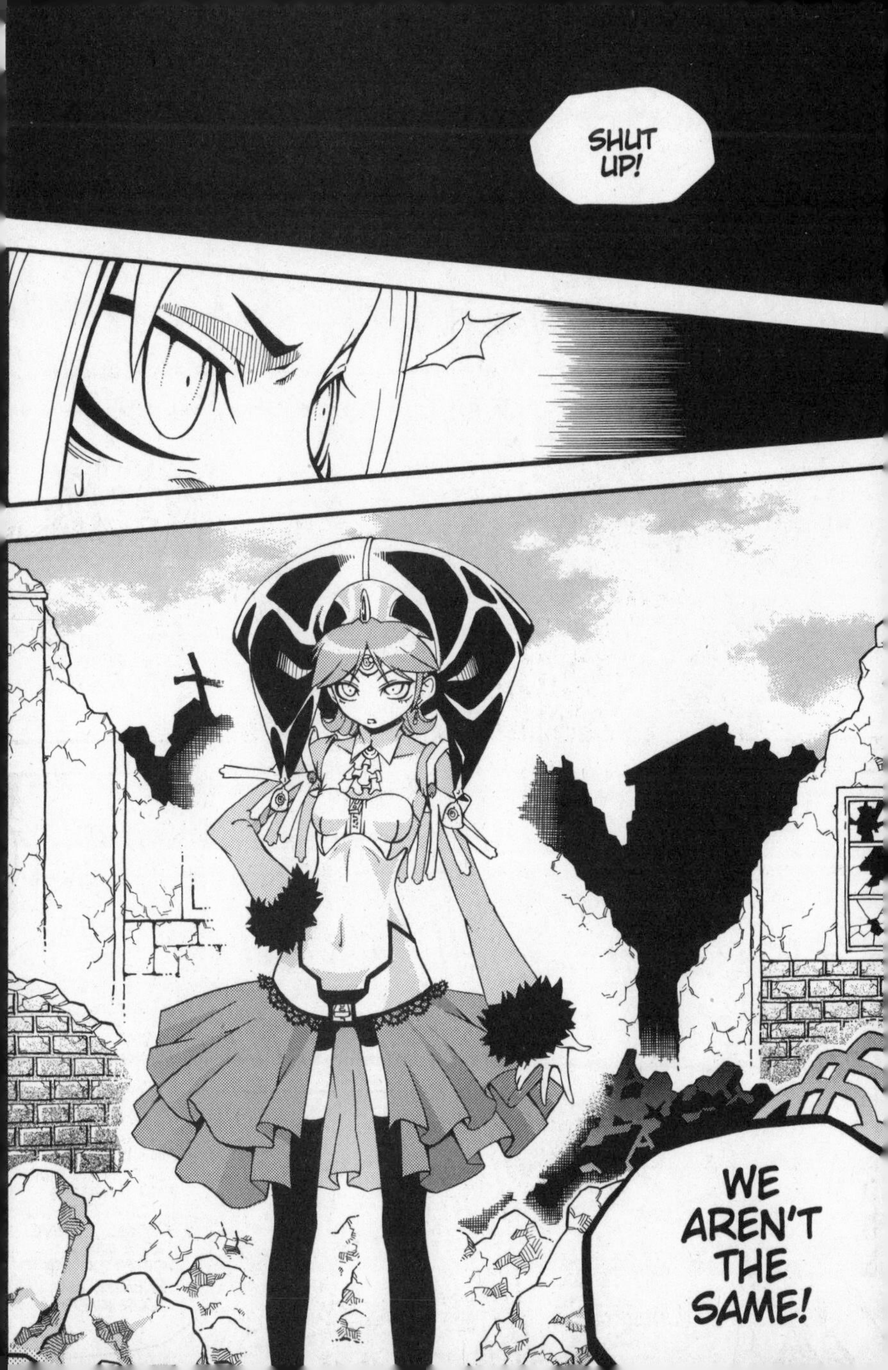
SHUT UP!
WE AREN'T THE SAME!

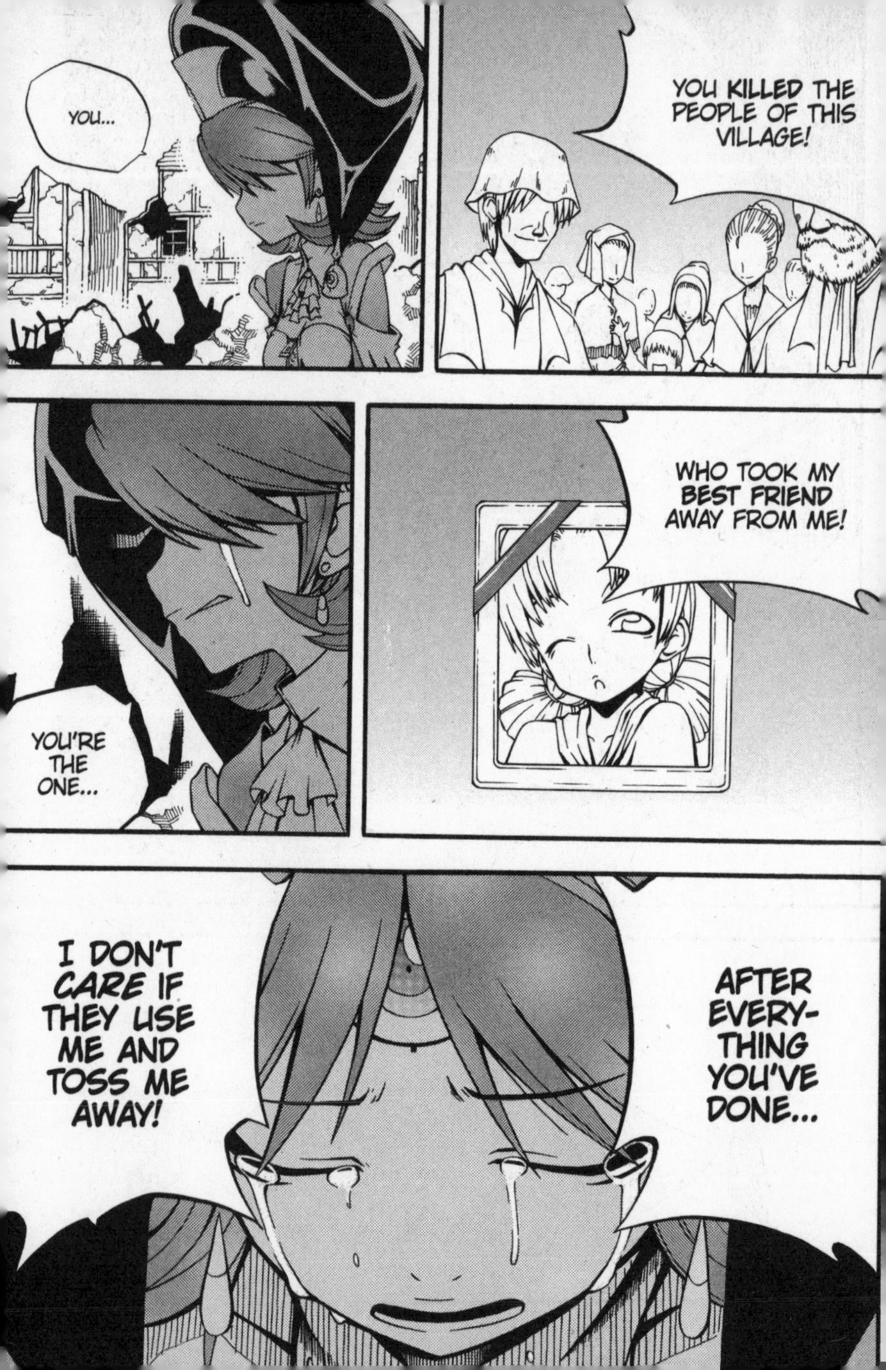
YOU...
YOU KILLED THE PEOPLE OF THIS VILLAGE!
YOU'RE THE ONE...
WHO TOOK MY BEST FRIEND AWAY FROM ME!
I DON'T CARE IF THEY USE ME AND TOSS ME AWAY!
AFTER EVERY-THING YOU'VE DONE...

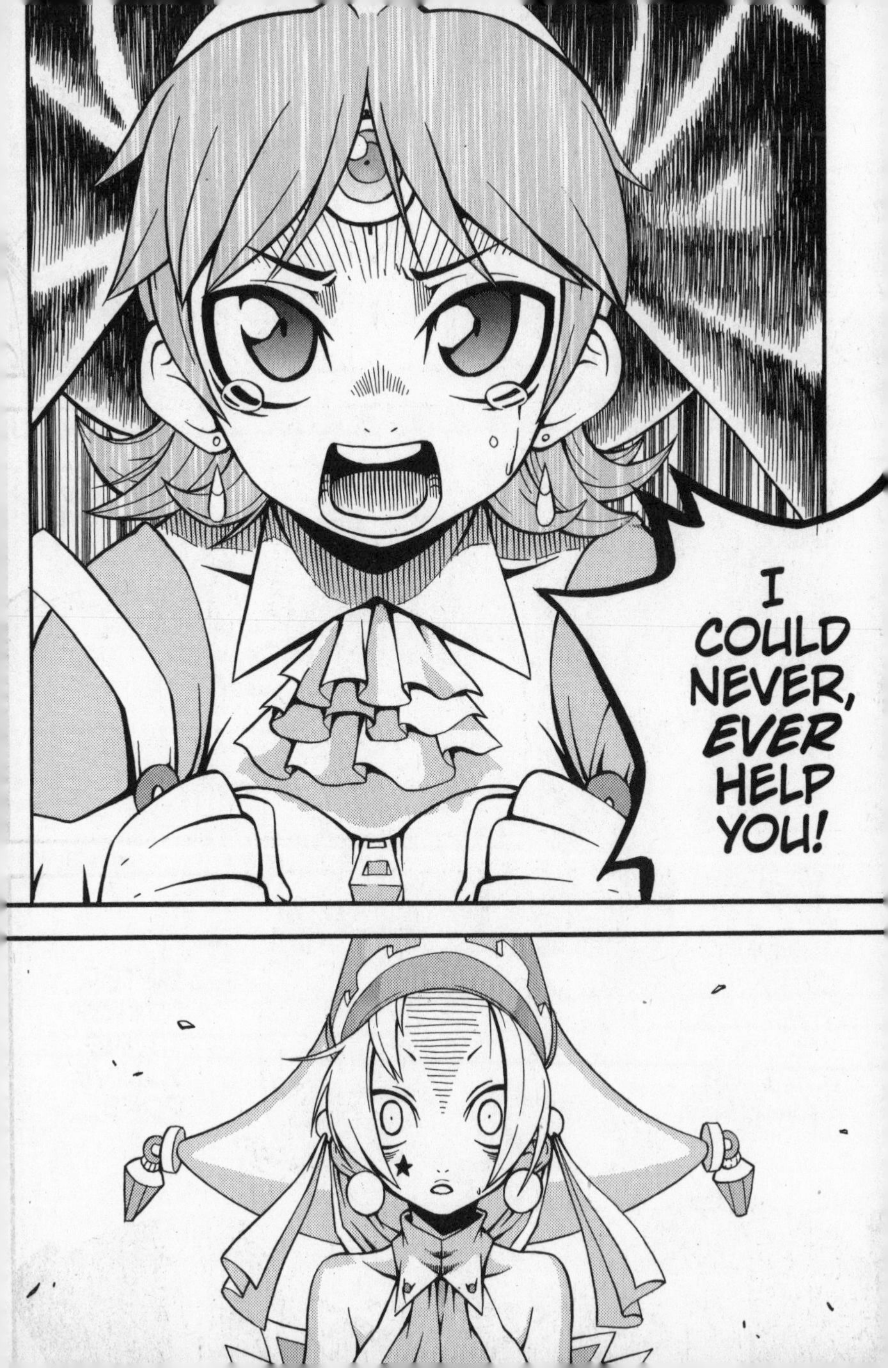
I COULD NEVER, EVER HELP YOU!

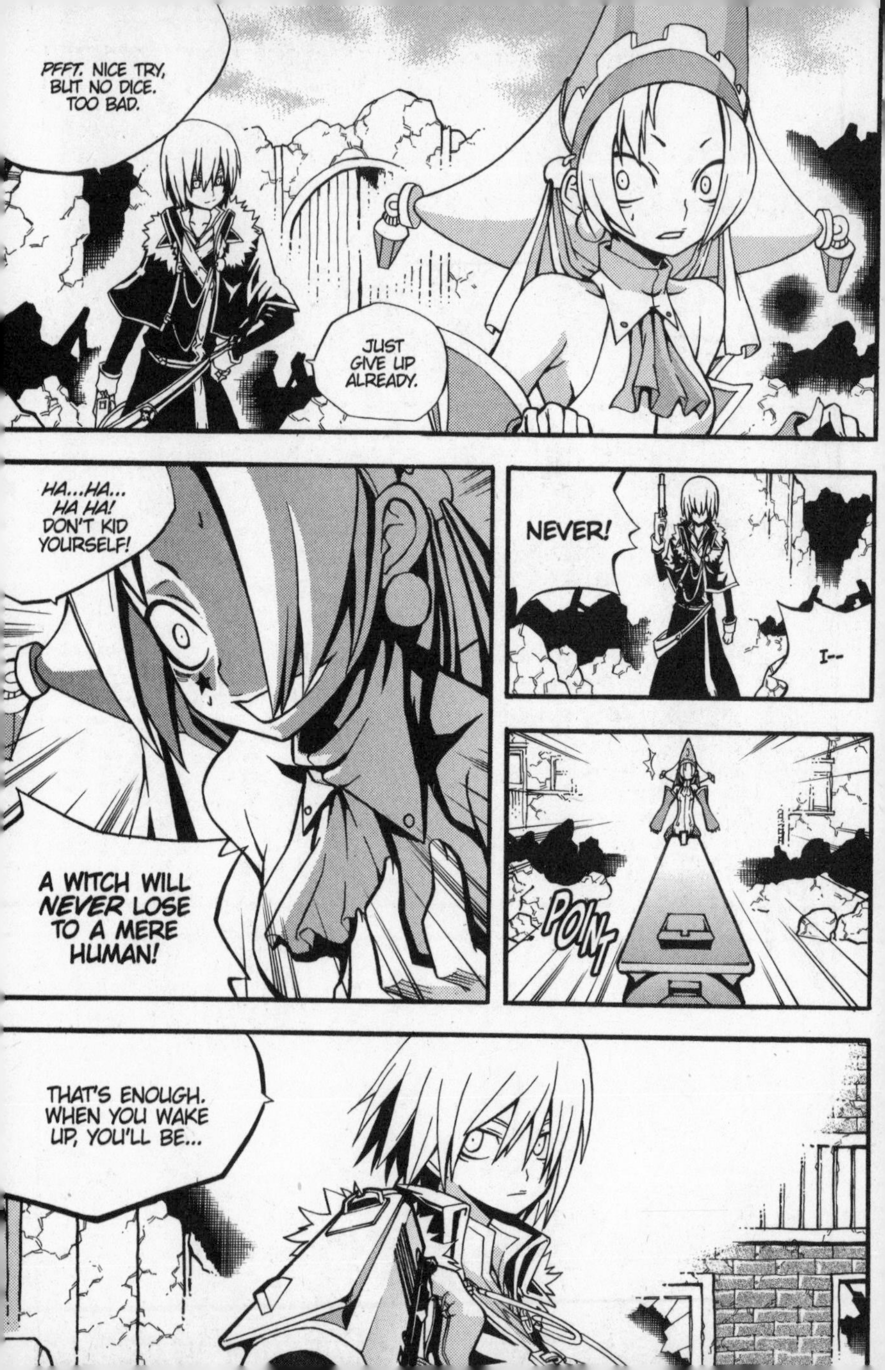
PFFT. NICE TRY, BUT NO DICE. TOO BAD.
JUST GIVE UP ALREADY.
HA...HA... HA HA! DON'T KID YOURSELF!
A WITCH WILL NEVER LOSE TO A MERE HUMAN!
NEVER!
I--
POINT
THAT'S ENOUGH. WHEN YOU WAKE UP, YOU'LL BE...

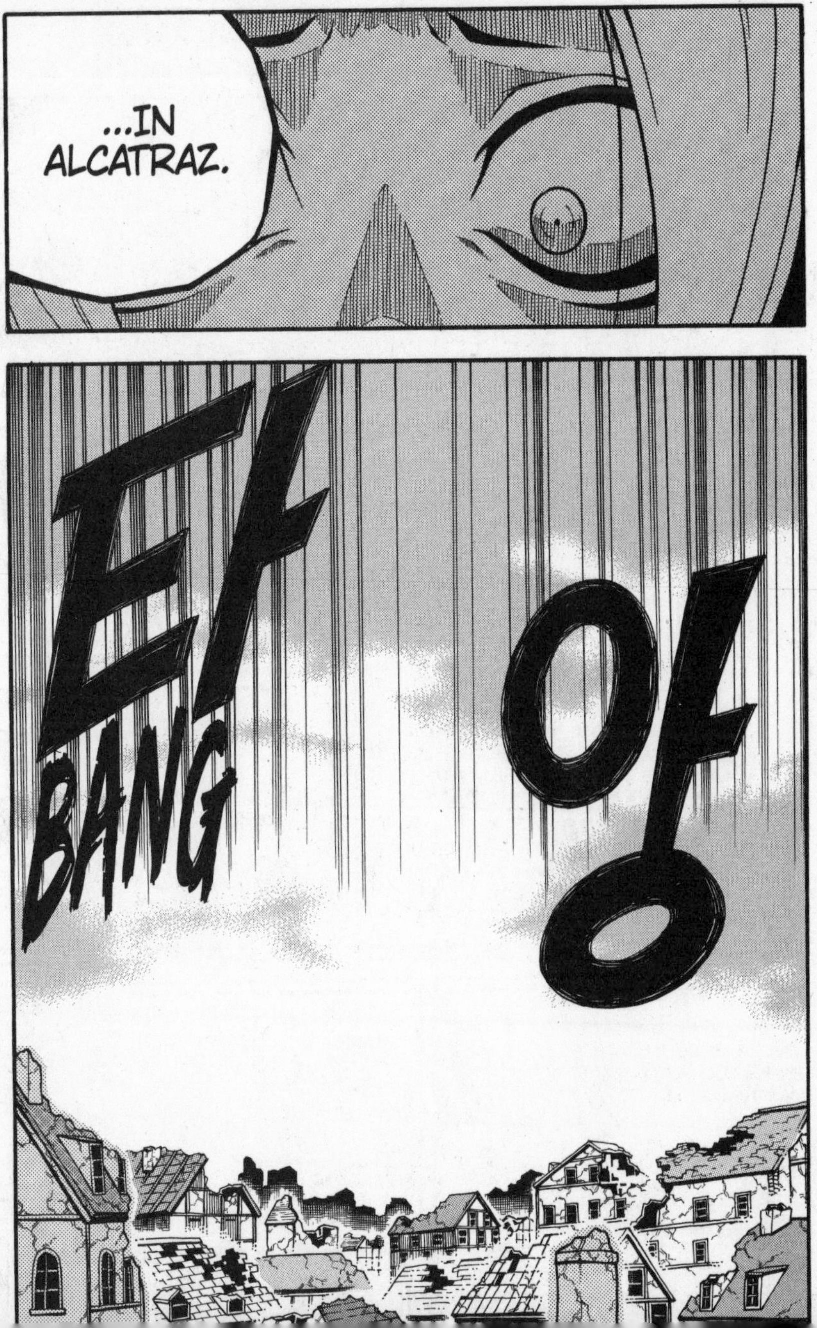
...IN ALCATRAZ.
BANG

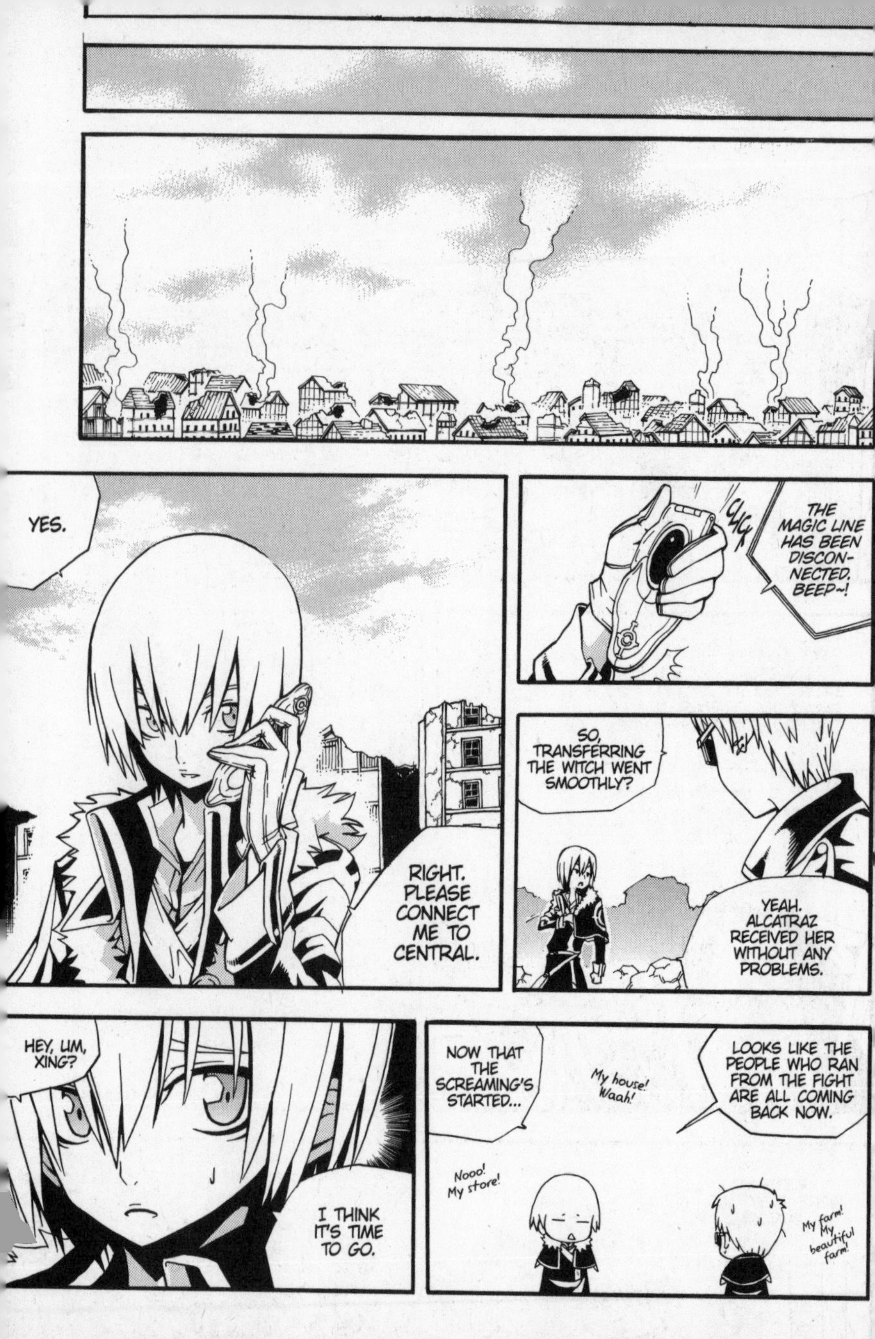
CLICK
THE MAGIC LINE HAS BEEN DISCONNECTED. BEEP~!
SO, TRANSFERRING THE WITCH WENT SMOOTHLY?
YEAH. ALCATRAZ RECEIVED HER WITHOUT ANY PROBLEMS.
YES.
RIGHT. PLEASE CONNECT ME TO CENTRAL.
LOOKS LIKE THE PEOPLE WHO RAN FROM THE FIGHT ARE ALL COMING BACK NOW.
My house! Waah!
NOW THAT THE SCREAMING'S STARTED...
My farm! My beautiful farm!
Nooo! My store!
HEY, UM, XING?
I THINK IT'S TIME TO GO.

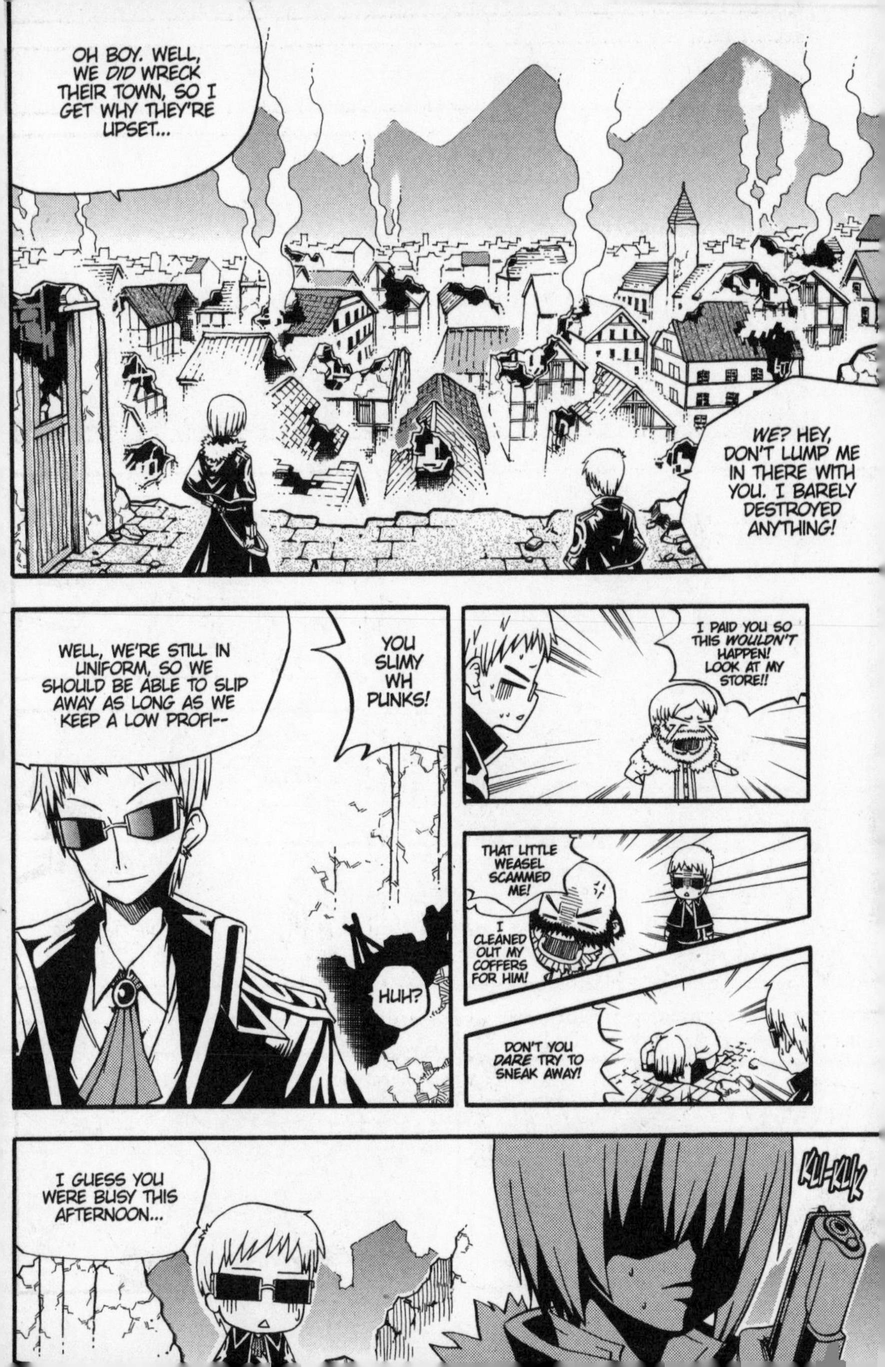
OH BOY. WELL, WE DID WRECK THEIR TOWN, SO I GET WHY THEY'RE UPSET...
WE? HEY, DON'T LUMP ME IN THERE WITH YOU. I BARELY DESTROYED ANYTHING!
WELL, WE'RE STILL IN UNIFORM, SO WE SHOULD BE ABLE TO SLIP AWAY AS LONG AS WE KEEP A LOW PROFI--
YOU SLIMY WH PUNKS!
HUH?
I PAID YOU SO THIS WOULDN'T HAPPEN! LOOK AT MY STORE!!
THAT LITTLE WEASEL SCAMMED ME!
I CLEANED OUT MY COFFERS FOR HIM!
DON'T YOU DARE TRY TO SNEAK AWAY!
I GUESS YOU WERE BUSY THIS AFTERNOON...
KLI-KLIK

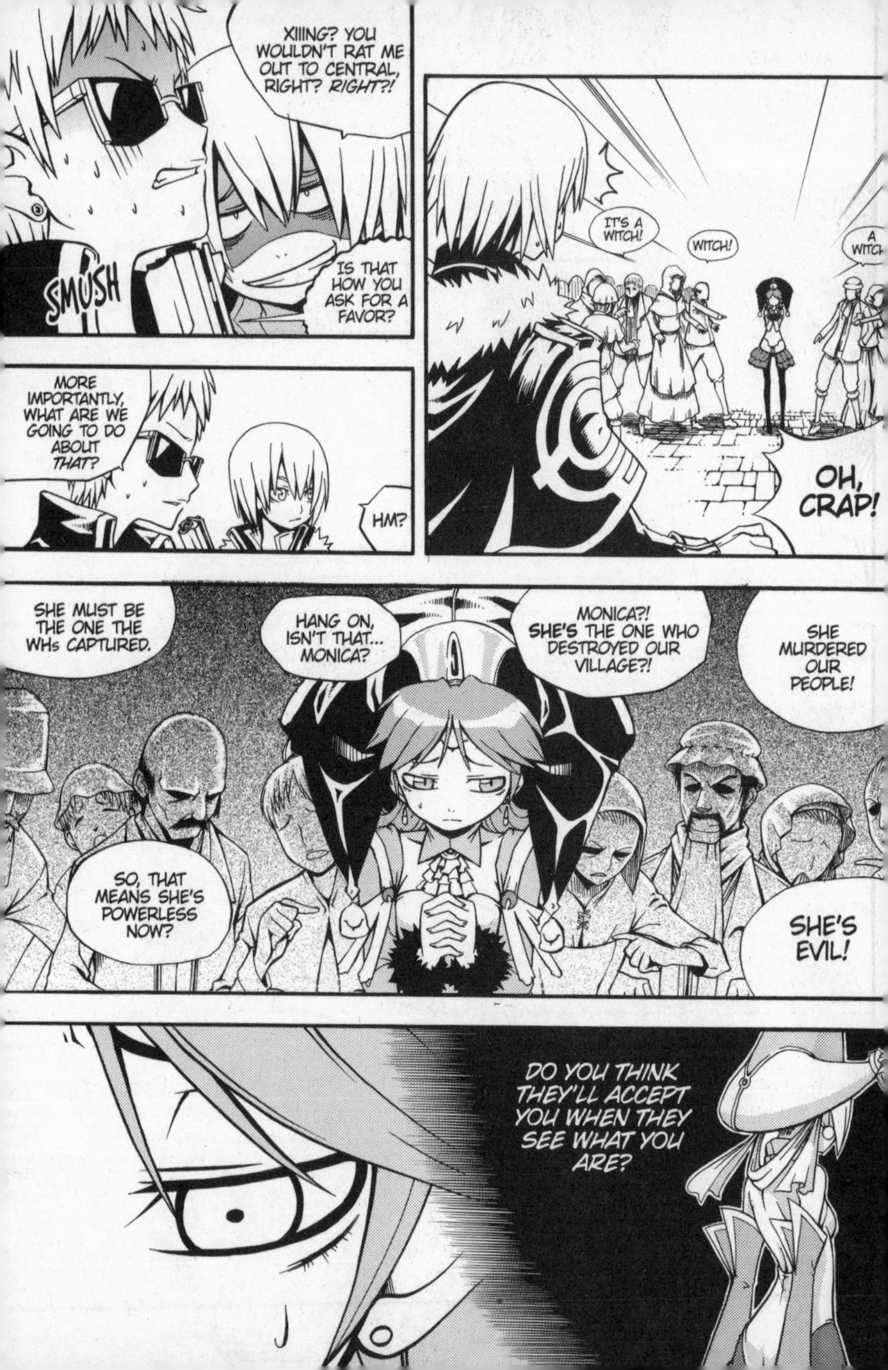
XIIING? YOU WOULDN'T RAT ME OUT TO CENTRAL, RIGHT? *RIGHT?!*
SMUSH
IS THAT HOW YOU ASK FOR A FAVOR?
MORE IMPORTANTLY, WHAT ARE WE GOING TO DO ABOUT *THAT?*
HM?
IT'S A WITCH!
WITCH!
A WITCH
OH, CRAP!
SHE MUST BE THE ONE THE WHs CAPTURED.
HANG ON, ISN'T THAT... MONICA?
MONICA?! SHE'S THE ONE WHO DESTROYED OUR VILLAGE?!
SHE MURDERED OUR PEOPLE!
SO, THAT MEANS SHE'S POWERLESS NOW?
SHE'S EVIL!
DO YOU THINK THEY'LL ACCEPT YOU WHEN THEY SEE WHAT YOU ARE?

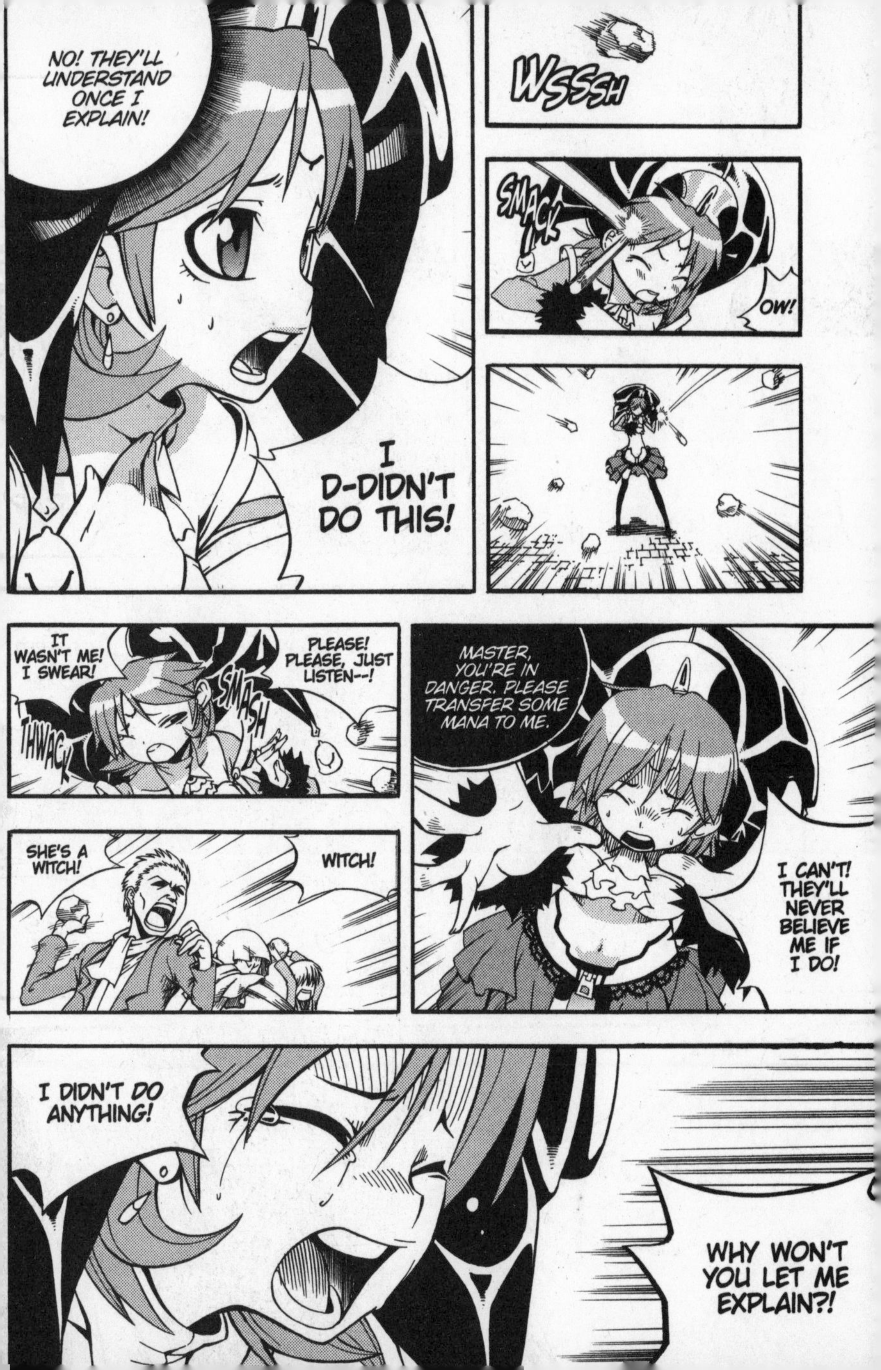

NO! THEY'LL UNDERSTAND ONCE I EXPLAIN!
I D-DIDN'T DO THIS!
WSSSH
SMACK
OW!
MASTER, YOU'RE IN DANGER. PLEASE TRANSFER SOME MANA TO ME.
I CAN'T! THEY'LL NEVER BELIEVE ME IF I DO!
PLEASE! PLEASE, JUST LISTEN--!
SMASH
IT WASN'T ME! I SWEAR!
THWACK
WITCH!
SHE'S A WITCH!
WHY WON'T YOU LET ME EXPLAIN?!
I DIDN'T DO ANYTHING!

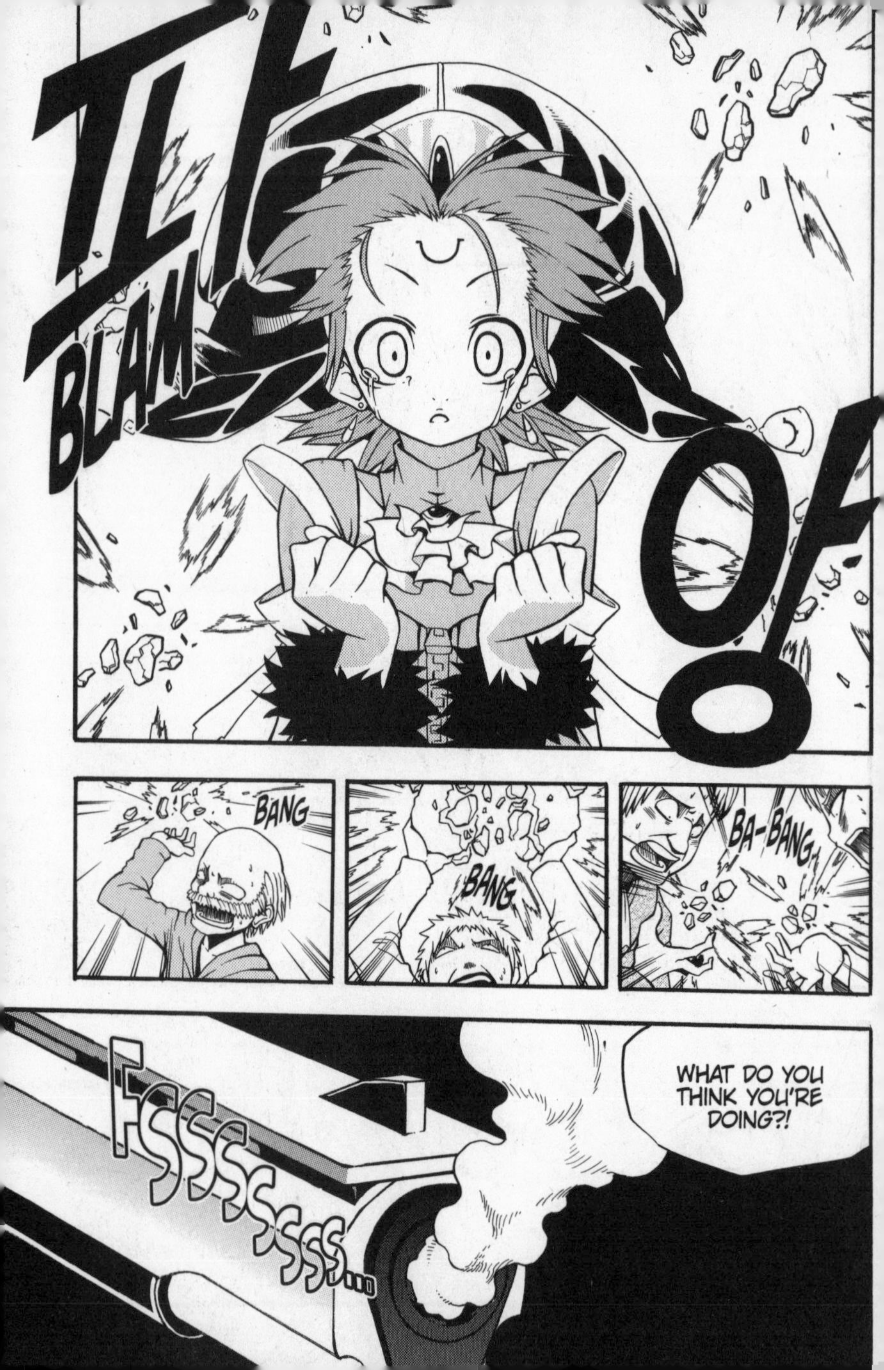
BLAM
BA-BANG
BANG
BANG
WHAT DO YOU THINK YOU'RE DOING?!
FSSSSsss...

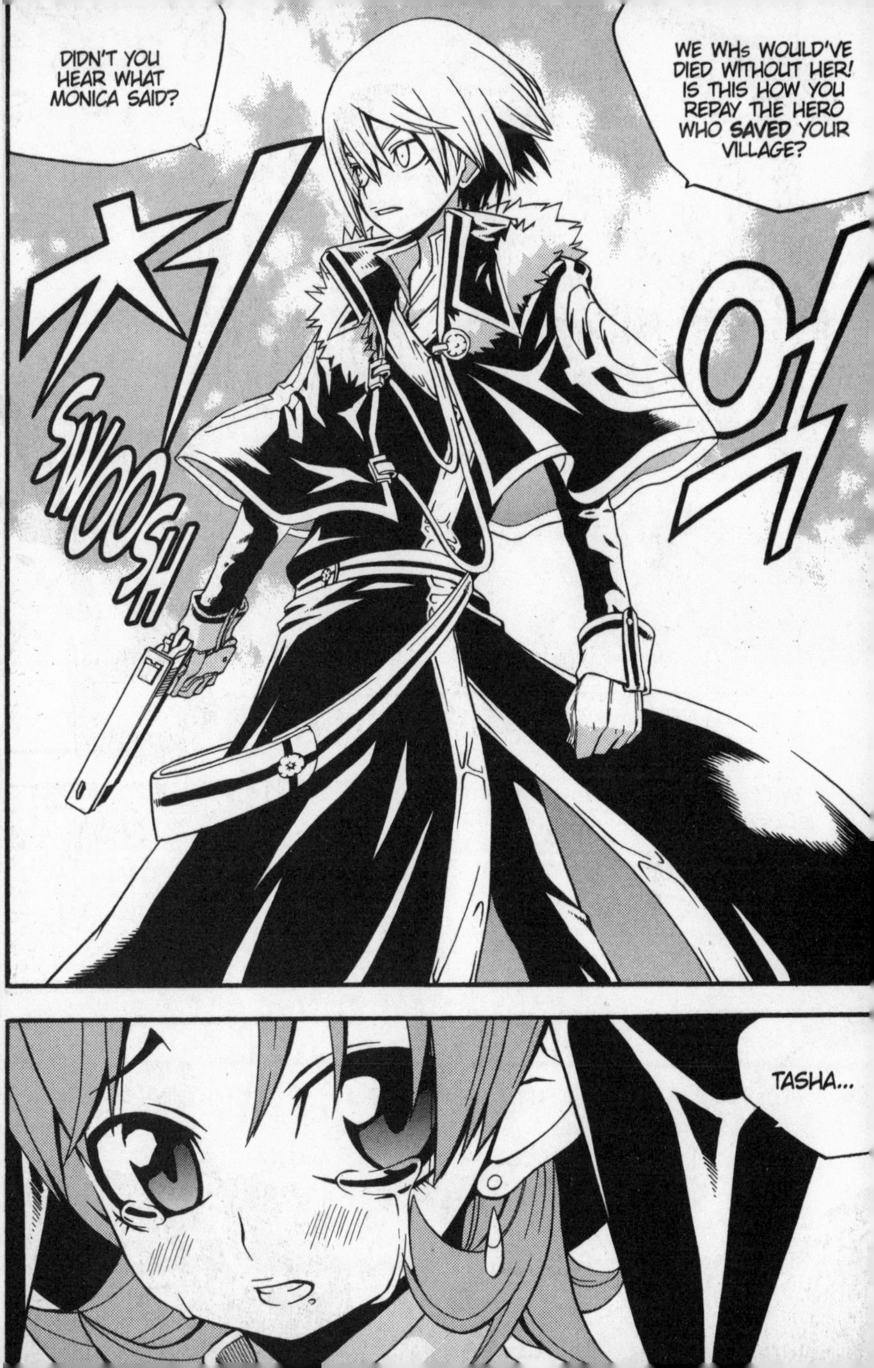
WE WHs WOULD'VE DIED WITHOUT HER! IS THIS HOW YOU REPAY THE HERO WHO **SAVED** YOUR VILLAGE?
DIDN'T YOU HEAR WHAT MONICA SAID?
SWOOSH
TASHA...

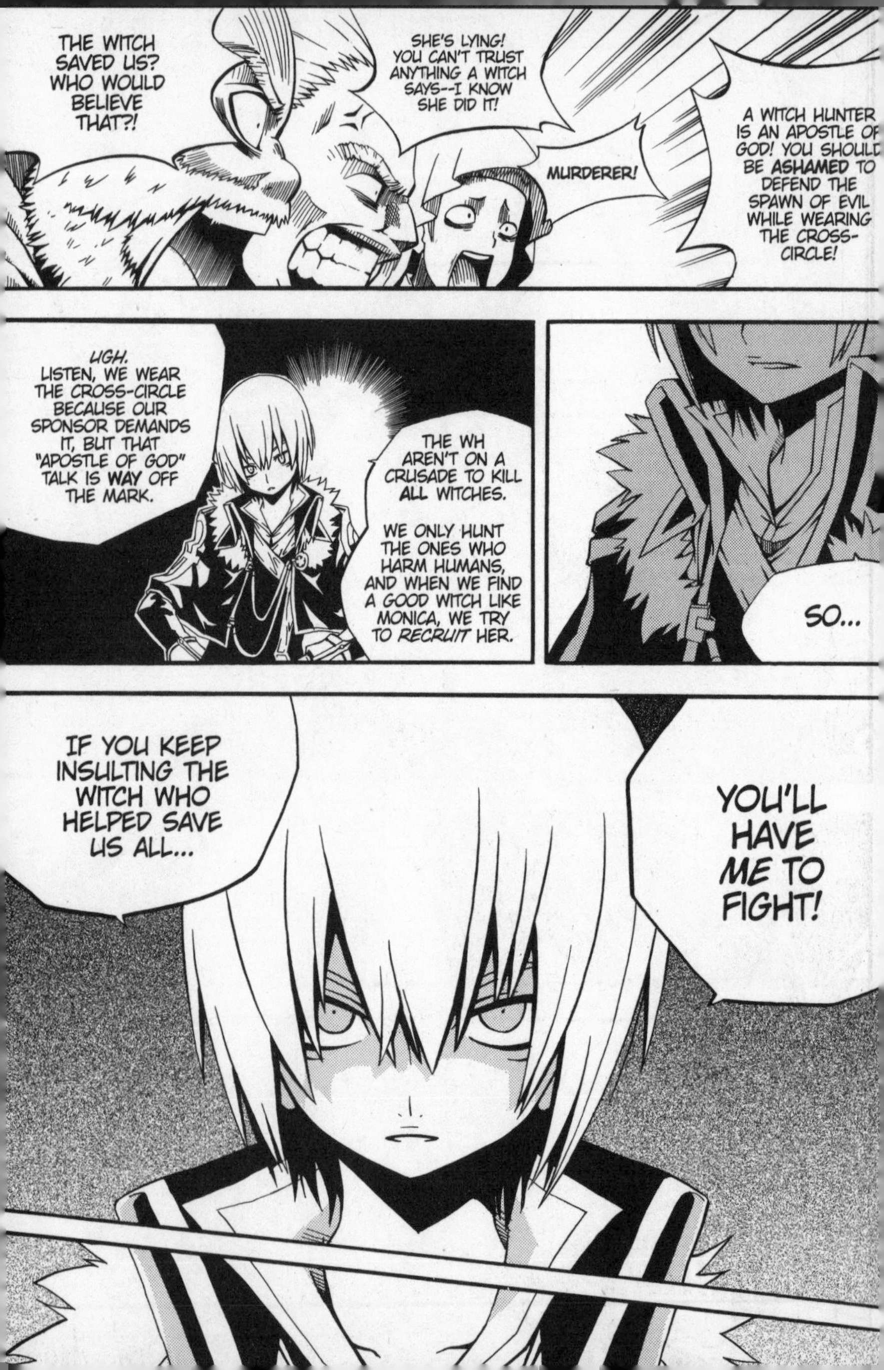
THE WITCH SAVED US? WHO WOULD BELIEVE THAT?!
SHE'S LYING! YOU CAN'T TRUST ANYTHING A WITCH SAYS--I KNOW SHE DID IT!
MURDERER!
A WITCH HUNTER IS AN APOSTLE OF GOD! YOU SHOULD BE ASHAMED TO DEFEND THE SPAWN OF EVIL WHILE WEARING THE CROSS-CIRCLE!
UGH. LISTEN, WE WEAR THE CROSS-CIRCLE BECAUSE OUR SPONSOR DEMANDS IT, BUT THAT "APOSTLE OF GOD" TALK IS WAY OFF THE MARK.
THE WH AREN'T ON A CRUSADE TO KILL ALL WITCHES.
WE ONLY HUNT THE ONES WHO HARM HUMANS, AND WHEN WE FIND A GOOD WITCH LIKE MONICA, WE TRY TO RECRUIT HER.
SO...
IF YOU KEEP INSULTING THE WITCH WHO HELPED SAVE US ALL...
YOU'LL HAVE ME TO FIGHT!

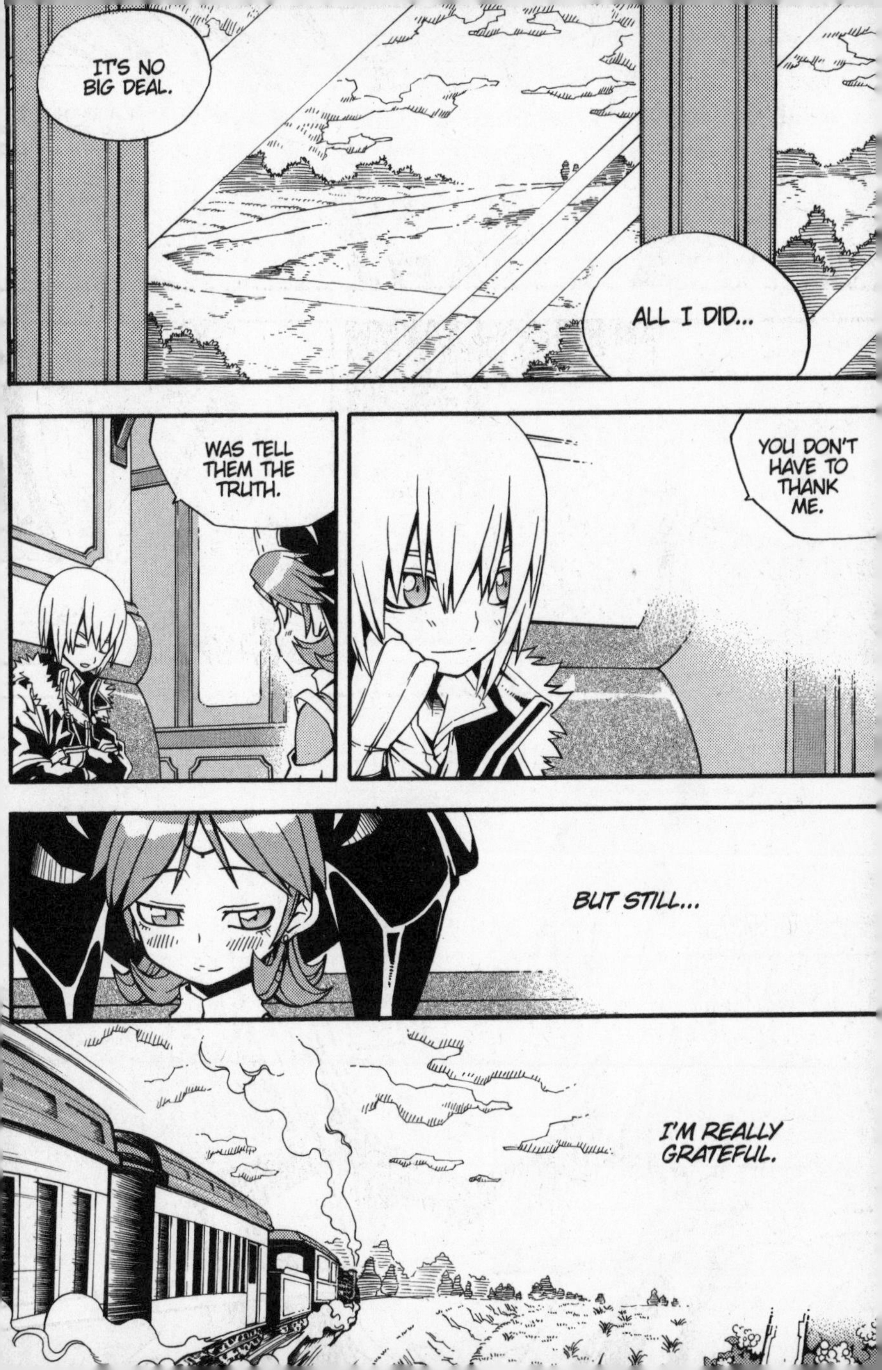
IT'S NO BIG DEAL.
ALL I DID...
WAS TELL THEM THE TRUTH.
YOU DON'T HAVE TO THANK ME.
BUT STILL...
I'M REALLY GRATEFUL.

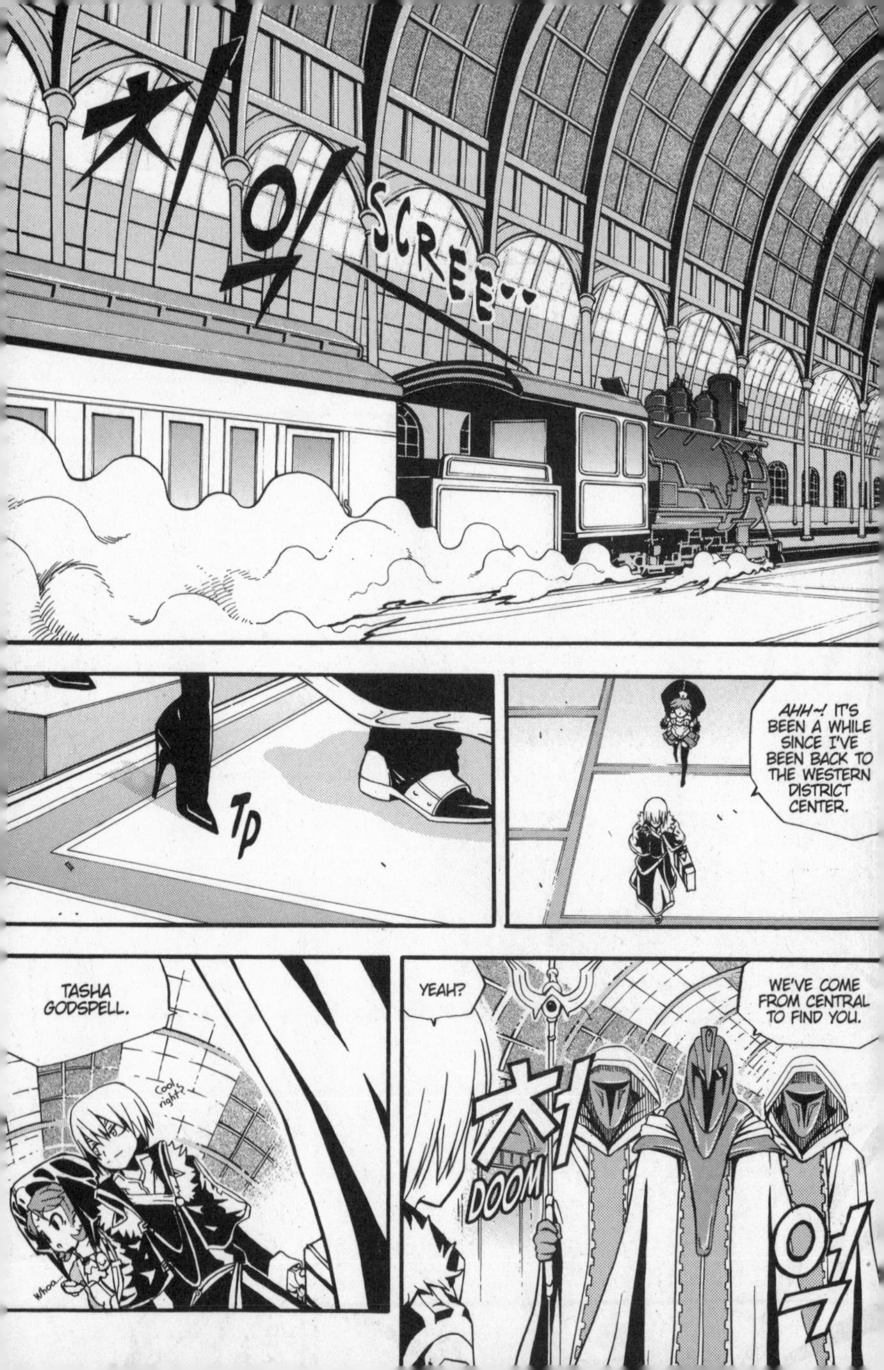
SCREE--
TP
AHH~! IT'S BEEN A WHILE SINCE I'VE BEEN BACK TO THE WESTERN DISTRICT CENTER.
TASHA GODSPELL.
cool, right?
whoa...
YEAH?
WE'VE COME FROM CENTRAL TO FIND YOU.
DOOM

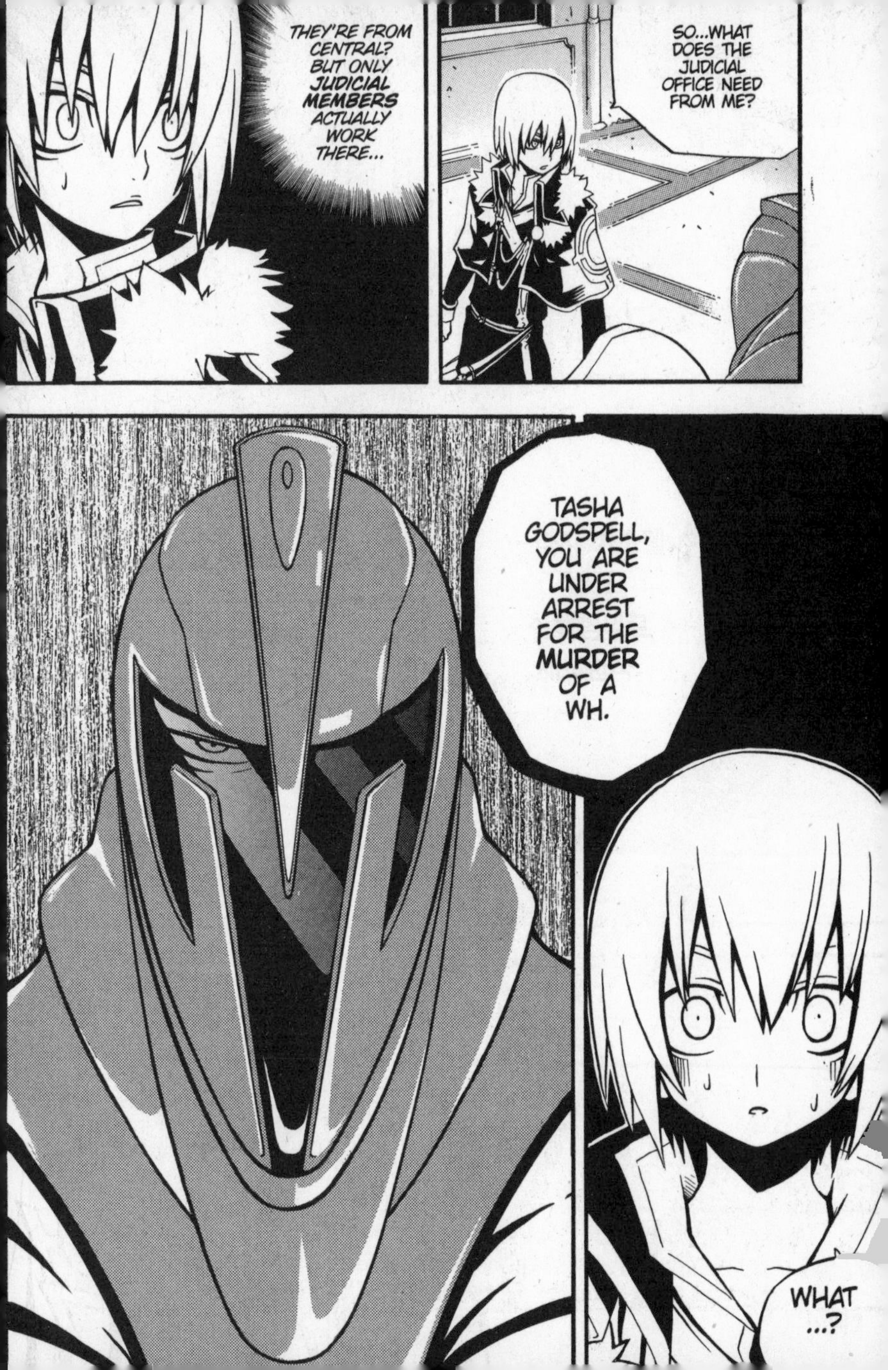
THEY'RE FROM CENTRAL? BUT ONLY JUDICIAL MEMBERS ACTUALLY WORK THERE...
SO...WHAT DOES THE JUDICIAL OFFICE NEED FROM ME?
TASHA GODSPELL, YOU ARE UNDER ARREST FOR THE MURDER OF A WH.
WHAT ...?

IF THEY DIDN'T BECOME WHS...

LOAN SHARK.
PAY UP NOW, BEFORE THINGS GET... UNPLEAS-ANT.
FLASH SPEED DELIVERY!
SELLS HIS OWN LINE OF SCANNERS!
Scanner
NOTHING BEATS EARTH SCAN!
AND HALLOWEEN...

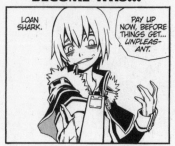

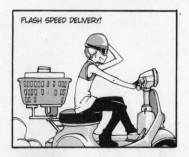

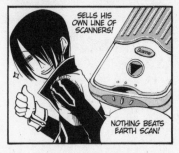

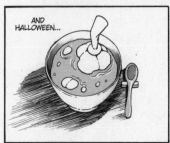

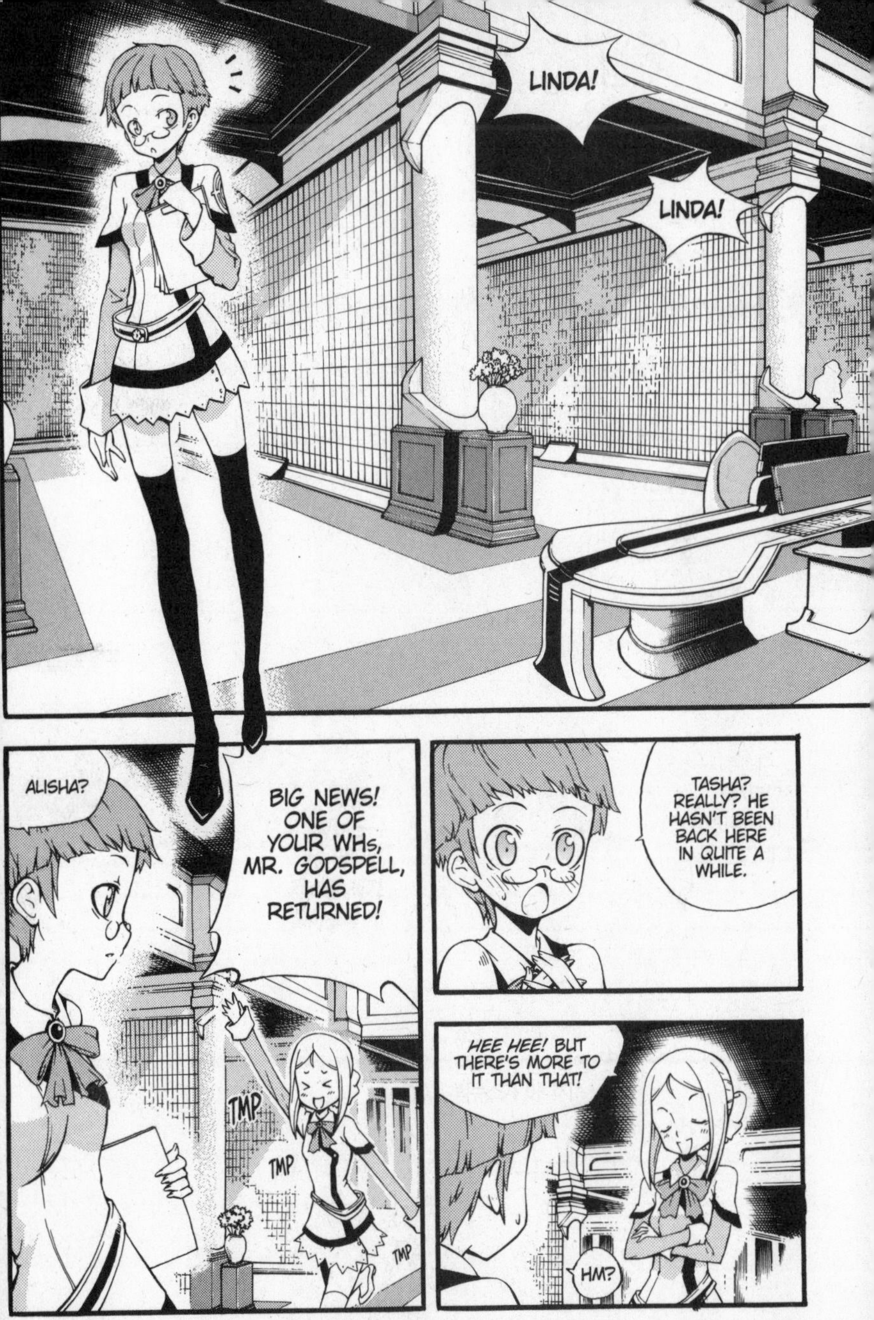
LINDA!
LINDA!
ALISHA?
BIG NEWS! ONE OF YOUR WHs, MR. GODSPELL, HAS RETURNED!
TMP
TMP
TMP
TASHA? REALLY? HE HASN'T BEEN BACK HERE IN QUITE A WHILE.
HEE HEE! BUT THERE'S MORE TO IT THAN THAT!
HM?

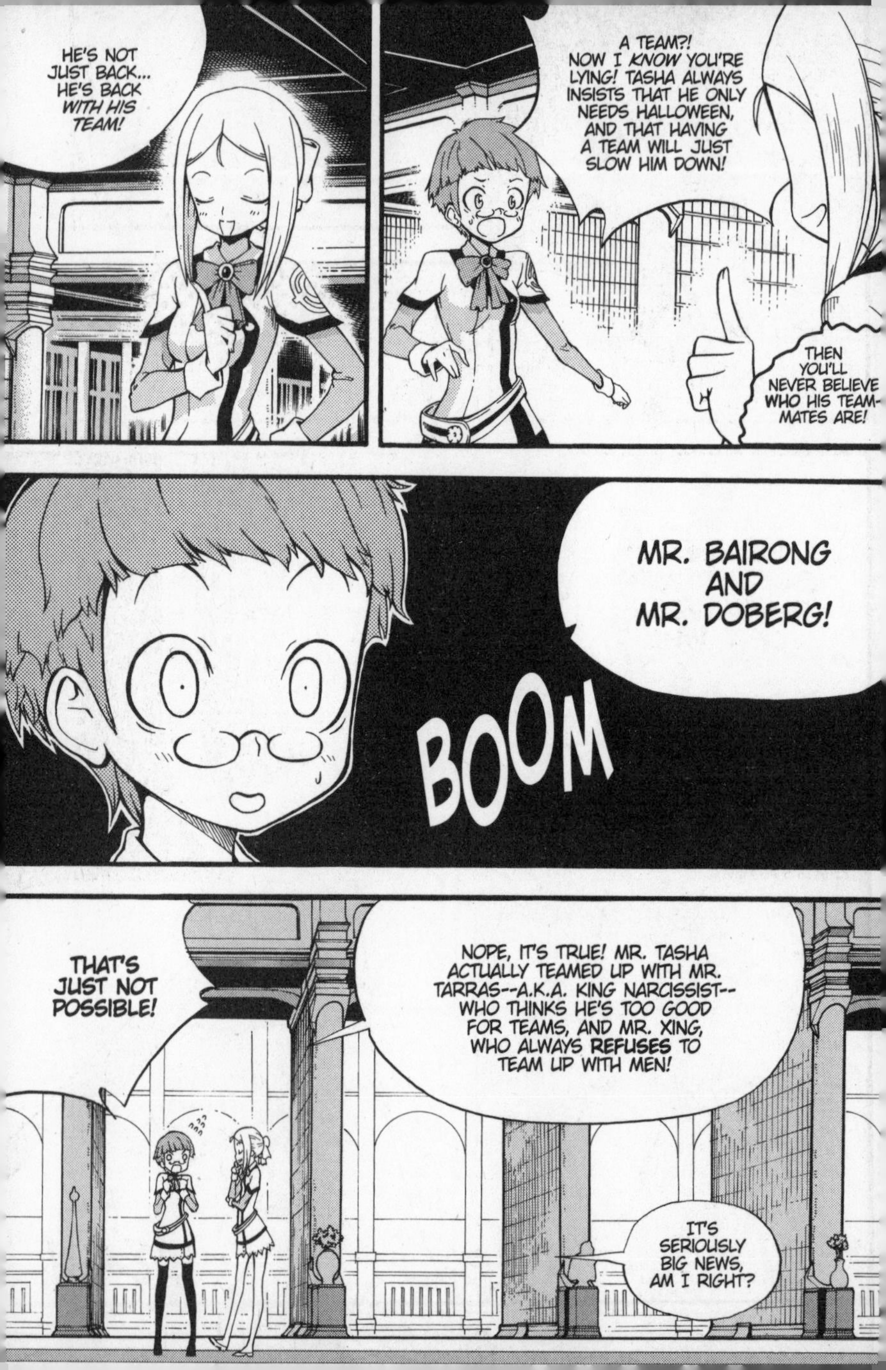
HE'S NOT JUST BACK... HE'S BACK WITH HIS TEAM!
A TEAM?! NOW I KNOW YOU'RE LYING! TASHA ALWAYS INSISTS THAT HE ONLY NEEDS HALLOWEEN, AND THAT HAVING A TEAM WILL JUST SLOW HIM DOWN!
THEN YOU'LL NEVER BELIEVE WHO HIS TEAM-MATES ARE!
MR. BAIRONG AND MR. DOBERG!
BOOM
THAT'S JUST NOT POSSIBLE!
NOPE, IT'S TRUE! MR. TASHA ACTUALLY TEAMED UP WITH MR. TARRAS--A.K.A. KING NARCISSIST--WHO THINKS HE'S TOO GOOD FOR TEAMS, AND MR. XING, WHO ALWAYS REFUSES TO TEAM UP WITH MEN!
IT'S SERIOUSLY BIG NEWS, AM I RIGHT?

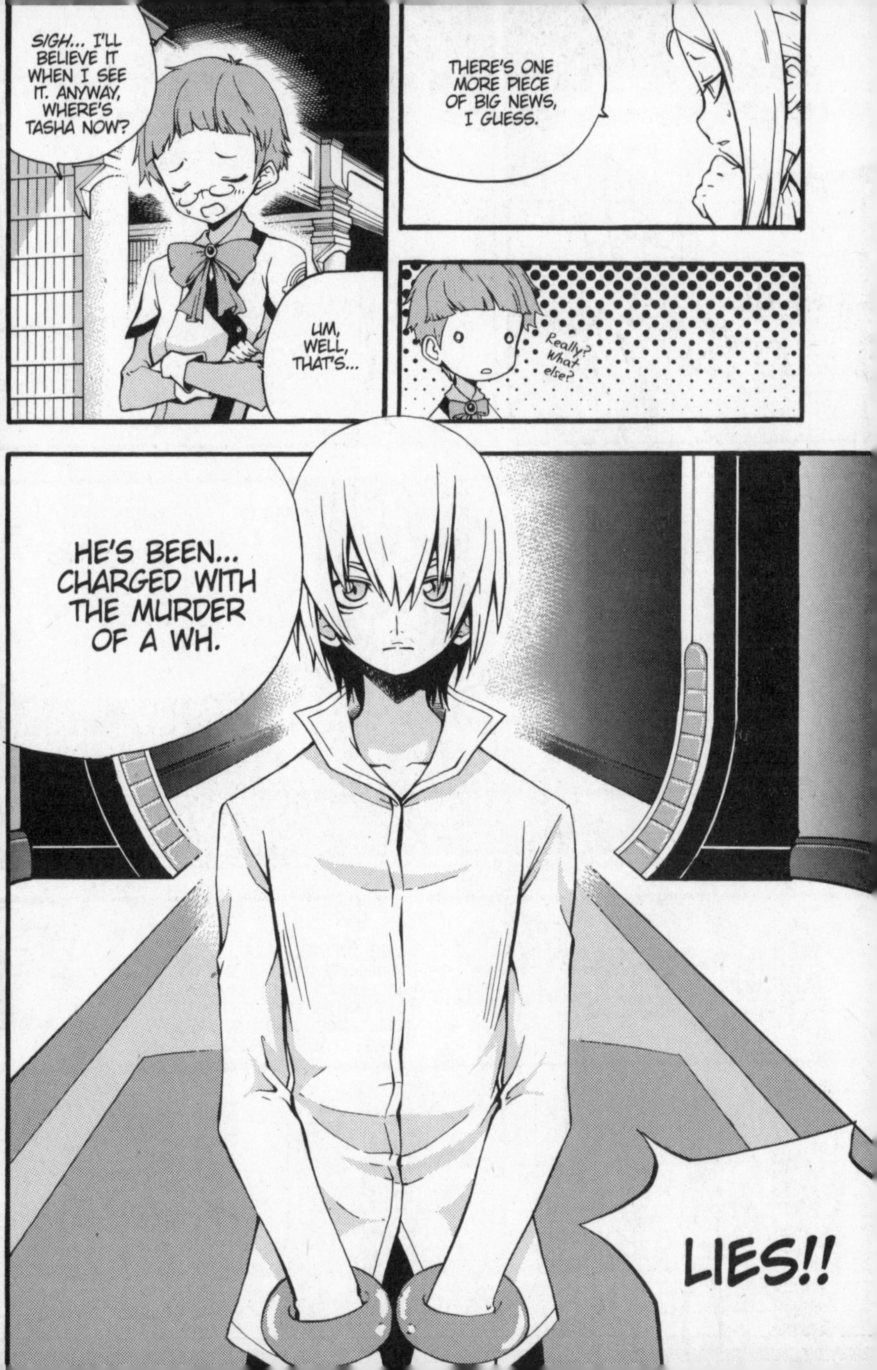
THERE'S ONE MORE PIECE OF BIG NEWS, I GUESS.
SIGH... I'LL BELIEVE IT WHEN I SEE IT. ANYWAY, WHERE'S TASHA NOW?
Really? What else?
UM, WELL, THAT'S...
HE'S BEEN... CHARGED WITH THE MURDER OF A WH.
LIES!!

10. EVIDENCE/PROOF

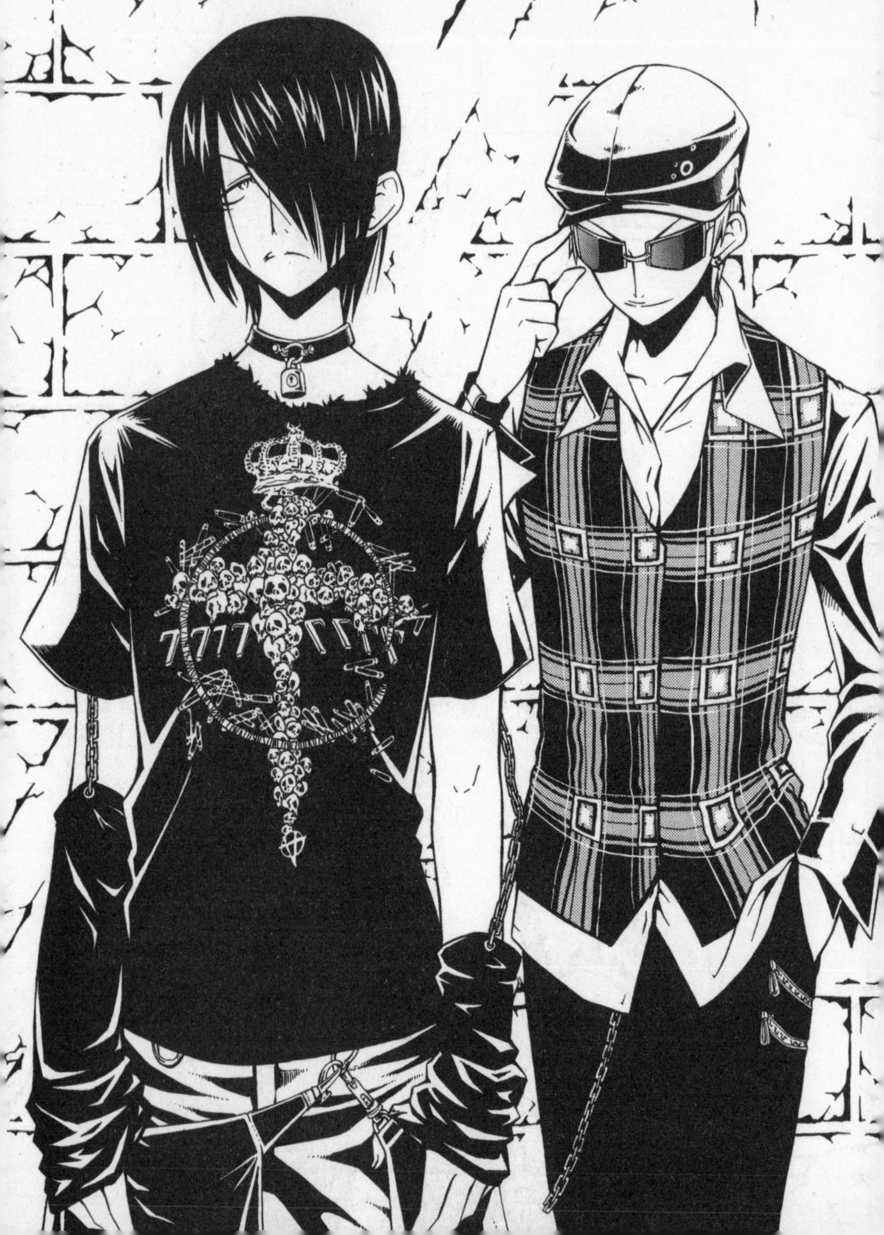

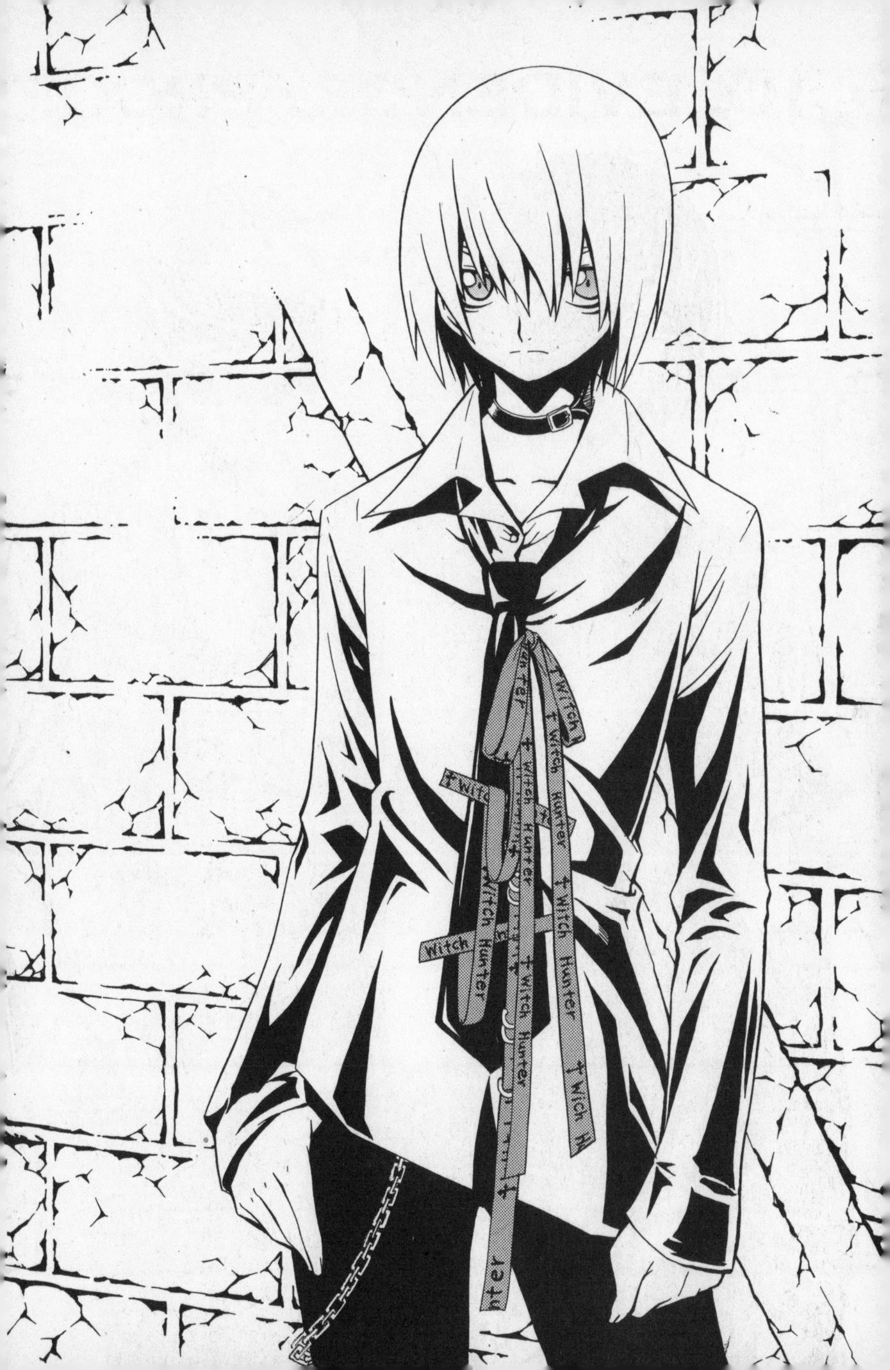

Witch Hunter

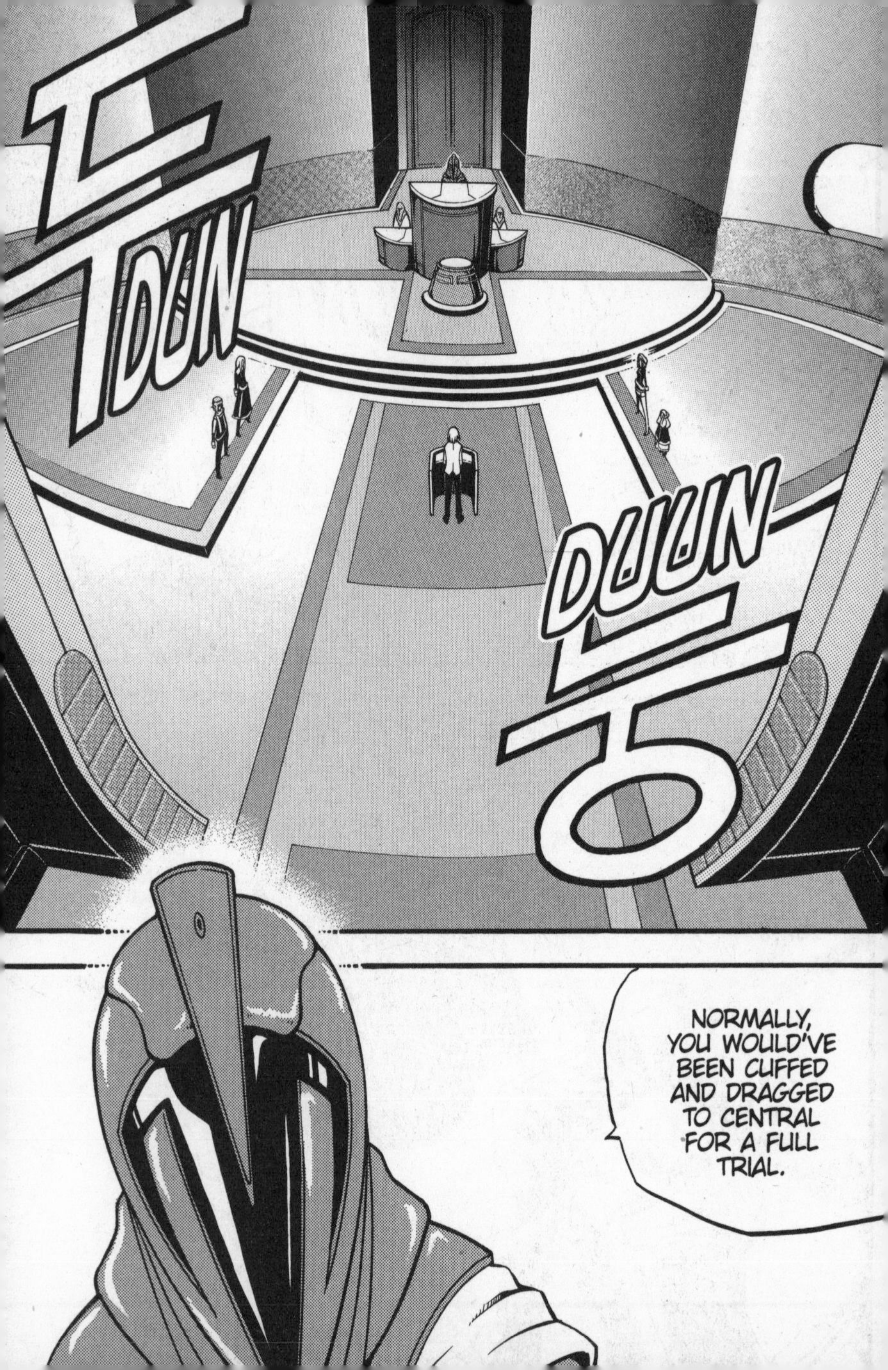
DUN
DUUN
NORMALLY, YOU WOULD'VE BEEN CUFFED AND DRAGGED TO CENTRAL FOR A FULL TRIAL.

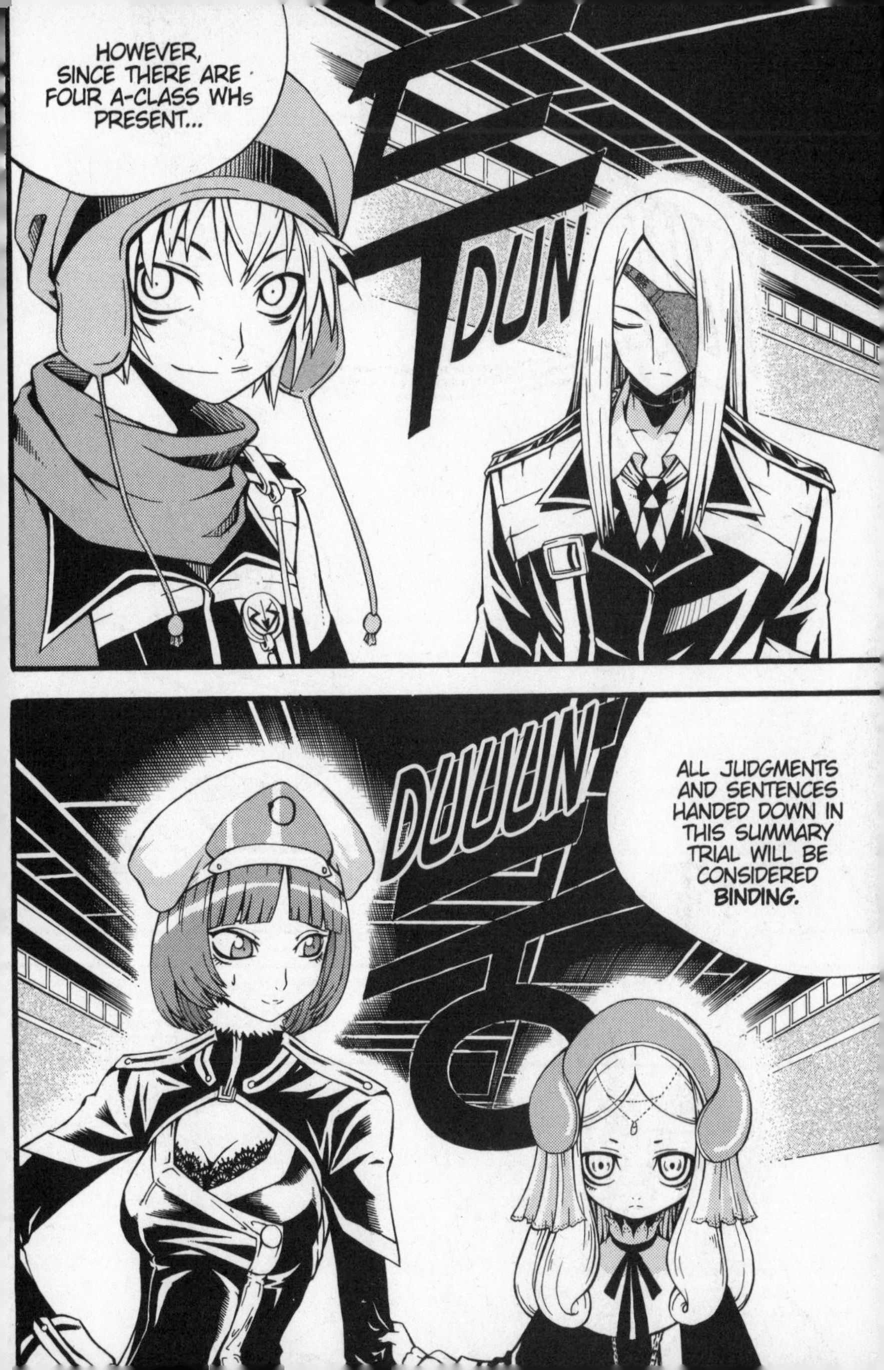
HOWEVER, SINCE THERE ARE FOUR A-CLASS WHs PRESENT...
DUN
DUUUN
ALL JUDGMENTS AND SENTENCES HANDED DOWN IN THIS SUMMARY TRIAL WILL BE CONSIDERED BINDING.

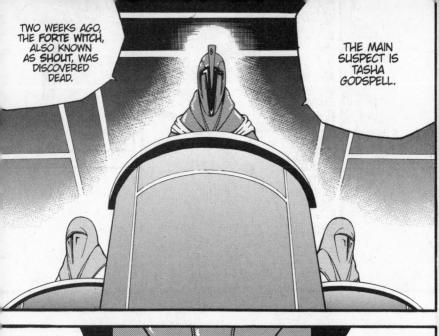

TWO WEEKS AGO, THE FORTE WITCH, ALSO KNOWN AS SHOUT, WAS DISCOVERED DEAD.

THE MAIN SUSPECT IS TASHA GODSPELL.

ANY OBJECTIONS...

TASHA GODSPELL?

HMPH. THIS IS ABSURD.

WHEN WHs DIE, IT'S ALWAYS A WITCH. WHY ARE YOU TRYING TO BLAME THIS ON ME?

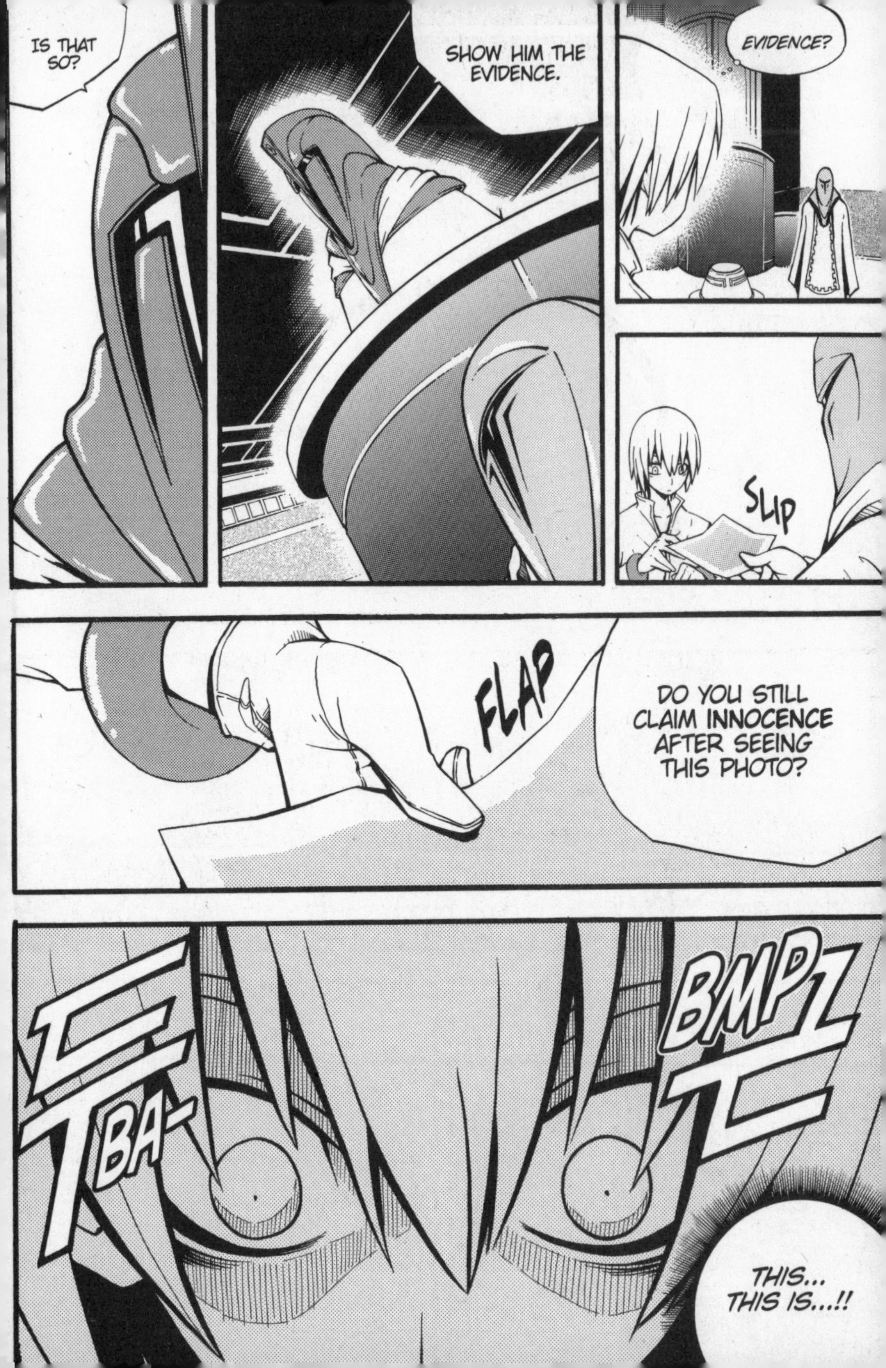
IS THAT SO?
SHOW HIM THE EVIDENCE.
EVIDENCE?
SLIP
FLAP
DO YOU STILL CLAIM INNOCENCE AFTER SEEING THIS PHOTO?
BA-BMP
THIS... THIS IS...!!

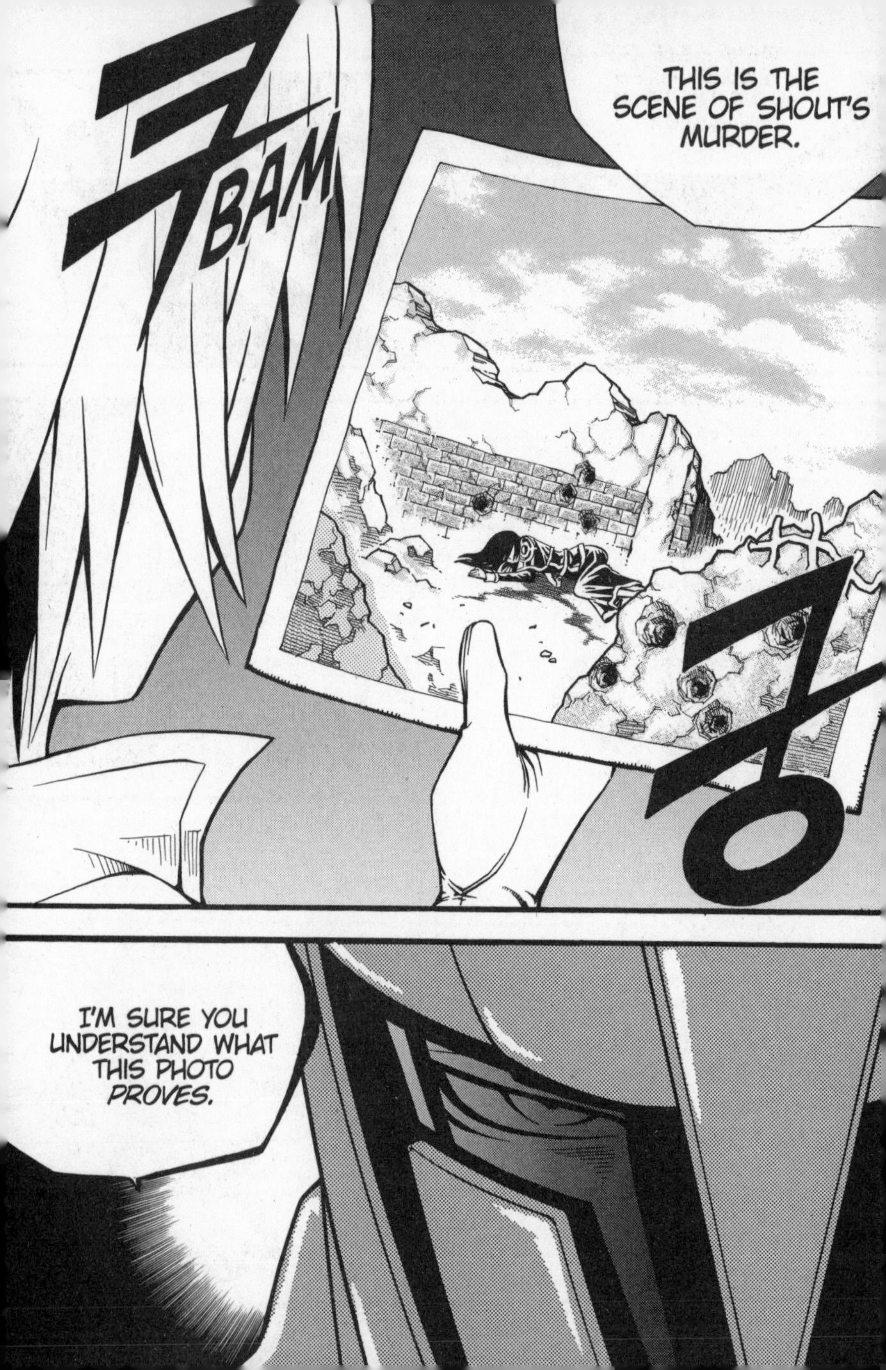
THIS IS THE SCENE OF SHOUT'S MURDER.
BAM
I'M SURE YOU UNDERSTAND WHAT THIS PHOTO *PROVES.*

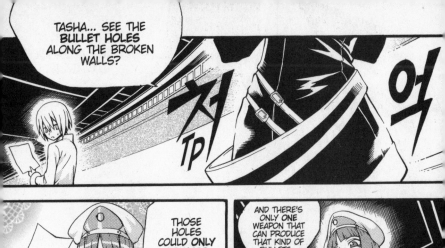

TASHA... SEE THE BULLET HOLES ALONG THE BROKEN WALLS?

THOSE HOLES COULD ONLY BE MADE BY HIGH LEVEL MAGIC.

AND THERE'S ONLY ONE WEAPON THAT CAN PRODUCE THAT KIND OF BULLETS...

FLICK

WHIP

THIS MANA GUN.

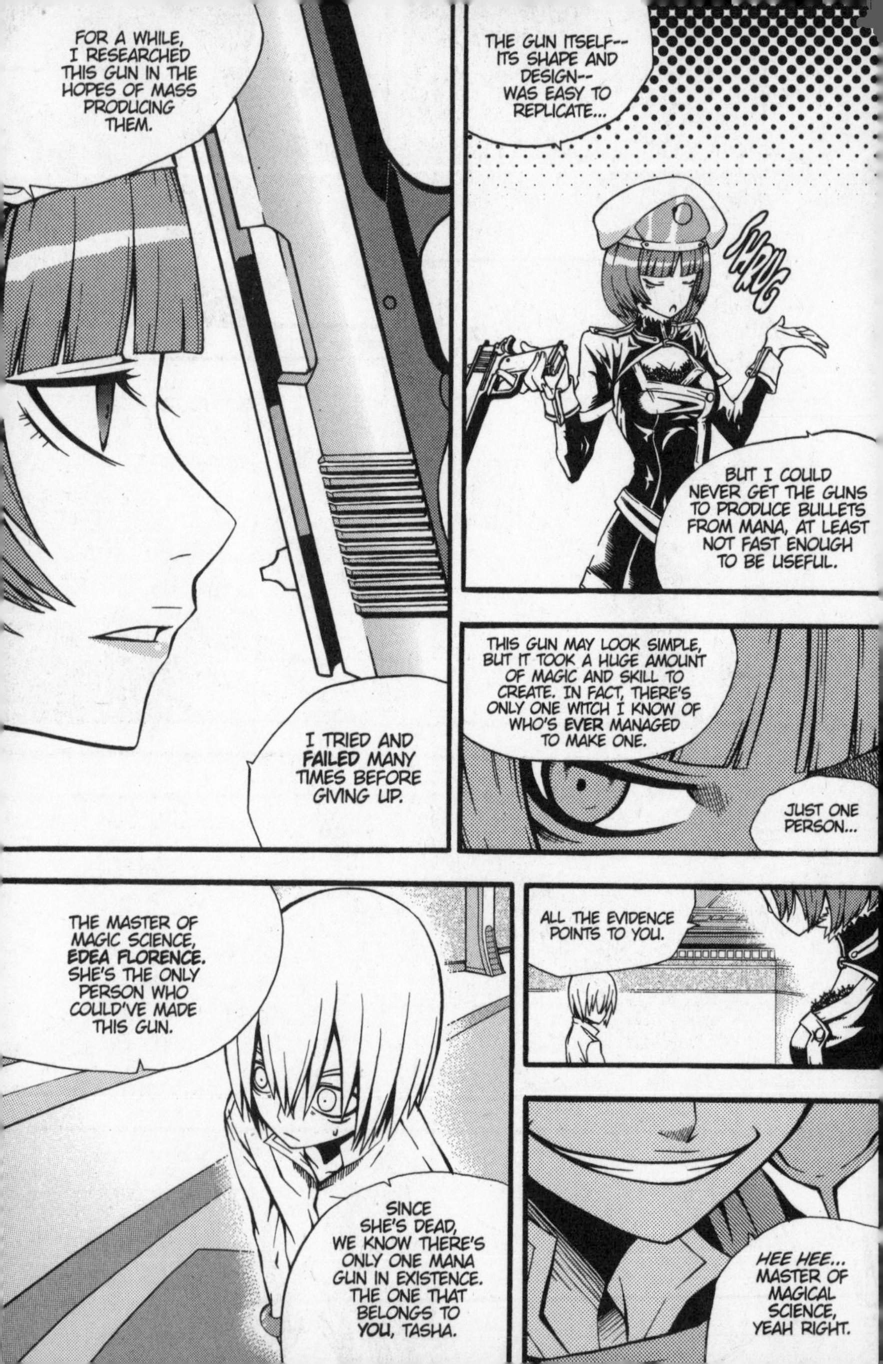
FOR A WHILE, I RESEARCHED THIS GUN IN THE HOPES OF MASS PRODUCING THEM.
THE GUN ITSELF-- ITS SHAPE AND DESIGN-- WAS EASY TO REPLICATE...
SHRUG
BUT I COULD NEVER GET THE GUNS TO PRODUCE BULLETS FROM MANA, AT LEAST NOT FAST ENOUGH TO BE USEFUL.
I TRIED AND FAILED MANY TIMES BEFORE GIVING UP.
THIS GUN MAY LOOK SIMPLE, BUT IT TOOK A HUGE AMOUNT OF MAGIC AND SKILL TO CREATE. IN FACT, THERE'S ONLY ONE WITCH I KNOW OF WHO'S EVER MANAGED TO MAKE ONE.
JUST ONE PERSON...
THE MASTER OF MAGIC SCIENCE, EDEA FLORENCE. SHE'S THE ONLY PERSON WHO COULD'VE MADE THIS GUN.
ALL THE EVIDENCE POINTS TO YOU.
SINCE SHE'S DEAD, WE KNOW THERE'S ONLY ONE MANA GUN IN EXISTENCE. THE ONE THAT BELONGS TO YOU, TASHA.
HEE HEE... MASTER OF MAGICAL SCIENCE, YEAH RIGHT.

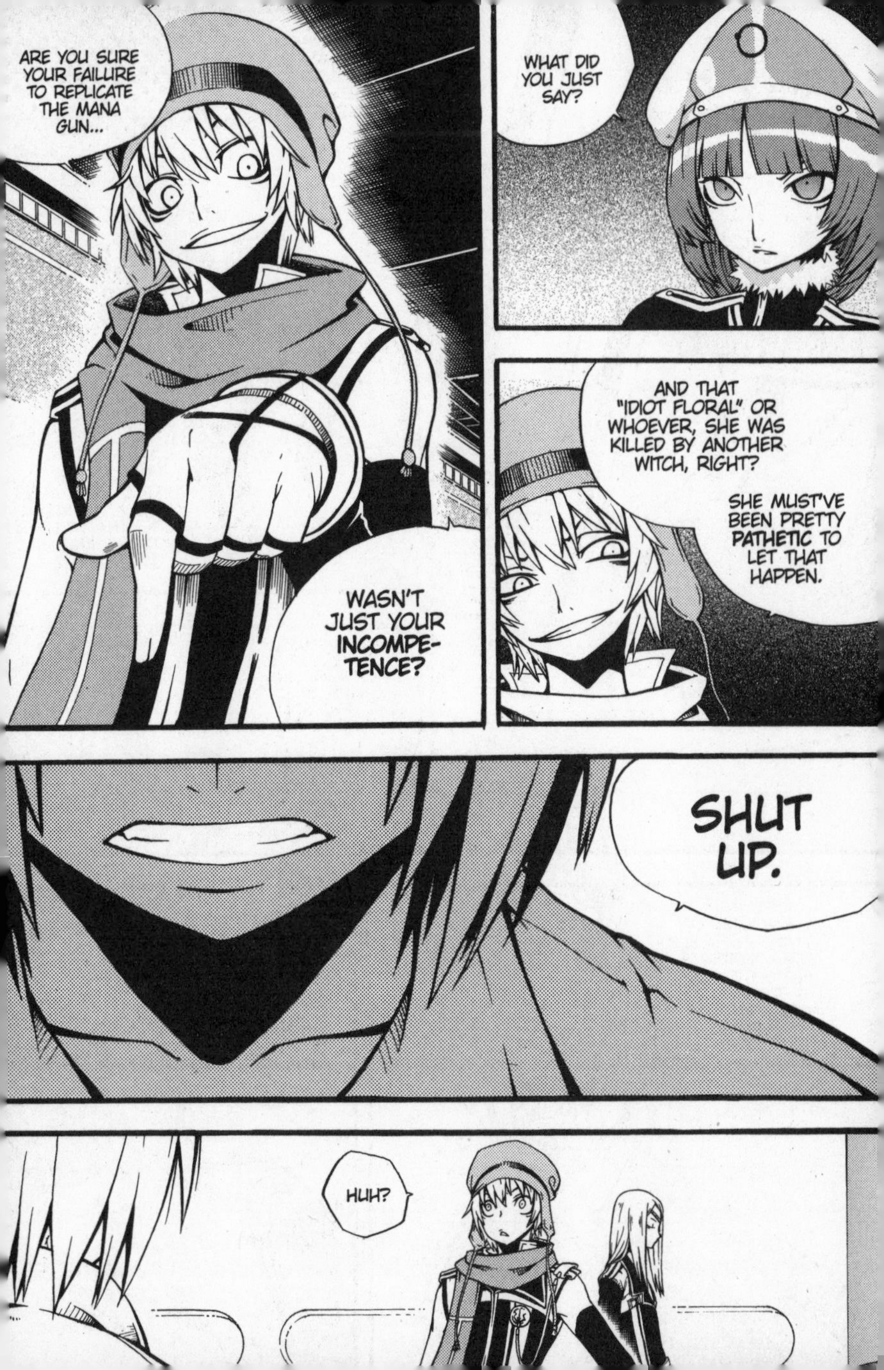
ARE YOU SURE YOUR FAILURE TO REPLICATE THE MANA GUN...
WASN'T JUST YOUR INCOMPE- TENCE?
WHAT DID YOU JUST SAY?
AND THAT "IDIOT FLORAL" OR WHOEVER, SHE WAS KILLED BY ANOTHER WITCH, RIGHT?
SHE MUST'VE BEEN PRETTY PATHETIC TO LET THAT HAPPEN.
SHUT UP.
HUH?

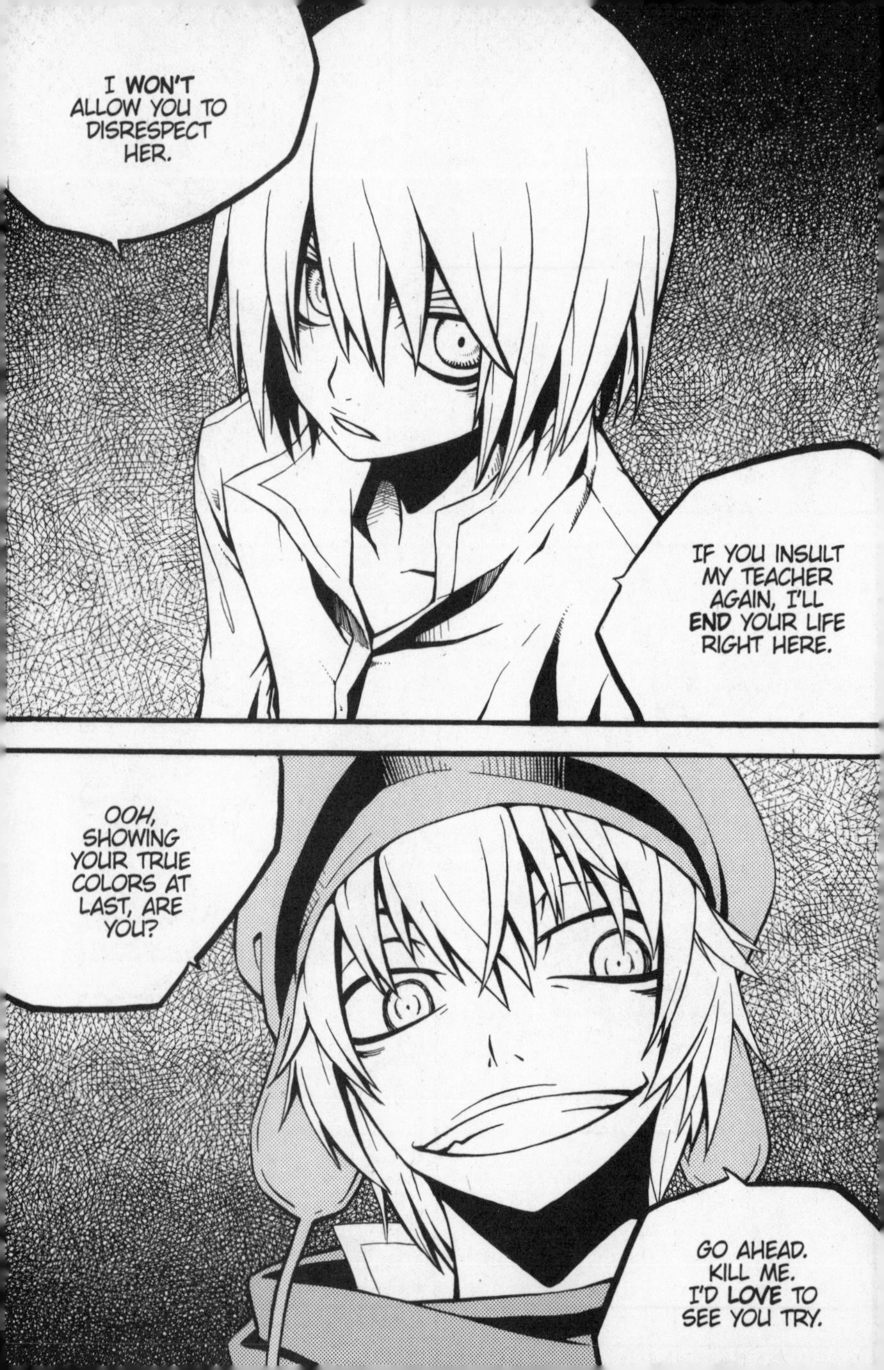
I WON'T ALLOW YOU TO DISRESPECT HER.
IF YOU INSULT MY TEACHER AGAIN, I'LL END YOUR LIFE RIGHT HERE.
OOH, SHOWING YOUR TRUE COLORS AT LAST, ARE YOU?
GO AHEAD. KILL ME. I'D LOVE TO SEE YOU TRY.

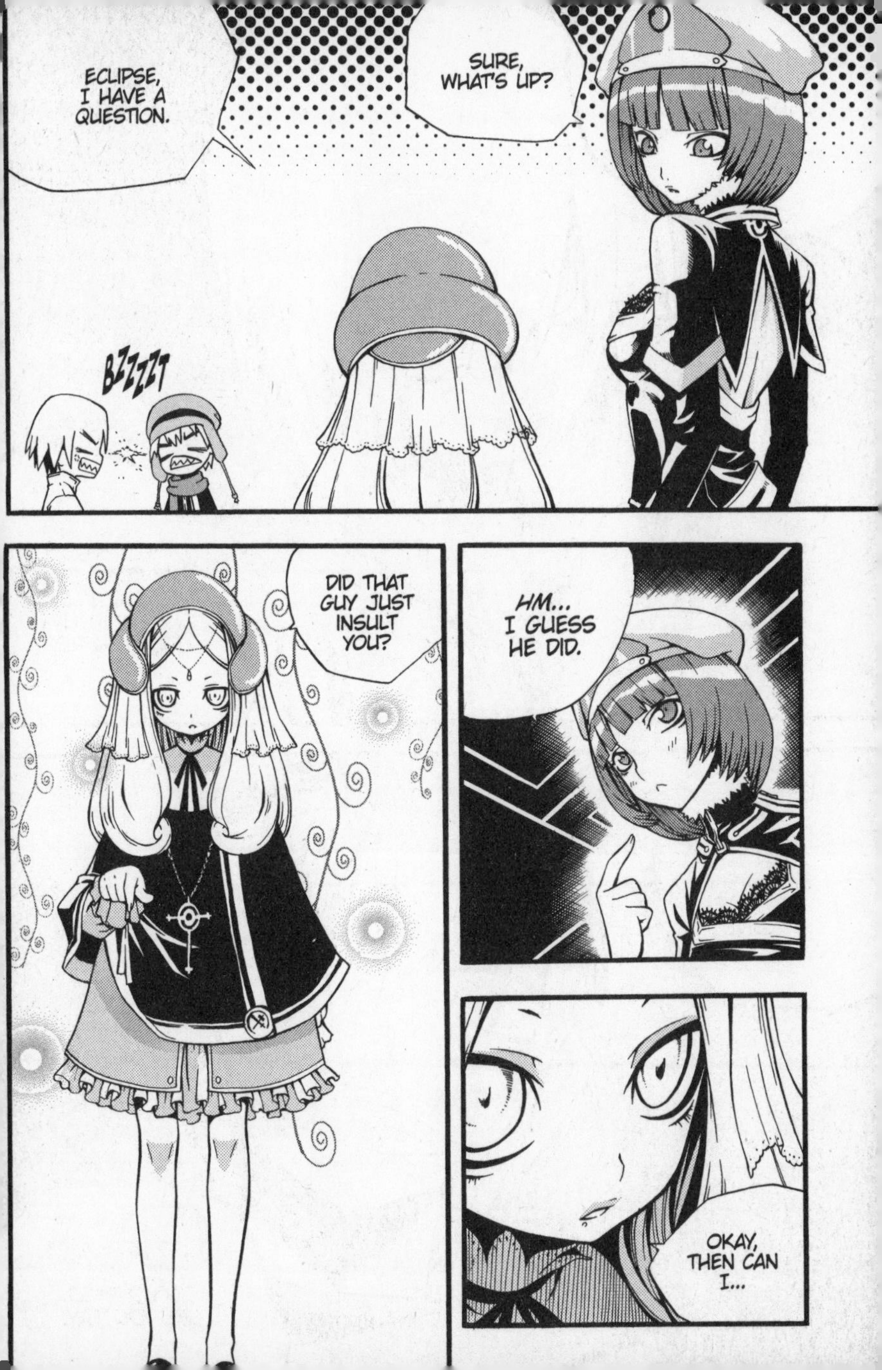
SURE, WHAT'S UP?
ECLIPSE, I HAVE A QUESTION.
BZZZZT
HM... I GUESS HE DID.
DID THAT GUY JUST INSULT YOU?
OKAY, THEN CAN I...

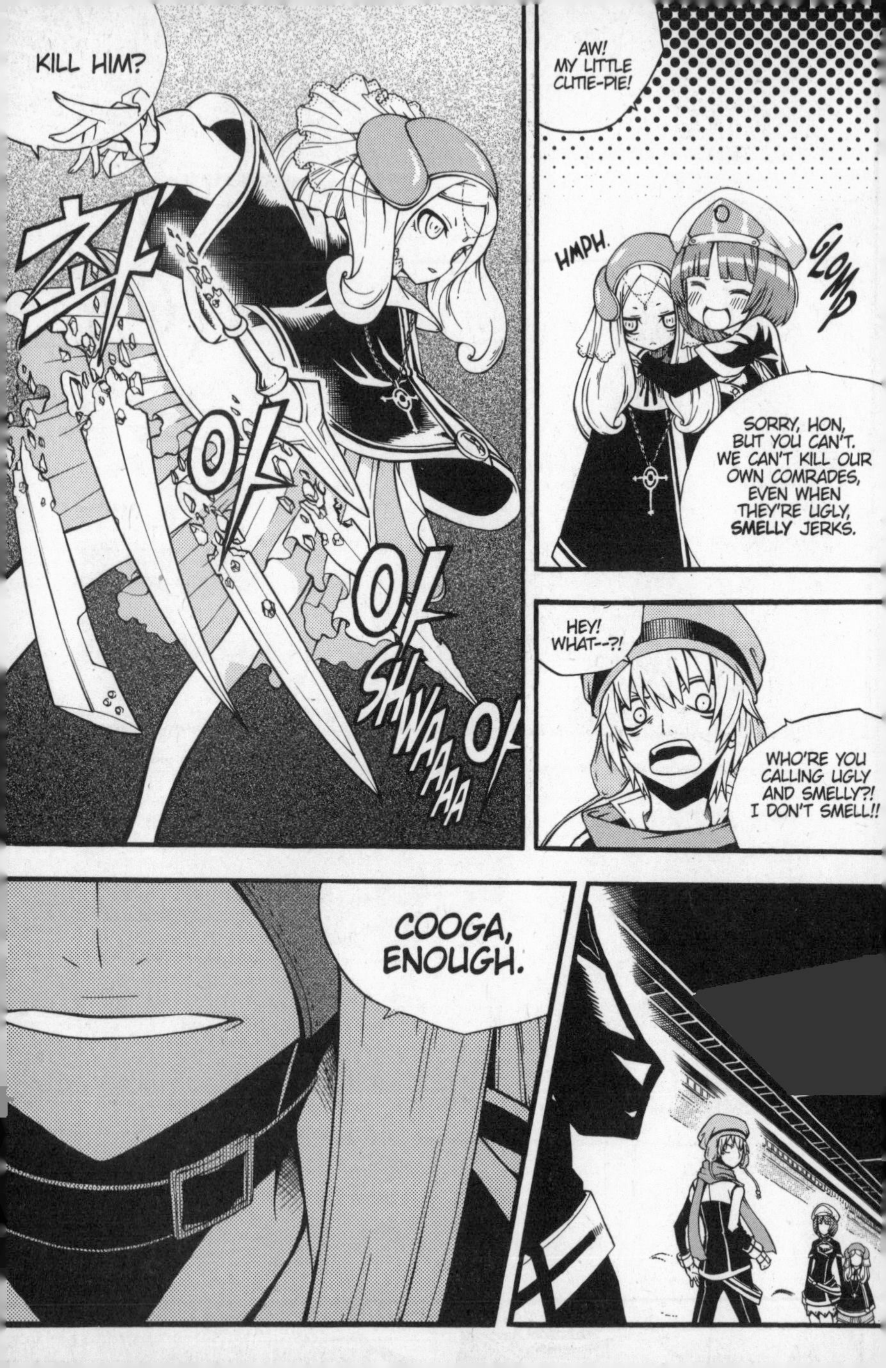

KILL HIM?
SHWAAAA
AW! MY LITTLE CUTIE-PIE!
HMPH.
GLOMP
SORRY, HON, BUT YOU CAN'T. WE CAN'T KILL OUR OWN COMRADES, EVEN WHEN THEY'RE UGLY, SMELLY JERKS.
HEY! WHAT--?!
WHO'RE YOU CALLING UGLY AND SMELLY?! I DON'T SMELL!!
COOGA, ENOUGH.

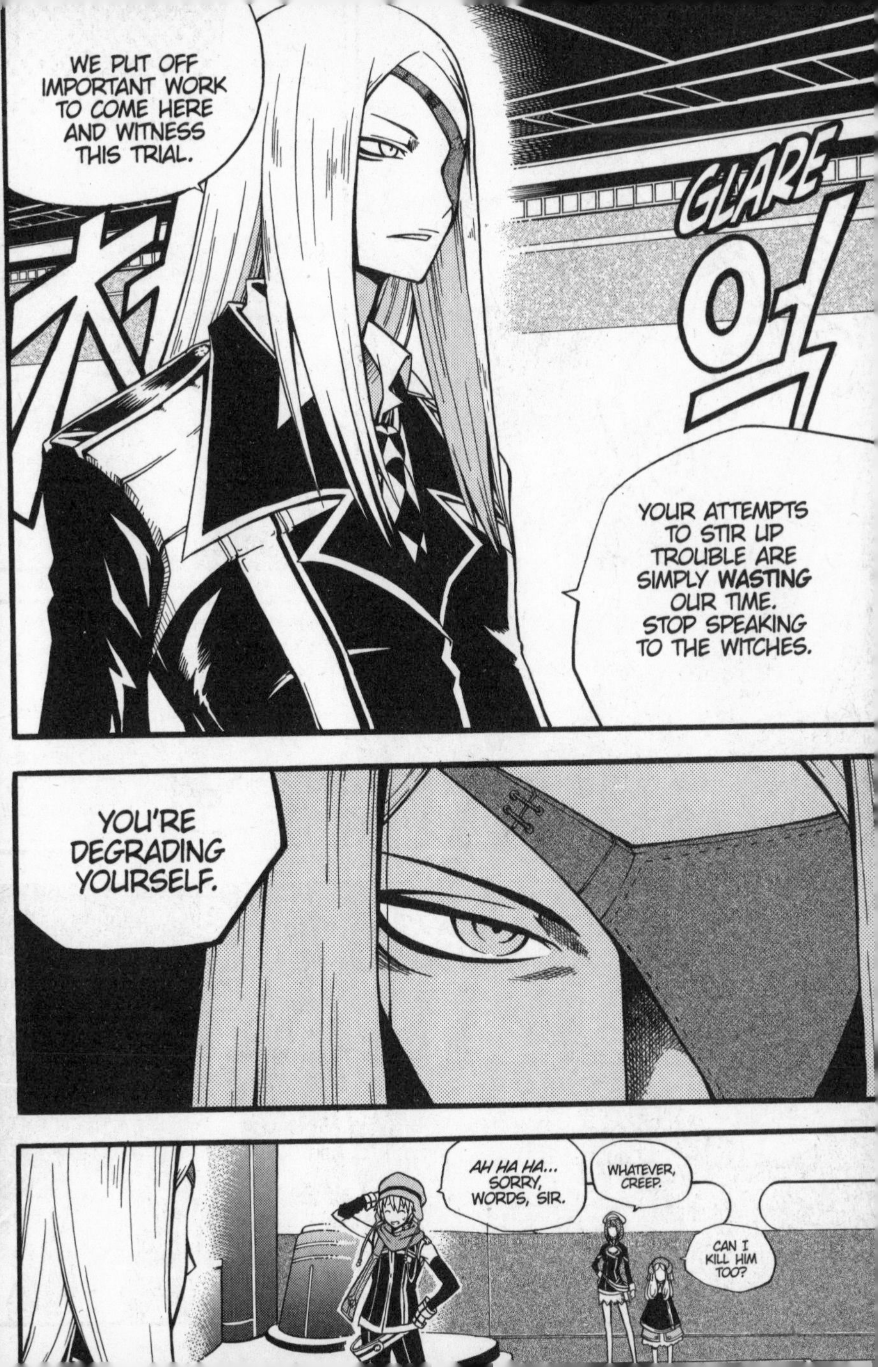
WE PUT OFF IMPORTANT WORK TO COME HERE AND WITNESS THIS TRIAL.
GLARE
YOUR ATTEMPTS TO STIR UP TROUBLE ARE SIMPLY WASTING OUR TIME. STOP SPEAKING TO THE WITCHES.
YOU'RE DEGRADING YOURSELF.
AH HA HA... SORRY, WORDS, SIR.
WHATEVER, CREEP.
CAN I KILL HIM TOO?

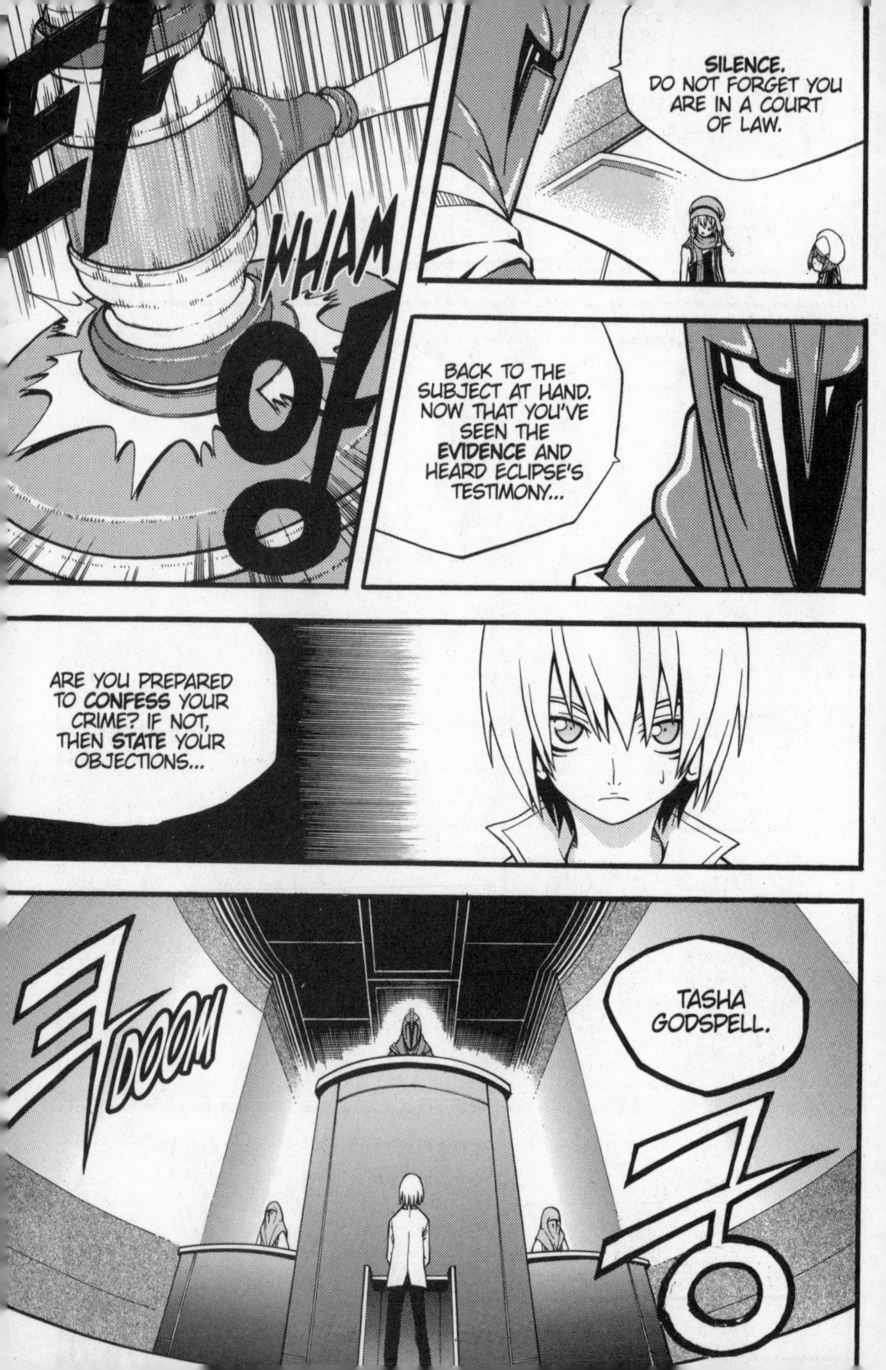
WHAM
SILENCE. DO NOT FORGET YOU ARE IN A COURT OF LAW.
BACK TO THE SUBJECT AT HAND. NOW THAT YOU'VE SEEN THE EVIDENCE AND HEARD ECLIPSE'S TESTIMONY...
ARE YOU PREPARED TO CONFESS YOUR CRIME? IF NOT, THEN STATE YOUR OBJECTIONS...
DOOM
TASHA GODSPELL.

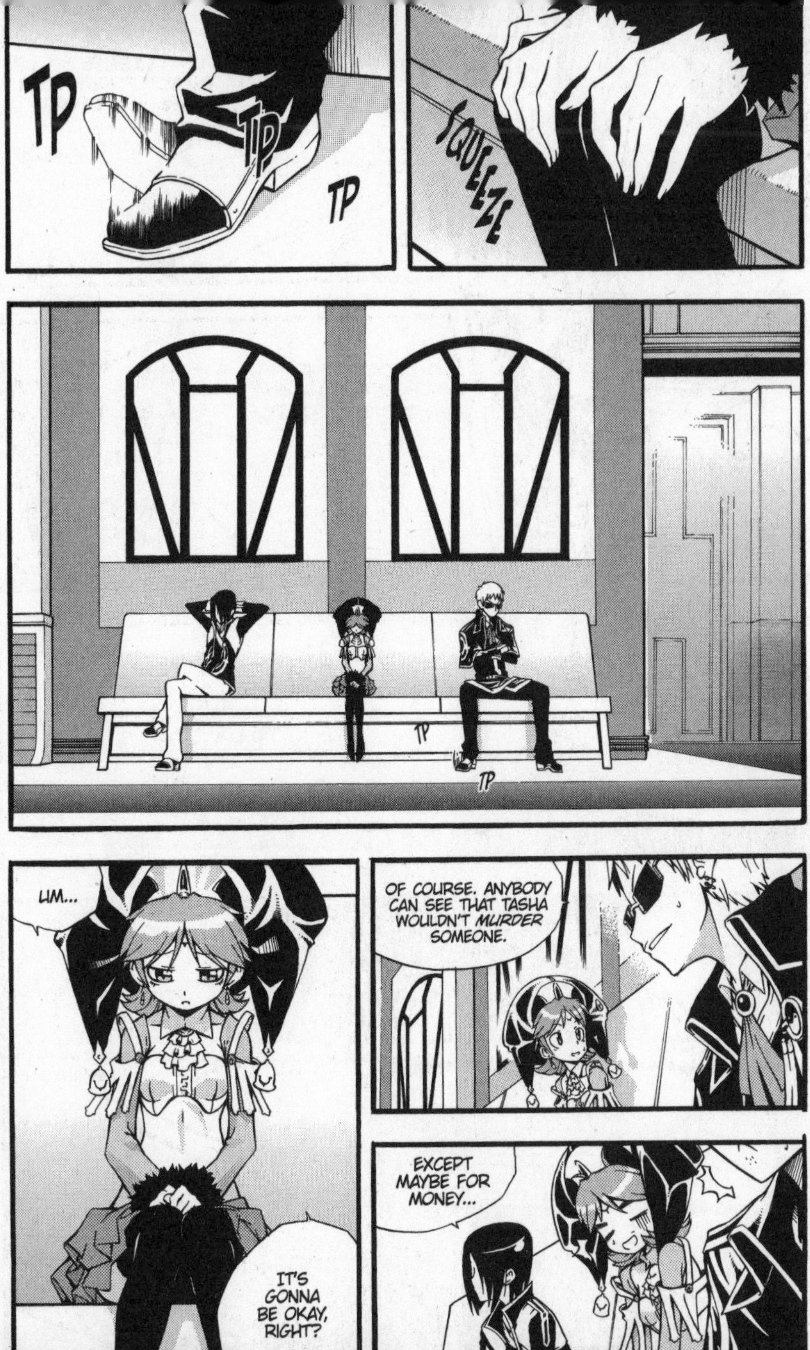
TP
TP
TP
SQUEEZE
TP
TP
UM...
IT'S GONNA BE OKAY, RIGHT?
OF COURSE. ANYBODY CAN SEE THAT TASHA WOULDN'T *MURDER* SOMEONE.
EXCEPT MAYBE FOR MONEY...

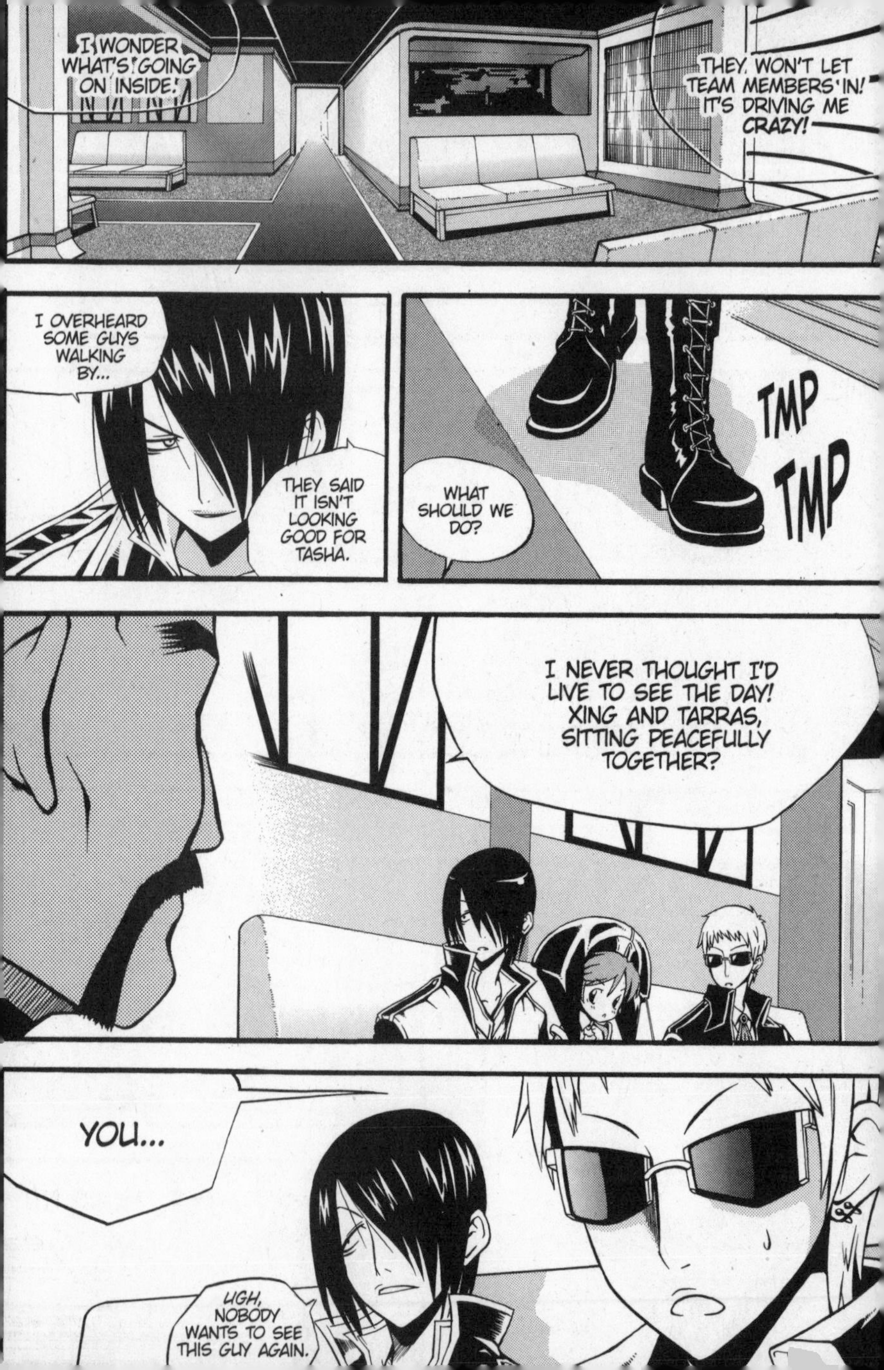
I WONDER WHAT'S GOING ON INSIDE!
THEY WON'T LET TEAM MEMBERS IN! IT'S DRIVING ME CRAZY!
I OVERHEARD SOME GUYS WALKING BY...
THEY SAID IT ISN'T LOOKING GOOD FOR TASHA.
WHAT SHOULD WE DO?
TMP TMP
I NEVER THOUGHT I'D LIVE TO SEE THE DAY! XING AND TARRAS, SITTING PEACEFULLY TOGETHER?
YOU...
UGH, NOBODY WANTS TO SEE THIS GUY AGAIN.

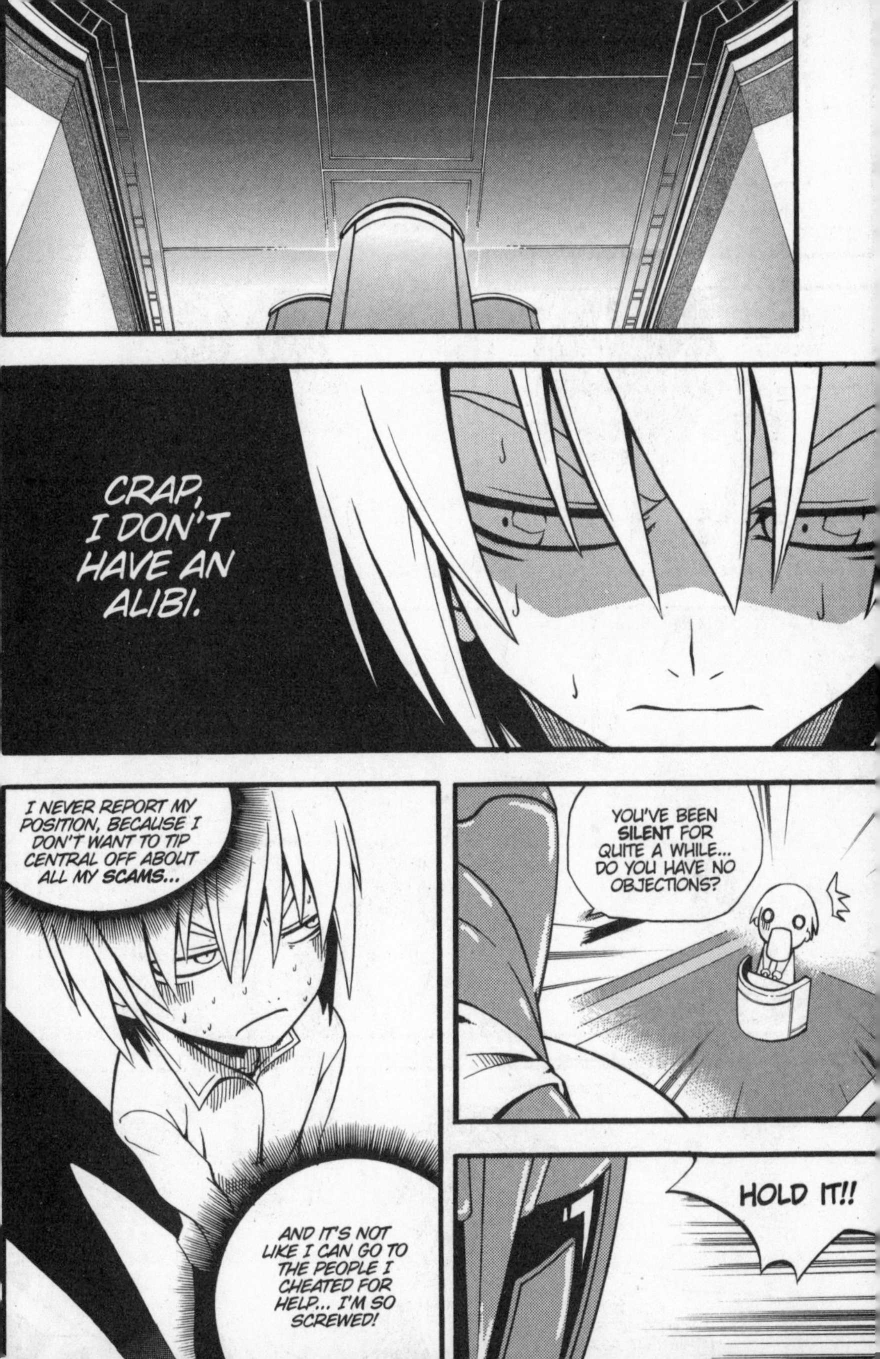
CRAP, I DON'T HAVE AN ALIBI.
I NEVER REPORT MY POSITION, BECAUSE I DON'T WANT TO TIP CENTRAL OFF ABOUT ALL MY SCAMS...
AND IT'S NOT LIKE I CAN GO TO THE PEOPLE I CHEATED FOR HELP... I'M SO SCREWED!
YOU'VE BEEN SILENT FOR QUITE A WHILE... DO YOU HAVE NO OBJECTIONS?
HOLD IT!!

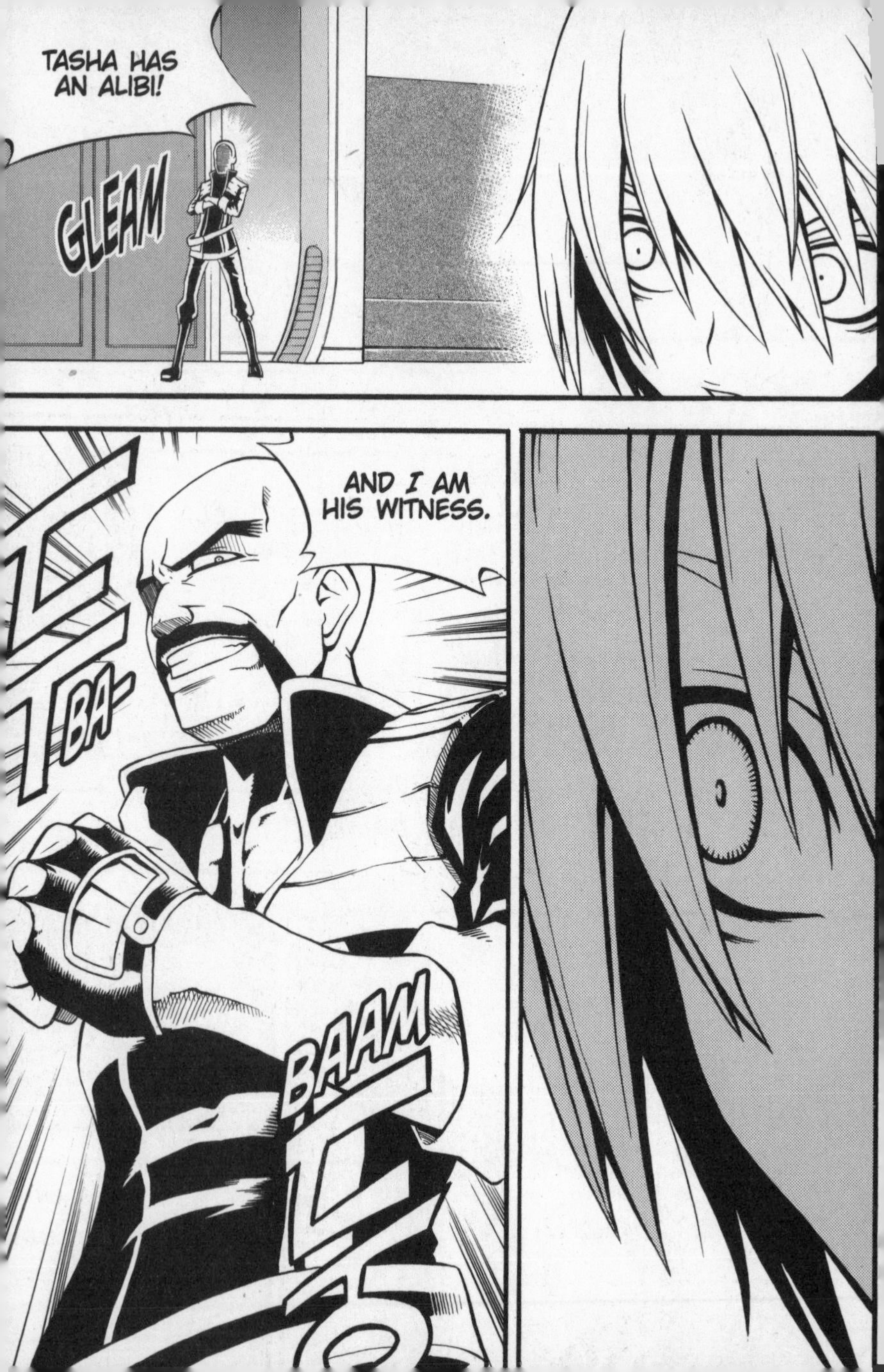
TASHA HAS
AN ALIBI!
GLEAM
AND I AM
HIS WITNESS.
BA-
BAAM

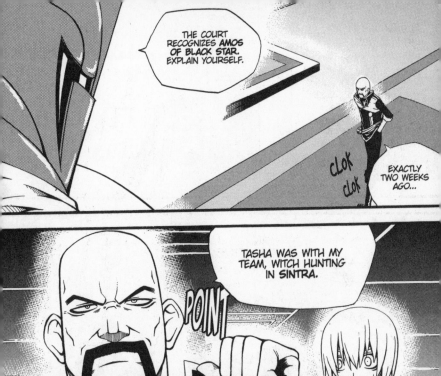

THE COURT RECOGNIZES AMOS OF BLACK STAR. EXPLAIN YOURSELF.

CLOk CLOk

EXACTLY TWO WEEKS AGO...

TASHA WAS WITH MY TEAM, WITCH HUNTING IN SINTRA.

POINT

...?

THERE WAS A WITCH HIDING AT SINTRA AND WE HAD SOME TROUBLE TAKING HER DOWN. LUCKILY, TASHA WAS IN THE AREA, SO WE INITIATED HELP.

WE KNEW TASHA'S BATTLEFIELD COULD DETECT THE HIDDEN WITCH.

IF YOU DON'T BELIEVE ME, SEND SOMEONE TO SINTRA. THERE SHOULD STILL BE REMNANTS OF TASHA'S BULLETS TO BE FOUND.

WE DIDN'T REPORT THIS EARLIER BECAUSE WE FAILED TO CAPTURE THE WITCH. HOWEVER, SINTRA AND THE PLACE YOU FOUND SHOUT'S BODY ARE NOWHERE NEAR EACH OTHER.

TO BE IN **BOTH** PLACES ON THE SAME DAY, HE'D NEED TO USE MAGIC PORTALS.

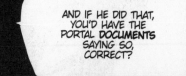

AND IF HE DID THAT, YOU'D HAVE THE PORTAL **DOCUMENTS** SAYING SO, CORRECT?

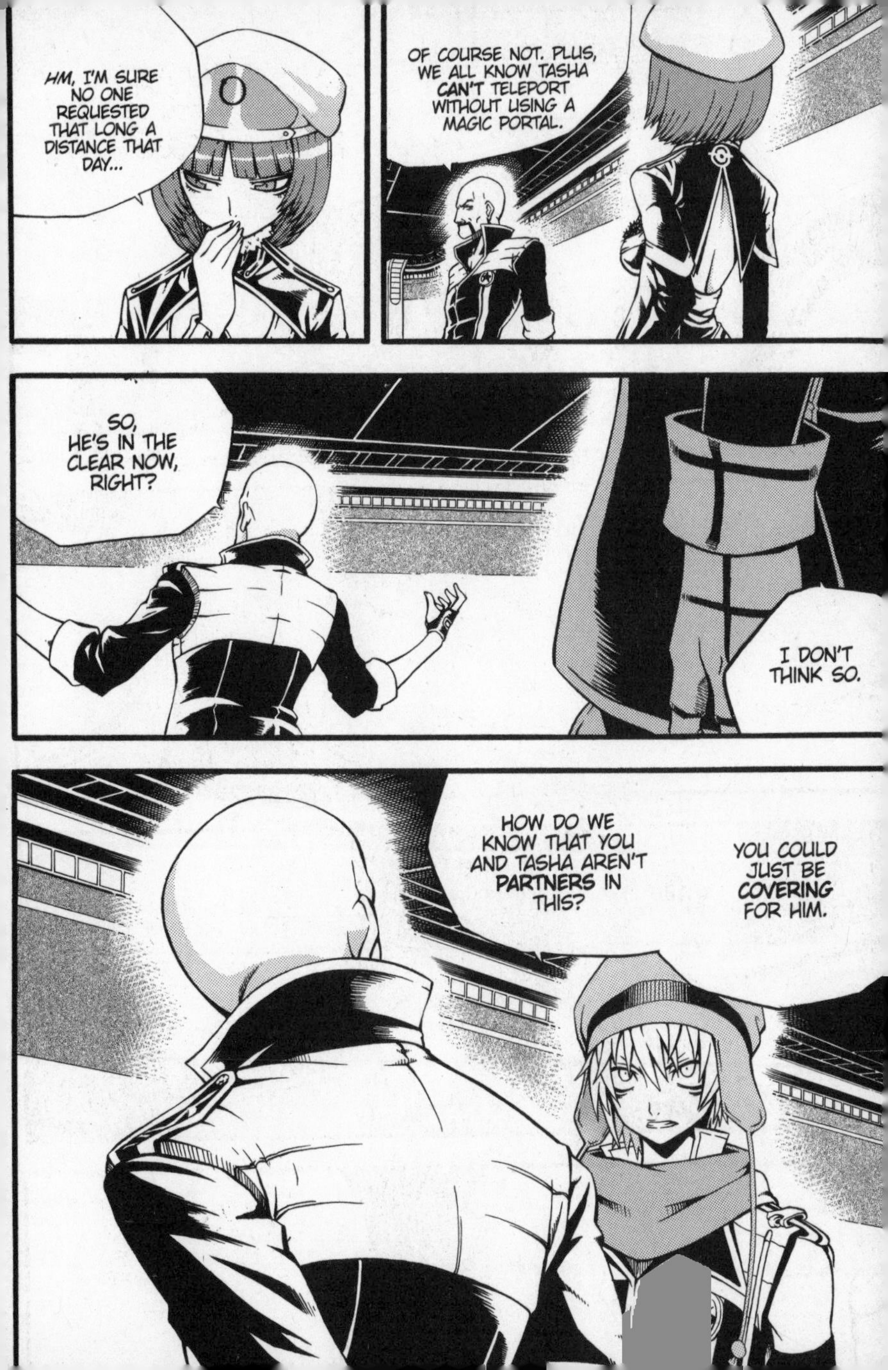
HM, I'M SURE NO ONE REQUESTED THAT LONG A DISTANCE THAT DAY...
OF COURSE NOT. PLUS, WE ALL KNOW TASHA CAN'T TELEPORT WITHOUT USING A MAGIC PORTAL.
SO, HE'S IN THE CLEAR NOW, RIGHT?
I DON'T THINK SO.
HOW DO WE KNOW THAT YOU AND TASHA AREN'T PARTNERS IN THIS?
YOU COULD JUST BE COVERING FOR HIM.

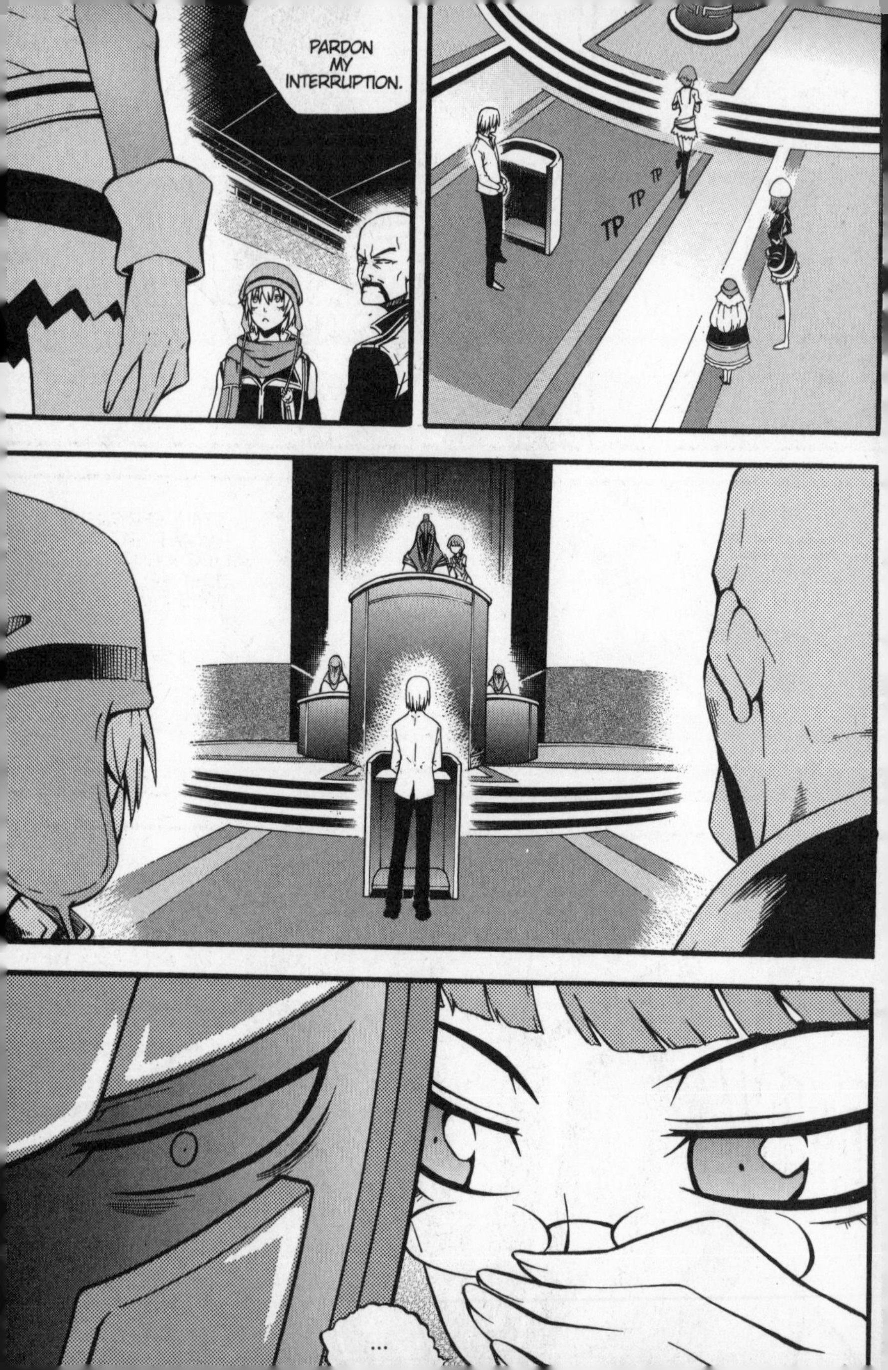
PARDON MY INTERRUPTION.
TP TP TP
...

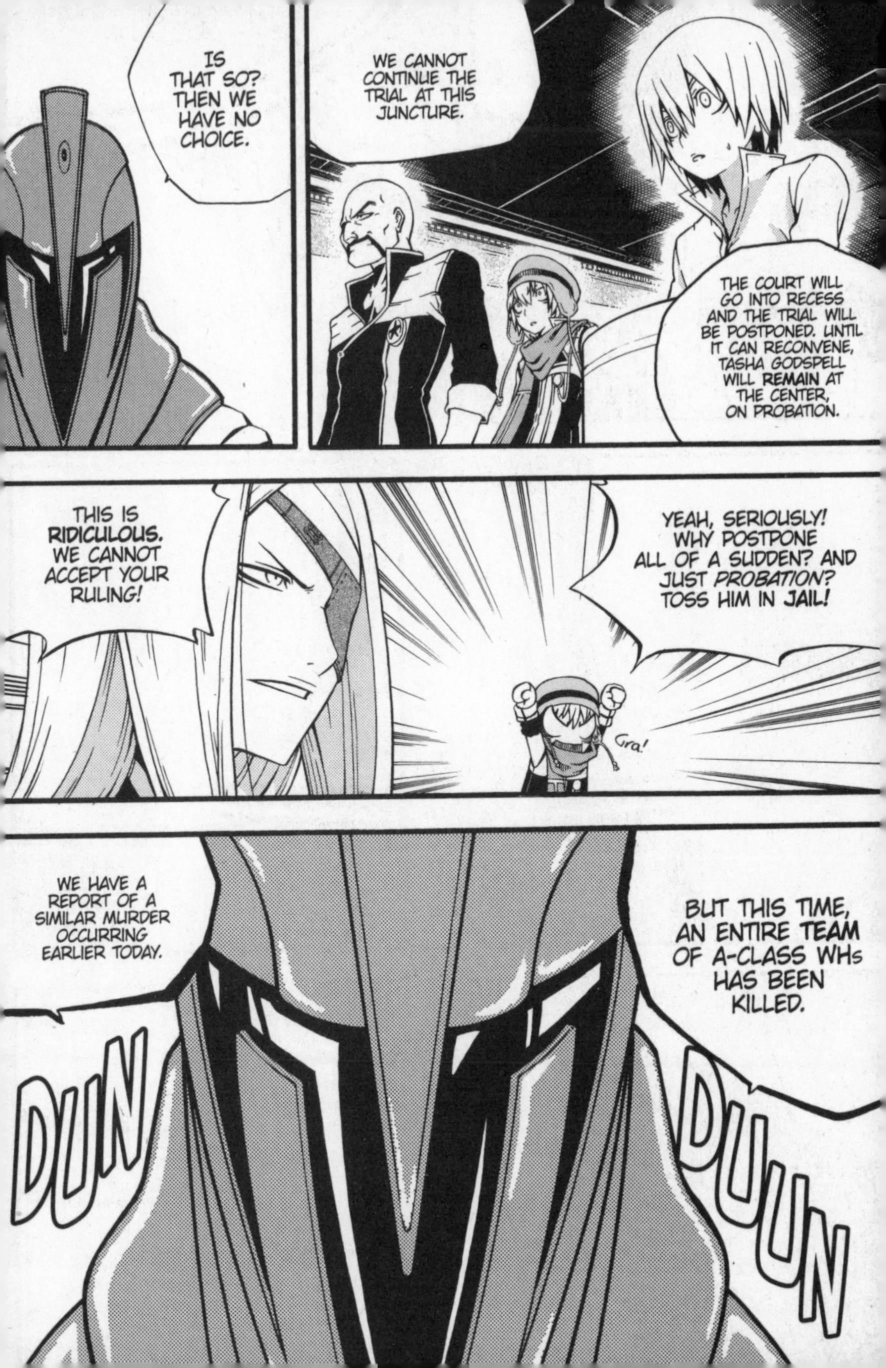
IS THAT SO? THEN WE HAVE NO CHOICE.
WE CANNOT CONTINUE THE TRIAL AT THIS JUNCTURE.
THE COURT WILL GO INTO RECESS AND THE TRIAL WILL BE POSTPONED. UNTIL IT CAN RECONVENE, TASHA GODSPELL WILL **REMAIN** AT THE CENTER, ON PROBATION.
THIS IS **RIDICULOUS.** WE CANNOT ACCEPT YOUR RULING!
YEAH, SERIOUSLY! WHY POSTPONE ALL OF A SUDDEN? AND JUST *PROBATION*? TOSS HIM IN **JAIL!**
Gra!
WE HAVE A REPORT OF A SIMILAR MURDER OCCURRING EARLIER TODAY.
BUT THIS TIME, AN ENTIRE **TEAM** OF A-CLASS WHs HAS BEEN KILLED.
DUN
DUUN

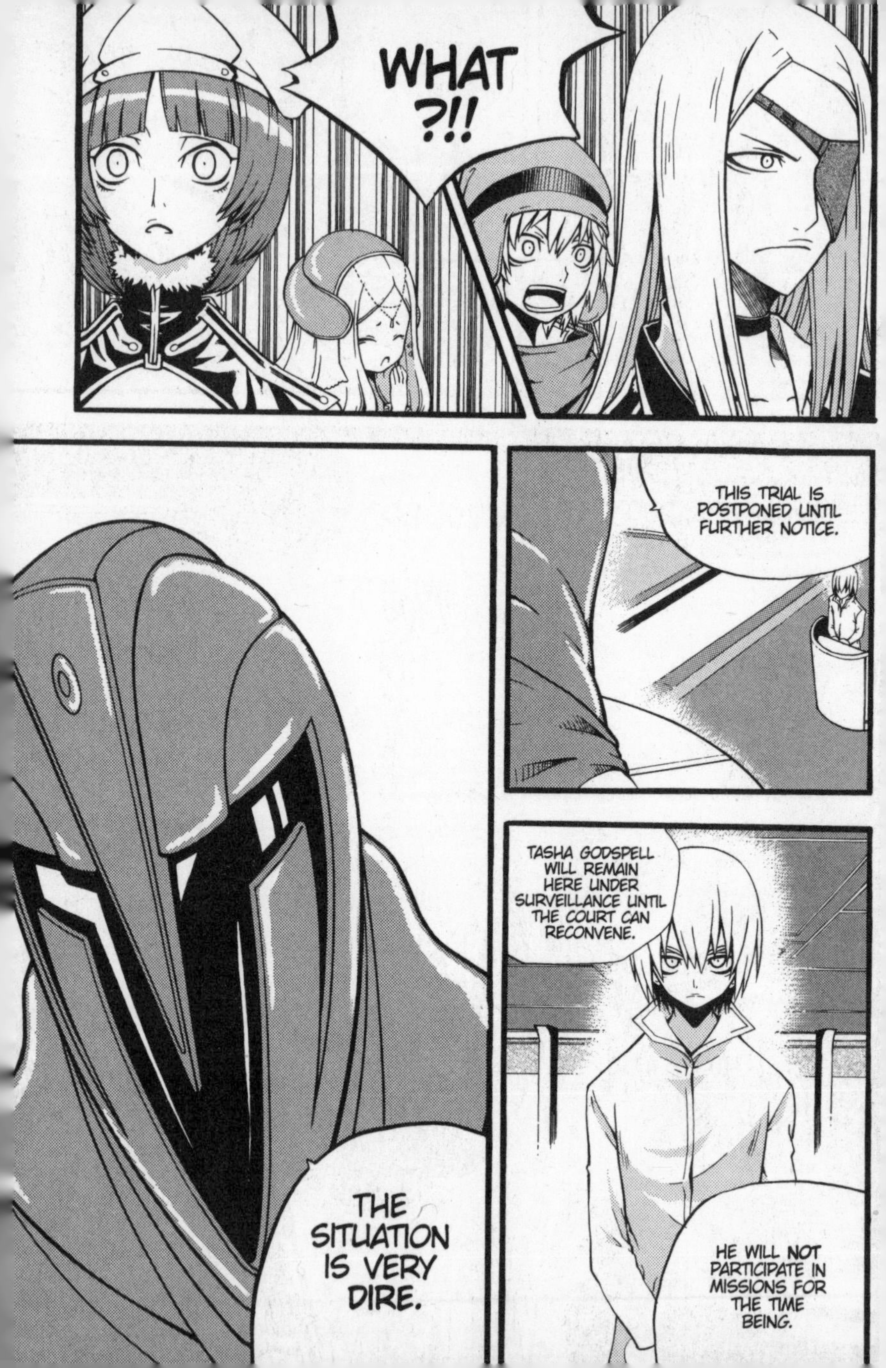
WHAT ?!!
THIS TRIAL IS POSTPONED UNTIL FURTHER NOTICE.
TASHA GODSPELL WILL REMAIN HERE UNDER SURVEILLANCE UNTIL THE COURT CAN RECONVENE.
HE WILL NOT PARTICIPATE IN MISSIONS FOR THE TIME BEING.
THE SITUATION IS VERY DIRE.

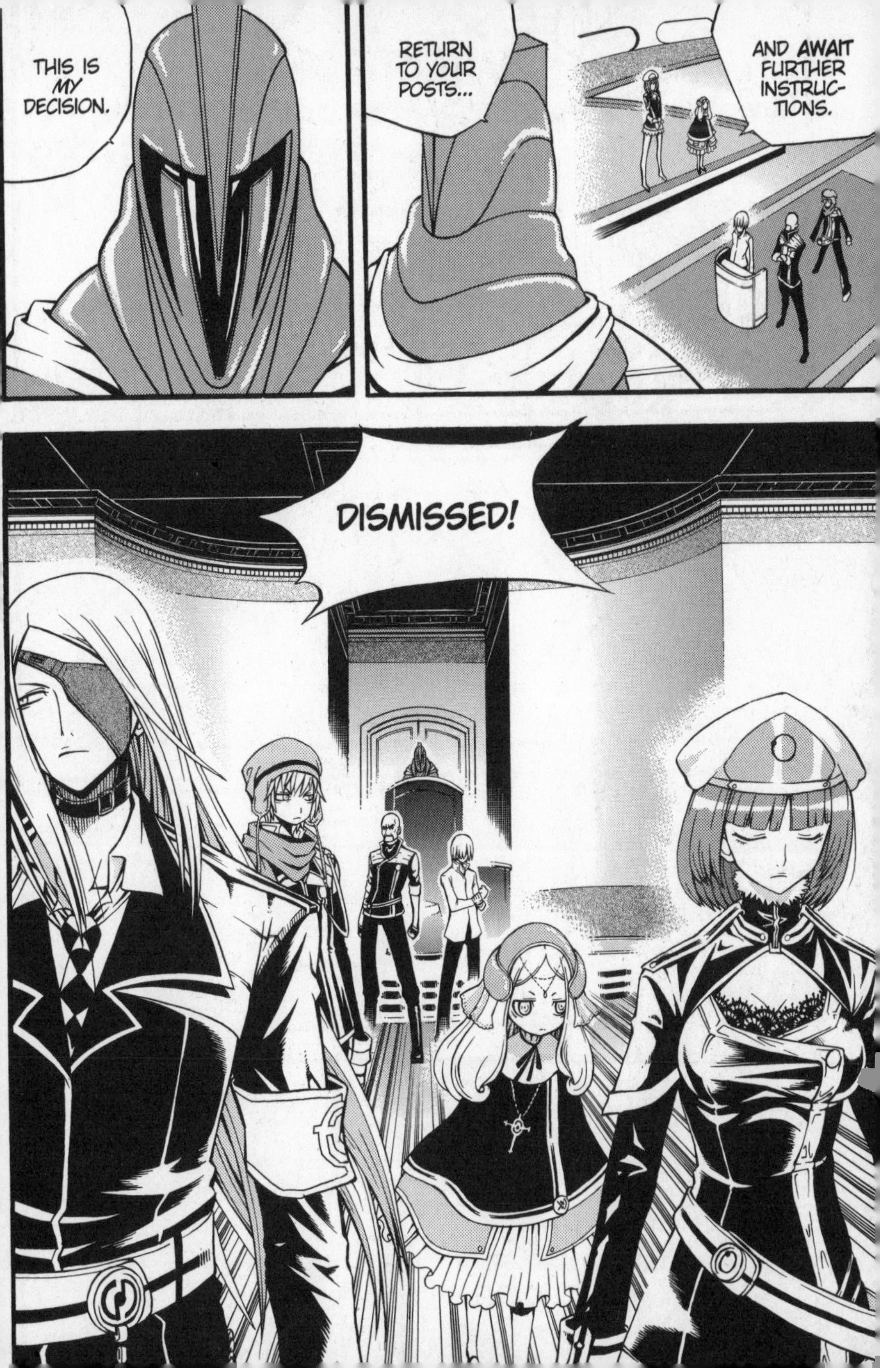
AND AWAIT FURTHER INSTRUC-TIONS.
RETURN TO YOUR POSTS...
THIS IS MY DECISION.
DISMISSED!

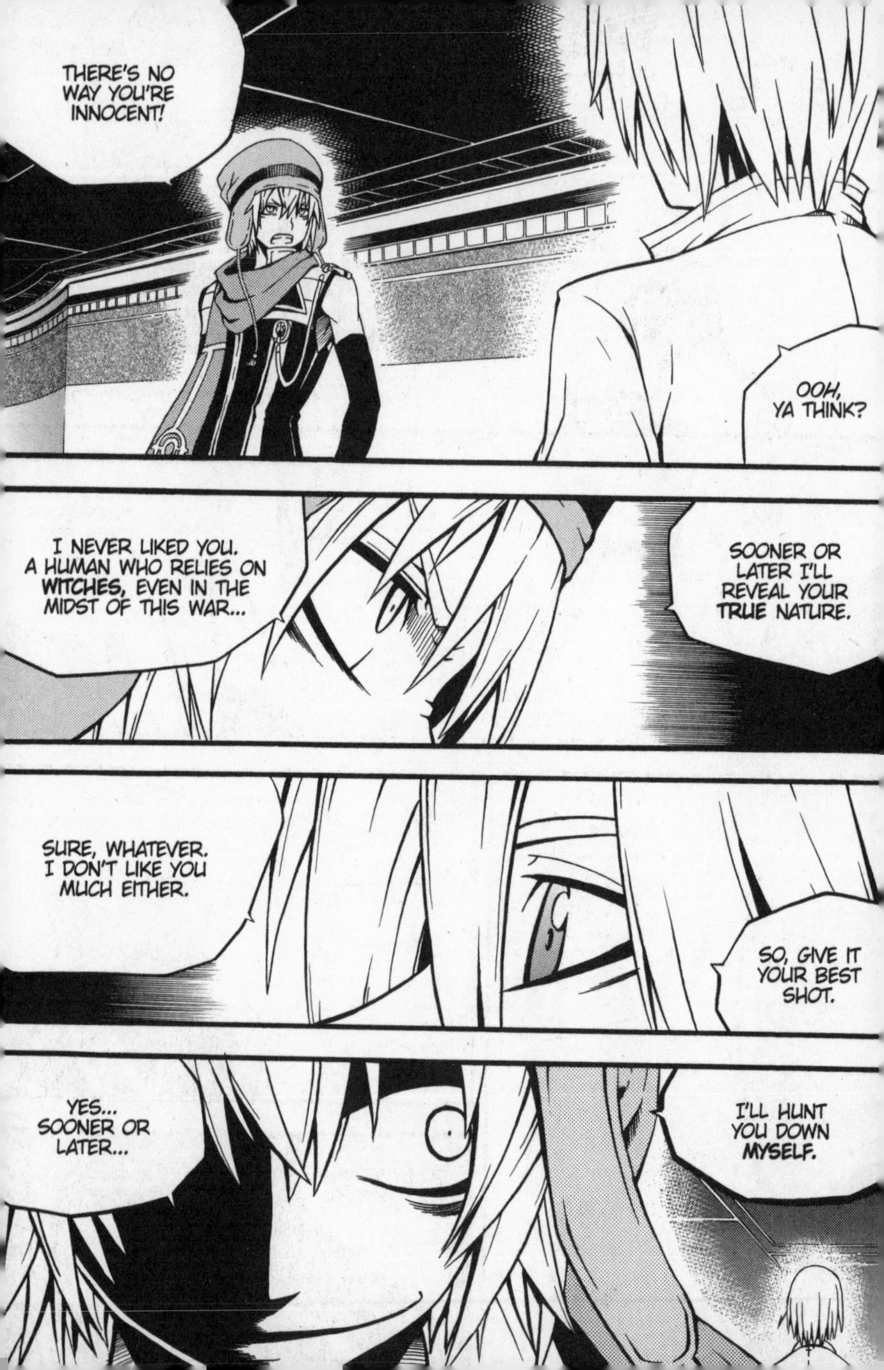
THERE'S NO WAY YOU'RE INNOCENT!
OOH, YA THINK?
I NEVER LIKED YOU. A HUMAN WHO RELIES ON WITCHES, EVEN IN THE MIDST OF THIS WAR...
SOONER OR LATER I'LL REVEAL YOUR TRUE NATURE.
SURE, WHATEVER. I DON'T LIKE YOU MUCH EITHER.
SO, GIVE IT YOUR BEST SHOT.
YES... SOONER OR LATER...
I'LL HUNT YOU DOWN MYSELF.

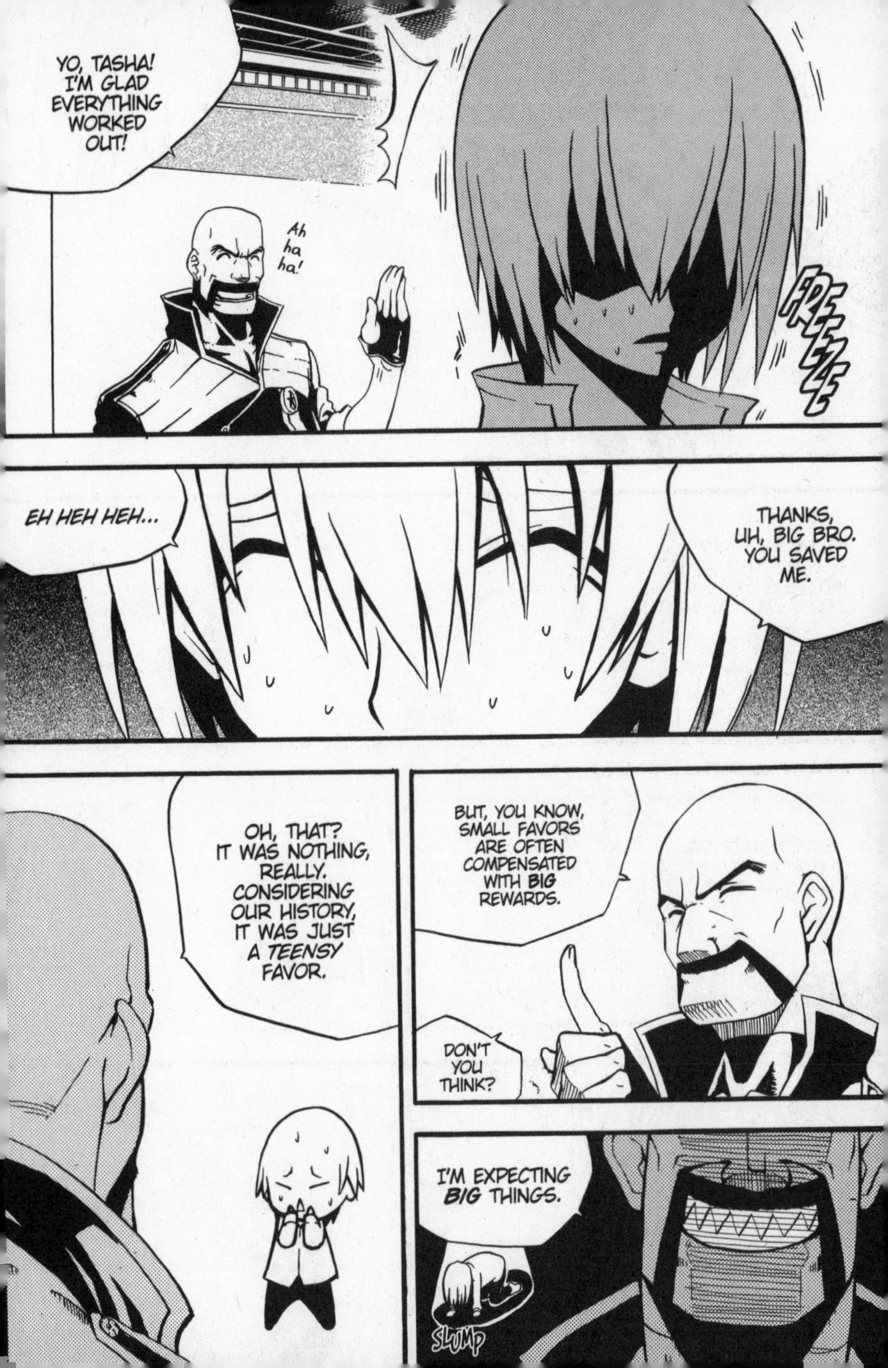
YO, TASHA! I'M GLAD EVERYTHING WORKED OUT!
Ah ha ha!
FREEZE
EH HEH HEH...
THANKS, UH, BIG BRO. YOU SAVED ME.
OH, THAT? IT WAS NOTHING, REALLY. CONSIDERING OUR HISTORY, IT WAS JUST A TEENSY FAVOR.
BUT, YOU KNOW, SMALL FAVORS ARE OFTEN COMPENSATED WITH BIG REWARDS.
DON'T YOU THINK?
I'M EXPECTING BIG THINGS.
SLUMP

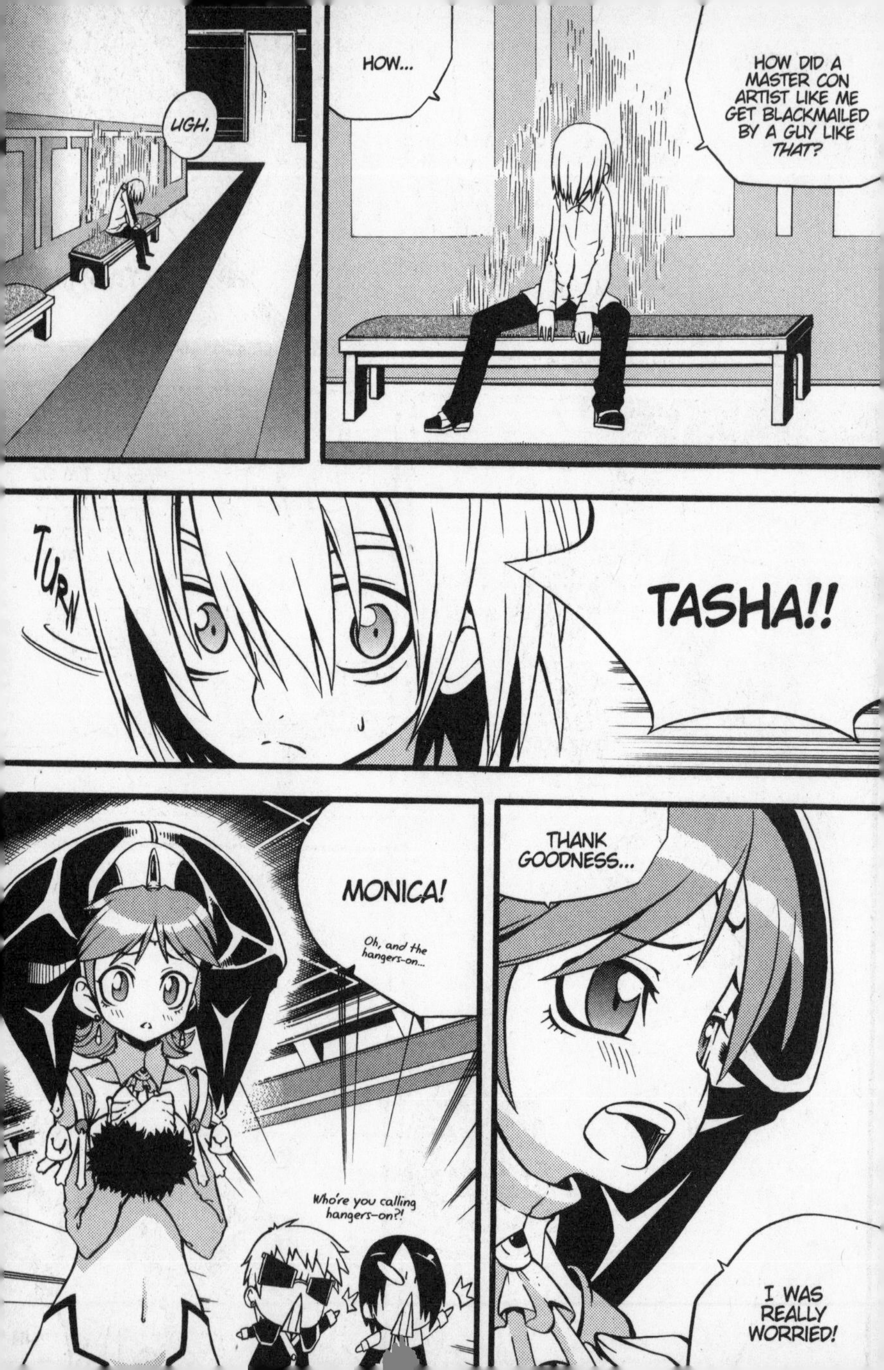

UGH.
HOW...
HOW DID A MASTER CON ARTIST LIKE ME GET BLACKMAILED BY A GUY LIKE THAT?
TURN
TASHA!!
MONICA!
Oh, and the hangers-on...
Who're you calling hangers-on?!
THANK GOODNESS...
I WAS REALLY WORRIED!

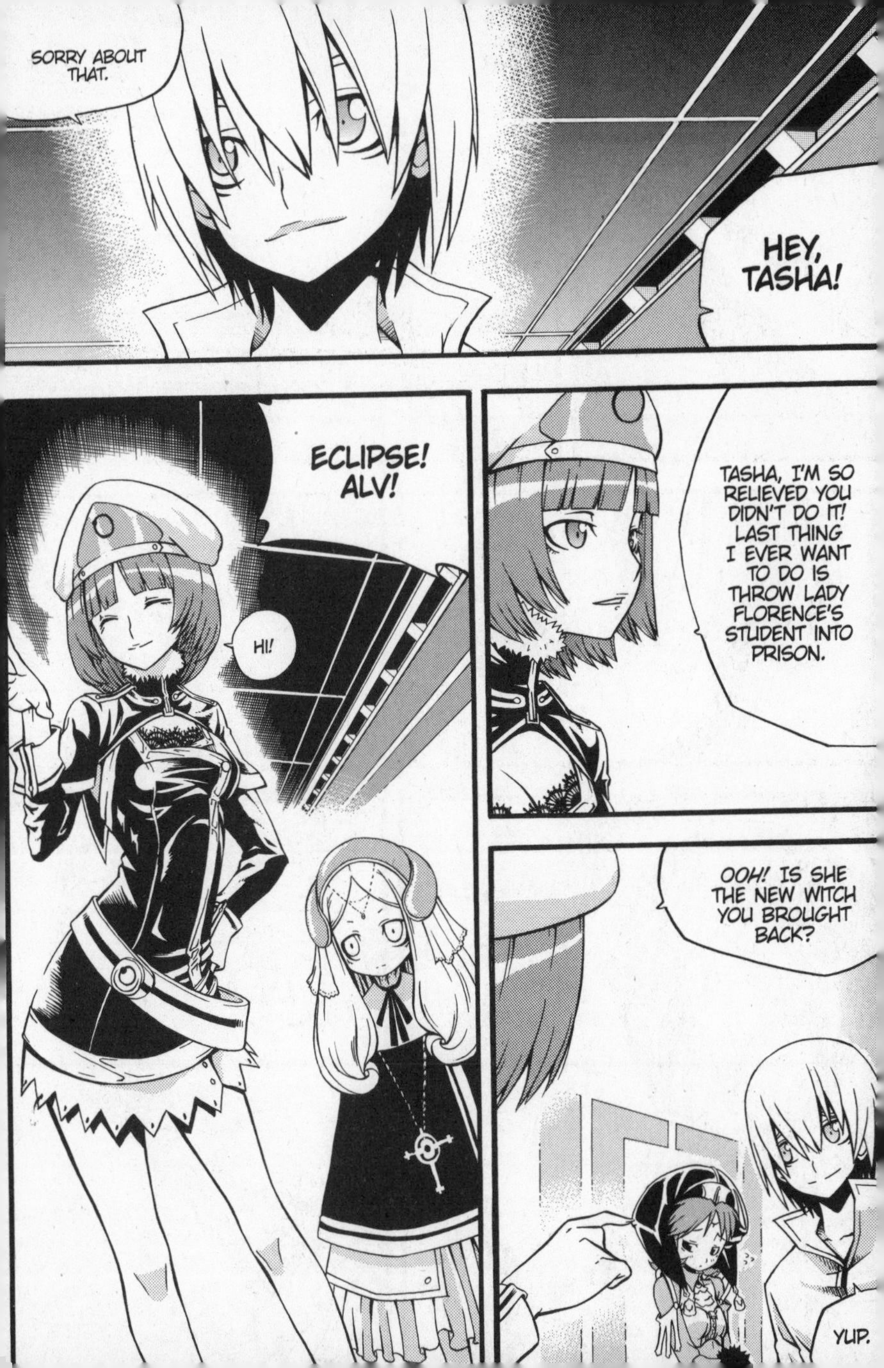
HEY, TASHA!
SORRY ABOUT THAT.
TASHA, I'M SO RELIEVED YOU DIDN'T DO IT! LAST THING I EVER WANT TO DO IS THROW LADY FLORENCE'S STUDENT INTO PRISON.
ECLIPSE! ALV!
HI!
OOH! IS SHE THE NEW WITCH YOU BROUGHT BACK?
YUP.

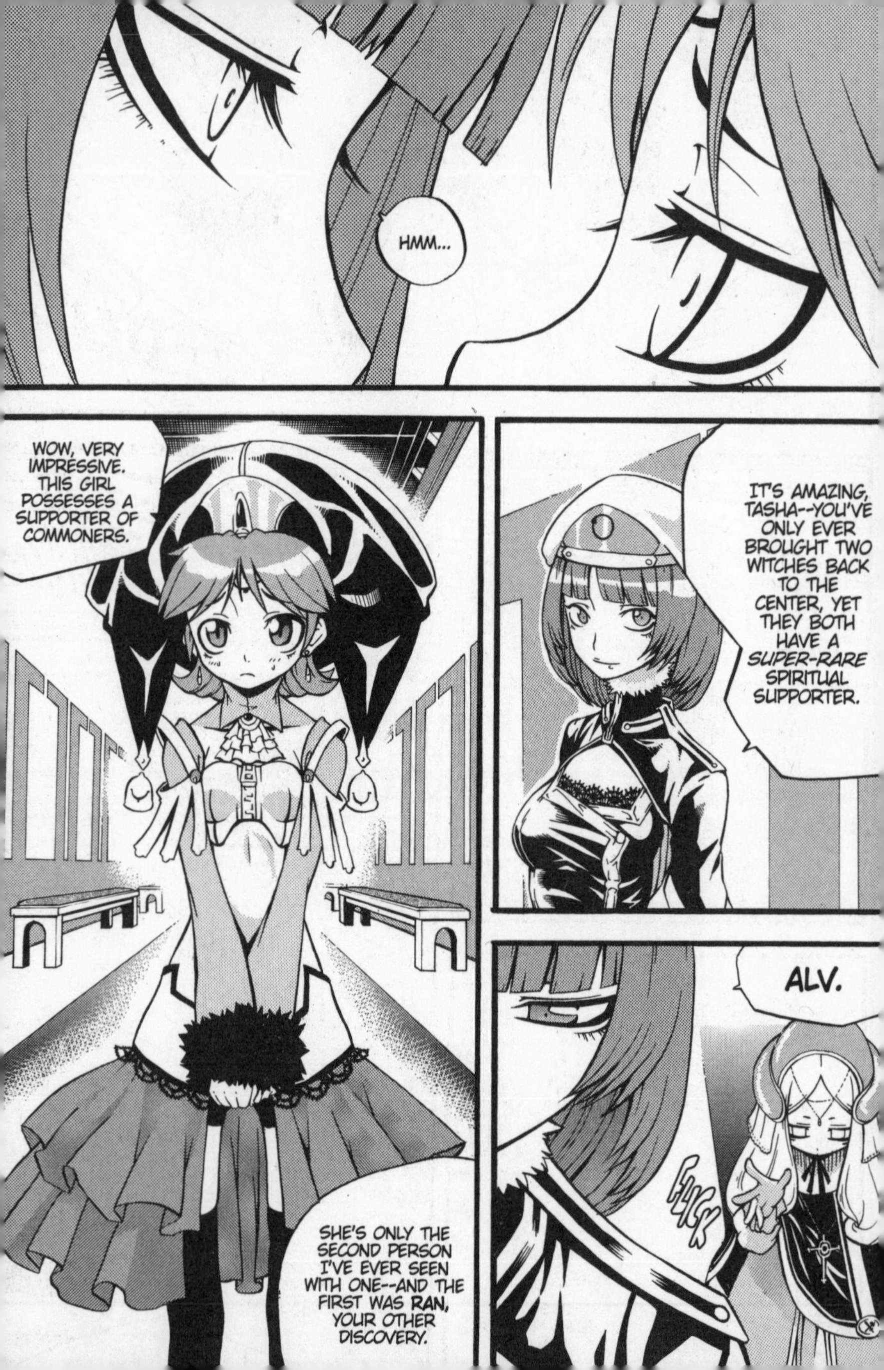
HMM...
IT'S AMAZING, TASHA--YOU'VE ONLY EVER BROUGHT TWO WITCHES BACK TO THE CENTER, YET THEY BOTH HAVE A SUPER-RARE SPIRITUAL SUPPORTER.
WOW, VERY IMPRESSIVE. THIS GIRL POSSESSES A SUPPORTER OF COMMONERS.
ALV.
FLICK
SHE'S ONLY THE SECOND PERSON I'VE EVER SEEN WITH ONE--AND THE FIRST WAS RAN, YOUR OTHER DISCOVERY.

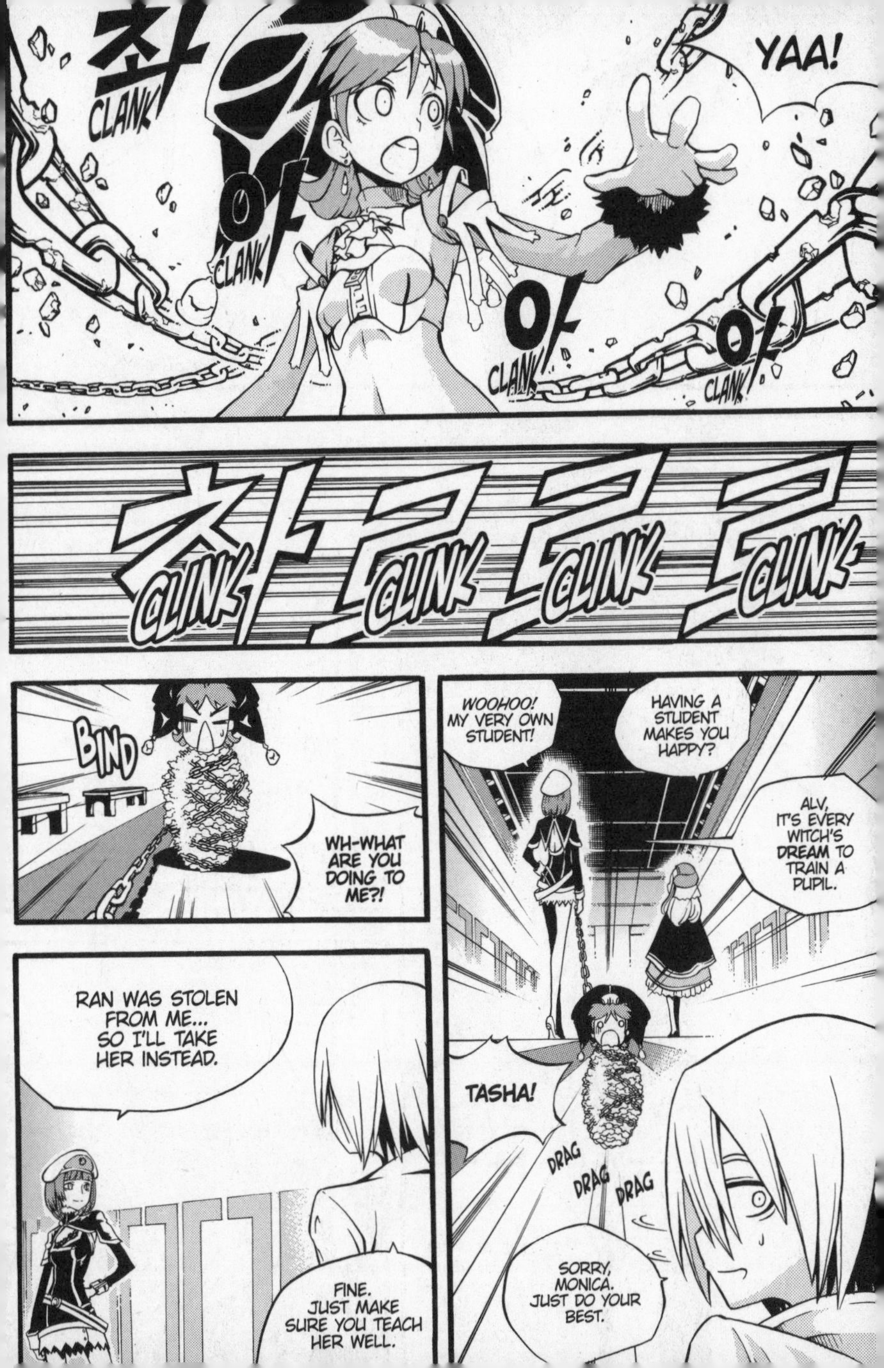
CLANK
CLANK
YAA!
CLANK
CLANK
CLINK
CLINK
CLINK
CLINK
BIND
WH-WHAT ARE YOU DOING TO ME?!
WOOHOO! MY VERY OWN STUDENT!
HAVING A STUDENT MAKES YOU HAPPY?
ALV, IT'S EVERY WITCH'S DREAM TO TRAIN A PUPIL.
RAN WAS STOLEN FROM ME... SO I'LL TAKE HER INSTEAD.
FINE. JUST MAKE SURE YOU TEACH HER WELL.
TASHA!
DRAG
DRAG
DRAG
SORRY, MONICA. JUST DO YOUR BEST.

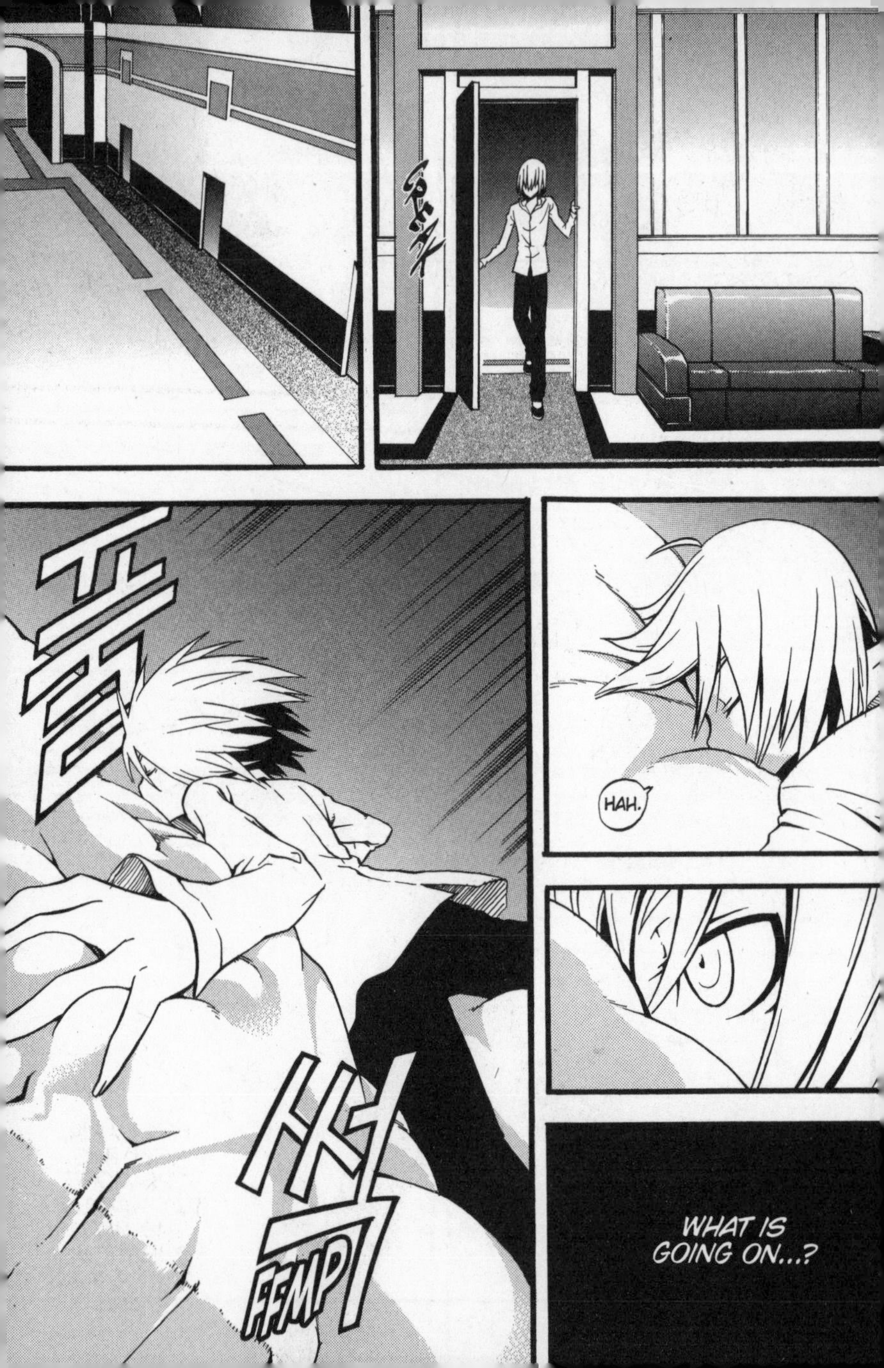
CREAK
HAH.
FFMP
WHAT IS GOING ON...?

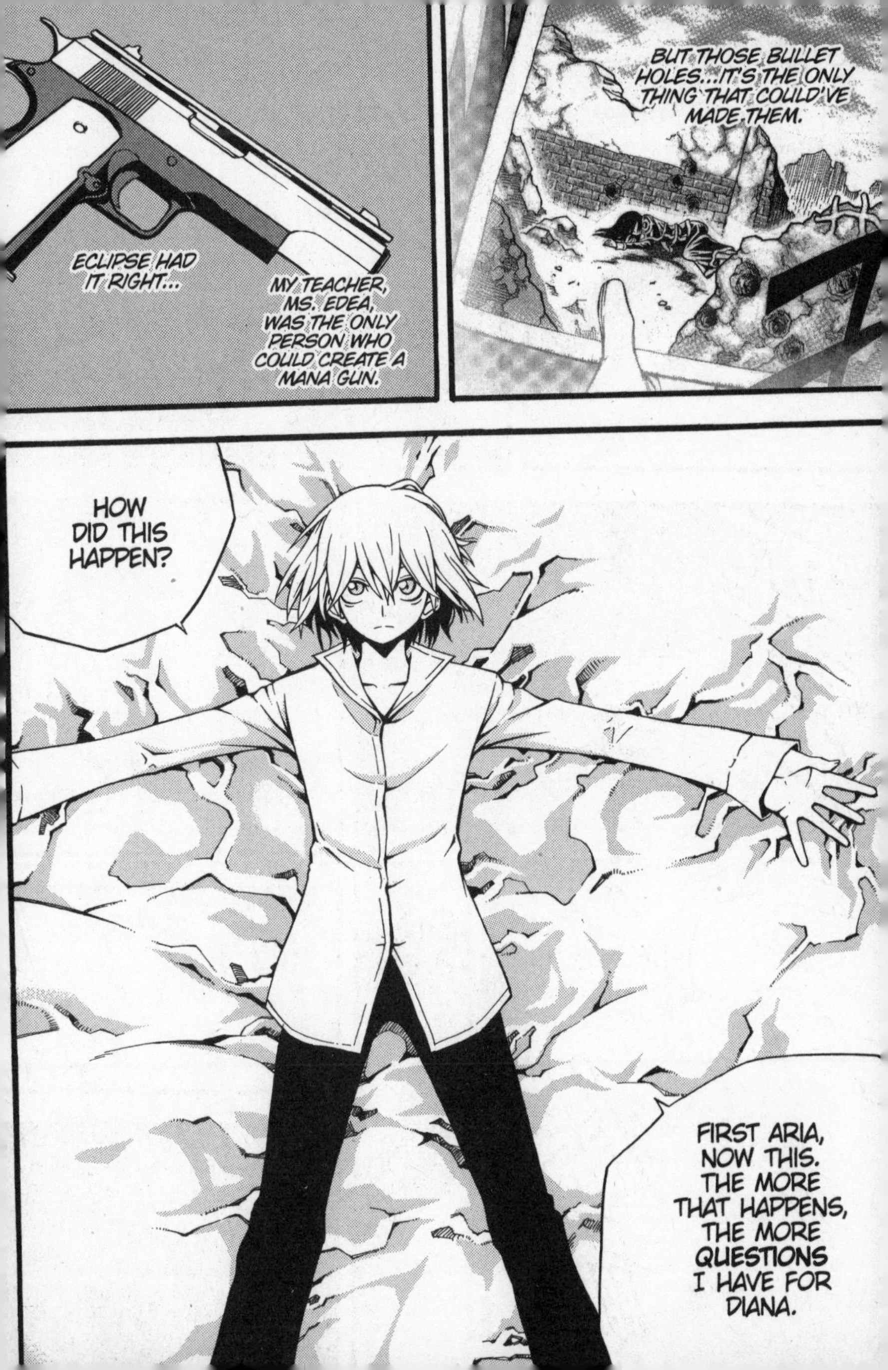
BUT THOSE BULLET HOLES...IT'S THE ONLY THING THAT COULD'VE MADE THEM.
ECLIPSE HAD IT RIGHT...
MY TEACHER, MS. EDEA, WAS THE ONLY PERSON WHO COULD CREATE A MANA GUN.
FIRST ARIA, NOW THIS. THE MORE THAT HAPPENS, THE MORE QUESTIONS I HAVE FOR DIANA.
HOW DID THIS HAPPEN?

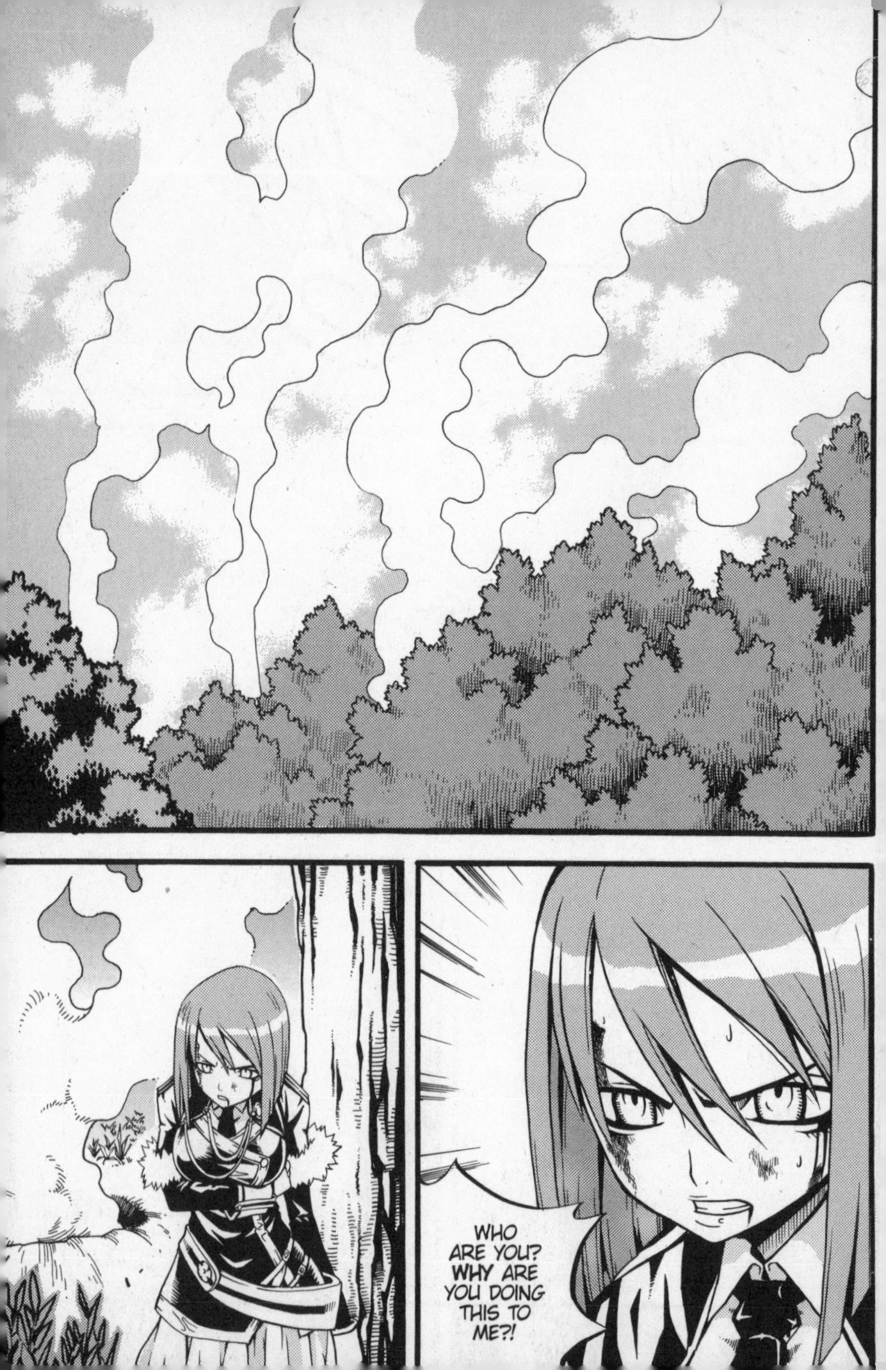
WHO ARE YOU? WHY ARE YOU DOING THIS TO ME?!

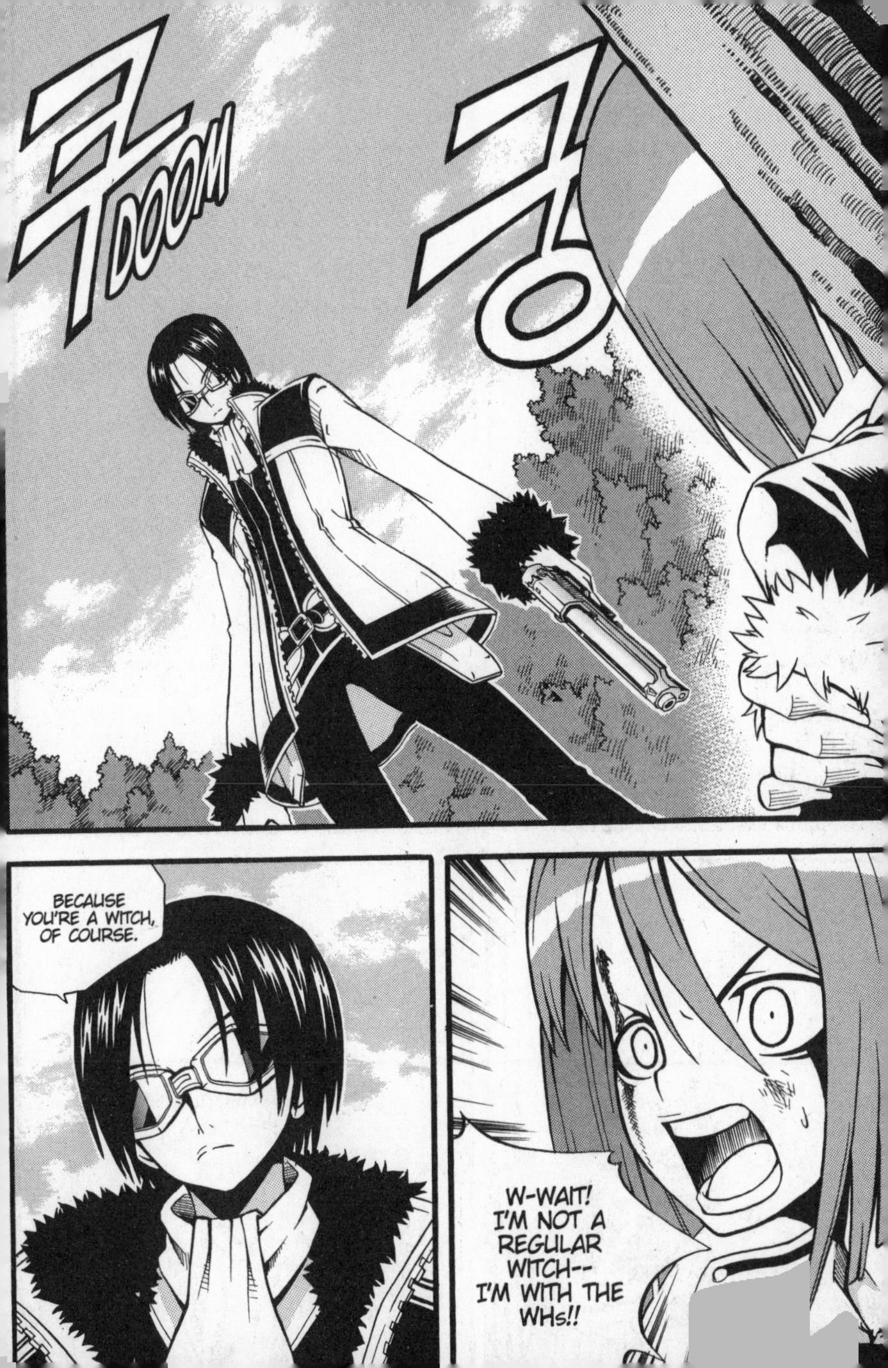
DOOM
BECAUSE YOU'RE A WITCH, OF COURSE.
W-WAIT! I'M NOT A REGULAR WITCH-- I'M WITH THE WHs!!

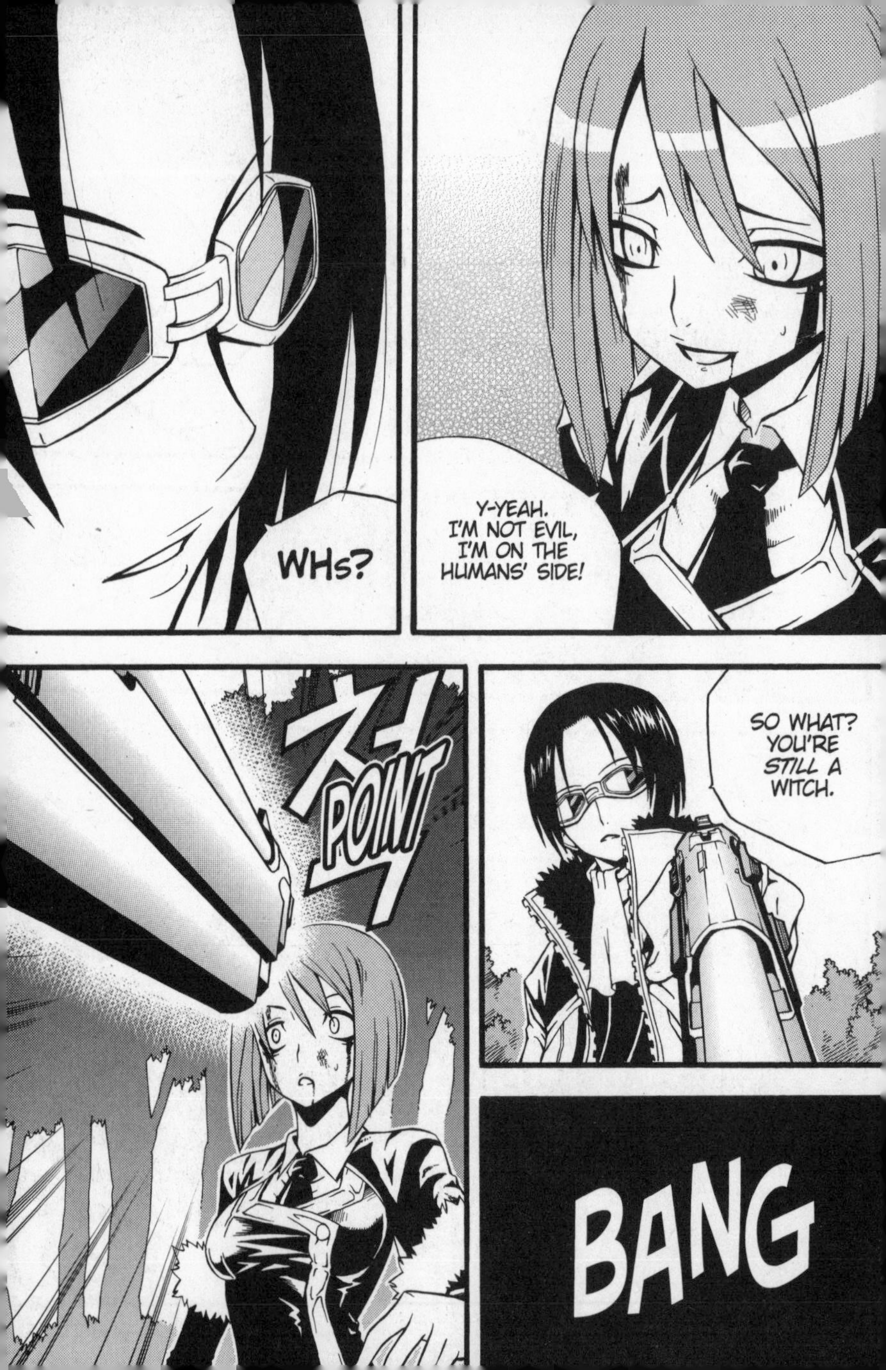
Y-YEAH. I'M NOT EVIL, I'M ON THE HUMANS' SIDE!
WHs?
SO WHAT? YOU'RE STILL A WITCH.
POINT
BANG

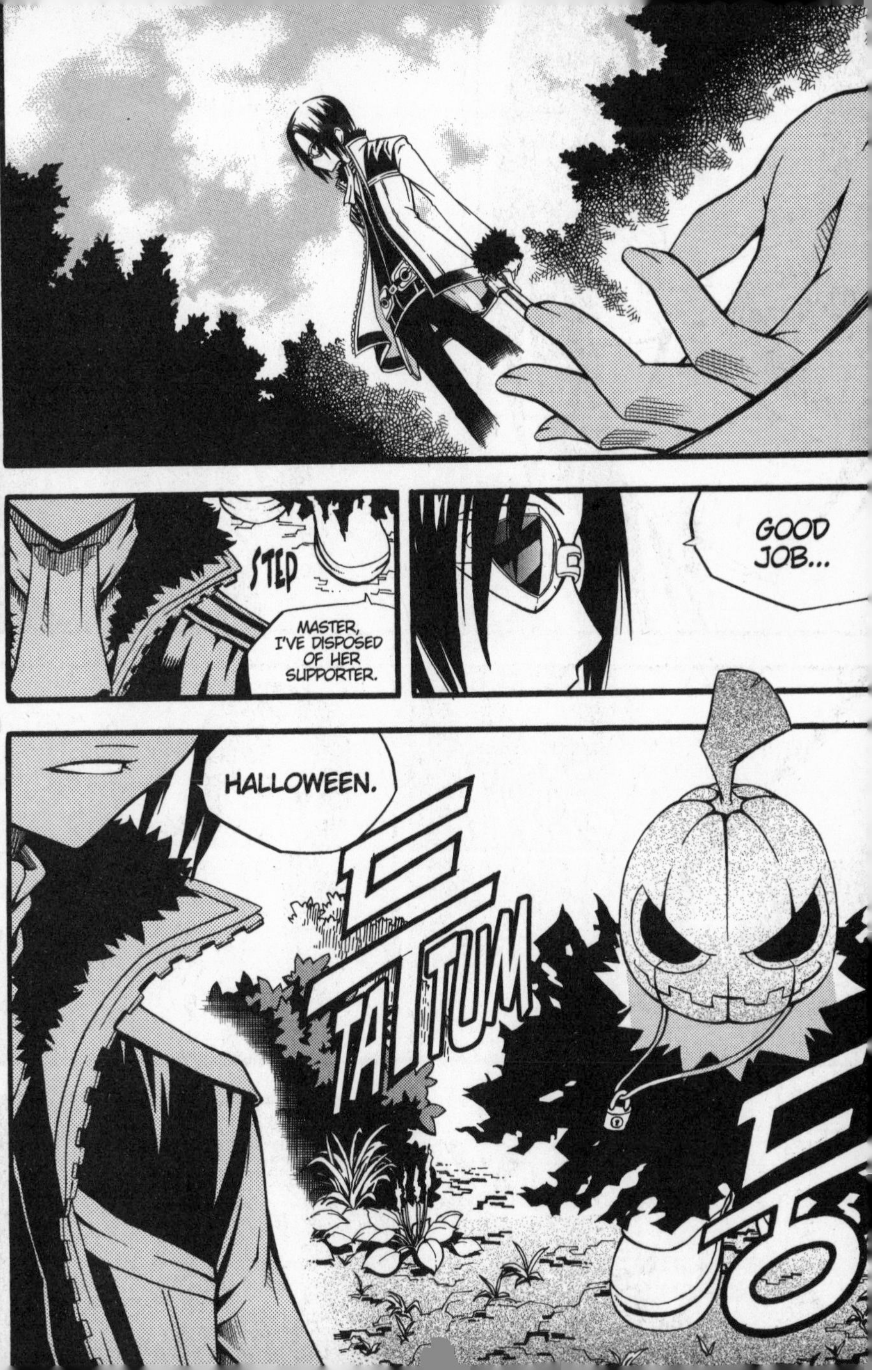
STEP
MASTER, I'VE DISPOSED OF HER SUPPORTER.
GOOD JOB...
HALLOWEEN.
TA TUM

PEOPLE WHO LIKE TASHA

THE SHY ONES.

THE OUTGOING ONES.

HOW-
EVER
...

WHAT THE HELL? YOU'RE ALL AS FLAT AS THE WALL! NO WONDER TASHA HAS NO INTEREST IN GIRLS.

SHOCK

THOSE WERE XING'S FINAL RECORDED WORDS. HE WAS NEVER SEEN AGAIN.

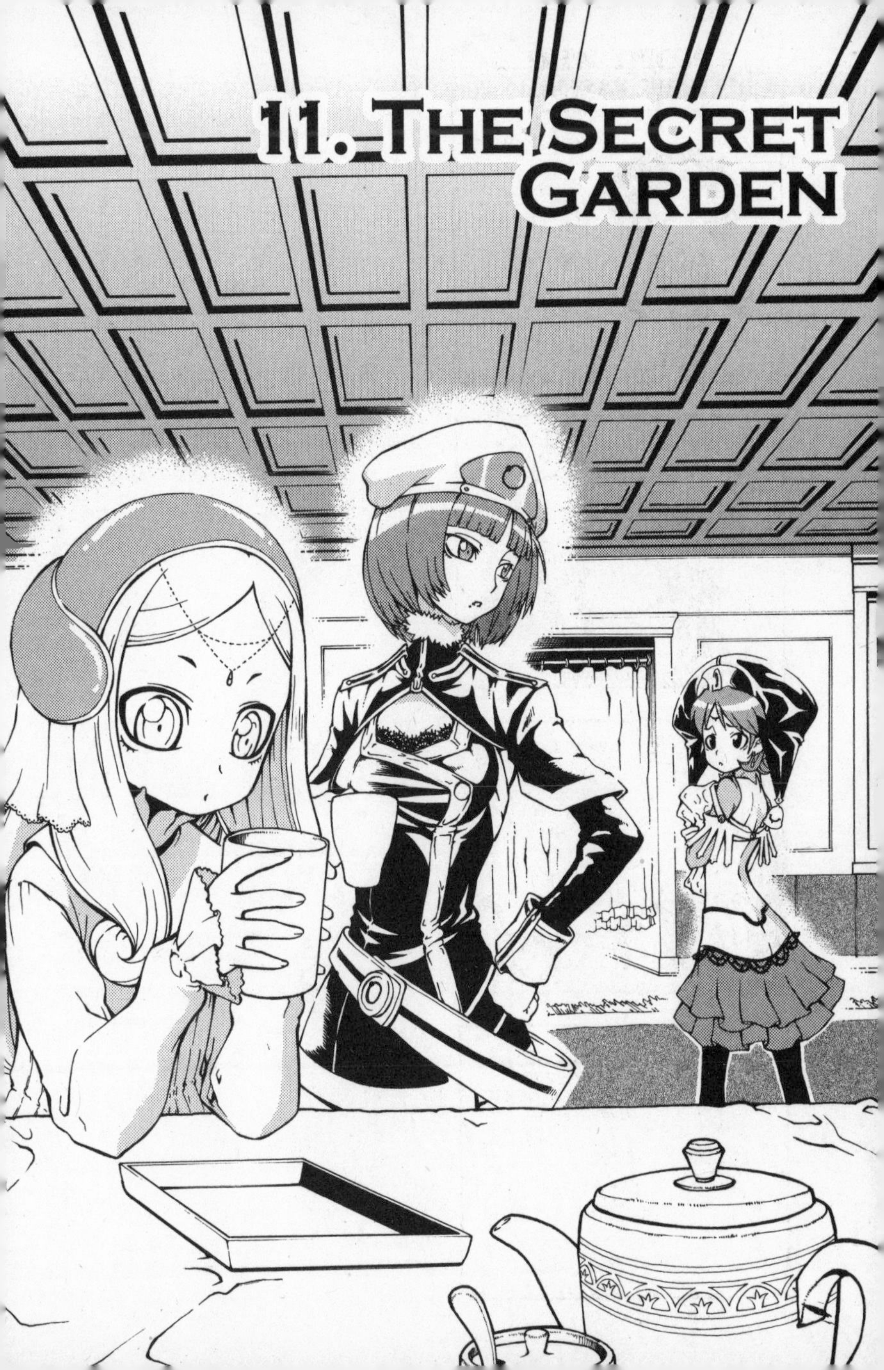
11. The Secret Garden

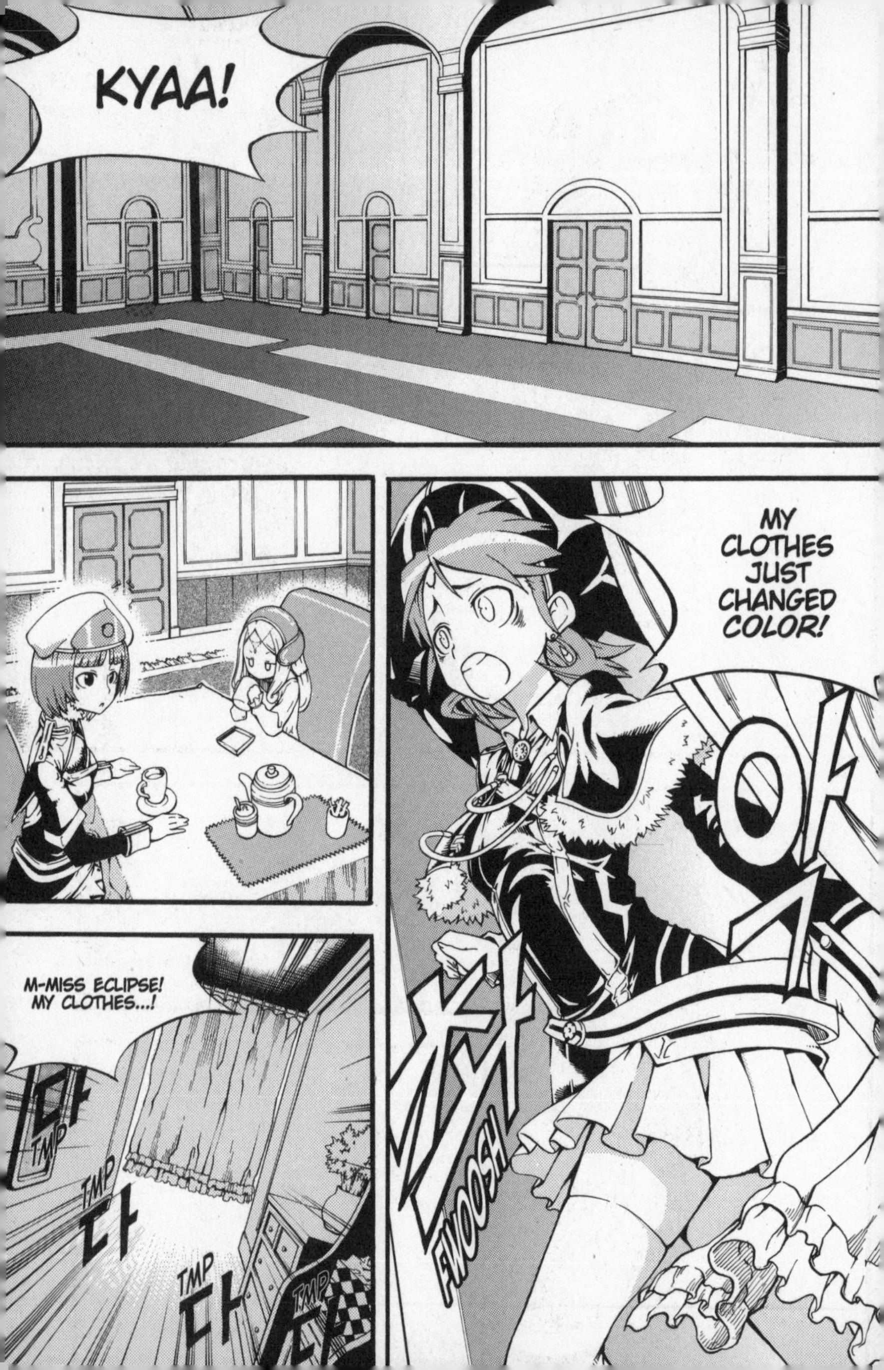
KYAA!
MY CLOTHES JUST CHANGED COLOR!
FWOOSH
M-MISS ECLIPSE! MY CLOTHES...!
TMP
TMP
TMP
TMP

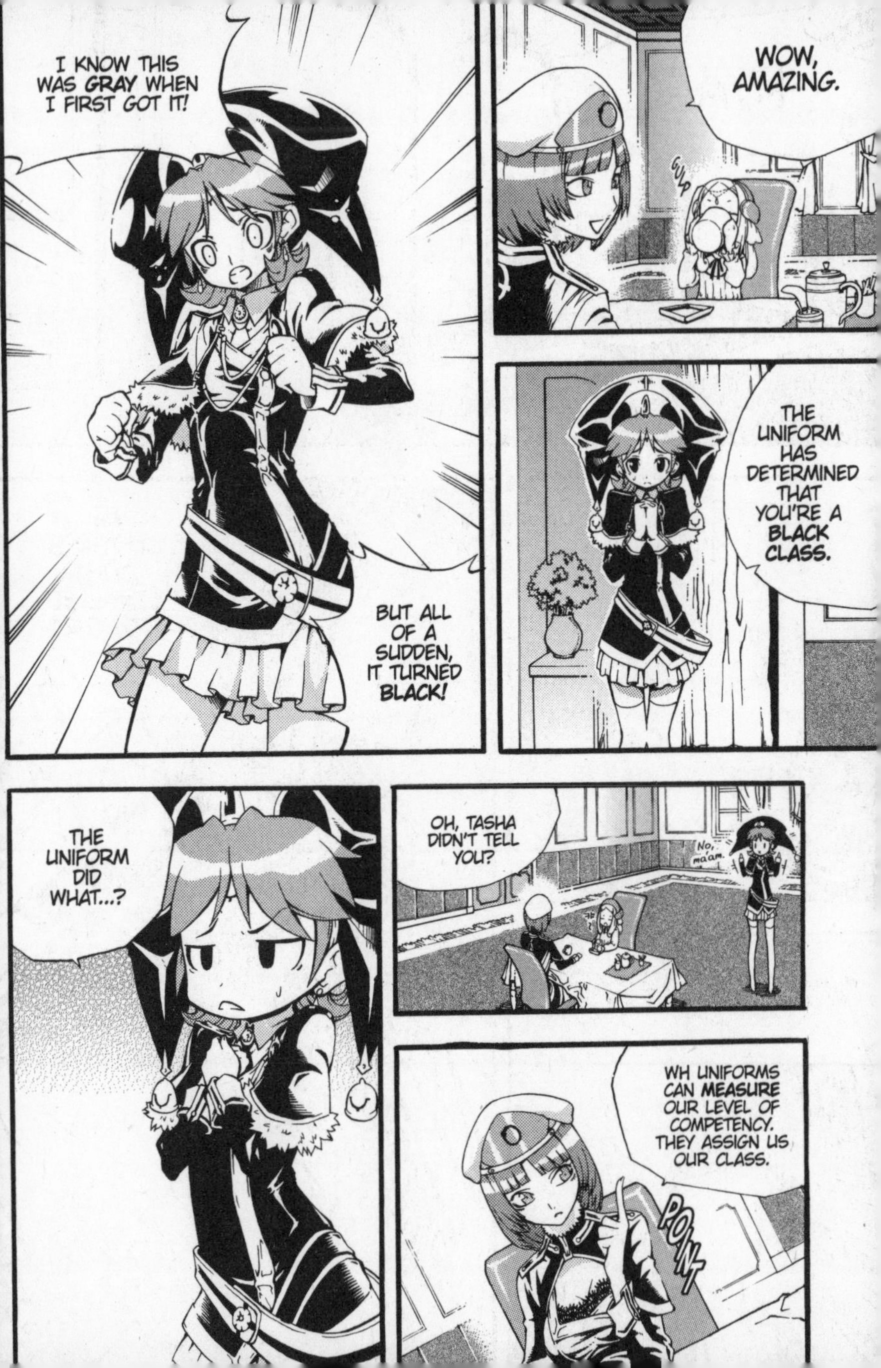
WOW, AMAZING.
GULP
THE UNIFORM HAS DETERMINED THAT YOU'RE A BLACK CLASS.
I KNOW THIS WAS GRAY WHEN I FIRST GOT IT!
BUT ALL OF A SUDDEN, IT TURNED BLACK!
OH, TASHA DIDN'T TELL YOU?
No, ma'am.
THE UNIFORM DID WHAT...?
WH UNIFORMS CAN MEASURE OUR LEVEL OF COMPETENCY. THEY ASSIGN US OUR CLASS.
POINT

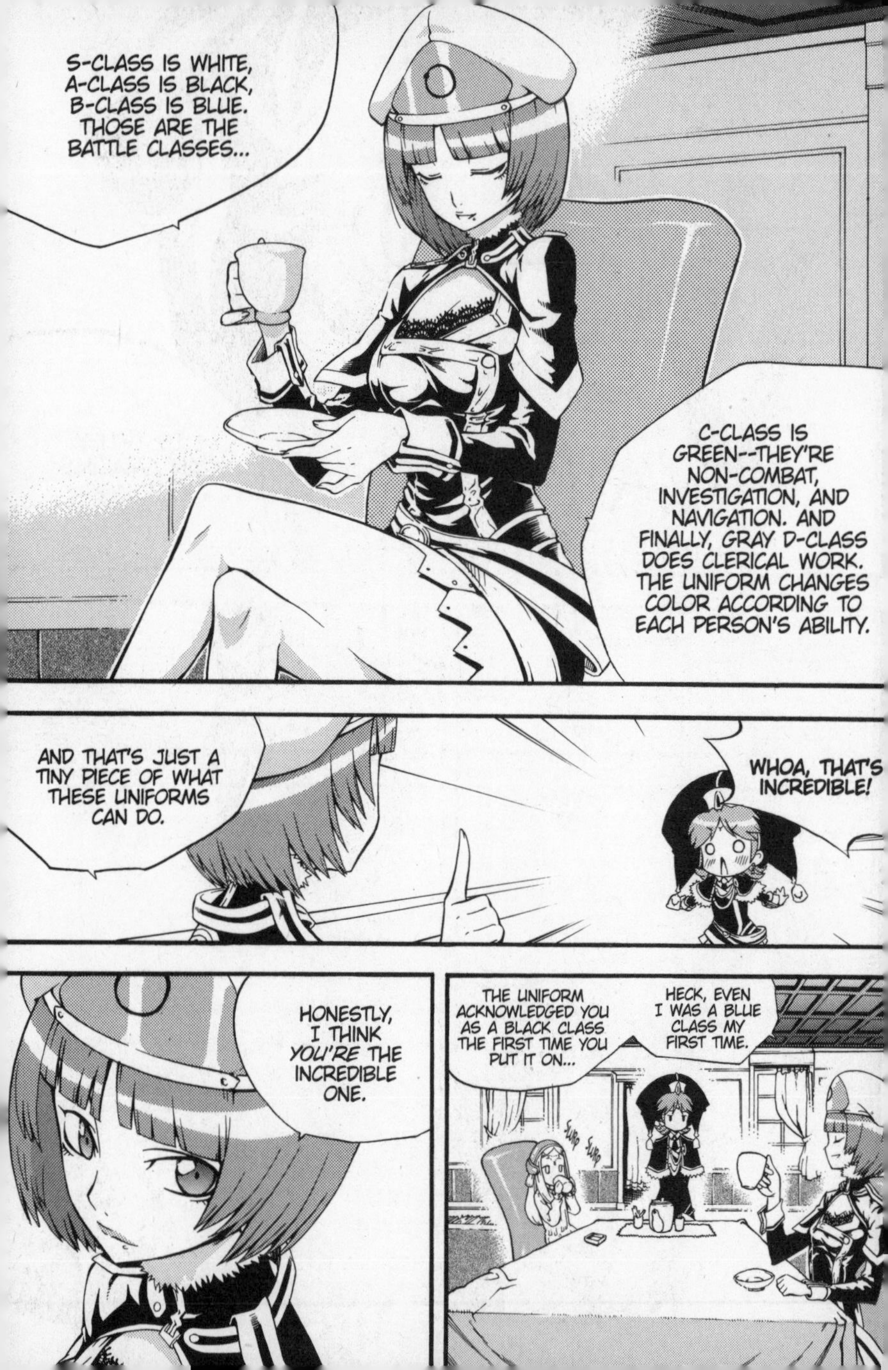
S-CLASS IS WHITE, A-CLASS IS BLACK, B-CLASS IS BLUE. THOSE ARE THE BATTLE CLASSES...
C-CLASS IS GREEN--THEY'RE NON-COMBAT, INVESTIGATION, AND NAVIGATION. AND FINALLY, GRAY D-CLASS DOES CLERICAL WORK. THE UNIFORM CHANGES COLOR ACCORDING TO EACH PERSON'S ABILITY.
WHOA, THAT'S INCREDIBLE!
AND THAT'S JUST A TINY PIECE OF WHAT THESE UNIFORMS CAN DO.
HONESTLY, I THINK *YOU'RE* THE INCREDIBLE ONE.
THE UNIFORM ACKNOWLEDGED YOU AS A BLACK CLASS THE FIRST TIME YOU PUT IT ON...
HECK, EVEN I WAS A BLUE CLASS MY FIRST TIME.
SLURP
SLURP

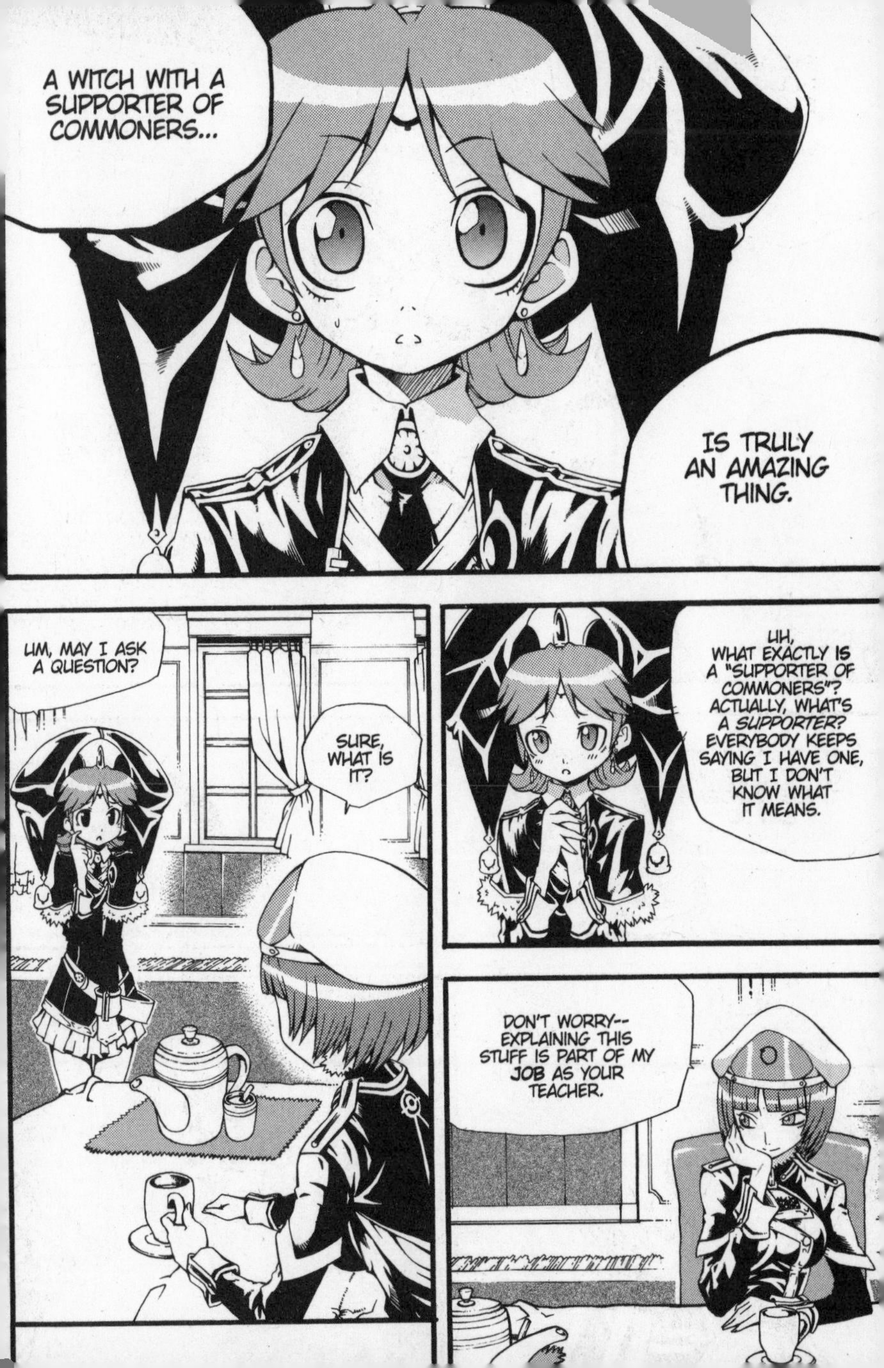
A WITCH WITH A SUPPORTER OF COMMONERS...
IS TRULY AN AMAZING THING.
UM, MAY I ASK A QUESTION?
SURE, WHAT IS IT?
UH, WHAT EXACTLY IS A "SUPPORTER OF COMMONERS"? ACTUALLY, WHAT'S A *SUPPORTER*? EVERYBODY KEEPS SAYING I HAVE ONE, BUT I DON'T KNOW WHAT IT MEANS.
DON'T WORRY-- EXPLAINING THIS STUFF IS PART OF MY JOB AS YOUR TEACHER.

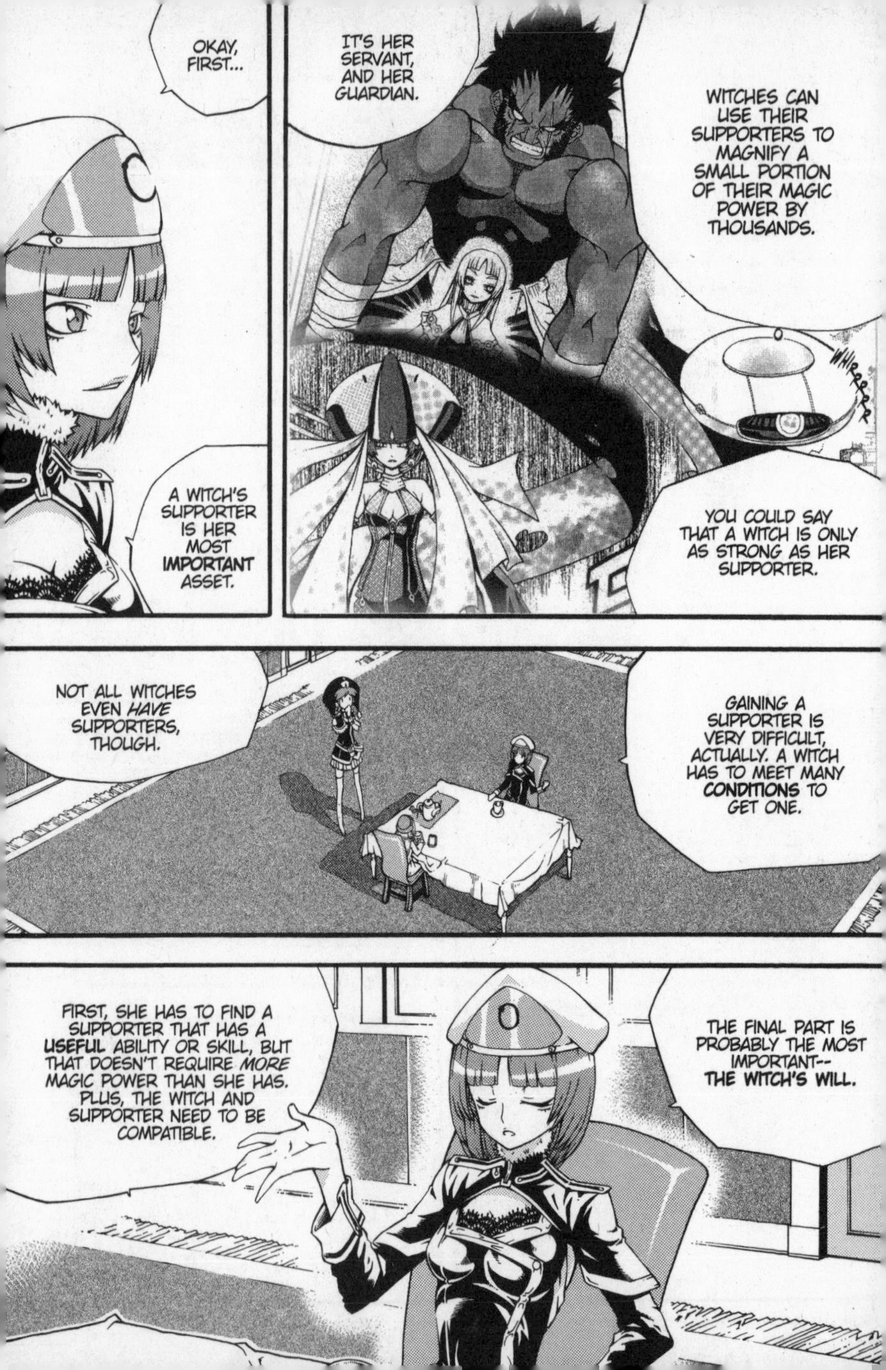
OKAY, FIRST...
A WITCH'S SUPPORTER IS HER MOST **IMPORTANT** ASSET.
IT'S HER SERVANT, AND HER GUARDIAN.
WITCHES CAN USE THEIR SUPPORTERS TO MAGNIFY A SMALL PORTION OF THEIR MAGIC POWER BY THOUSANDS.
WHIRRRRR
YOU COULD SAY THAT A WITCH IS ONLY AS STRONG AS HER SUPPORTER.
NOT ALL WITCHES EVEN *HAVE* SUPPORTERS, THOUGH.
GAINING A SUPPORTER IS VERY DIFFICULT, ACTUALLY. A WITCH HAS TO MEET MANY **CONDITIONS** TO GET ONE.
FIRST, SHE HAS TO FIND A SUPPORTER THAT HAS A **USEFUL** ABILITY OR SKILL, BUT THAT DOESN'T REQUIRE *MORE* MAGIC POWER THAN SHE HAS. PLUS, THE WITCH AND SUPPORTER NEED TO BE COMPATIBLE.
THE FINAL PART IS PROBABLY THE MOST IMPORTANT-- **THE WITCH'S WILL.**

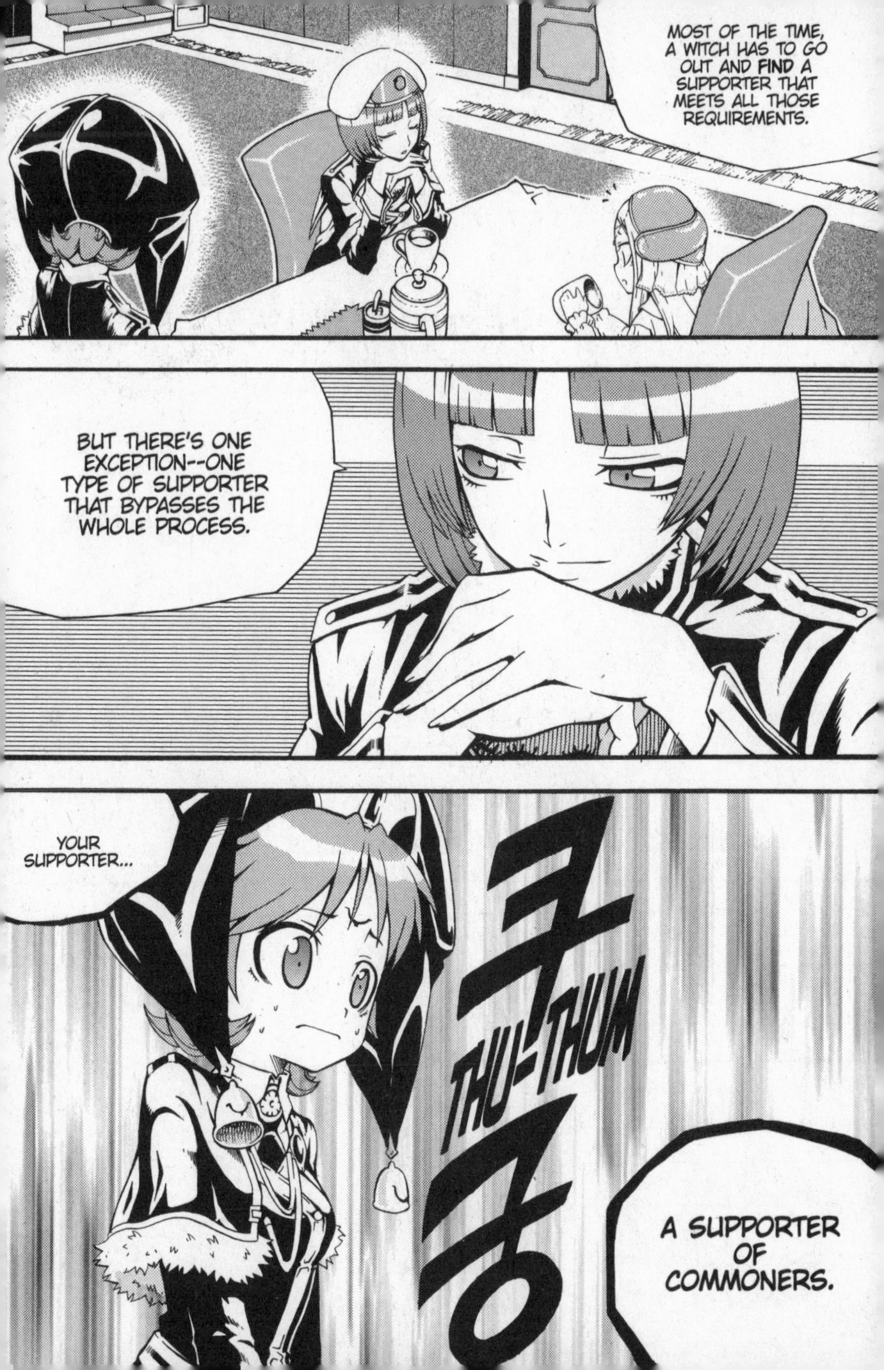
MOST OF THE TIME, A WITCH HAS TO GO OUT AND FIND A SUPPORTER THAT MEETS ALL THOSE REQUIREMENTS.
BUT THERE'S ONE EXCEPTION--ONE TYPE OF SUPPORTER THAT BYPASSES THE WHOLE PROCESS.
YOUR SUPPORTER...
THU-THUM
A SUPPORTER OF COMMONERS.

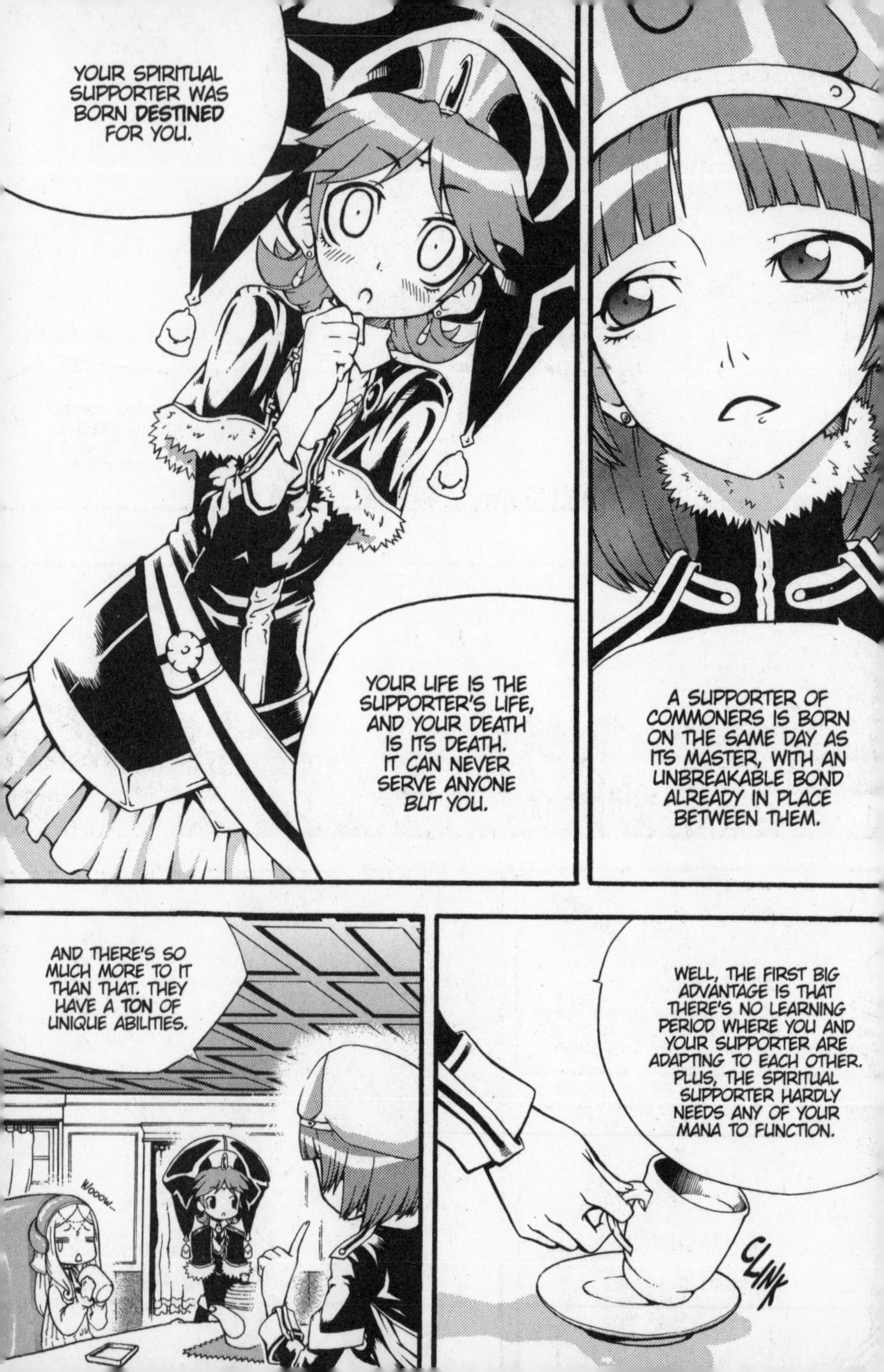
A SUPPORTER OF COMMONERS IS BORN ON THE SAME DAY AS ITS MASTER, WITH AN UNBREAKABLE BOND ALREADY IN PLACE BETWEEN THEM.
YOUR SPIRITUAL SUPPORTER WAS BORN DESTINED FOR YOU.
YOUR LIFE IS THE SUPPORTER'S LIFE, AND YOUR DEATH IS ITS DEATH. IT CAN NEVER SERVE ANYONE BUT YOU.
WELL, THE FIRST BIG ADVANTAGE IS THAT THERE'S NO LEARNING PERIOD WHERE YOU AND YOUR SUPPORTER ARE ADAPTING TO EACH OTHER. PLUS, THE SPIRITUAL SUPPORTER HARDLY NEEDS ANY OF YOUR MANA TO FUNCTION.
CLINK
AND THERE'S SO MUCH MORE TO IT THAN THAT. THEY HAVE A TON OF UNIQUE ABILITIES.
WOOOW...

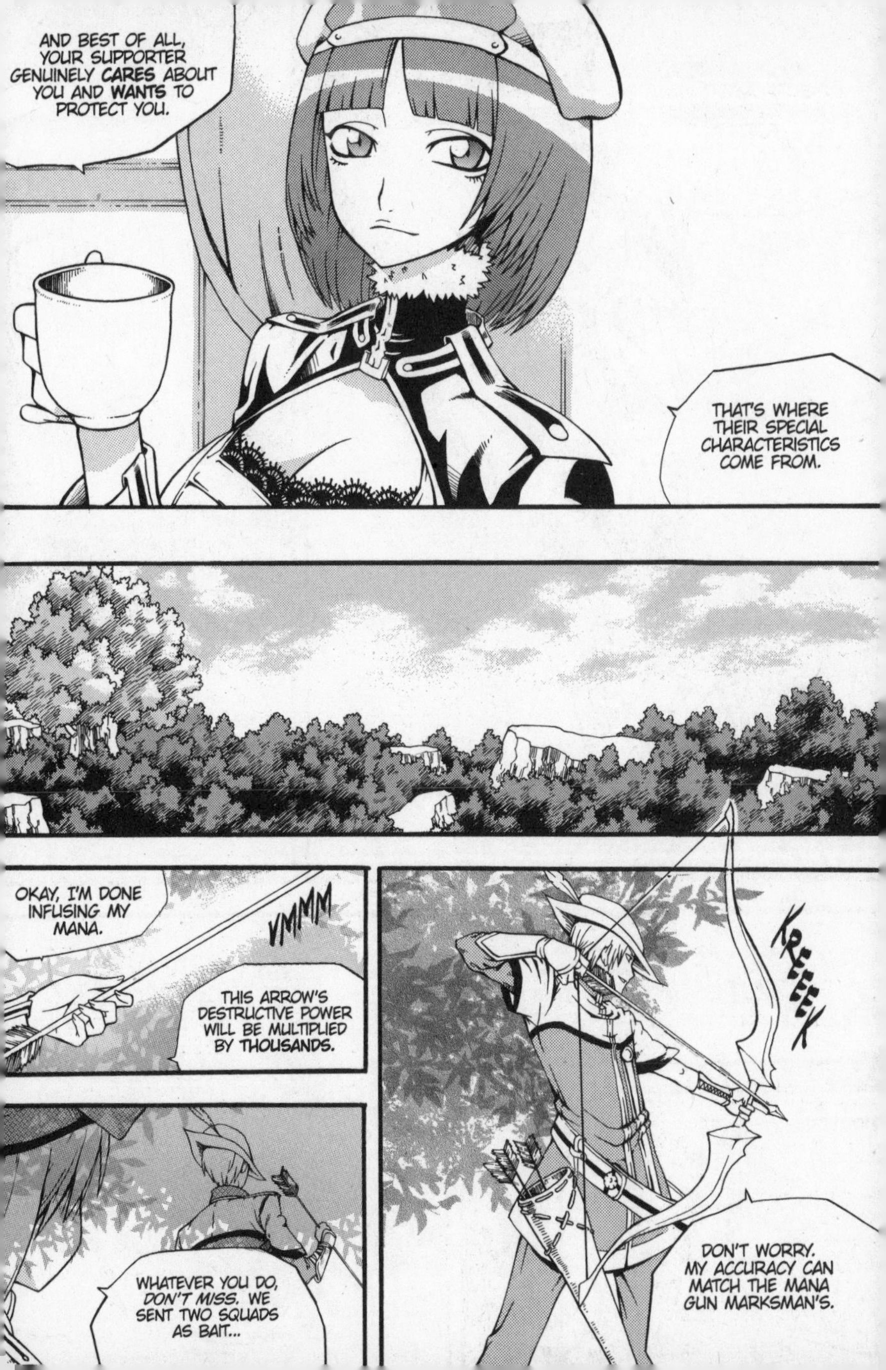
AND BEST OF ALL, YOUR SUPPORTER GENUINELY CARES ABOUT YOU AND WANTS TO PROTECT YOU.
THAT'S WHERE THEIR SPECIAL CHARACTERISTICS COME FROM.
KREEEK
OKAY, I'M DONE INFUSING MY MANA.
VMMM
THIS ARROW'S DESTRUCTIVE POWER WILL BE MULTIPLIED BY THOUSANDS.
DON'T WORRY. MY ACCURACY CAN MATCH THE MANA GUN MARKSMAN'S.
WHATEVER YOU DO, DON'T MISS. WE SENT TWO SQUADS AS BAIT...

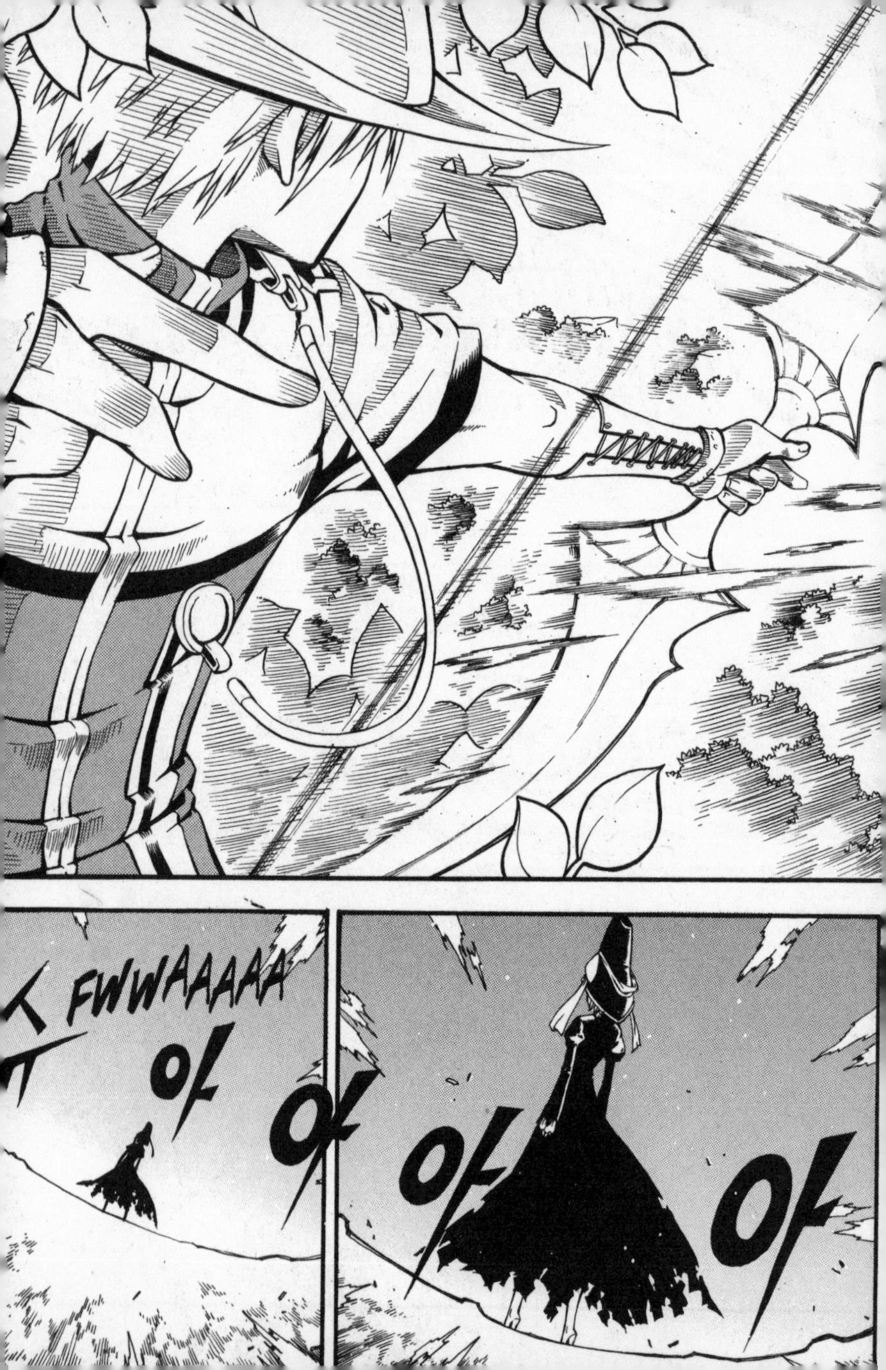

FWWAAAAA

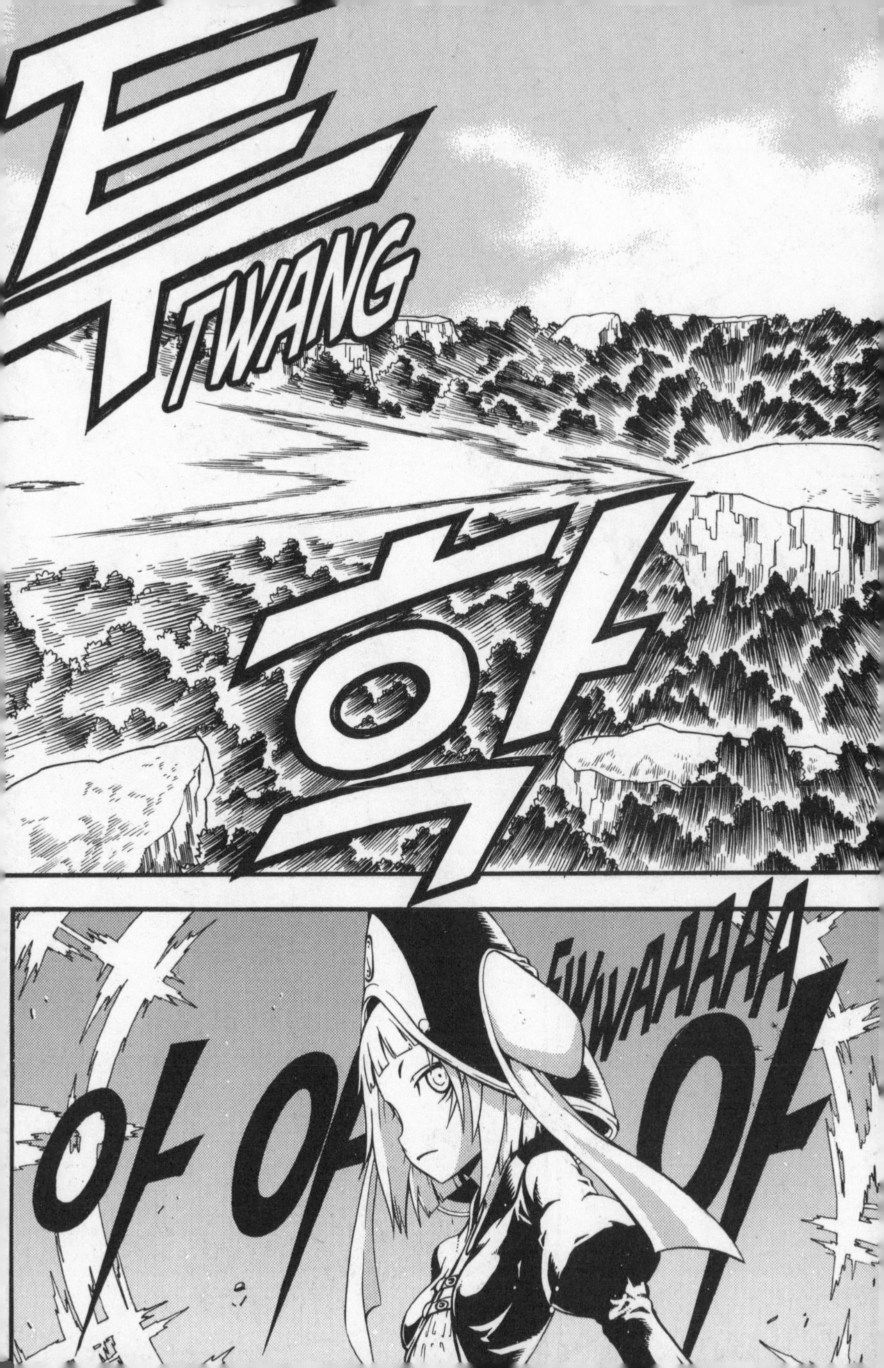
TWANG
SWAAAAAA
아아아

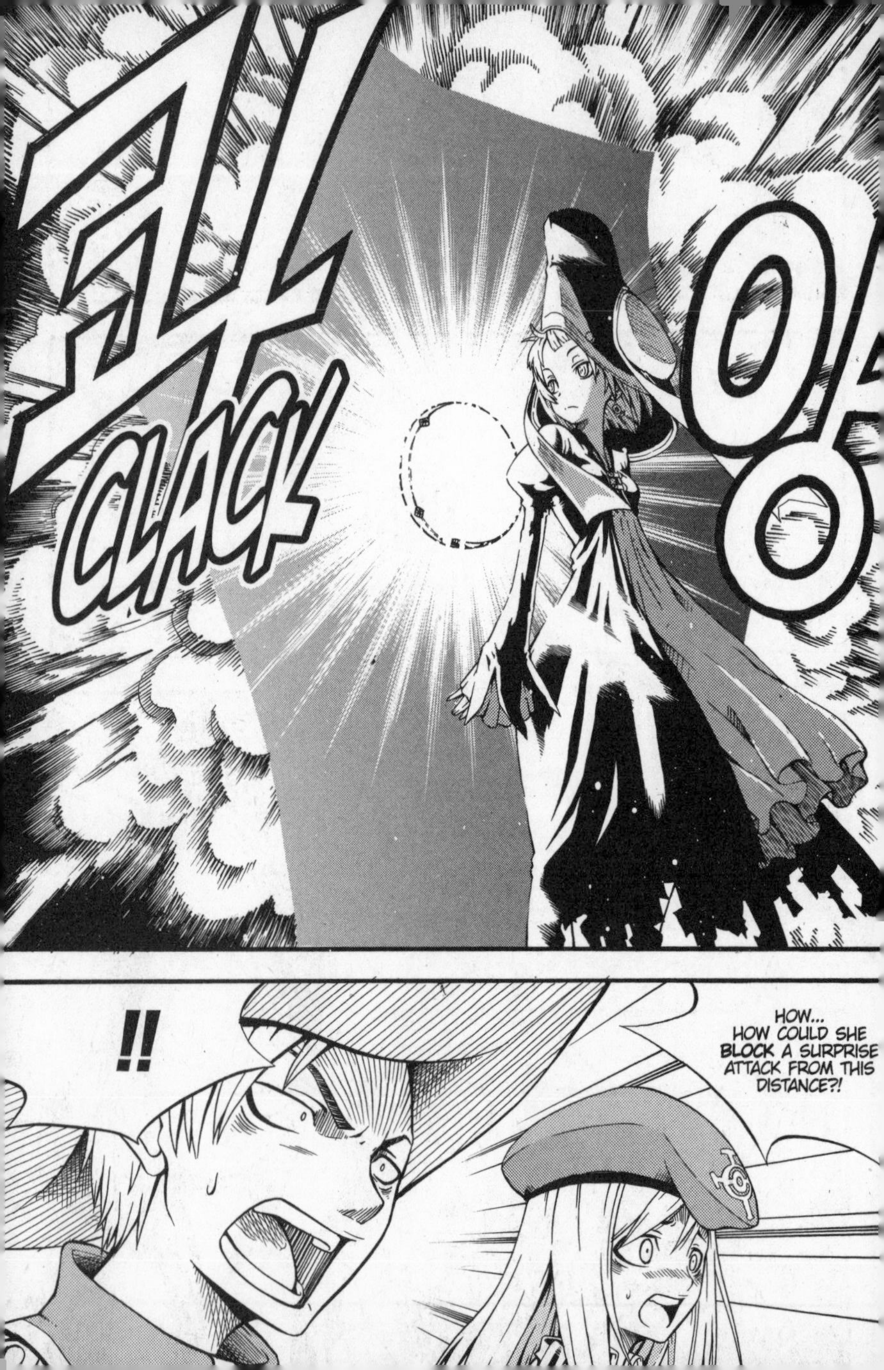
ZA!
CLACK
O...
!!
HOW...
HOW COULD SHE BLOCK A SURPRISE ATTACK FROM THIS DISTANCE?!

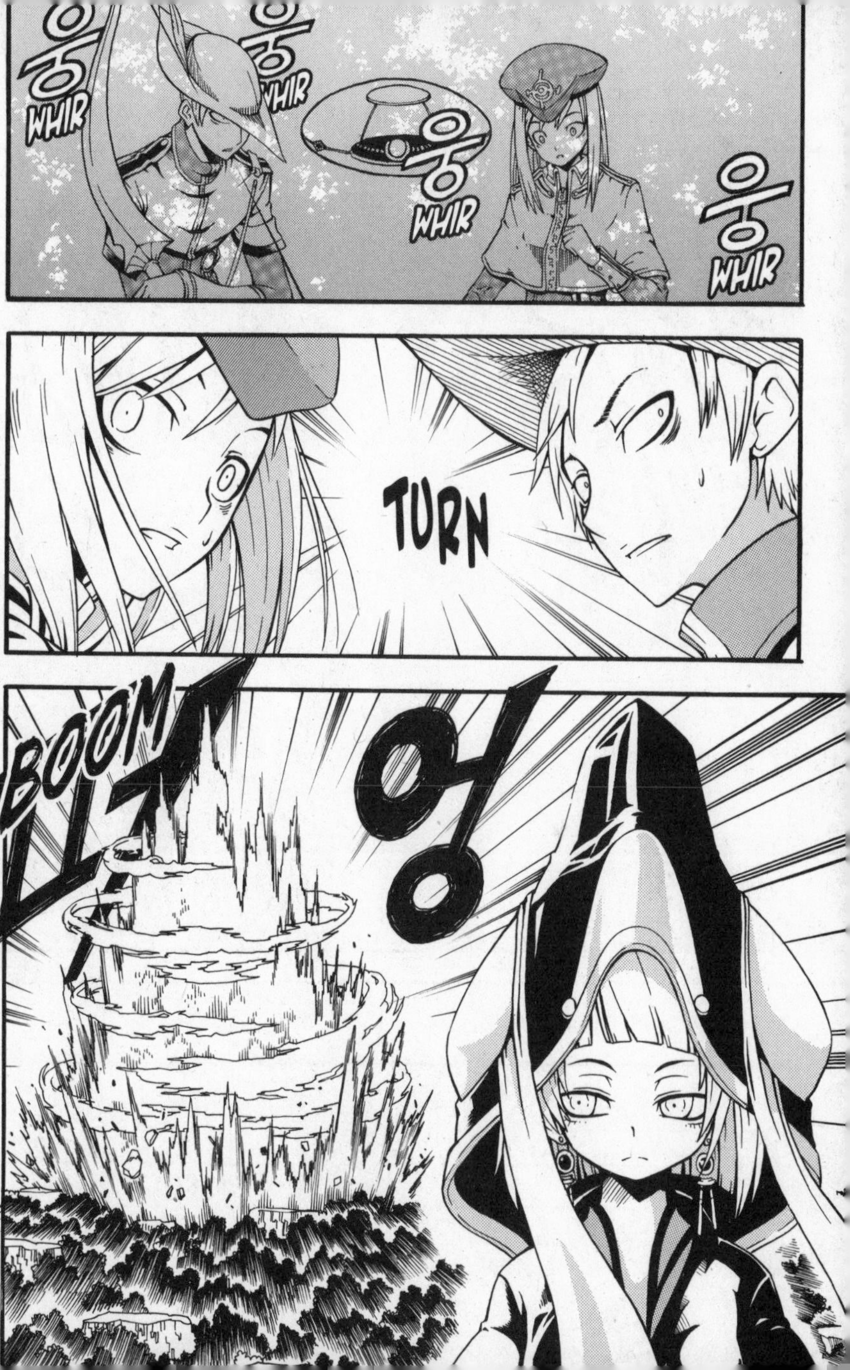
웅
WHIR
웅
WHIR
웅
WHIR
웅
WHIR
TURN
BOOM

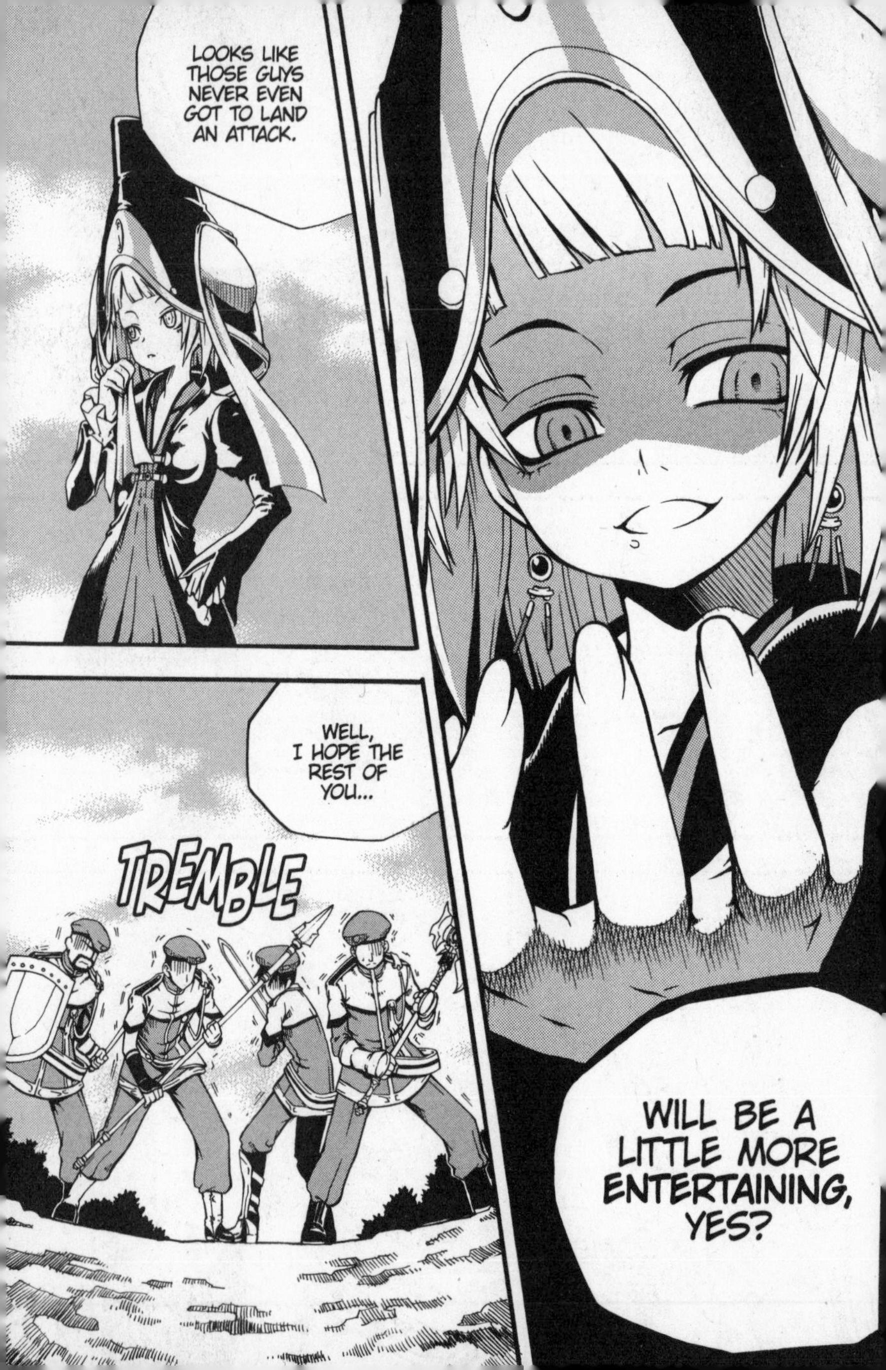
LOOKS LIKE THOSE GUYS NEVER EVEN GOT TO LAND AN ATTACK.
WELL, I HOPE THE REST OF YOU...
TREMBLE
WILL BE A LITTLE MORE ENTERTAINING, YES?

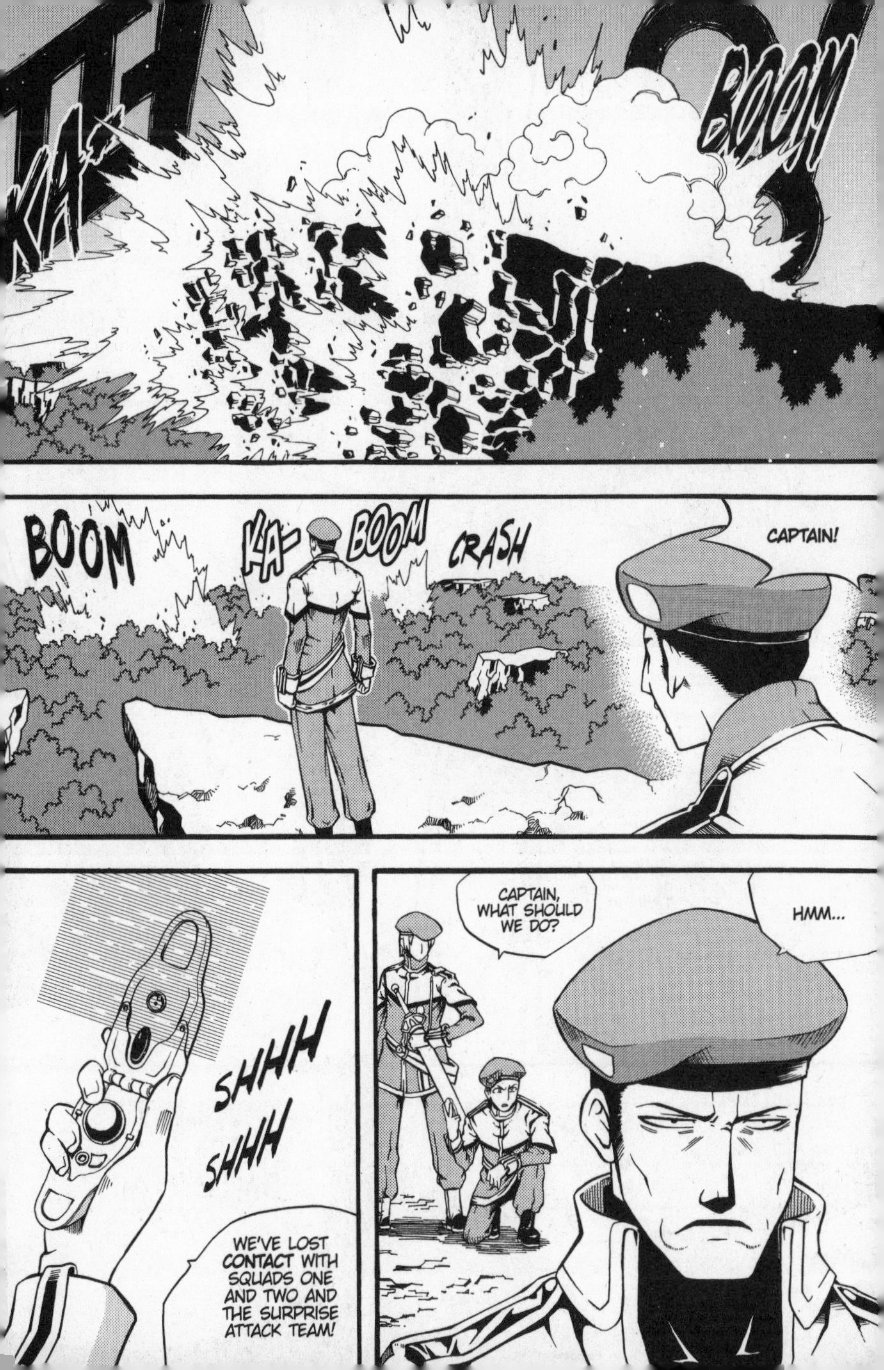
KA-THH
BOOM
BOOM
KA-BOOM
CRASH
CAPTAIN!
WE'VE LOST CONTACT WITH SQUADS ONE AND TWO AND THE SURPRISE ATTACK TEAM!
SHHH
SHHH
CAPTAIN, WHAT SHOULD WE DO?
HMM...

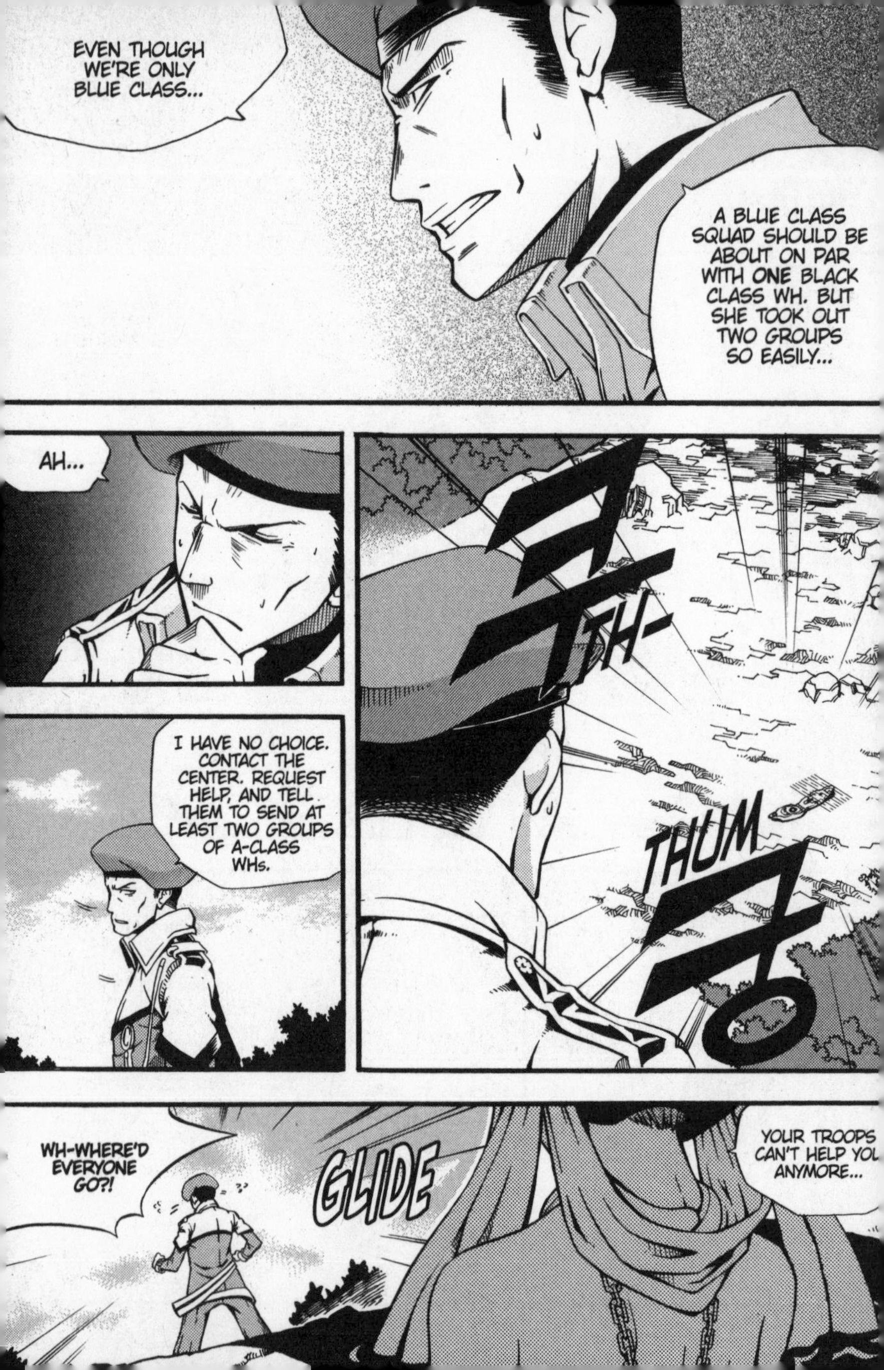
EVEN THOUGH WE'RE ONLY BLUE CLASS...
A BLUE CLASS SQUAD SHOULD BE ABOUT ON PAR WITH ONE BLACK CLASS WH. BUT SHE TOOK OUT TWO GROUPS SO EASILY...
AH...
TH-
THUM
I HAVE NO CHOICE. CONTACT THE CENTER. REQUEST HELP, AND TELL THEM TO SEND AT LEAST TWO GROUPS OF A-CLASS WHs.
WH-WHERE'D EVERYONE GO?!
GLIDE
YOUR TROOPS CAN'T HELP YOU ANYMORE...

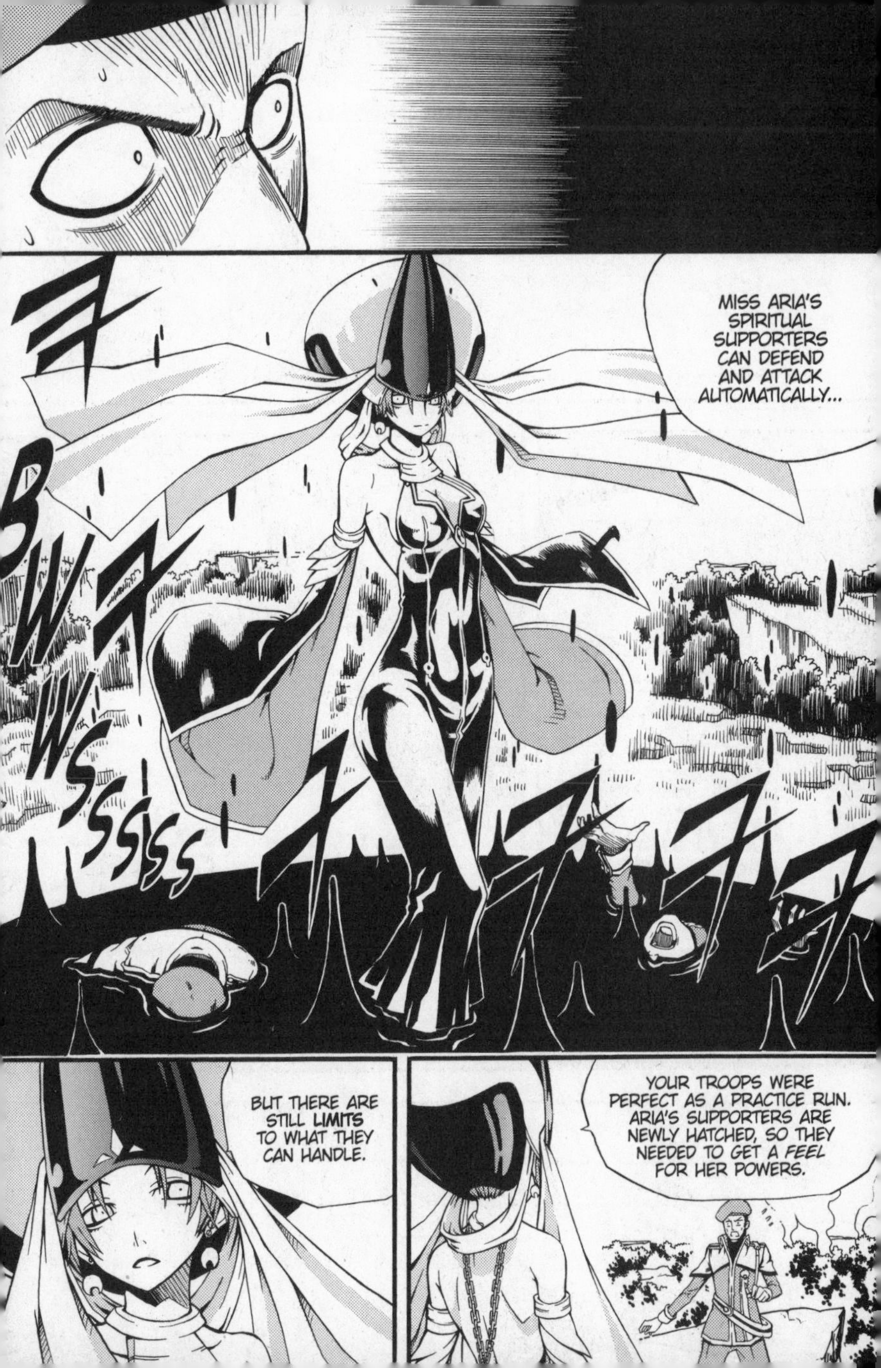

MISS ARIA'S SPIRITUAL SUPPORTERS CAN DEFEND AND ATTACK AUTOMATICALLY...
BWWSSSSS
BUT THERE ARE STILL LIMITS TO WHAT THEY CAN HANDLE.
YOUR TROOPS WERE PERFECT AS A PRACTICE RUN. ARIA'S SUPPORTERS ARE NEWLY HATCHED, SO THEY NEEDED TO GET A FEEL FOR HER POWERS.

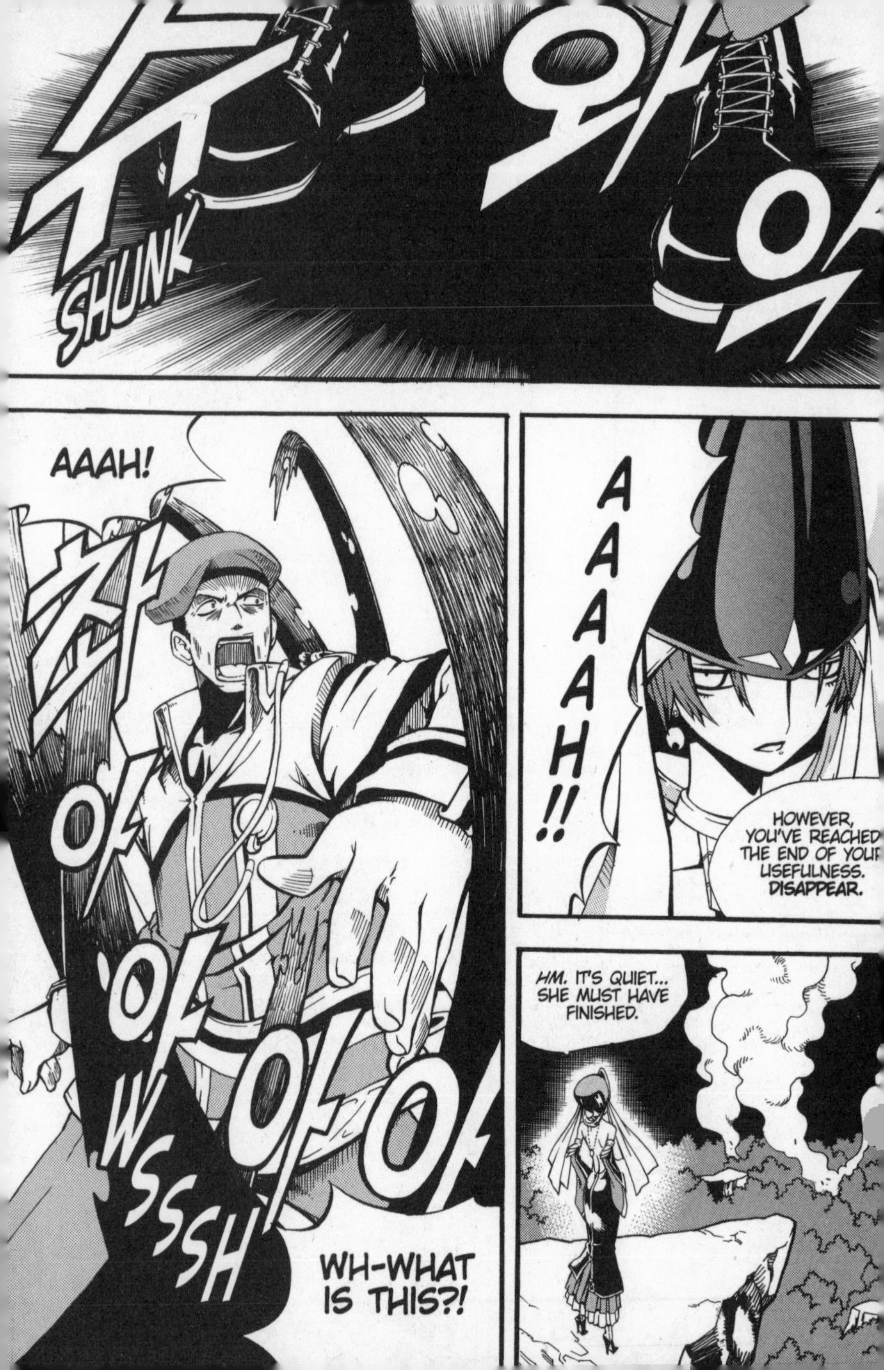

SHUNK
AAAAAH!!
HOWEVER, YOU'VE REACHED THE END OF YOUR USEFULNESS. DISAPPEAR.
AAAH!
WSSSH
WH-WHAT IS THIS?!
HM. IT'S QUIET... SHE MUST HAVE FINISHED.

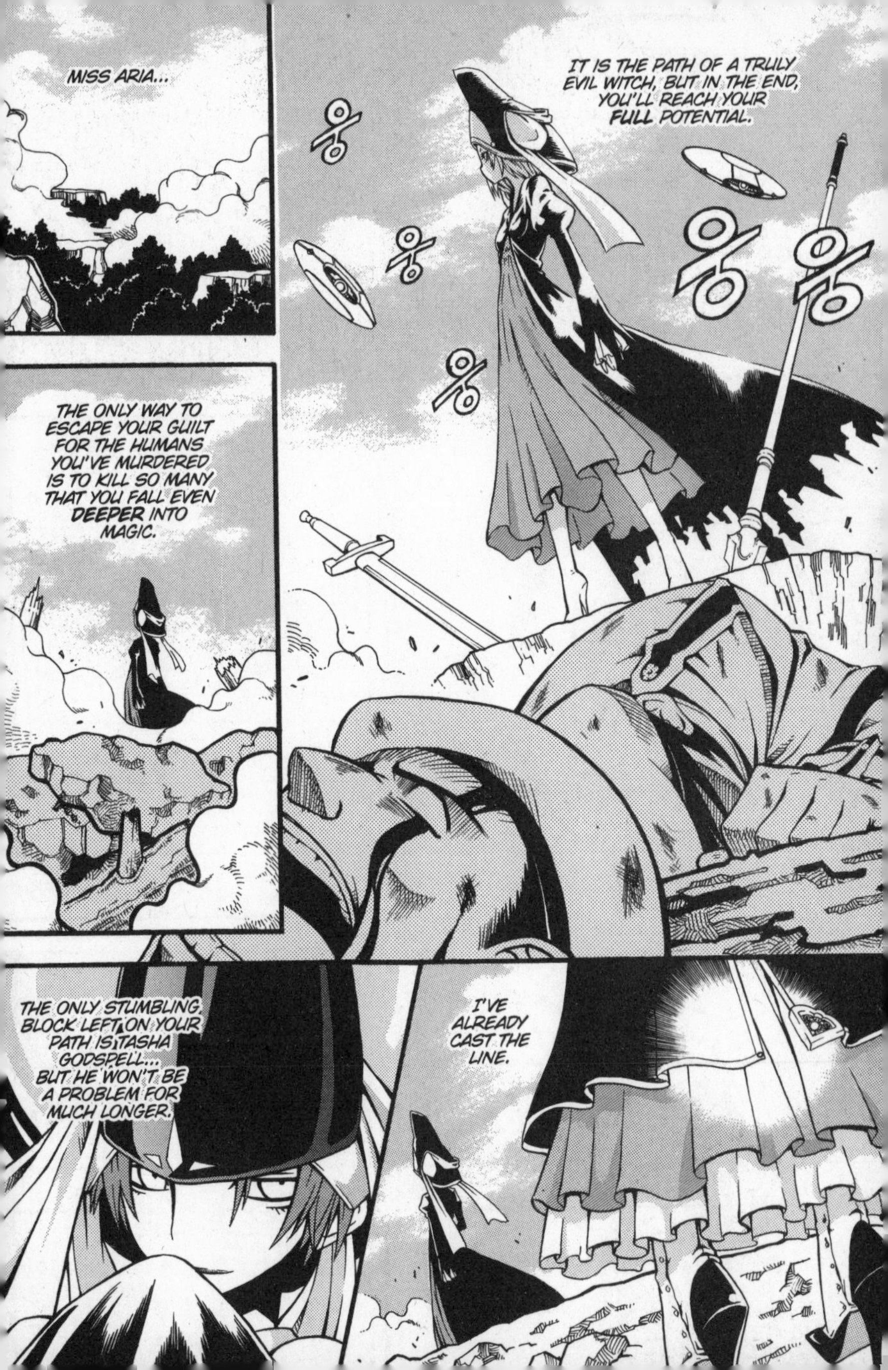
IT IS THE PATH OF A TRULY EVIL WITCH, BUT IN THE END, YOU'LL REACH YOUR FULL POTENTIAL.
MISS ARIA...
THE ONLY WAY TO ESCAPE YOUR GUILT FOR THE HUMANS YOU'VE MURDERED IS TO KILL SO MANY THAT YOU FALL EVEN DEEPER INTO MAGIC.
I'VE ALREADY CAST THE LINE.
THE ONLY STUMBLING BLOCK LEFT ON YOUR PATH IS TASHA GODSPELL... BUT HE WON'T BE A PROBLEM FOR MUCH LONGER.

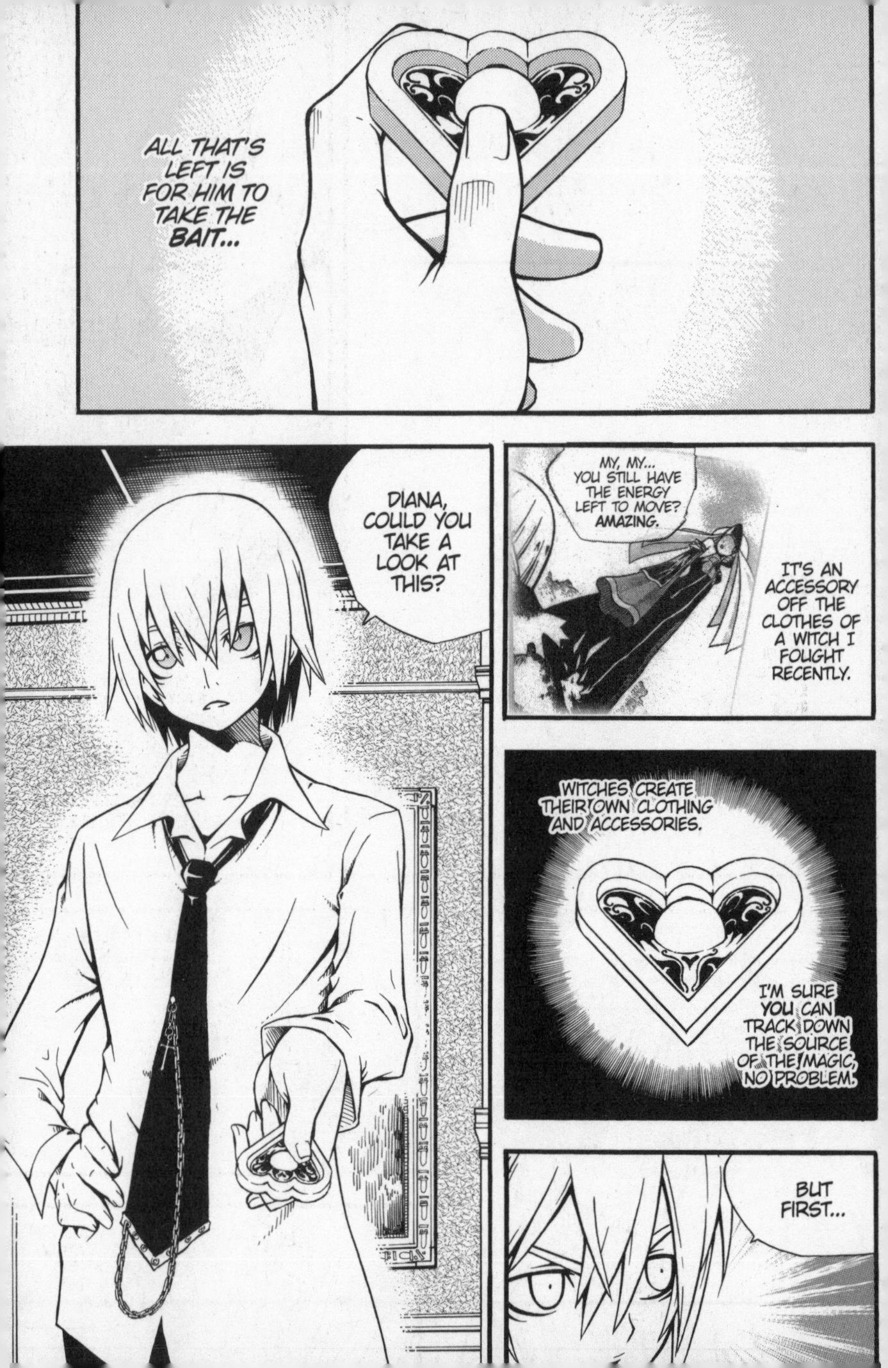
ALL THAT'S LEFT IS FOR HIM TO TAKE THE BAIT...
MY, MY... YOU STILL HAVE THE ENERGY LEFT TO MOVE? AMAZING.
IT'S AN ACCESSORY OFF THE CLOTHES OF A WITCH I FOUGHT RECENTLY.
DIANA, COULD YOU TAKE A LOOK AT THIS?
WITCHES CREATE THEIR OWN CLOTHING AND ACCESSORIES.
I'M SURE YOU CAN TRACK DOWN THE SOURCE OF THE MAGIC, NO PROBLEM.
BUT FIRST...

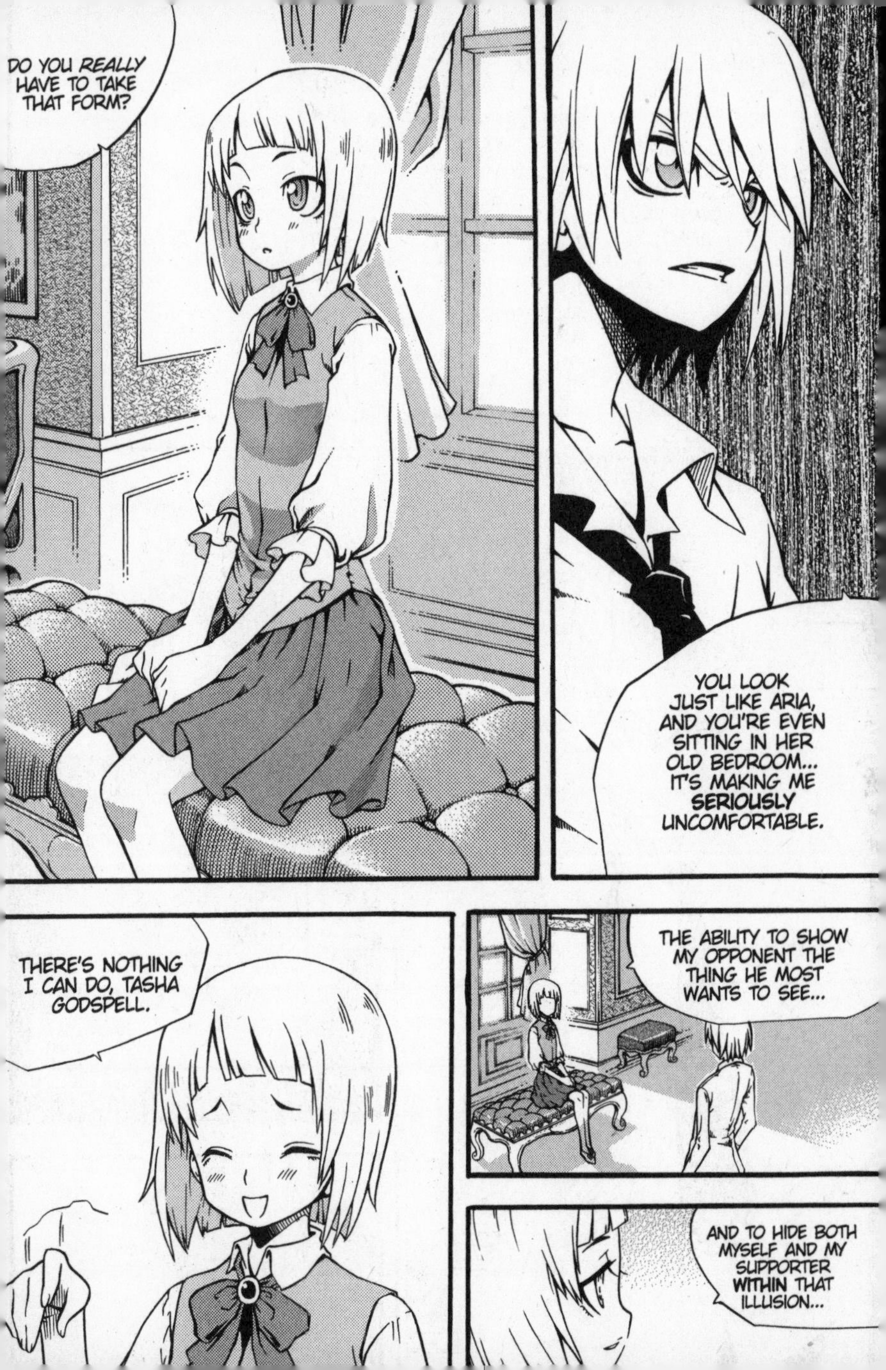
DO YOU *REALLY* HAVE TO TAKE THAT FORM?
YOU LOOK JUST LIKE ARIA, AND YOU'RE EVEN SITTING IN HER OLD BEDROOM... IT'S MAKING ME **SERIOUSLY** UNCOMFORTABLE.
THERE'S NOTHING I CAN DO, TASHA GODSPELL.
THE ABILITY TO SHOW MY OPPONENT THE THING HE MOST WANTS TO SEE...
AND TO HIDE BOTH MYSELF AND MY SUPPORTER **WITHIN** THAT ILLUSION...

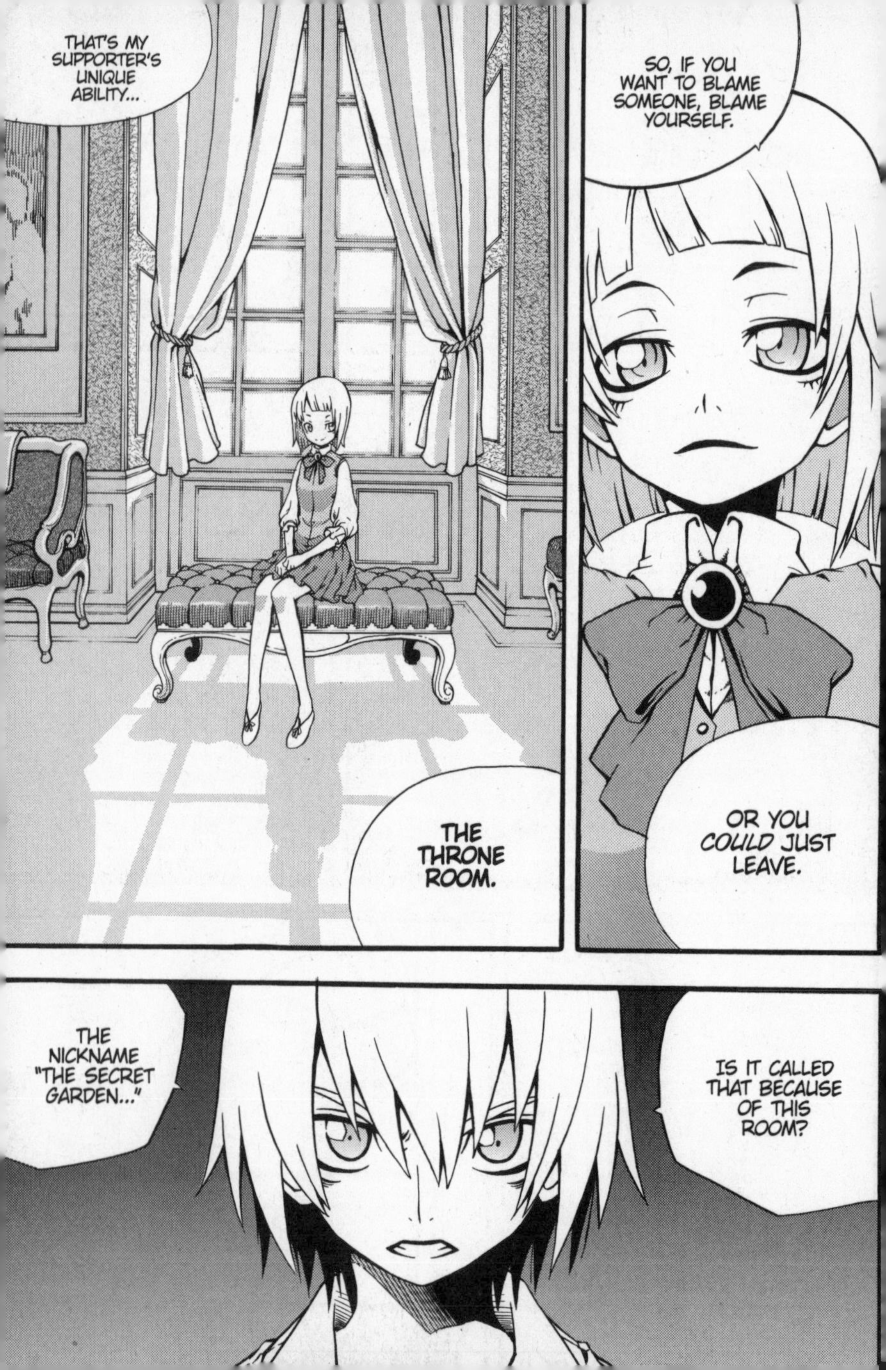
THAT'S MY SUPPORTER'S UNIQUE ABILITY...
THE THRONE ROOM.
SO, IF YOU WANT TO BLAME SOMEONE, BLAME YOURSELF.
OR YOU *COULD* JUST LEAVE.
THE NICKNAME "THE SECRET GARDEN..."
IS IT CALLED THAT BECAUSE OF THIS ROOM?

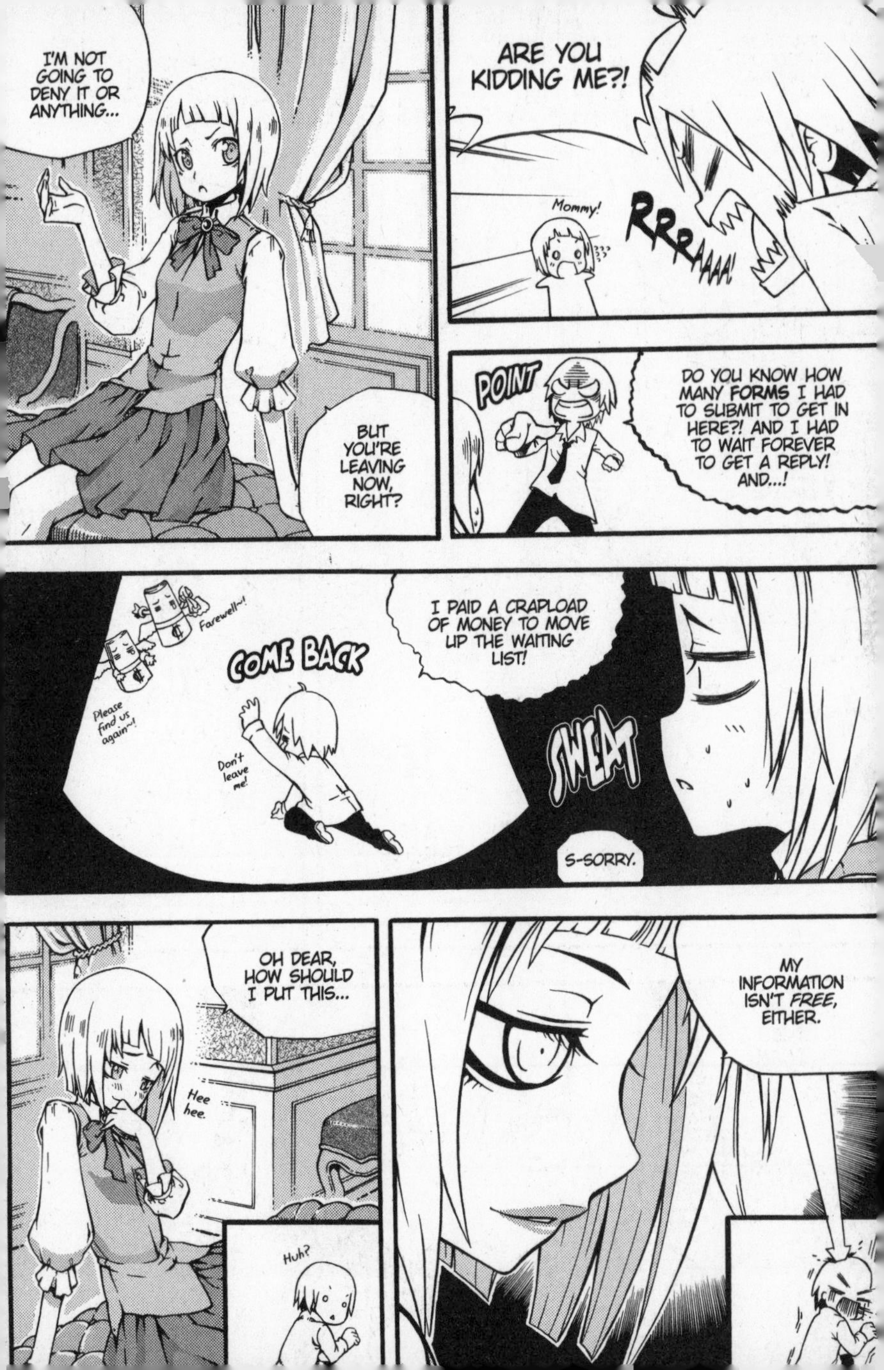

ARE YOU KIDDING ME?!
RRRAAAA!
Mommy!
I'M NOT GOING TO DENY IT OR ANYTHING...
DO YOU KNOW HOW MANY FORMS I HAD TO SUBMIT TO GET IN HERE?! AND I HAD TO WAIT FOREVER TO GET A REPLY! AND...!
POINT
BUT YOU'RE LEAVING NOW, RIGHT?
I PAID A CRAPLOAD OF MONEY TO MOVE UP THE WAITING LIST!
Farewell~!
Please find us again~!
COME BACK
Don't leave me!
SWEAT
S-SORRY.
MY INFORMATION ISN'T FREE, EITHER.
OH DEAR, HOW SHOULD I PUT THIS...
Hee hee.
Huh?

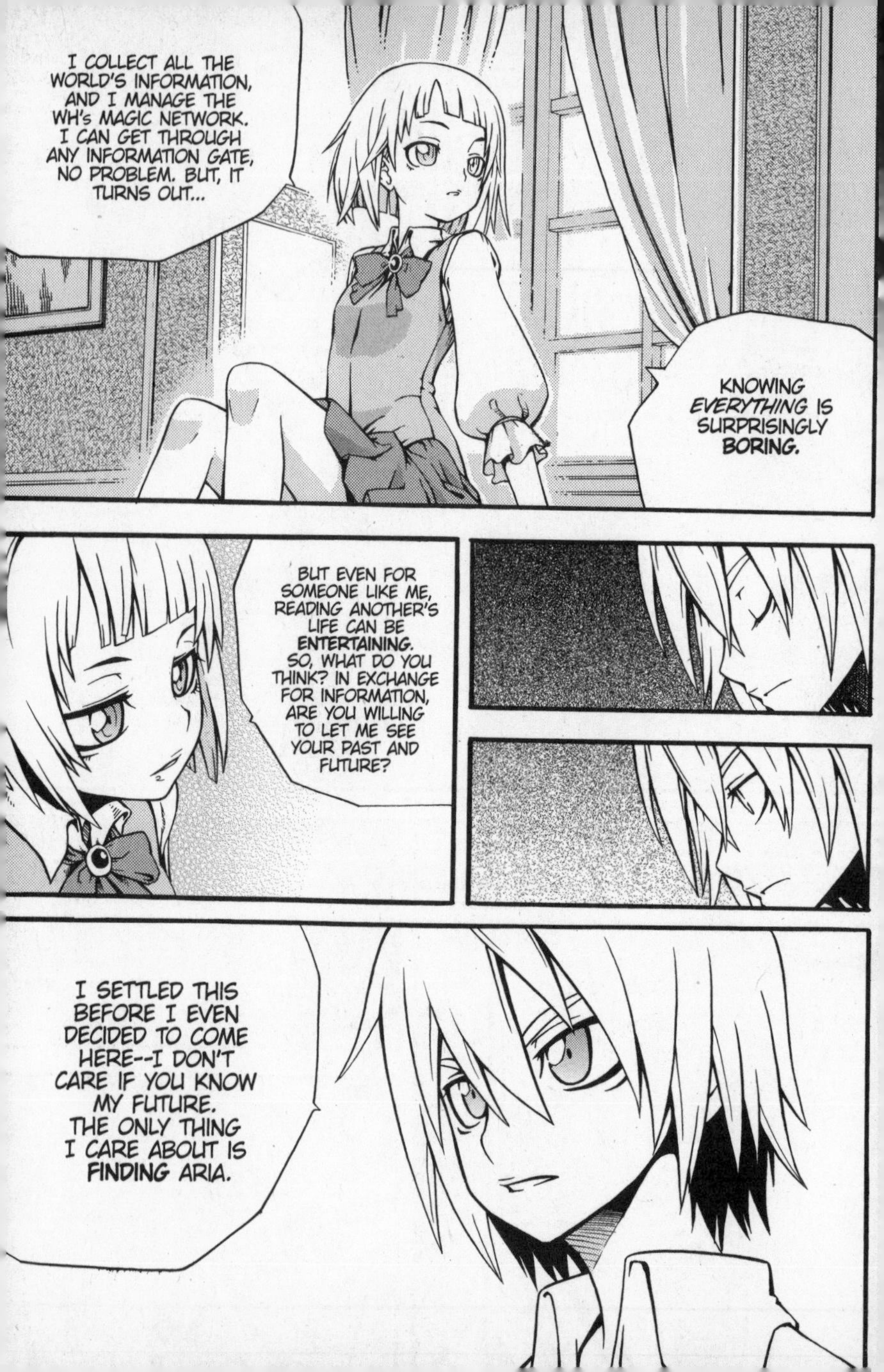
I COLLECT ALL THE WORLD'S INFORMATION, AND I MANAGE THE WH's MAGIC NETWORK. I CAN GET THROUGH ANY INFORMATION GATE, NO PROBLEM. BUT, IT TURNS OUT...
KNOWING *EVERYTHING* IS SURPRISINGLY **BORING.**
BUT EVEN FOR SOMEONE LIKE ME, READING ANOTHER'S LIFE CAN BE **ENTERTAINING.** SO, WHAT DO YOU THINK? IN EXCHANGE FOR INFORMATION, ARE YOU WILLING TO LET ME SEE YOUR PAST AND FUTURE?
I SETTLED THIS BEFORE I EVEN DECIDED TO COME HERE--I DON'T CARE IF YOU KNOW MY FUTURE. THE ONLY THING I CARE ABOUT IS **FINDING ARIA.**

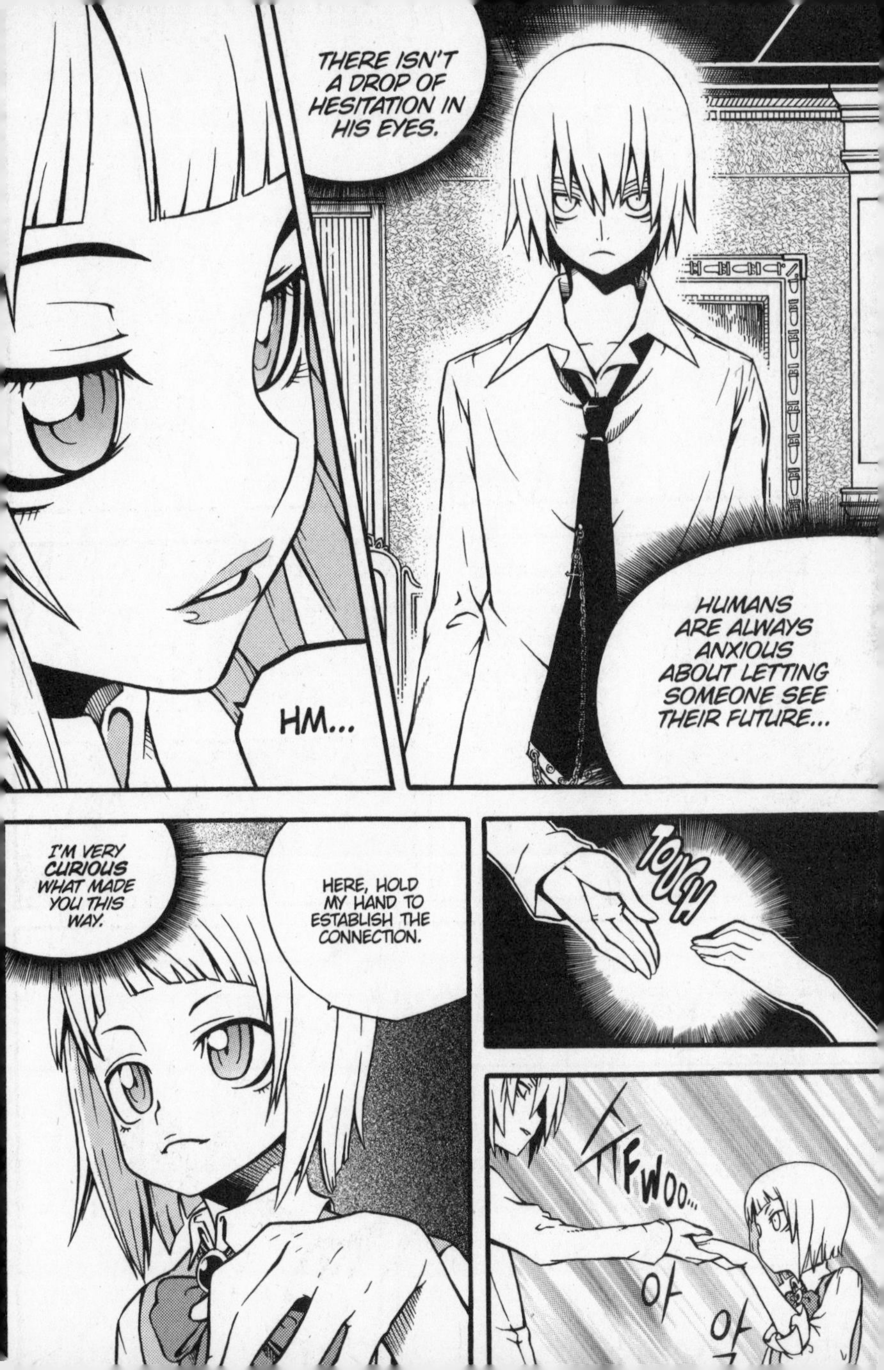
THERE ISN'T A DROP OF HESITATION IN HIS EYES.
HUMANS ARE ALWAYS ANXIOUS ABOUT LETTING SOMEONE SEE THEIR FUTURE...
HM...
HERE, HOLD MY HAND TO ESTABLISH THE CONNECTION.
I'M VERY CURIOUS WHAT MADE YOU THIS WAY.
TOUCH
FWOO...

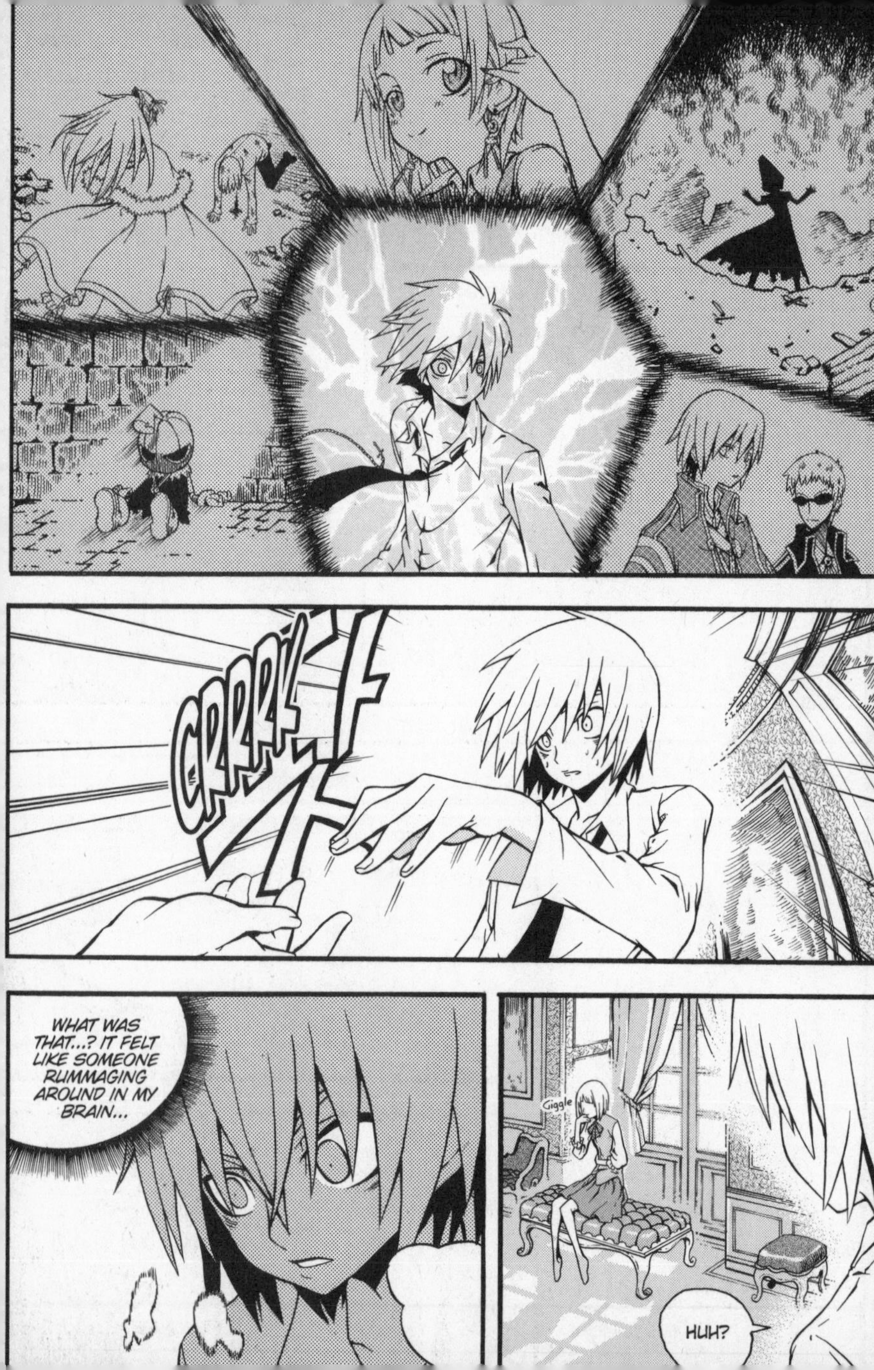
WHAT WAS THAT...? IT FELT LIKE SOMEONE RUMMAGING AROUND IN MY BRAIN...
Giggle
HUH?

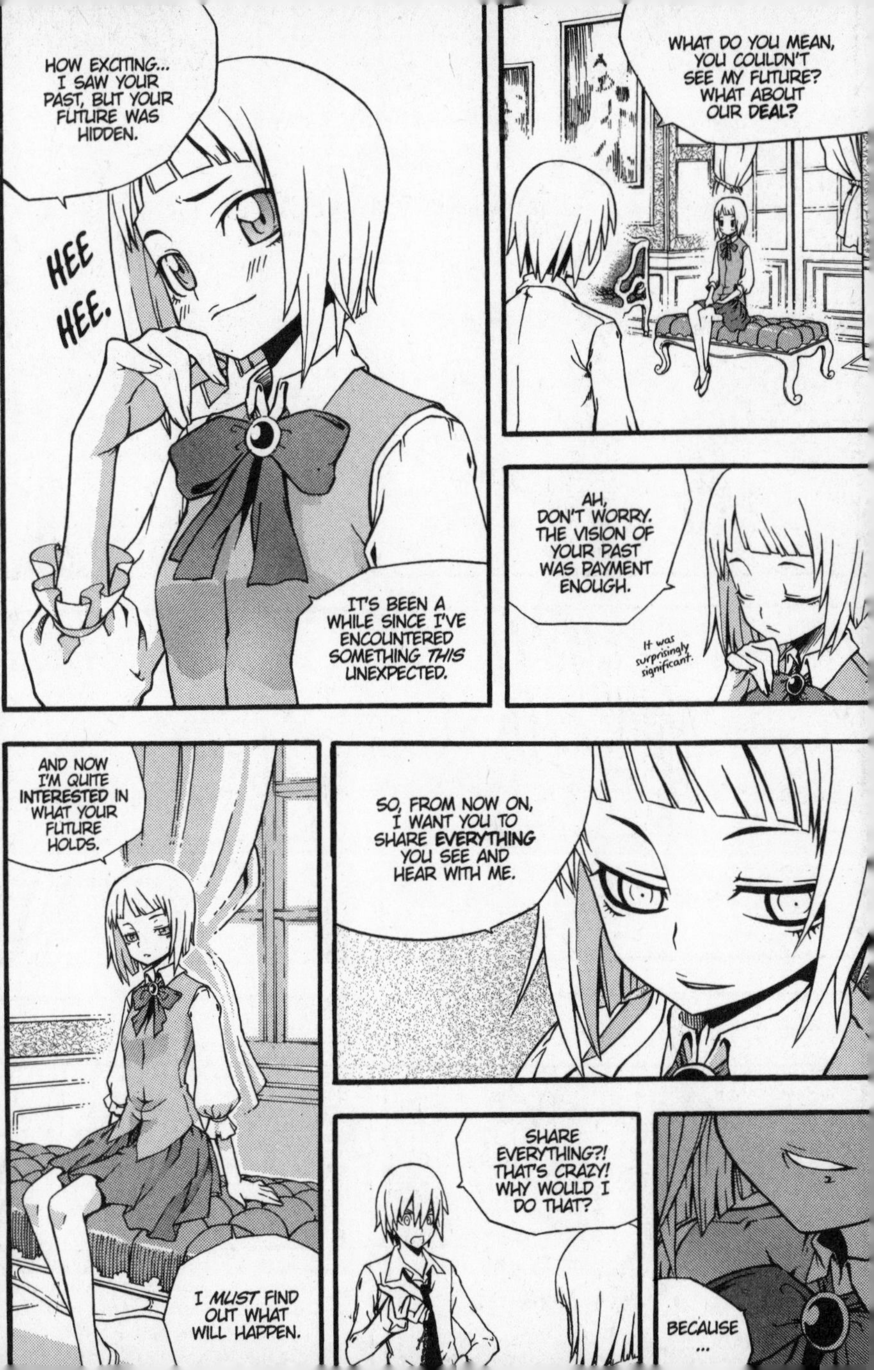

HOW EXCITING... I SAW YOUR PAST, BUT YOUR FUTURE WAS HIDDEN.
HEE HEE.
IT'S BEEN A WHILE SINCE I'VE ENCOUNTERED SOMETHING *THIS* UNEXPECTED.
WHAT DO YOU MEAN, YOU COULDN'T SEE MY FUTURE? WHAT ABOUT OUR DEAL?
AH, DON'T WORRY. THE VISION OF YOUR PAST WAS PAYMENT ENOUGH.
It was surprisingly significant.
AND NOW I'M QUITE INTERESTED IN WHAT YOUR FUTURE HOLDS.
I *MUST* FIND OUT WHAT WILL HAPPEN.
SO, FROM NOW ON, I WANT YOU TO SHARE **EVERYTHING** YOU SEE AND HEAR WITH ME.
SHARE EVERYTHING?! THAT'S CRAZY! WHY WOULD I DO THAT?
BECAUSE ...

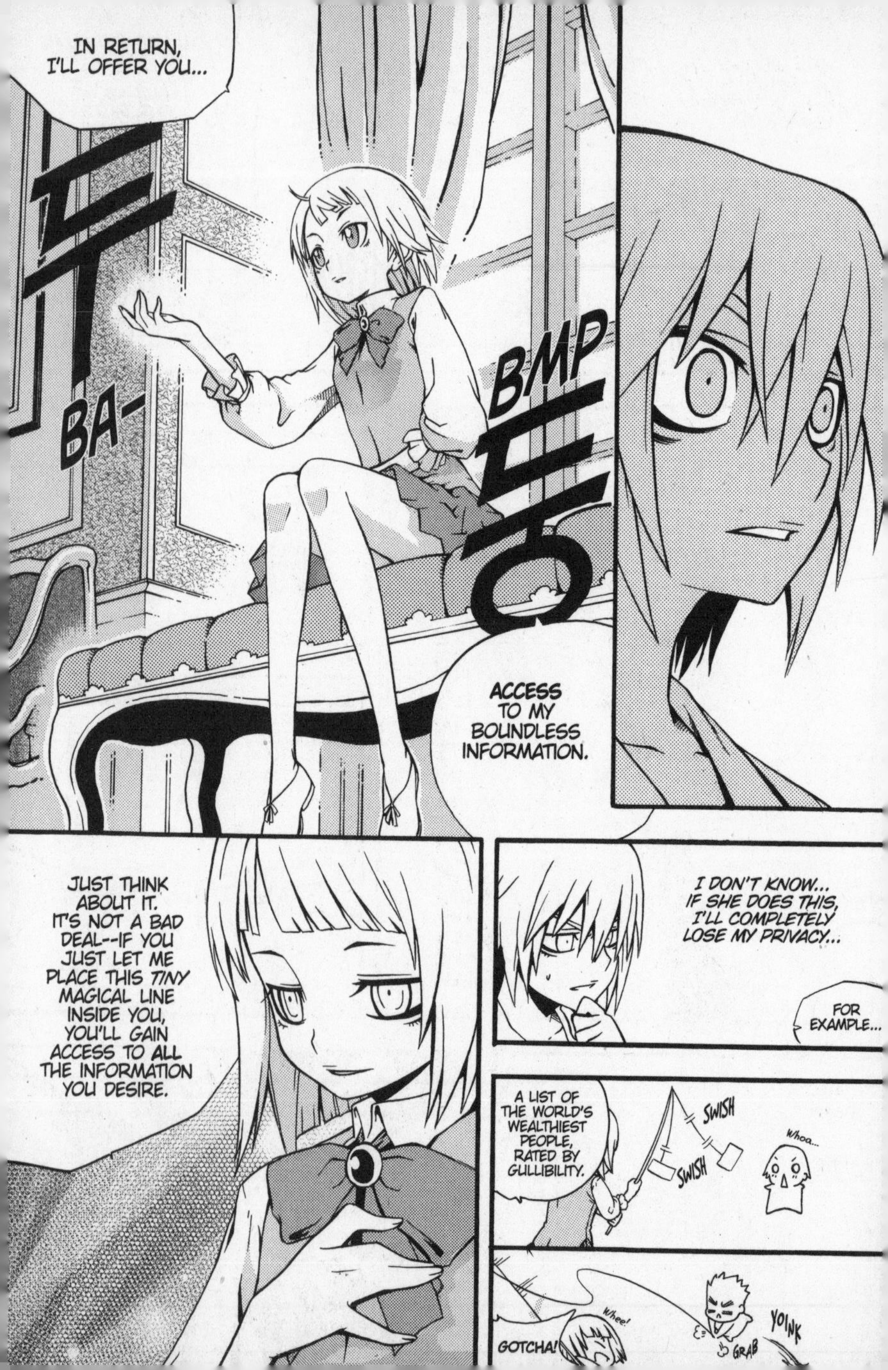
IN RETURN, I'LL OFFER YOU...
BA-
BMP
ACCESS TO MY BOUNDLESS INFORMATION.
JUST THINK ABOUT IT. IT'S NOT A BAD DEAL--IF YOU JUST LET ME PLACE THIS *TINY* MAGICAL LINE INSIDE YOU, YOU'LL GAIN ACCESS TO ALL THE INFORMATION YOU DESIRE.
I DON'T KNOW... IF SHE DOES THIS, I'LL COMPLETELY LOSE MY PRIVACY...
FOR EXAMPLE...
A LIST OF THE WORLD'S WEALTHIEST PEOPLE, RATED BY GULLIBILITY.
SWISH
SWISH
Whoa...
Whee!
GOTCHA!
GRAB
YOINK

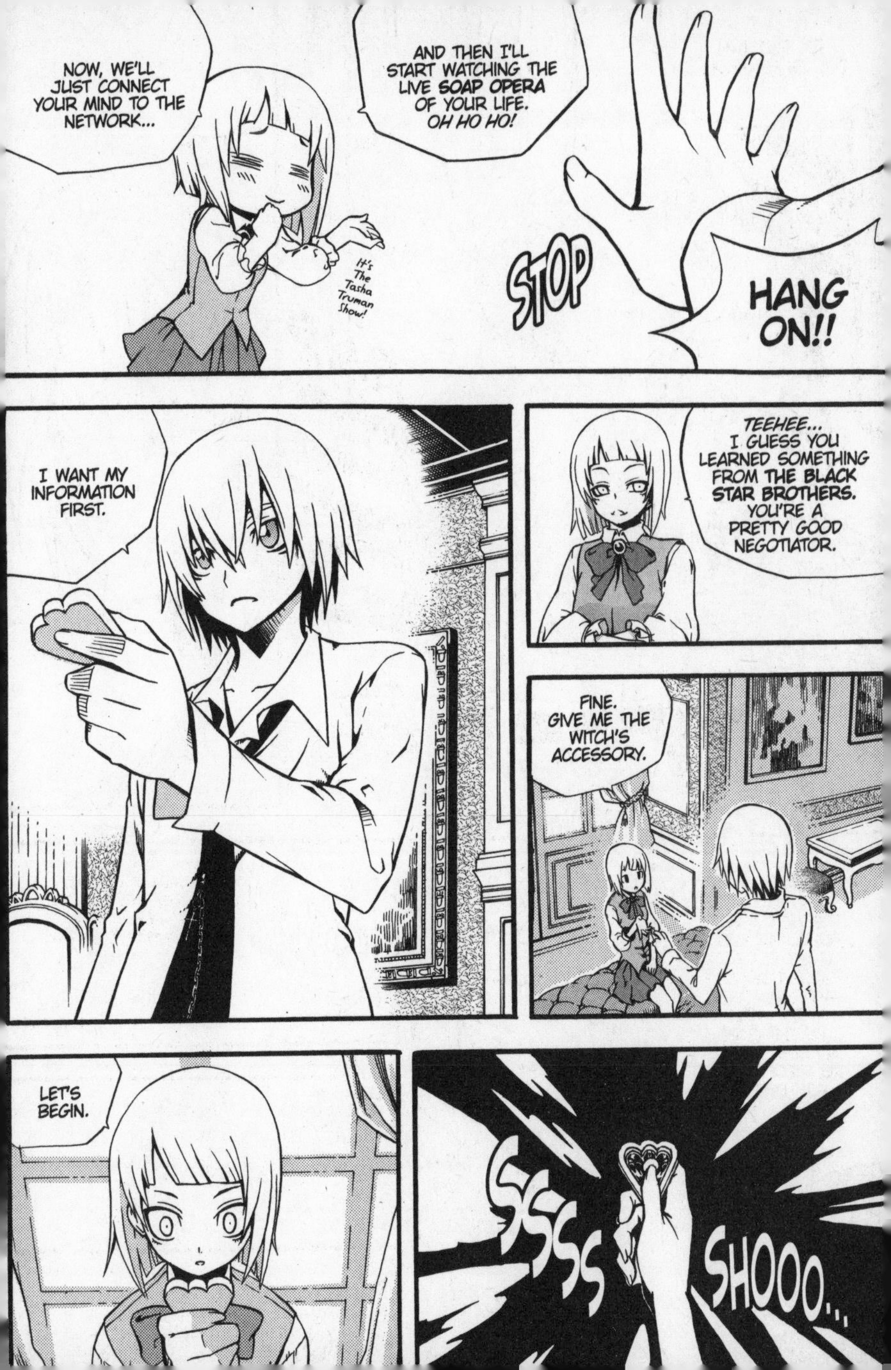
NOW, WE'LL JUST CONNECT YOUR MIND TO THE NETWORK...
AND THEN I'LL START WATCHING THE LIVE SOAP OPERA OF YOUR LIFE. OH HO HO!
It's The Tasha Truman Show!
STOP
HANG ON!!
I WANT MY INFORMATION FIRST.
TEEHEE... I GUESS YOU LEARNED SOMETHING FROM THE BLACK STAR BROTHERS. YOU'RE A PRETTY GOOD NEGOTIATOR.
FINE. GIVE ME THE WITCH'S ACCESSORY.
LET'S BEGIN.
SSSS
SHOOO...

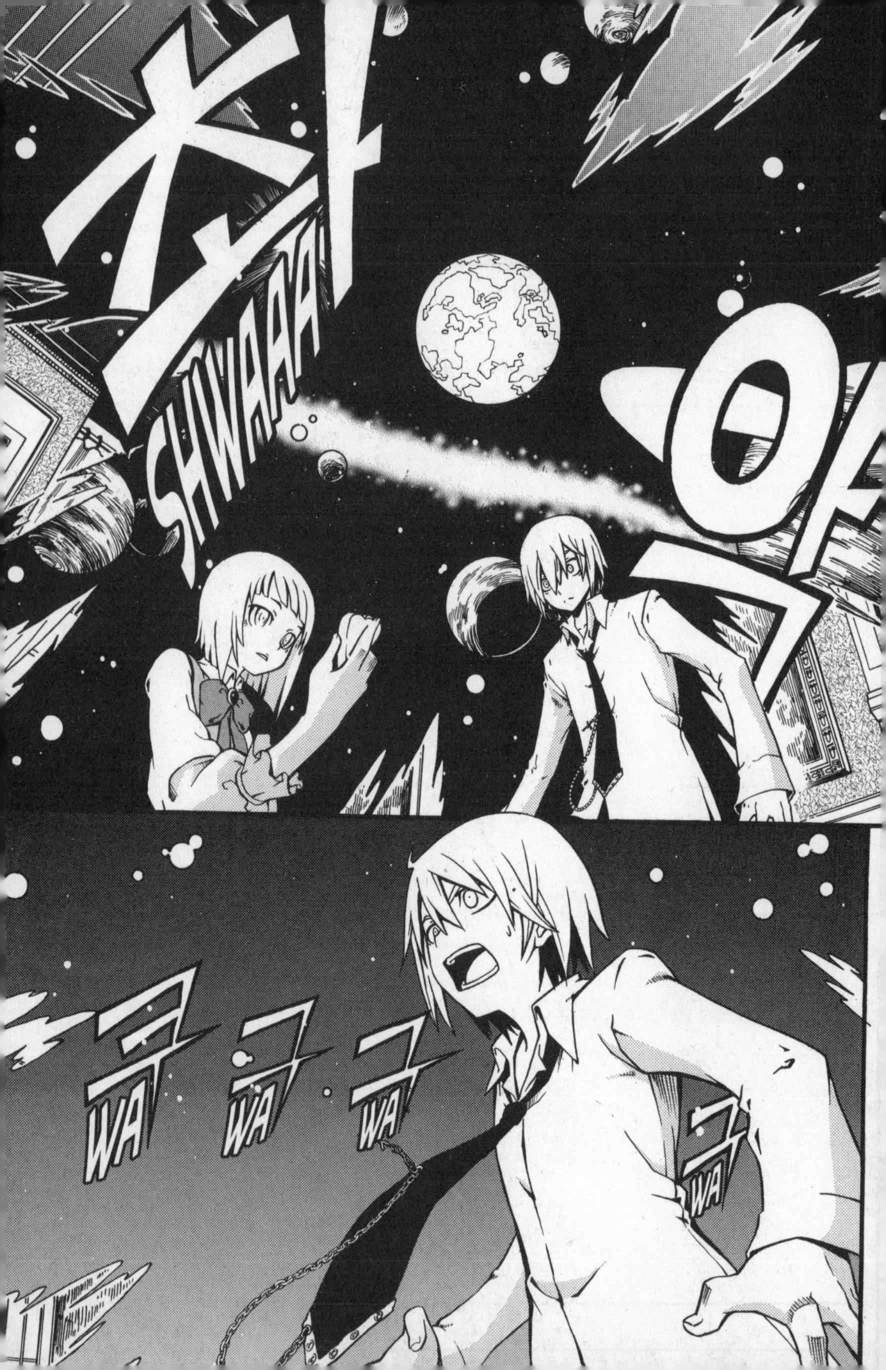
SHWAAAA
WA
WA
WA
WA

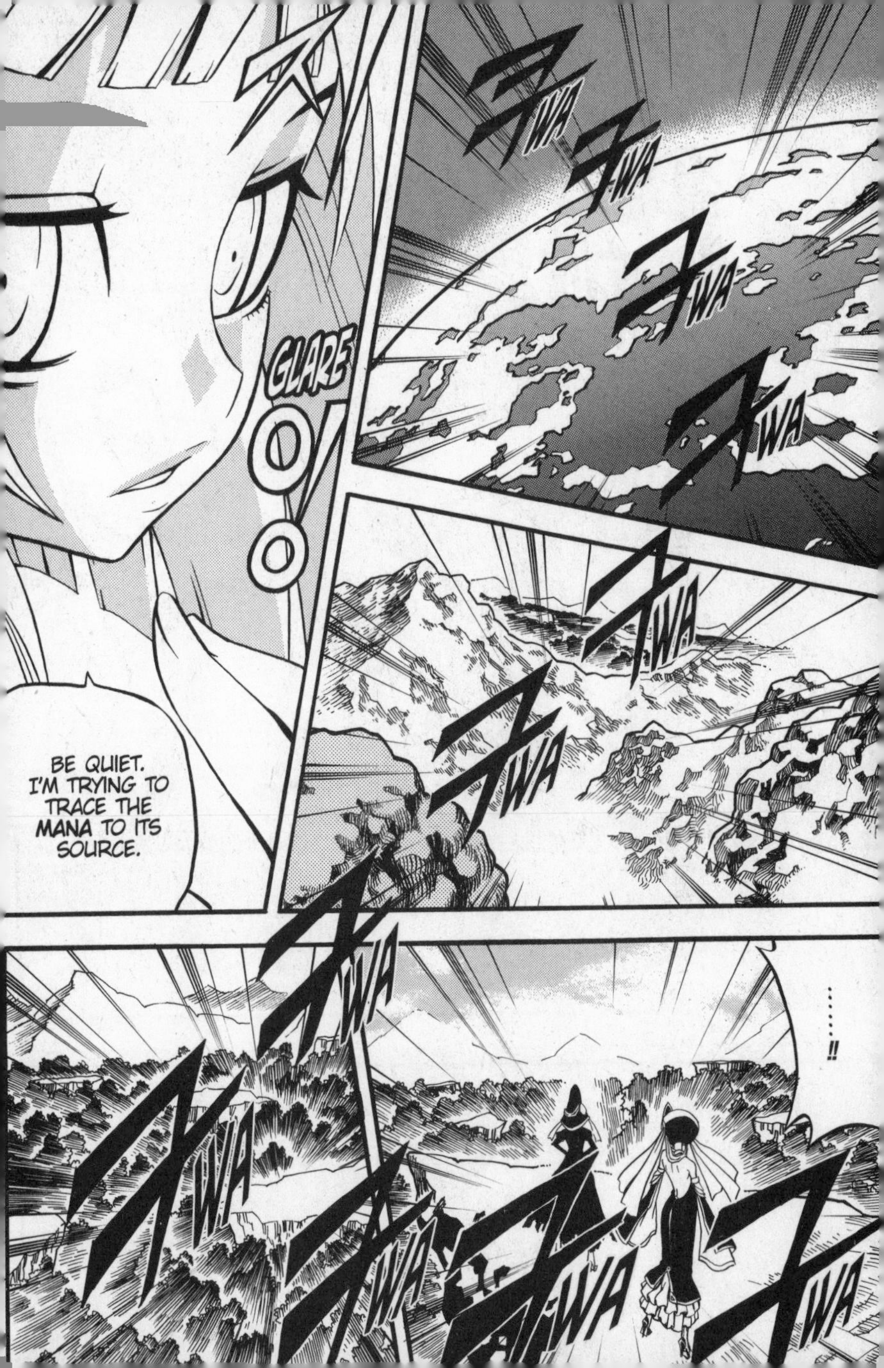
WA
WA
WA
WA
GLARE
WA
WA
BE QUIET. I'M TRYING TO TRACE THE MANA TO ITS SOURCE.
......!!
WA
WA
WA
WA
WA
WA

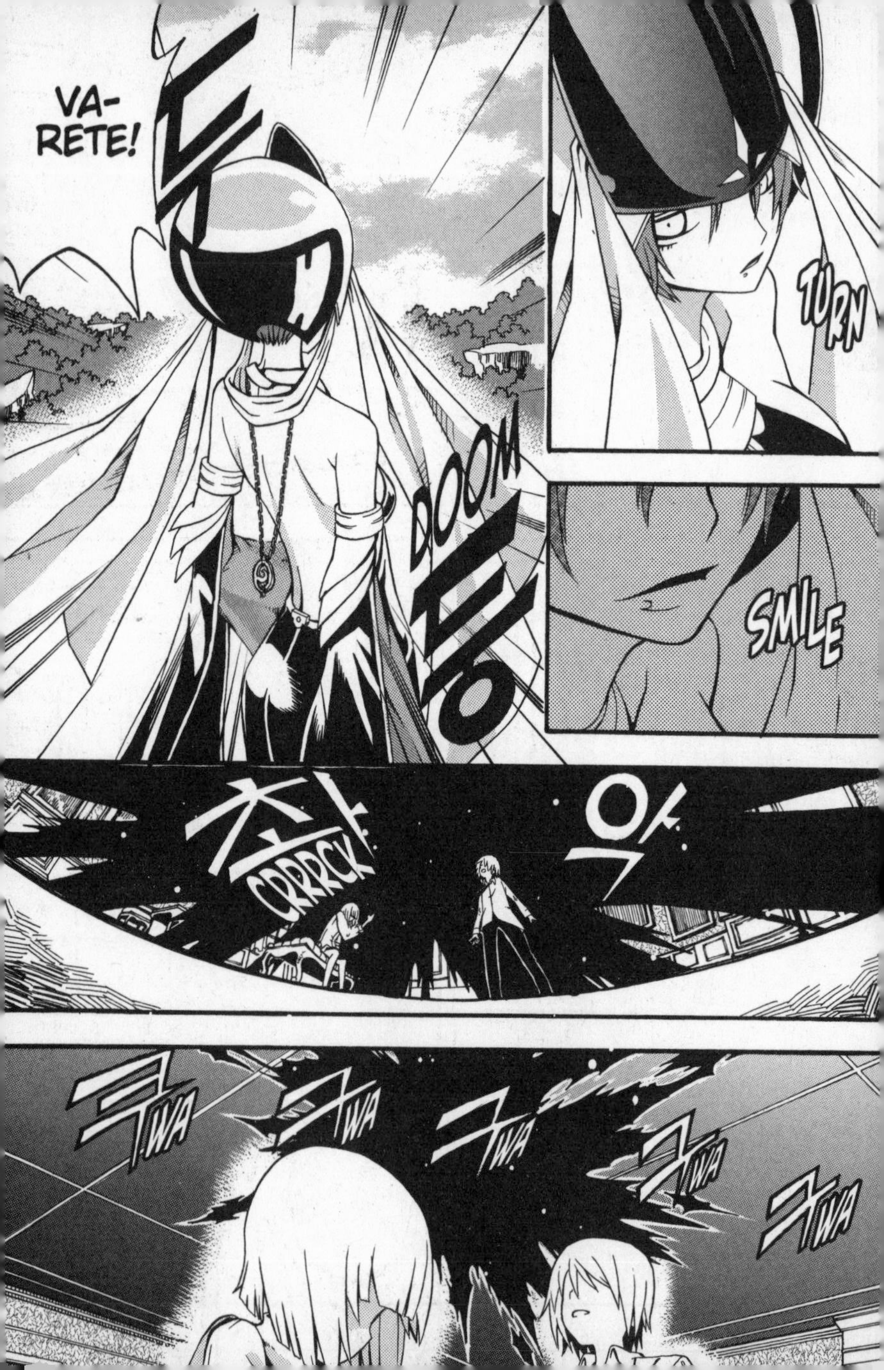
TURN
SMILE
VA-RETE!
DOOM
CRRRCK
WA
WA
WA
WA
WA

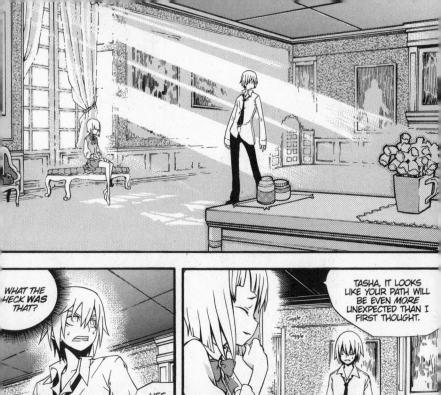

WHAT THE HECK **WAS** THAT?

HEE HEE...

TASHA, IT LOOKS LIKE YOUR PATH WILL BE EVEN *MORE* UNEXPECTED THAN I FIRST THOUGHT.

SHE MANAGED TO ESCAPE FROM MY INFORMATION RADAR. SHE'S A FORCE TO BE RECKONED WITH.

DID IT FAIL?

ARE YOU SERIOUS? I DON'T JUST *FAIL*.

IF YOU COMPLETE YOUR NEXT MISSION, I'LL GIVE YOU YOUR ANSWER WHEN YOU GET BACK.

WHAT MISSION?

OH, YOU'LL HEAR ABOUT IT SOON ENOUGH.

AH, THERE IT IS...

BEEP BEEP BEEP

FLIP

POP

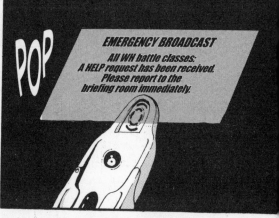

EMERGENCY BROADCAST

All WH battle classes: A HELP request has been received. Please report to the briefing room immediately.

GET GOING! YOU NEED ALL THE WITCHES' HATS YOU CAN GET, RIGHT?

I'LL TAKE CARE OF YOUR PROBATION.

YOU KNEW THIS WOULD HAPPEN...? YOU WEREN'T KIDDING ABOUT BEING MASTER OF THE NETWORK.

TURN

WAIT, HOLD ON.

HUH?

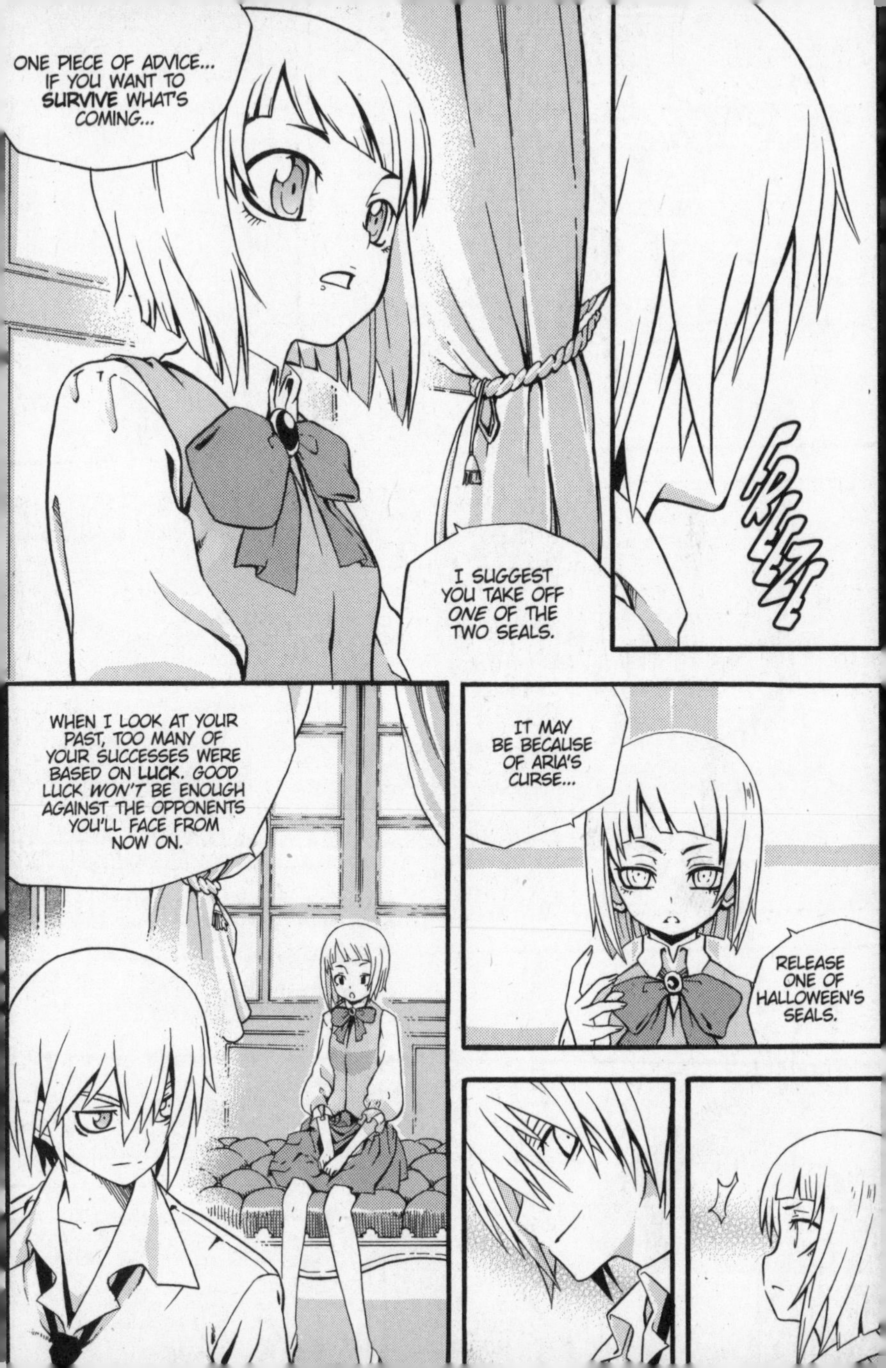
ONE PIECE OF ADVICE... IF YOU WANT TO SURVIVE WHAT'S COMING...
FREEZE
I SUGGEST YOU TAKE OFF ONE OF THE TWO SEALS.
IT MAY BE BECAUSE OF ARIA'S CURSE...
RELEASE ONE OF HALLOWEEN'S SEALS.
WHEN I LOOK AT YOUR PAST, TOO MANY OF YOUR SUCCESSES WERE BASED ON LUCK. GOOD LUCK WON'T BE ENOUGH AGAINST THE OPPONENTS YOU'LL FACE FROM NOW ON.

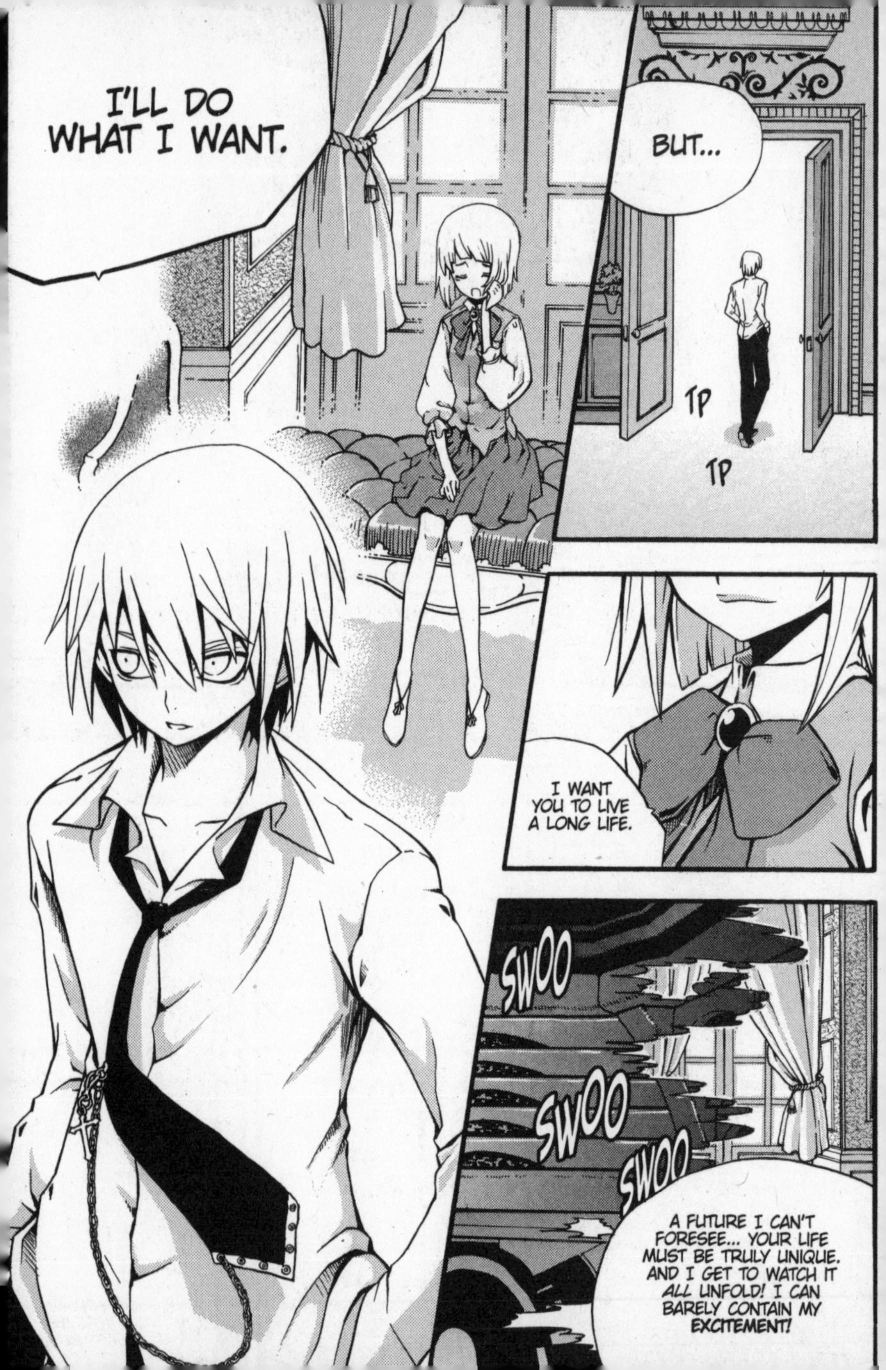
I'LL DO WHAT I WANT.
BUT...
TP
TP
I WANT YOU TO LIVE A LONG LIFE.
SWOO
SWOO
SWOO
A FUTURE I CAN'T FORESEE... YOUR LIFE MUST BE TRULY UNIQUE. AND I GET TO WATCH IT ALL UNFOLD! I CAN BARELY CONTAIN MY EXCITEMENT!

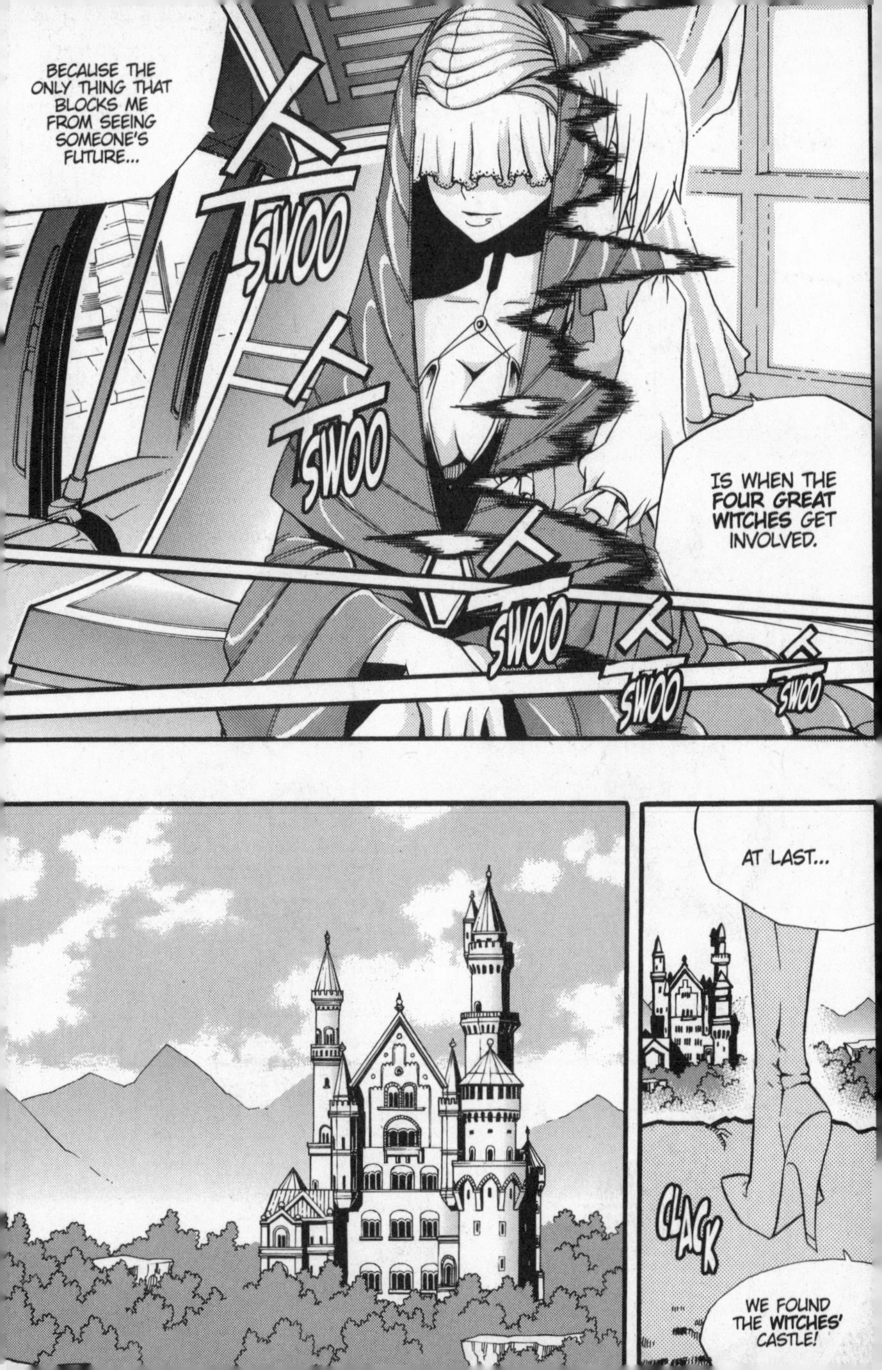
BECAUSE THE ONLY THING THAT BLOCKS ME FROM SEEING SOMEONE'S FUTURE...
SWOO
SWOO
IS WHEN THE FOUR GREAT WITCHES GET INVOLVED.
SWOO
SWOO
SWOO
AT LAST...
CLACK
WE FOUND THE WITCHES' CASTLE!

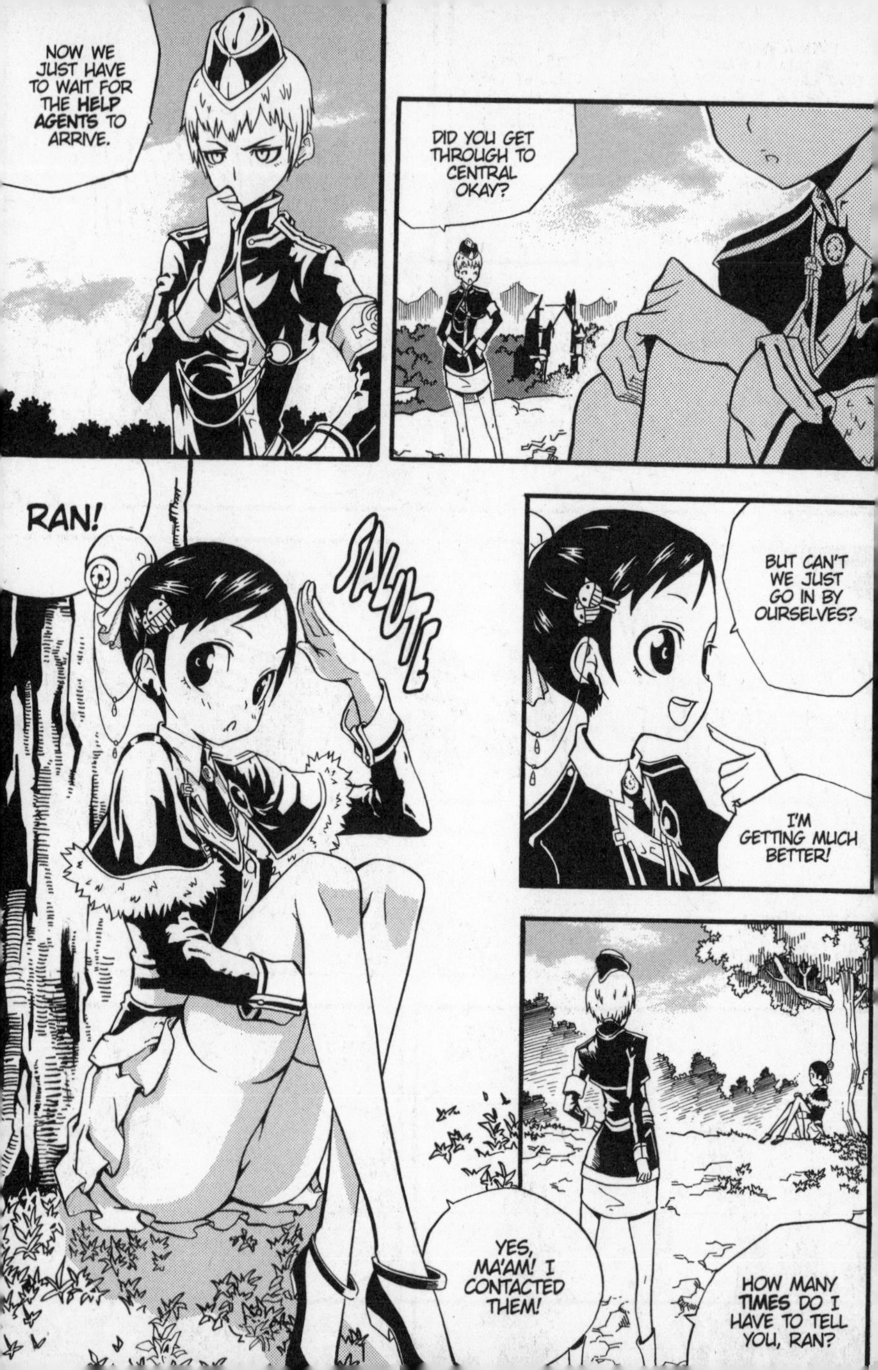
DID YOU GET THROUGH TO CENTRAL OKAY?
YES, MA'AM! I CONTACTED THEM!
SALUTE
NOW WE JUST HAVE TO WAIT FOR THE HELP AGENTS TO ARRIVE.
BUT CAN'T WE JUST GO IN BY OURSELVES?
I'M GETTING MUCH BETTER!
HOW MANY TIMES DO I HAVE TO TELL YOU, RAN?
RAN!

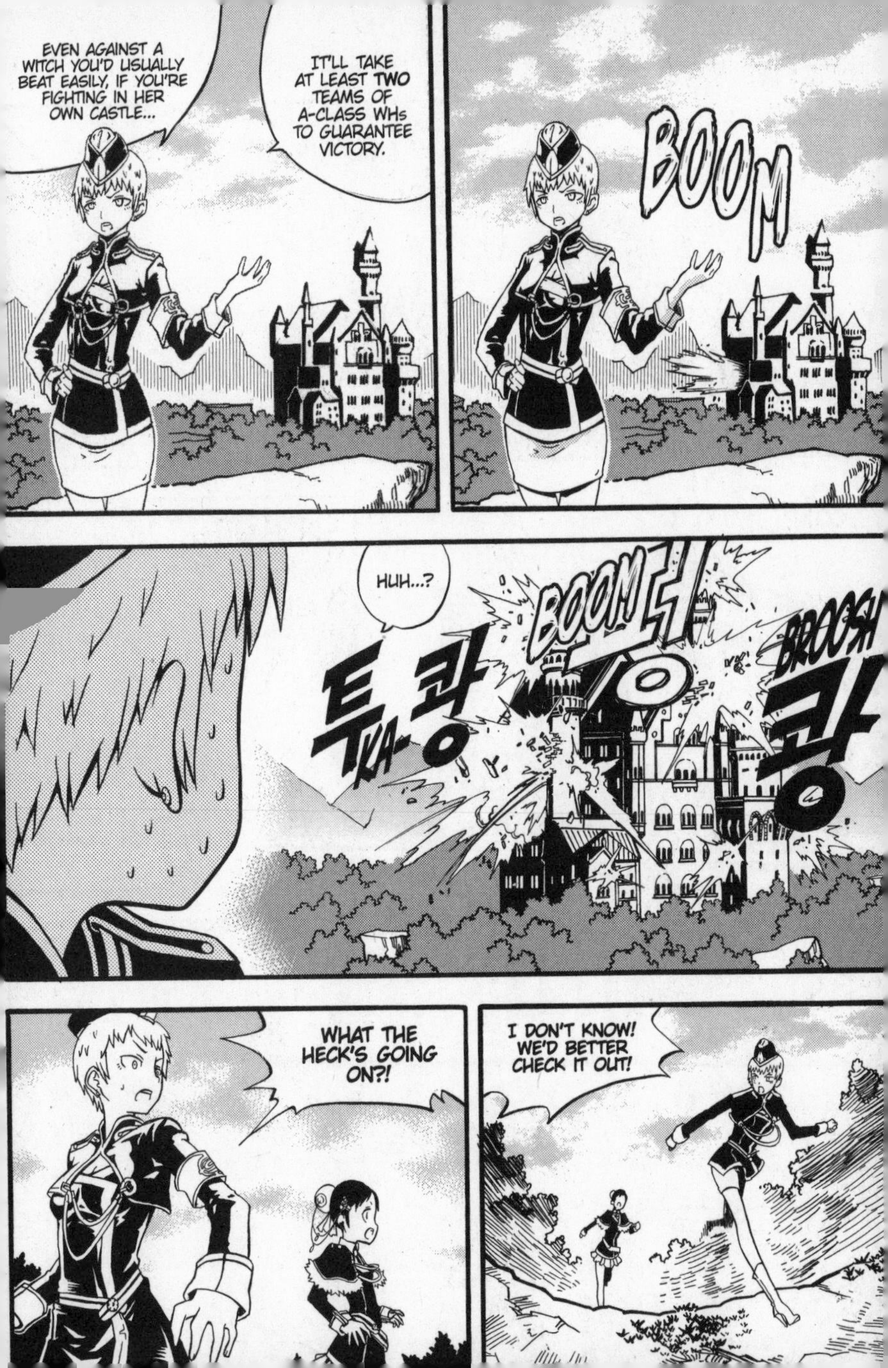

EVEN AGAINST A WITCH YOU'D USUALLY BEAT EASILY, IF YOU'RE FIGHTING IN HER OWN CASTLE...
IT'LL TAKE AT LEAST TWO TEAMS OF A-CLASS WHs TO GUARANTEE VICTORY.
BOOM
HUH...?
BOOM!!
KA-
BROOSH
WHAT THE HECK'S GOING ON?!
I DON'T KNOW! WE'D BETTER CHECK IT OUT!

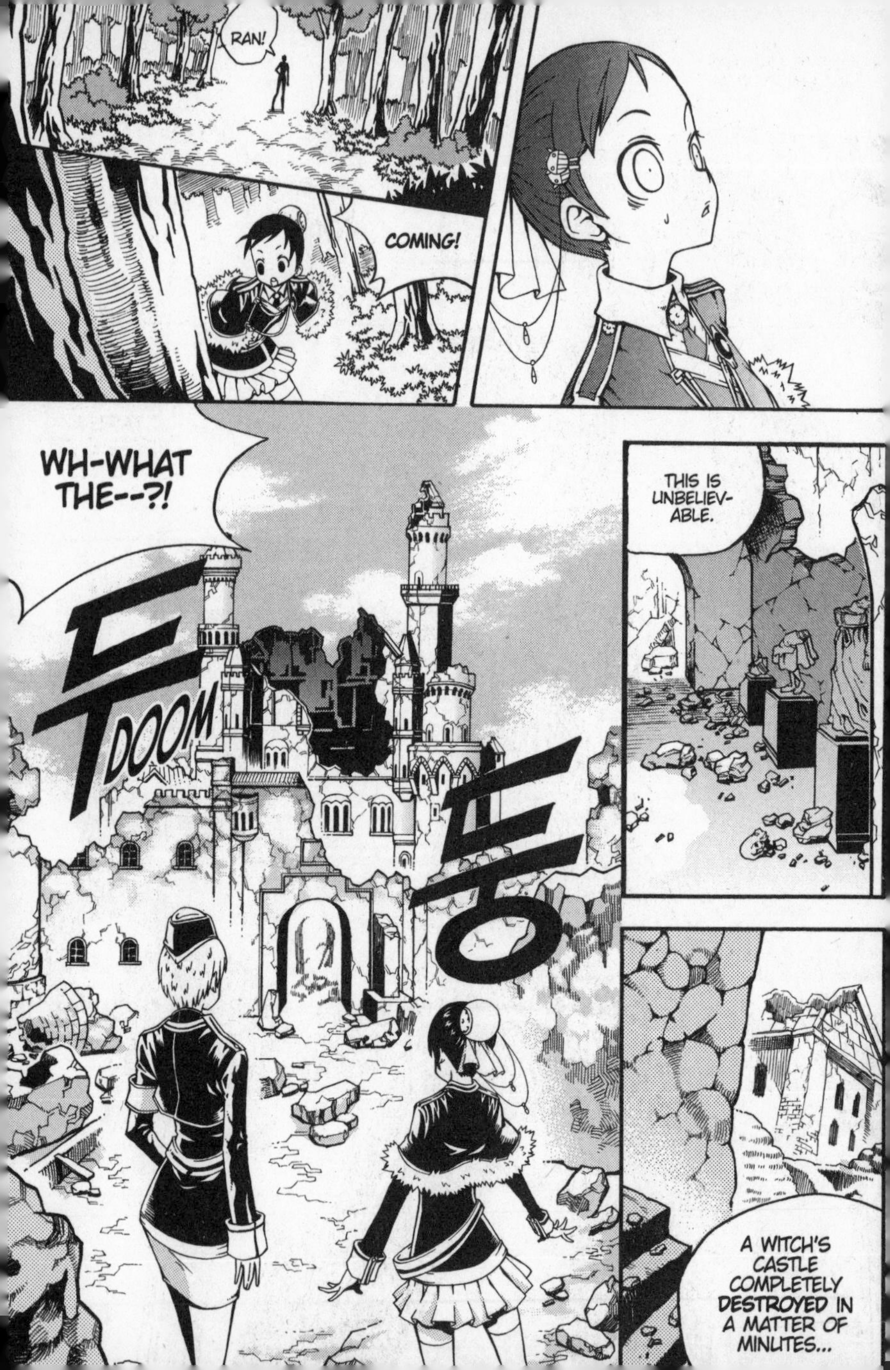
RAN!
COMING!
WH-WHAT THE--?!
FDOOM
THIS IS UNBELIEVABLE.
A WITCH'S CASTLE COMPLETELY DESTROYED IN A MATTER OF MINUTES...

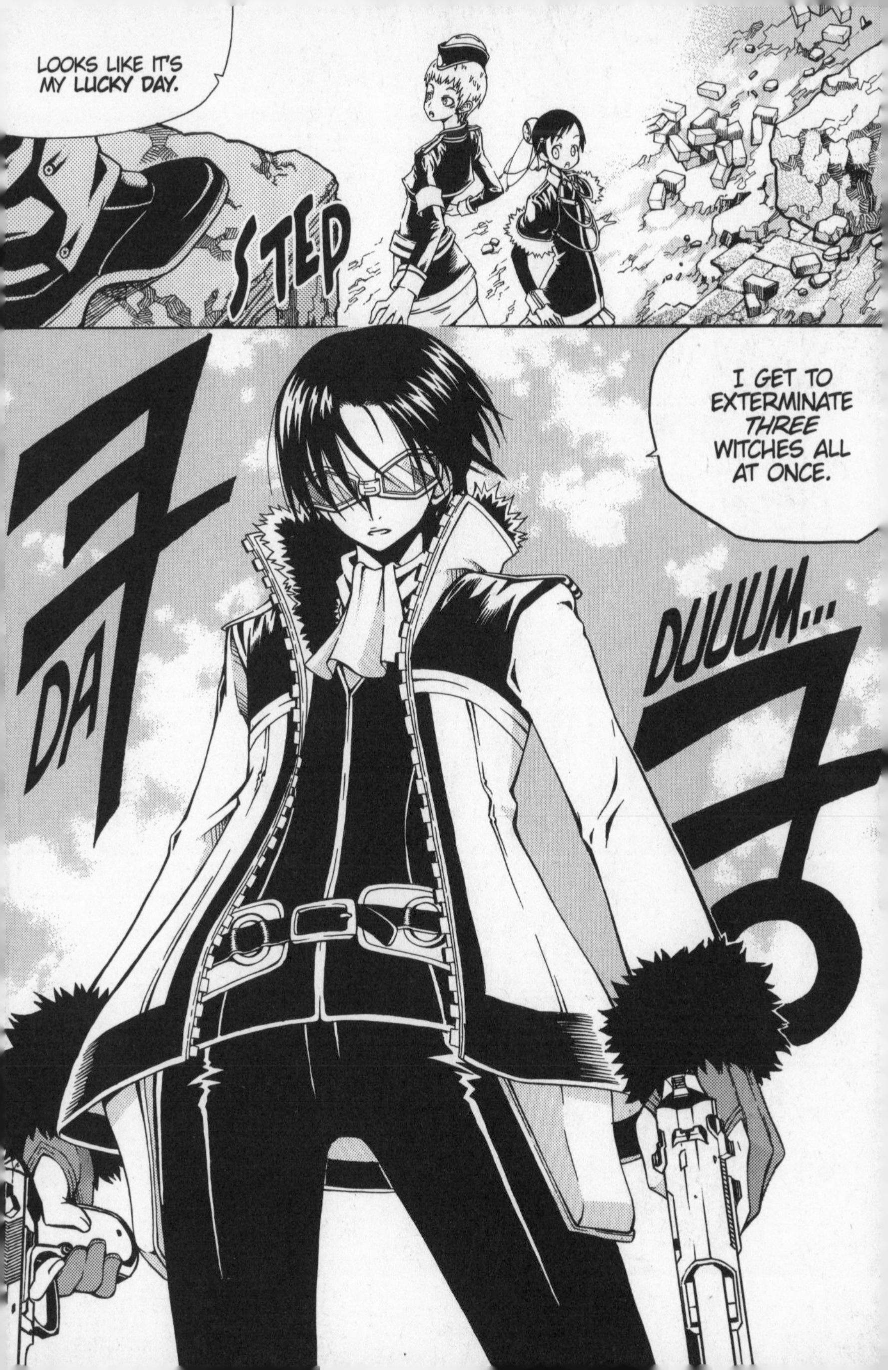
LOOKS LIKE IT'S MY LUCKY DAY.
STEP
I GET TO EXTERMINATE THREE WITCHES ALL AT ONCE.
DUUUM...
DA

OPTION

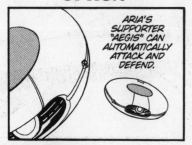

ARIA'S SUPPORTER "AEGIS" CAN AUTOMATICALLY ATTACK AND DEFEND.

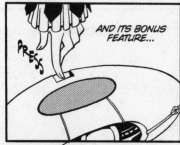

AND ITS BONUS FEATURE...

PRESS

I THINK WE NEED SOME NEW FIGHT MUSIC TODAY.

CLICK

CD PLAYER OPTION ?!!

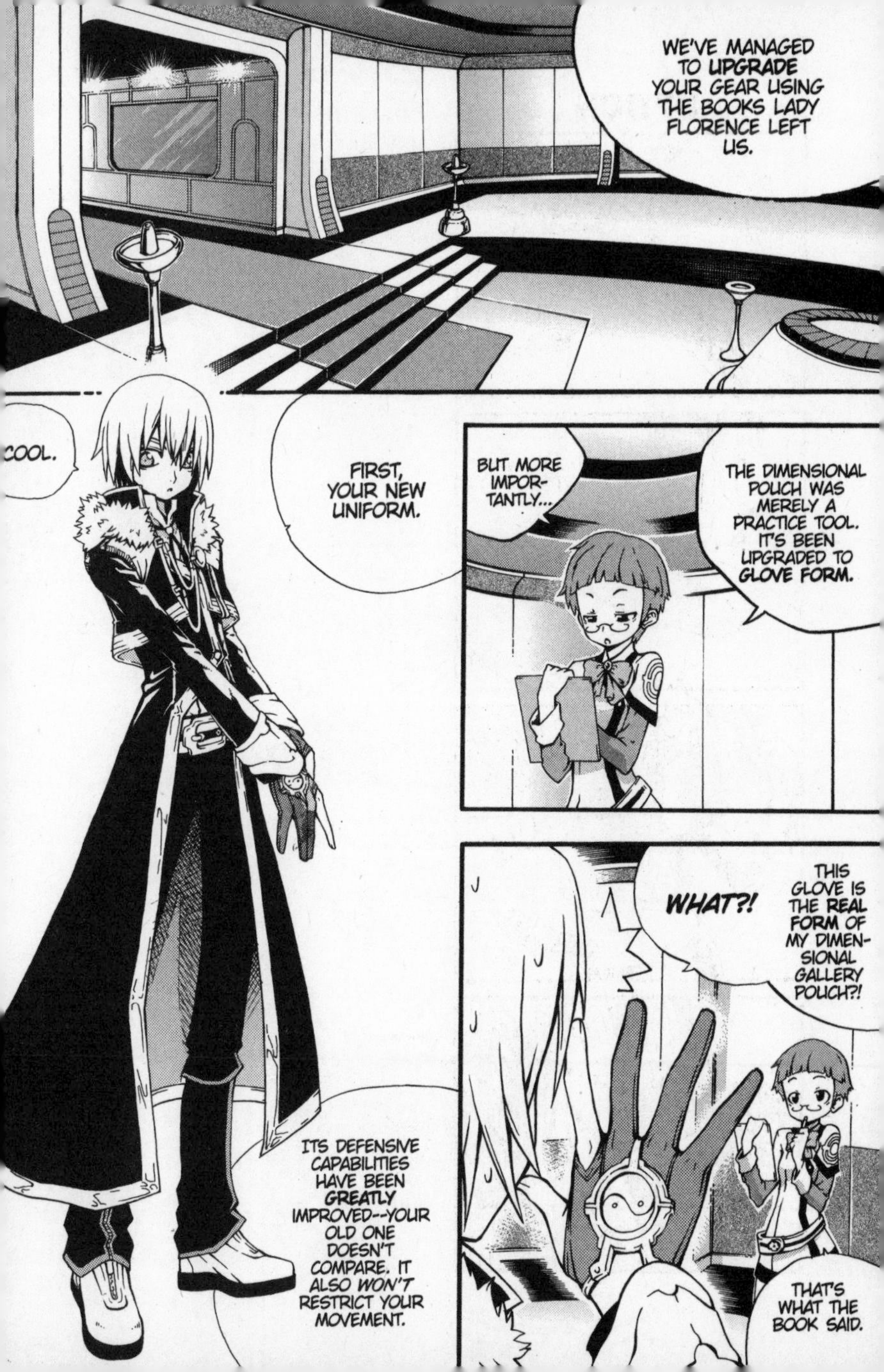
WE'VE MANAGED TO UPGRADE YOUR GEAR USING THE BOOKS LADY FLORENCE LEFT US.
FIRST, YOUR NEW UNIFORM.
COOL.
ITS DEFENSIVE CAPABILITIES HAVE BEEN GREATLY IMPROVED--YOUR OLD ONE DOESN'T COMPARE. IT ALSO WON'T RESTRICT YOUR MOVEMENT.
THE DIMENSIONAL POUCH WAS MERELY A PRACTICE TOOL. IT'S BEEN UPGRADED TO GLOVE FORM.
BUT MORE IMPORTANTLY...
THIS GLOVE IS THE REAL FORM OF MY DIMENSIONAL GALLERY POUCH?!
WHAT?!
THAT'S WHAT THE BOOK SAID.

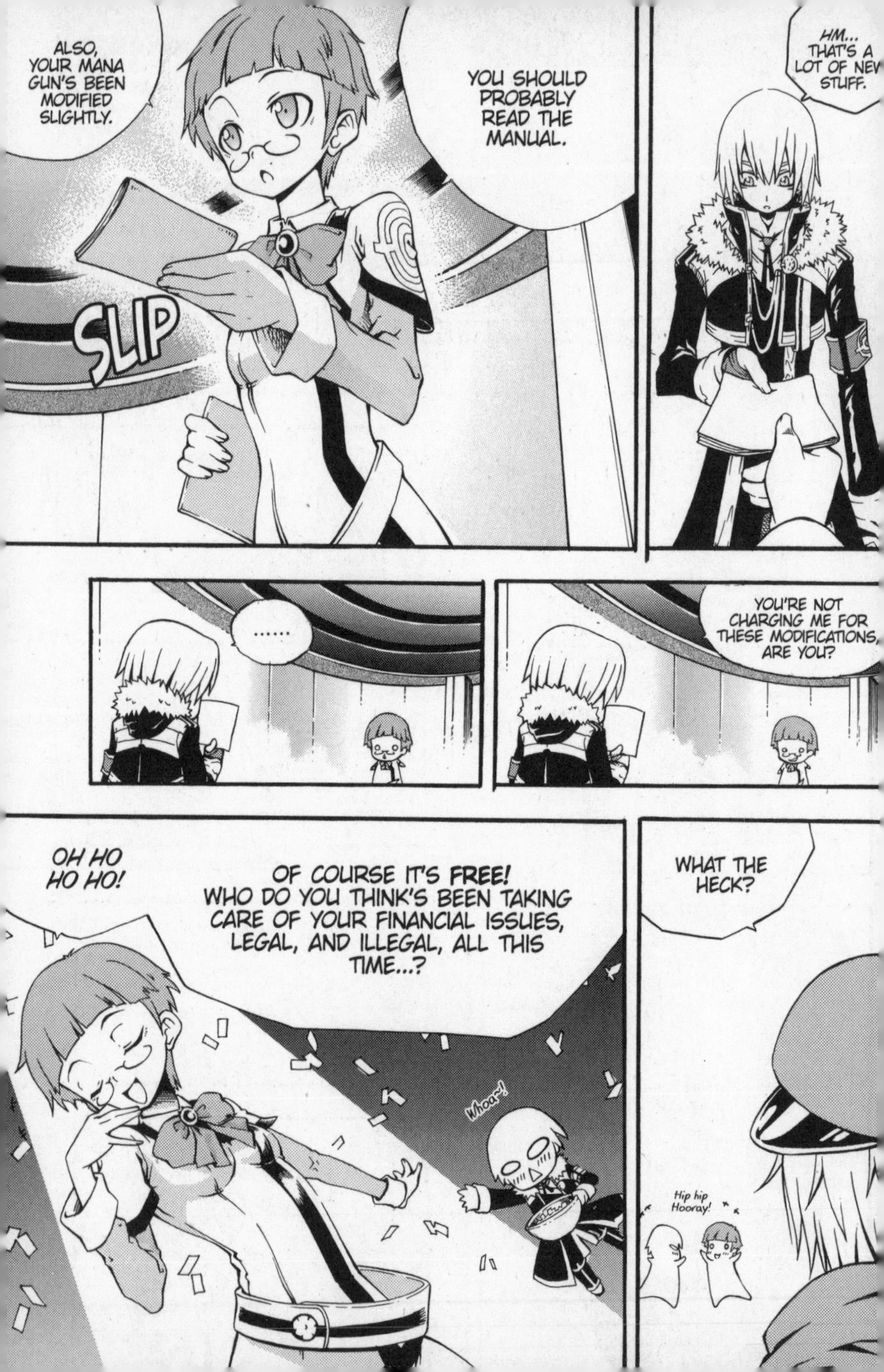
ALSO, YOUR MANA GUN'S BEEN MODIFIED SLIGHTLY.
YOU SHOULD PROBABLY READ THE MANUAL.
SLIP
HM... THAT'S A LOT OF NEW STUFF.
......
YOU'RE NOT CHARGING ME FOR THESE MODIFICATIONS, ARE YOU?
OH HO HO HO!
OF COURSE IT'S FREE! WHO DO YOU THINK'S BEEN TAKING CARE OF YOUR FINANCIAL ISSUES, LEGAL, AND ILLEGAL, ALL THIS TIME...?
Whoa~!
WHAT THE HECK?
Hip hip Hooray!

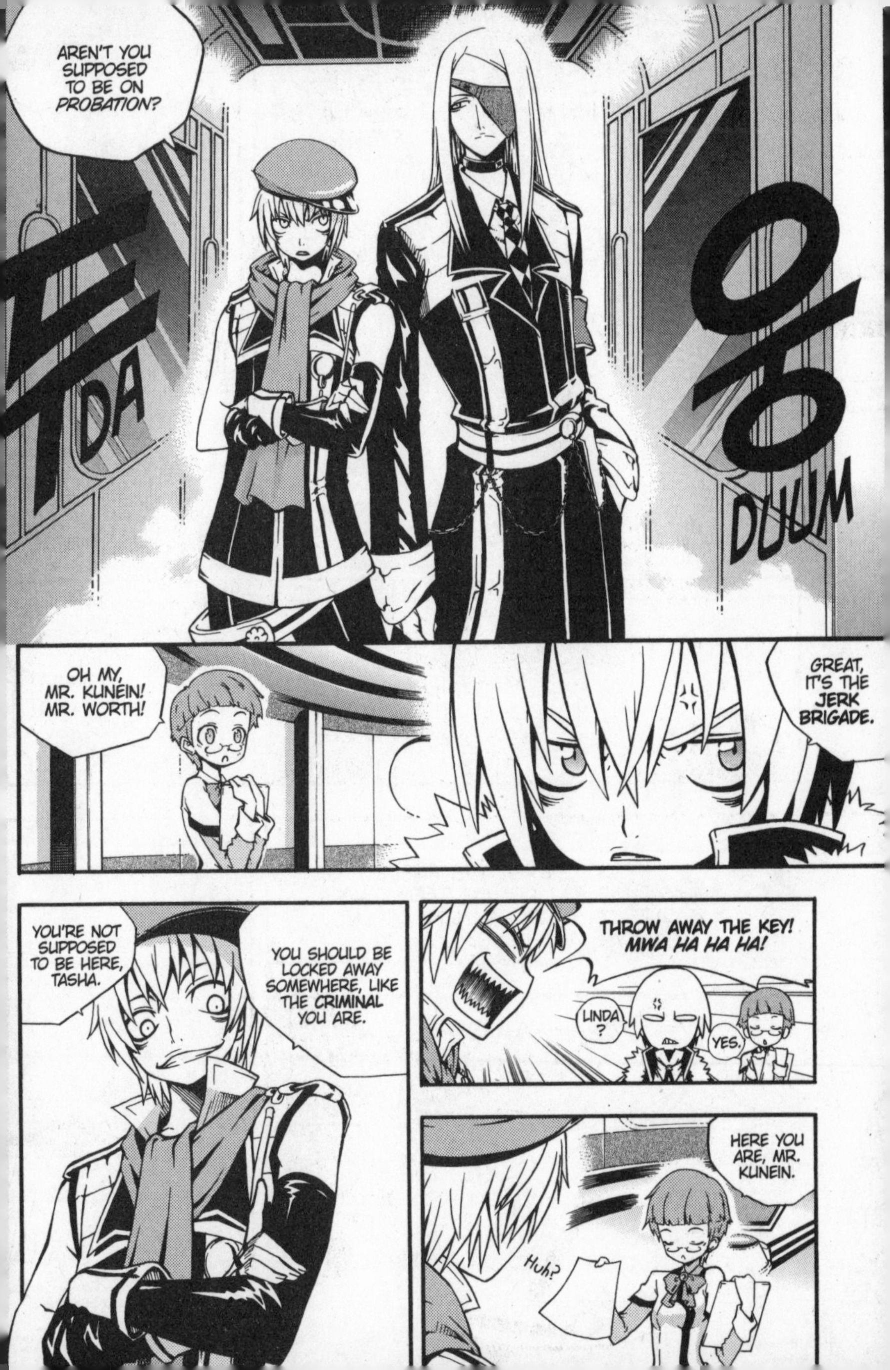
ARE'NT YOU SUPPOSED TO BE ON *PROBATION*?
DA
DUUM
OH MY, MR. KUNEIN! MR. WORTH!
GREAT, IT'S THE **JERK BRIGADE**.
YOU'RE NOT SUPPOSED TO BE HERE, TASHA.
YOU SHOULD BE LOCKED AWAY SOMEWHERE, LIKE THE CRIMINAL YOU ARE.
THROW AWAY THE KEY! *MWA HA HA HA!*
LINDA?
YES.
HERE YOU ARE, MR. KUNEIN.
Huh?

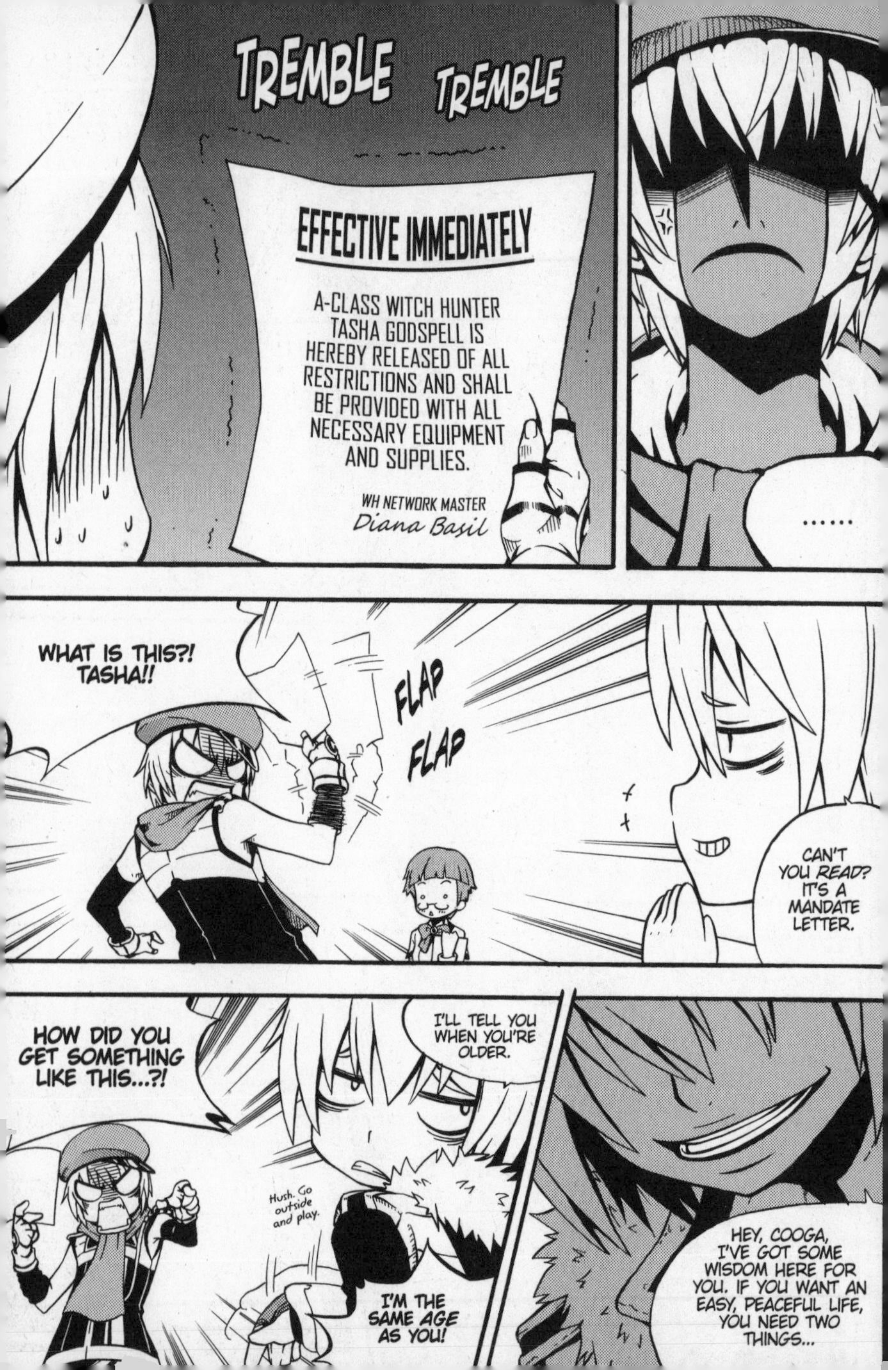
TREMBLE
TREMBLE
EFFECTIVE IMMEDIATELY
A-CLASS WITCH HUNTER TASHA GODSPELL IS HEREBY RELEASED OF ALL RESTRICTIONS AND SHALL BE PROVIDED WITH ALL NECESSARY EQUIPMENT AND SUPPLIES.
WH NETWORK MASTER
Diana Basil
......
WHAT IS THIS?! TASHA!!
FLAP
FLAP
CAN'T YOU READ? IT'S A MANDATE LETTER.
HOW DID YOU GET SOMETHING LIKE THIS...?!
I'LL TELL YOU WHEN YOU'RE OLDER.
Hush. Go outside and play.
I'M THE SAME AGE AS YOU!
HEY, COOGA, I'VE GOT SOME WISDOM HERE FOR YOU. IF YOU WANT AN EASY, PEACEFUL LIFE, YOU NEED TWO THINGS...

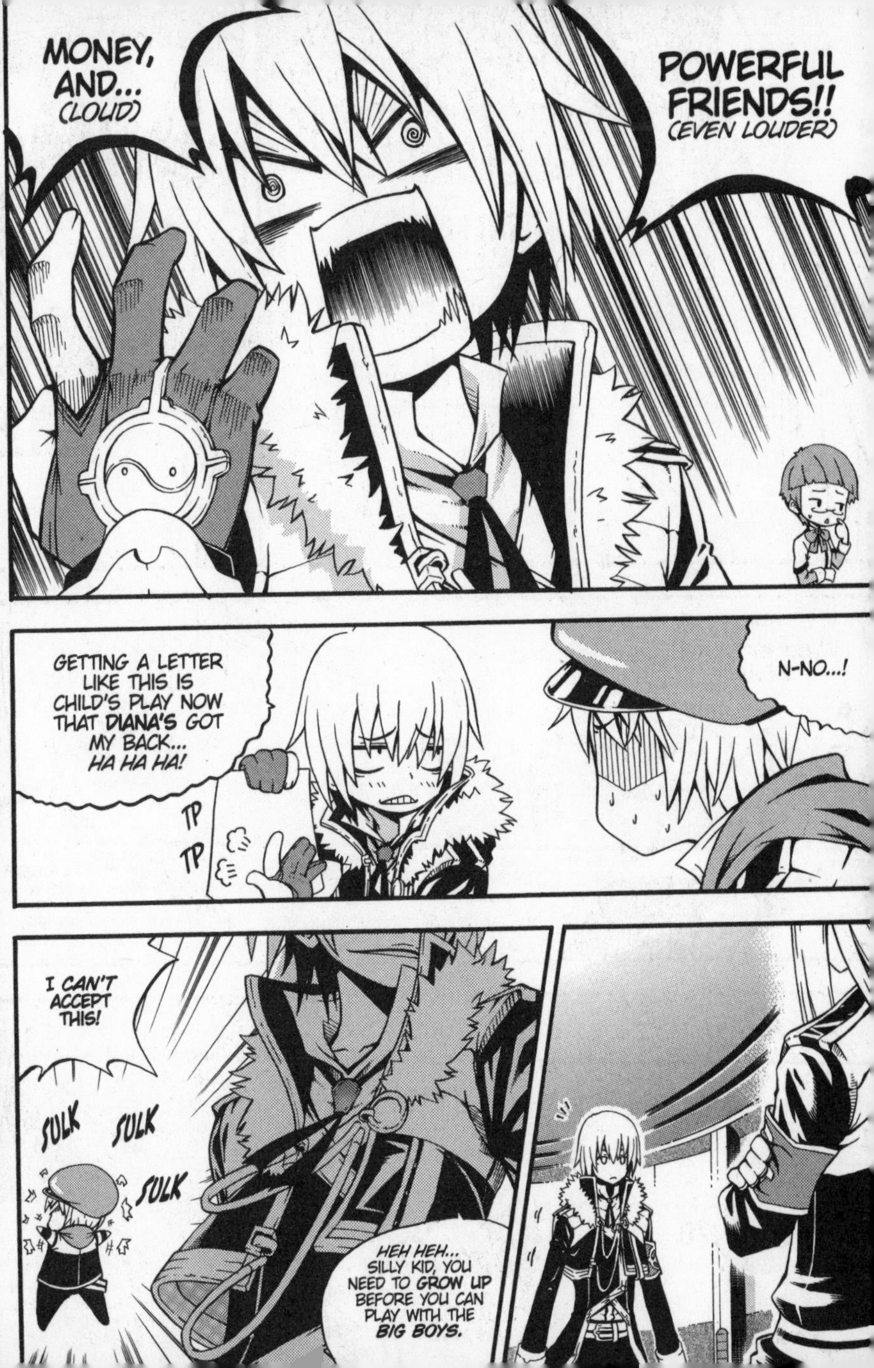
POWERFUL FRIENDS!!
(EVEN LOUDER)
MONEY, AND...
(LOUD)
N-NO...!
GETTING A LETTER LIKE THIS IS CHILD'S PLAY NOW THAT DIANA'S GOT MY BACK... HA HA HA!
TP
TP
I CAN'T ACCEPT THIS!
SULK
SULK
SULK
HEH HEH... SILLY KID, YOU NEED TO GROW UP BEFORE YOU CAN PLAY WITH THE BIG BOYS.

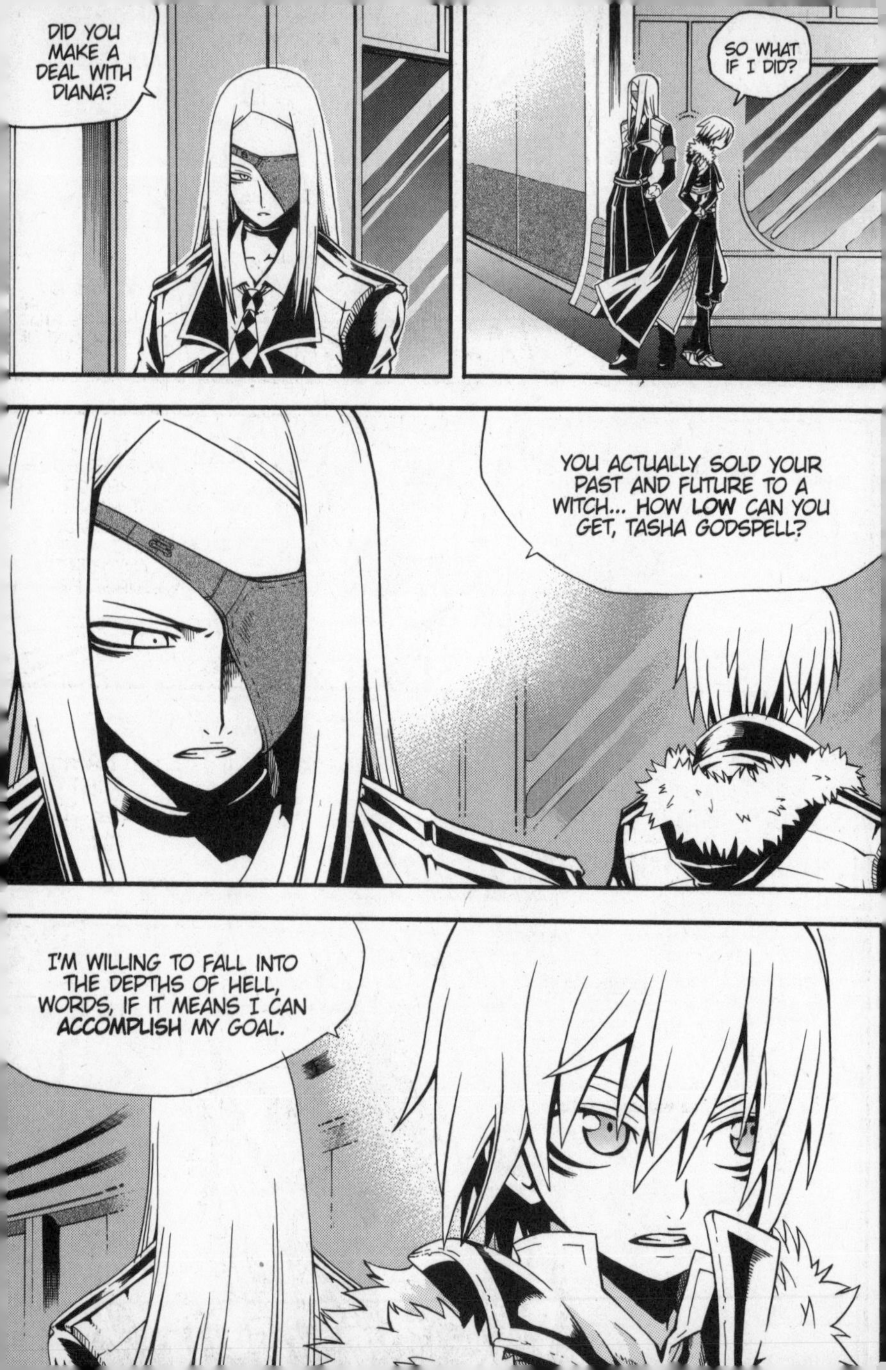
DID YOU MAKE A DEAL WITH DIANA?
SO WHAT IF I DID?
YOU ACTUALLY SOLD YOUR PAST AND FUTURE TO A WITCH... HOW LOW CAN YOU GET, TASHA GODSPELL?
I'M WILLING TO FALL INTO THE DEPTHS OF HELL, WORDS, IF IT MEANS I CAN ACCOMPLISH MY GOAL.

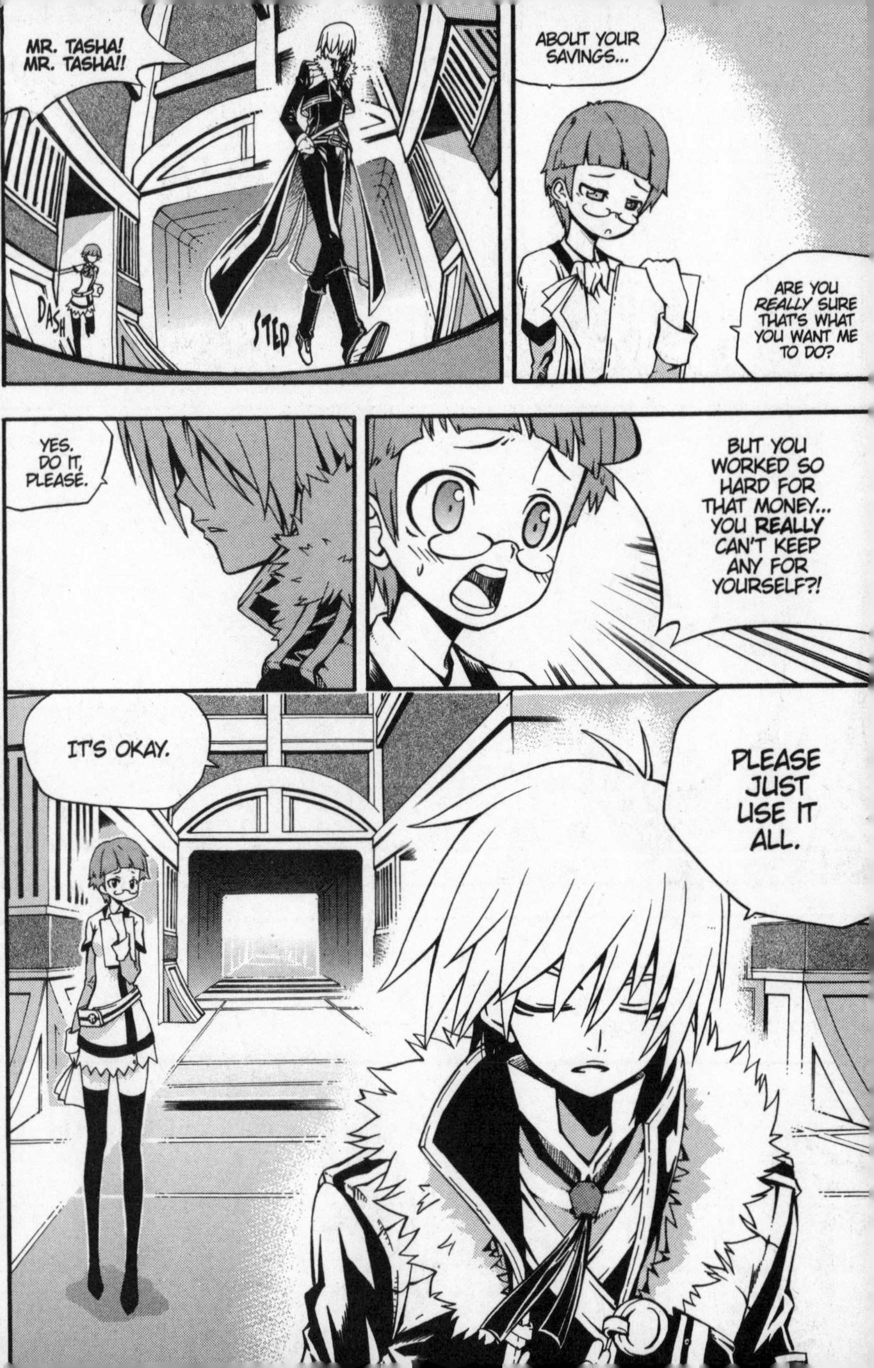
MR. TASHA! MR. TASHA!!
DASH
STEP
ABOUT YOUR SAVINGS...
ARE YOU REALLY SURE THAT'S WHAT YOU WANT ME TO DO?
YES. DO IT, PLEASE.
BUT YOU WORKED SO HARD FOR THAT MONEY... YOU REALLY CAN'T KEEP ANY FOR YOURSELF?!
IT'S OKAY.
PLEASE JUST USE IT ALL.

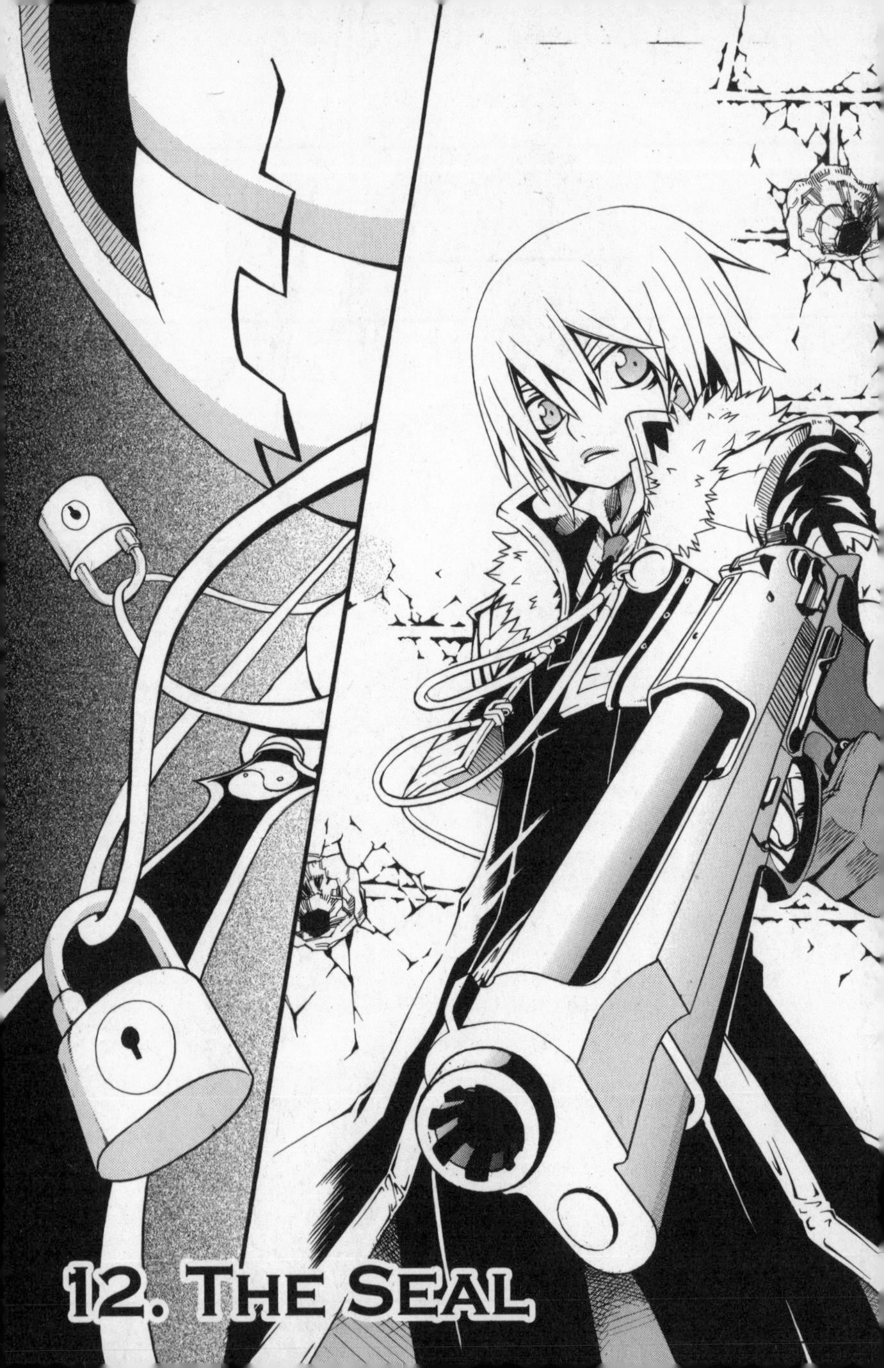
12. The Seal

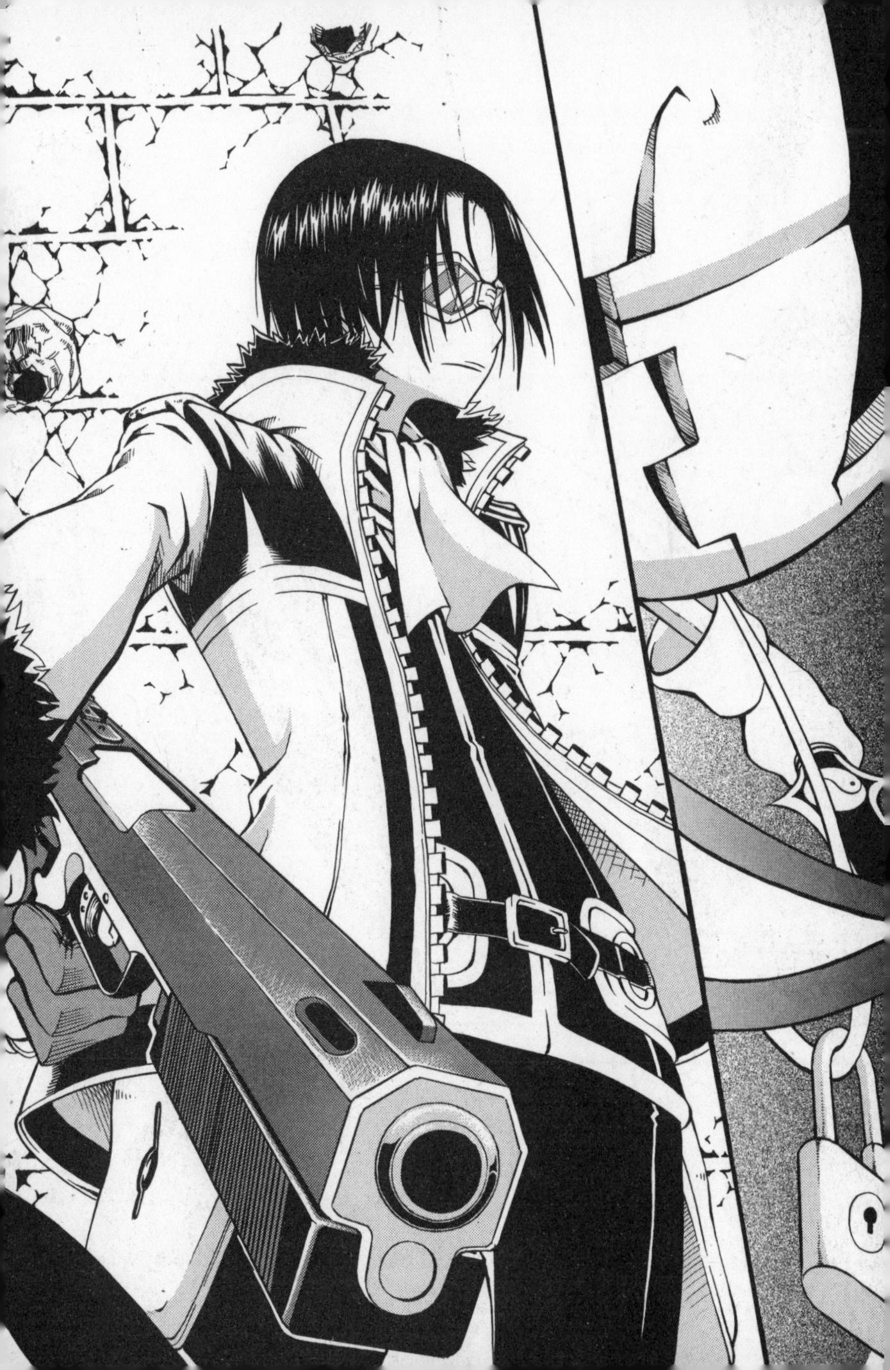

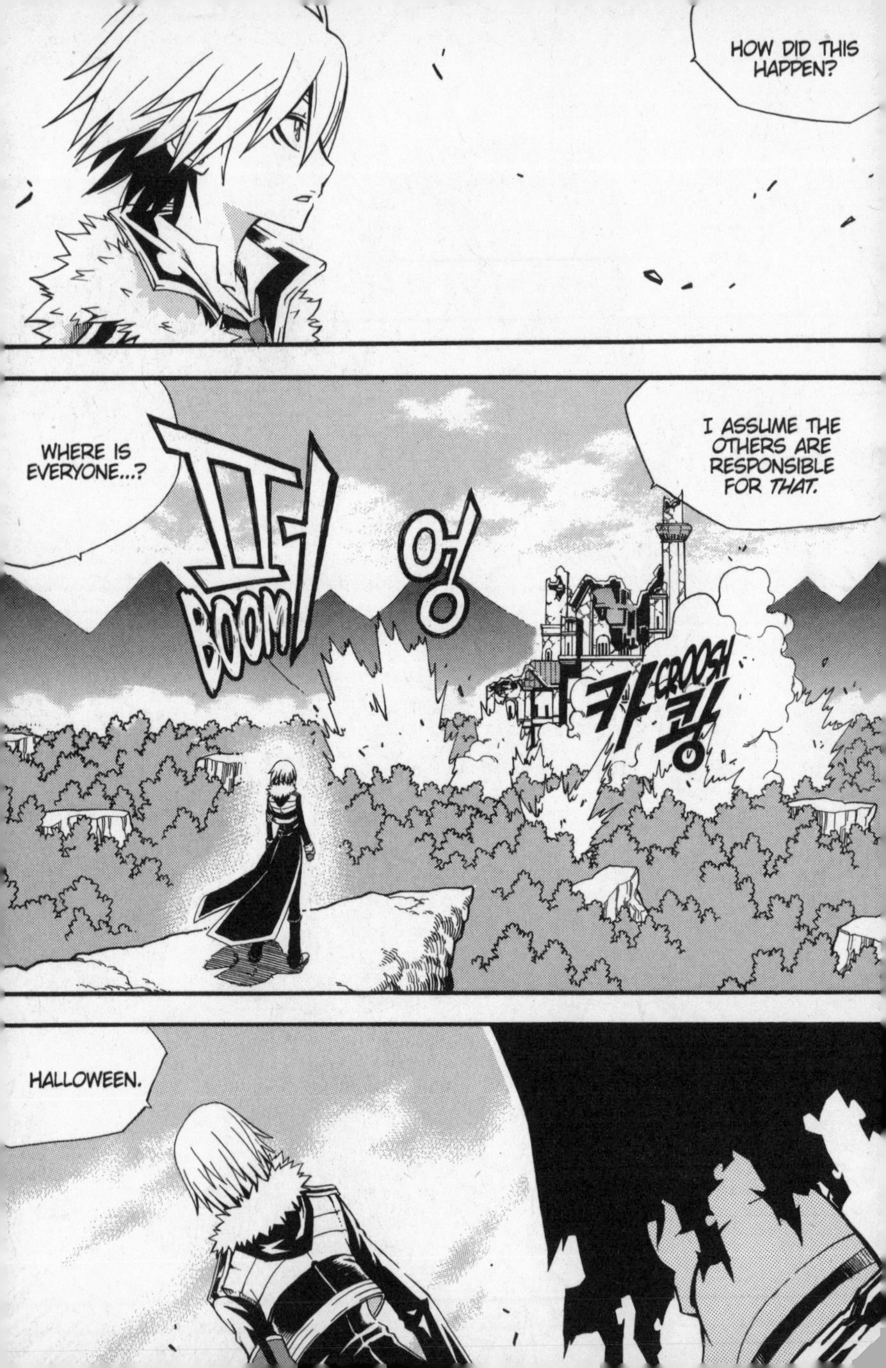
HOW DID THIS HAPPEN?
I ASSUME THE OTHERS ARE RESPONSIBLE FOR *THAT.*
WHERE IS EVERYONE...?
펑
BOOM
카광
CROOSH
HALLOWEEN.

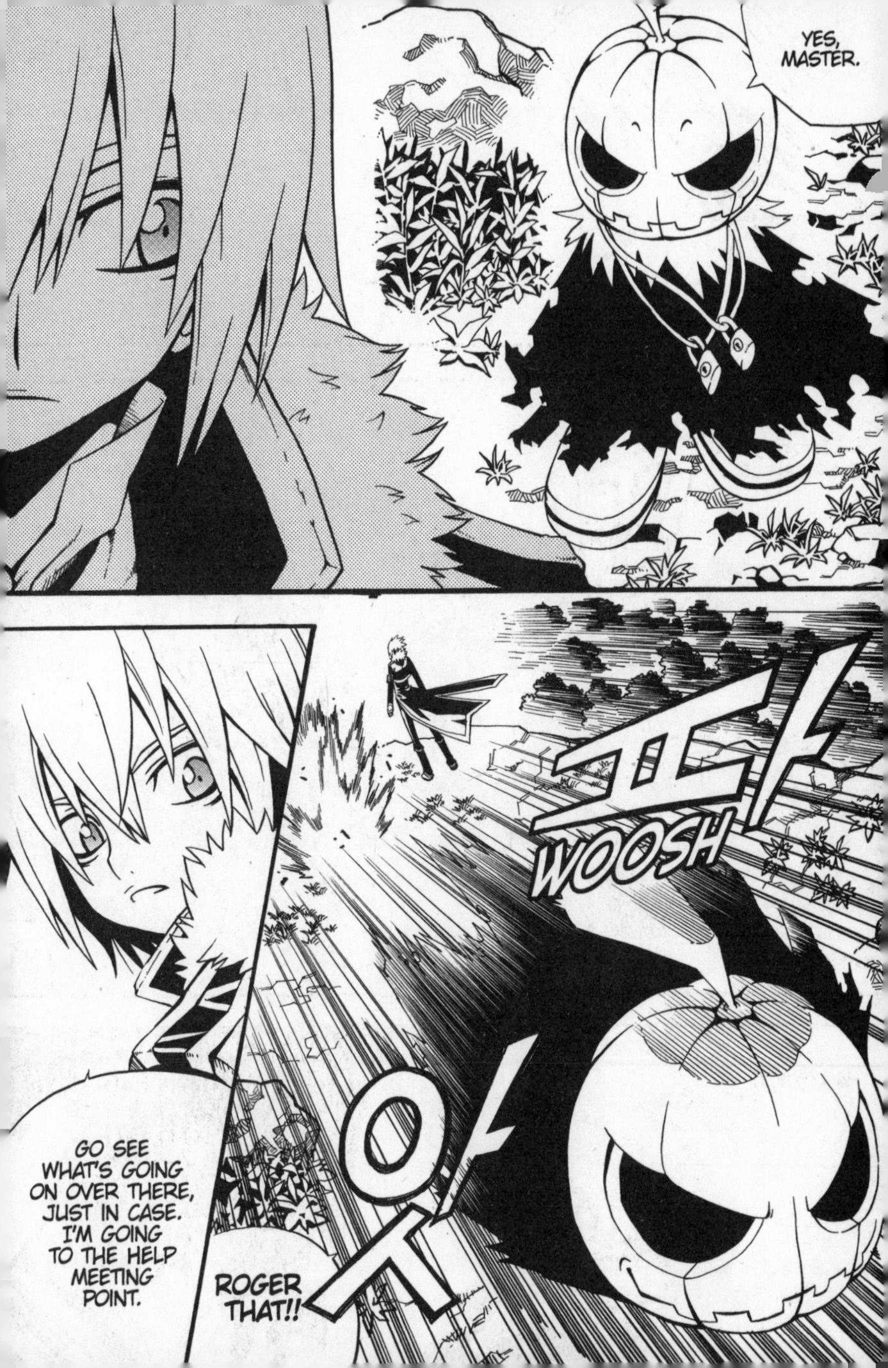

YES, MASTER.
WOOSH
GO SEE WHAT'S GOING ON OVER THERE, JUST IN CASE. I'M GOING TO THE HELP MEETING POINT.
ROGER THAT!!

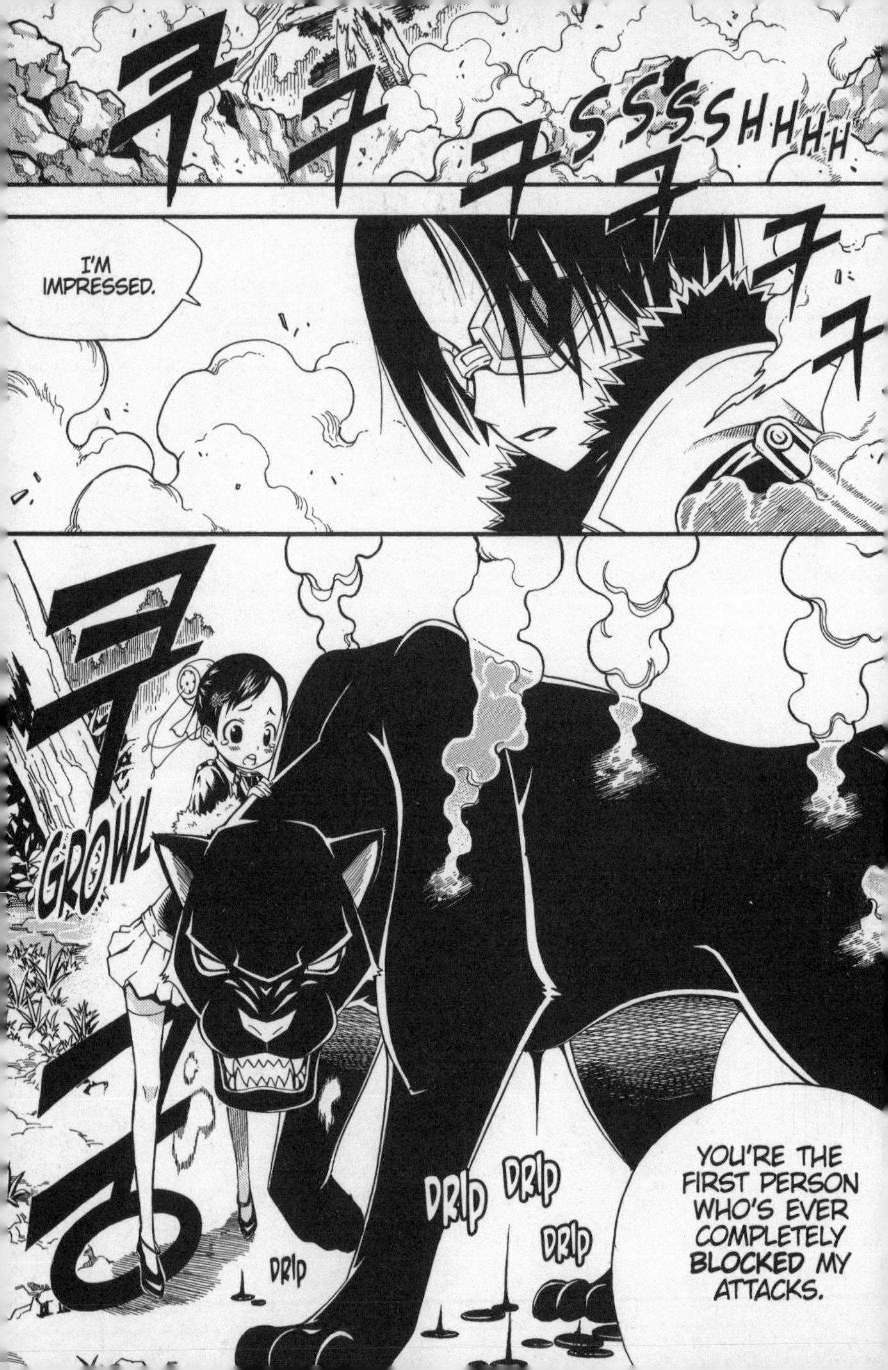
SSSSHHHH
I'M IMPRESSED.
GROWL
DRIP DRIP
DRIP
DRIP
YOU'RE THE FIRST PERSON WHO'S EVER COMPLETELY BLOCKED MY ATTACKS.

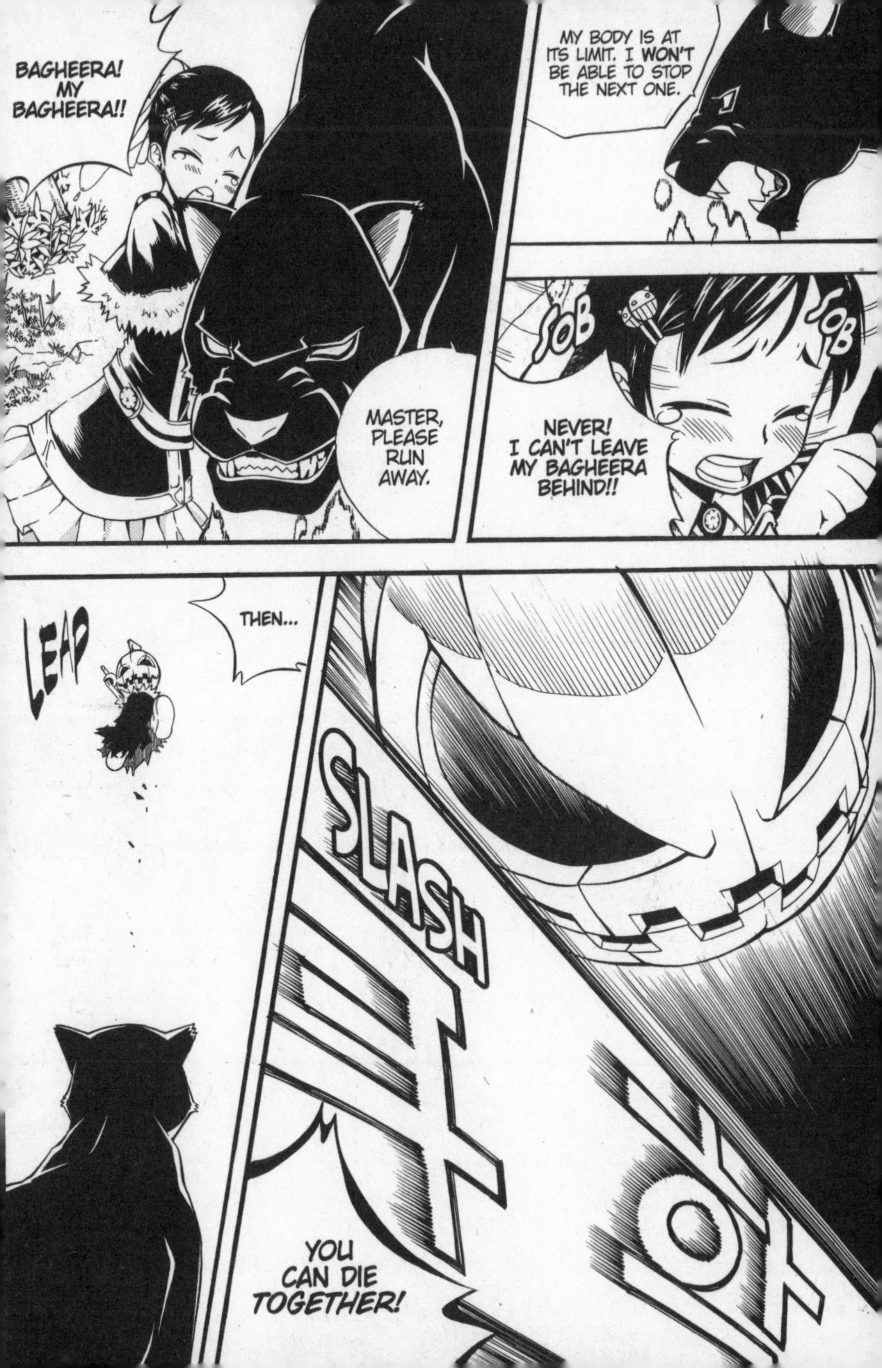
MY BODY IS AT ITS LIMIT. I WON'T BE ABLE TO STOP THE NEXT ONE.
BAGHEERA! MY BAGHEERA!!
MASTER, PLEASE RUN AWAY.
SOB
SOB
NEVER! I CAN'T LEAVE MY BAGHEERA BEHIND!!
THEN...
LEAP
SLASH
YOU CAN DIE TOGETHER!

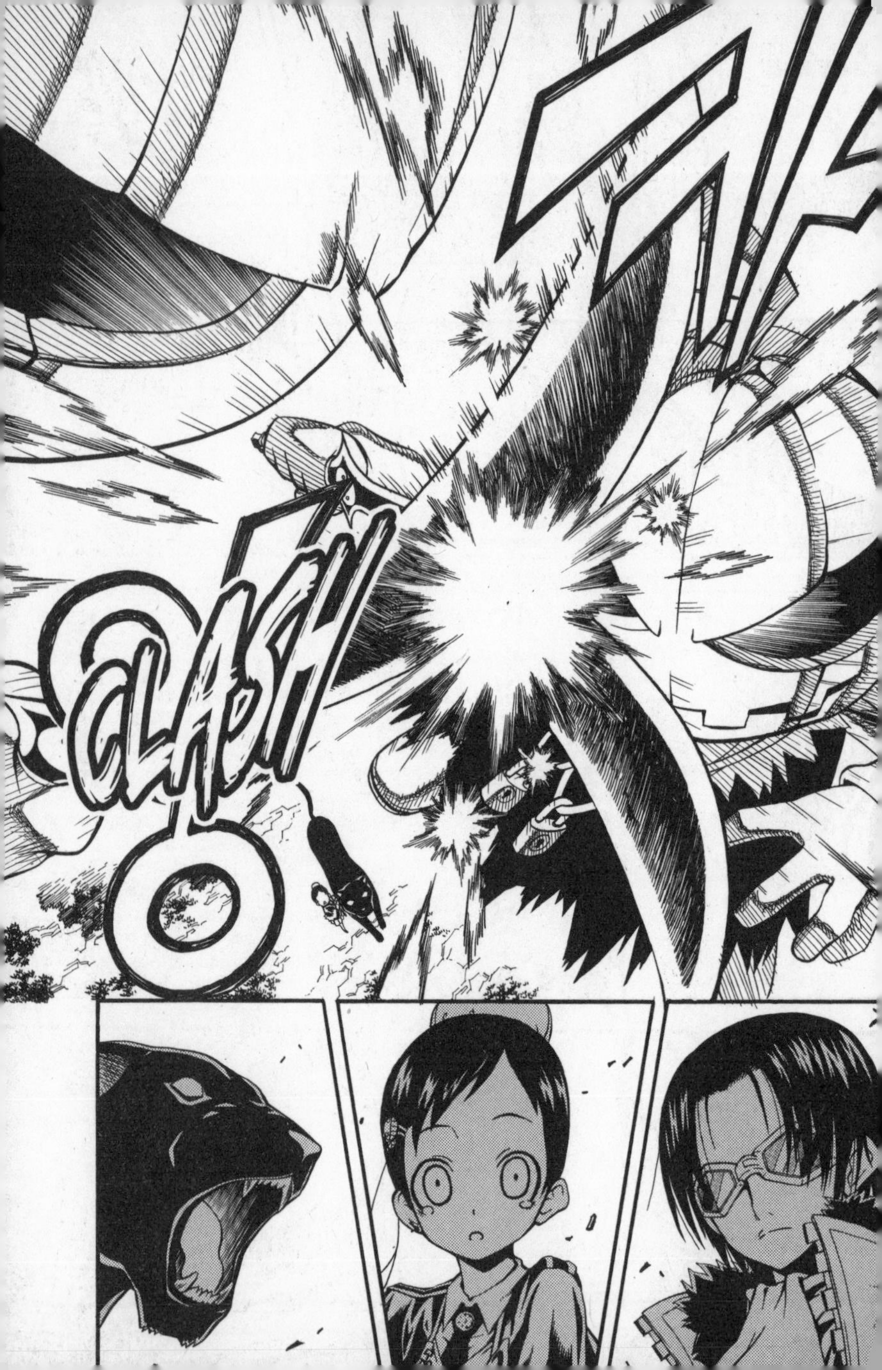
CLASH

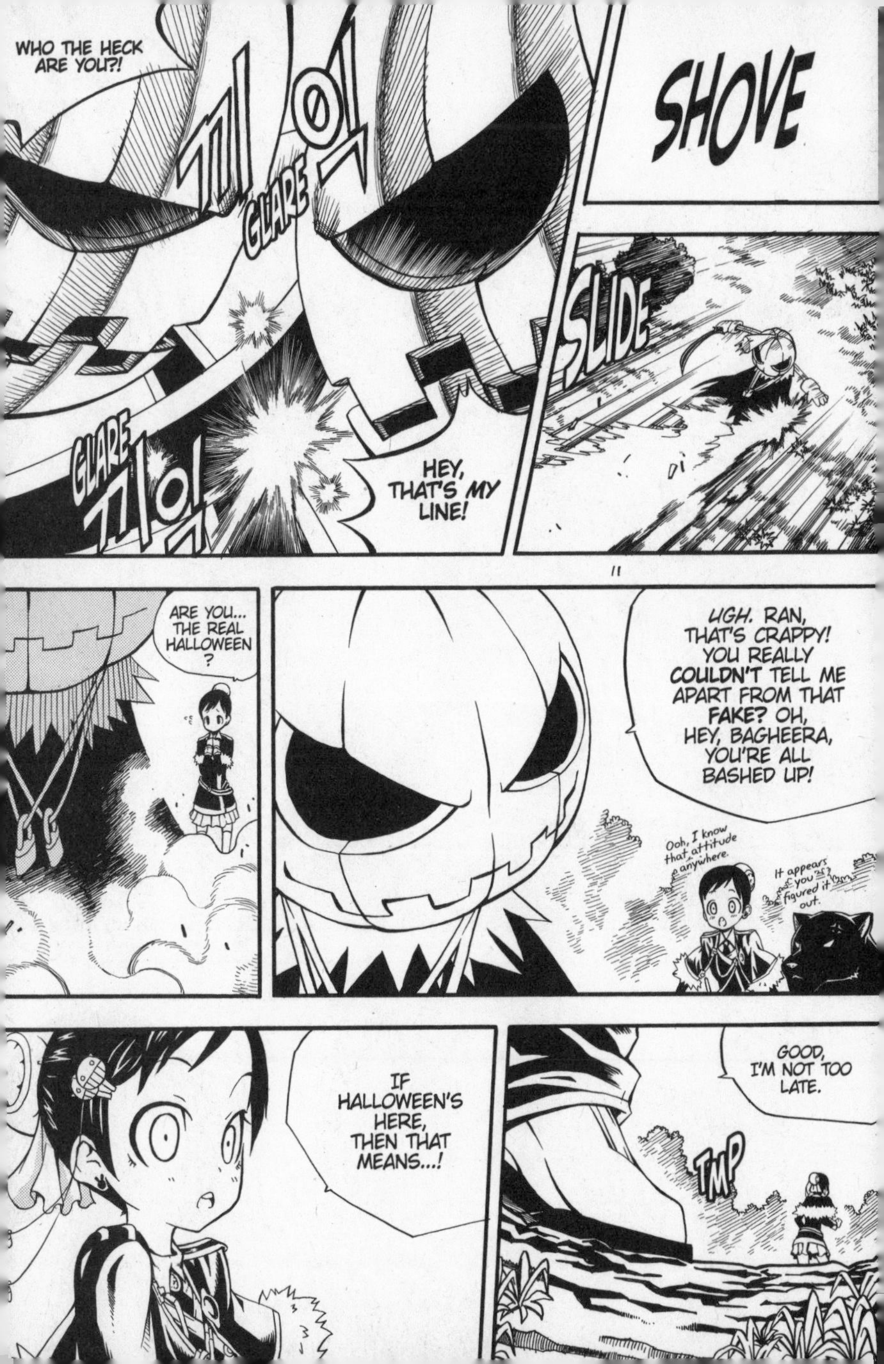
WHO THE HECK ARE YOU?!
GLARE
GLARE
HEY, THAT'S MY LINE!
SHOVE
SLIDE
ARE YOU... THE REAL HALLOWEEN?
UGH. RAN, THAT'S CRAPPY! YOU REALLY COULDN'T TELL ME APART FROM THAT FAKE? OH, HEY, BAGHEERA, YOU'RE ALL BASHED UP!
Ooh, I know that attitude anywhere.
It appears you've figured it out.
IF HALLOWEEN'S HERE, THEN THAT MEANS...!
TMP
GOOD, I'M NOT TOO LATE.

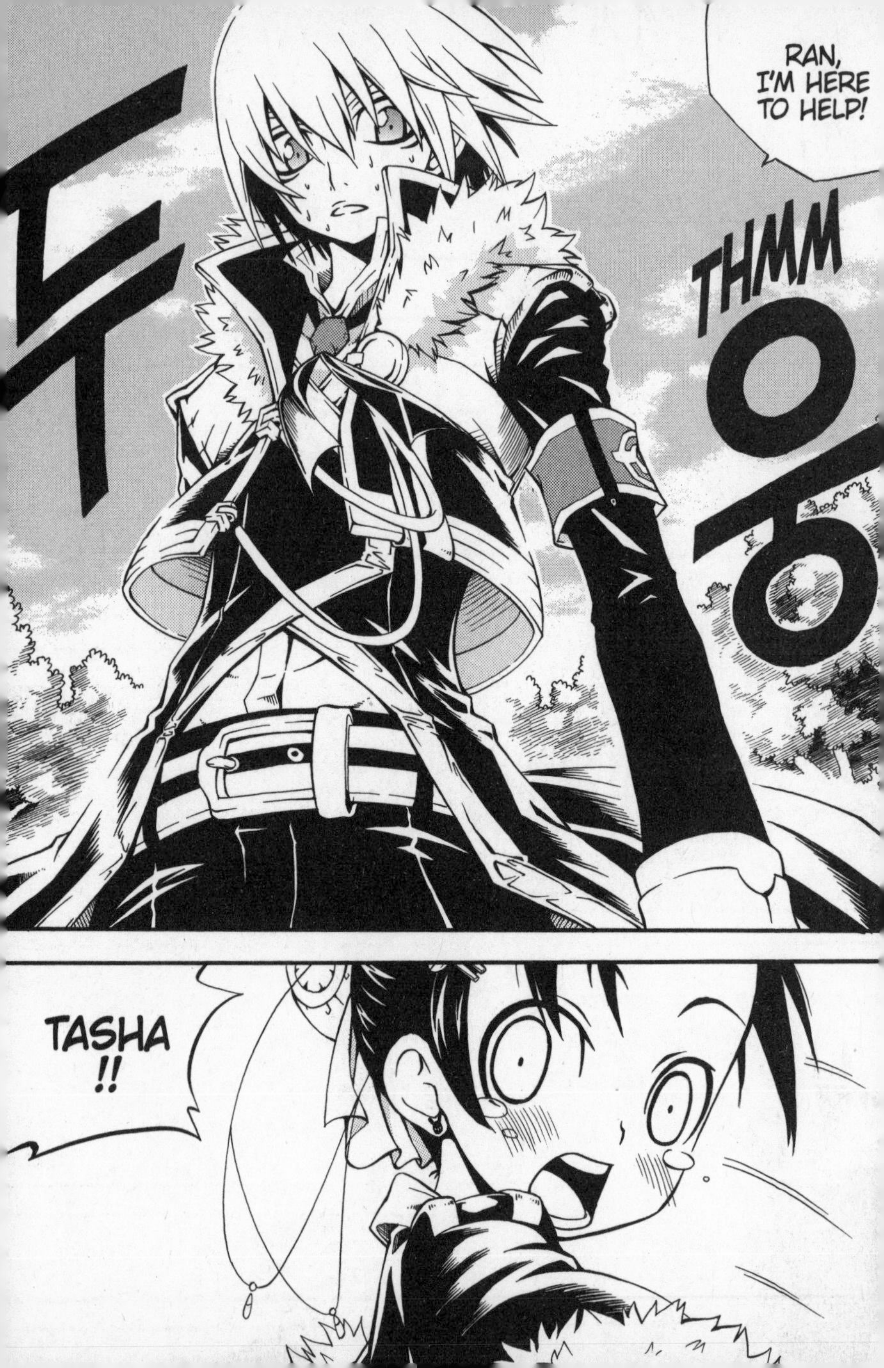
RAN, I'M HERE TO HELP!
THMM
TASHA !!

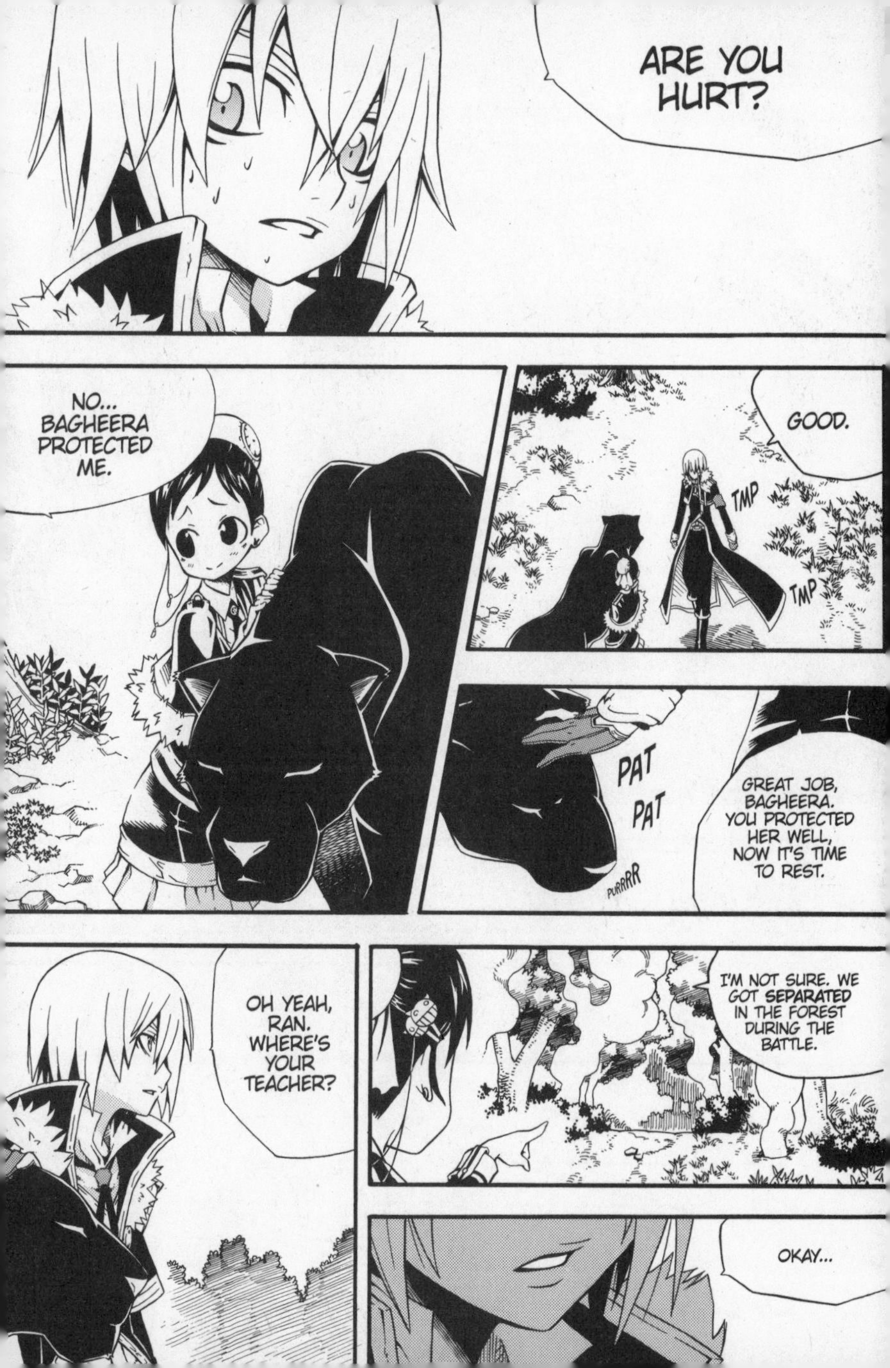
ARE YOU HURT?
GOOD.
TMP
TMP
NO... BAGHEERA PROTECTED ME.
GREAT JOB, BAGHEERA. YOU PROTECTED HER WELL, NOW IT'S TIME TO REST.
PAT
PAT
PURRRR
I'M NOT SURE. WE GOT SEPARATED IN THE FOREST DURING THE BATTLE.
OH YEAH, RAN. WHERE'S YOUR TEACHER?
OKAY...

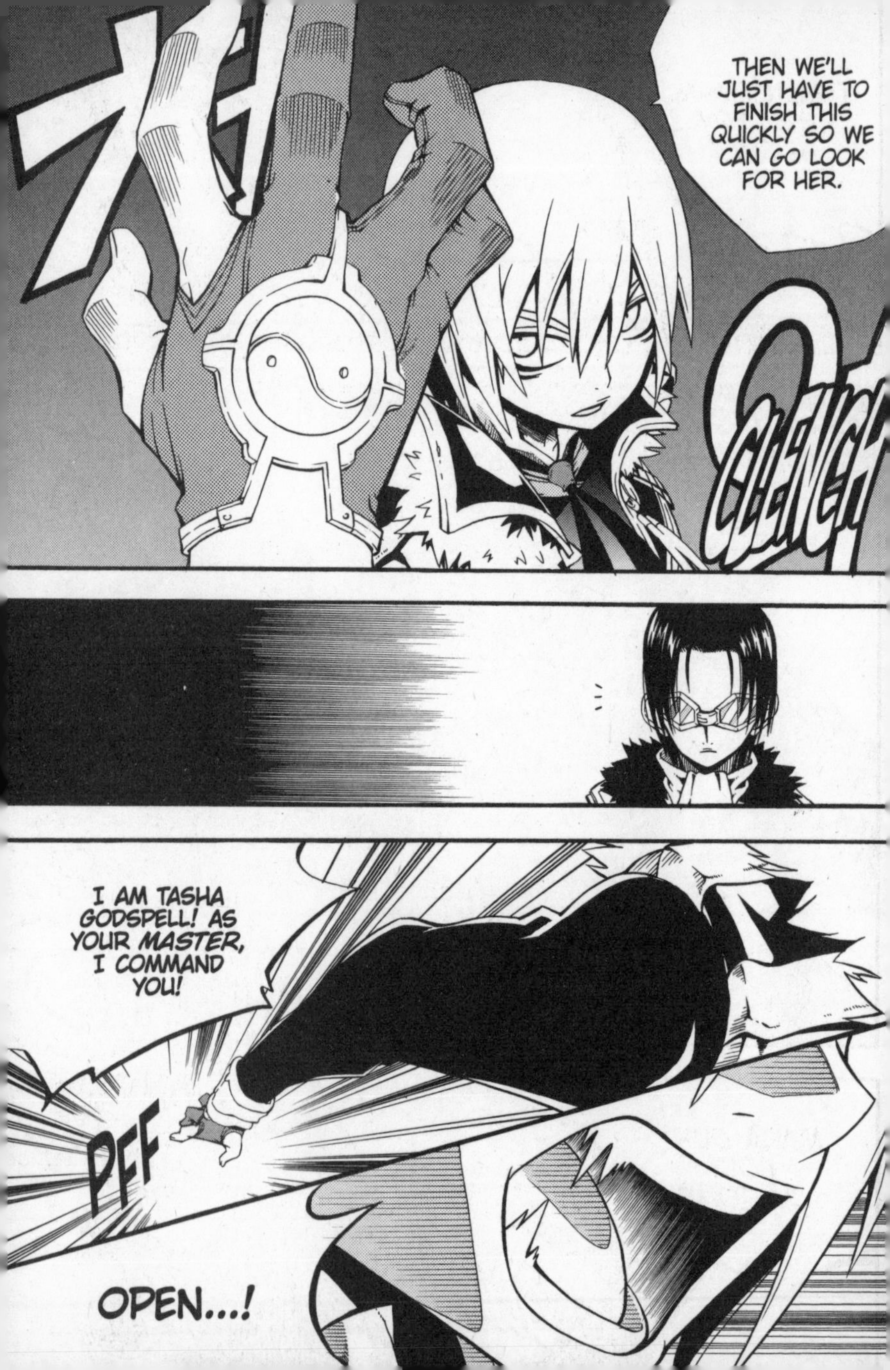
THEN WE'LL JUST HAVE TO FINISH THIS QUICKLY SO WE CAN GO LOOK FOR HER.
CLENCH
I AM TASHA GODSPELL! AS YOUR *MASTER*, I COMMAND YOU!
PFF
OPEN...!

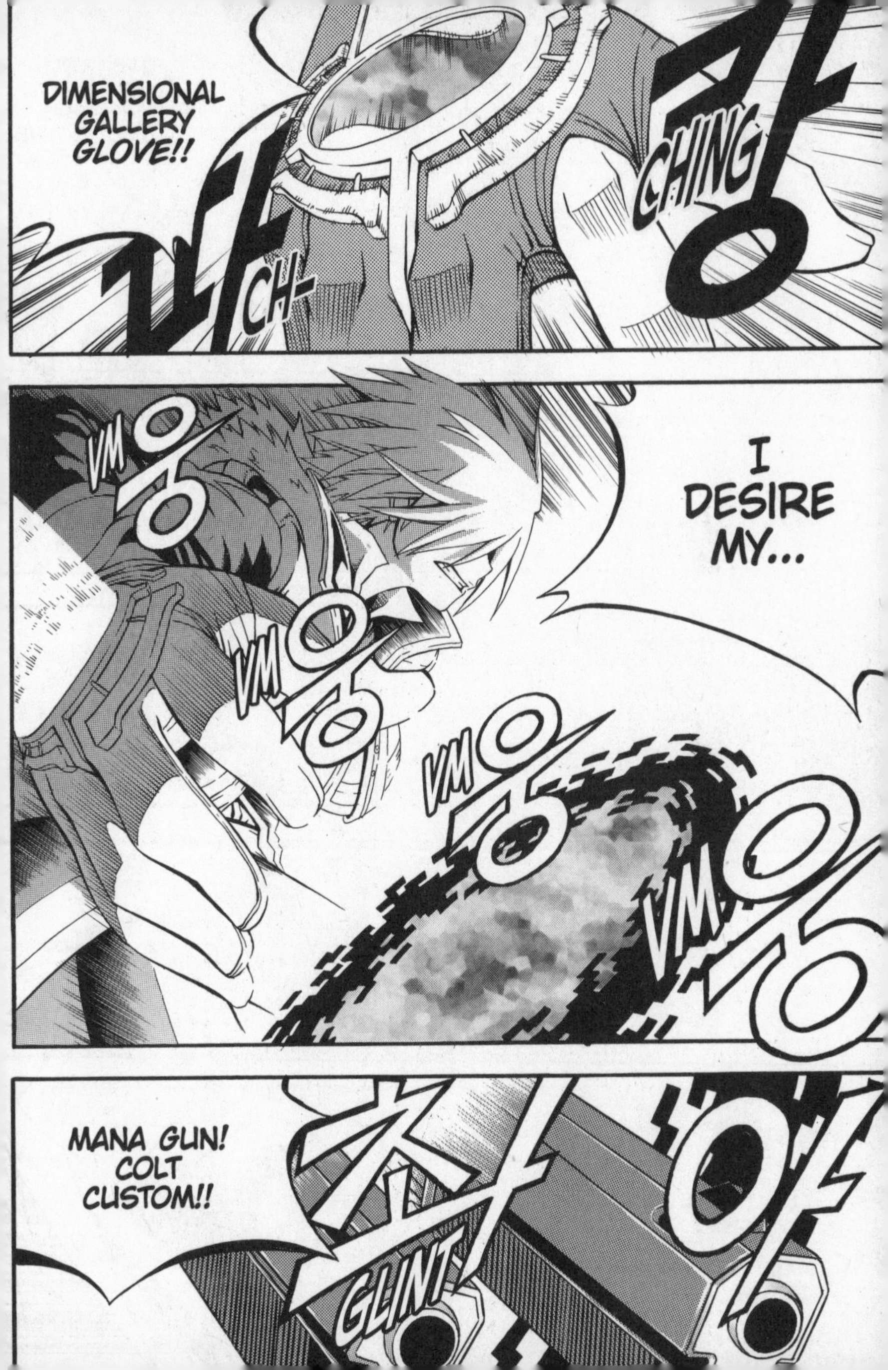
CHING
DIMENSIONAL GALLERY GLOVE!!
CH-
I DESIRE MY...
VM
VM
VM
VM
VM
GLINT
MANA GUN! COLT CUSTOM!!

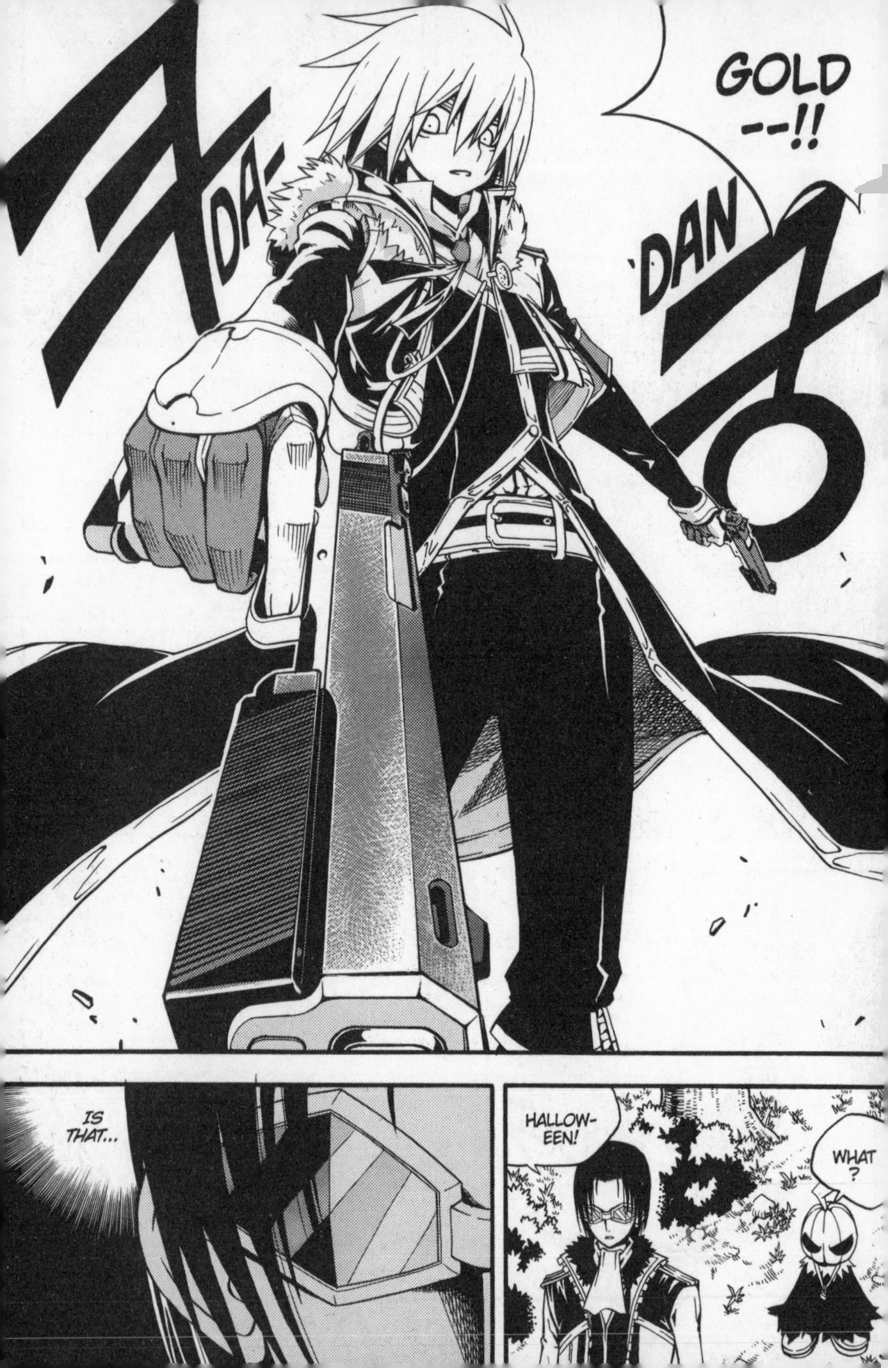
GOLD --!!
DA- DAN
WHAT ?
HALLOW-EEN!
IS THAT...

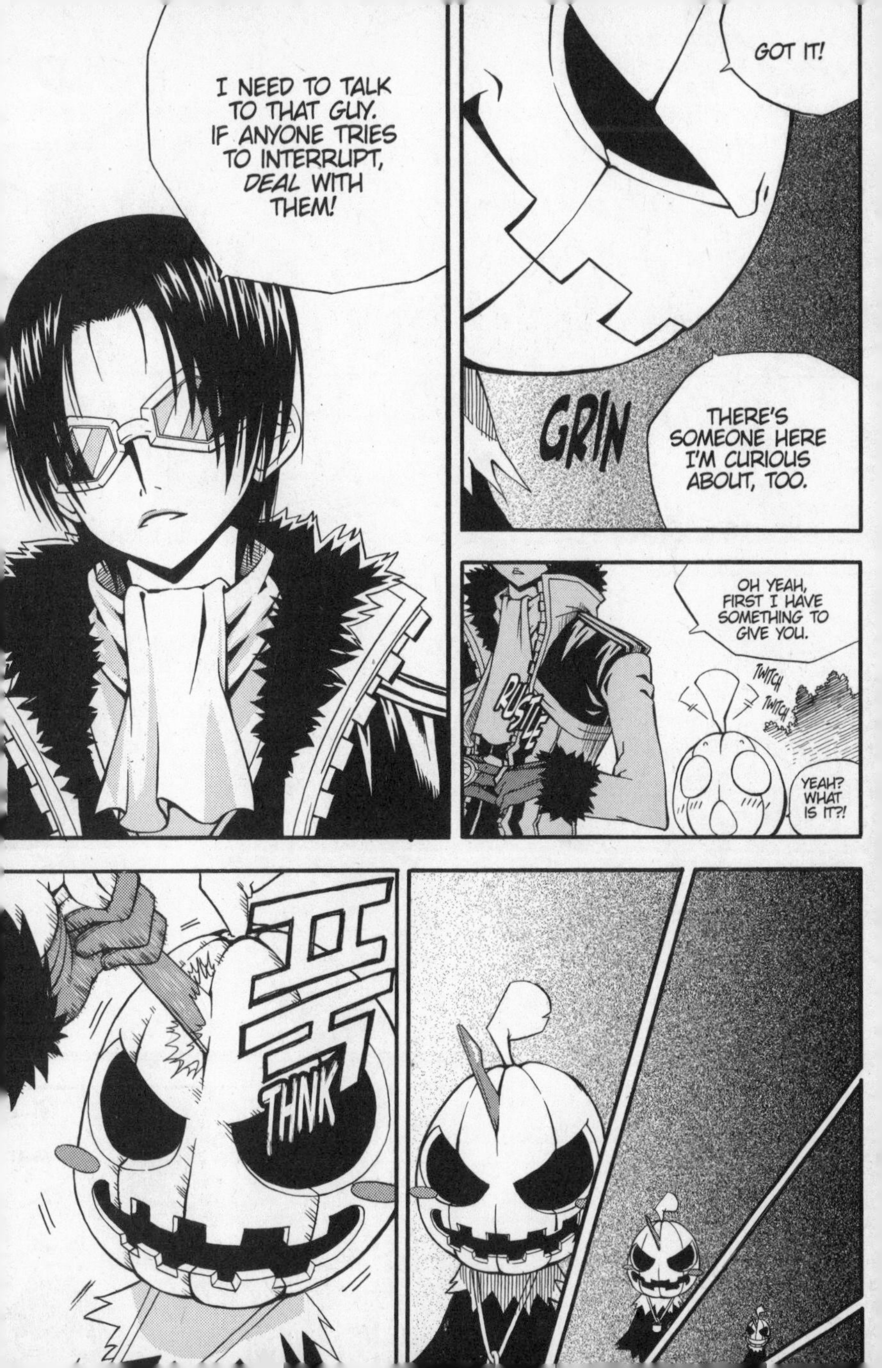

I NEED TO TALK TO THAT GUY. IF ANYONE TRIES TO INTERRUPT, DEAL WITH THEM!
GOT IT!
GRIN
THERE'S SOMEONE HERE I'M CURIOUS ABOUT, TOO.
OH YEAH, FIRST I HAVE SOMETHING TO GIVE YOU.
RUSTLE
TWITCH
TWITCH
YEAH? WHAT IS IT?!
THNK

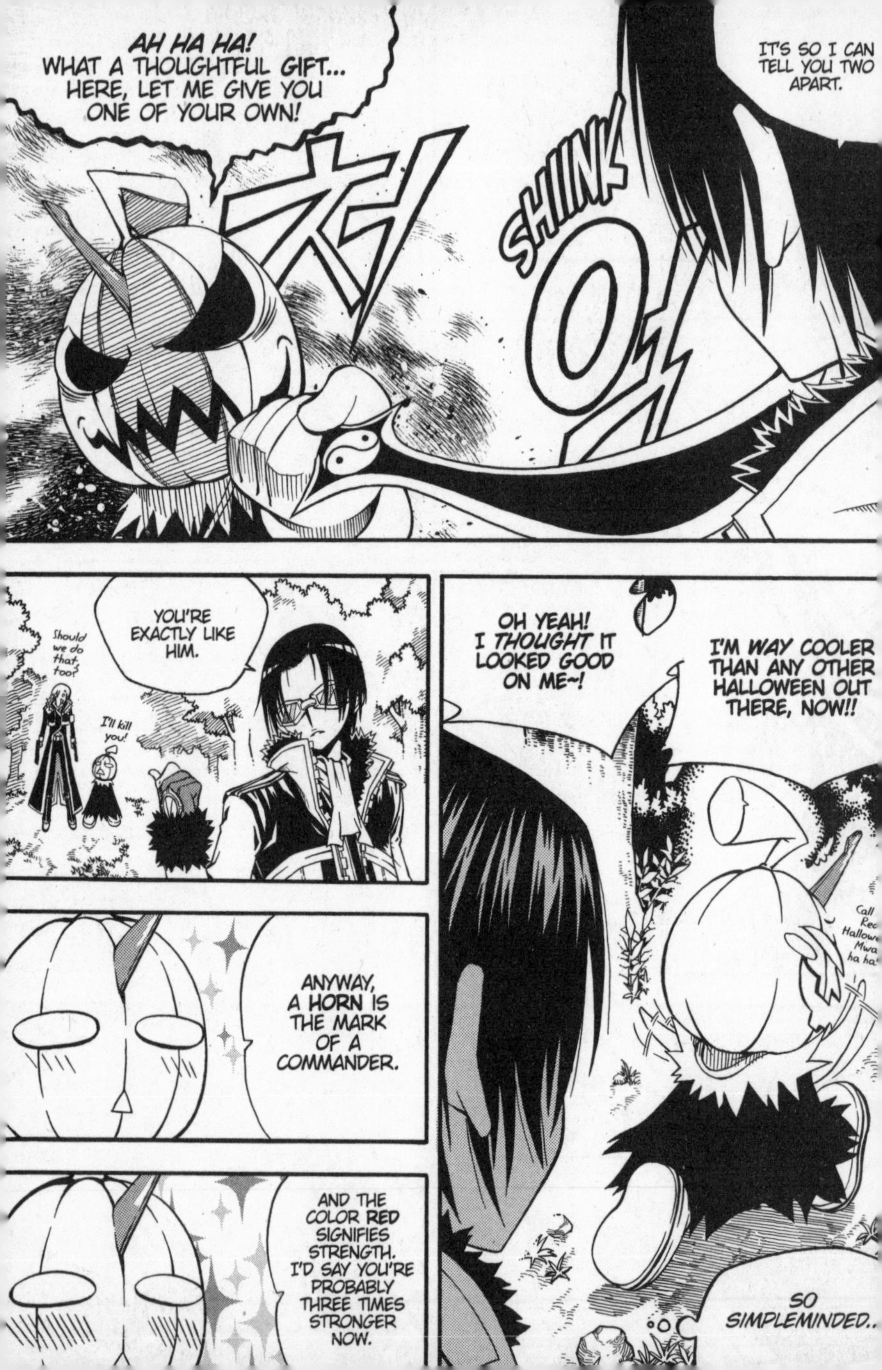
IT'S SO I CAN TELL YOU TWO APART.
SHIINK
AH HA HA! WHAT A THOUGHTFUL GIFT... HERE, LET ME GIVE YOU ONE OF YOUR OWN!
OH YEAH! I THOUGHT IT LOOKED GOOD ON ME~!
I'M WAY COOLER THAN ANY OTHER HALLOWEEN OUT THERE, NOW!!
SO SIMPLEMINDED...
YOU'RE EXACTLY LIKE HIM.
Should we do that, too?
I'll kill you!
ANYWAY, A HORN IS THE MARK OF A COMMANDER.
AND THE COLOR RED SIGNIFIES STRENGTH. I'D SAY YOU'RE PROBABLY THREE TIMES STRONGER NOW.

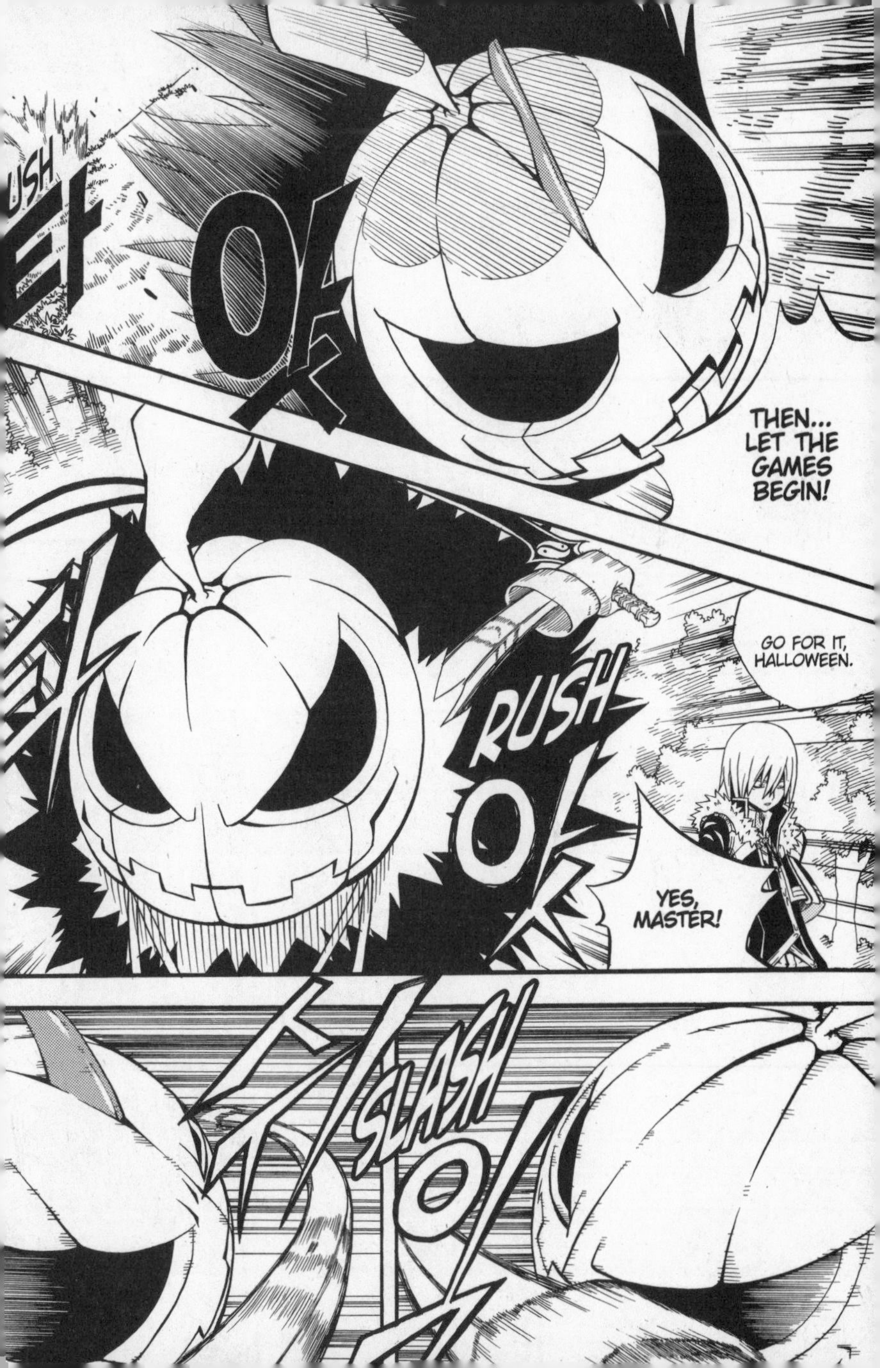
USH
THEN... LET THE GAMES BEGIN!
GO FOR IT, HALLOWEEN.
YES, MASTER!
RUSH
SLASH

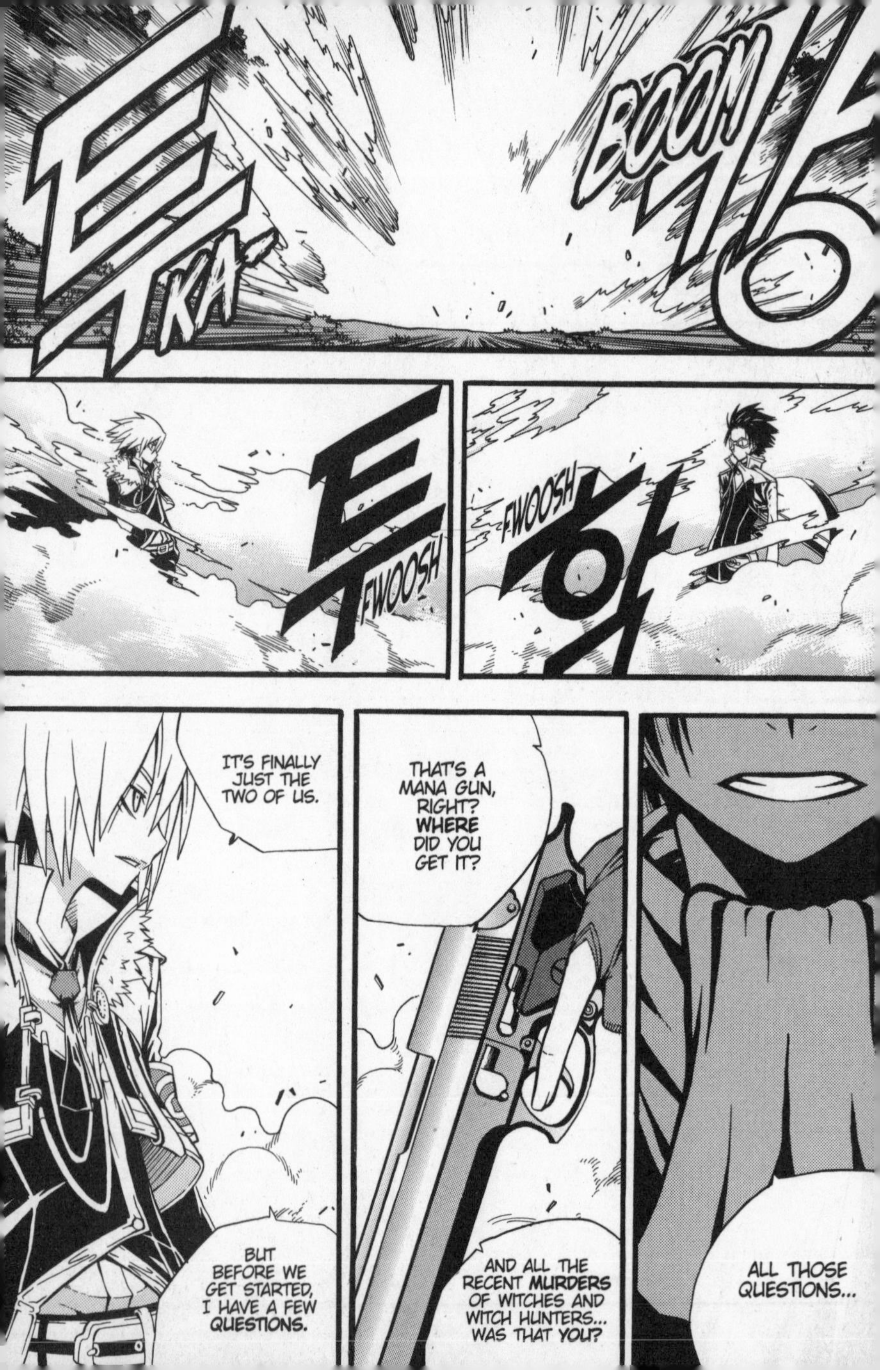
KA-
BOOM
FWOOSH
FWOOSH
IT'S FINALLY JUST THE TWO OF US.
BUT BEFORE WE GET STARTED, I HAVE A FEW QUESTIONS.
THAT'S A MANA GUN, RIGHT? WHERE DID YOU GET IT?
AND ALL THE RECENT MURDERS OF WITCHES AND WITCH HUNTERS... WAS THAT YOU?
ALL THOSE QUESTIONS...

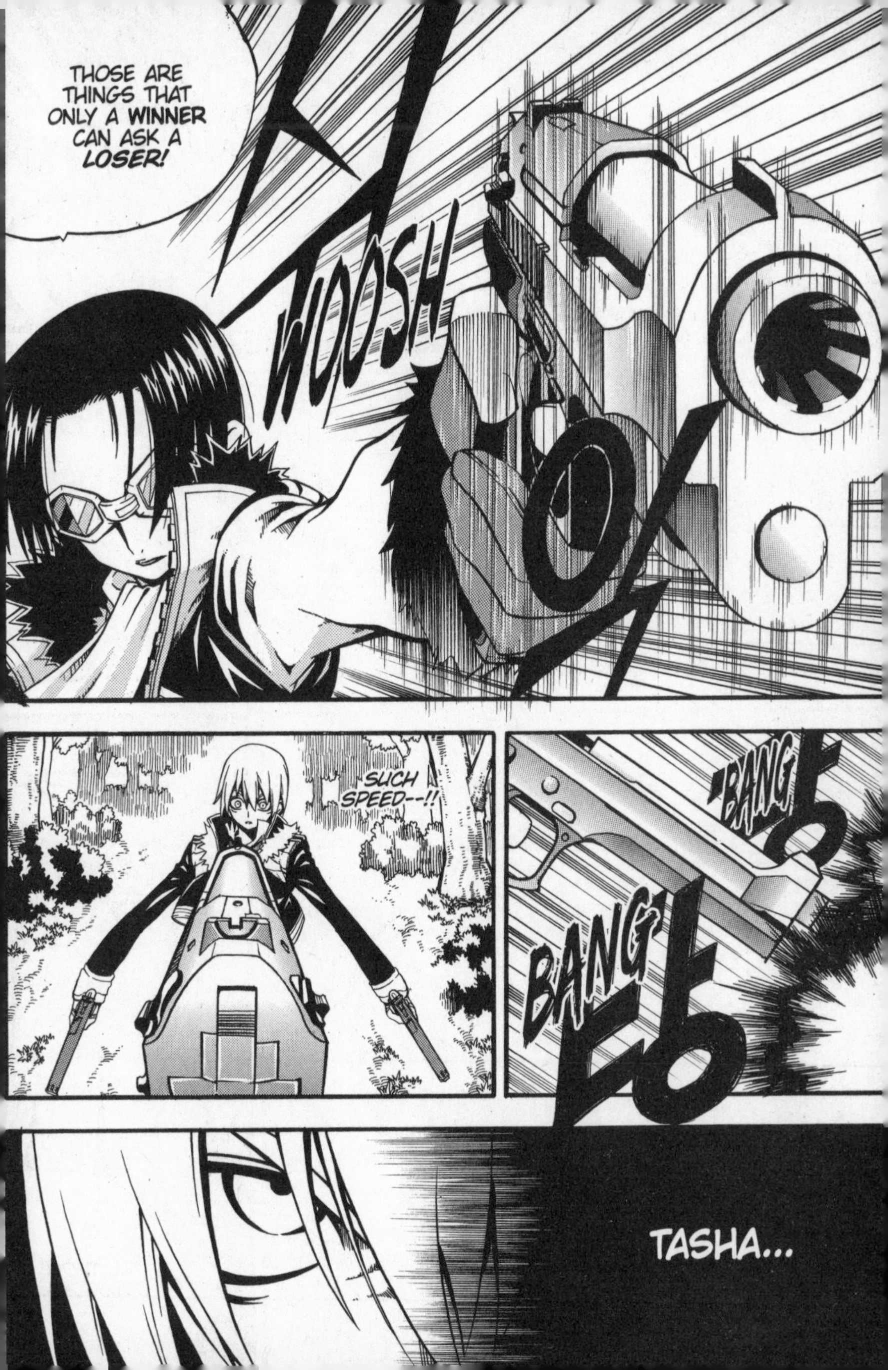
THOSE ARE THINGS THAT ONLY A WINNER CAN ASK A LOSER!
WOOSH
SUCH SPEED--!!
BANG
BANG
TASHA...

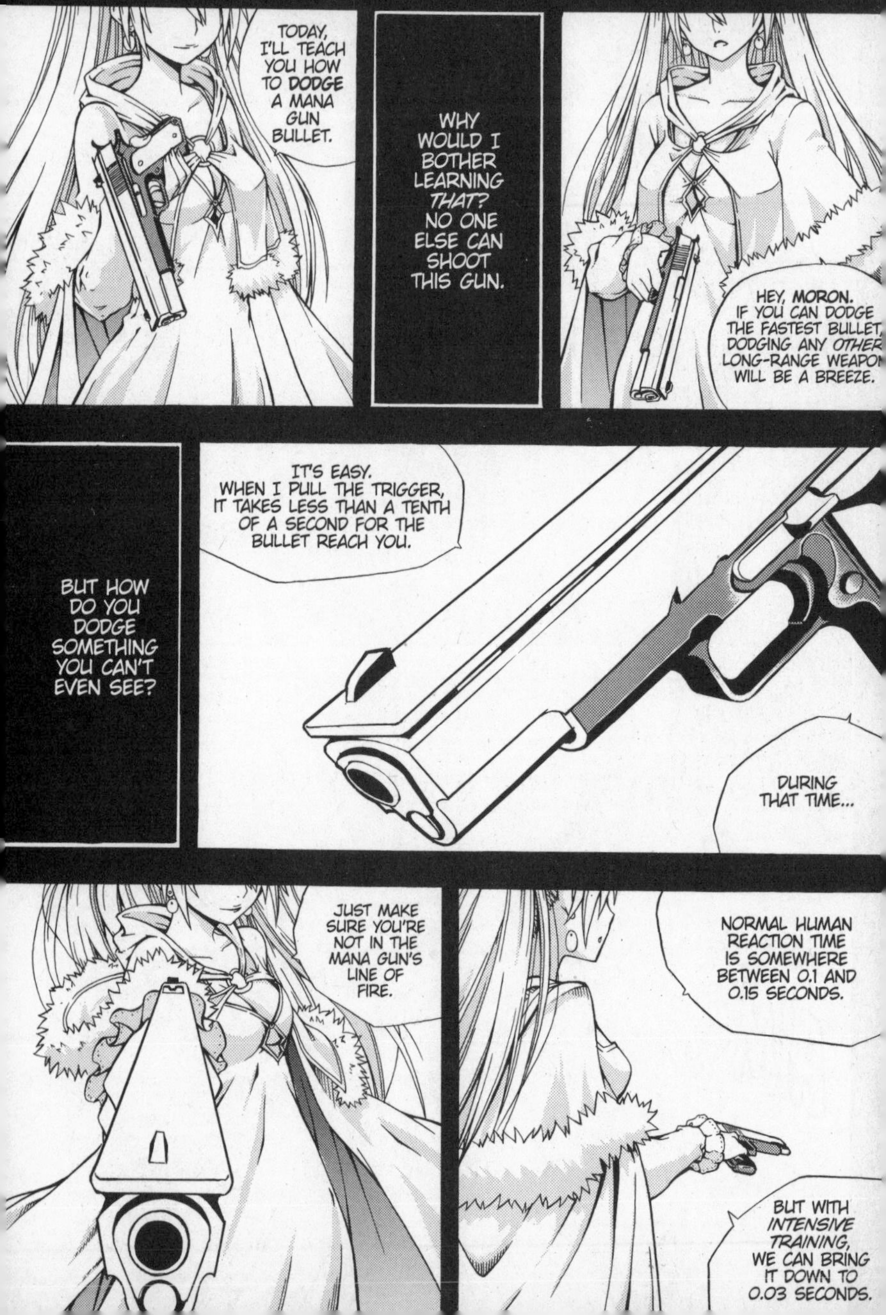
TODAY, I'LL TEACH YOU HOW TO DODGE A MANA GUN BULLET.
WHY WOULD I BOTHER LEARNING *THAT?* NO ONE ELSE CAN SHOOT THIS GUN.
HEY, MORON. IF YOU CAN DODGE THE FASTEST BULLET, DODGING ANY *OTHER* LONG-RANGE WEAPO WILL BE A BREEZE.
BUT HOW DO YOU DODGE SOMETHING YOU CAN'T EVEN SEE?
IT'S EASY. WHEN I PULL THE TRIGGER, IT TAKES LESS THAN A TENTH OF A SECOND FOR THE BULLET REACH YOU.
DURING THAT TIME...
JUST MAKE SURE YOU'RE NOT IN THE MANA GUN'S LINE OF FIRE.
NORMAL HUMAN REACTION TIME IS SOMEWHERE BETWEEN 0.1 AND 0.15 SECONDS.
BUT WITH *INTENSIVE TRAINING,* WE CAN BRING IT DOWN TO 0.03 SECONDS.

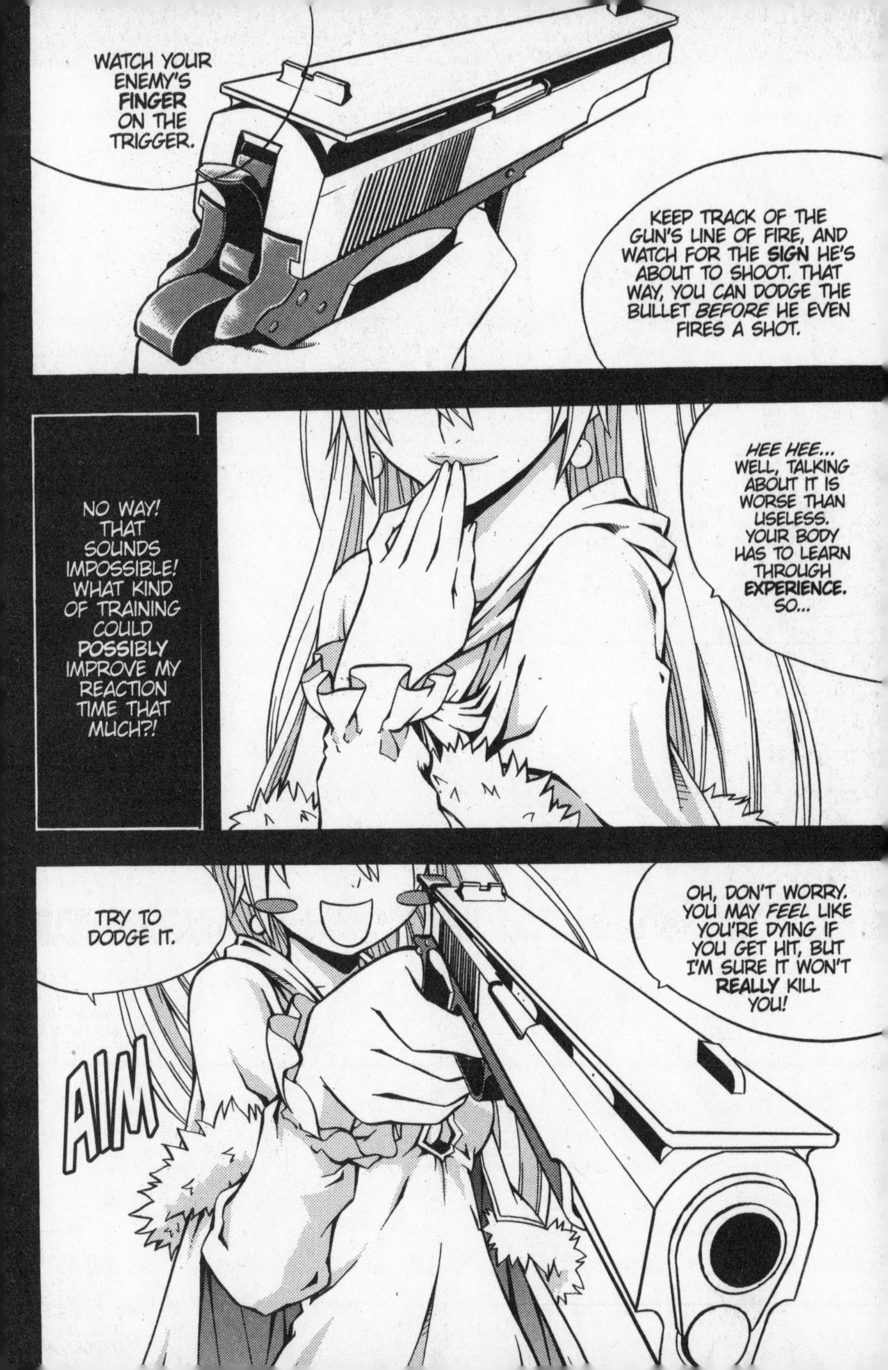
WATCH YOUR ENEMY'S **FINGER** ON THE TRIGGER.
KEEP TRACK OF THE GUN'S LINE OF FIRE, AND WATCH FOR THE **SIGN** HE'S ABOUT TO SHOOT. THAT WAY, YOU CAN DODGE THE BULLET *BEFORE* HE EVEN FIRES A SHOT.
HEE HEE... WELL, TALKING ABOUT IT IS WORSE THAN USELESS. YOUR BODY HAS TO LEARN THROUGH **EXPERIENCE.** SO...
NO WAY! THAT SOUNDS IMPOSSIBLE! WHAT KIND OF TRAINING COULD **POSSIBLY** IMPROVE MY REACTION TIME THAT MUCH?!
OH, DON'T WORRY. YOU MAY *FEEL* LIKE YOU'RE DYING IF YOU GET HIT, BUT I'M SURE IT WON'T **REALLY** KILL YOU!
TRY TO DODGE IT.
AIM

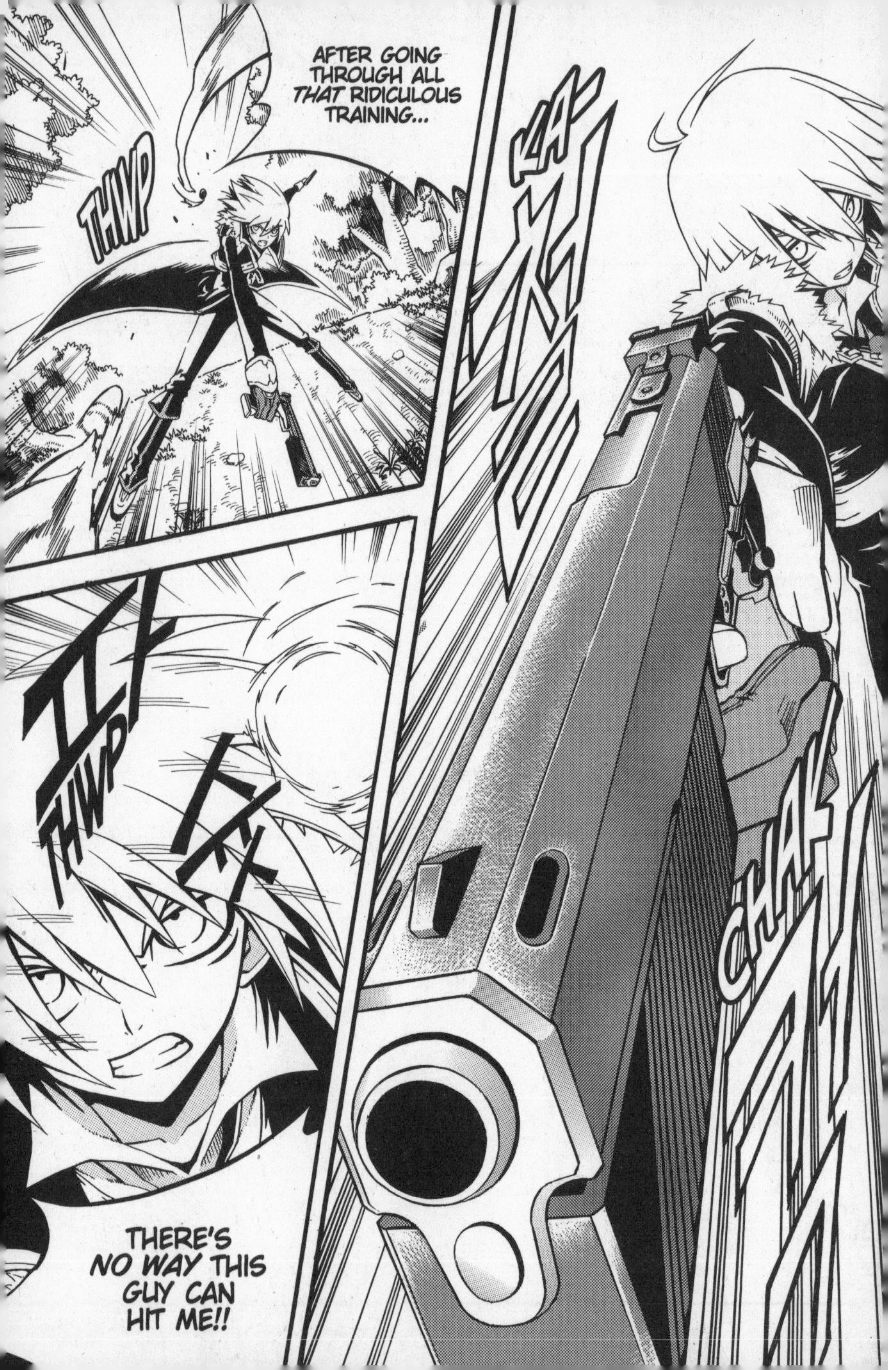
KA
CHAK
AFTER GOING THROUGH ALL *THAT* RIDICULOUS TRAINING...
THWP
THWP
THERE'S *NO WAY* THIS GUY CAN HIT ME!!

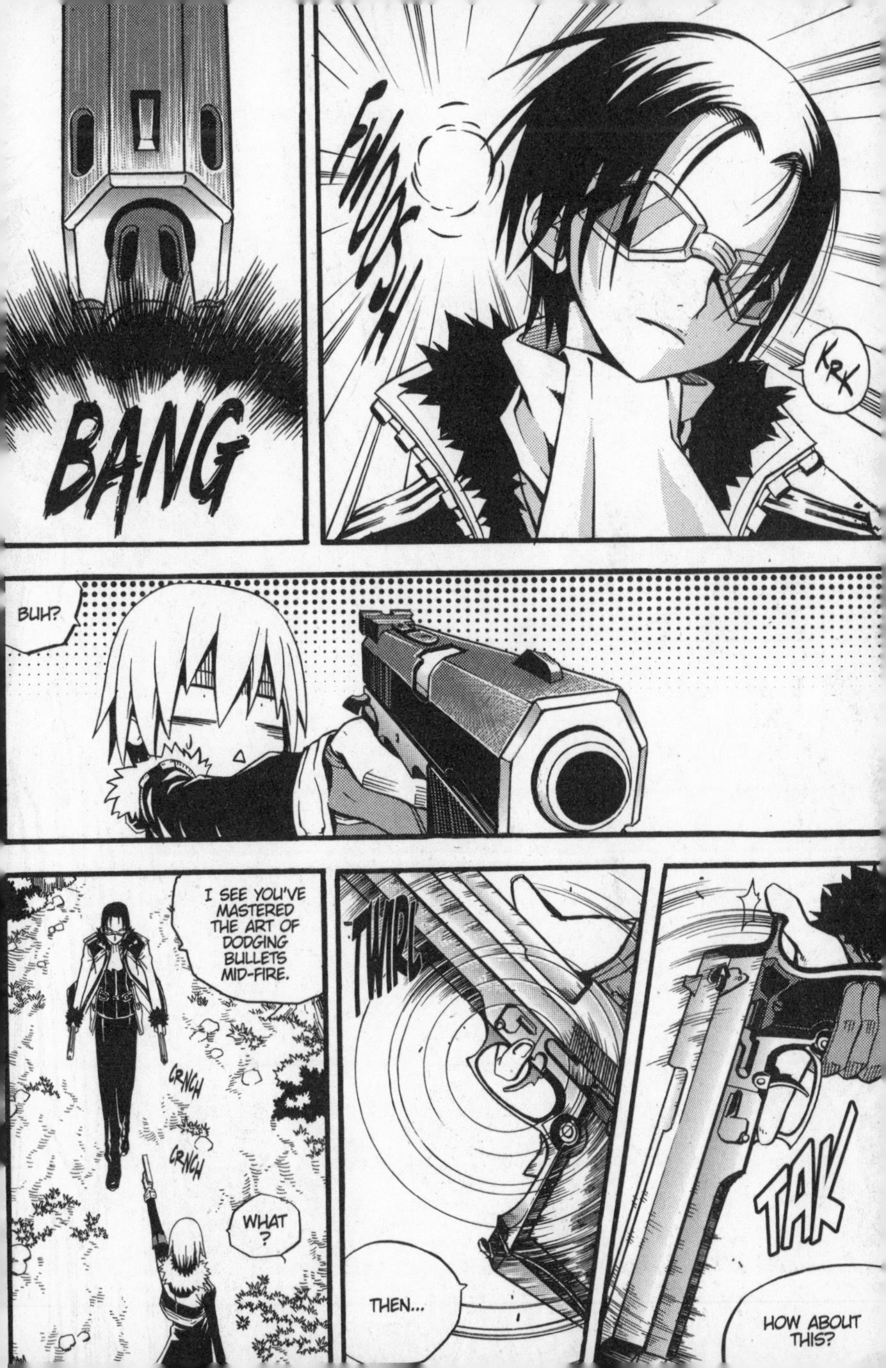
BANG
FWOOSH
KRK
BUH?
I SEE YOU'VE MASTERED THE ART OF DODGING BULLETS MID-FIRE.
CRNCH
CRNCH
WHAT?
TWIRL
THEN...
TAK
HOW ABOUT THIS?

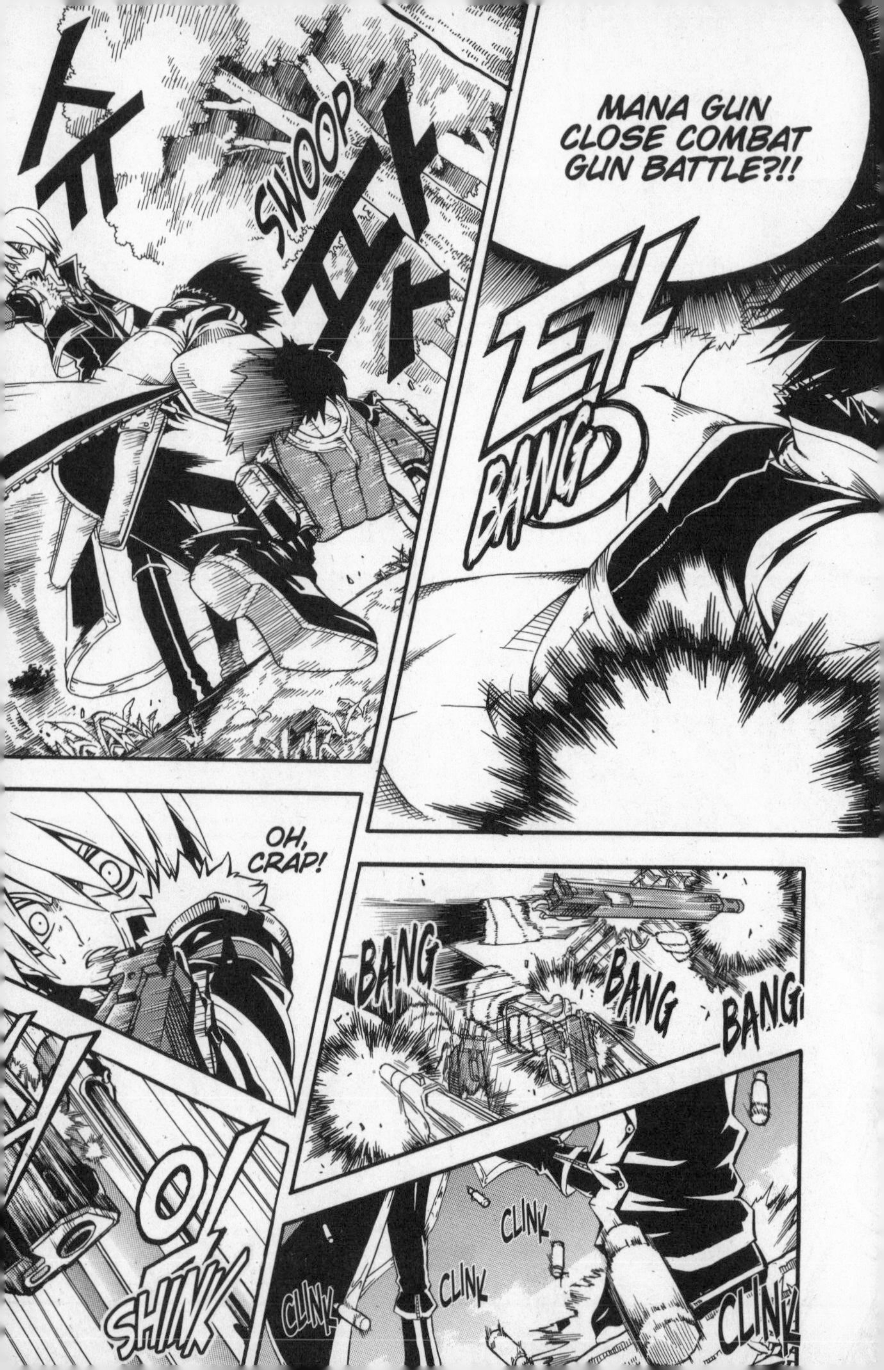
MANA GUN CLOSE COMBAT GUN BATTLE?!!
BANG
SWOOP
OH, CRAP!
BANG
BANG
BANG
SHINK
CLINK
CLINK
CLINK
CLINK

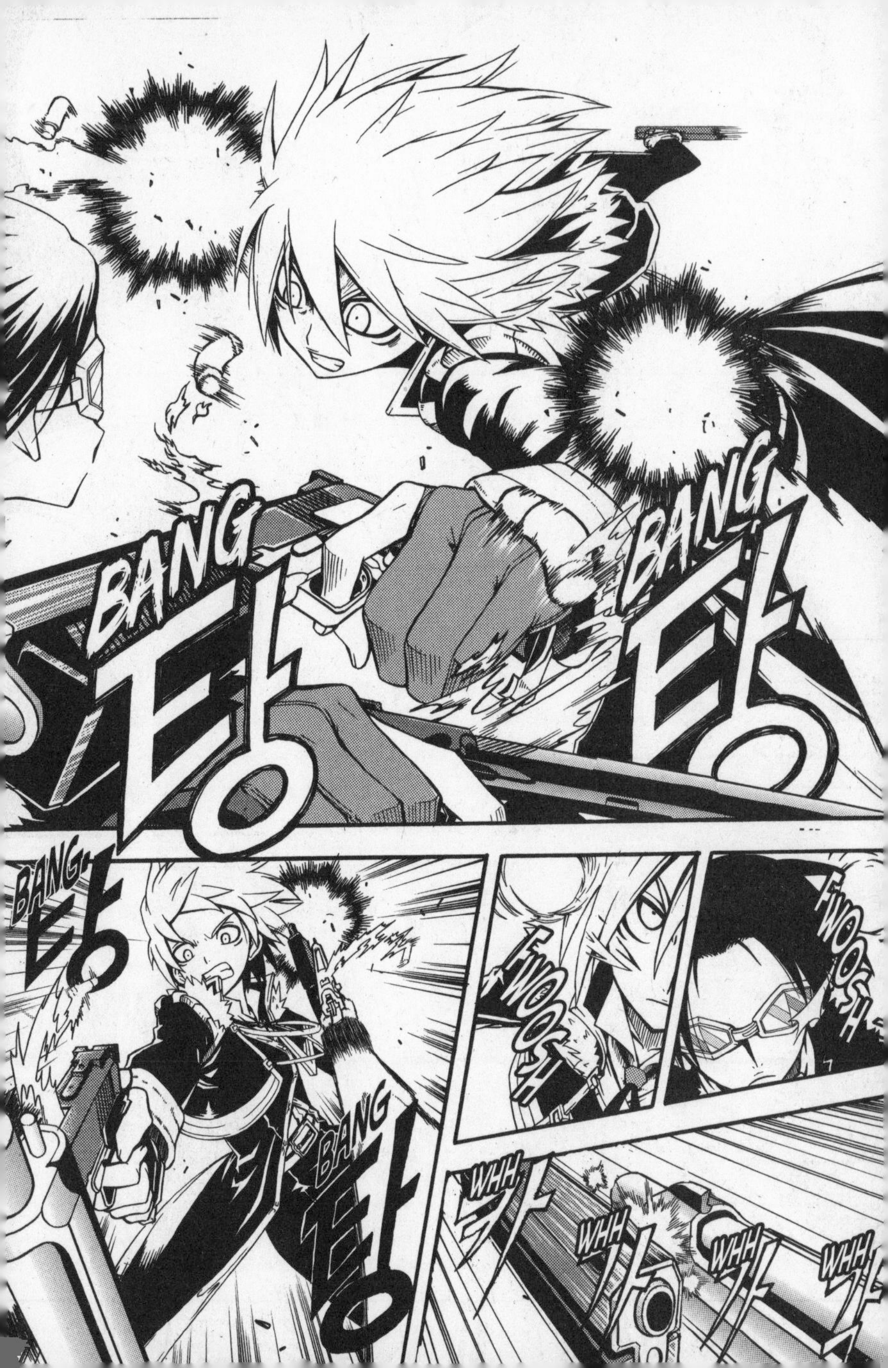
BANG
BANG
FWOOSH
FWOOSH
BANG
BANG
WHH
WHH
WHH
WHH

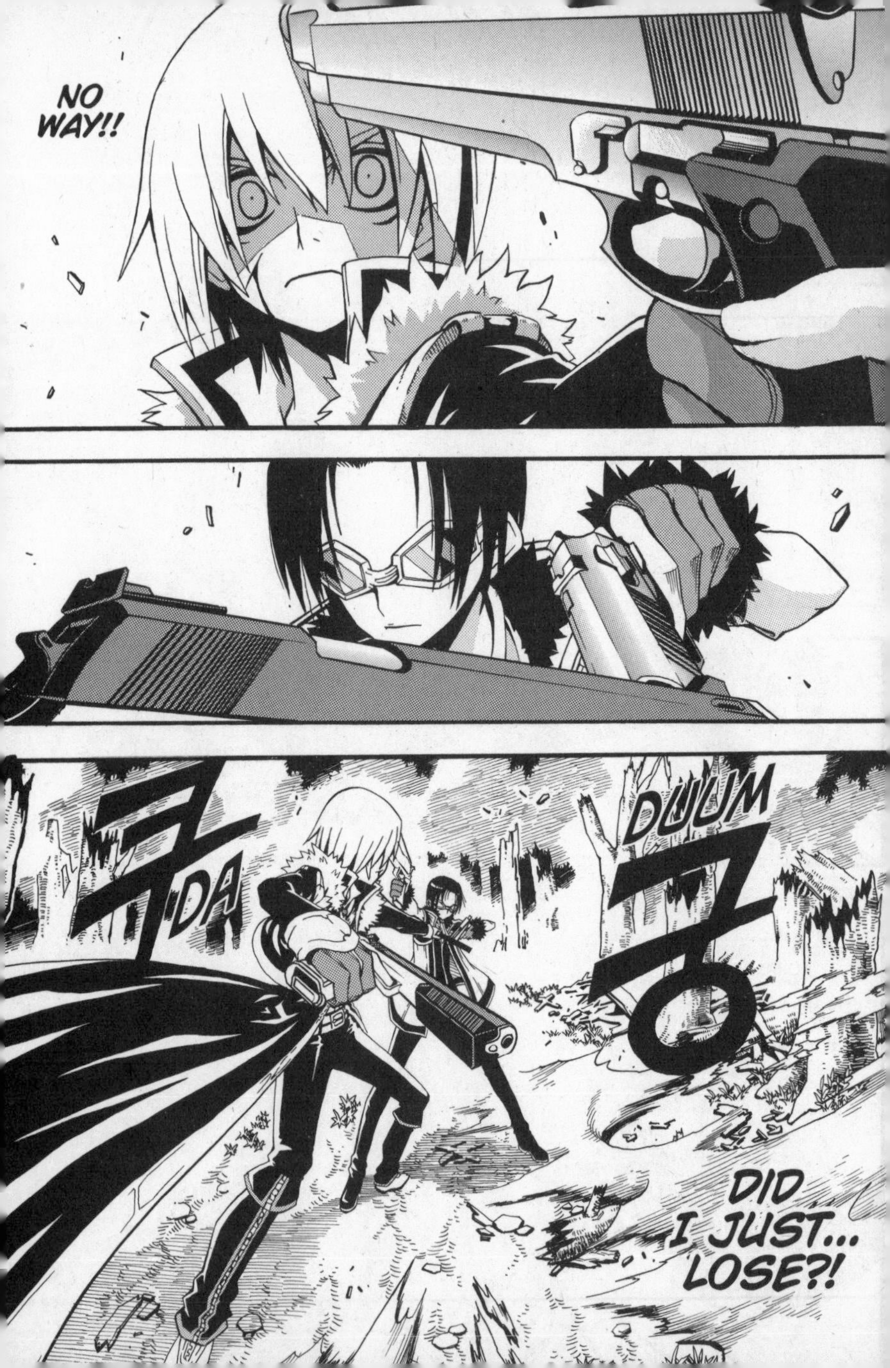
NO WAY!!
DUUM
DA
DID I JUST... LOSE?!

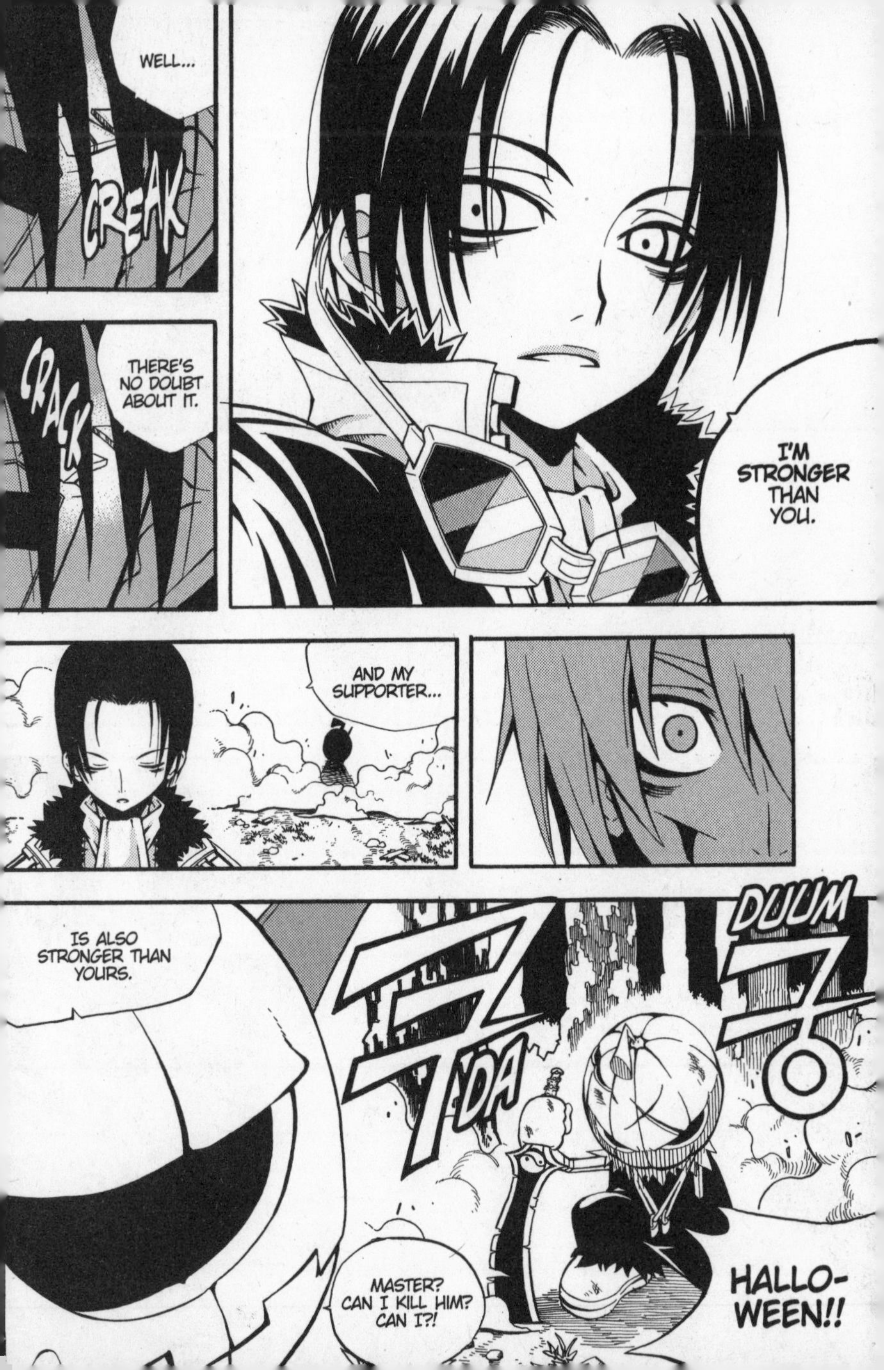
WELL...
CREAK
THERE'S NO DOUBT ABOUT IT.
CRACK
I'M STRONGER THAN YOU.
AND MY SUPPORTER...
IS ALSO STRONGER THAN YOURS.
DA
DUUM
MASTER? CAN I KILL HIM? CAN I?!
HALLO-WEEN!!

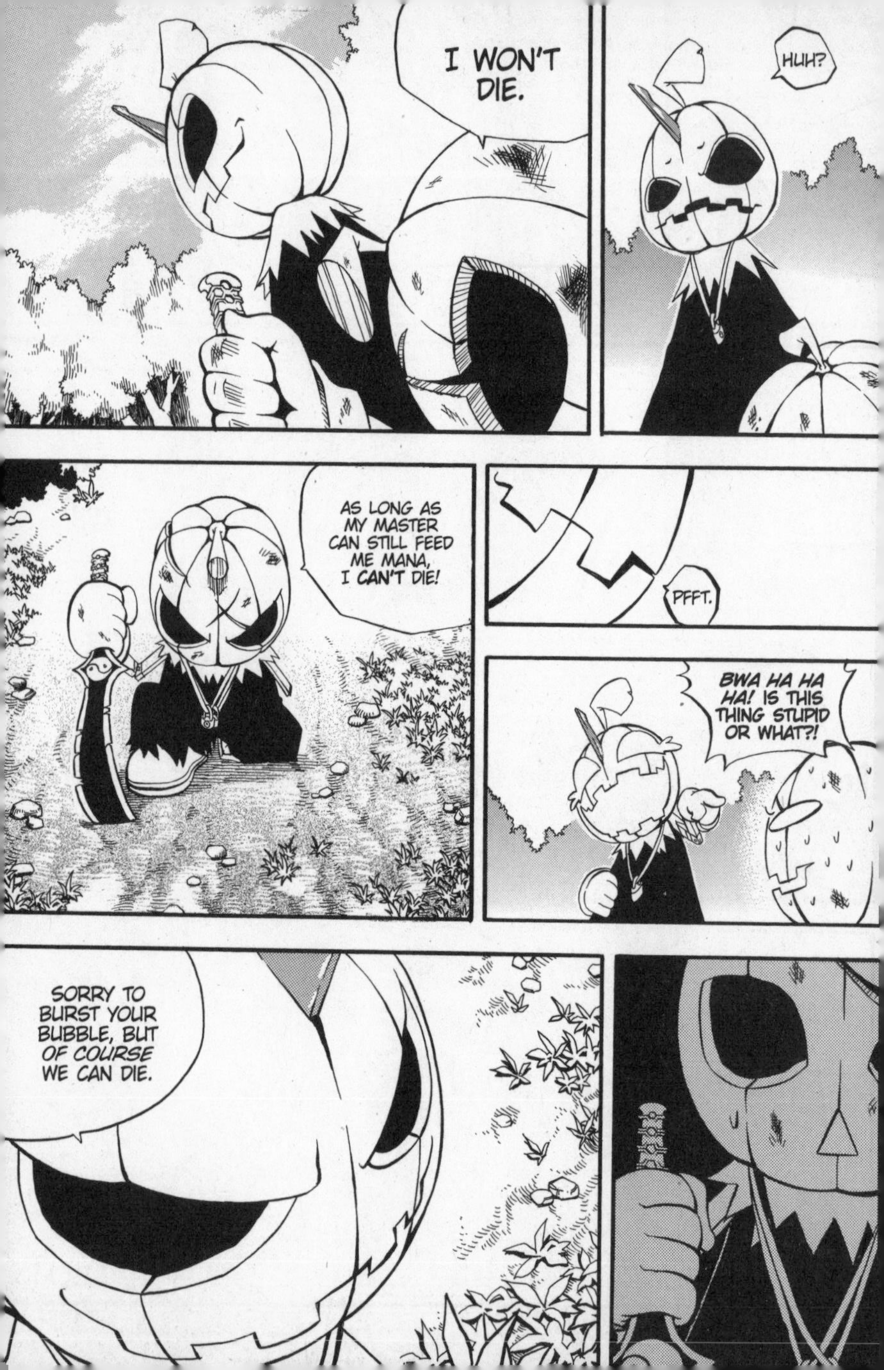

I WON'T DIE.
HUH?
AS LONG AS MY MASTER CAN STILL FEED ME MANA, I CAN'T DIE!
PFFT.
BWA HA HA HA! IS THIS THING STUPID OR WHAT?!
SORRY TO BURST YOUR BUBBLE, BUT OF COURSE WE CAN DIE.

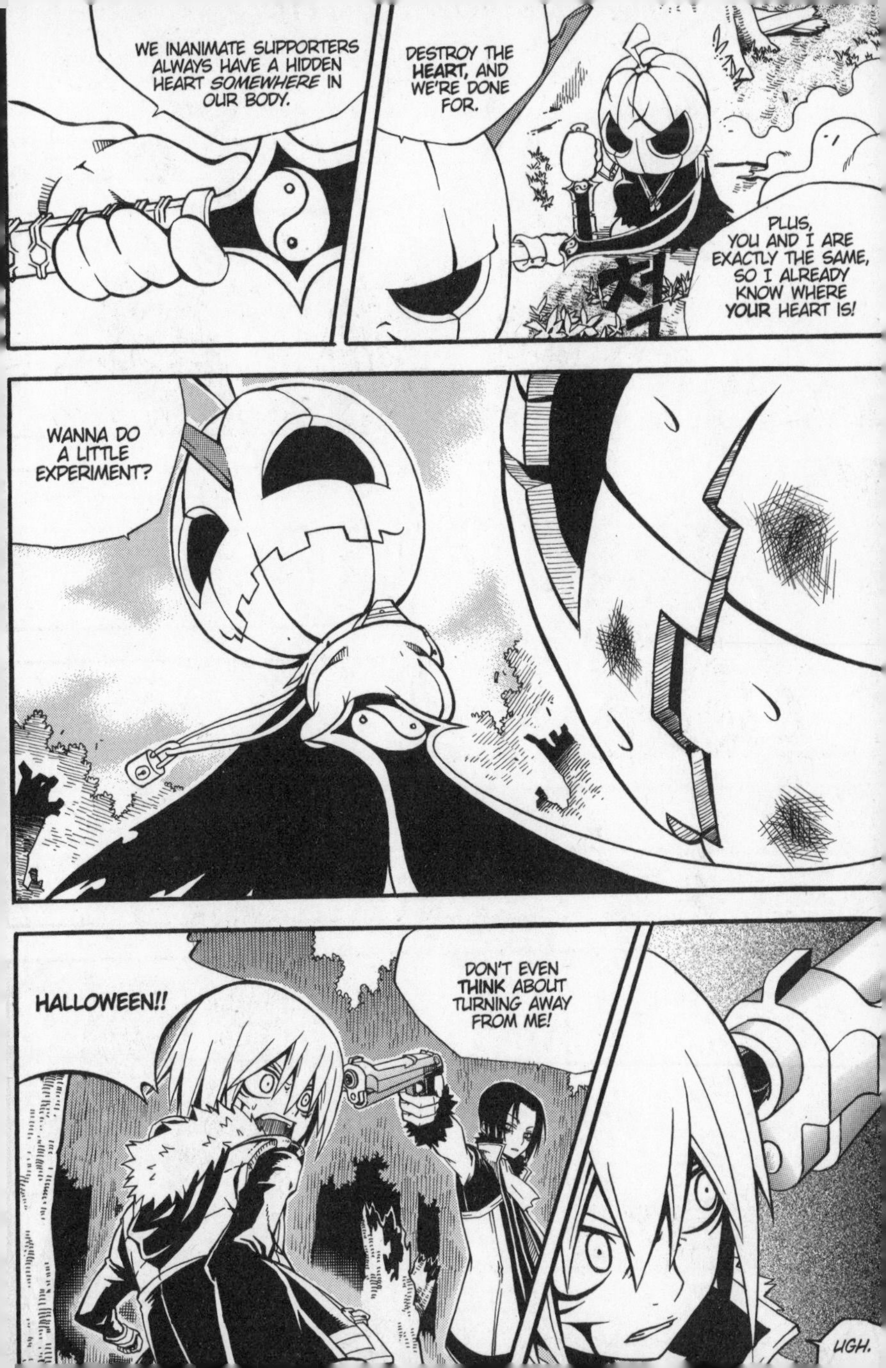
WE INANIMATE SUPPORTERS ALWAYS HAVE A HIDDEN HEART SOMEWHERE IN OUR BODY.
DESTROY THE HEART, AND WE'RE DONE FOR.
PLUS, YOU AND I ARE EXACTLY THE SAME, SO I ALREADY KNOW WHERE YOUR HEART IS!
WANNA DO A LITTLE EXPERIMENT?
HALLOWEEN!!
DON'T EVEN THINK ABOUT TURNING AWAY FROM ME!
UGH.

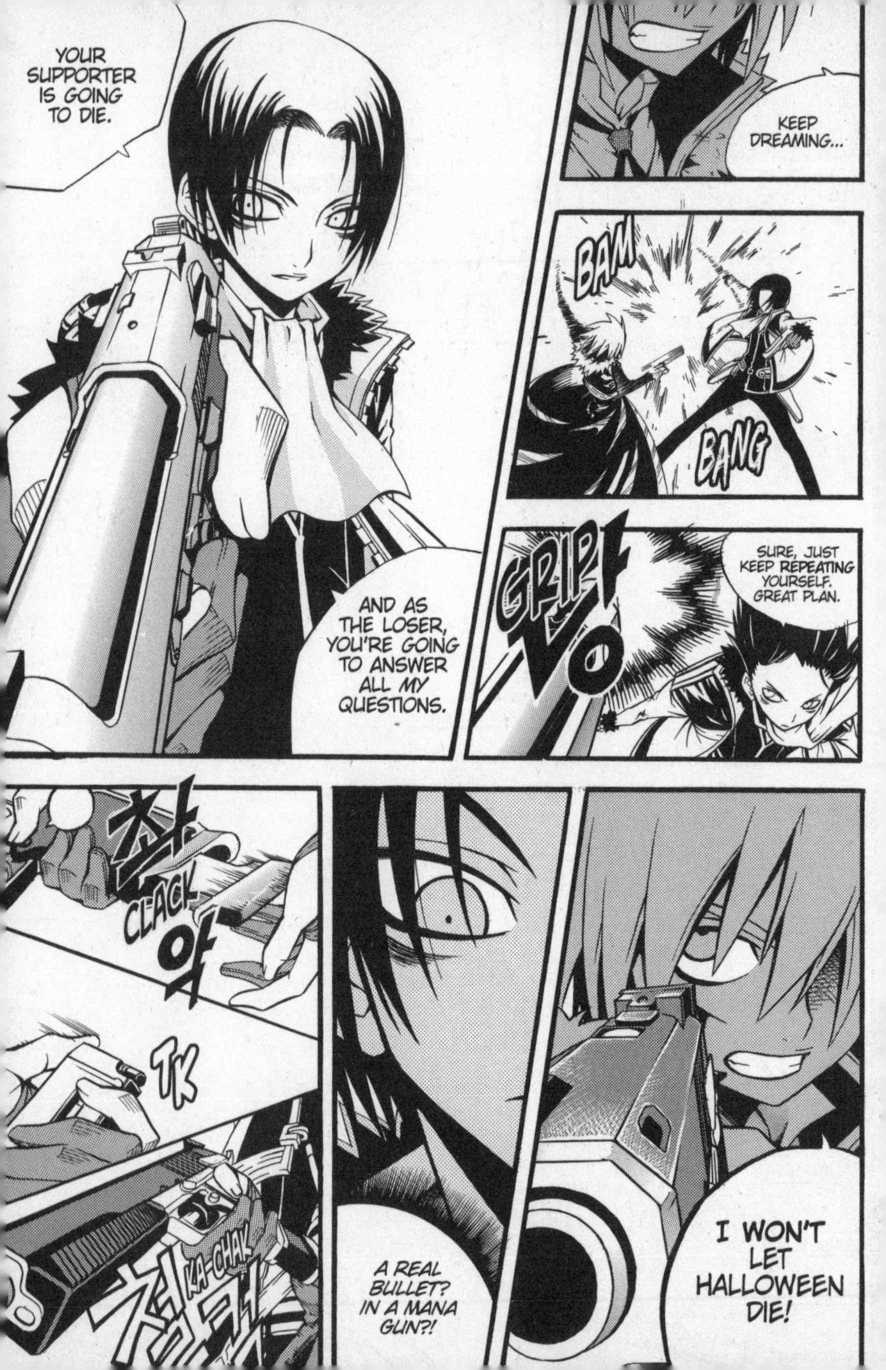
YOUR SUPPORTER IS GOING TO DIE.
AND AS THE LOSER, YOU'RE GOING TO ANSWER ALL MY QUESTIONS.
KEEP DREAMING...
BAM
BANG
GRIP
SURE, JUST KEEP REPEATING YOURSELF. GREAT PLAN.
CLACK
TK
KA-CHAK
A REAL BULLET? IN A MANA GUN?!
I WON'T LET HALLOWEEN DIE!

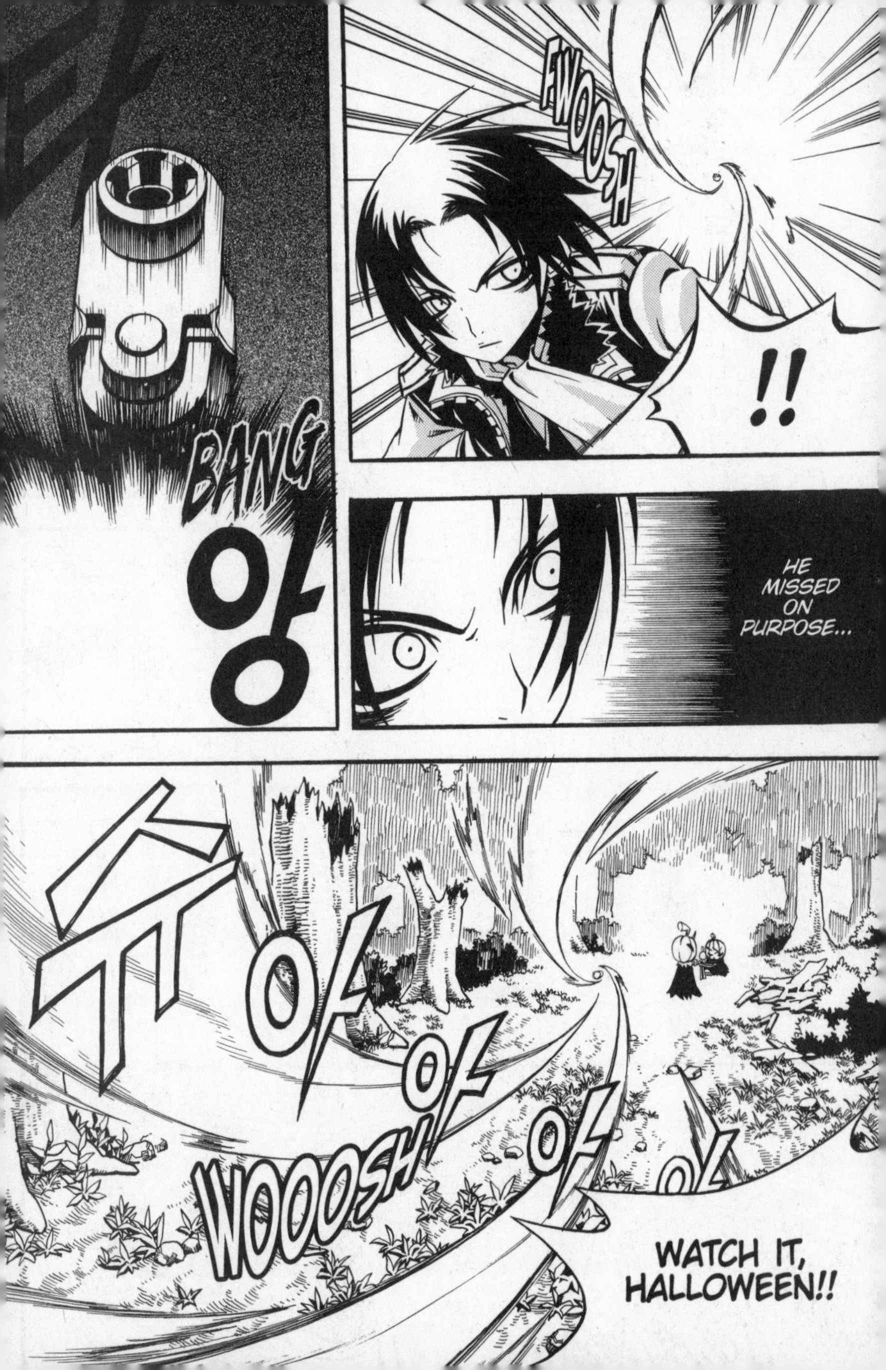
FWOOSH
!!
BANG
HE MISSED ON PURPOSE...
WOOOSH
WATCH IT, HALLOWEEN!!

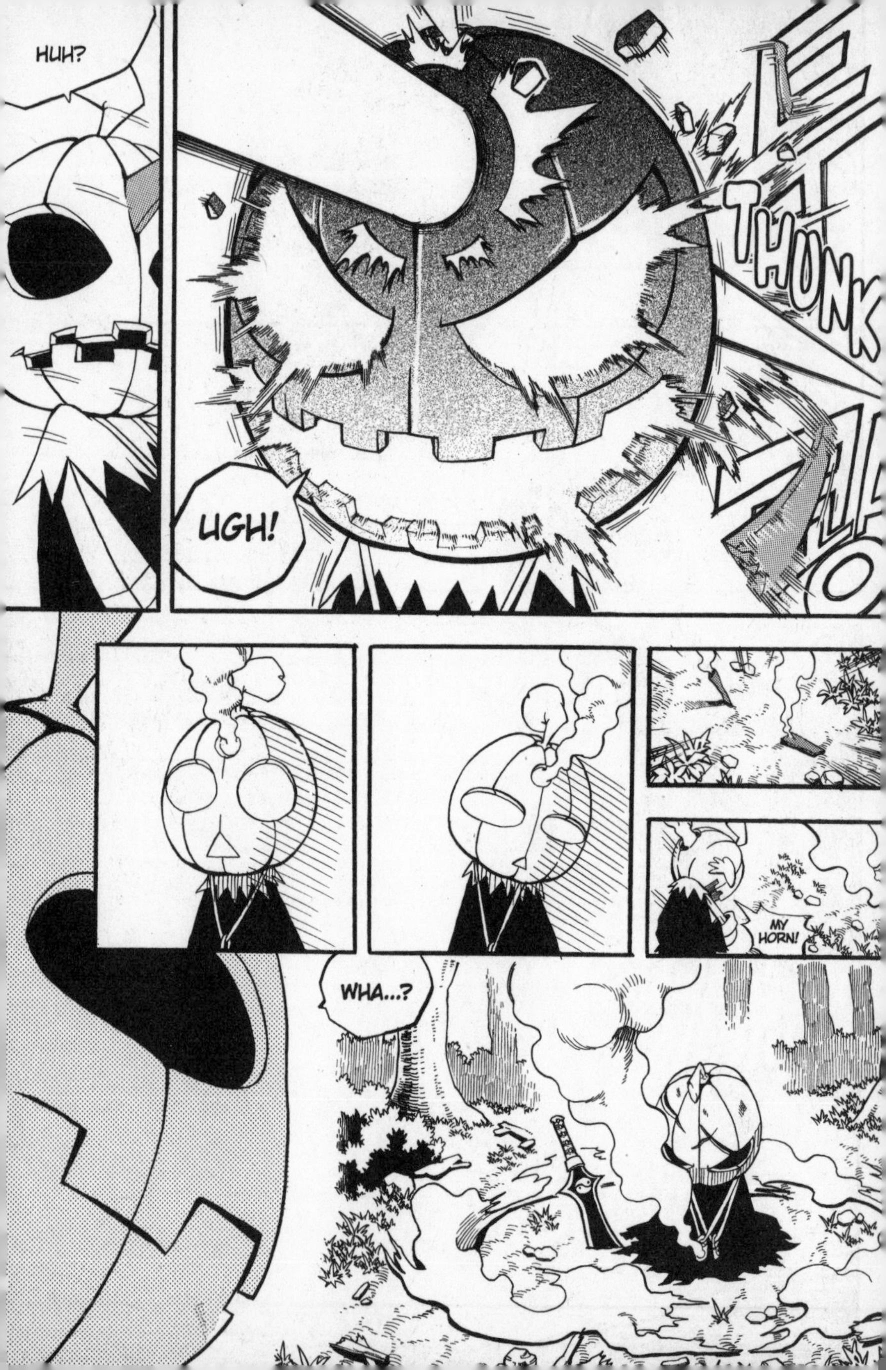

HUH?
THUNK
UGH!
MY HORN!
WHA...?

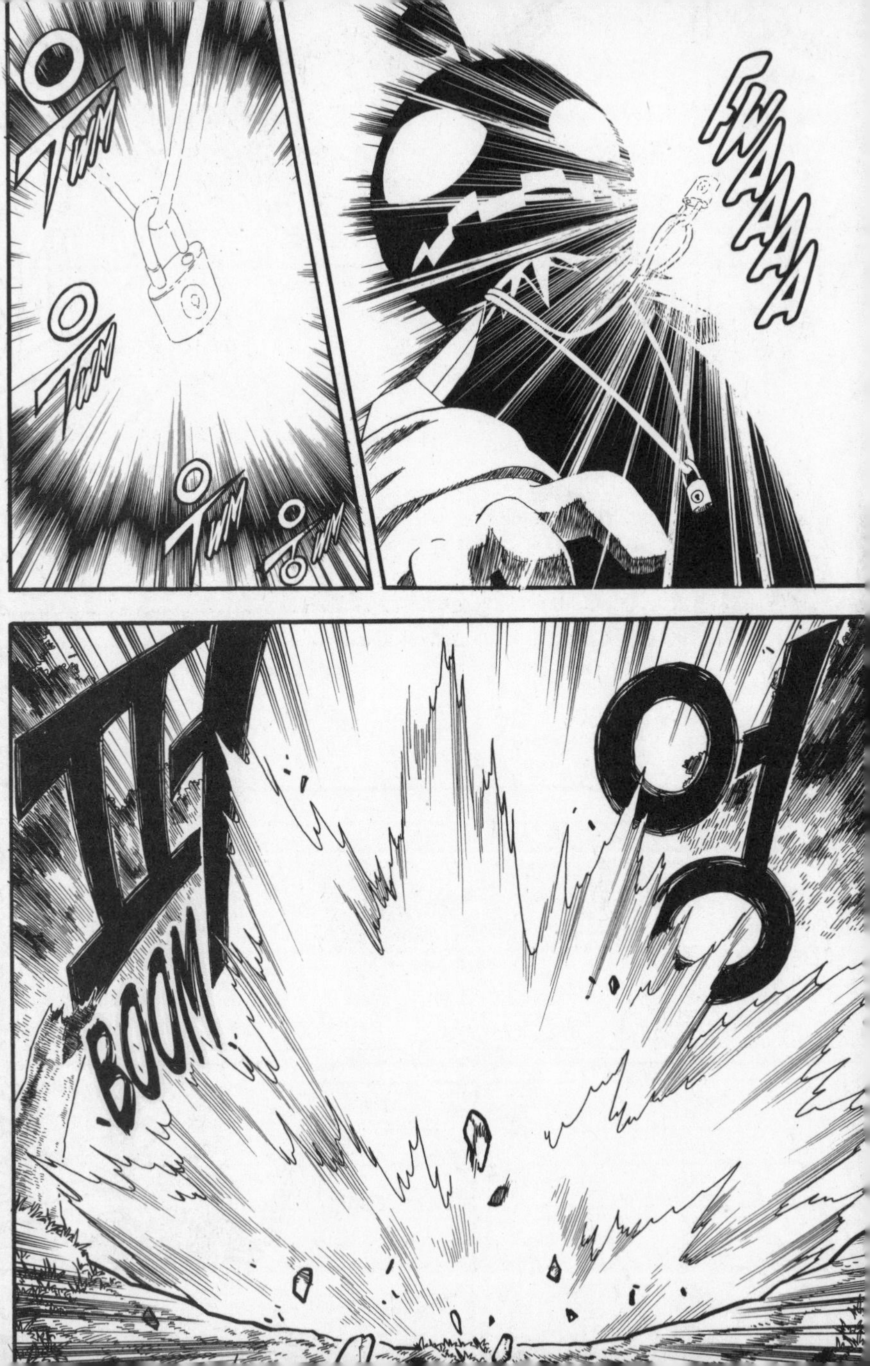
FWAAAA
BOOM

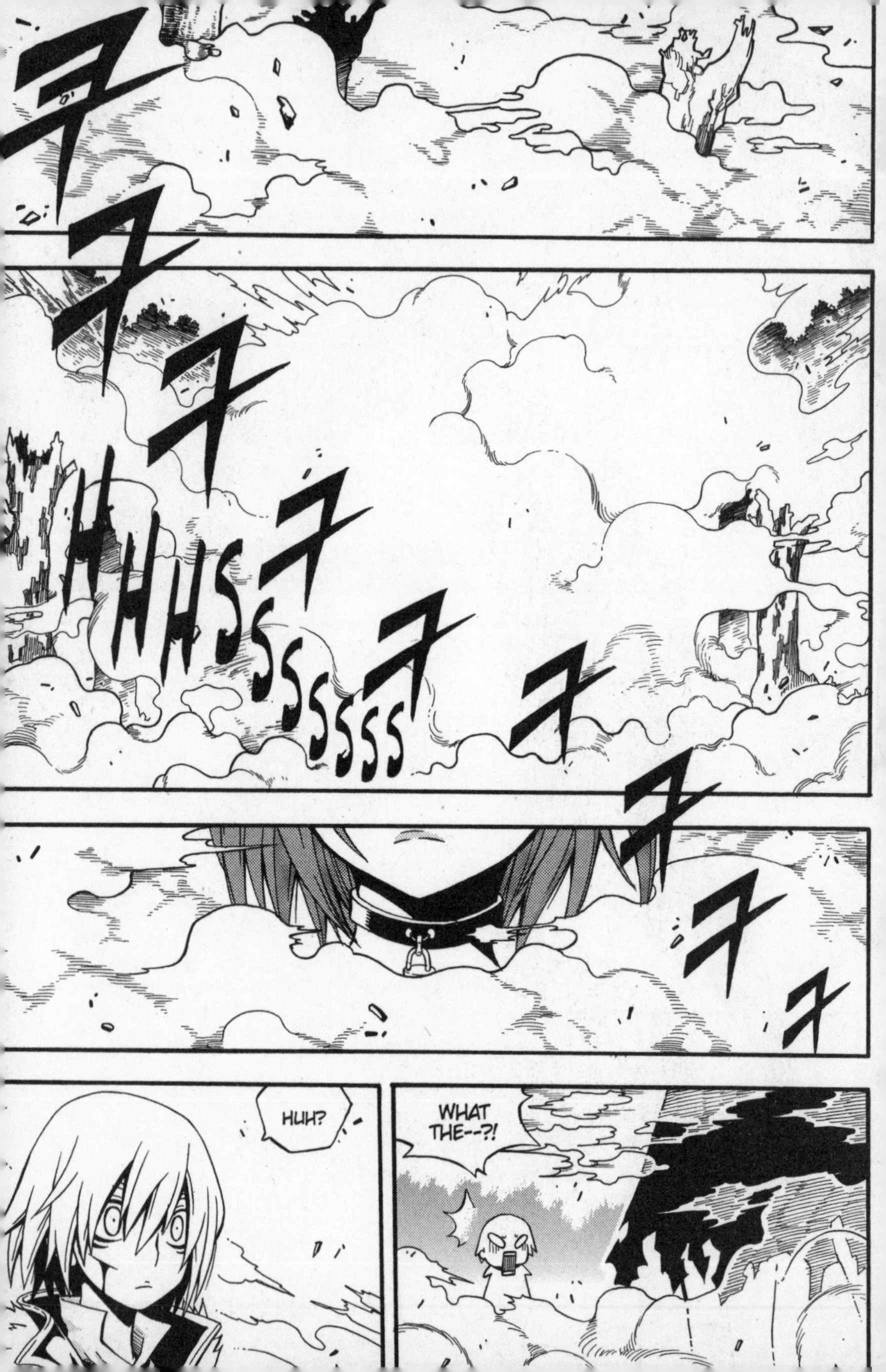
HHHSSSSSSS
HUH?
WHAT THE--?!

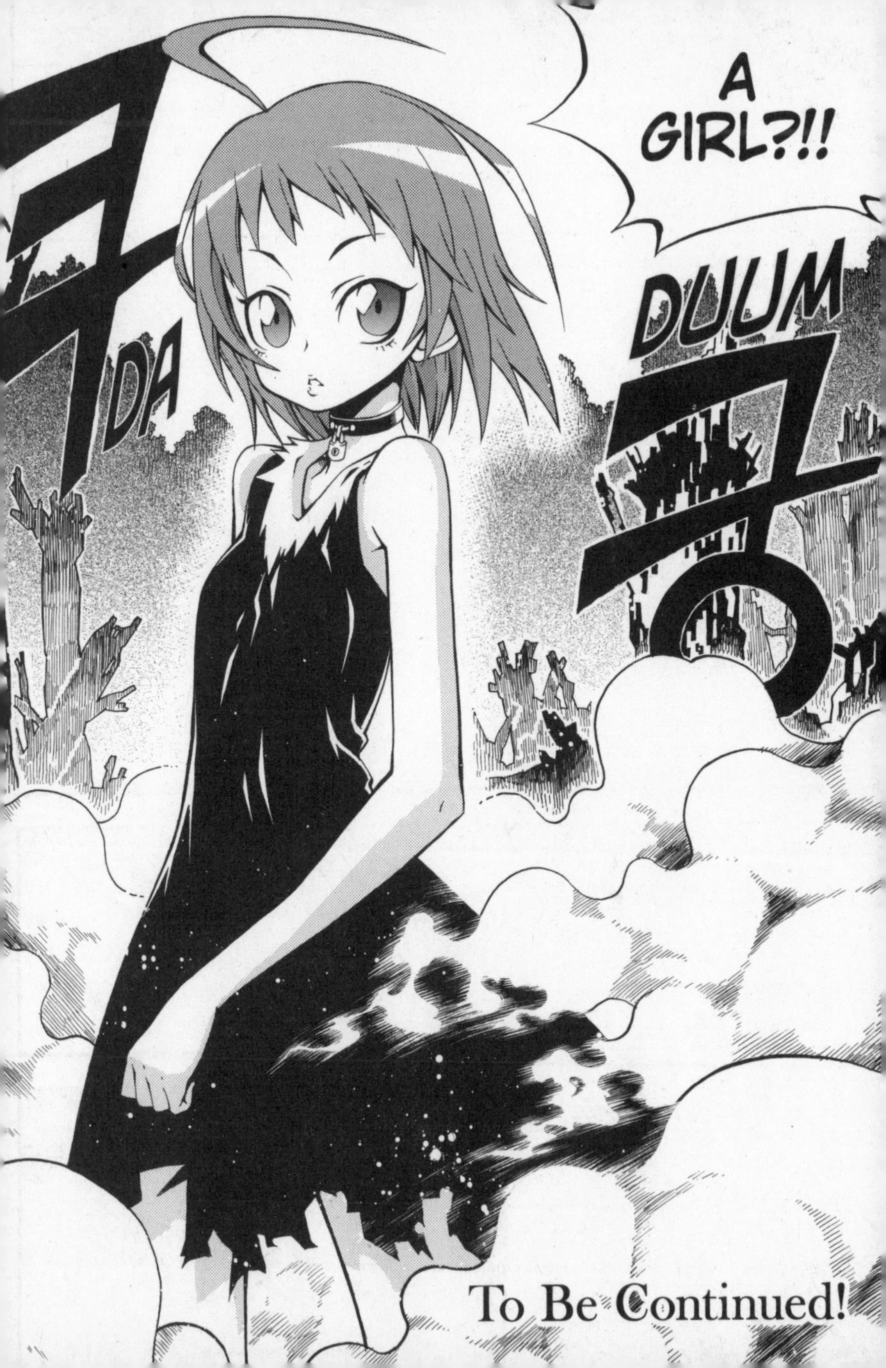
A GIRL?!!
DA
DUUM
To Be Continued!

WITCH BUSTER

BOOK

Brother

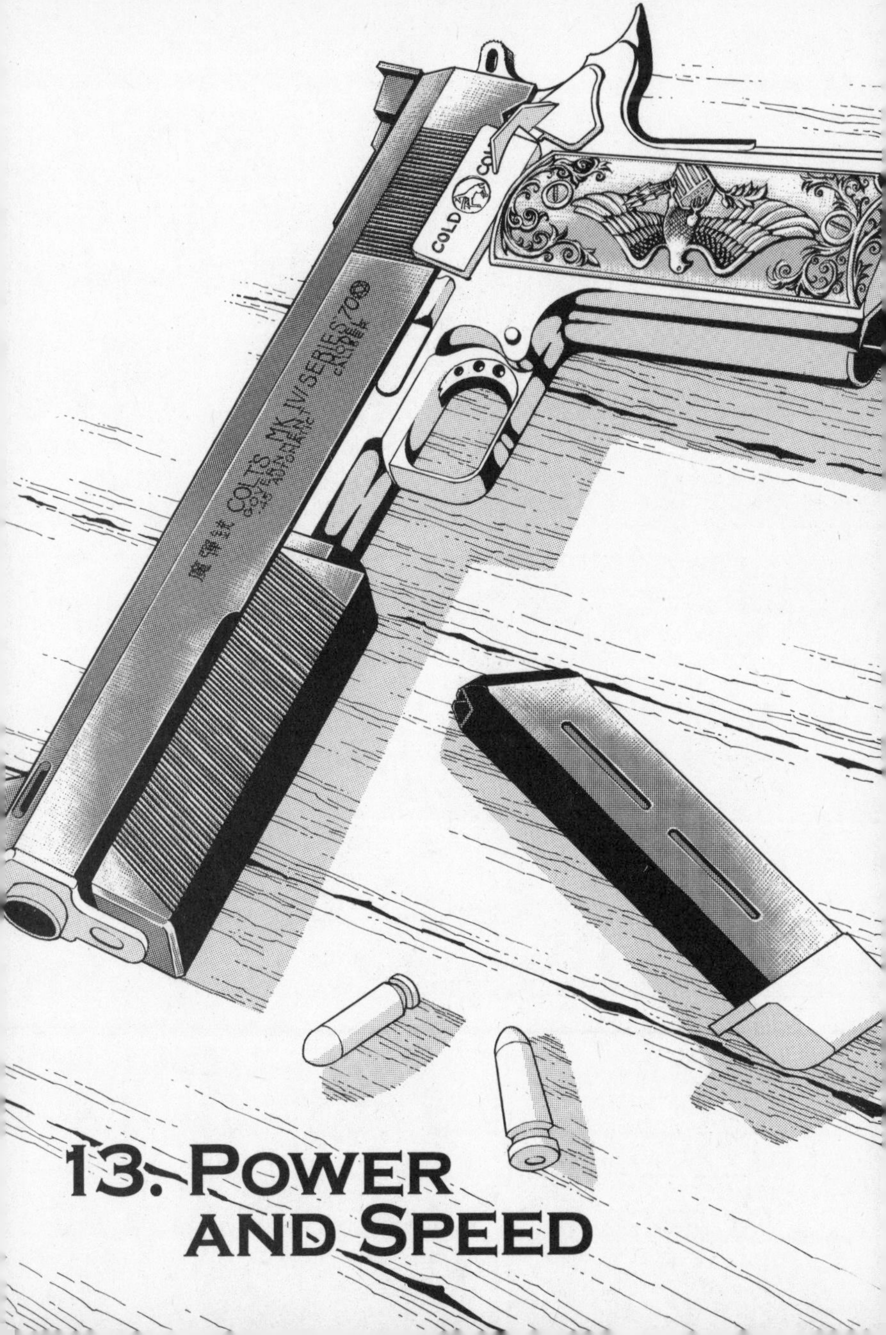
COLD
COLTS MK IV/SERIES'70

13. Power and Speed

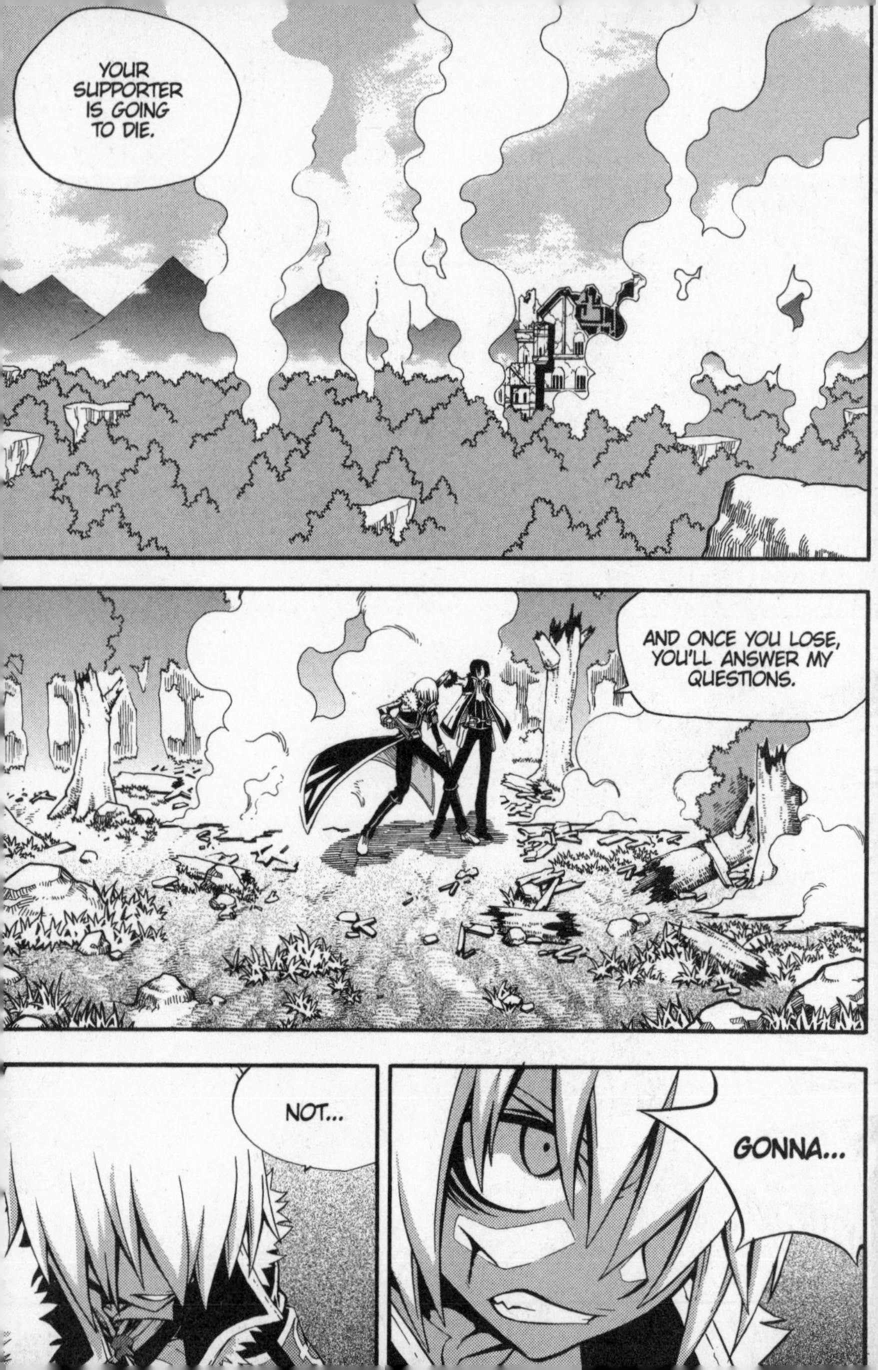
YOUR SUPPORTER IS GOING TO DIE.
AND ONCE YOU LOSE, YOU'LL ANSWER MY QUESTIONS.
NOT...
GONNA...

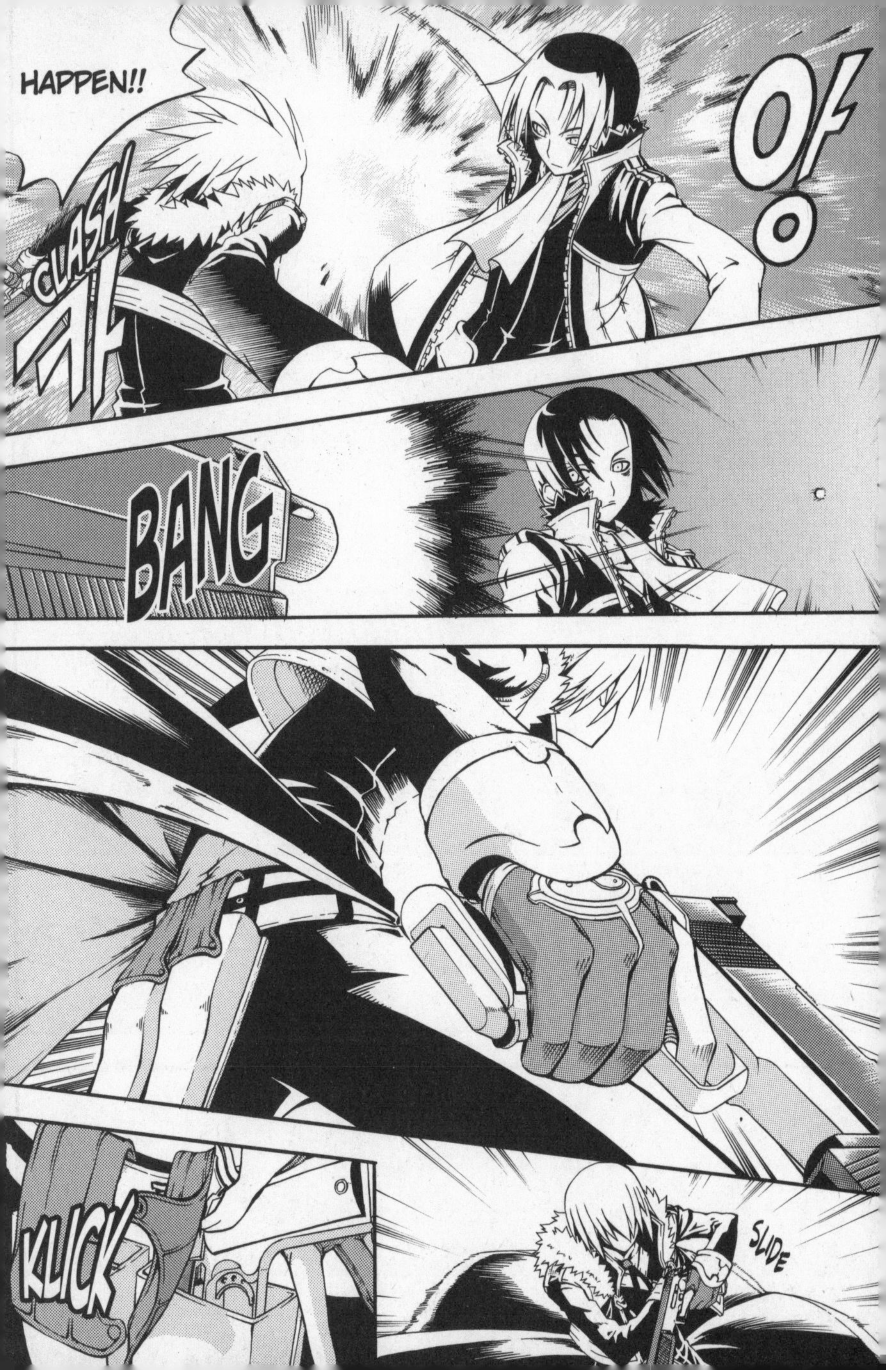
HAPPEN!!
CLASH
BANG
KLICK
SLIDE

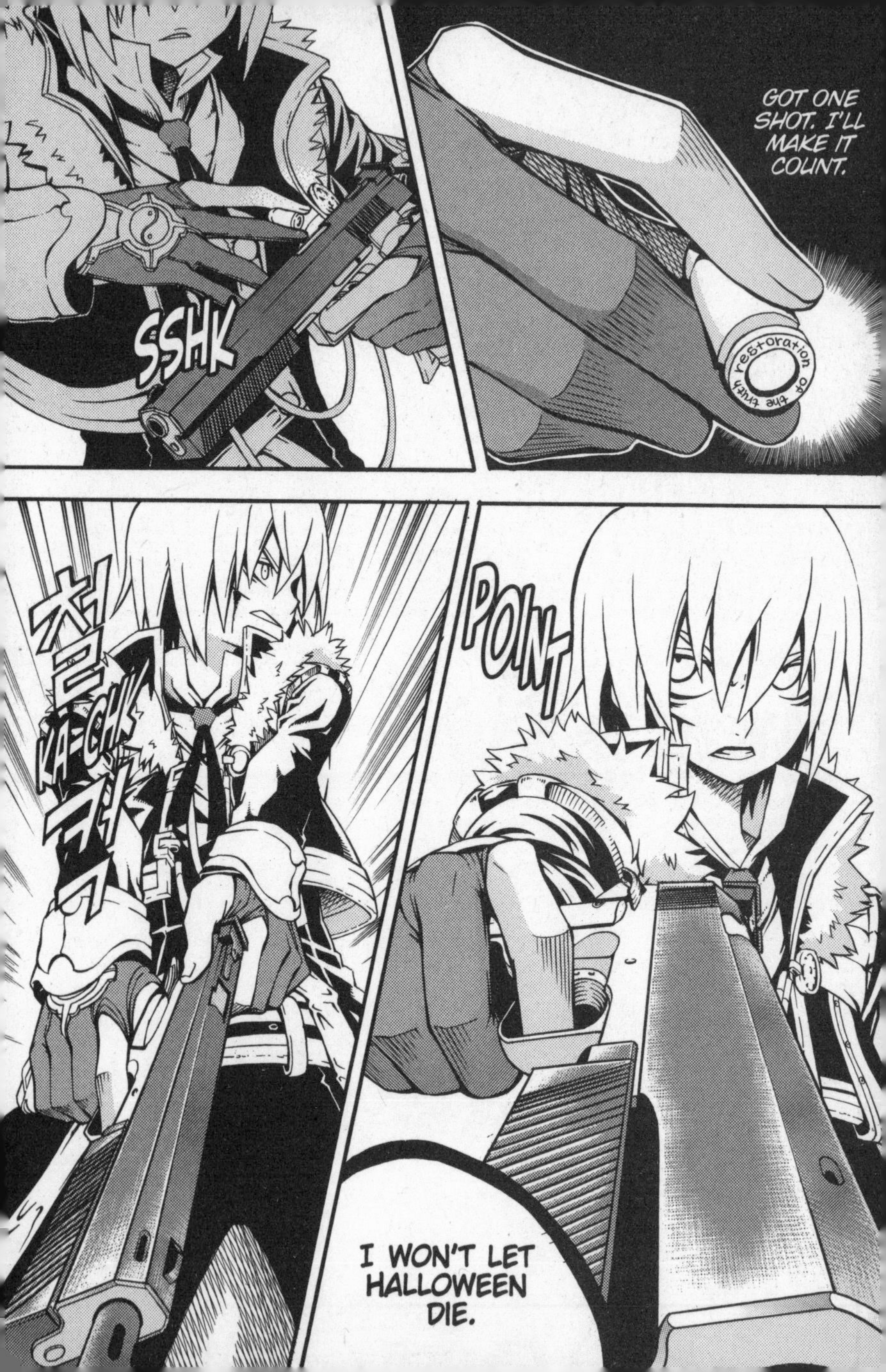
GOT ONE SHOT. I'LL MAKE IT COUNT.
restoration of the truth
SSHK
POINT
I WON'T LET HALLOWEEN DIE.
KA-CHK

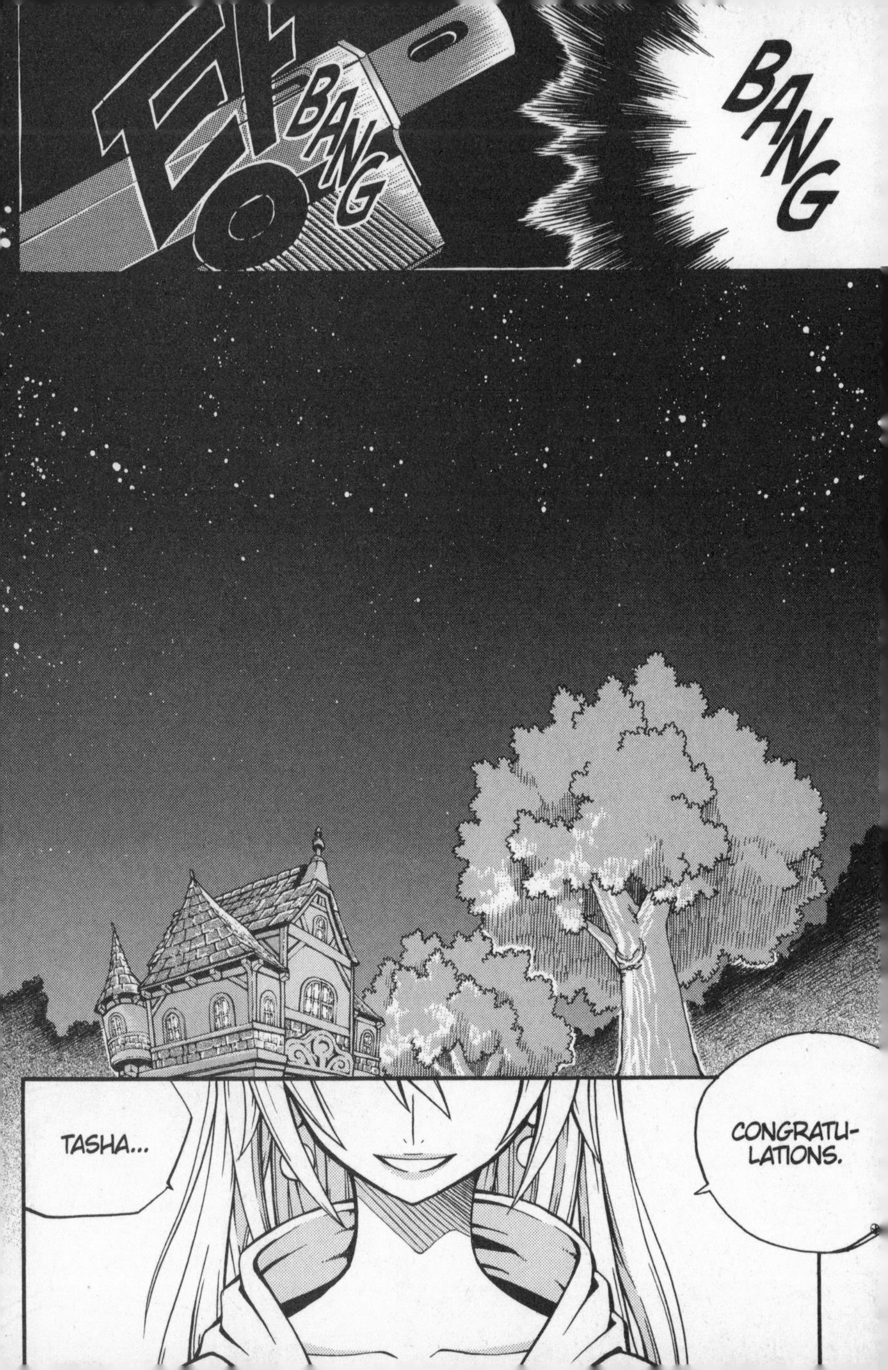
BANG
BANG
TASHA...
CONGRATU-LATIONS.

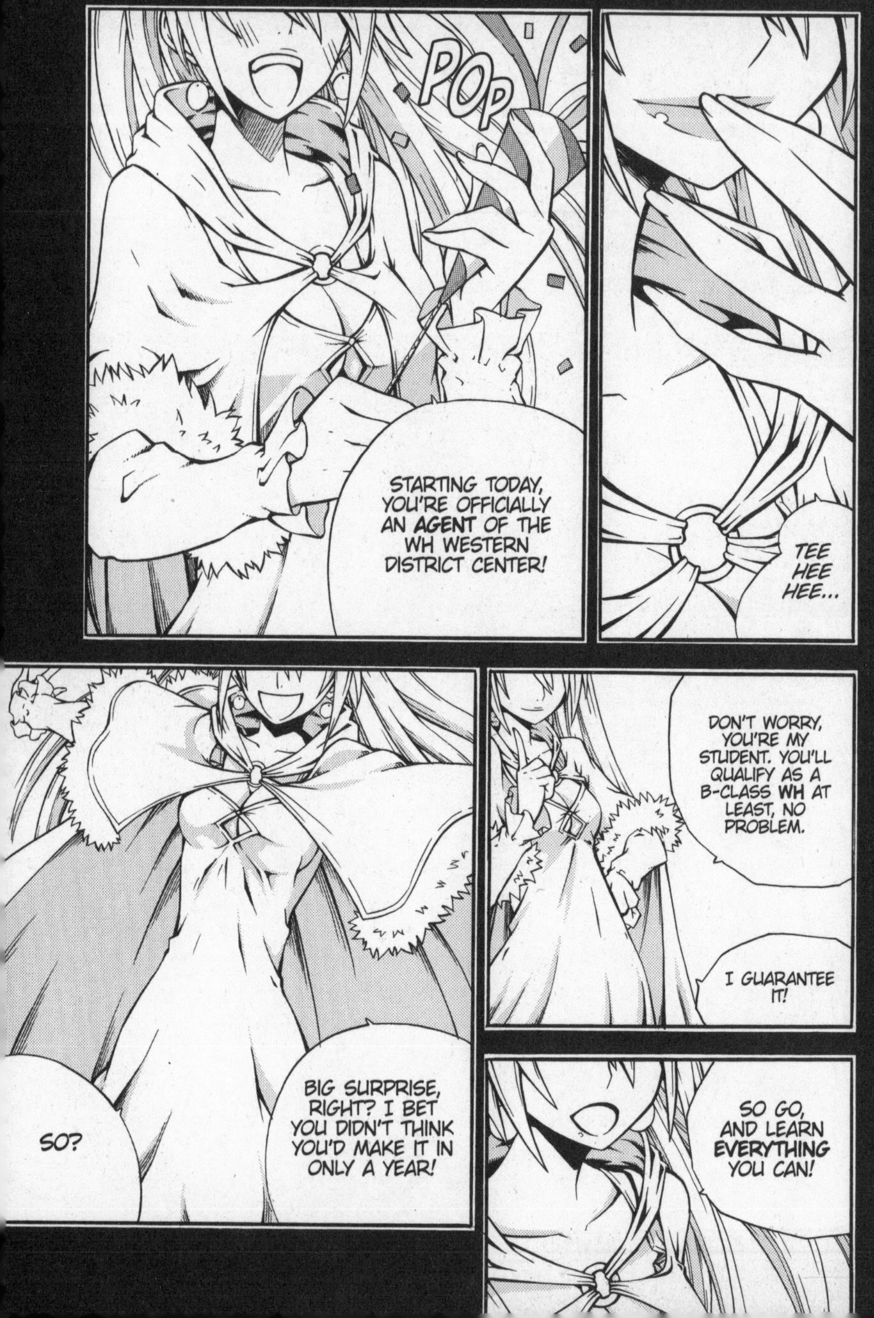
POP
STARTING TODAY, YOU'RE OFFICIALLY AN AGENT OF THE WH WESTERN DISTRICT CENTER!
TEE HEE HEE...
BIG SURPRISE, RIGHT? I BET YOU DIDN'T THINK YOU'D MAKE IT IN ONLY A YEAR!
SO?
DON'T WORRY, YOU'RE MY STUDENT. YOU'LL QUALIFY AS A B-CLASS WH AT LEAST, NO PROBLEM.
I GUARANTEE IT!
SO GO, AND LEARN EVERYTHING YOU CAN!

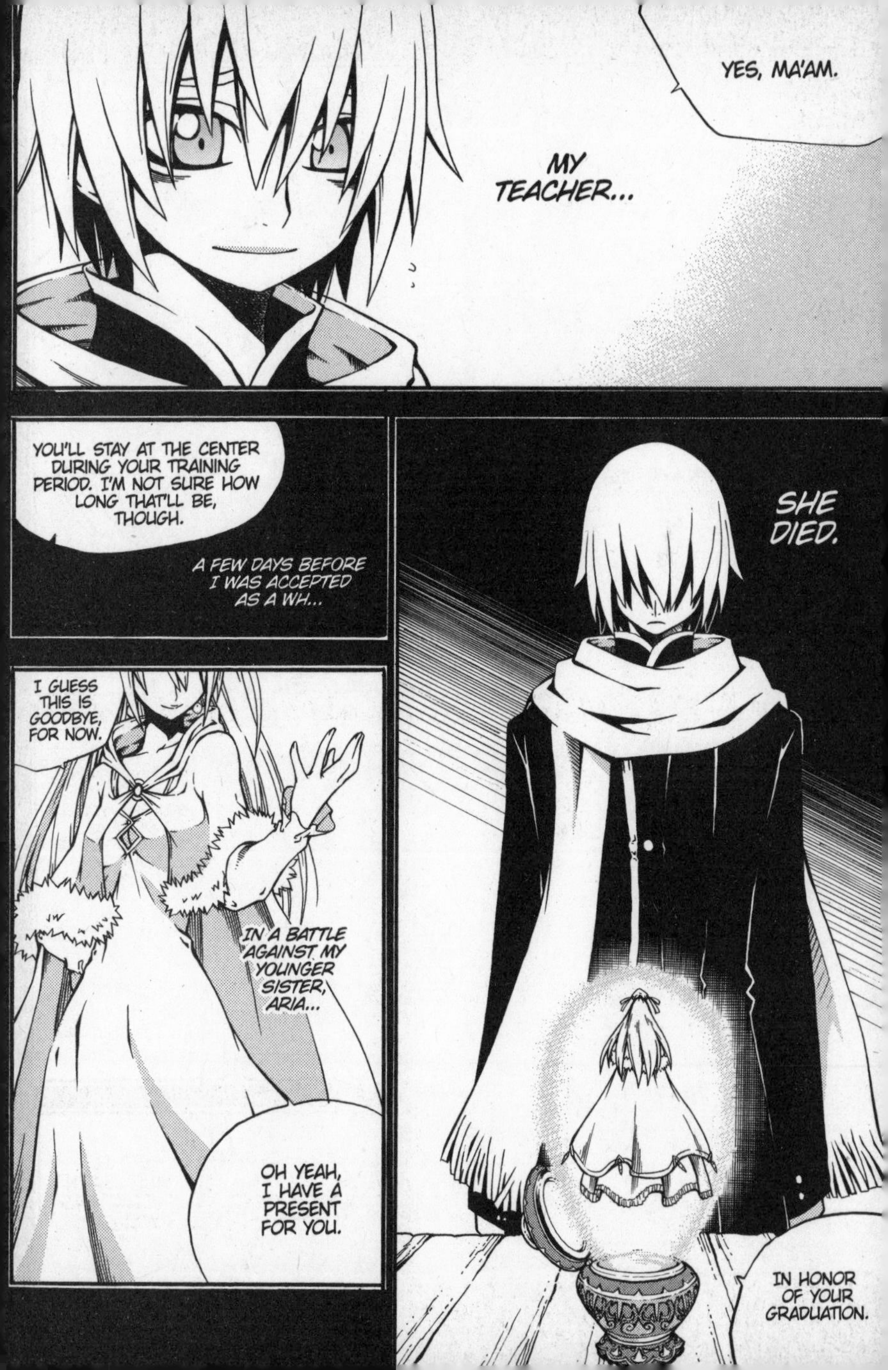
YES, MA'AM.
MY TEACHER...
YOU'LL STAY AT THE CENTER DURING YOUR TRAINING PERIOD. I'M NOT SURE HOW LONG THAT'LL BE, THOUGH.
A FEW DAYS BEFORE I WAS ACCEPTED AS A WH...
SHE DIED.
I GUESS THIS IS GOODBYE, FOR NOW.
IN A BATTLE AGAINST MY YOUNGER SISTER, ARIA...
OH YEAH, I HAVE A PRESENT FOR YOU.
IN HONOR OF YOUR GRADUATION.

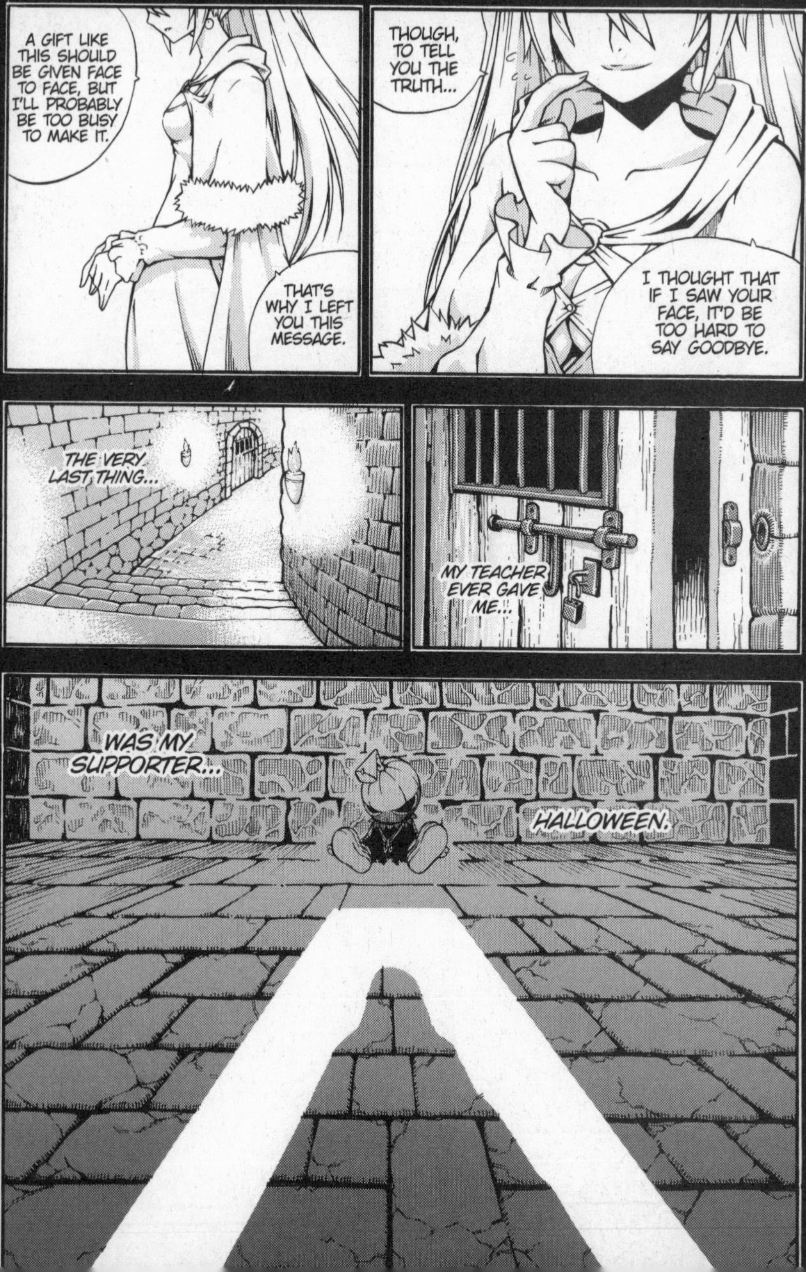
A GIFT LIKE THIS SHOULD BE GIVEN FACE TO FACE, BUT I'LL PROBABLY BE TOO BUSY TO MAKE IT.
THAT'S WHY I LEFT YOU THIS MESSAGE.
THOUGH, TO TELL YOU THE TRUTH...
I THOUGHT THAT IF I SAW YOUR FACE, IT'D BE TOO HARD TO SAY GOODBYE.
THE VERY LAST THING...
MY TEACHER EVER GAVE ME...
WAS MY SUPPORTER...
HALLOWEEN.

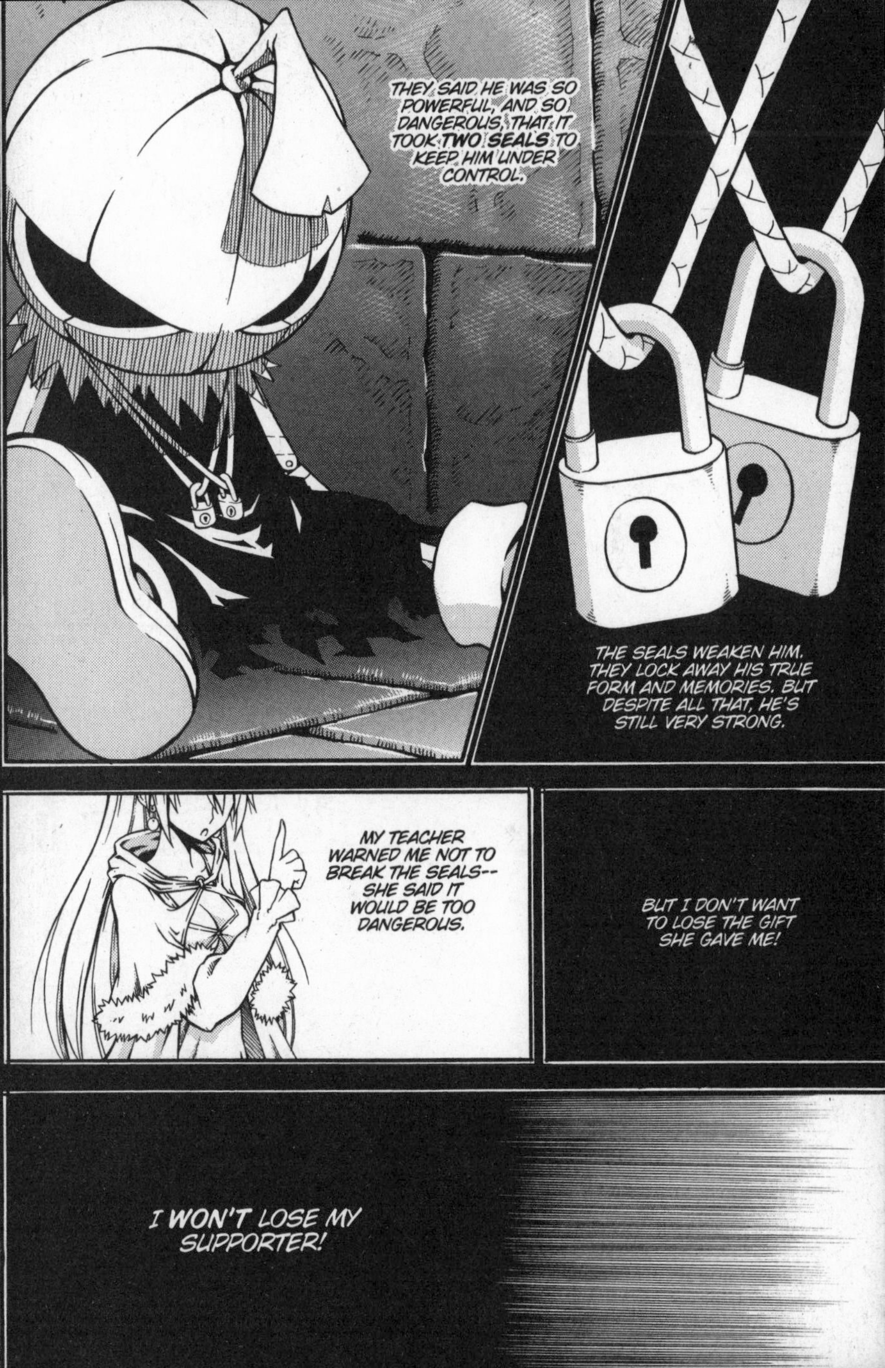
THEY SAID HE WAS SO POWERFUL, AND SO DANGEROUS, THAT IT TOOK TWO SEALS TO KEEP HIM UNDER CONTROL.
THE SEALS WEAKEN HIM. THEY LOCK AWAY HIS TRUE FORM AND MEMORIES. BUT DESPITE ALL THAT, HE'S STILL VERY STRONG.
MY TEACHER WARNED ME NOT TO BREAK THE SEALS-- SHE SAID IT WOULD BE TOO DANGEROUS.
BUT I DON'T WANT TO LOSE THE GIFT SHE GAVE ME!
I WON'T LOSE MY SUPPORTER!

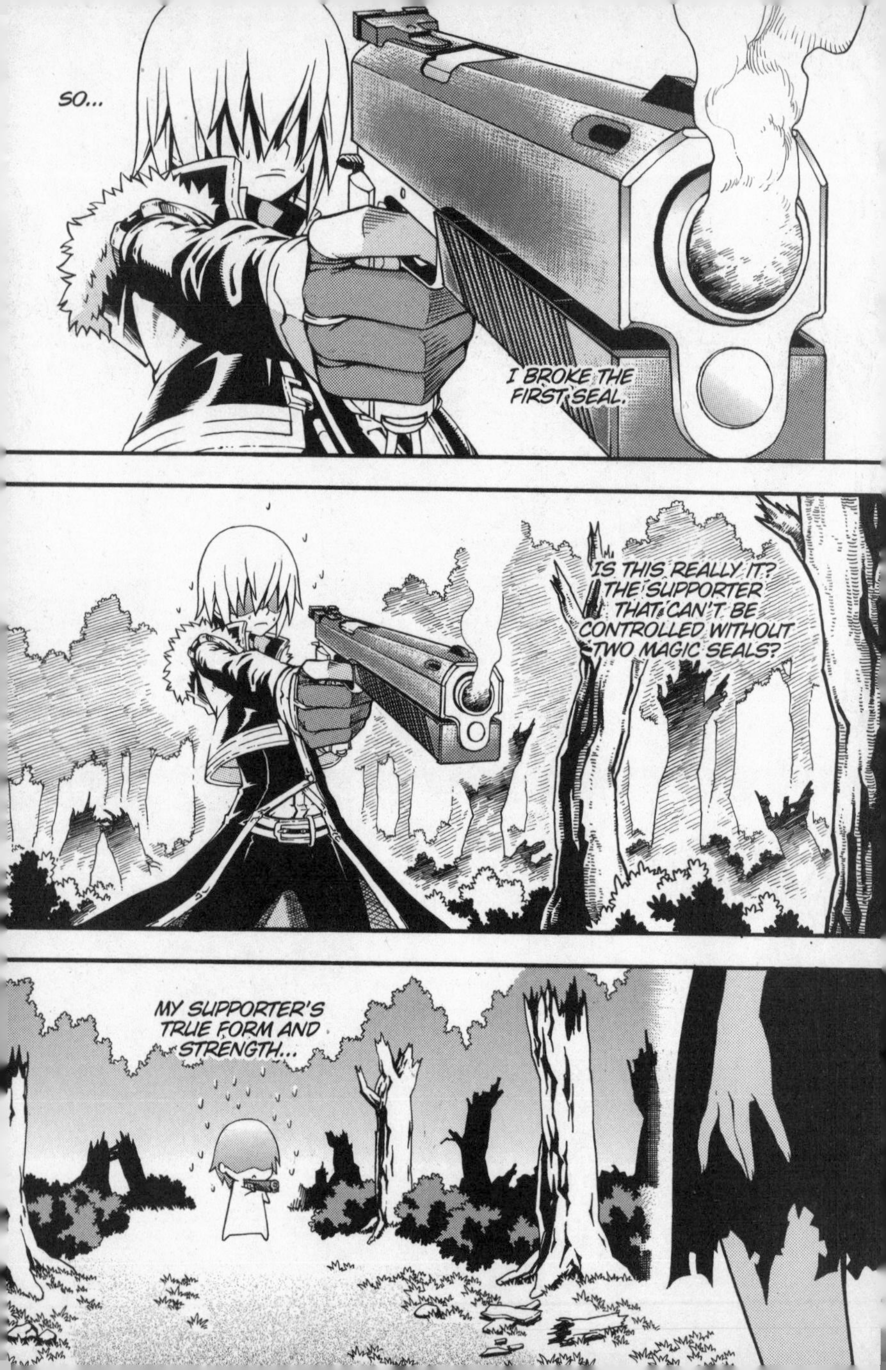
SO...
I BROKE THE FIRST SEAL.
IS THIS REALLY IT? THE SUPPORTER THAT CAN'T BE CONTROLLED WITHOUT TWO MAGIC SEALS?
MY SUPPORTER'S TRUE FORM AND STRENGTH...

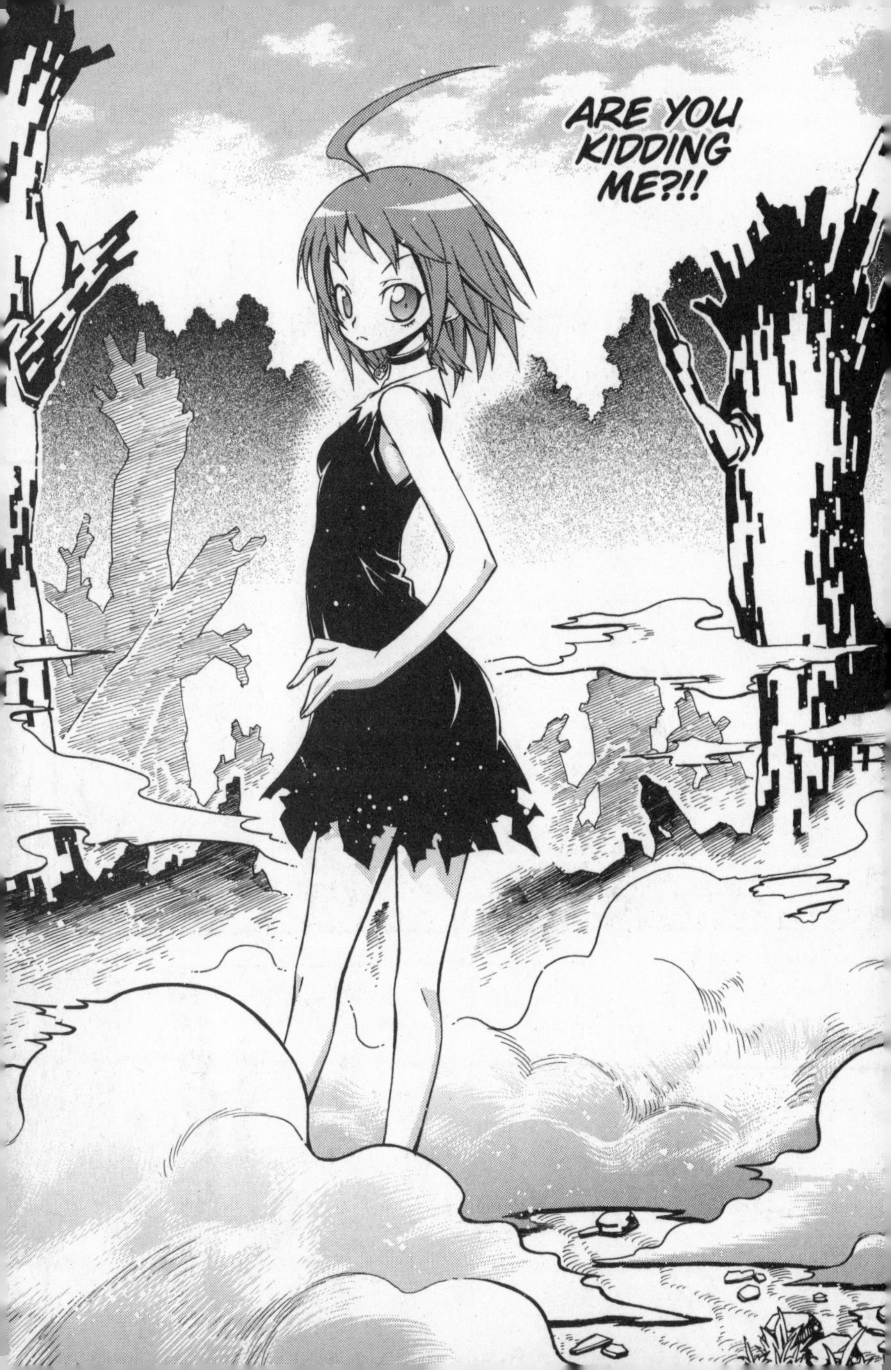
ARE YOU KIDDING ME?!!

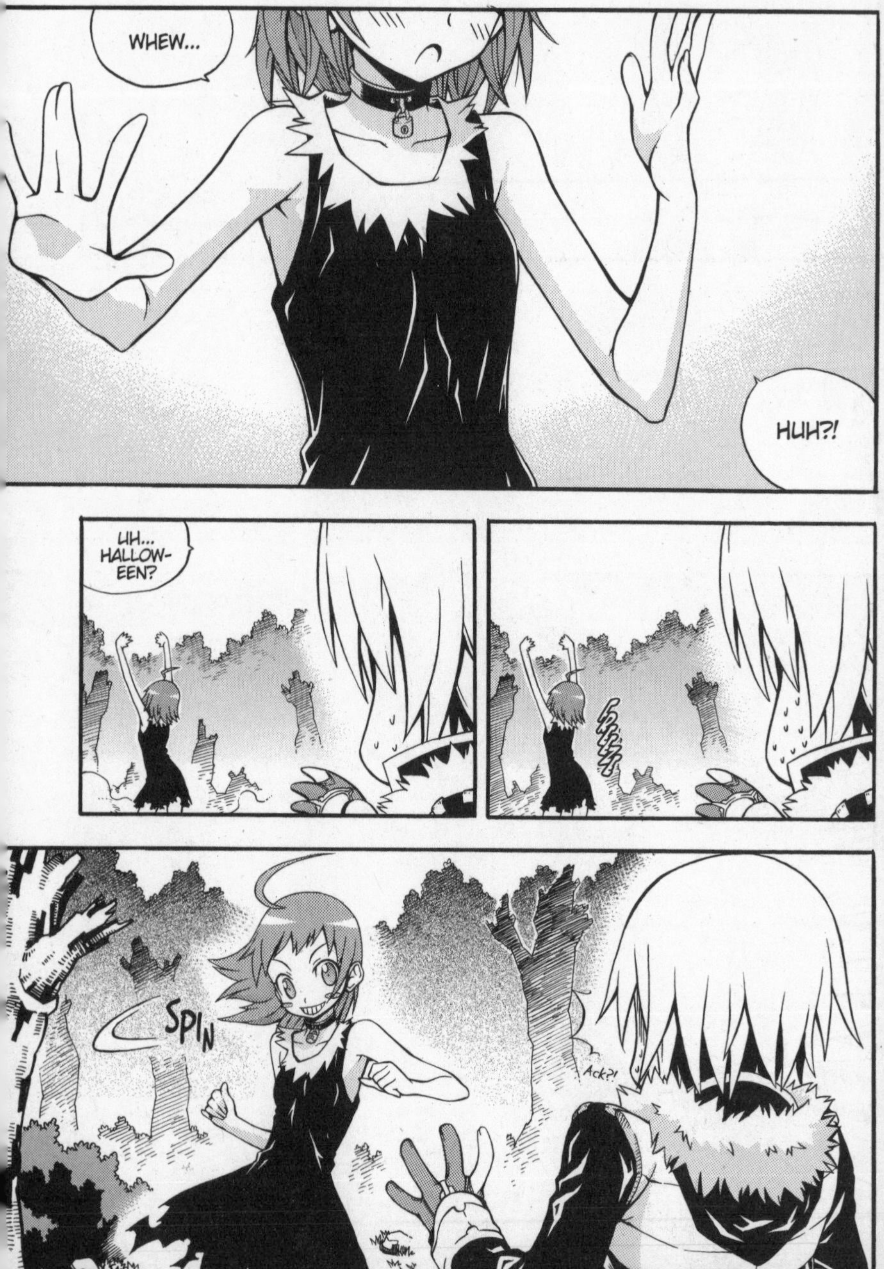
WHEW...
HUH?!
UH... HALLOW-EEN?
SPIN
Ack?!

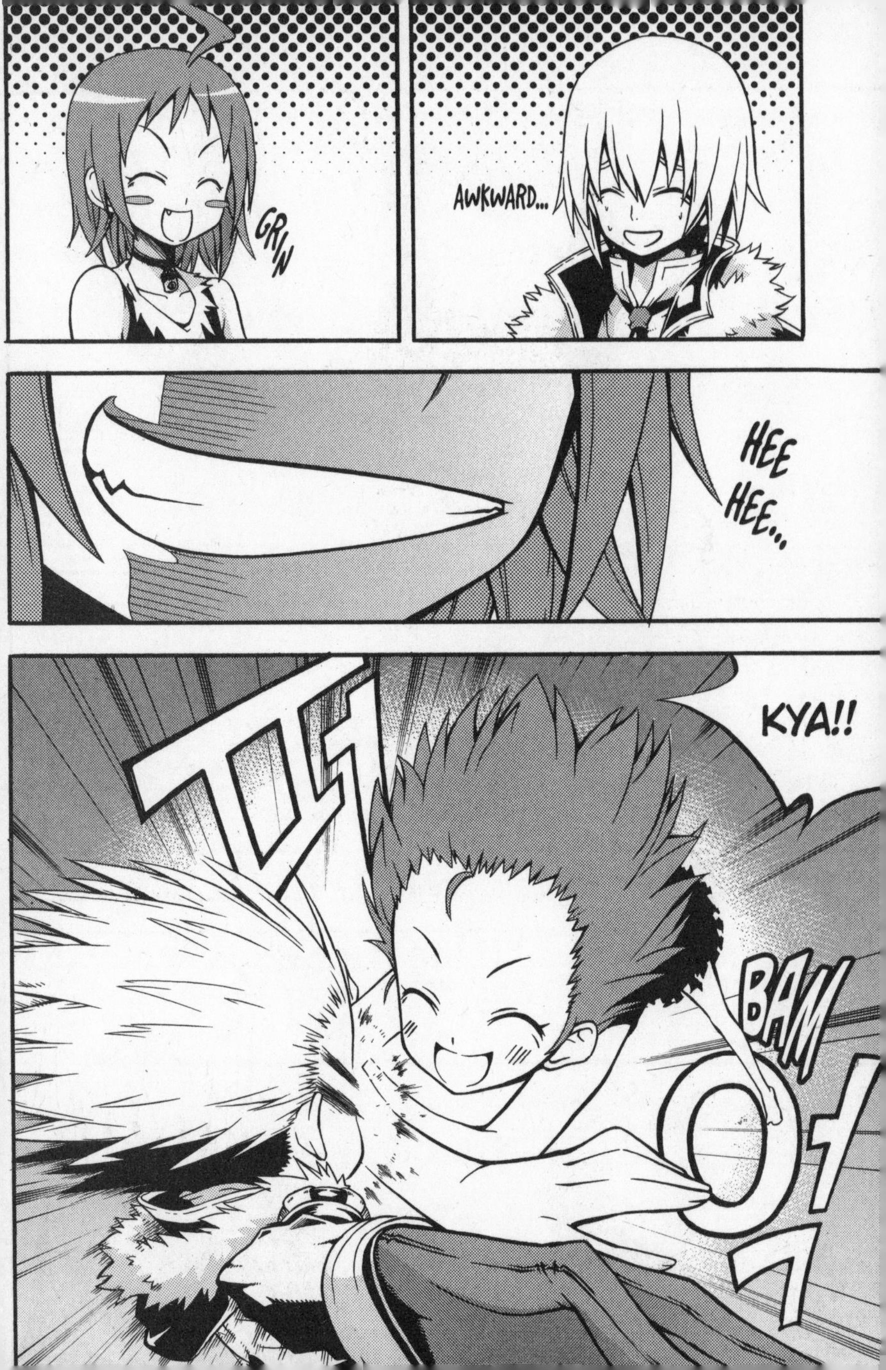
AWKWARD...
GRIN
HEE HEE...
KYA!!
BAM

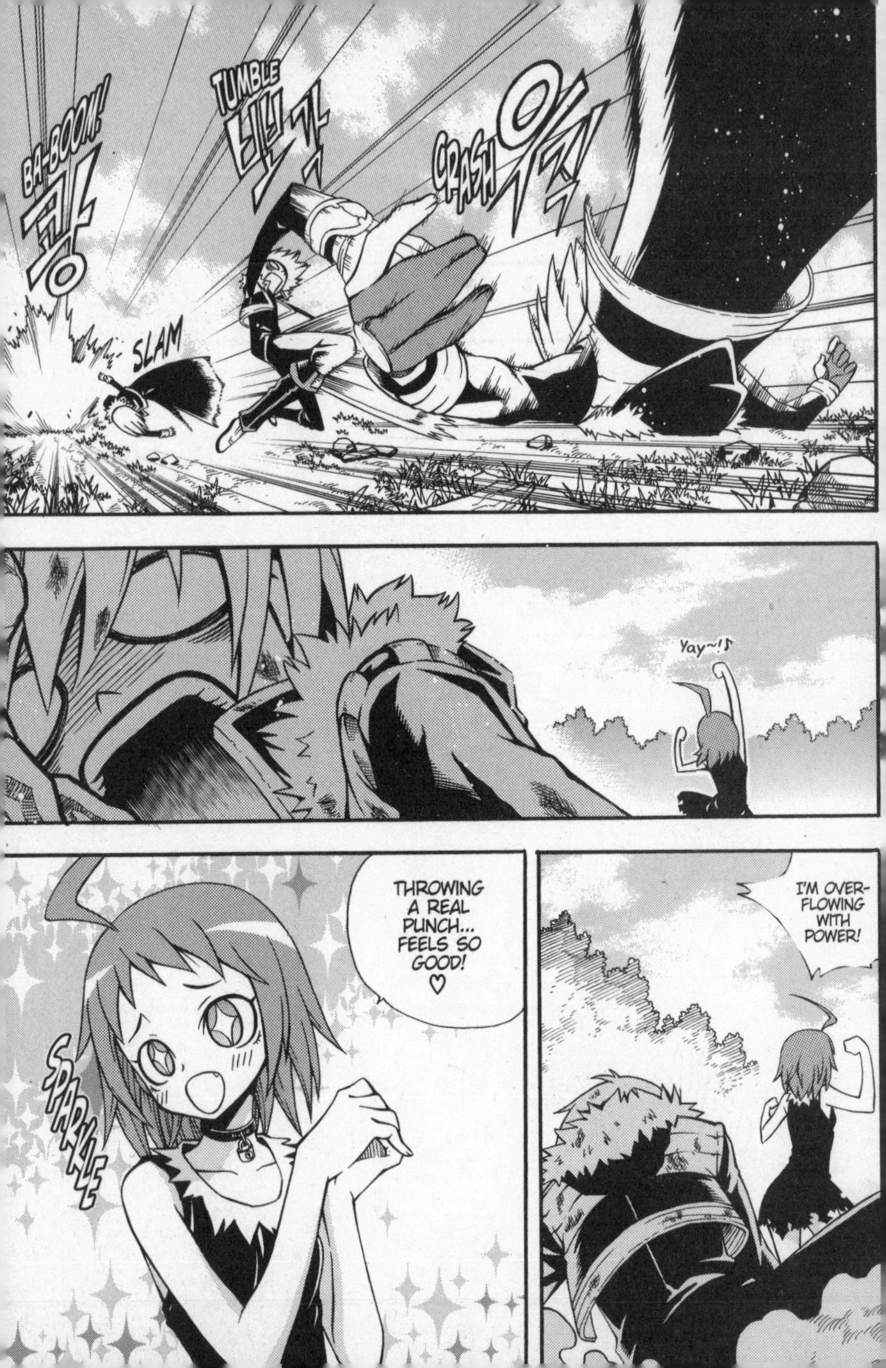
BA-BOOM!
TUMBLE
CRASH
SLAM
Yay~!♪
THROWING A REAL PUNCH... FEELS SO GOOD! ♡
SPARKLE
I'M OVER-FLOWING WITH POWER!

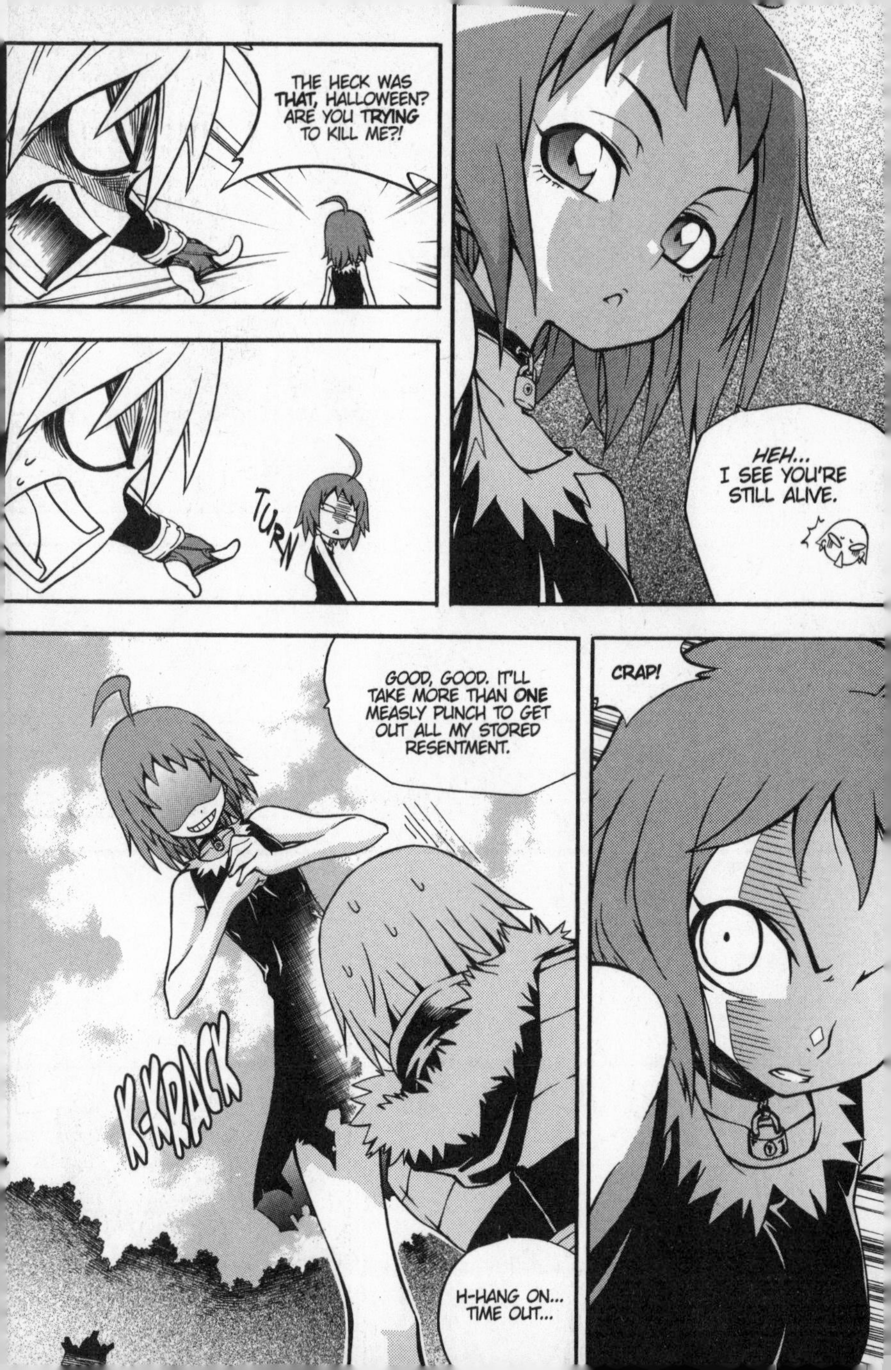
THE HECK WAS THAT, HALLOWEEN? ARE YOU TRYING TO KILL ME?!
TURN
HEH... I SEE YOU'RE STILL ALIVE.
GOOD, GOOD. IT'LL TAKE MORE THAN ONE MEASLY PUNCH TO GET OUT ALL MY STORED RESENTMENT.
CRAP!
H-HANG ON... TIME OUT...
K-KRACK

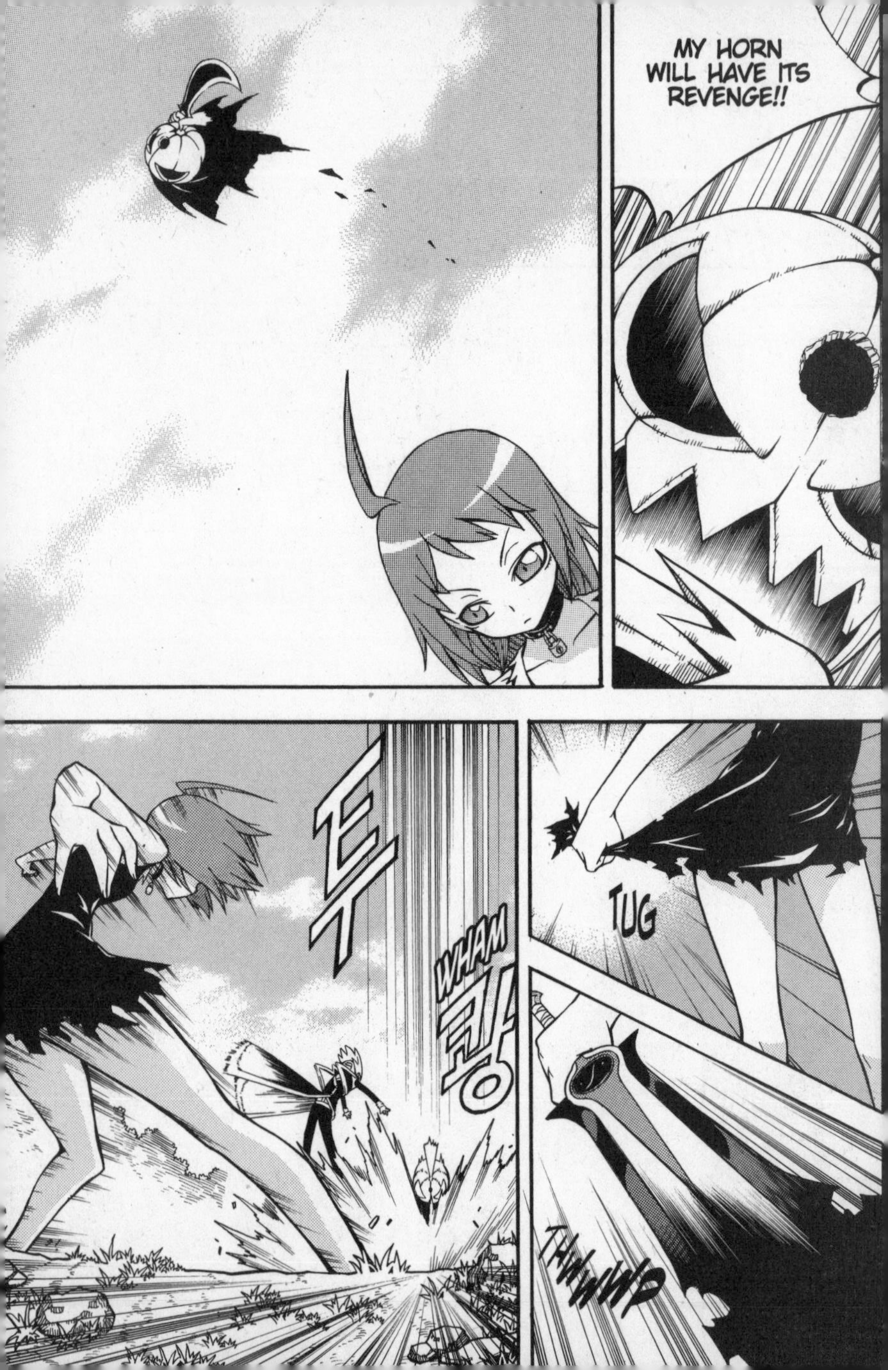
MY HORN WILL HAVE ITS REVENGE!!
TUG
THWWP
WHAM

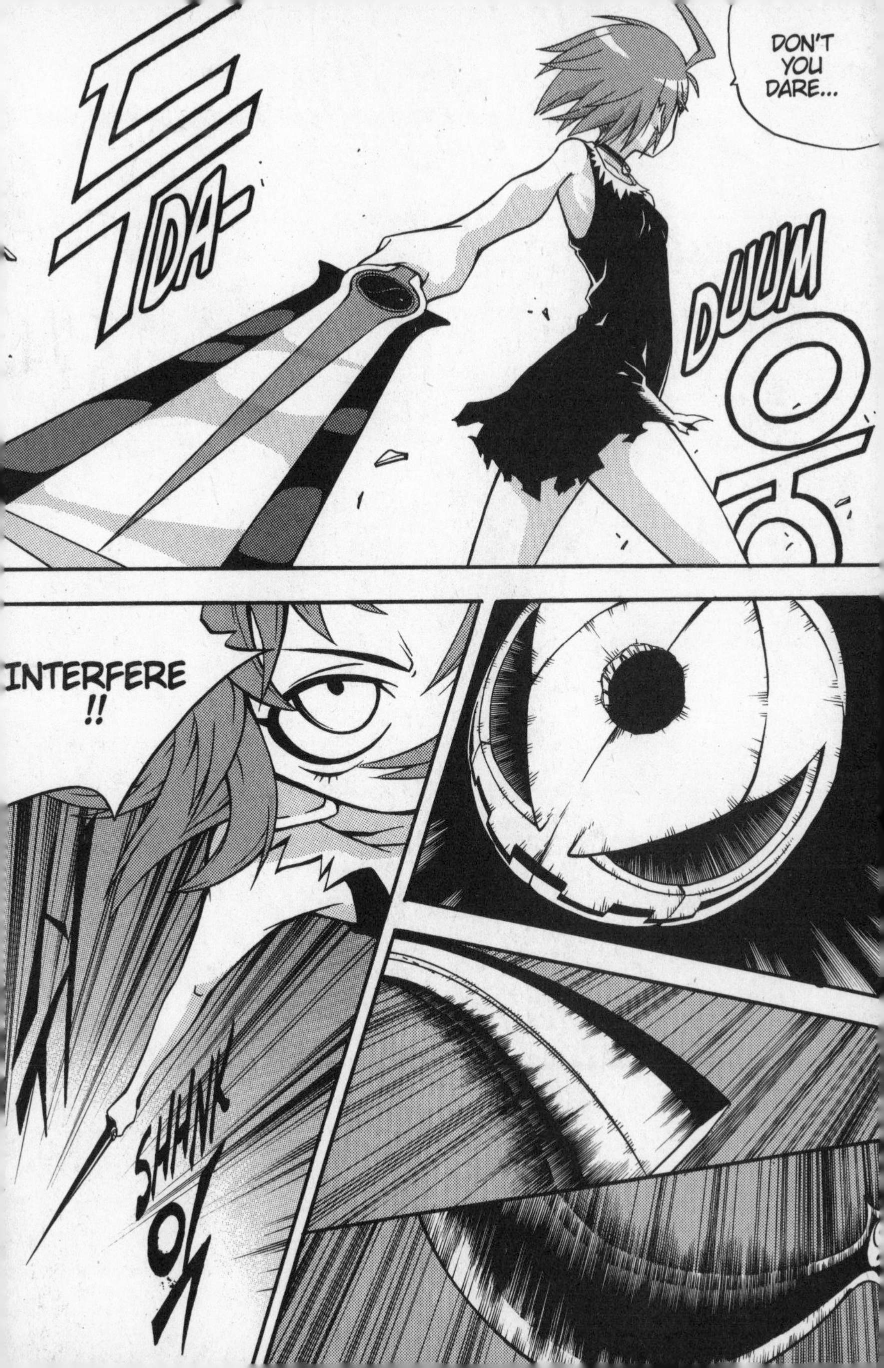
DON'T YOU DARE...
DA
DUUM
INTERFERE !!
SHHNK

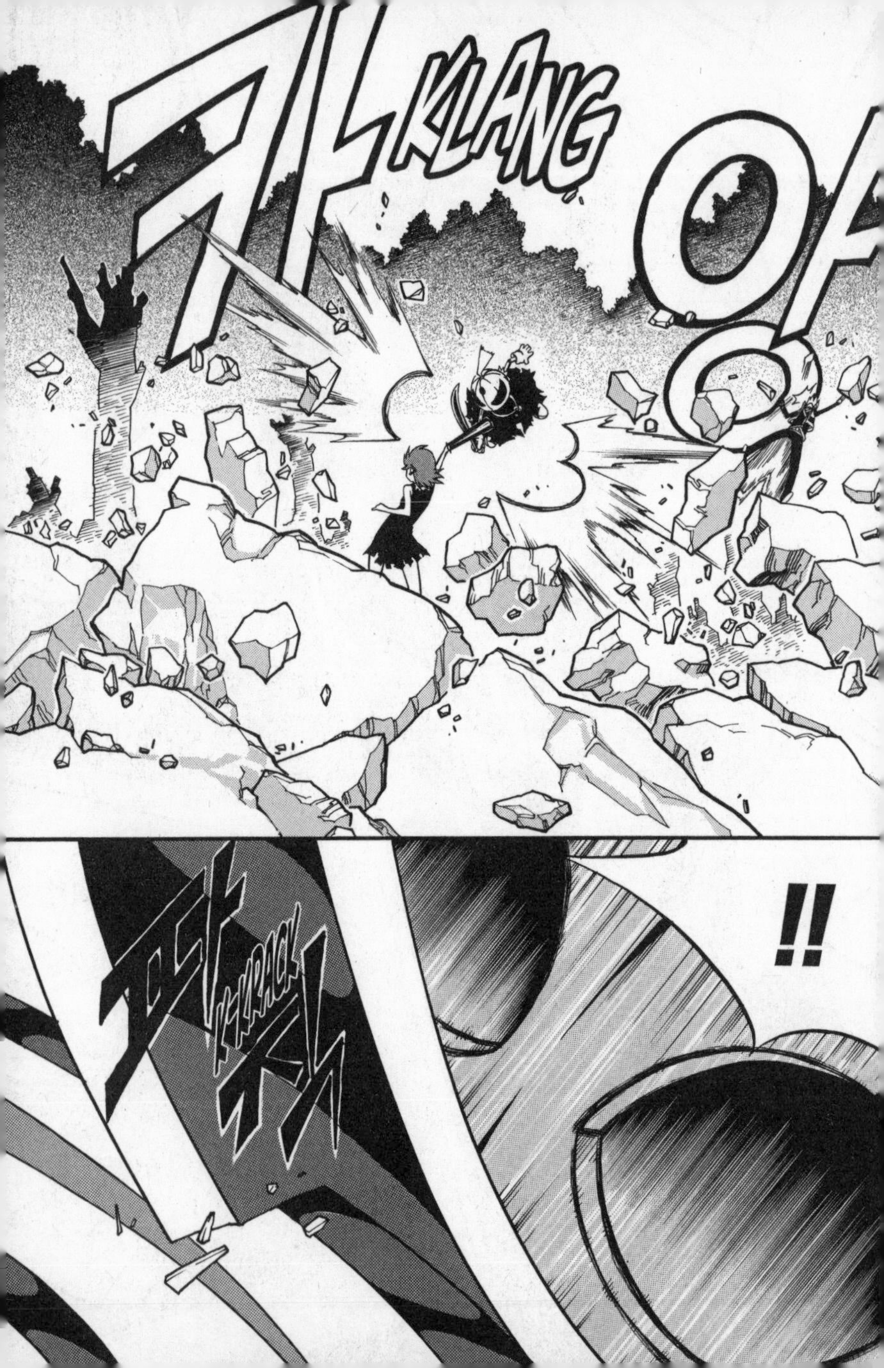
KLANG
K-KRACK
!!

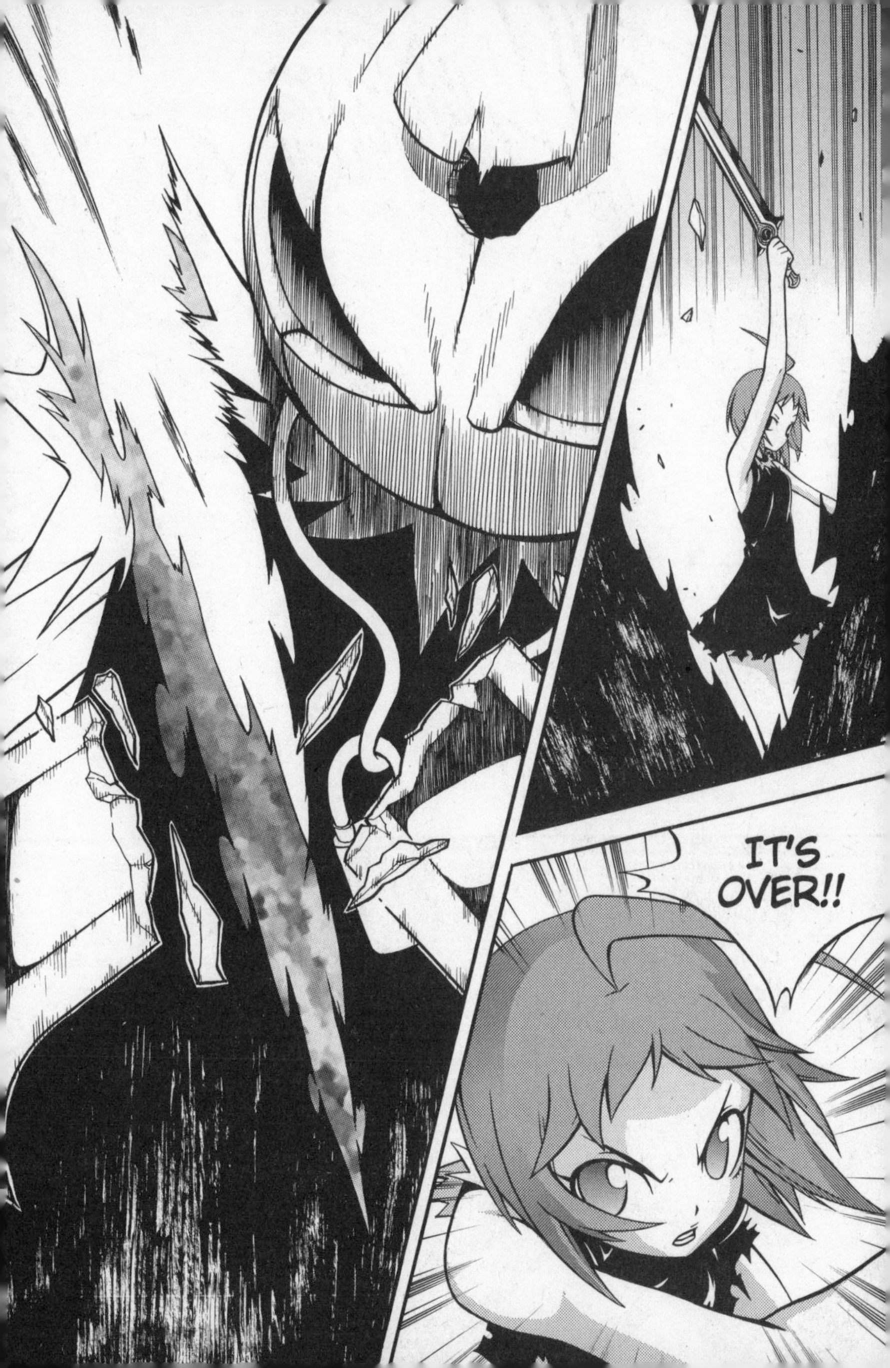
IT'S OVER!!

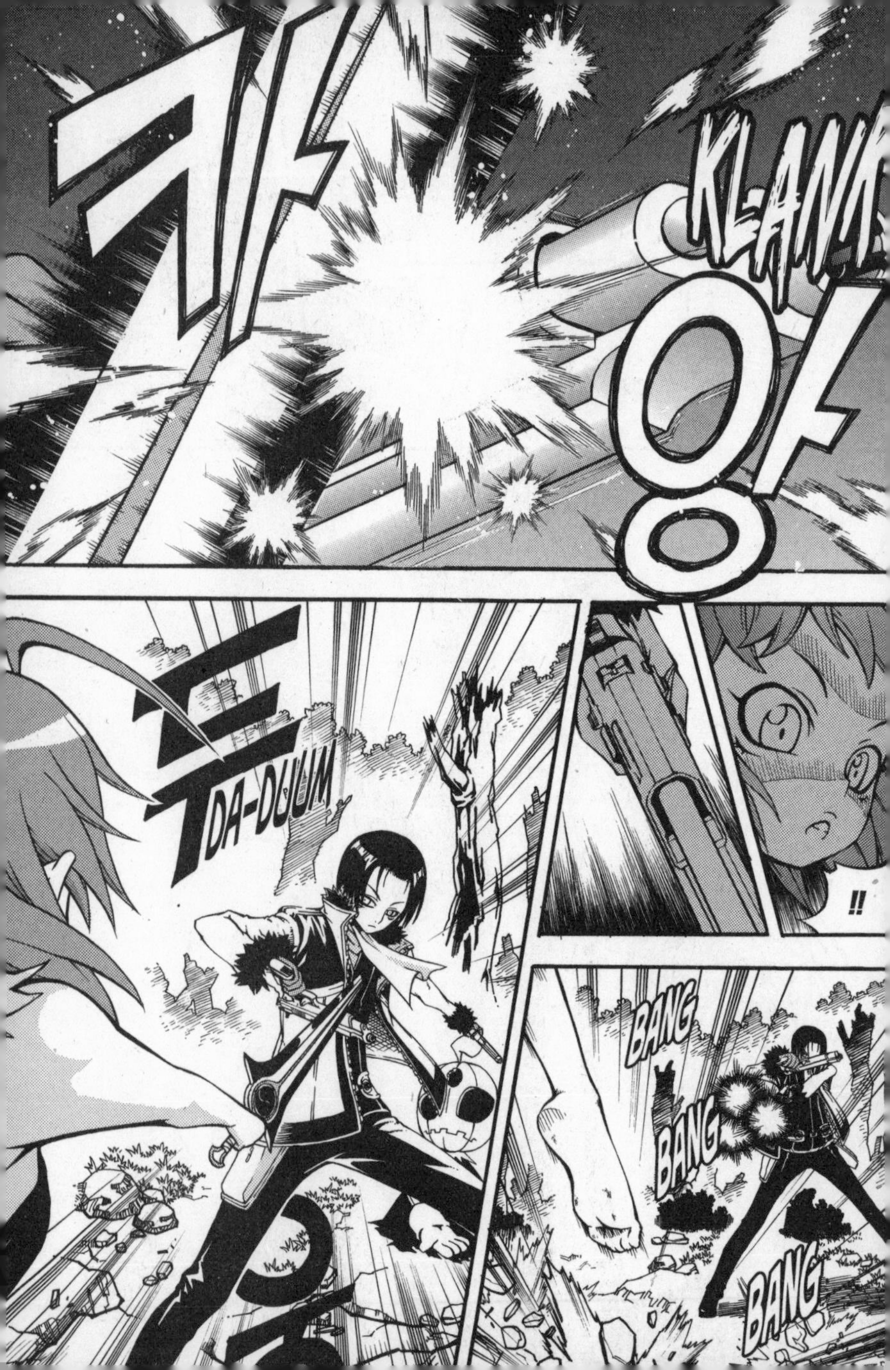
KLAN
!!
BANG
BANG
BANG
DA-DUUM

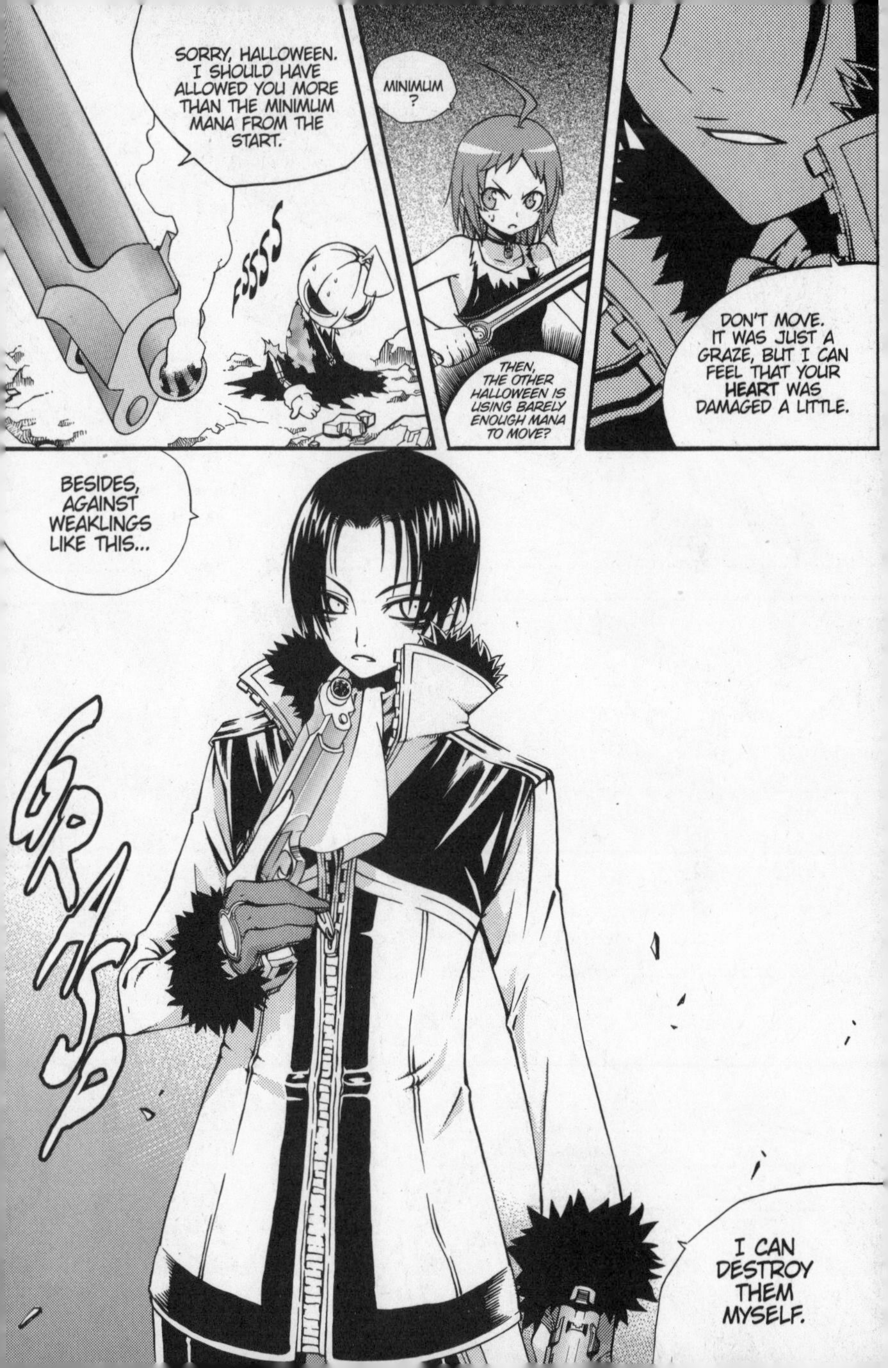
DON'T MOVE. IT WAS JUST A GRAZE, BUT I CAN FEEL THAT YOUR HEART WAS DAMAGED A LITTLE.
SORRY, HALLOWEEN. I SHOULD HAVE ALLOWED YOU MORE THAN THE MINIMUM MANA FROM THE START.
FSSSS
MINIMUM?
THEN, THE OTHER HALLOWEEN IS USING BARELY ENOUGH MANA TO MOVE?
BESIDES, AGAINST WEAKLINGS LIKE THIS...
GRASP
I CAN DESTROY THEM MYSELF.

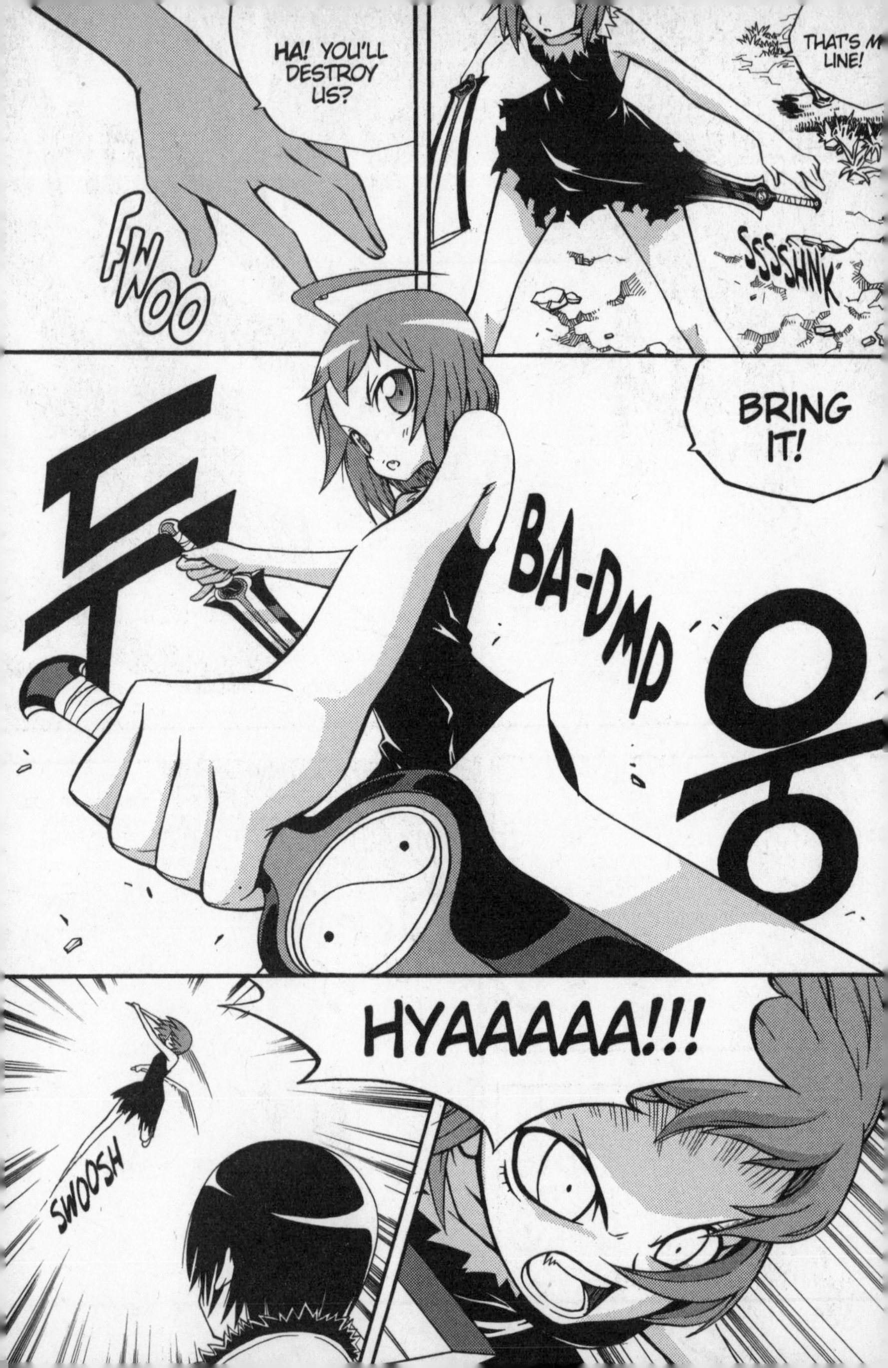
THAT'S MY LINE!
SSSSHNK
HA! YOU'LL DESTROY US?
FWOO
BRING IT!
BA-DMP
HYAAAAAA!!!
SWOOSH

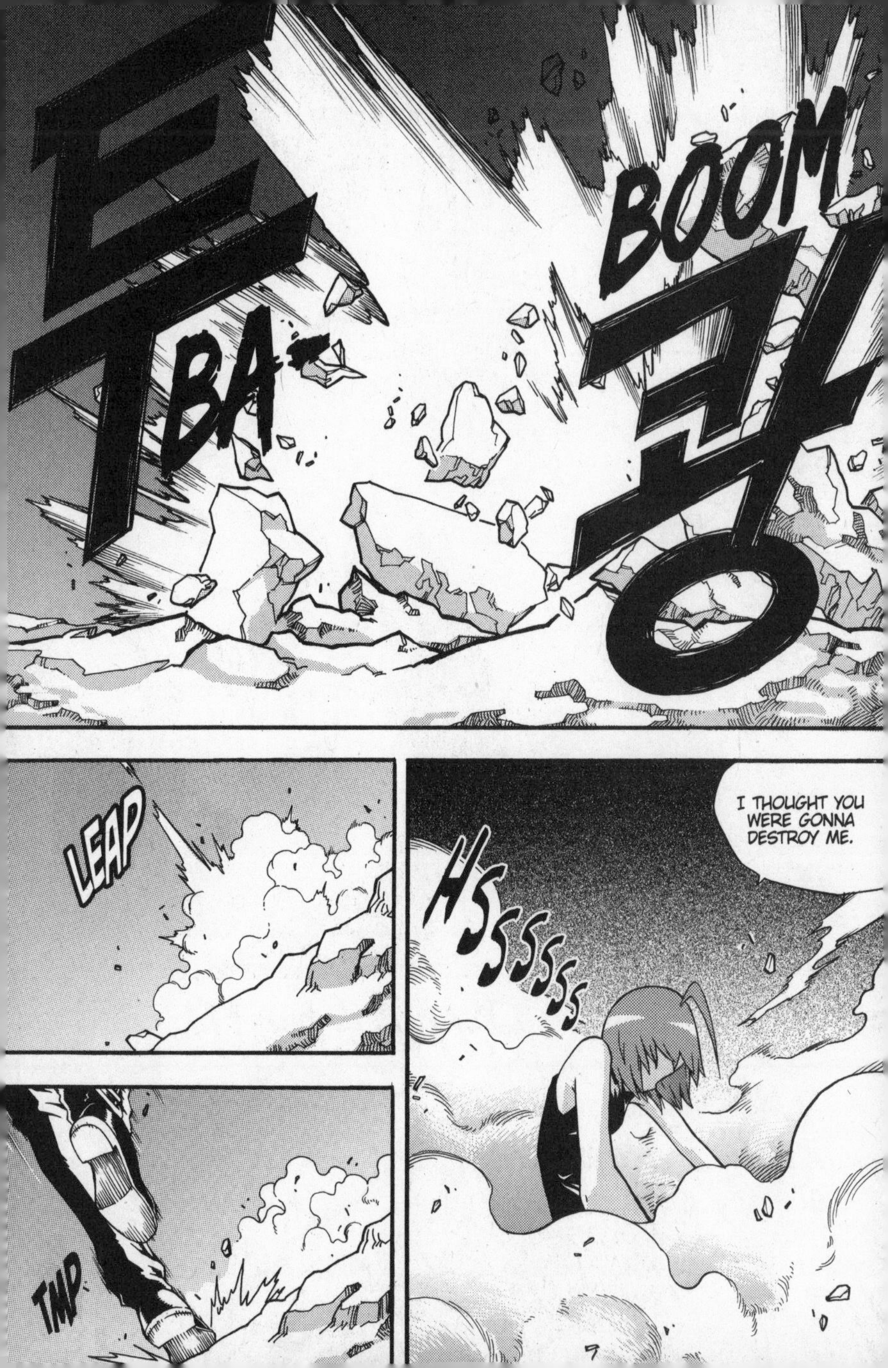
BA-BOOM
LEAP
TMP
HSSSSSS
I THOUGHT YOU WERE GONNA DESTROY ME.

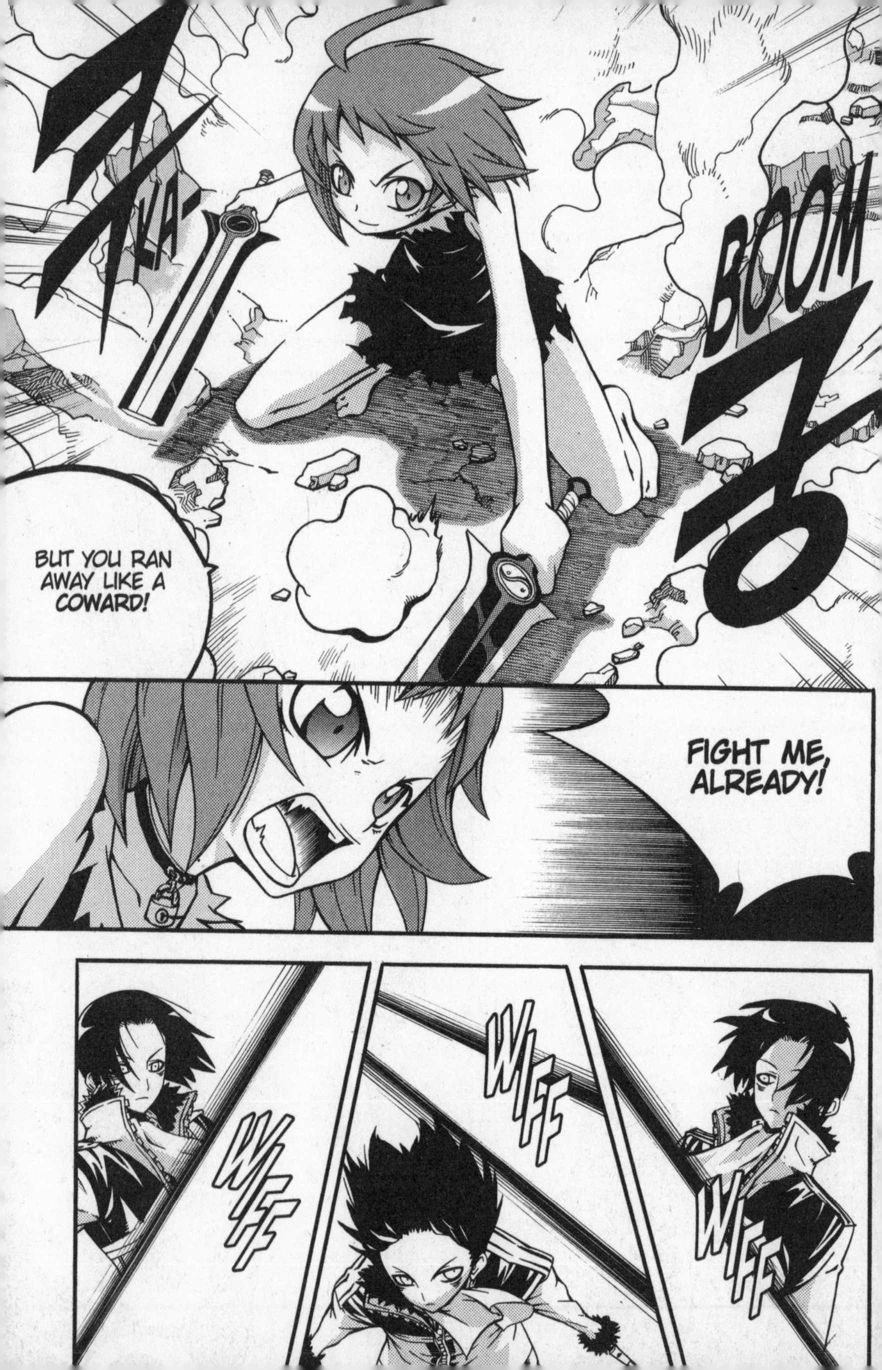
KA-
BOOM
BUT YOU RAN AWAY LIKE A COWARD!
FIGHT ME, ALREADY!
WIFF
WIFF
WIFF

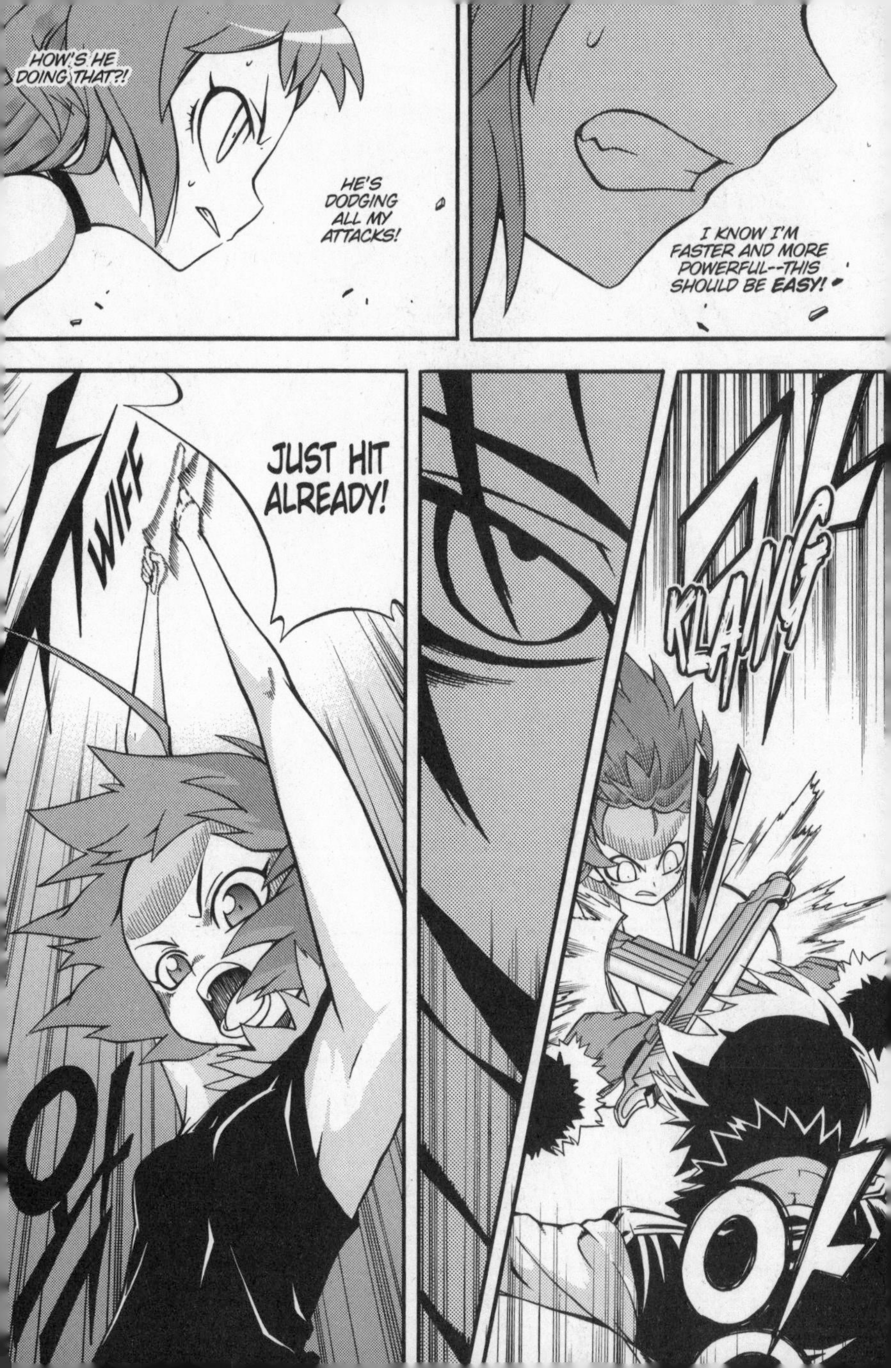
HOW'S HE DOING THAT?!
HE'S DODGING ALL MY ATTACKS!
I KNOW I'M FASTER AND MORE POWERFUL--THIS SHOULD BE EASY!
WIFF
JUST HIT ALREADY!
KLANG

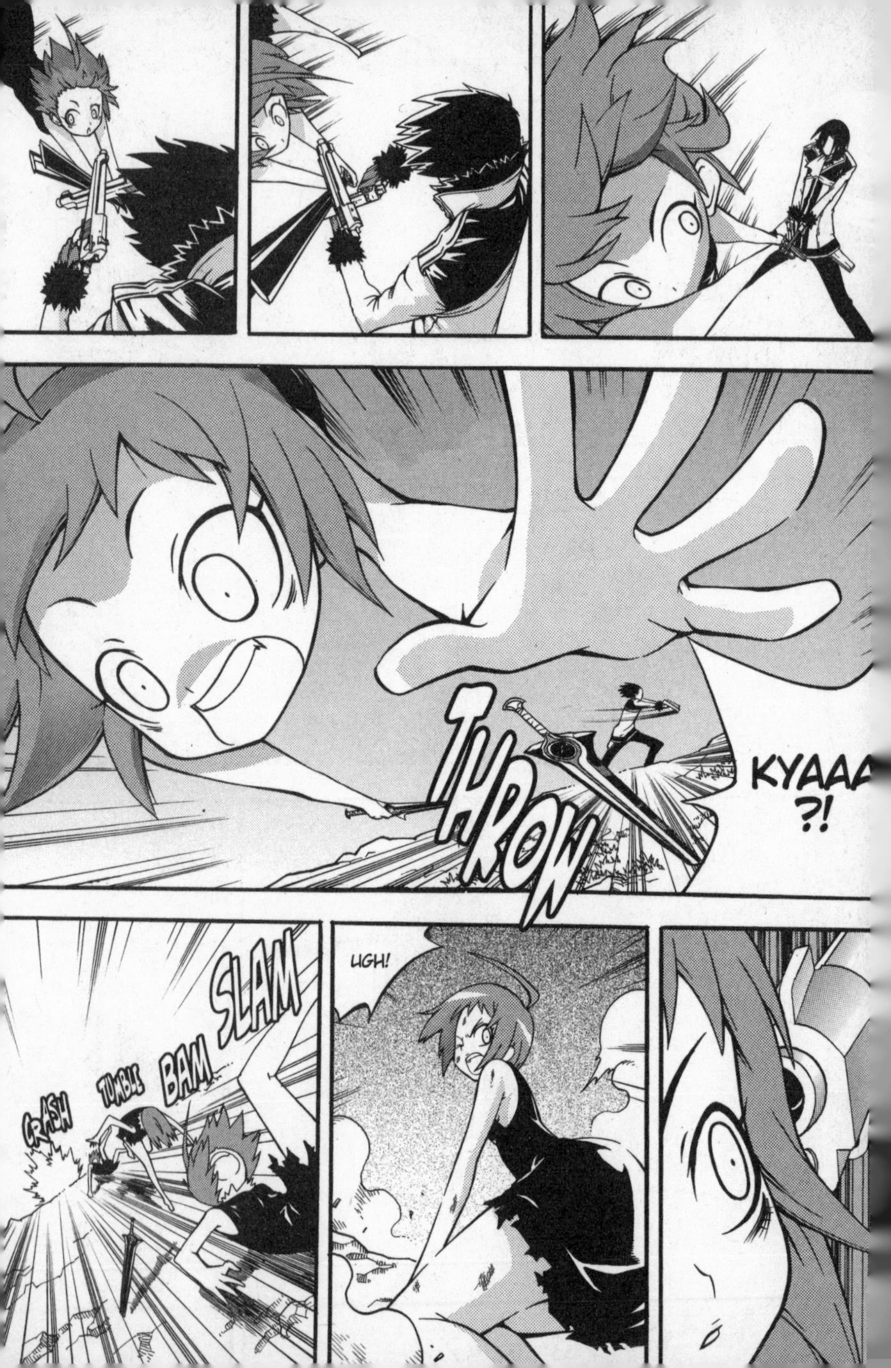

THROW
KYAAA ?!
UGH!
SLAM
BAM
TUMBLE
CRASH

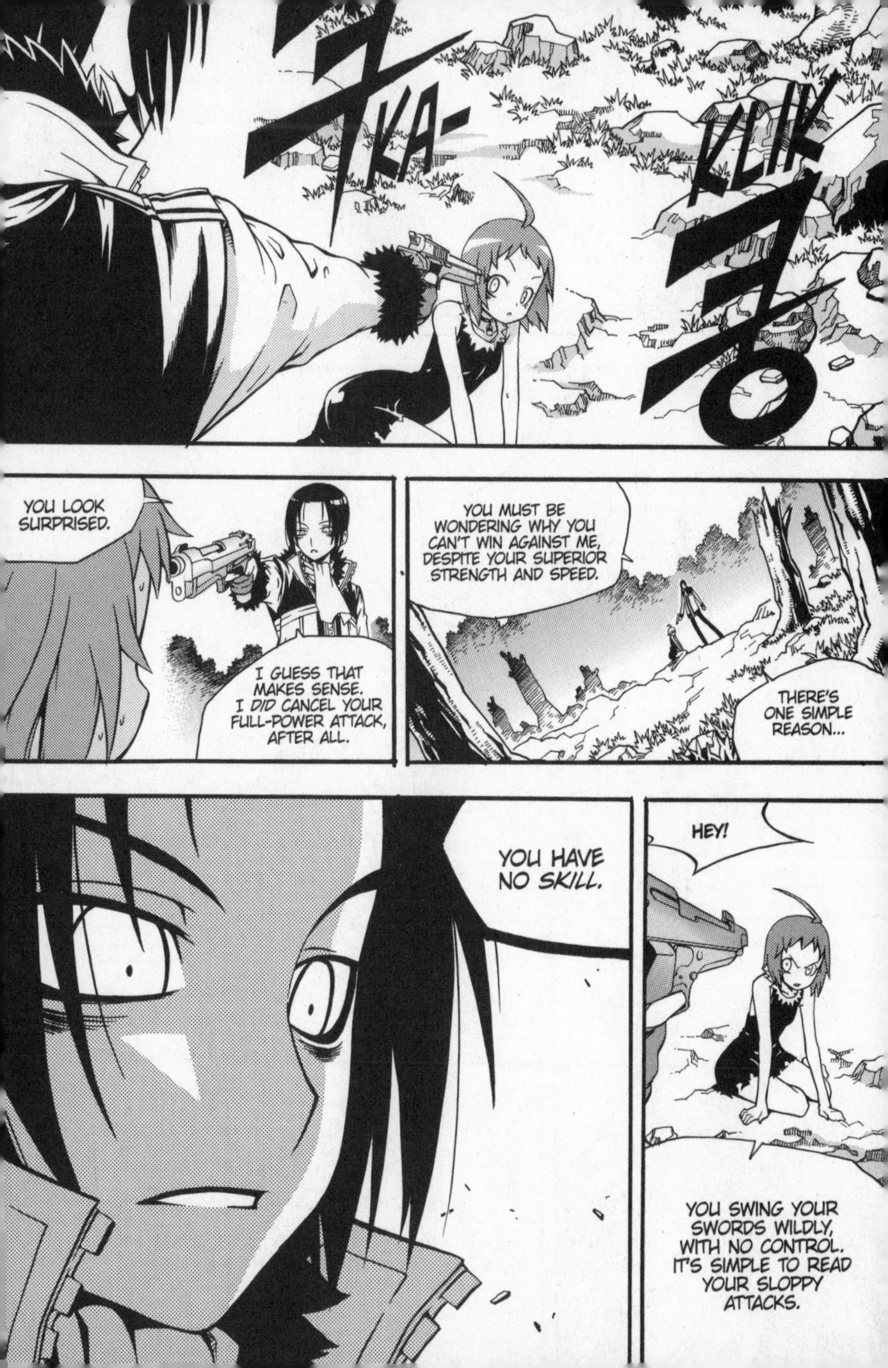
KLIK
KA-
YOU MUST BE WONDERING WHY YOU CAN'T WIN AGAINST ME, DESPITE YOUR SUPERIOR STRENGTH AND SPEED.
THERE'S ONE SIMPLE REASON...
YOU LOOK SURPRISED.
I GUESS THAT MAKES SENSE. I *DID* CANCEL YOUR FULL-POWER ATTACK, AFTER ALL.
HEY!
YOU SWING YOUR SWORDS WILDLY, WITH NO CONTROL. IT'S SIMPLE TO READ YOUR SLOPPY ATTACKS.
YOU HAVE NO *SKILL*.

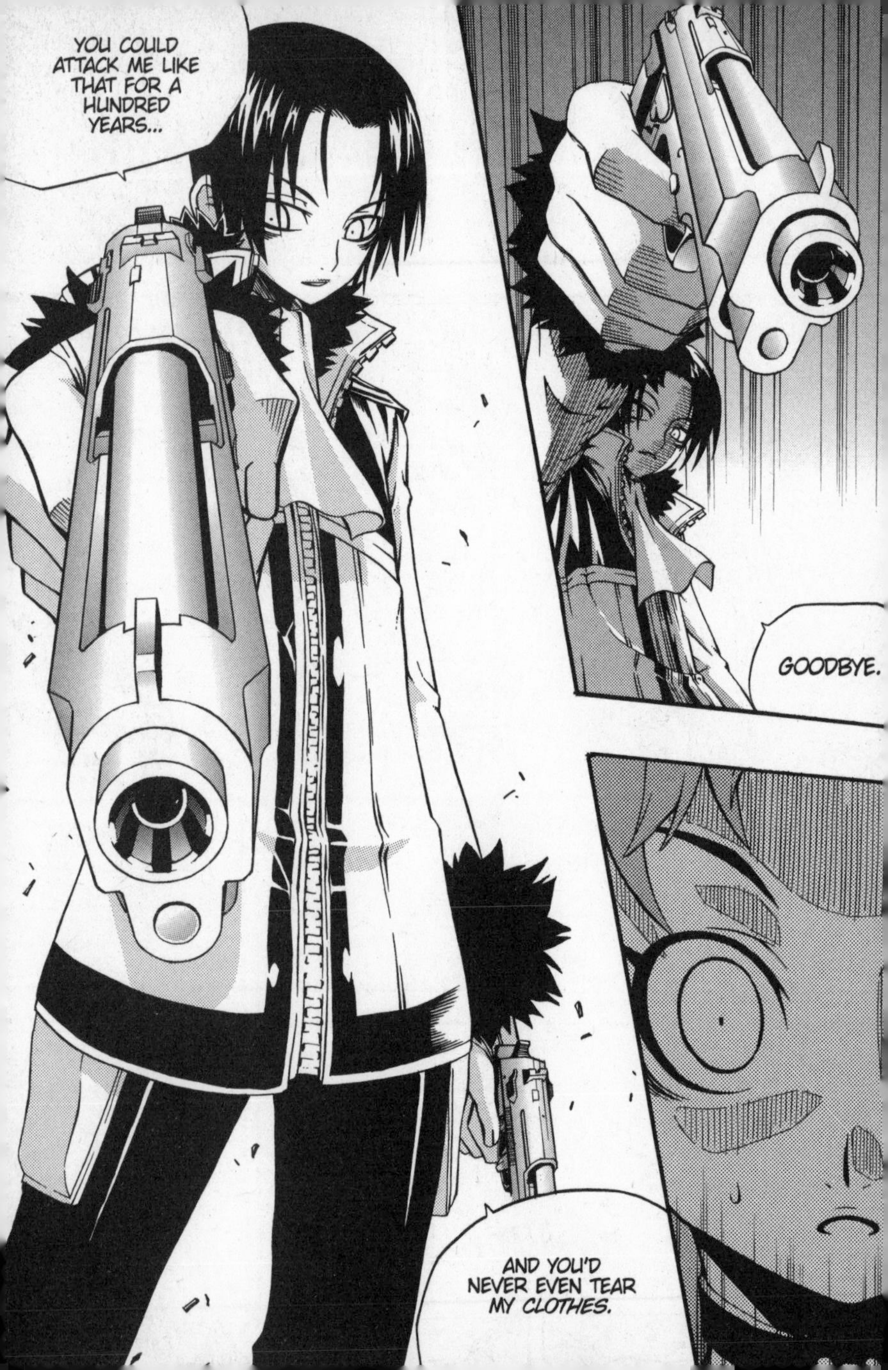
YOU COULD ATTACK ME LIKE THAT FOR A HUNDRED YEARS...
AND YOU'D NEVER EVEN TEAR MY CLOTHES.
GOODBYE.

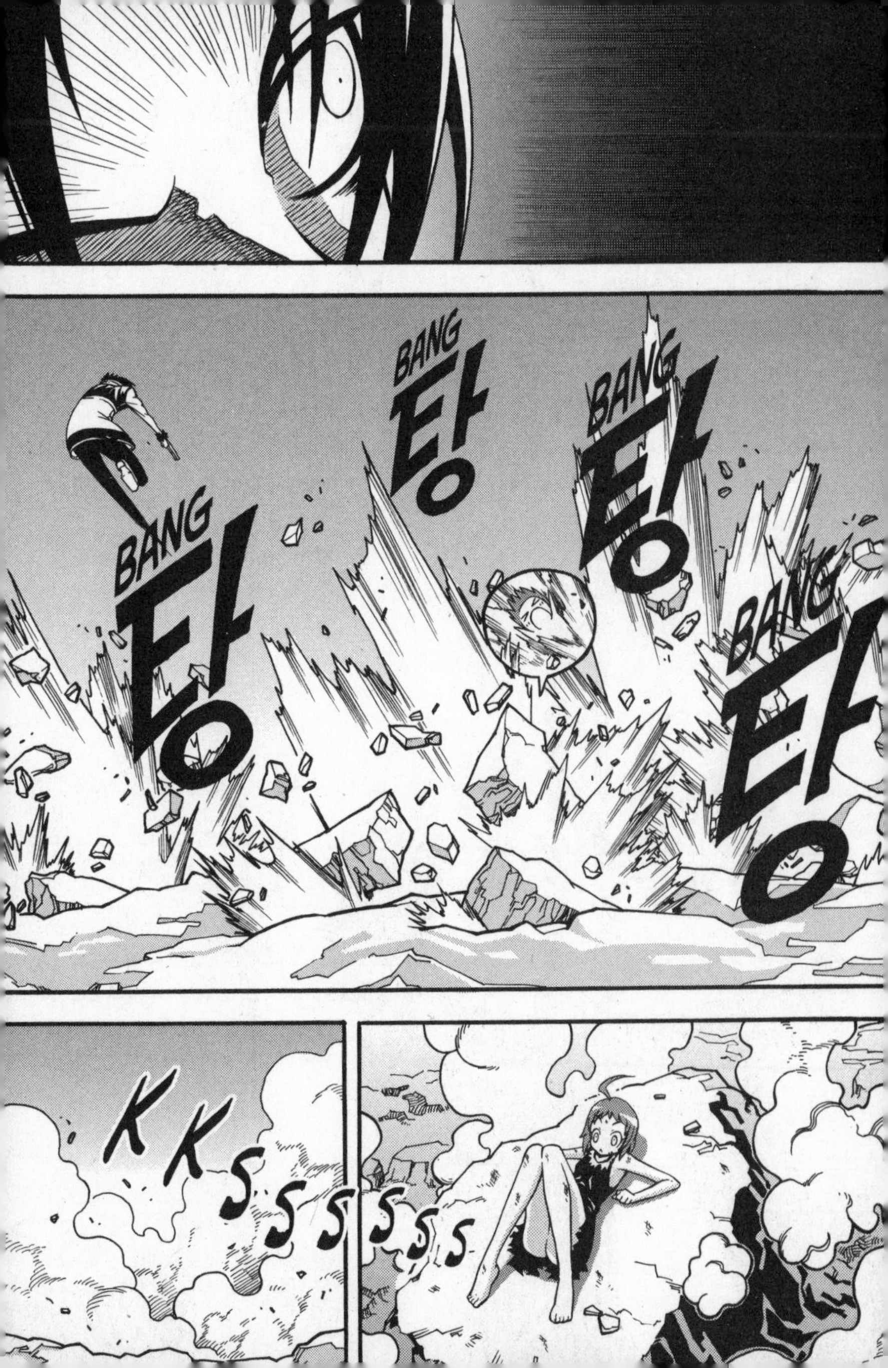
BANG
탕
BANG
탕
BANG
탕
BANG
탕
KKSSSSSSS

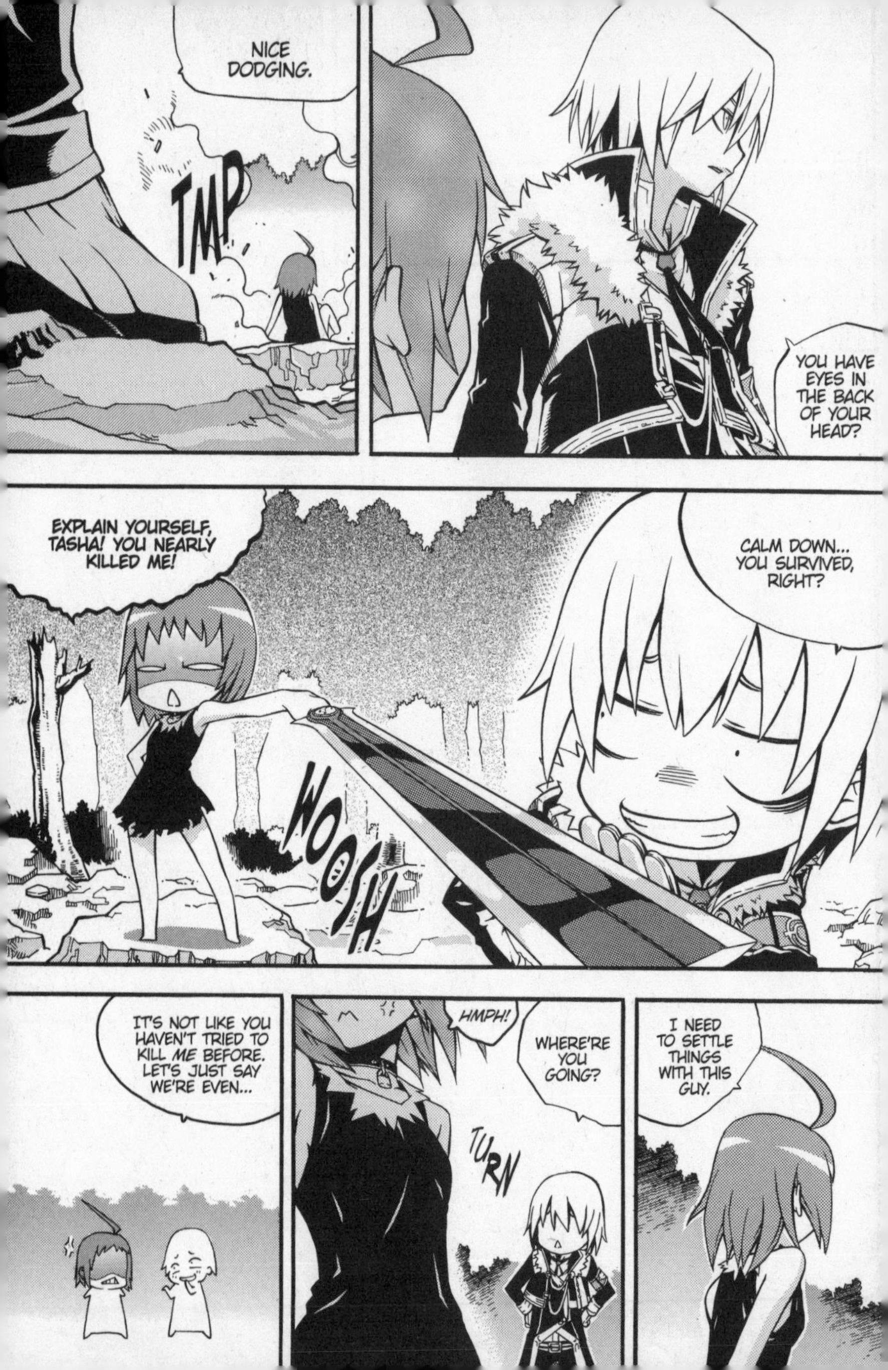
NICE DODGING.
TMP
YOU HAVE EYES IN THE BACK OF YOUR HEAD?
EXPLAIN YOURSELF, TASHA! YOU NEARLY KILLED ME!
CALM DOWN... YOU SURVIVED, RIGHT?
WOOSH
IT'S NOT LIKE YOU HAVEN'T TRIED TO KILL *ME* BEFORE. LET'S JUST SAY WE'RE EVEN...
HMPH!
WHERE'RE YOU GOING?
TURN
I NEED TO SETTLE THINGS WITH THIS GUY.

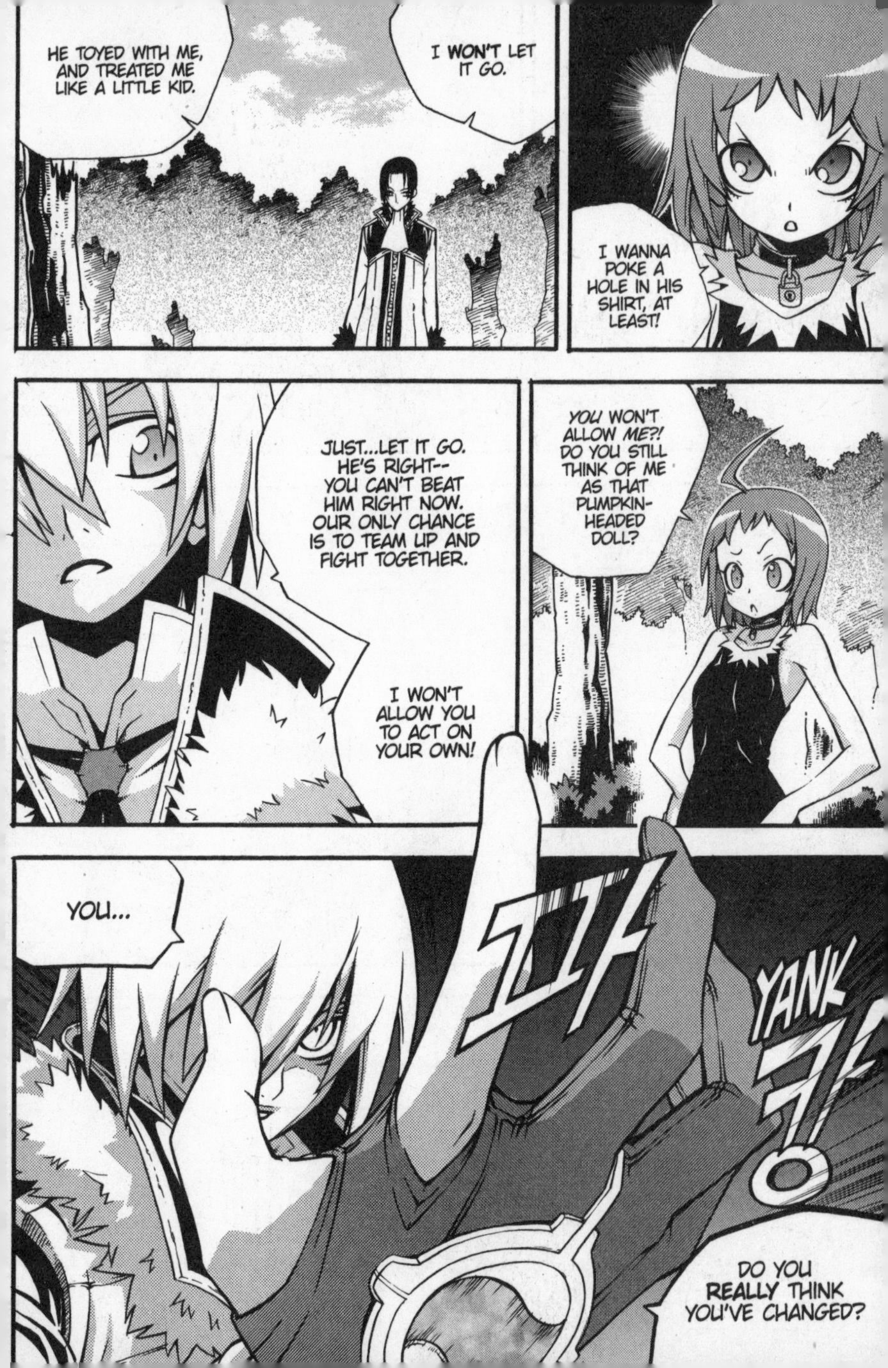
HE TOYED WITH ME, AND TREATED ME LIKE A LITTLE KID.
I WON'T LET IT GO.
I WANNA POKE A HOLE IN HIS SHIRT, AT LEAST!
JUST...LET IT GO. HE'S RIGHT-- YOU CAN'T BEAT HIM RIGHT NOW. OUR ONLY CHANCE IS TO TEAM UP AND FIGHT TOGETHER.
I WON'T ALLOW YOU TO ACT ON YOUR OWN!
YOU WON'T ALLOW *ME*?! DO YOU STILL THINK OF ME AS THAT PUMPKIN-HEADED DOLL?
YOU...
YANK
DO YOU **REALLY** THINK YOU'VE CHANGED?

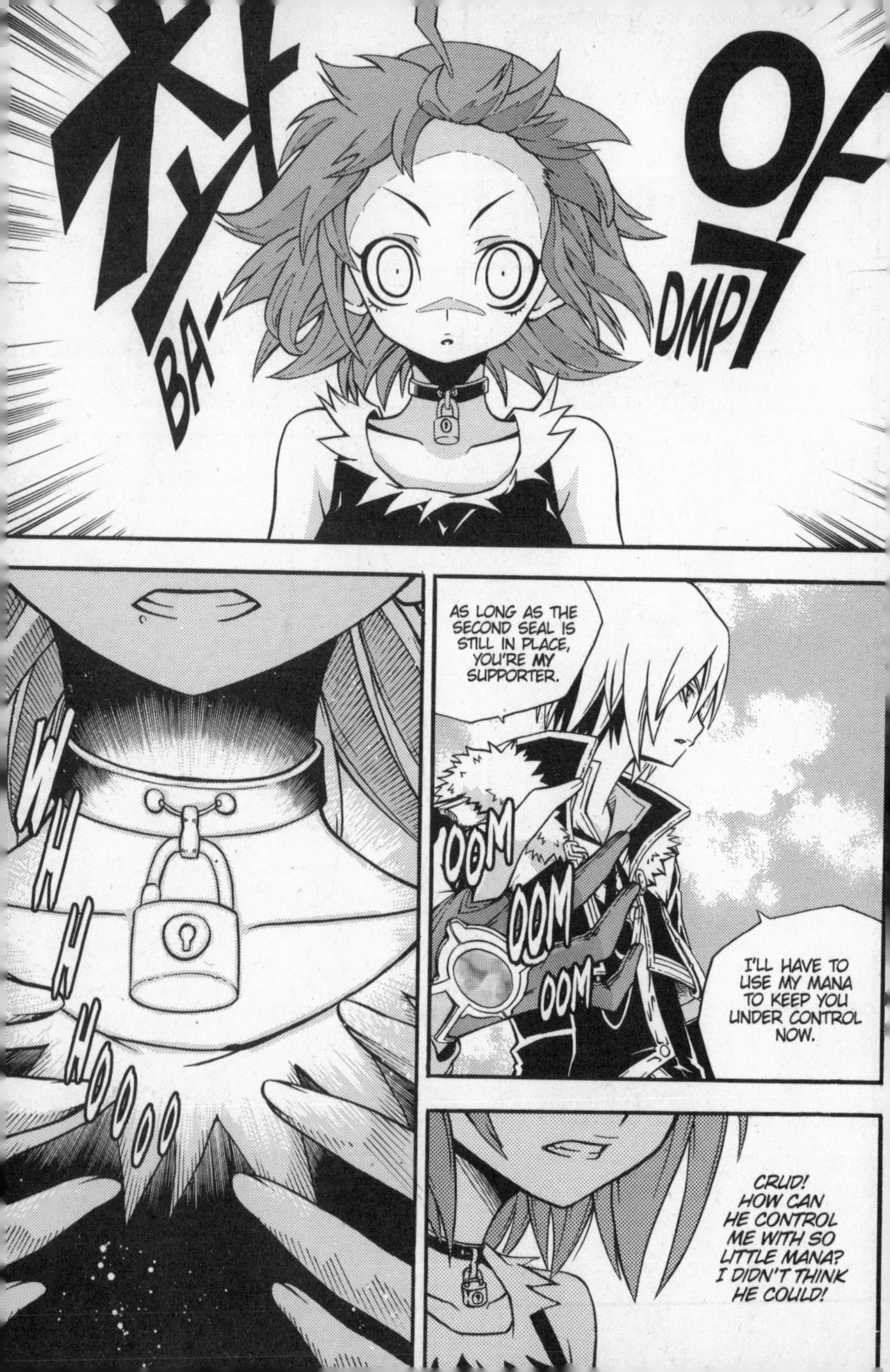
BA-DMP
AS LONG AS THE SECOND SEAL IS STILL IN PLACE, YOU'RE MY SUPPORTER.
OOM OOM OOM
I'LL HAVE TO USE MY MANA TO KEEP YOU UNDER CONTROL NOW.
WHHHOOOO
CRUD! HOW CAN HE CONTROL ME WITH SO LITTLE MANA? I DIDN'T THINK HE COULD!

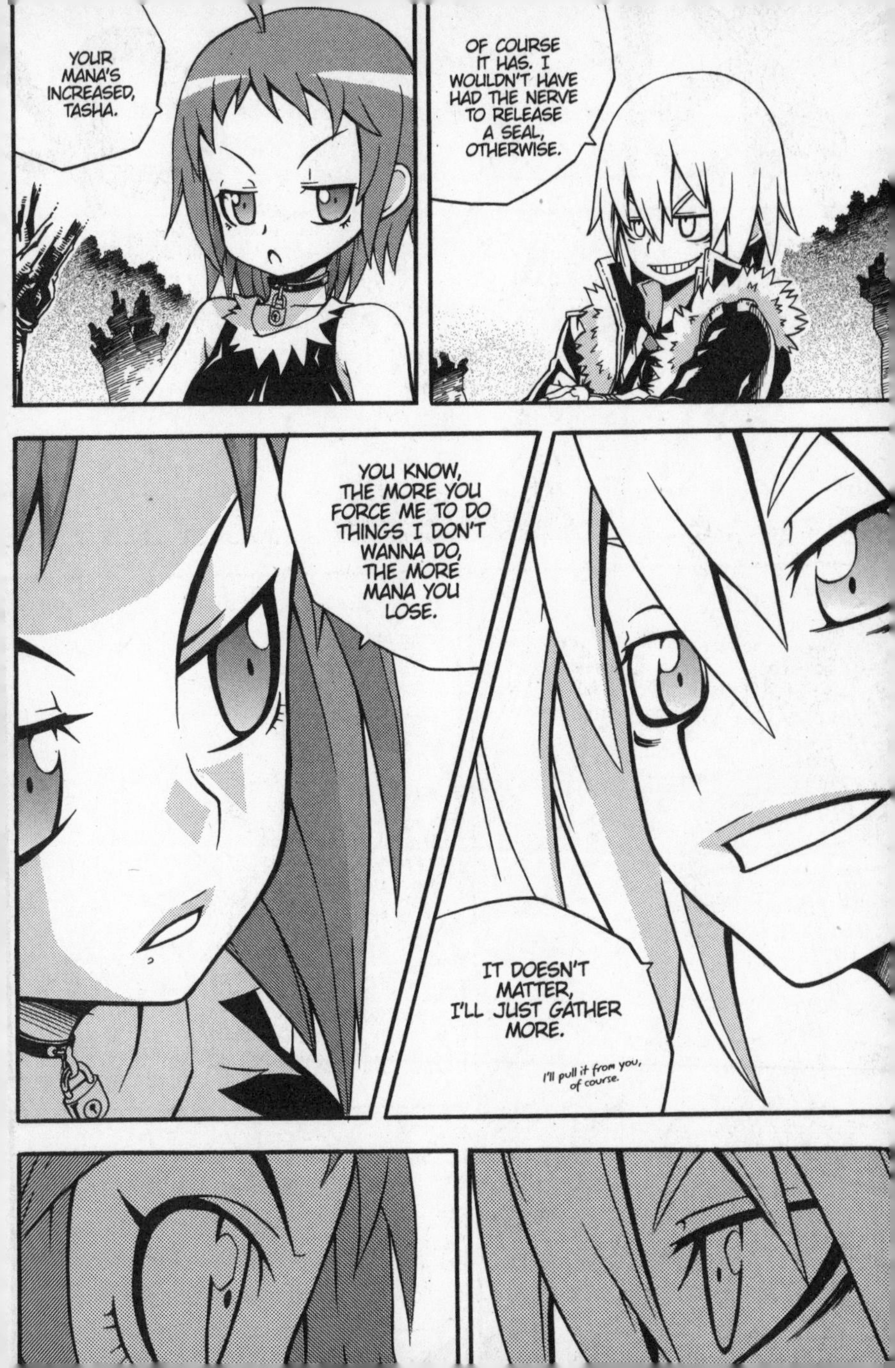
YOUR MANA'S INCREASED, TASHA.
OF COURSE IT HAS. I WOULDN'T HAVE HAD THE NERVE TO RELEASE A SEAL, OTHERWISE.
YOU KNOW, THE MORE YOU FORCE ME TO DO THINGS I DON'T WANNA DO, THE MORE MANA YOU LOSE.
IT DOESN'T MATTER, I'LL JUST GATHER MORE.
I'll pull it from you, of course.

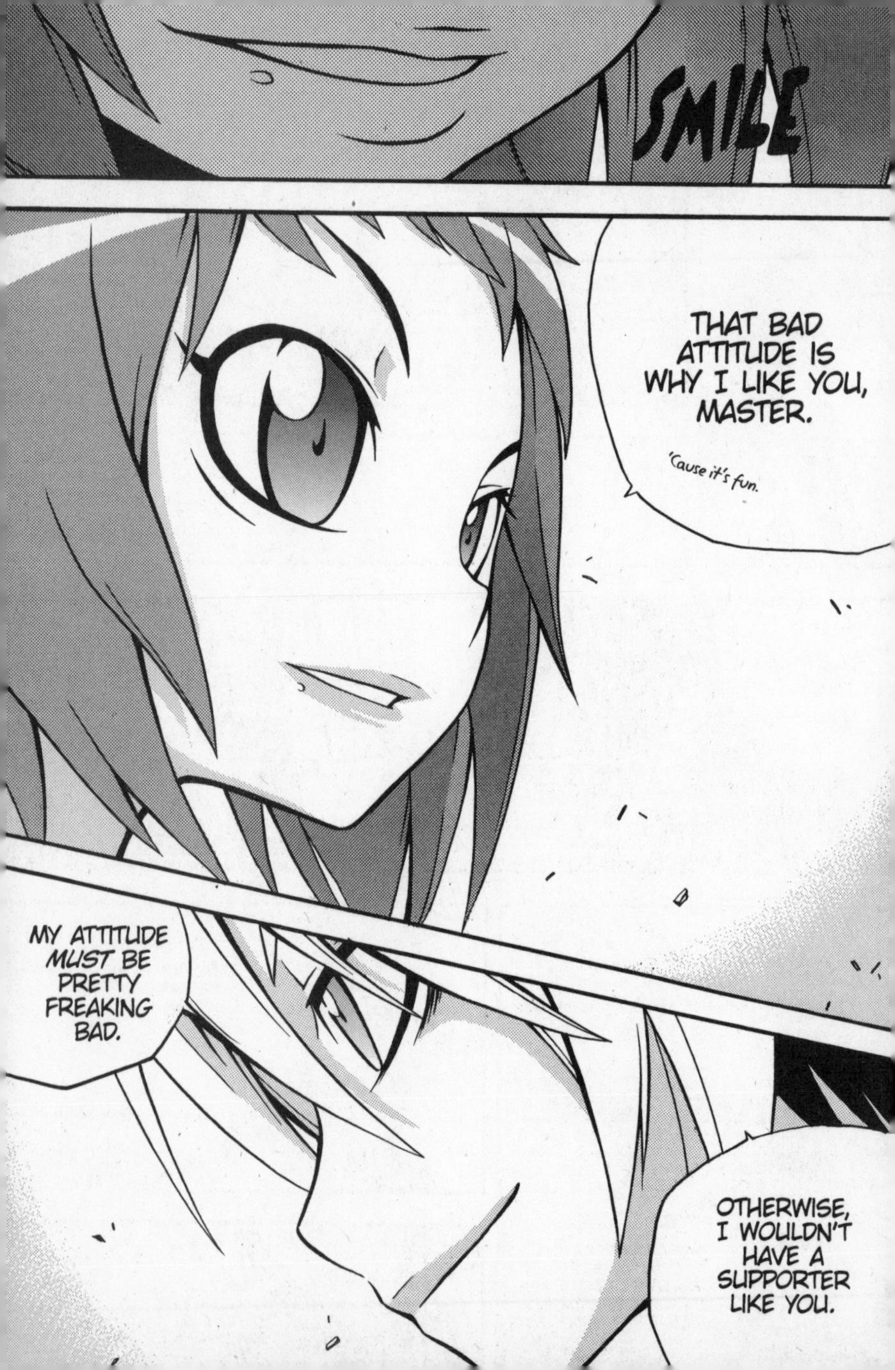
SMILE
THAT BAD ATTITUDE IS WHY I LIKE YOU, MASTER.
'Cause it's fun.
MY ATTITUDE *MUST* BE PRETTY FREAKING BAD.
OTHERWISE, I WOULDN'T HAVE A SUPPORTER LIKE YOU.

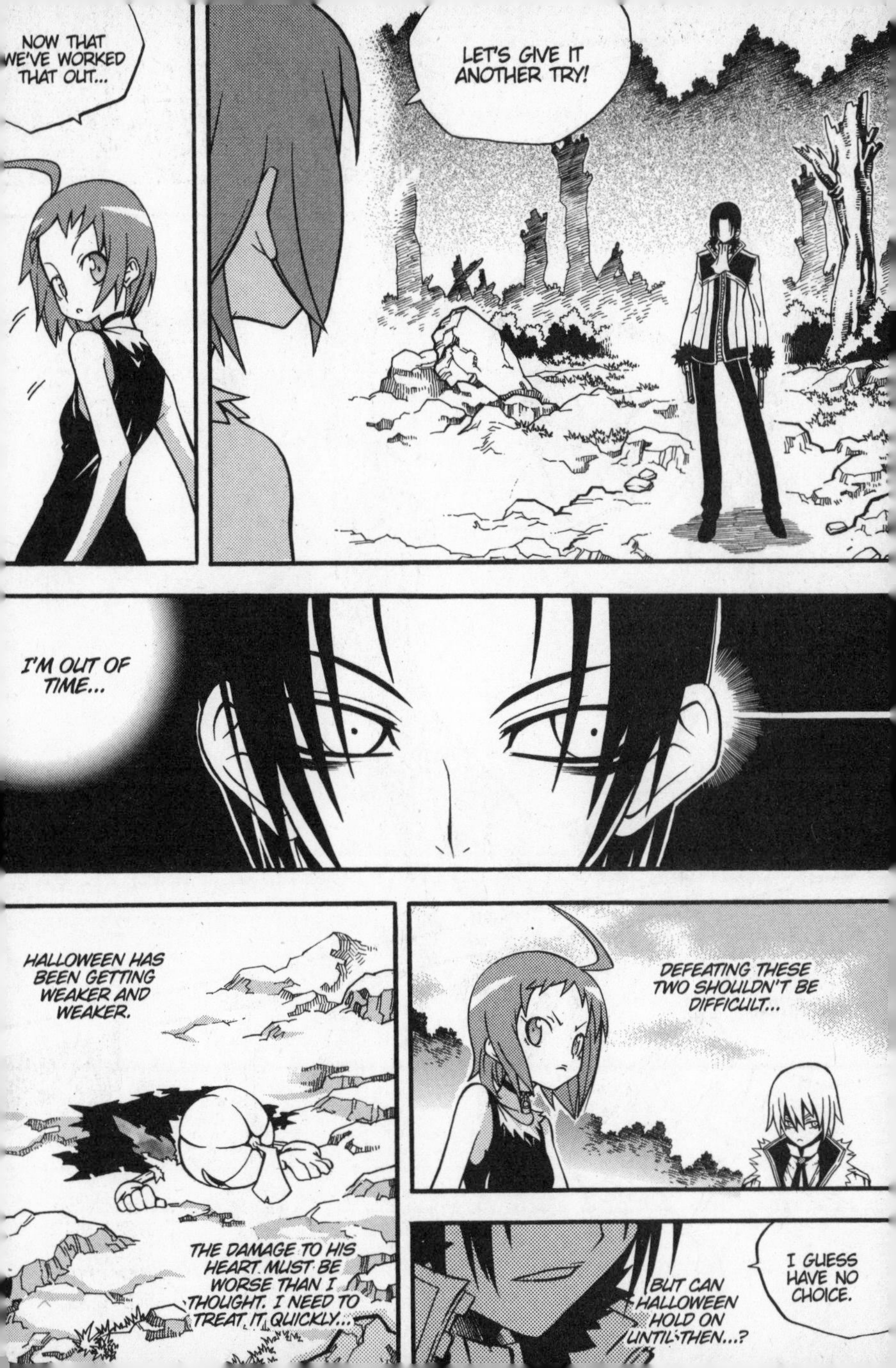
NOW THAT WE'VE WORKED THAT OUT...
LET'S GIVE IT ANOTHER TRY!
I'M OUT OF TIME...
HALLOWEEN HAS BEEN GETTING WEAKER AND WEAKER.
DEFEATING THESE TWO SHOULDN'T BE DIFFICULT...
THE DAMAGE TO HIS HEART MUST BE WORSE THAN I THOUGHT. I NEED TO TREAT IT QUICKLY...
BUT CAN HALLOWEEN HOLD ON UNTIL THEN...?
I GUESS HAVE NO CHOICE.

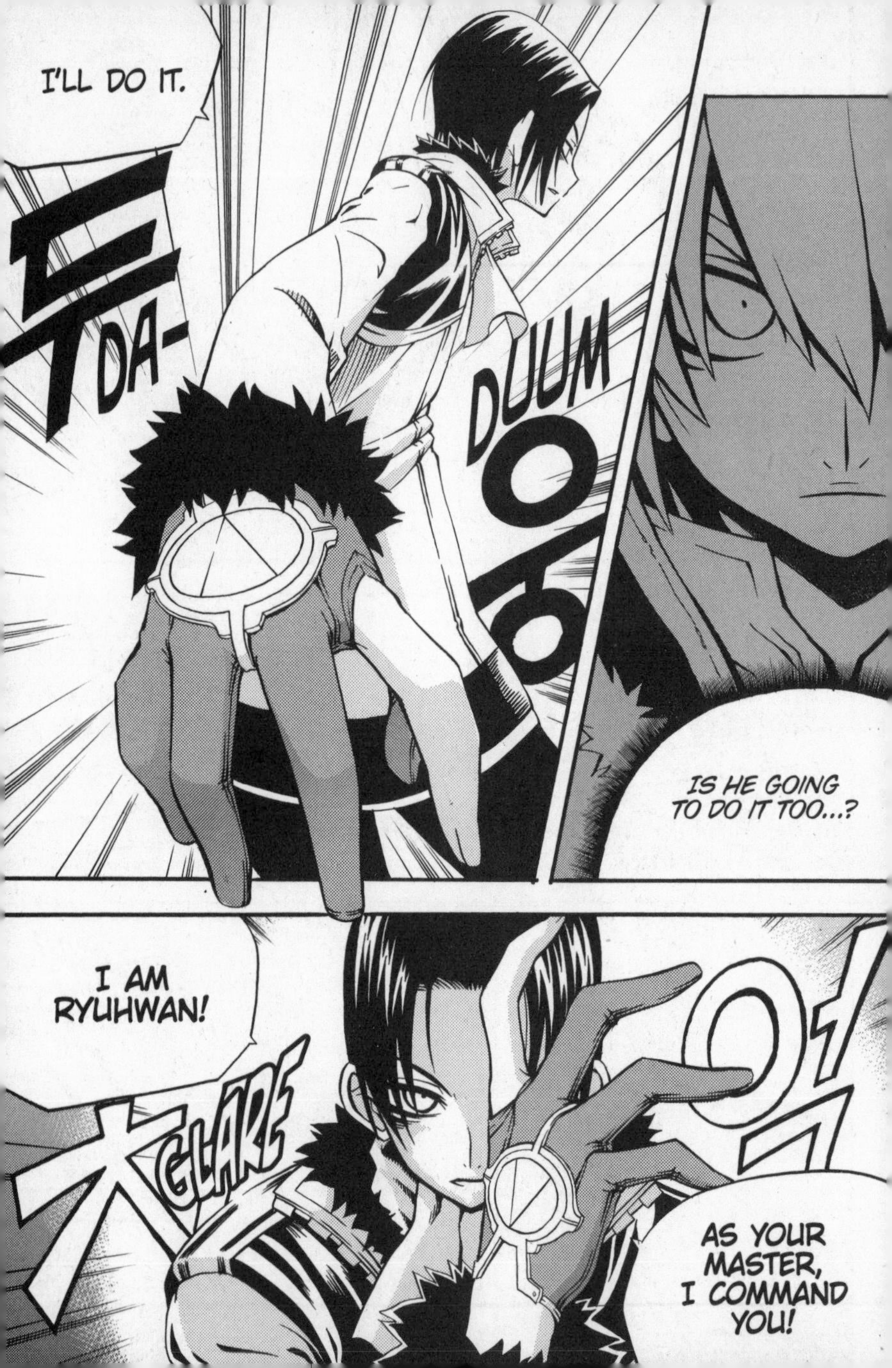
I'LL DO IT.
DA-
DUUM
IS HE GOING TO DO IT TOO...?
AS YOUR MASTER, I COMMAND YOU!
I AM RYUHWAN!
GLARE

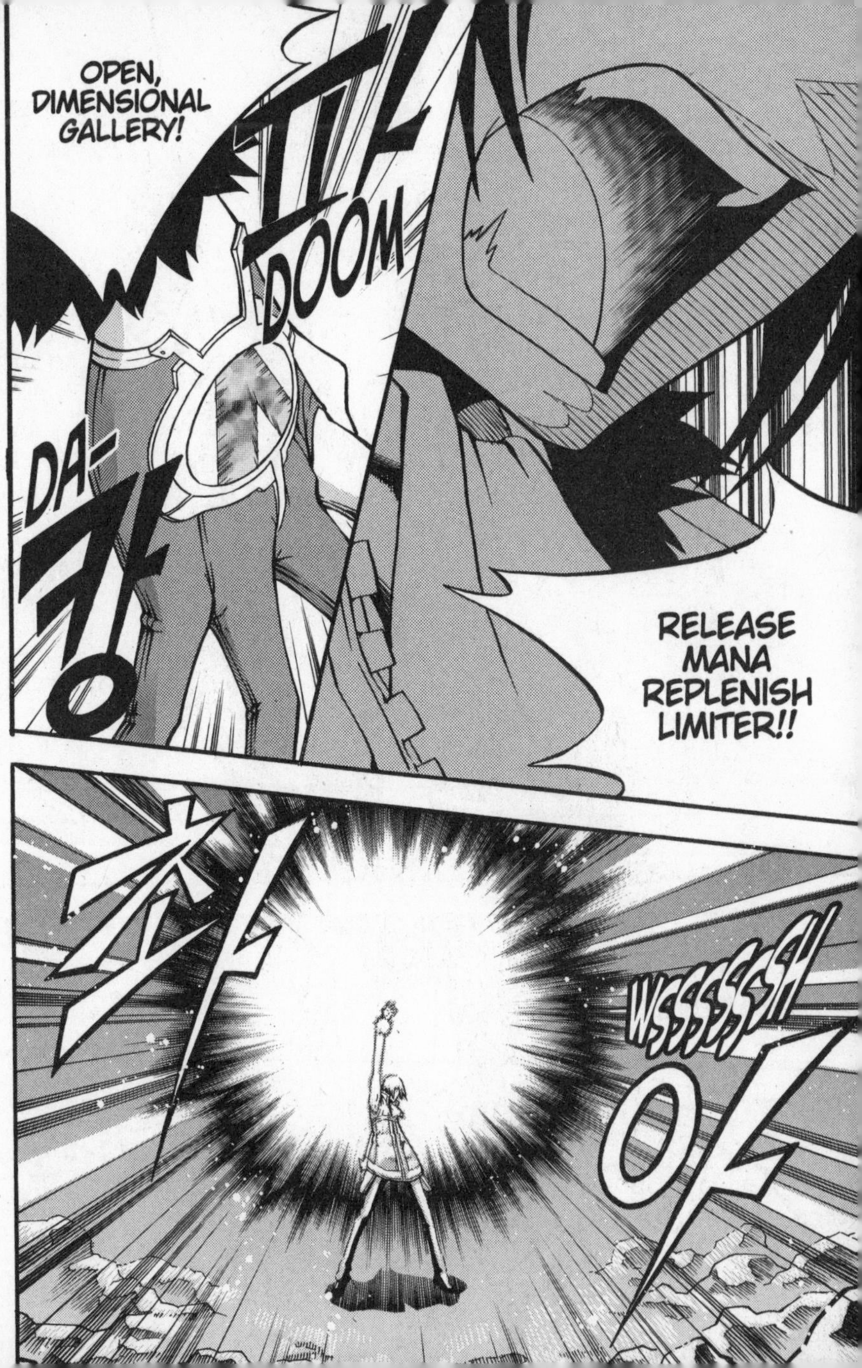
OPEN, DIMENSIONAL GALLERY!
DOOM
DA-
RELEASE MANA REPLENISH LIMITER!!
WSSSSSSH

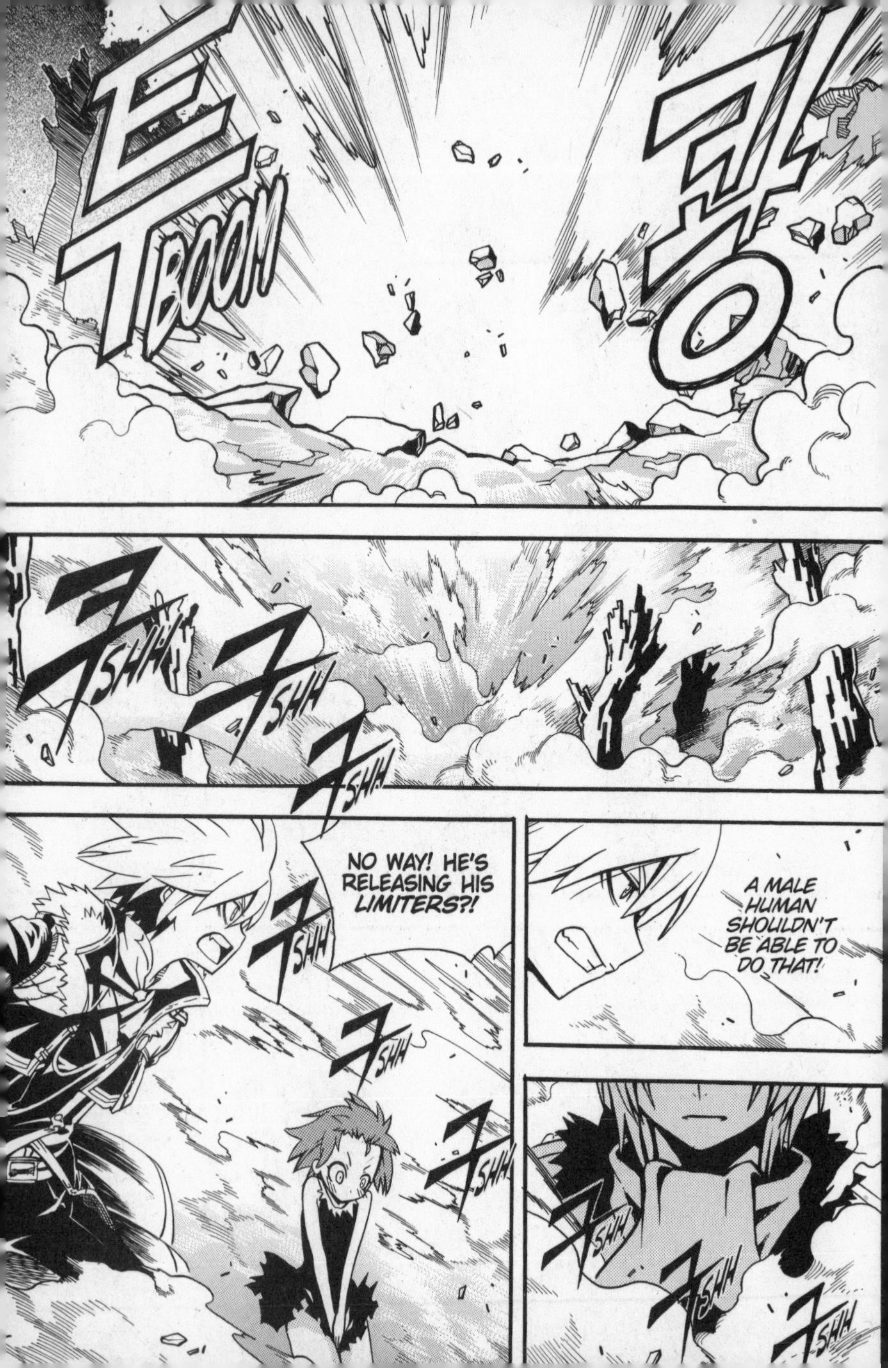

BOOM
SHH
SHH
SHH
NO WAY! HE'S RELEASING HIS LIMITERS?!
SHH
SHH
SHH
A MALE HUMAN SHOULDN'T BE ABLE TO DO THAT!
SHH
SHH
SHH

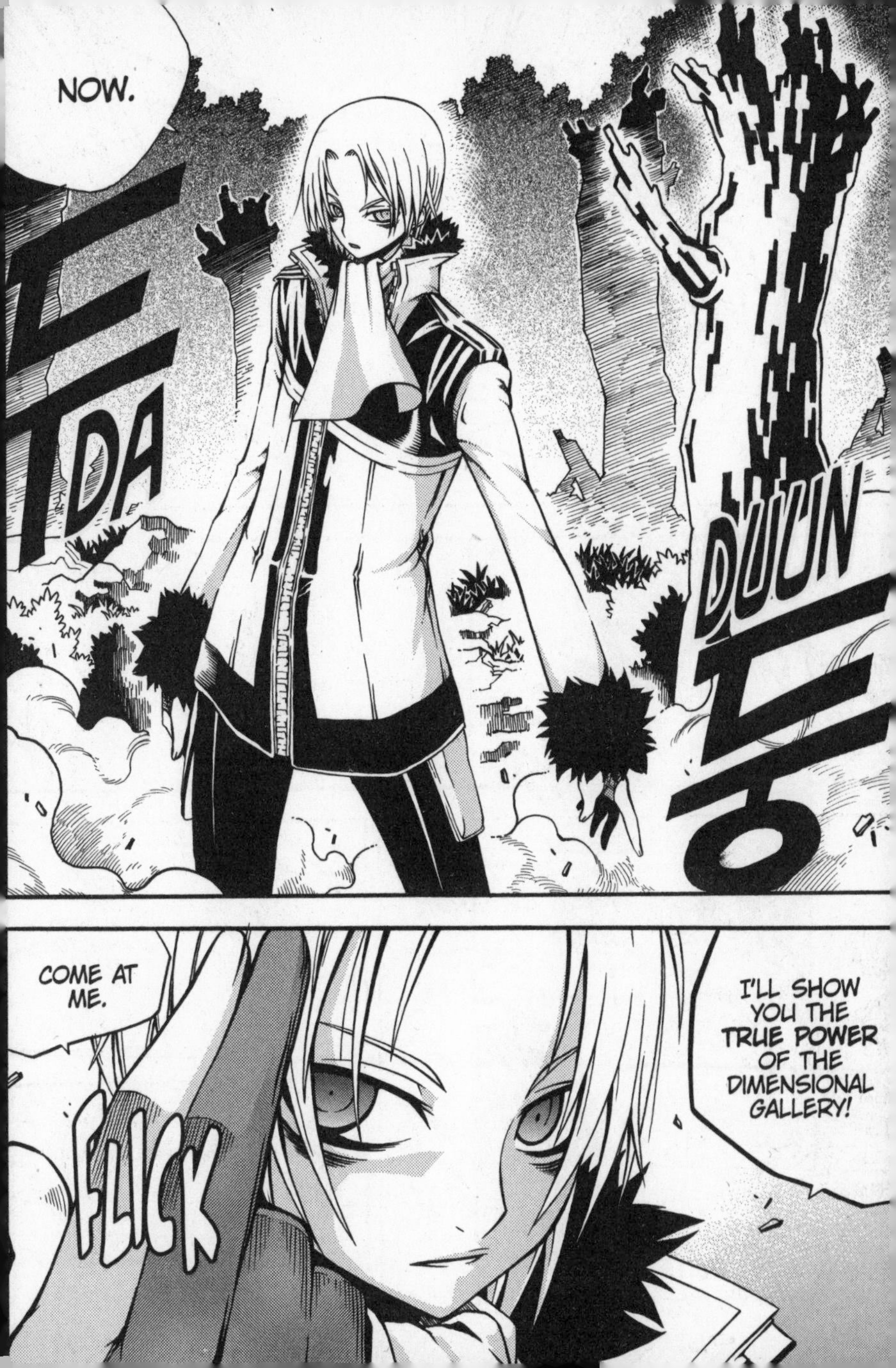
NOW.
DUUN
DA
I'LL SHOW YOU THE TRUE POWER OF THE DIMENSIONAL GALLERY!
COME AT ME.
FLICK

RIVAL [1]

FELICE FIDELIER, ASSIGNED TO COOGA.

THE CENTER CLASSIFIES MR. COOGA'S RELATIONSHIP WITH MR. TASHA AS A RIVALRY...

WHAT DO YOU THINK?

HA! THAT LOSER TASHA?

THEY THINK HE'S MY RIVAL? THAT'S FREAKIN' HILARIOUS. ANYWAY, DO THIS FOR ME.

A NEW UNIFORM REQUEST?

I DON'T WASTE MY TIME THINKING ABOUT SOMEBODY THAT FAR BENEATH ME.

SHOES

Shoes must be 6cm taller than Tasha's shoes.

RIGHT... YOU DON'T CARE ABOUT HIM AT ALL...

MANA IS POISON.

IT DESTROYS THE MIND AND BODY. THE ONLY ONES WHO CAN HANDLE IT ARE WITCHES--AND WITCHES ARE ALWAYS FEMALE.

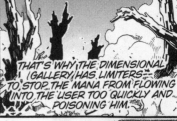

THAT'S WHY THE DIMENSIONAL GALLERY HAS LIMITERS-- TO STOP THE MANA FROM FLOWING INTO THE USER TOO QUICKLY AND POISONING HIM.

SO HOW THE HECK IS THIS GUY STILL OKAY, AFTER RELEASING THEM?!

HE'S CLEARLY NOT A FEMALE WITCH!

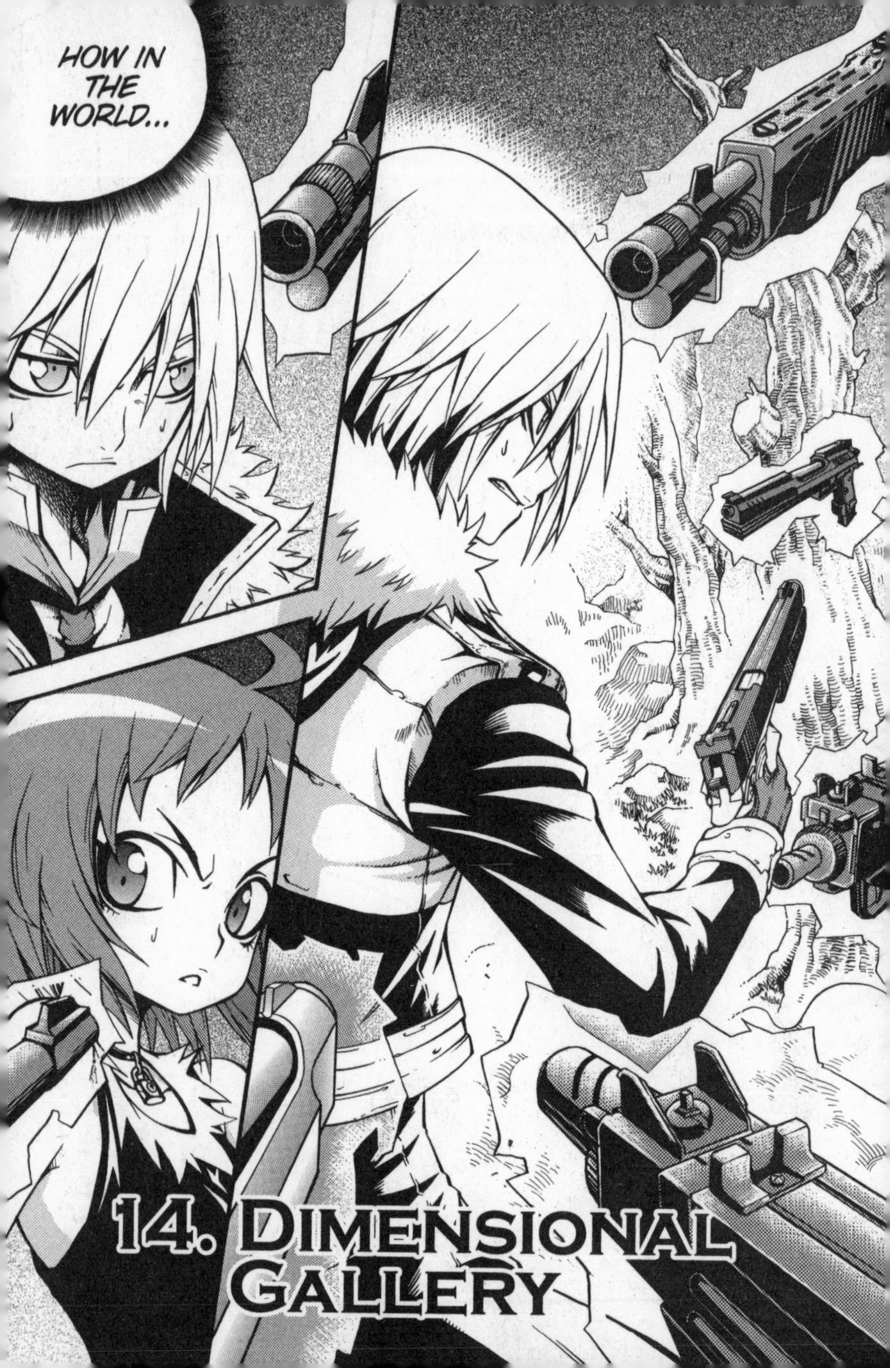
HOW IN THE WORLD...
14. DIMENSIONAL GALLERY

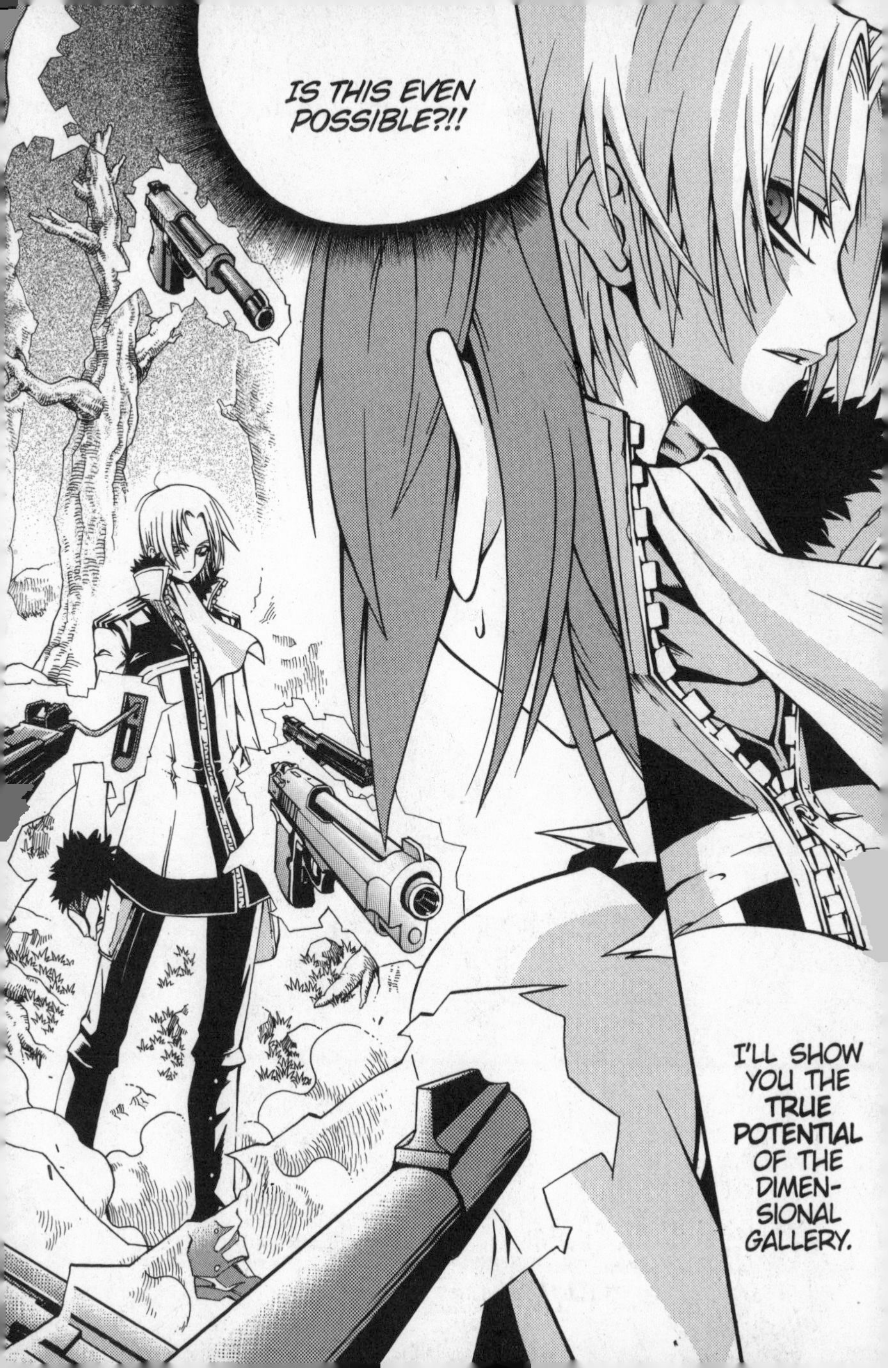
IS THIS EVEN POSSIBLE?!!
I'LL SHOW YOU THE TRUE POTENTIAL OF THE DIMEN-SIONAL GALLERY.

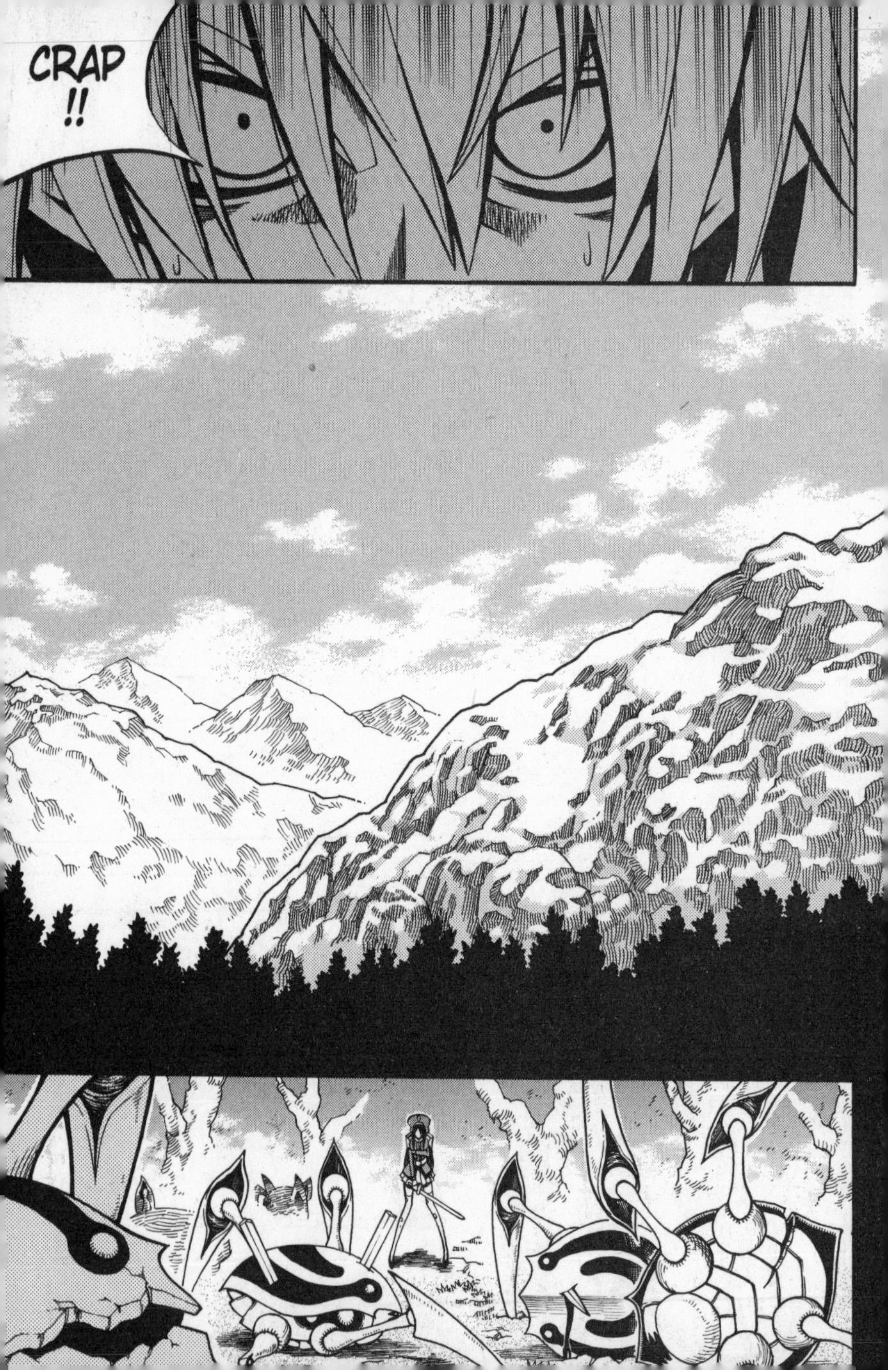
CRAP !!

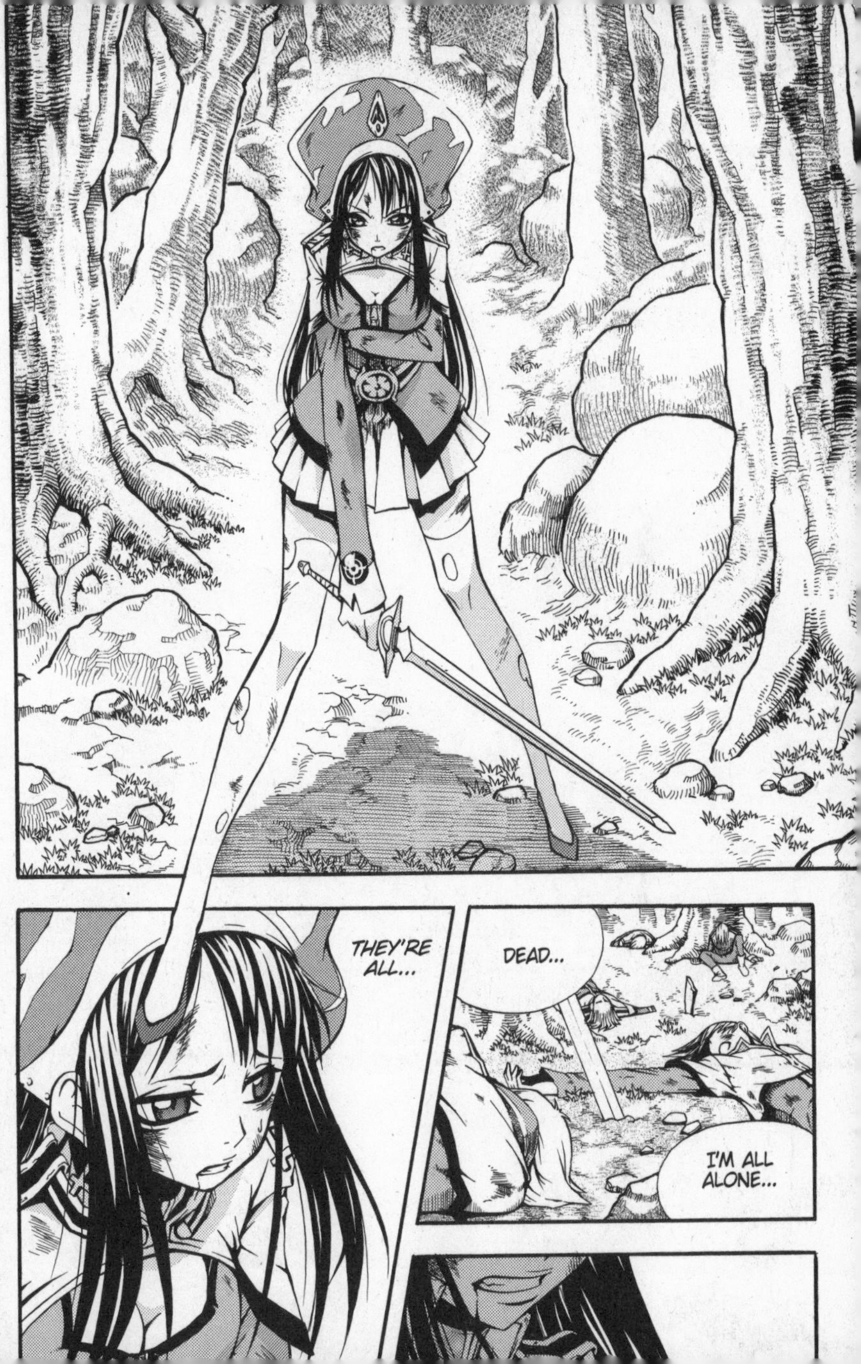
THEY'RE ALL...
DEAD...
I'M ALL ALONE...

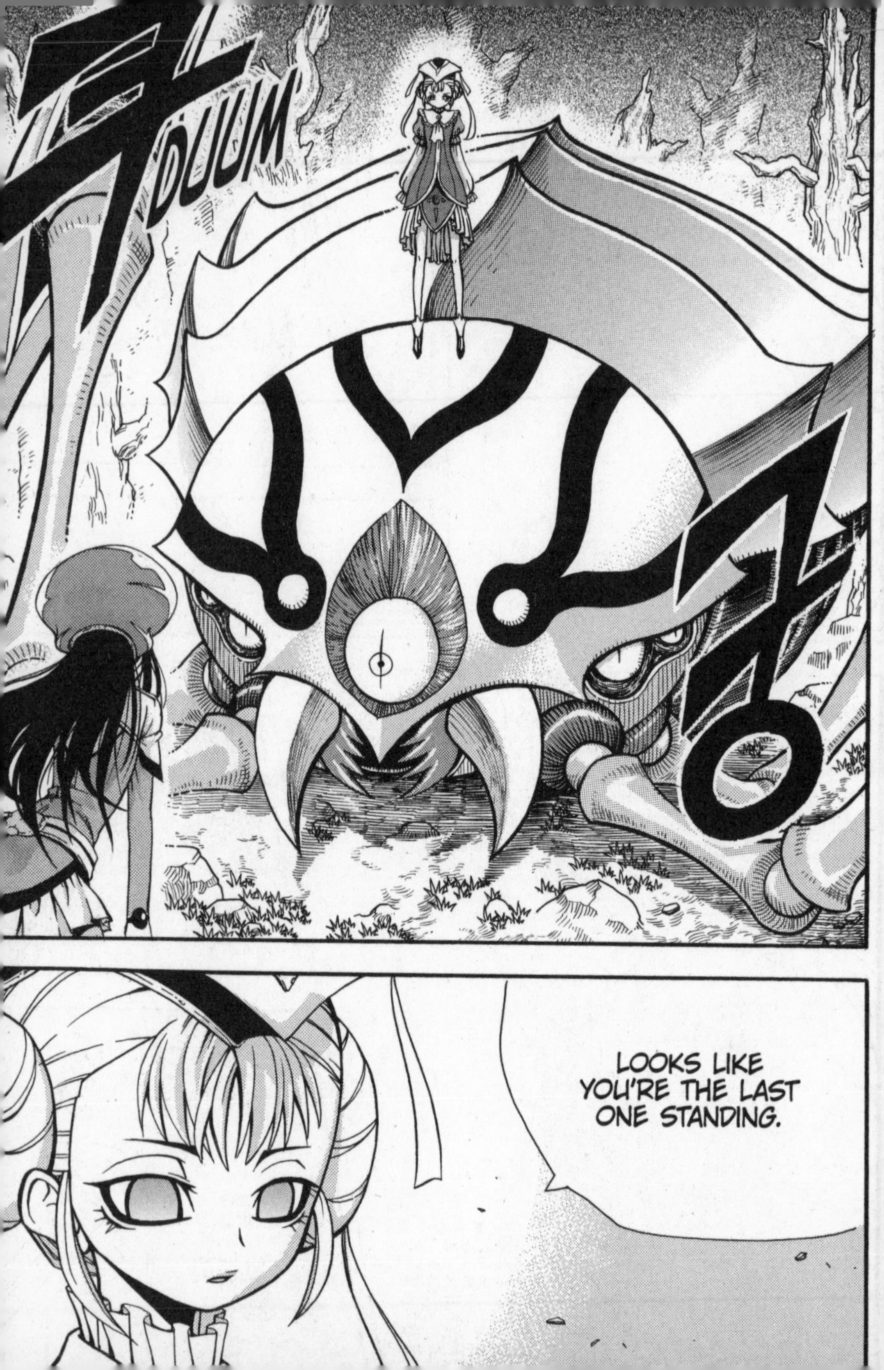
DUUM
LOOKS LIKE YOU'RE THE LAST ONE STANDING.

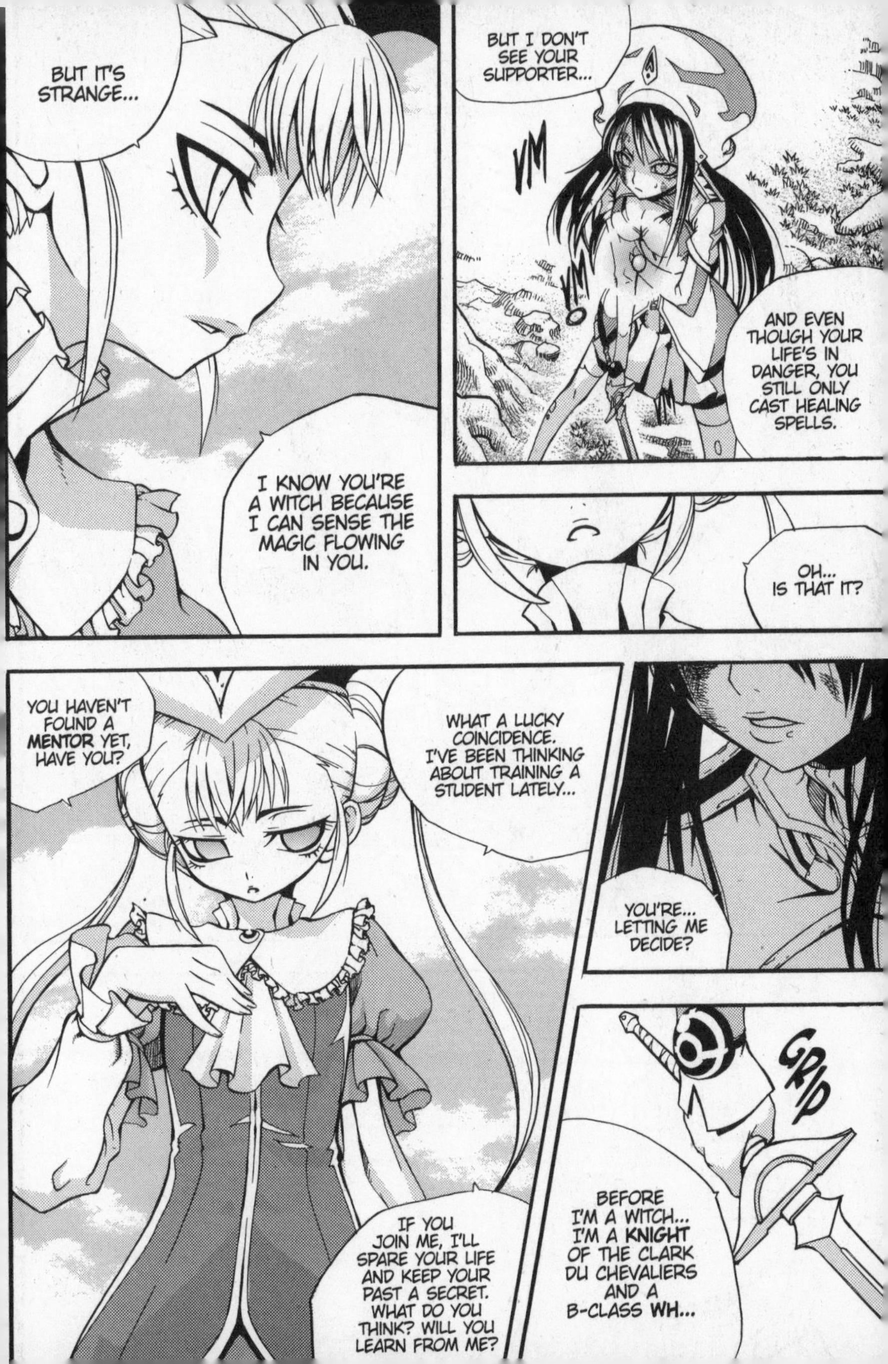
BUT IT'S STRANGE...
I KNOW YOU'RE A WITCH BECAUSE I CAN SENSE THE MAGIC FLOWING IN YOU.
BUT I DON'T SEE YOUR SUPPORTER...
VM
VM
AND EVEN THOUGH YOUR LIFE'S IN DANGER, YOU STILL ONLY CAST HEALING SPELLS.
OH... IS THAT IT?
YOU HAVEN'T FOUND A MENTOR YET, HAVE YOU?
WHAT A LUCKY COINCIDENCE. I'VE BEEN THINKING ABOUT TRAINING A STUDENT LATELY...
IF YOU JOIN ME, I'LL SPARE YOUR LIFE AND KEEP YOUR PAST A SECRET. WHAT DO YOU THINK? WILL YOU LEARN FROM ME?
YOU'RE... LETTING ME DECIDE?
GRIP
BEFORE I'M A WITCH... I'M A KNIGHT OF THE CLARK DU CHEVALIERS AND A B-CLASS WH...

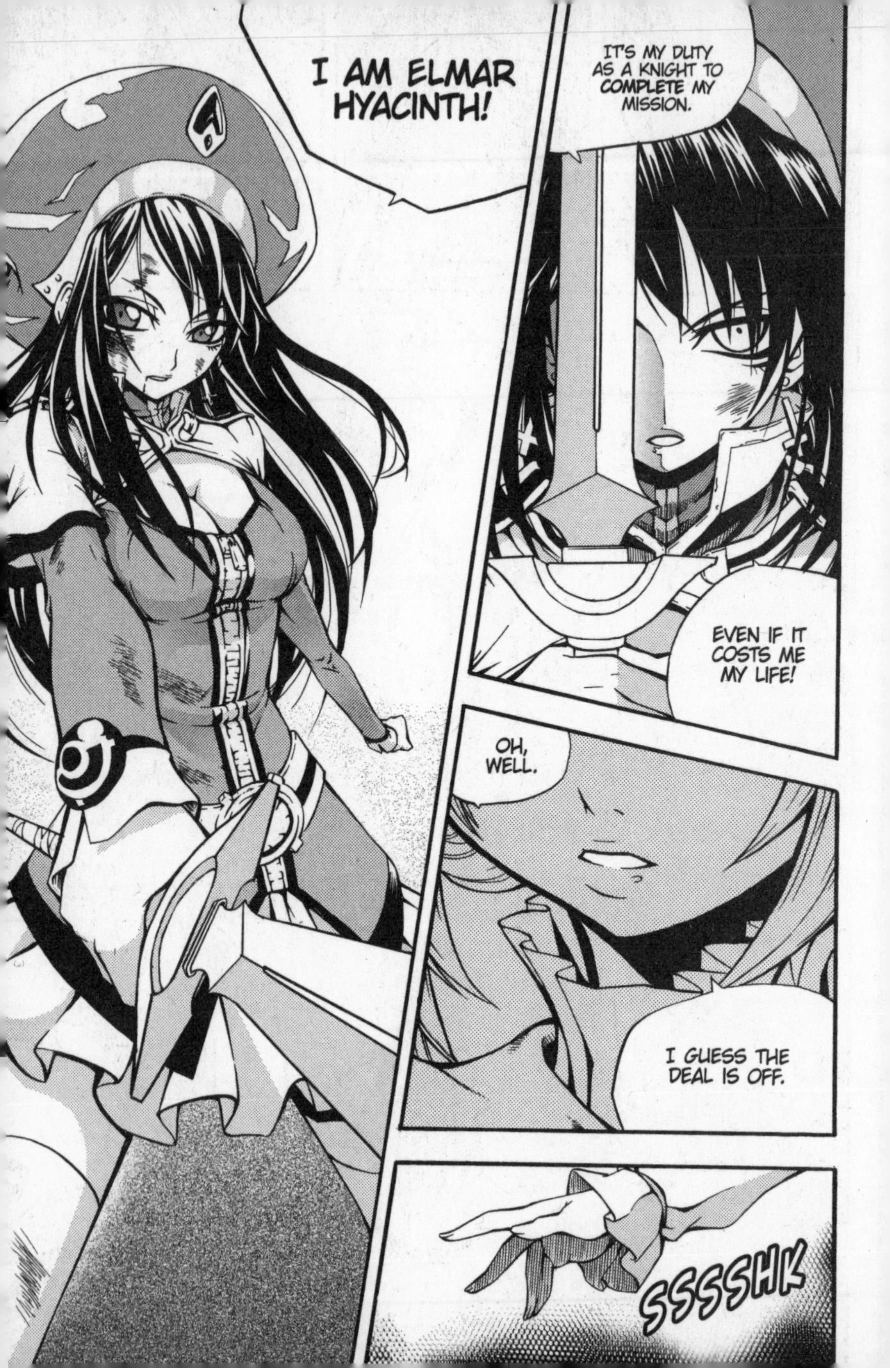
I AM ELMAR HYACINTH!
IT'S MY DUTY AS A KNIGHT TO COMPLETE MY MISSION.
EVEN IF IT COSTS ME MY LIFE!
OH, WELL.
I GUESS THE DEAL IS OFF.
SSSSHK

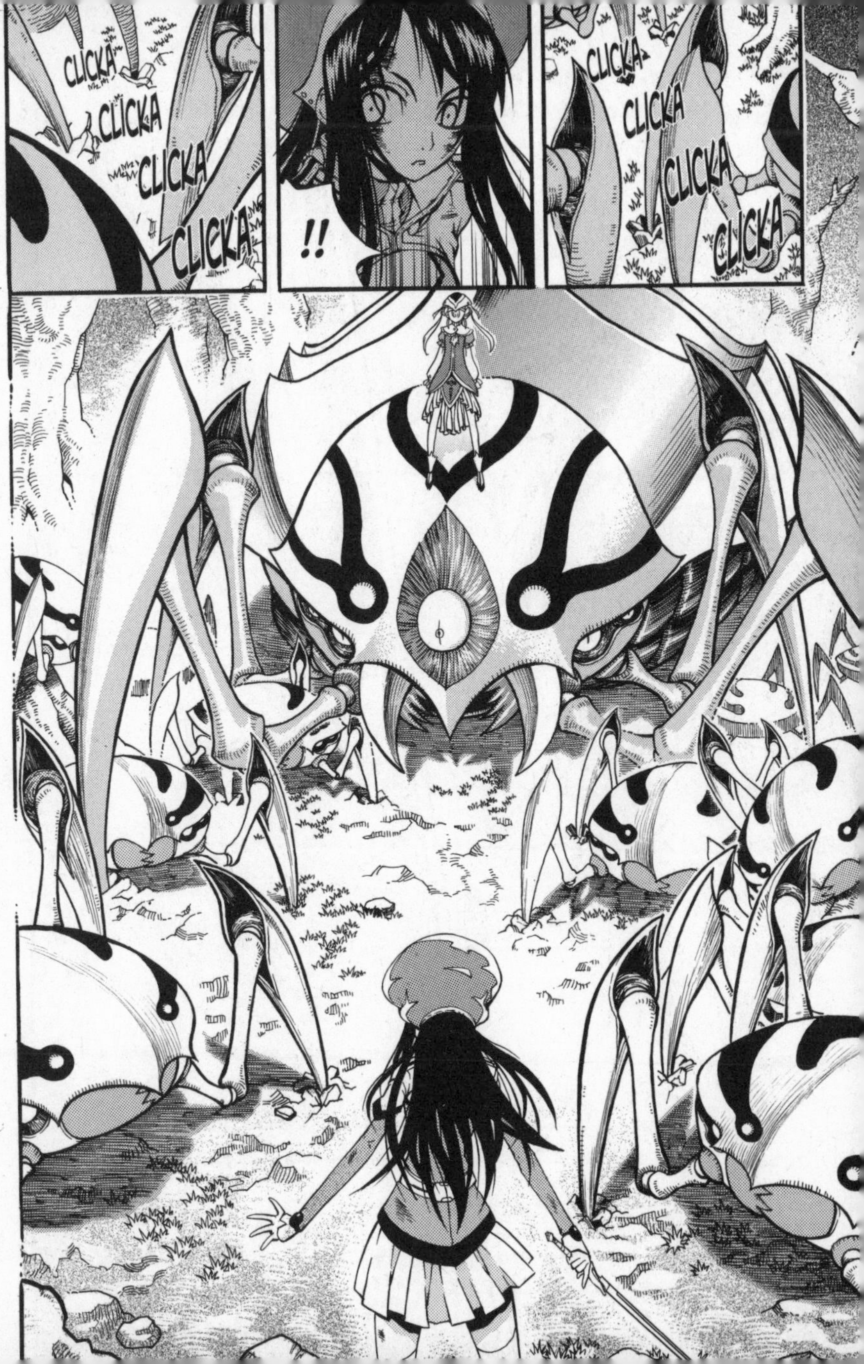
CLICKA
CLICKA
CLICKA
CLICKA
!!
CLICKA
CLICKA
CLICKA
CLICKA

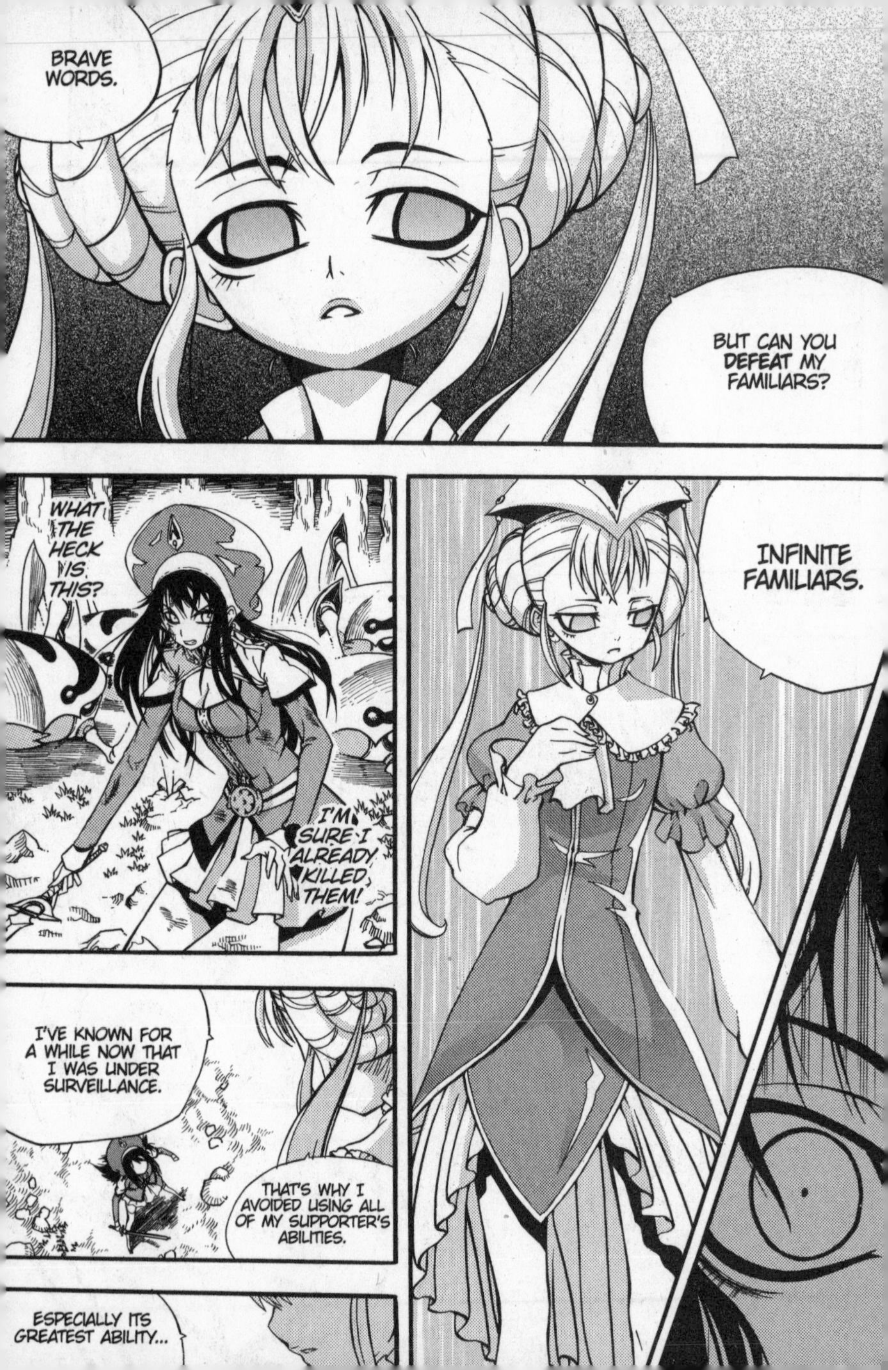
BRAVE WORDS.
BUT CAN YOU DEFEAT MY FAMILIARS?
WHAT THE HECK IS THIS?
I'M SURE I ALREADY KILLED THEM!
INFINITE FAMILIARS.
I'VE KNOWN FOR A WHILE NOW THAT I WAS UNDER SURVEILLANCE.
THAT'S WHY I AVOIDED USING ALL OF MY SUPPORTER'S ABILITIES.
ESPECIALLY ITS GREATEST ABILITY...

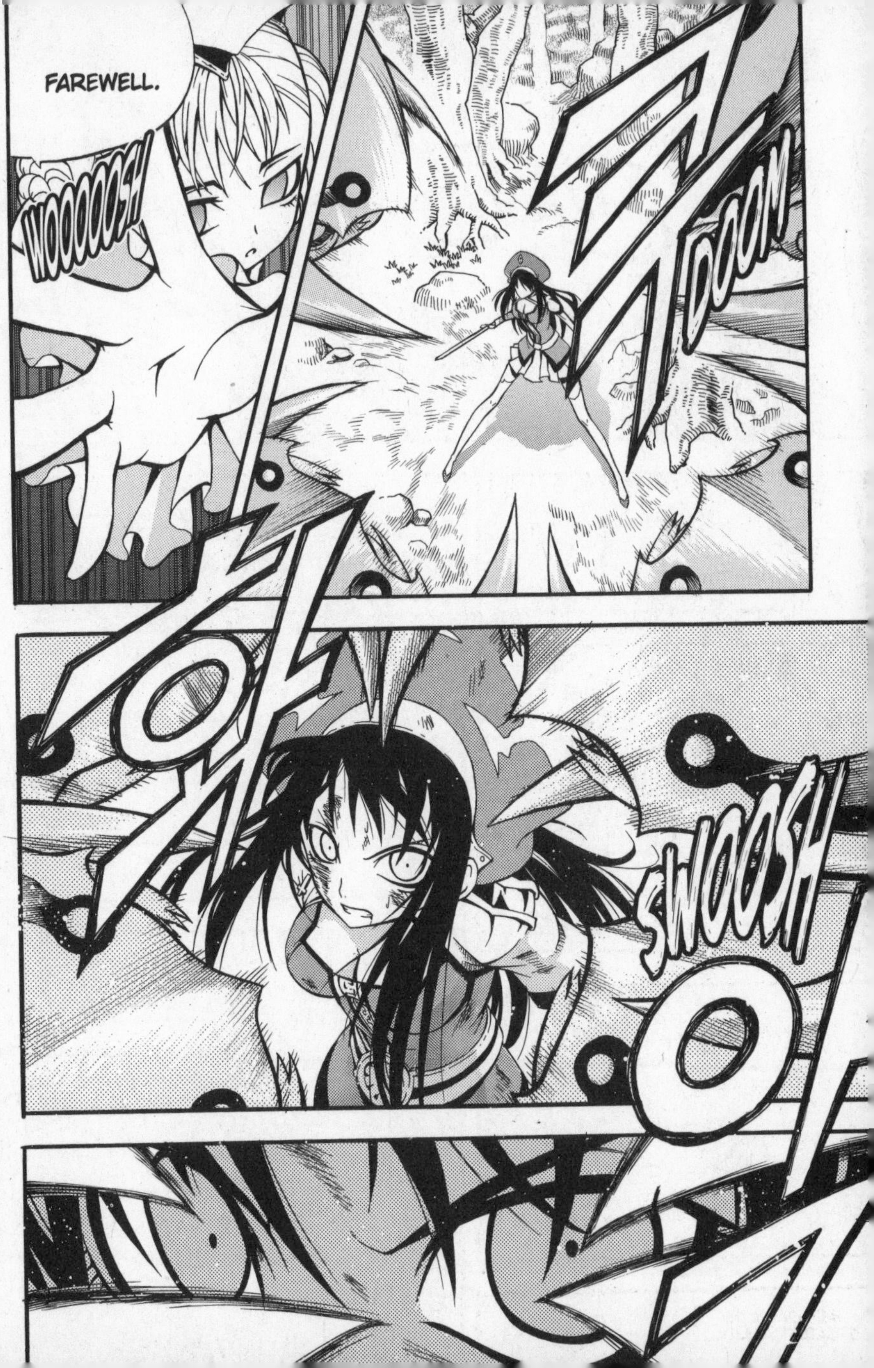
FAREWELL.
WOOOOOSH
DOOM
SWOOSH

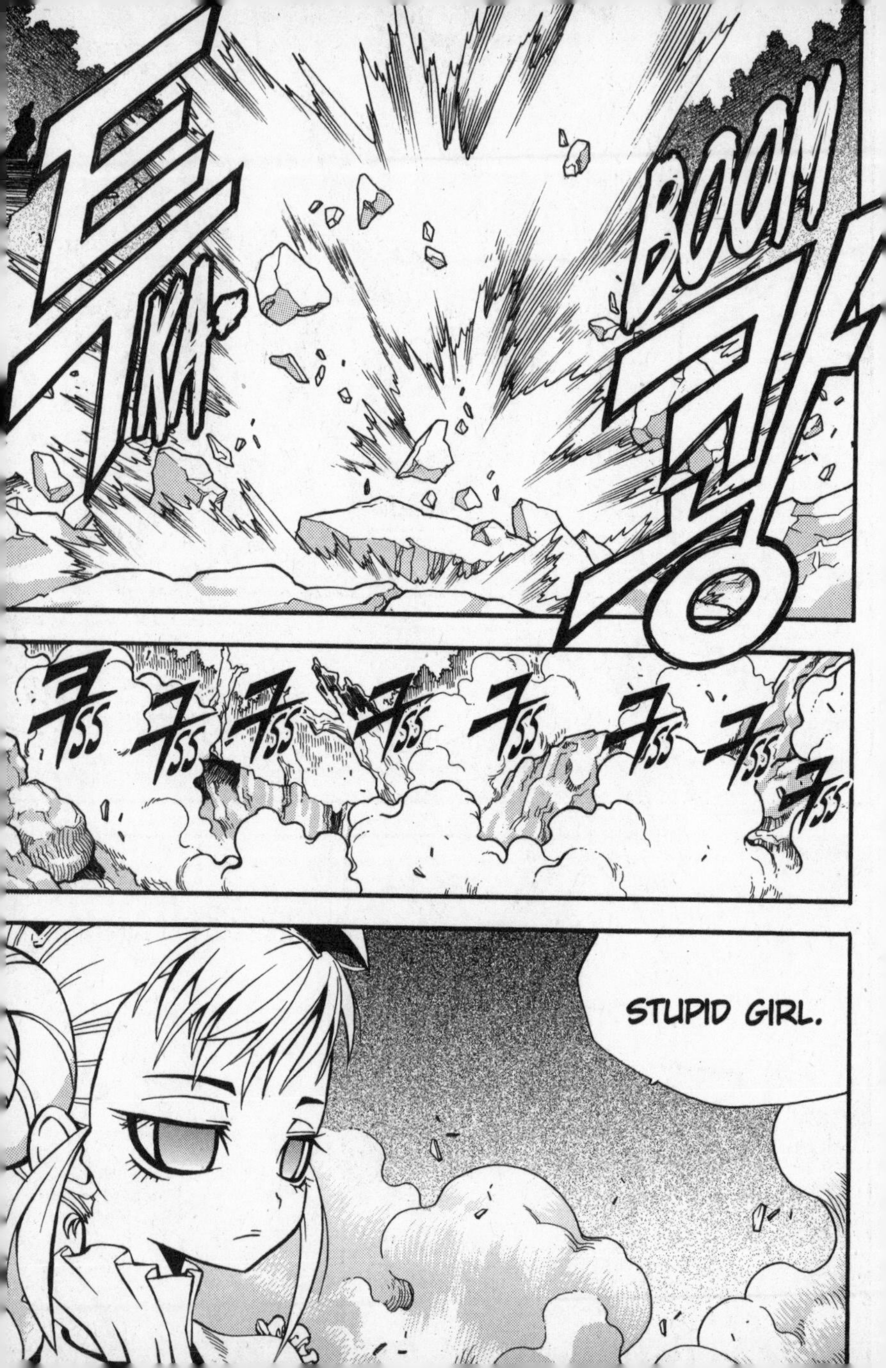
BOOM
STUPID GIRL.

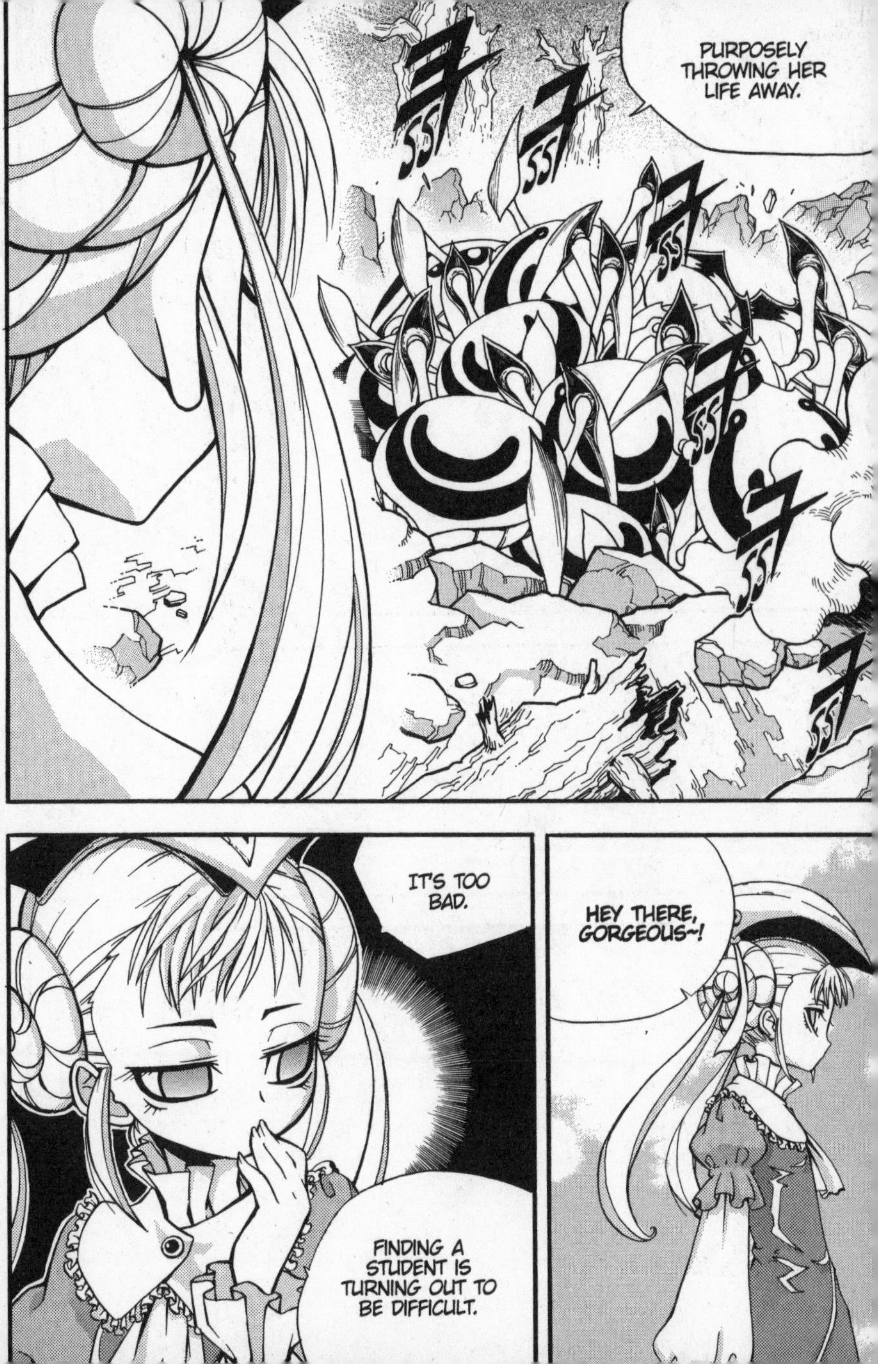
PURPOSELY THROWING HER LIFE AWAY.
HEY THERE, GORGEOUS~!
IT'S TOO BAD.
FINDING A STUDENT IS TURNING OUT TO BE DIFFICULT.

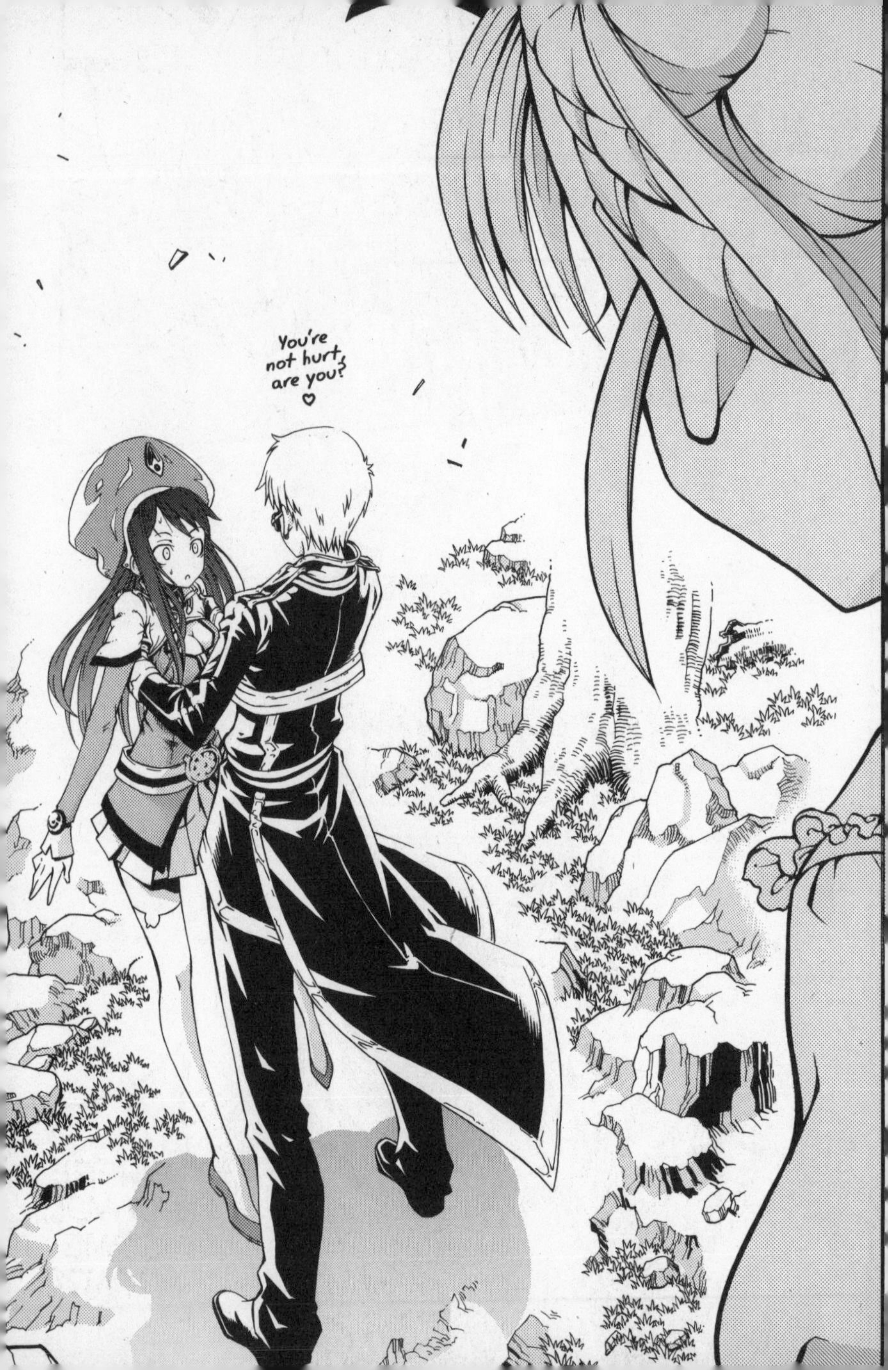
You're not hurt, are you? ♡

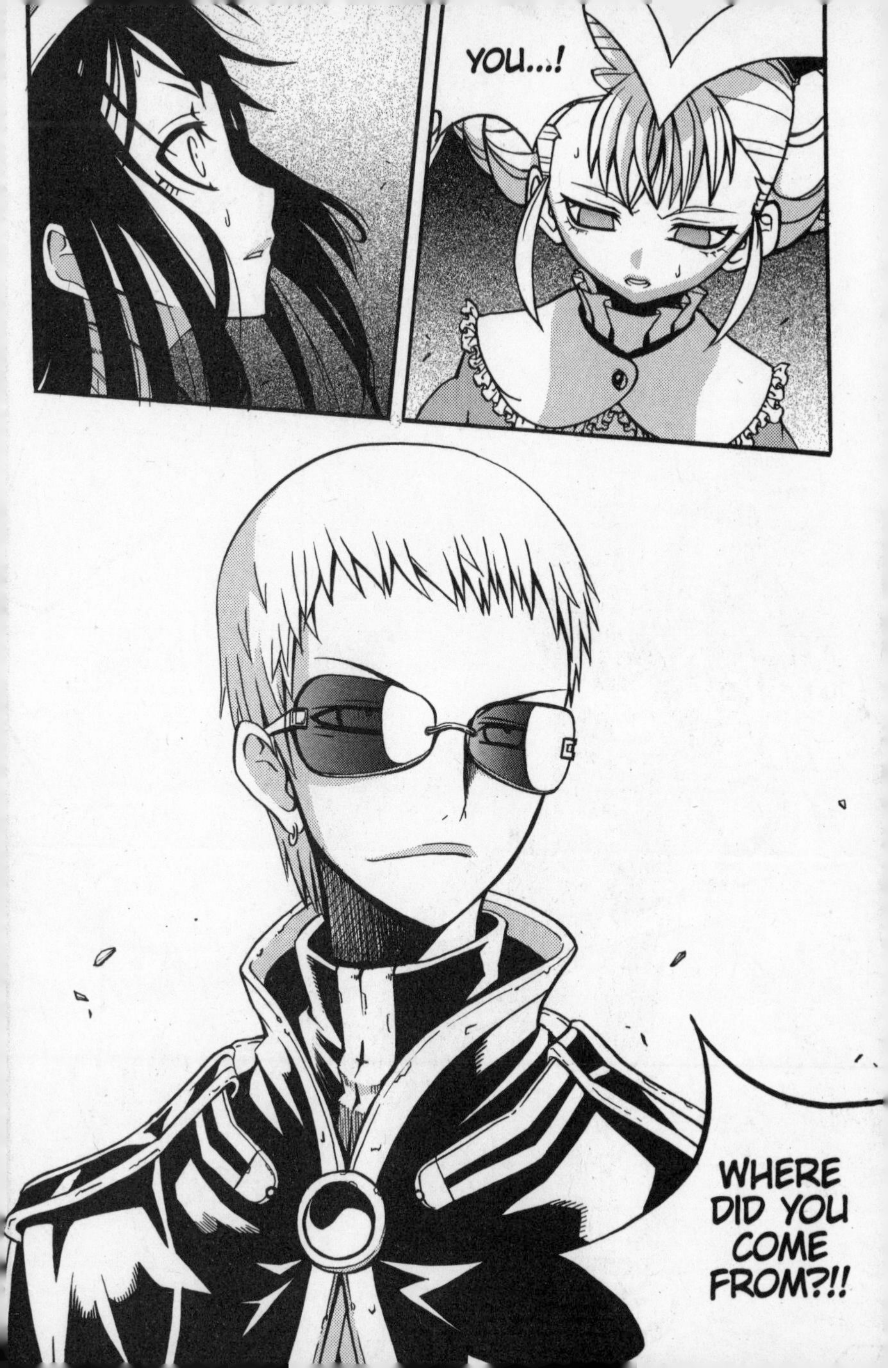
YOU...!
WHERE DID YOU COME FROM?!!

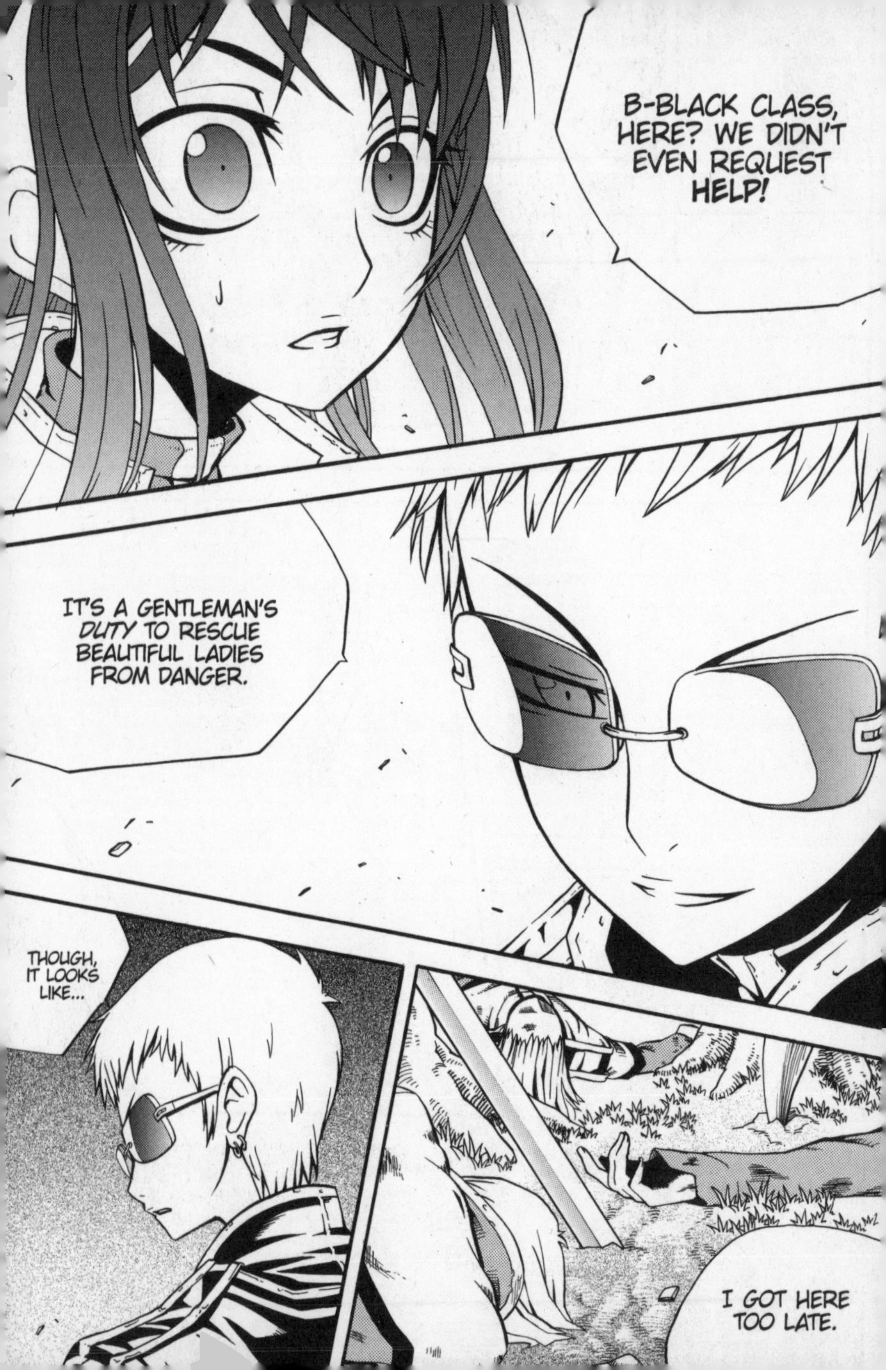

B-BLACK CLASS, HERE? WE DIDN'T EVEN REQUEST HELP!
IT'S A GENTLEMAN'S *DUTY* TO RESCUE BEAUTIFUL LADIES FROM DANGER.
THOUGH, IT LOOKS LIKE...
I GOT HERE TOO LATE.

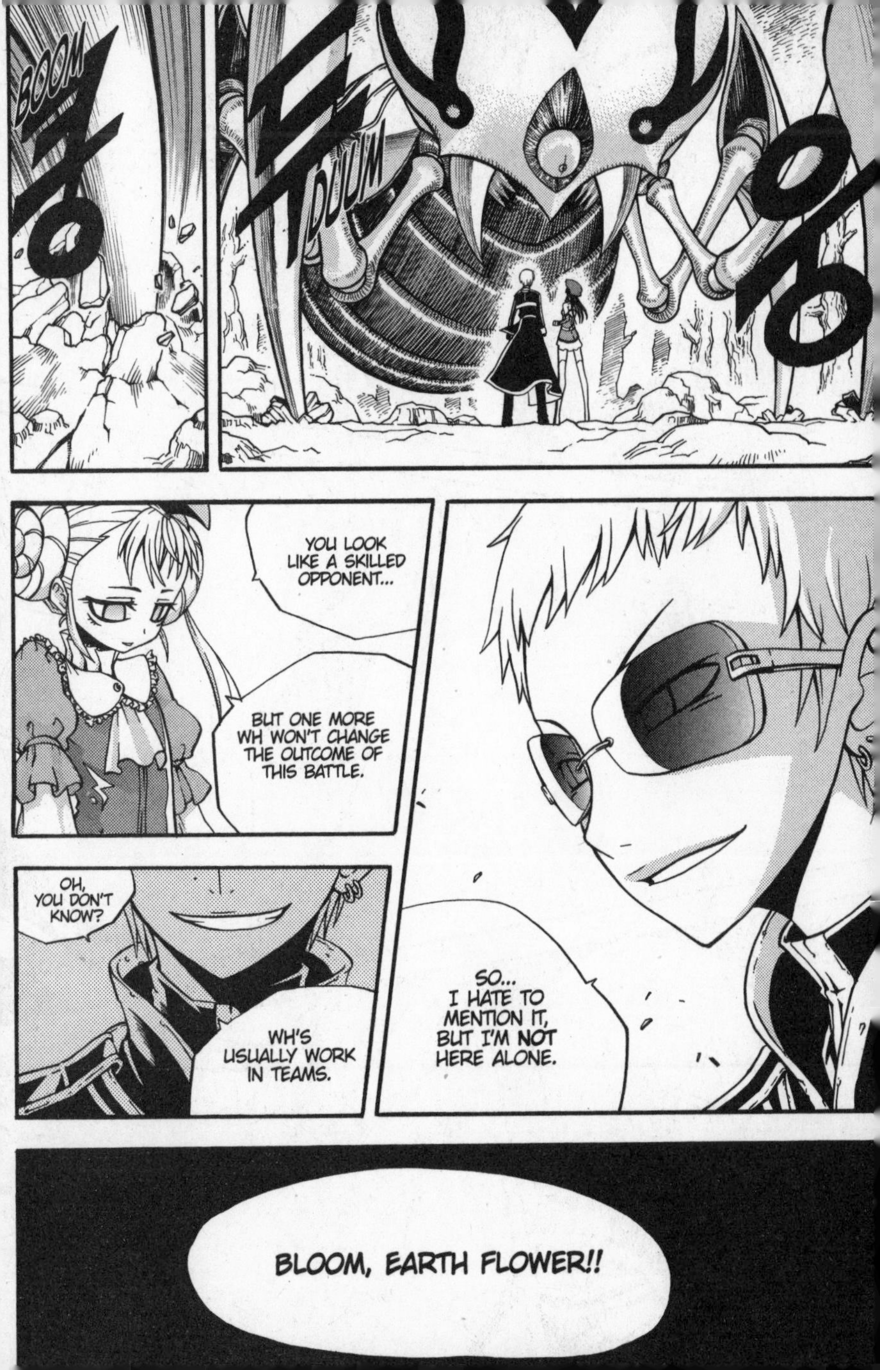
BOOM
DUUM
YOU LOOK LIKE A SKILLED OPPONENT...
BUT ONE MORE WH WON'T CHANGE THE OUTCOME OF THIS BATTLE.
OH, YOU DON'T KNOW?
WH'S USUALLY WORK IN TEAMS.
SO... I HATE TO MENTION IT, BUT I'M NOT HERE ALONE.
BLOOM, EARTH FLOWER!!

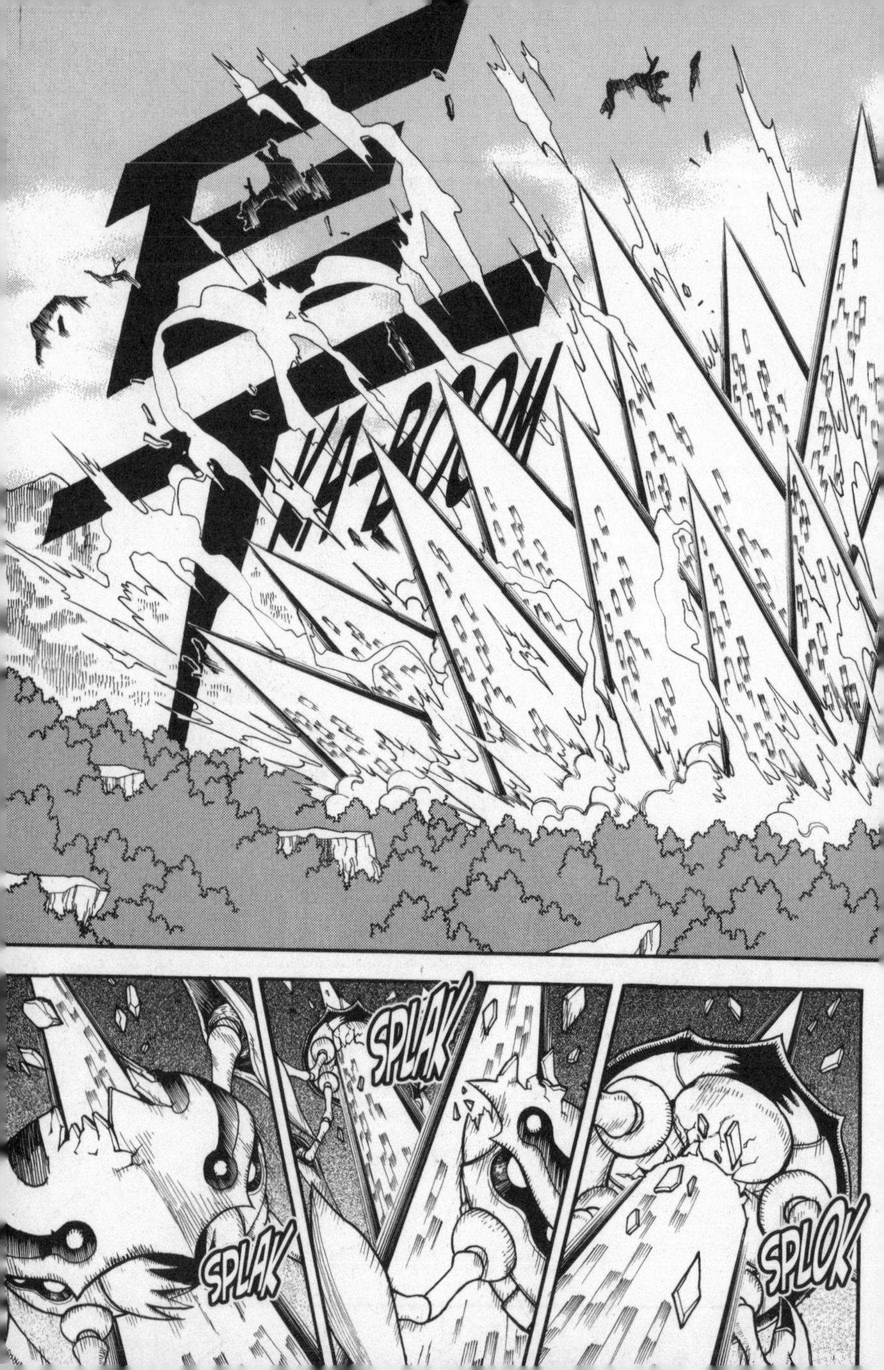
KA-BOOM
SPLAK
SPLAK
SPLOK

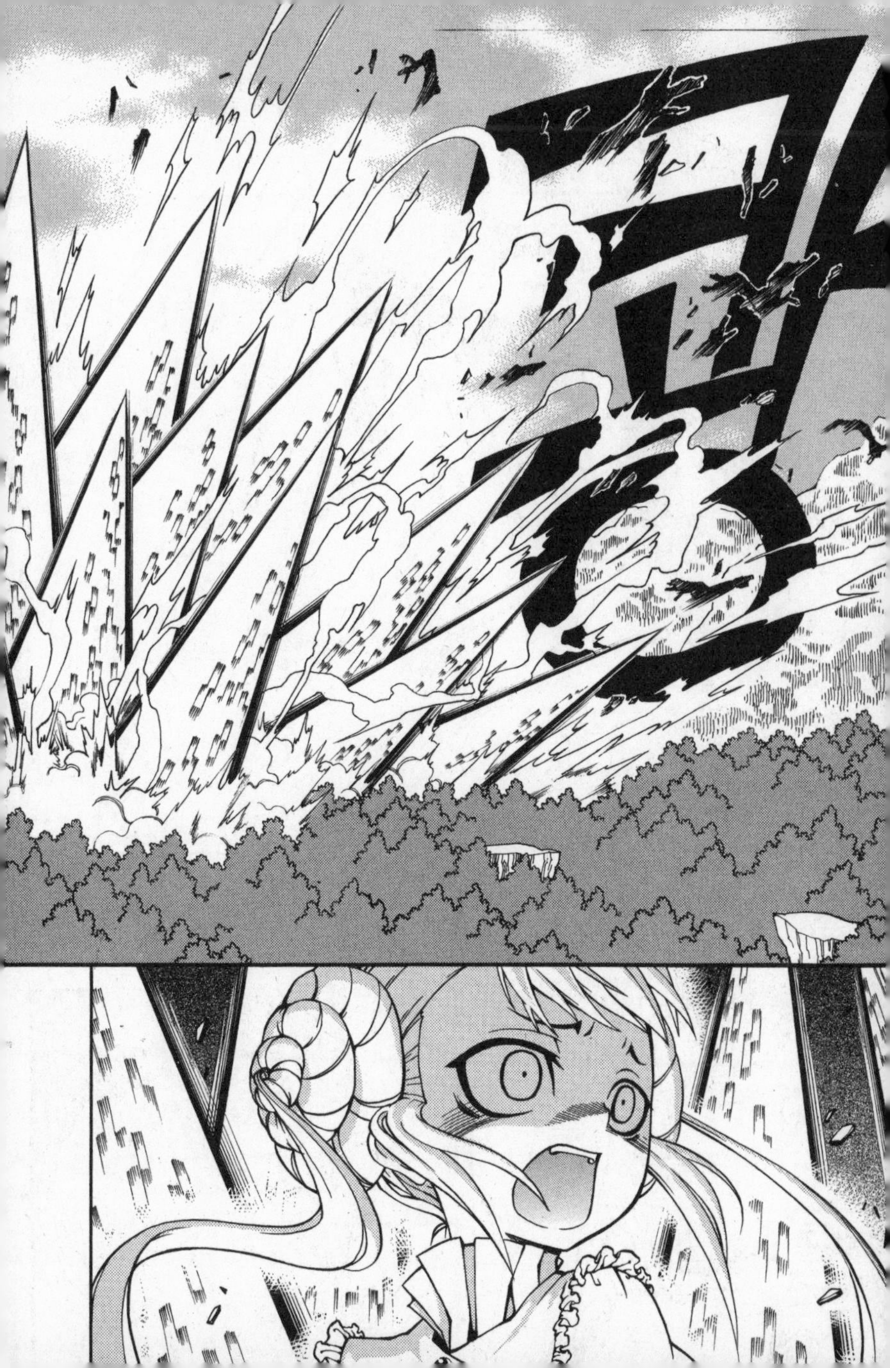

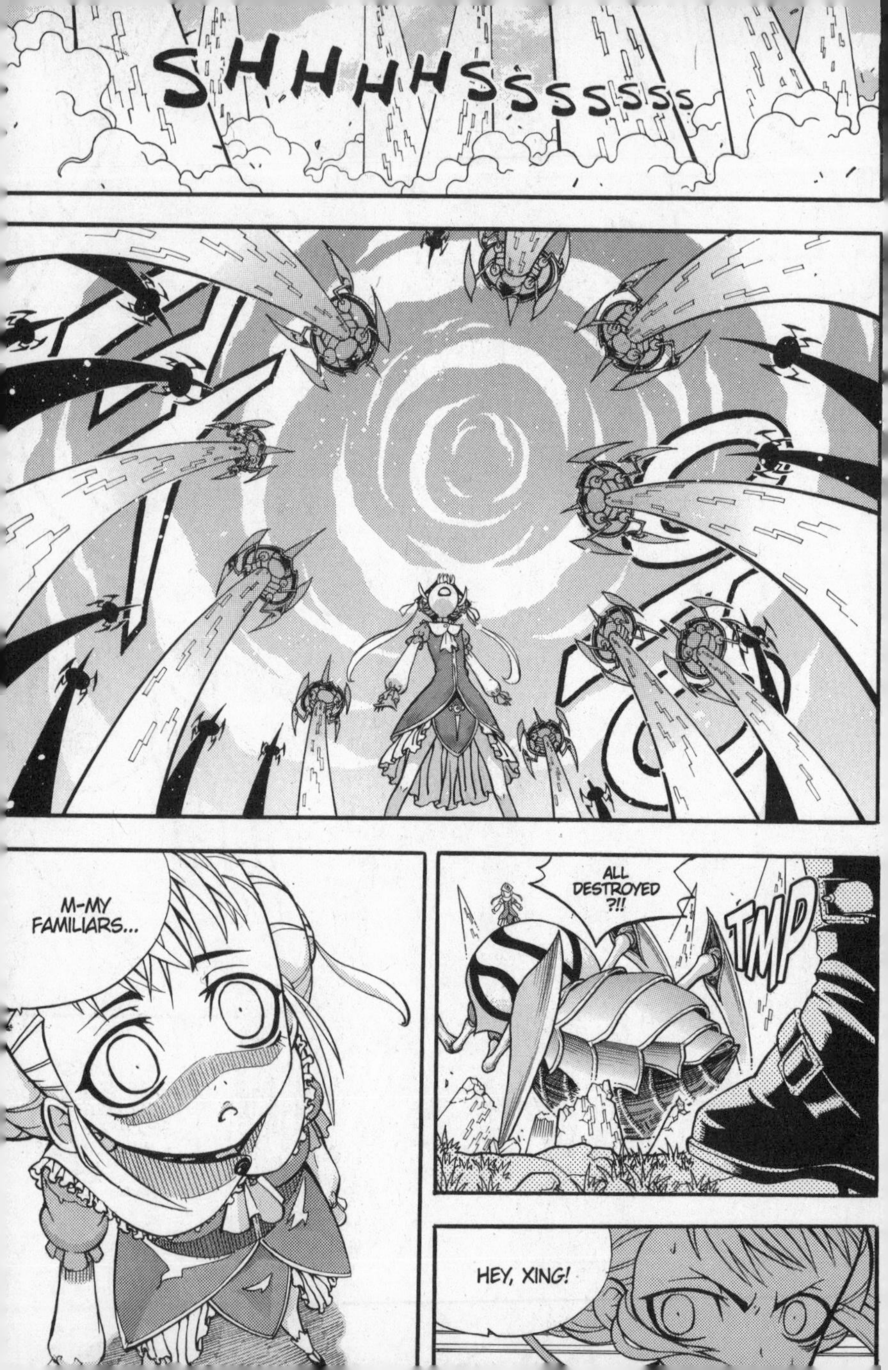
SHHHHSSSSSSSS
M-MY FAMILIARS...
ALL DESTROYED ?!!
TMP
HEY, XING!

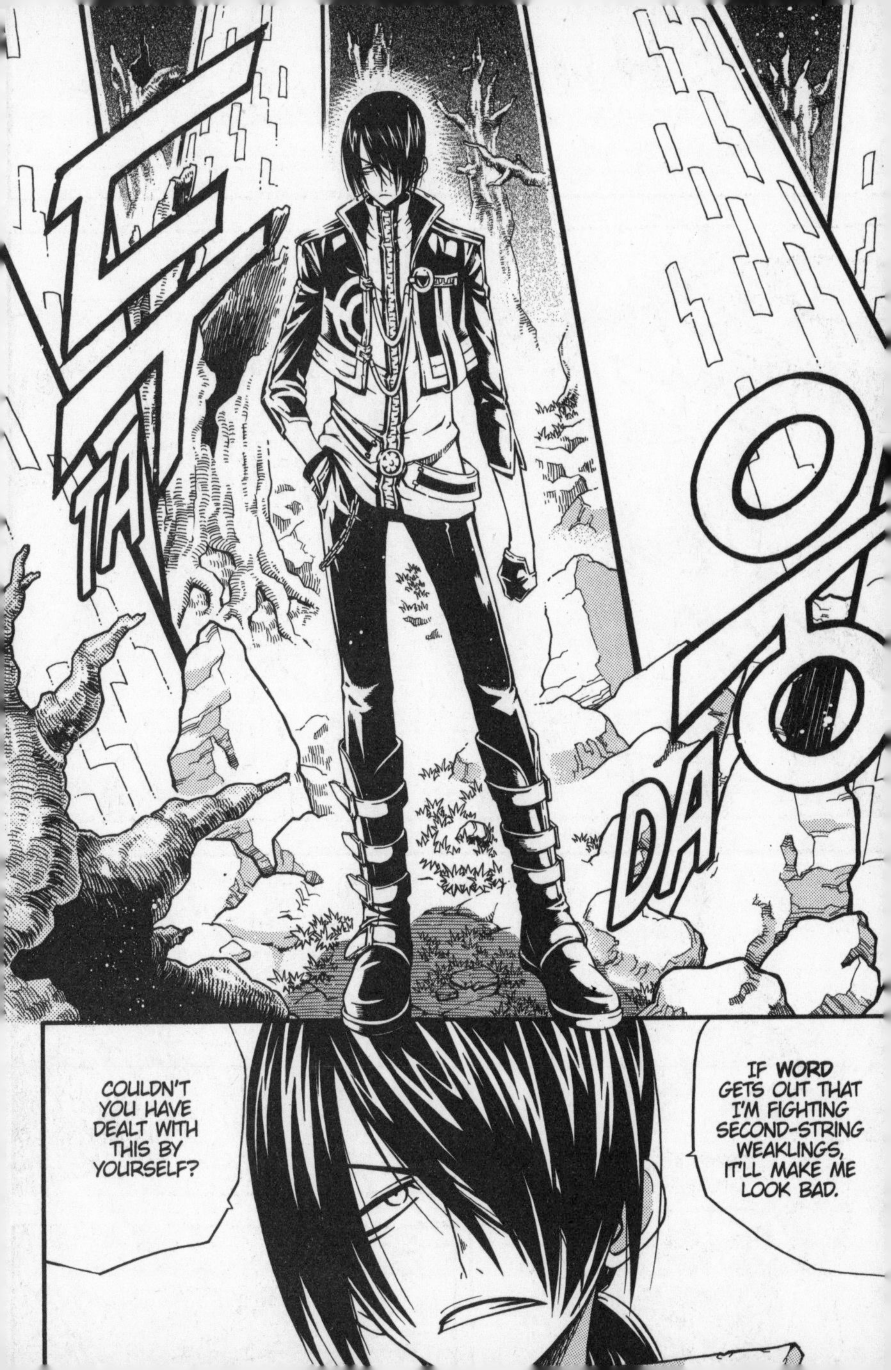

TA
DA
IF WORD GETS OUT THAT I'M FIGHTING SECOND-STRING WEAKLINGS, IT'LL MAKE ME LOOK BAD.
COULDN'T YOU HAVE DEALT WITH THIS BY YOURSELF?

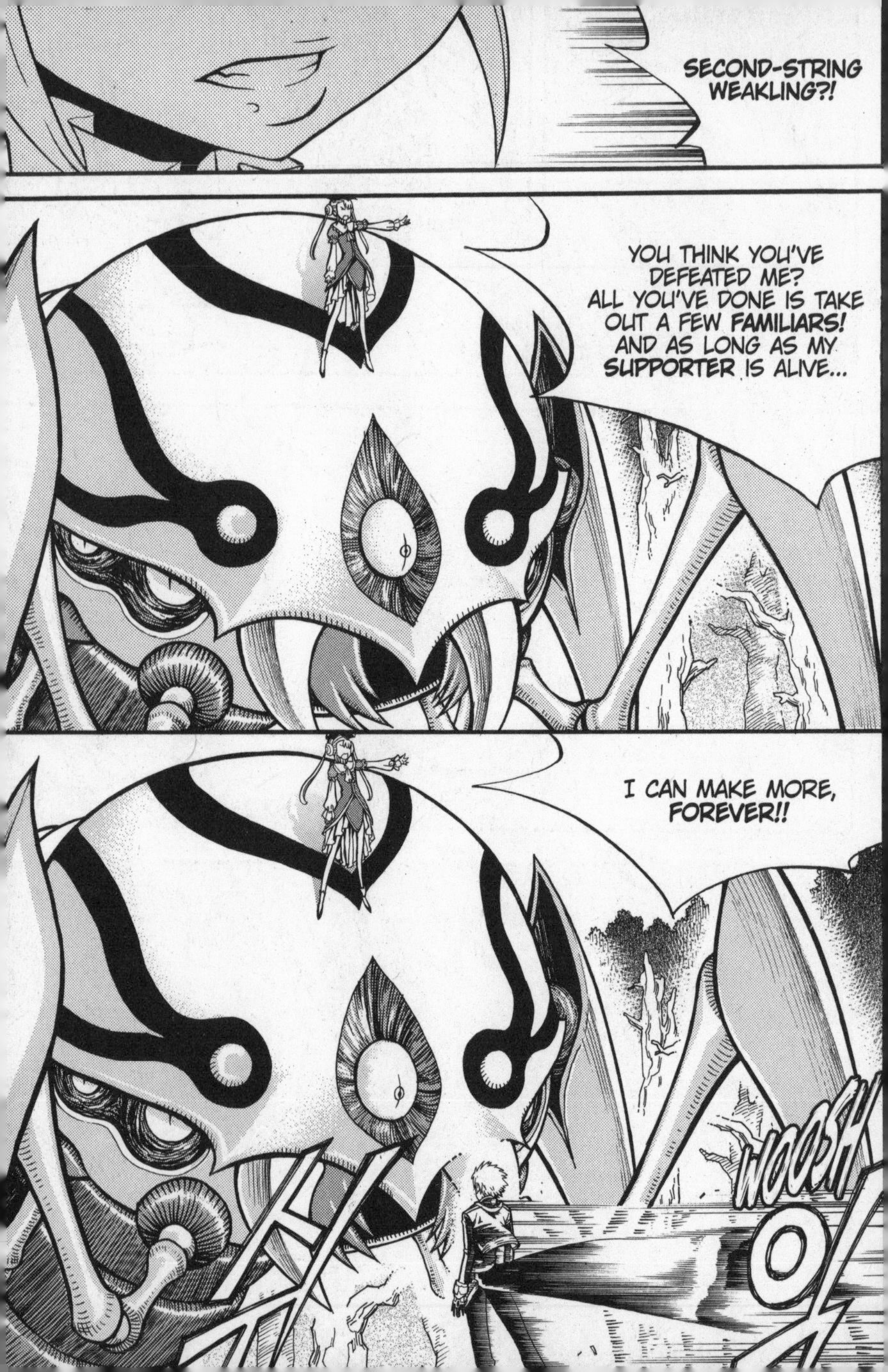
SECOND-STRING WEAKLING?!
YOU THINK YOU'VE DEFEATED ME? ALL YOU'VE DONE IS TAKE OUT A FEW FAMILIARS! AND AS LONG AS MY SUPPORTER IS ALIVE...
I CAN MAKE MORE, FOREVER!!
WOOSH

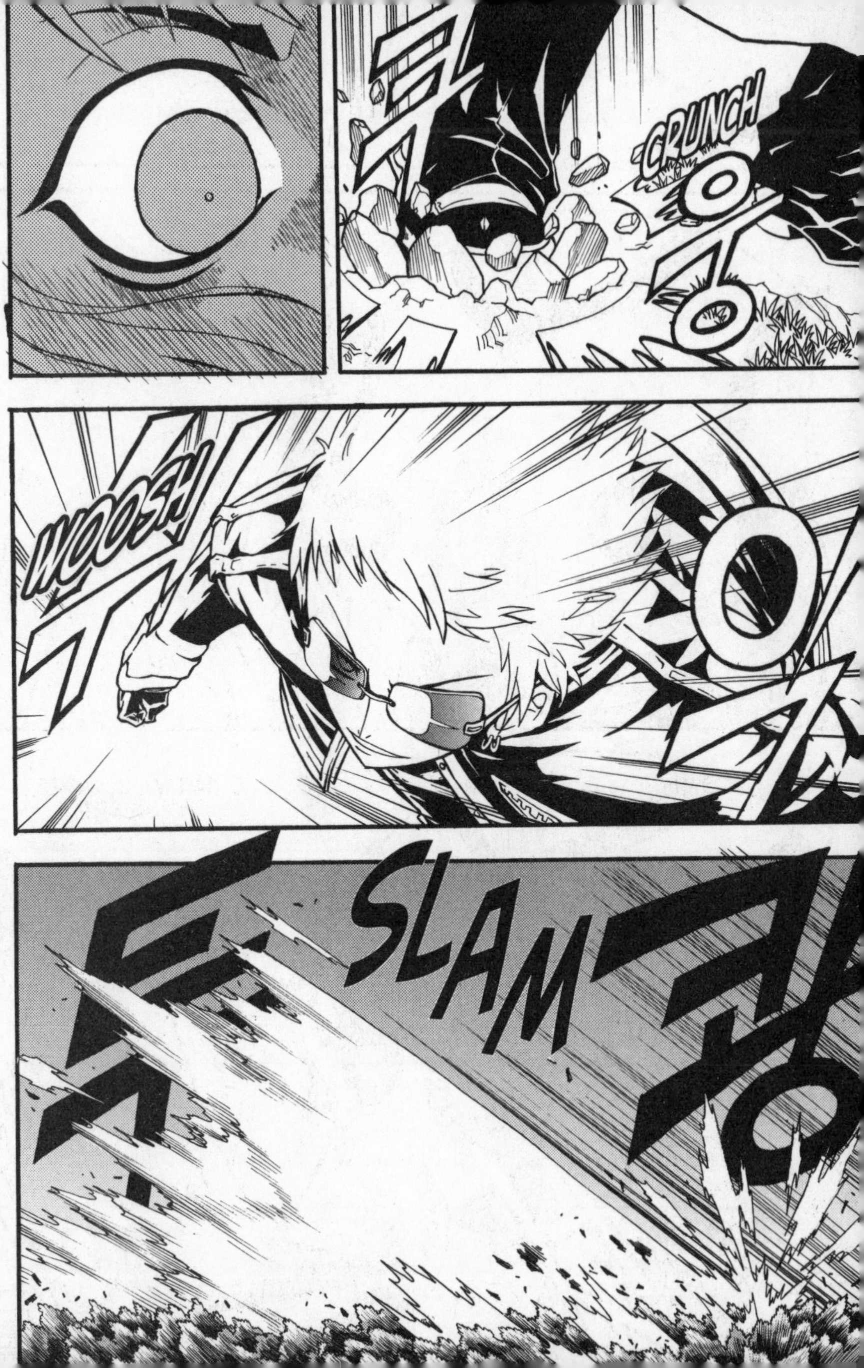
CRUNCH
WOOSH
SLAM

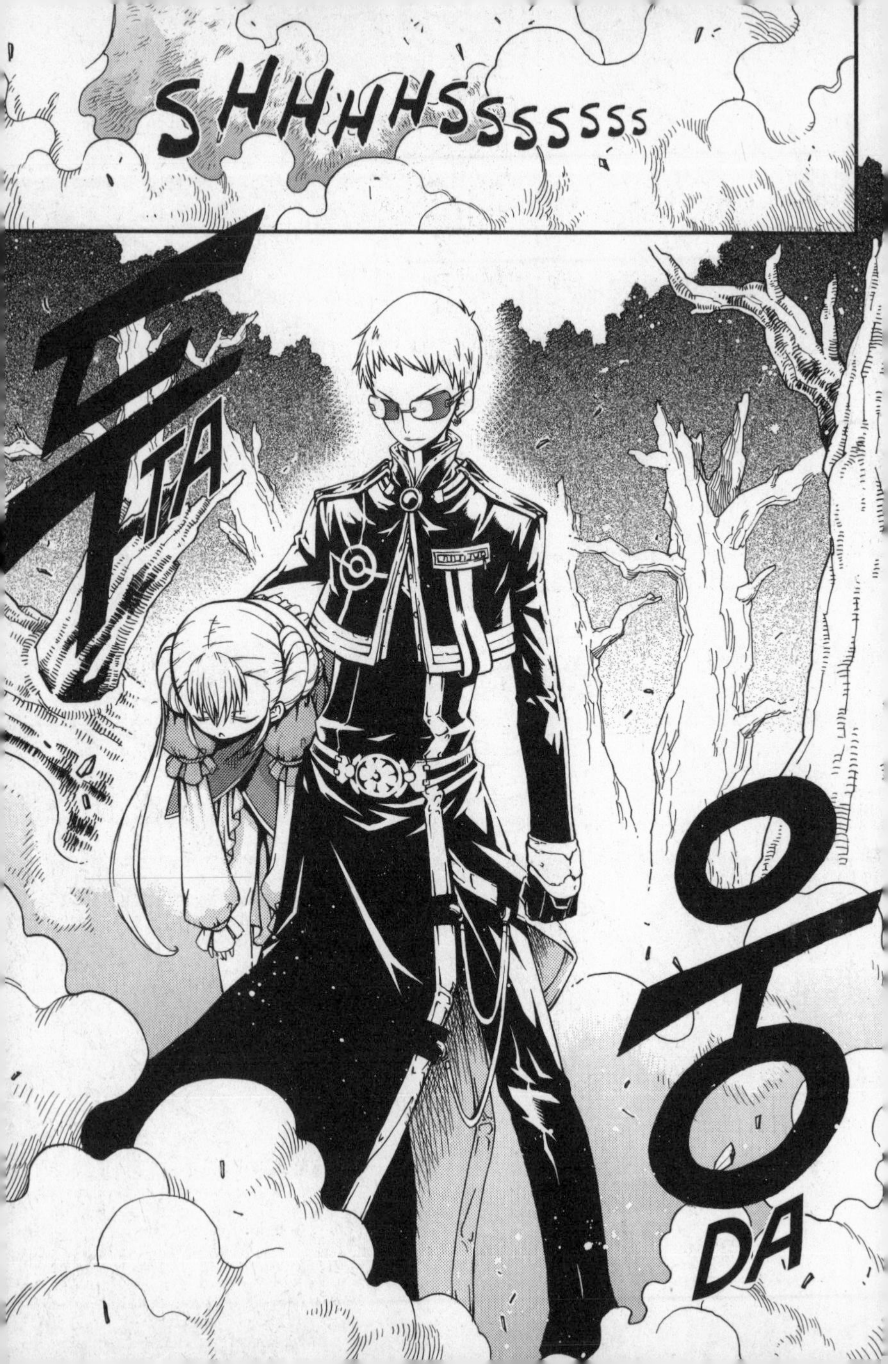
SHHHHSSSSSSS
TA
DA

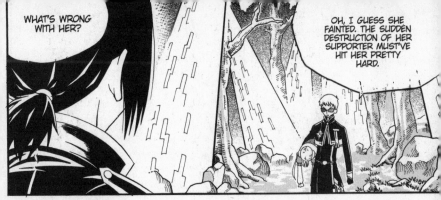

WHAT'S WRONG WITH HER?

OH, I GUESS SHE FAINTED. THE SUDDEN DESTRUCTION OF HER SUPPORTER MUST'VE HIT HER PRETTY HARD.

GOOD. NOW, HURRY AND TRANSFER HER SO WE CAN GET OUT OF HERE.

UGH, WHY IS A GREAT WH LIKE ME STUCK DOING THESE CRAPPY MISSIONS? THIS ISN'T EVEN WITCH HUNTING.

I KNOW I HAVE TO TRANSFER HER, YOU CAN KEEP YOUR IDIOTIC COMMENTS TO YOURSELF.

IF IT WEREN'T FOR THE ORDERS FROM WHITE CLASS WH VIHYUNGRANG, NOBODY WOULD EVER TEAM UP WITH YOU.

WHAT WAS THAT?!

A GUY LIKE YOU SHOULD BE HONORED TO TEAM UP WITH SOMEONE AS GLORIOUS AS ME!

WHAT'S SO GREAT ABOUT TEAMING UP WITH ANOTHER GUY?

And not even Tasha...

INCREDIBLE...

THIS IS THE POWER OF THE BLACK A-CLASS.

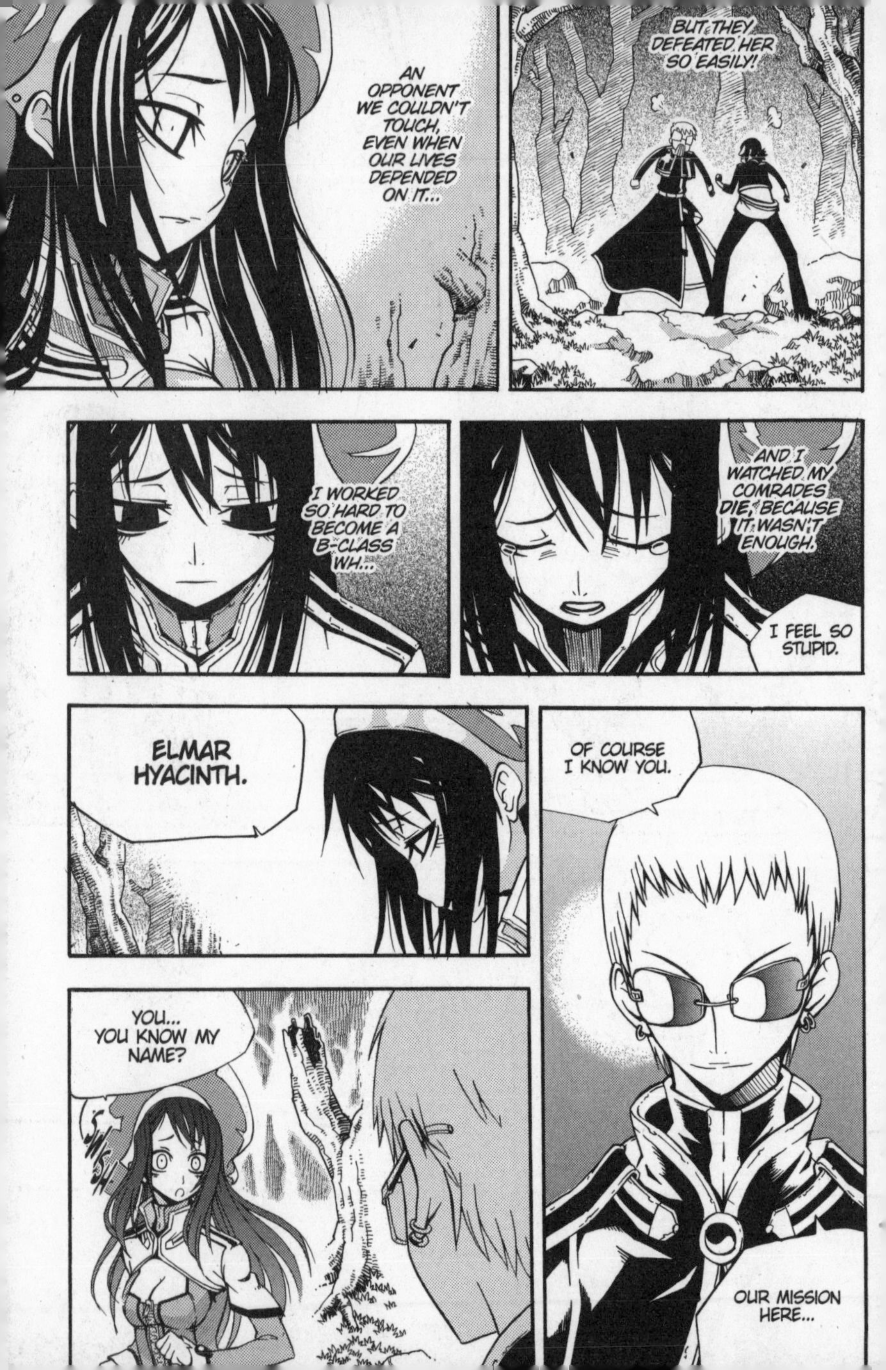
AN OPPONENT WE COULDN'T TOUCH, EVEN WHEN OUR LIVES DEPENDED ON IT...
BUT THEY DEFEATED HER SO EASILY!
I WORKED SO HARD TO BECOME A B-CLASS WH...
AND I WATCHED MY COMRADES DIE, BECAUSE IT WASN'T ENOUGH.
I FEEL SO STUPID.
ELMAR HYACINTH.
OF COURSE I KNOW YOU.
YOU... YOU KNOW MY NAME?
SWISH
OUR MISSION HERE...

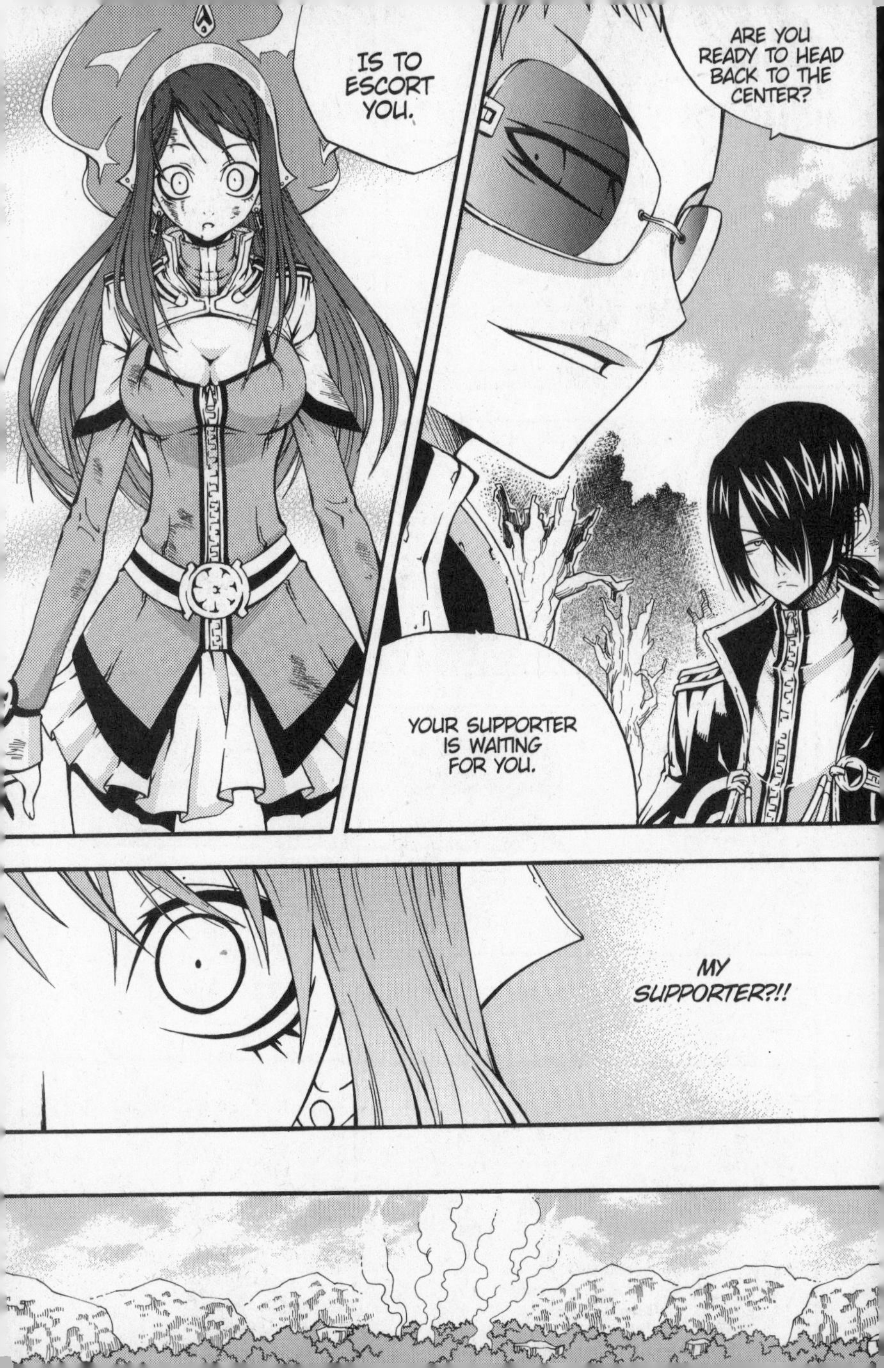
ARE YOU READY TO HEAD BACK TO THE CENTER?
IS TO ESCORT YOU.
YOUR SUPPORTER IS WAITING FOR YOU.
MY SUPPORTER?!!

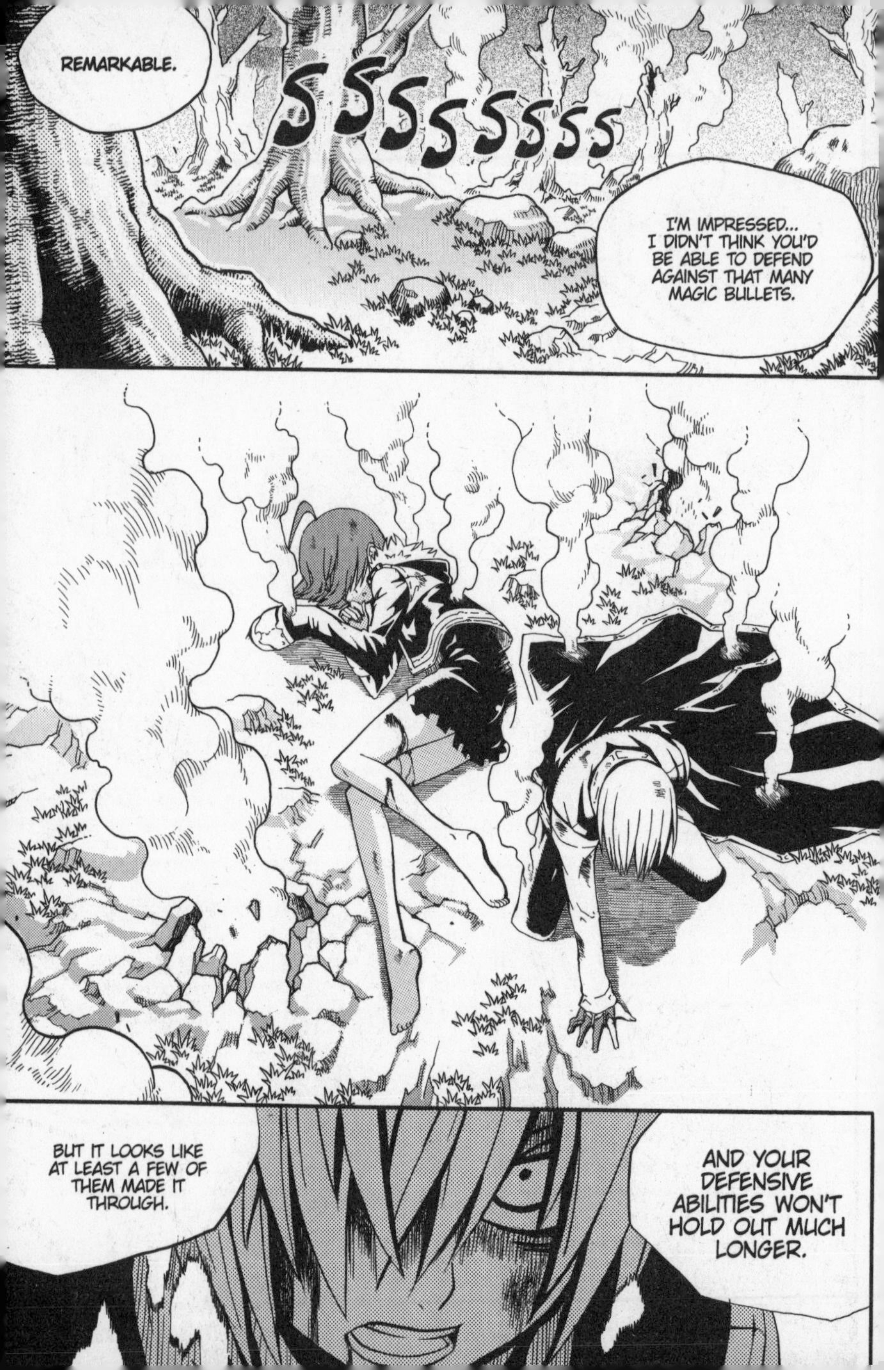
REMARKABLE.
SSSSSSSSS
I'M IMPRESSED... I DIDN'T THINK YOU'D BE ABLE TO DEFEND AGAINST THAT MANY MAGIC BULLETS.
AND YOUR DEFENSIVE ABILITIES WON'T HOLD OUT MUCH LONGER.
BUT IT LOOKS LIKE AT LEAST A FEW OF THEM MADE IT THROUGH.

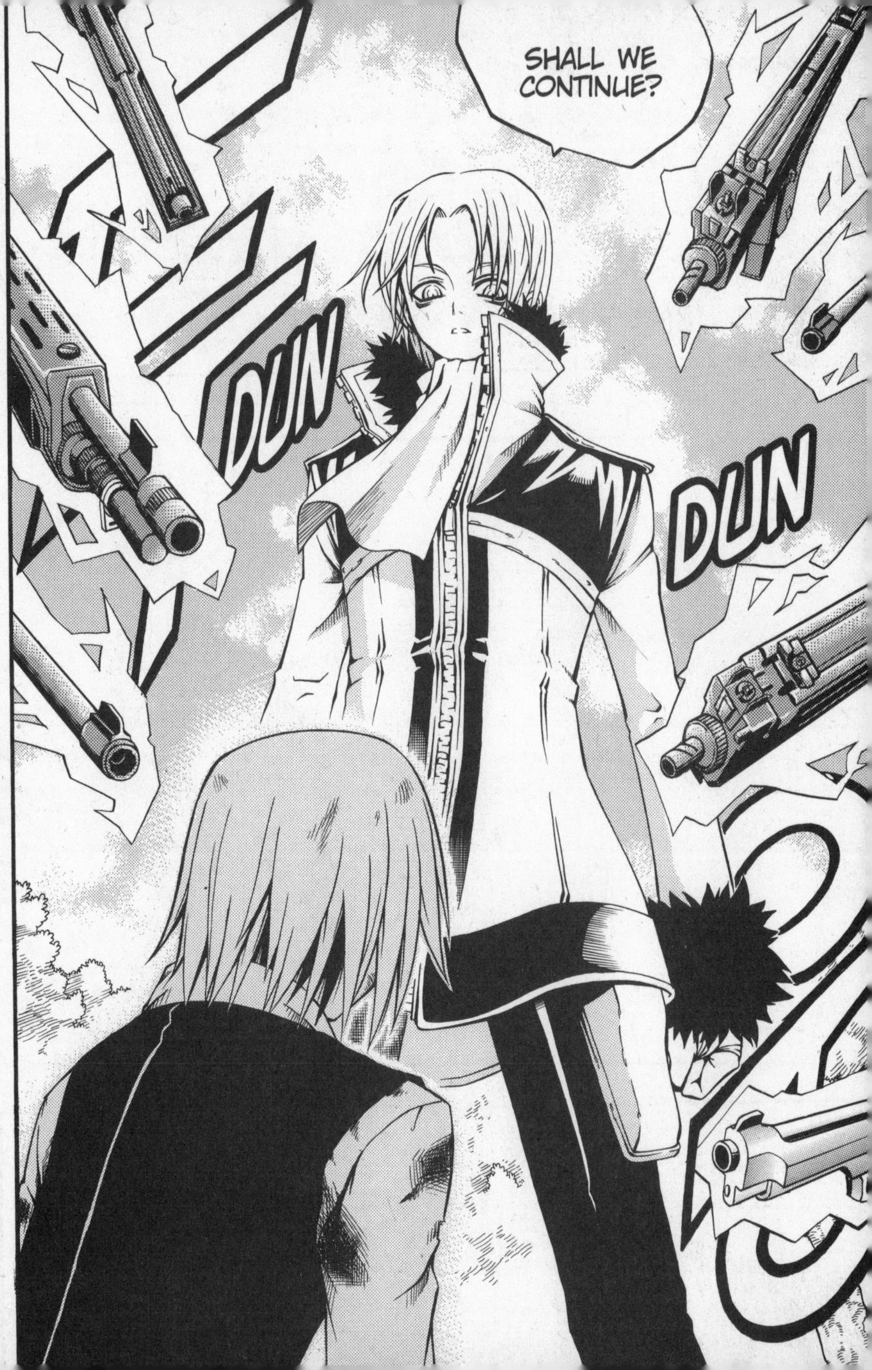
SHALL WE CONTINUE?
DUN
DUN

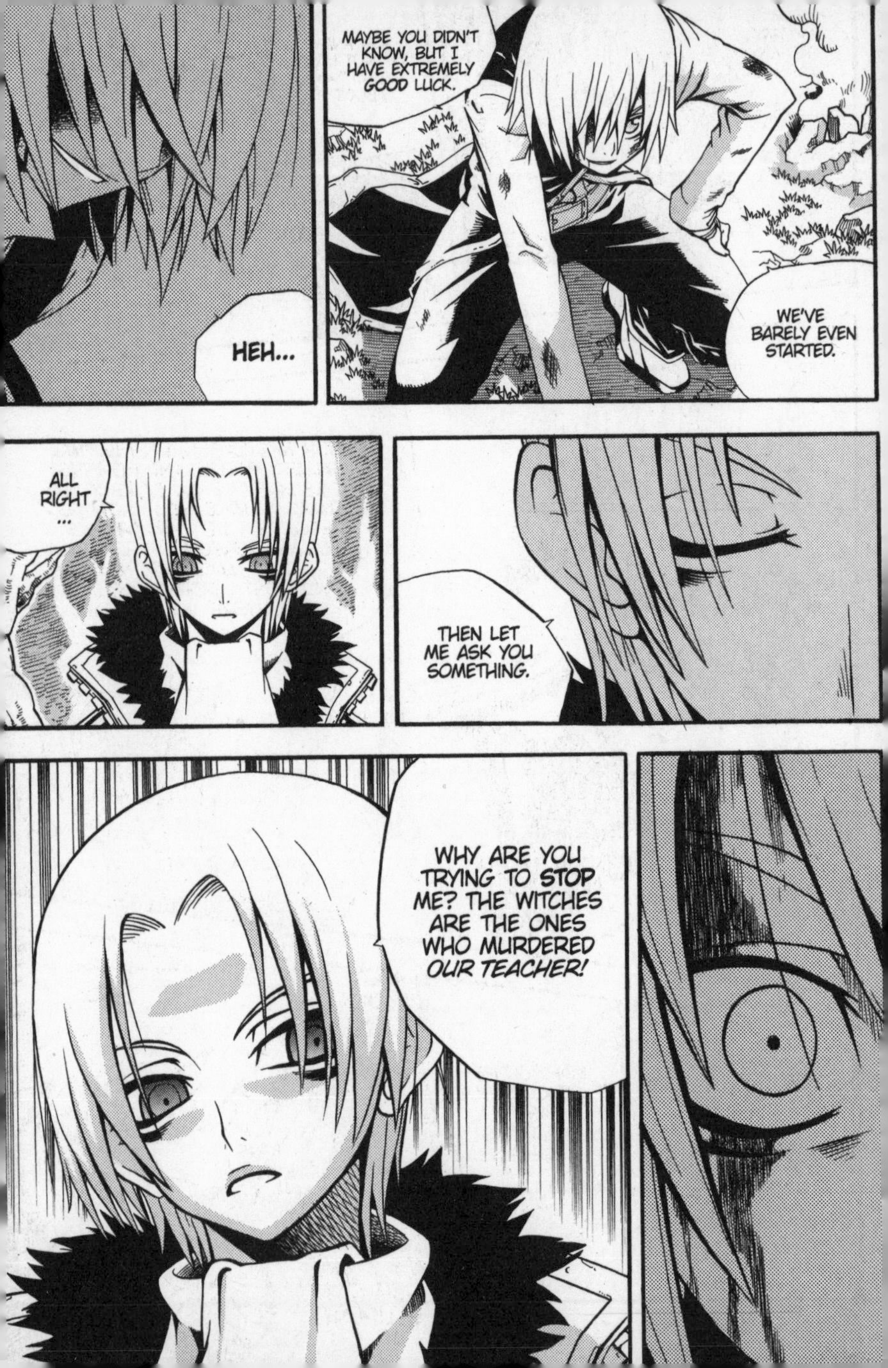
MAYBE YOU DIDN'T KNOW, BUT I HAVE EXTREMELY GOOD LUCK.
WE'VE BARELY EVEN STARTED.
HEH...
THEN LET ME ASK YOU SOMETHING.
ALL RIGHT ...
WHY ARE YOU TRYING TO STOP ME? THE WITCHES ARE THE ONES WHO MURDERED *OUR TEACHER!*

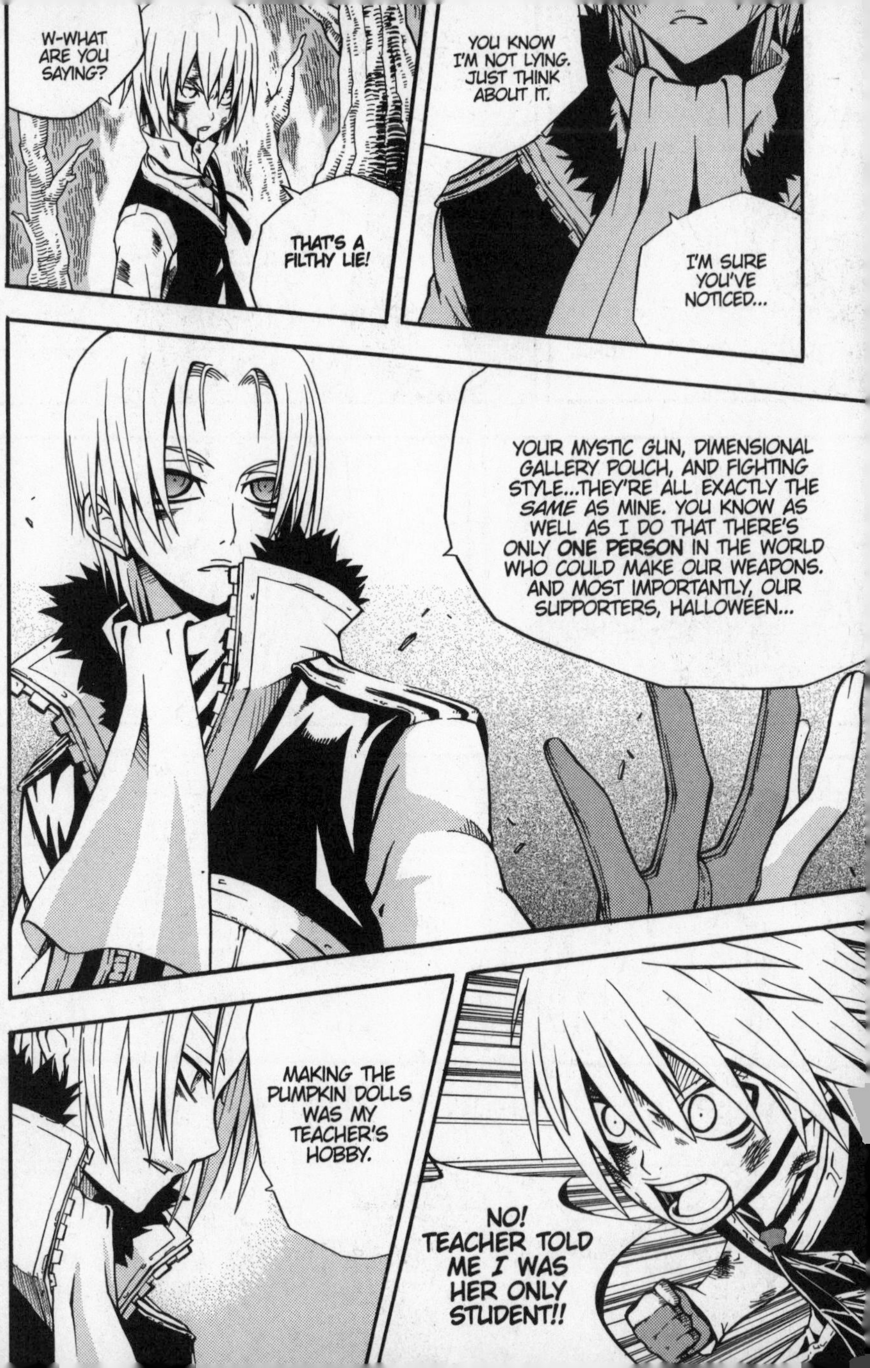
YOU KNOW I'M NOT LYING. JUST THINK ABOUT IT.
I'M SURE YOU'VE NOTICED...
W-WHAT ARE YOU SAYING?
THAT'S A FILTHY LIE!
YOUR MYSTIC GUN, DIMENSIONAL GALLERY POUCH, AND FIGHTING STYLE...THEY'RE ALL EXACTLY THE *SAME* AS MINE. YOU KNOW AS WELL AS I DO THAT THERE'S ONLY **ONE PERSON** IN THE WORLD WHO COULD MAKE OUR WEAPONS. AND MOST IMPORTANTLY, OUR SUPPORTERS, HALLOWEEN...
NO! TEACHER TOLD ME *I* WAS HER ONLY STUDENT!!
MAKING THE PUMPKIN DOLLS WAS MY TEACHER'S HOBBY.

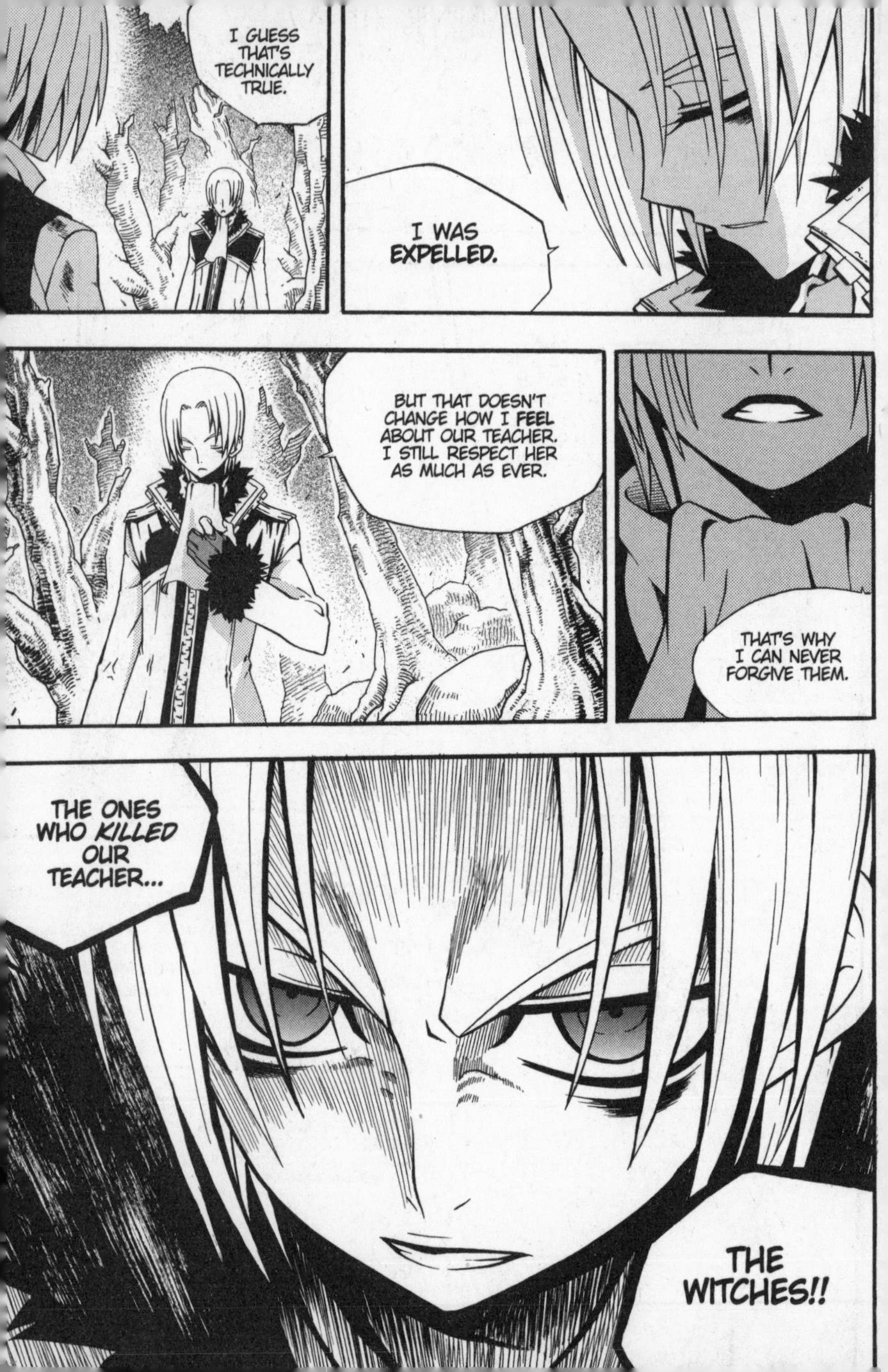
I GUESS THAT'S TECHNICALLY TRUE.
I WAS EXPELLED.
BUT THAT DOESN'T CHANGE HOW I FEEL ABOUT OUR TEACHER. I STILL RESPECT HER AS MUCH AS EVER.
THAT'S WHY I CAN NEVER FORGIVE THEM.
THE ONES WHO *KILLED* OUR TEACHER...
THE WITCHES!!

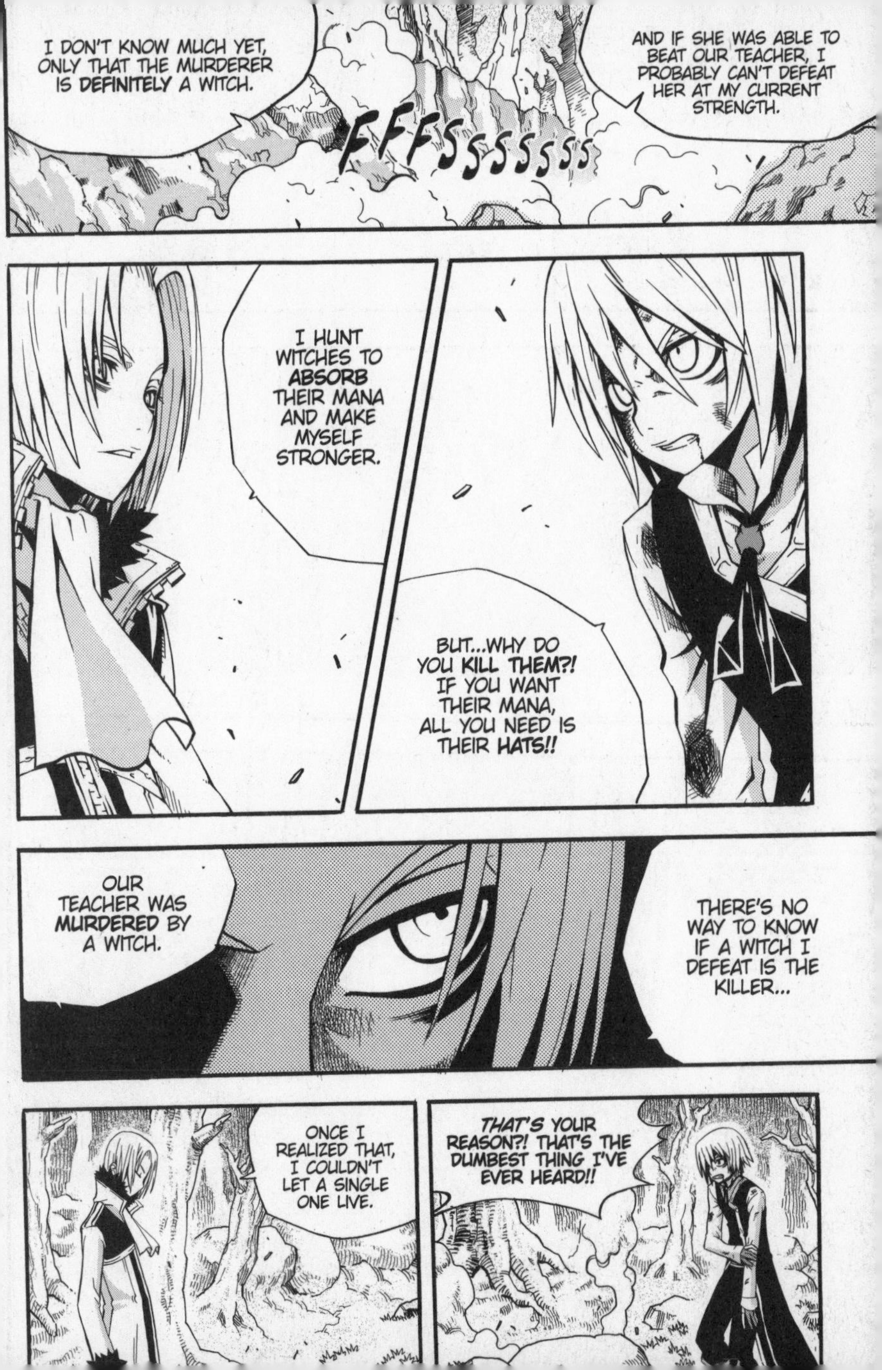
I DON'T KNOW MUCH YET, ONLY THAT THE MURDERER IS DEFINITELY A WITCH.
FFFSSSSSSSS
AND IF SHE WAS ABLE TO BEAT OUR TEACHER, I PROBABLY CAN'T DEFEAT HER AT MY CURRENT STRENGTH.
I HUNT WITCHES TO ABSORB THEIR MANA AND MAKE MYSELF STRONGER.
BUT...WHY DO YOU KILL THEM?! IF YOU WANT THEIR MANA, ALL YOU NEED IS THEIR HATS!!
OUR TEACHER WAS MURDERED BY A WITCH.
THERE'S NO WAY TO KNOW IF A WITCH I DEFEAT IS THE KILLER...
ONCE I REALIZED THAT, I COULDN'T LET A SINGLE ONE LIVE.
THAT'S YOUR REASON?! THAT'S THE DUMBEST THING I'VE EVER HEARD!!

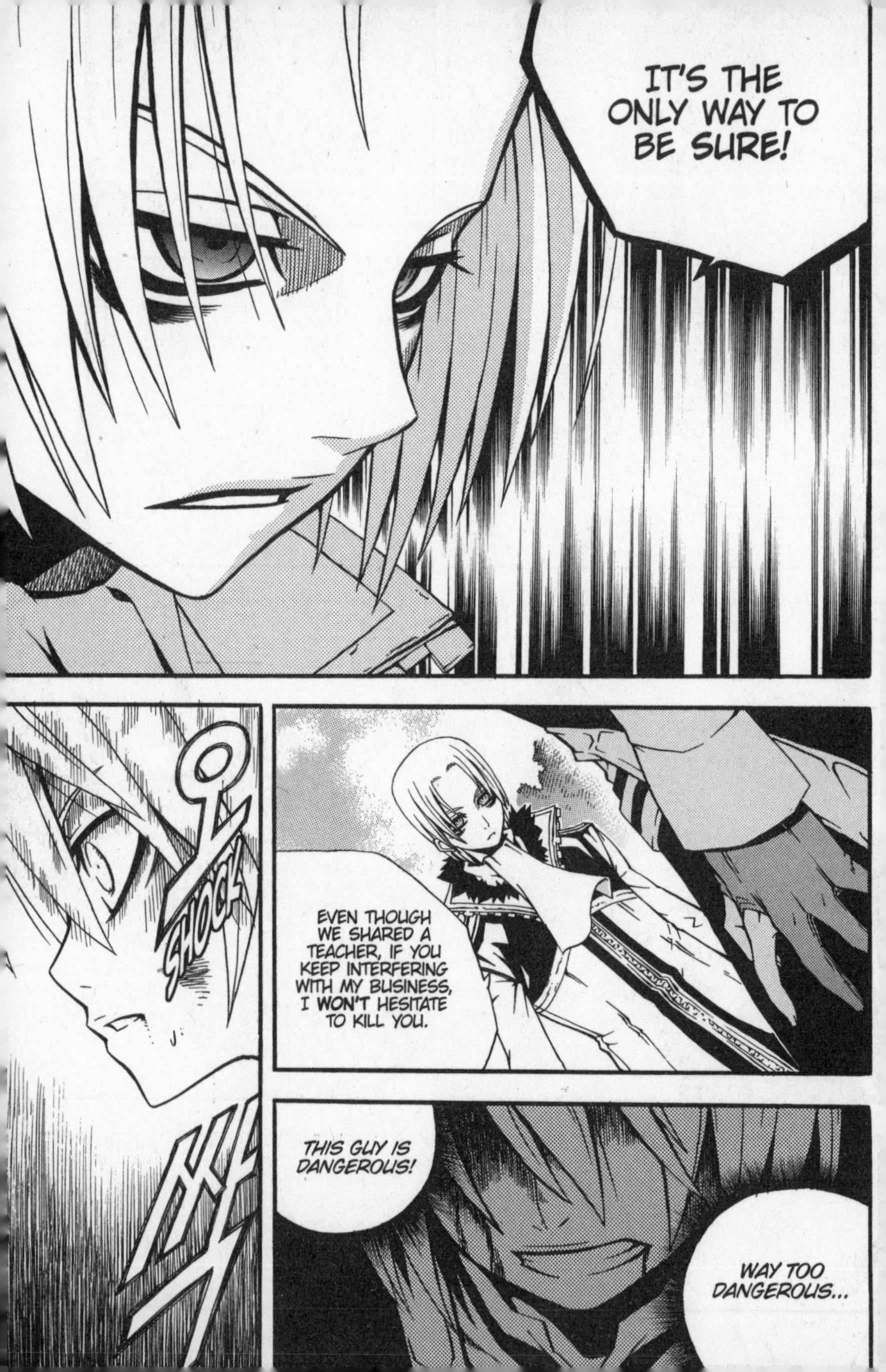
IT'S THE ONLY WAY TO BE SURE!
EVEN THOUGH WE SHARED A TEACHER, IF YOU KEEP INTERFERING WITH MY BUSINESS, I WON'T HESITATE TO KILL YOU.
SHOCK
THIS GUY IS DANGEROUS!
WAY TOO DANGEROUS...

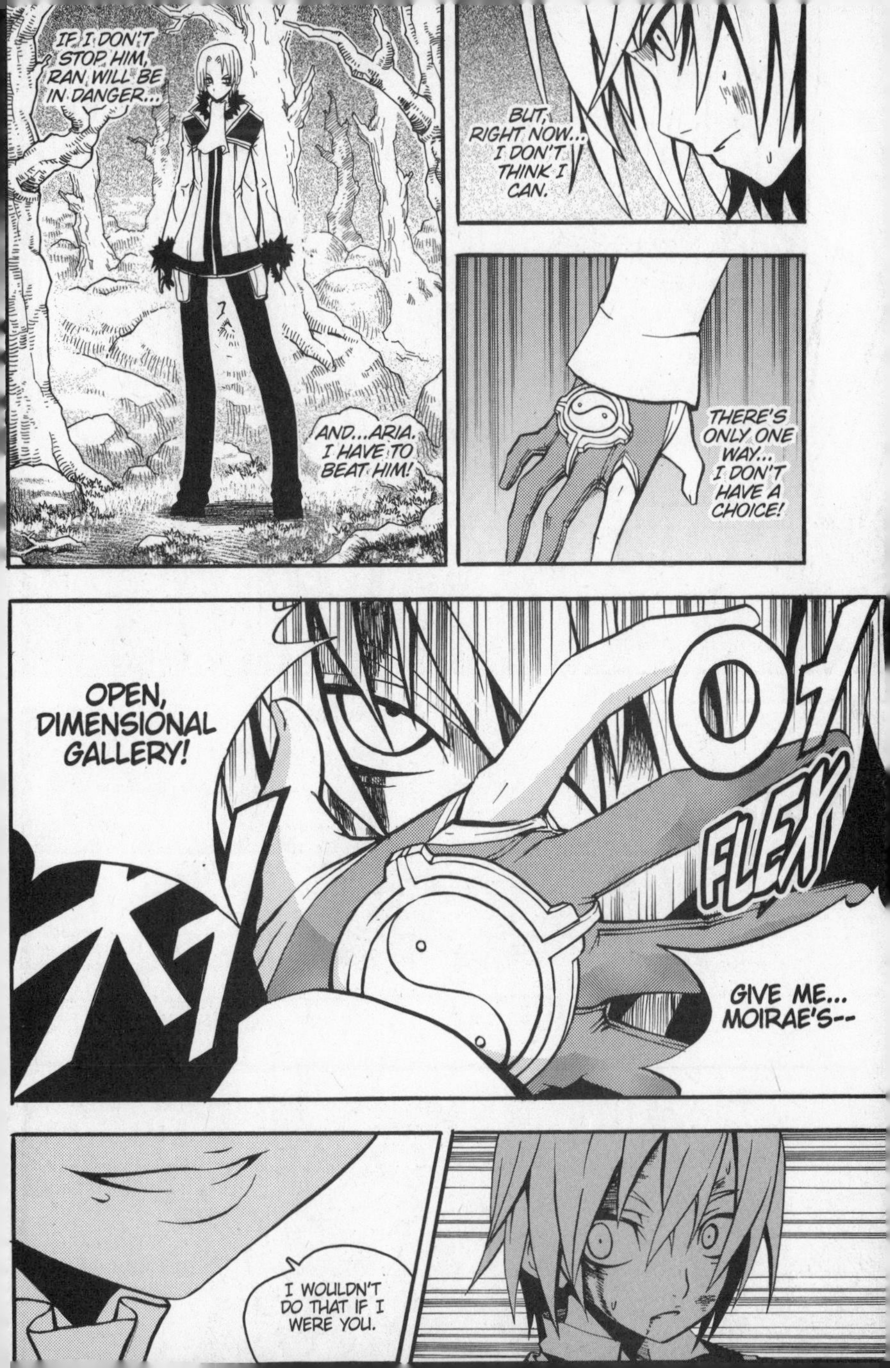

BUT, RIGHT NOW... I DON'T THINK I CAN.
IF I DON'T STOP HIM, RAN WILL BE IN DANGER...
AND...ARIA. I HAVE TO BEAT HIM!
THERE'S ONLY ONE WAY... I DON'T HAVE A CHOICE!
FLEX
OPEN, DIMENSIONAL GALLERY!
GIVE ME... MOIRAE'S--
I WOULDN'T DO THAT IF I WERE YOU.

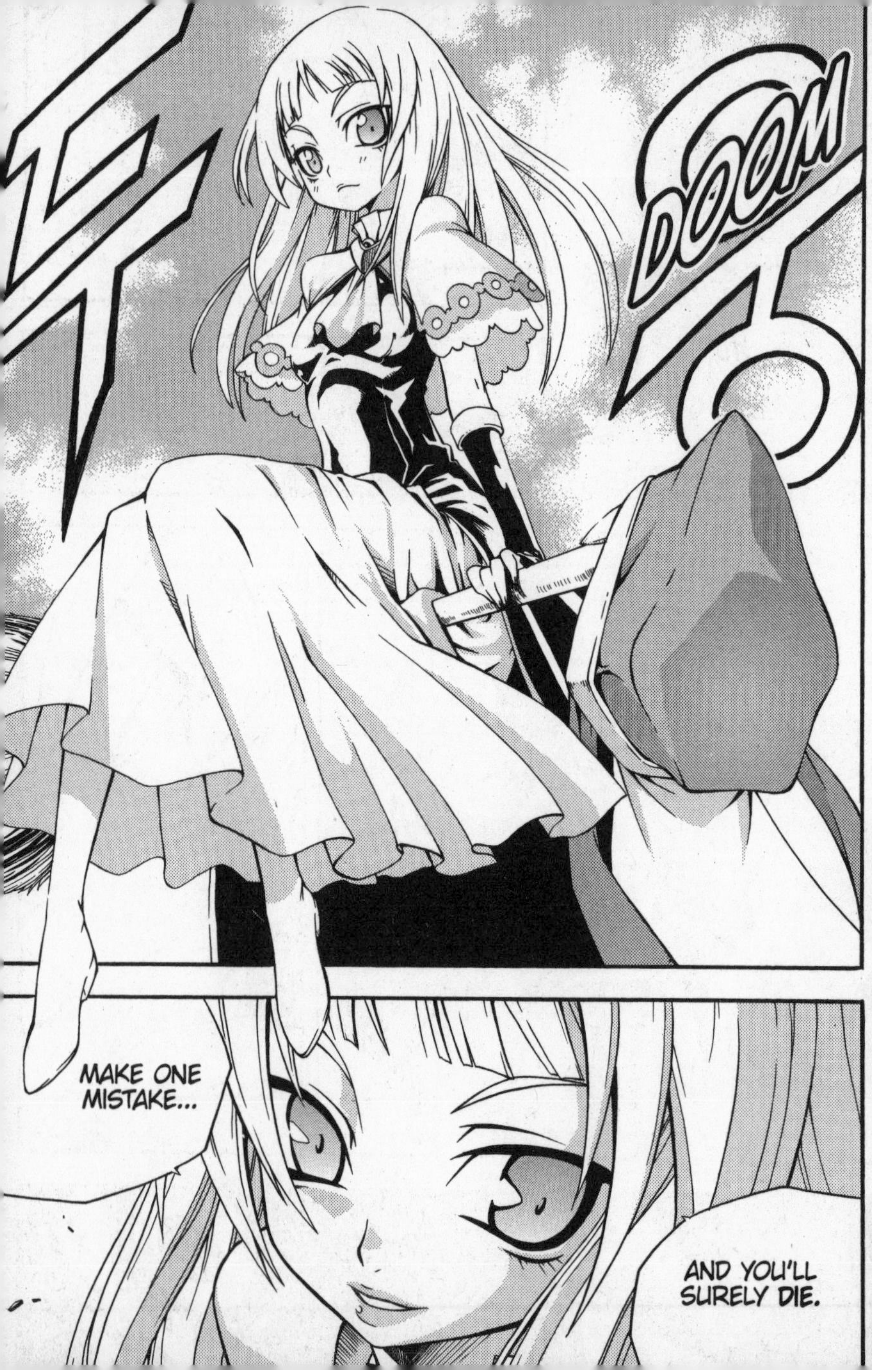
DOOM
MAKE ONE MISTAKE...
AND YOU'LL SURELY DIE.

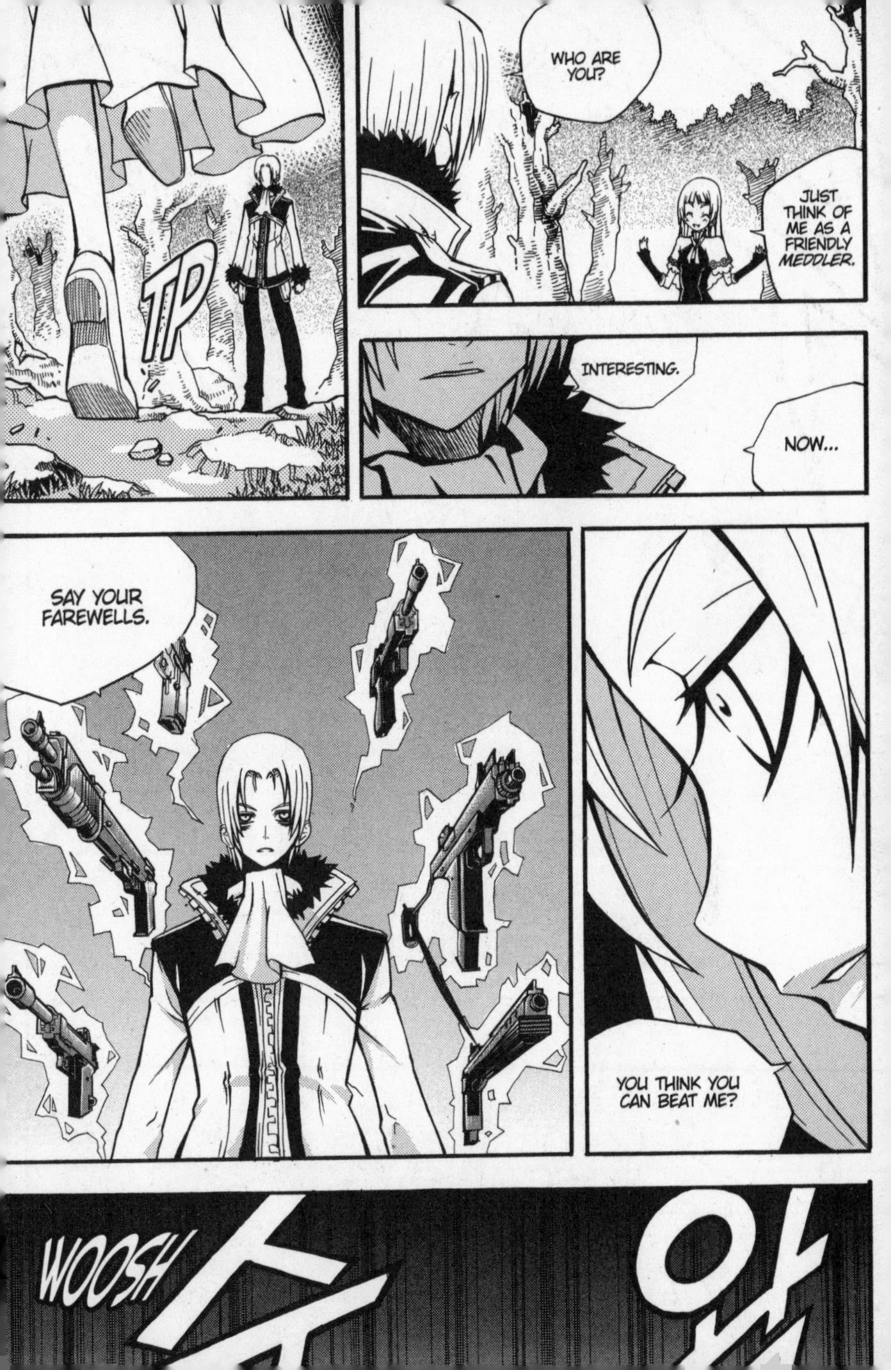
WHO ARE YOU?
JUST THINK OF ME AS A FRIENDLY *MEDDLER.*
INTERESTING.
NOW...
TP
YOU THINK YOU CAN BEAT ME?
SAY YOUR FAREWELLS.
WOOSH

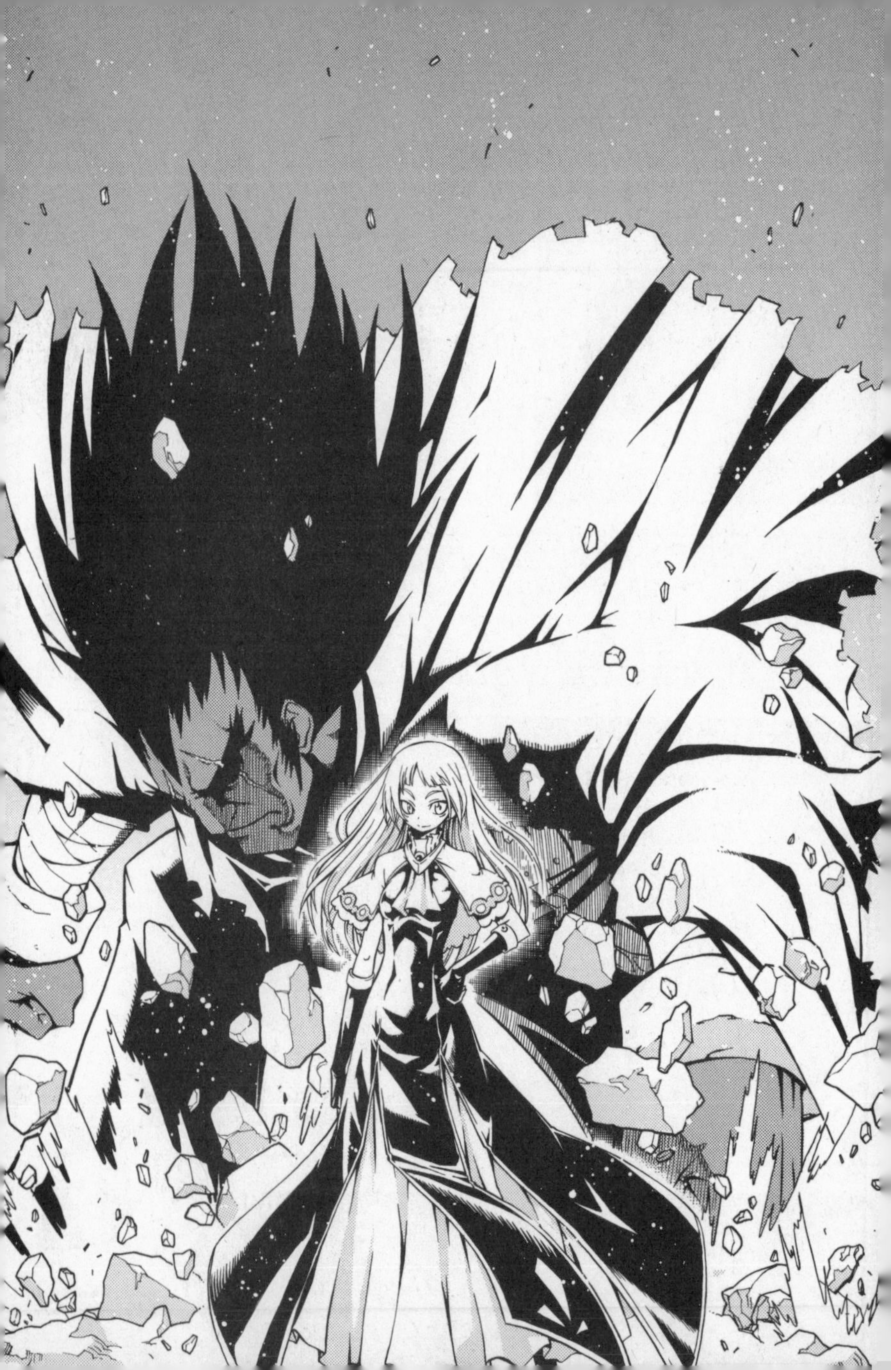

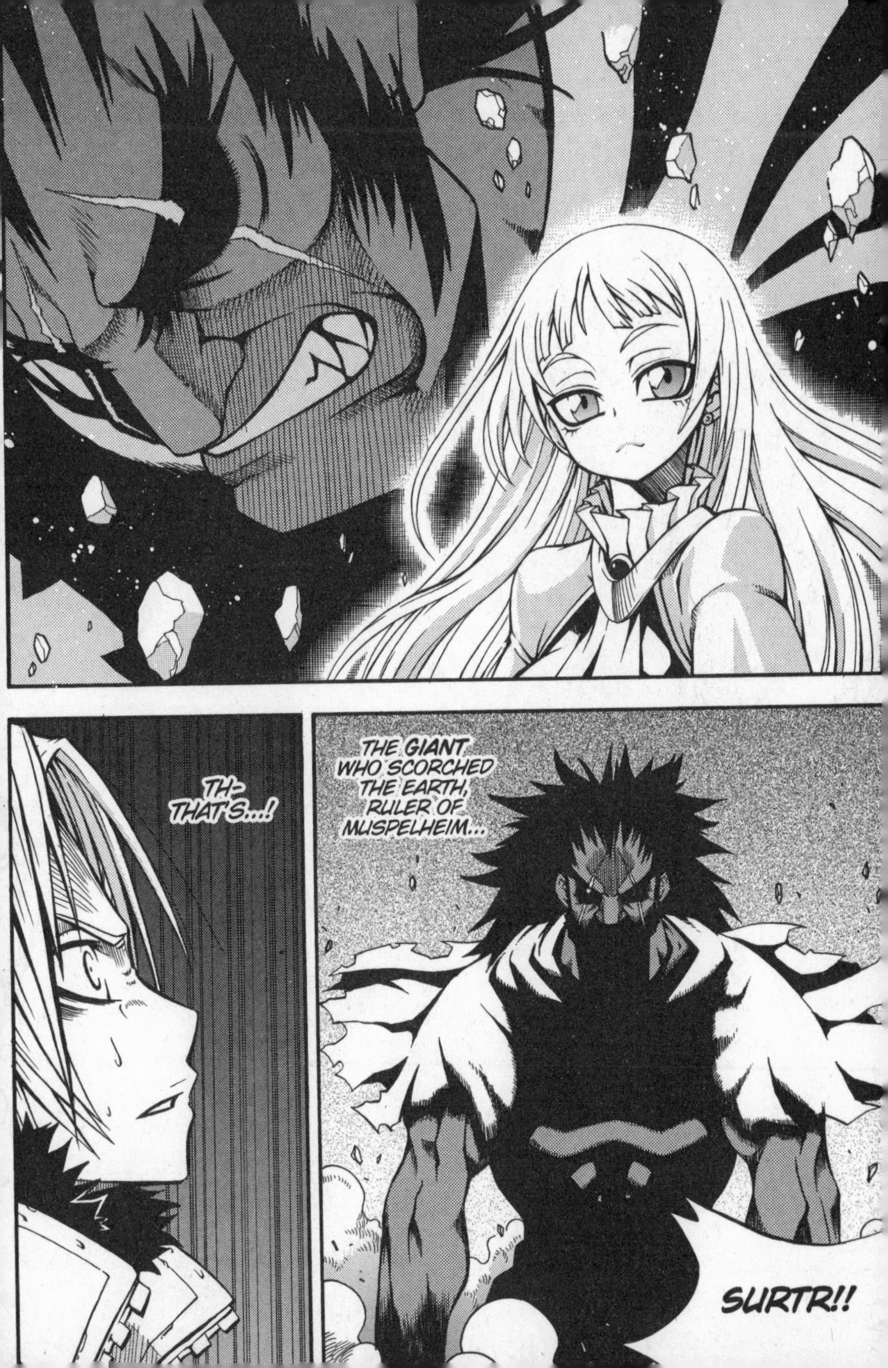
THE GIANT WHO SCORCHED THE EARTH, RULER OF MUSPELHEIM...
TH-THAT'S...!
SURTR!!

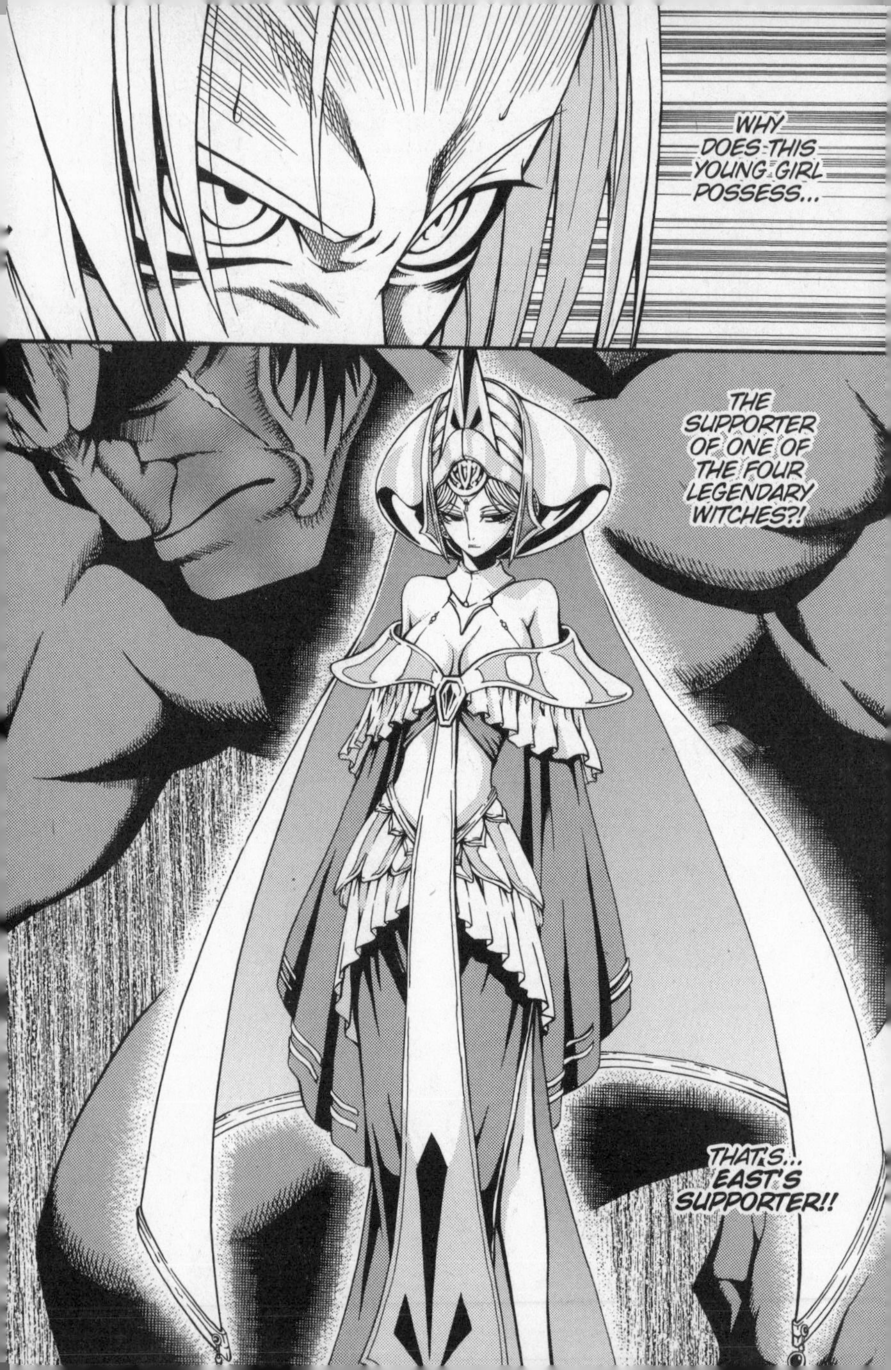
WHY DOES THIS YOUNG GIRL POSSESS...
THE SUPPORTER OF ONE OF THE FOUR LEGENDARY WITCHES?!
THAT'S... EAST'S SUPPORTER!!

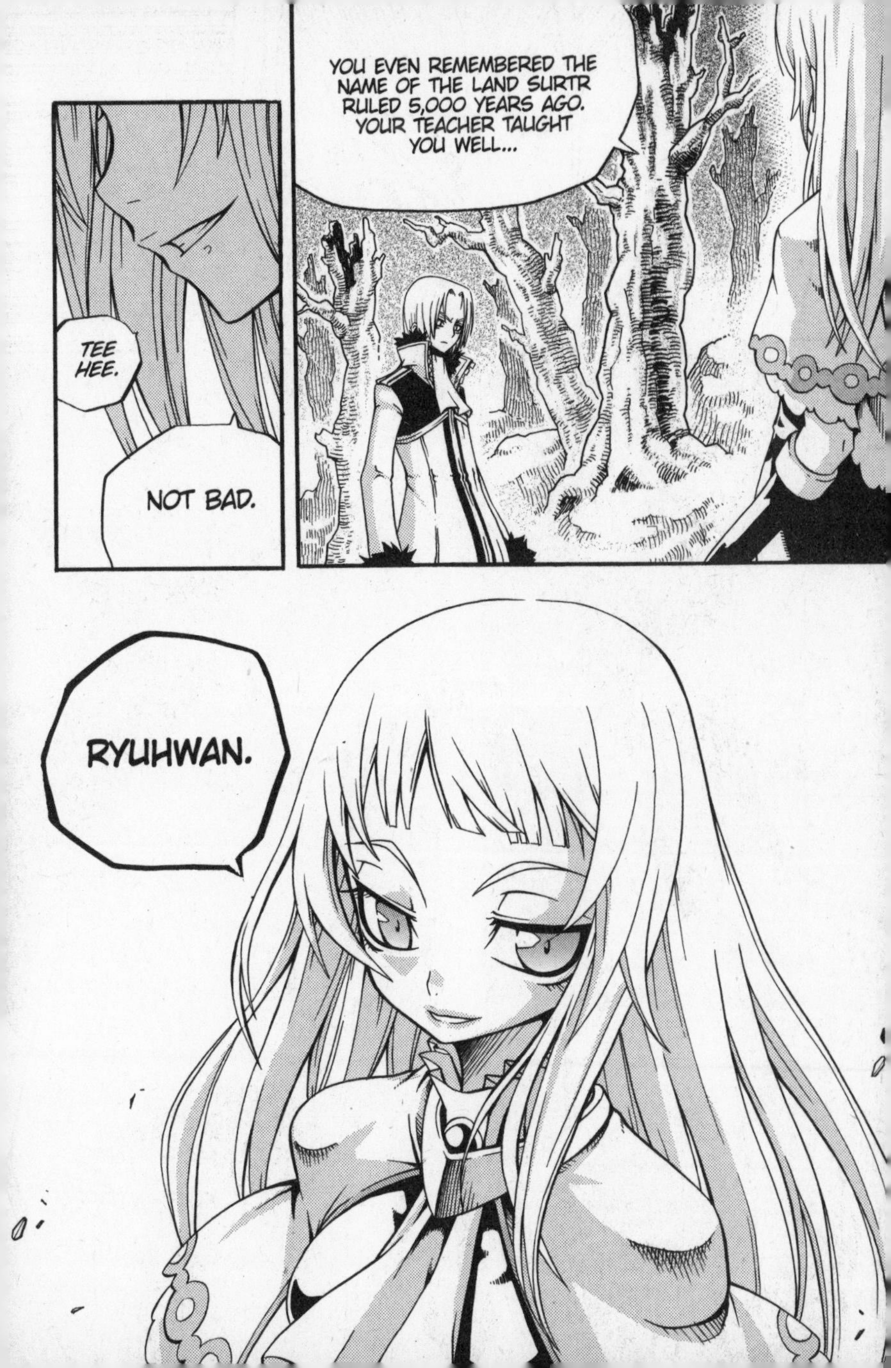
YOU EVEN REMEMBERED THE NAME OF THE LAND SURTR RULED 5,000 YEARS AGO. YOUR TEACHER TAUGHT YOU WELL...
TEE HEE.
NOT BAD.
RYUHWAN.

SENSITIVE

You're not hurt, are you?
LIGHT TOUCH
GYA HA HA! THAT TICKLES!!
ONCE AGAIN, XING RUINS HIS OWN COOL ENTRANCE.

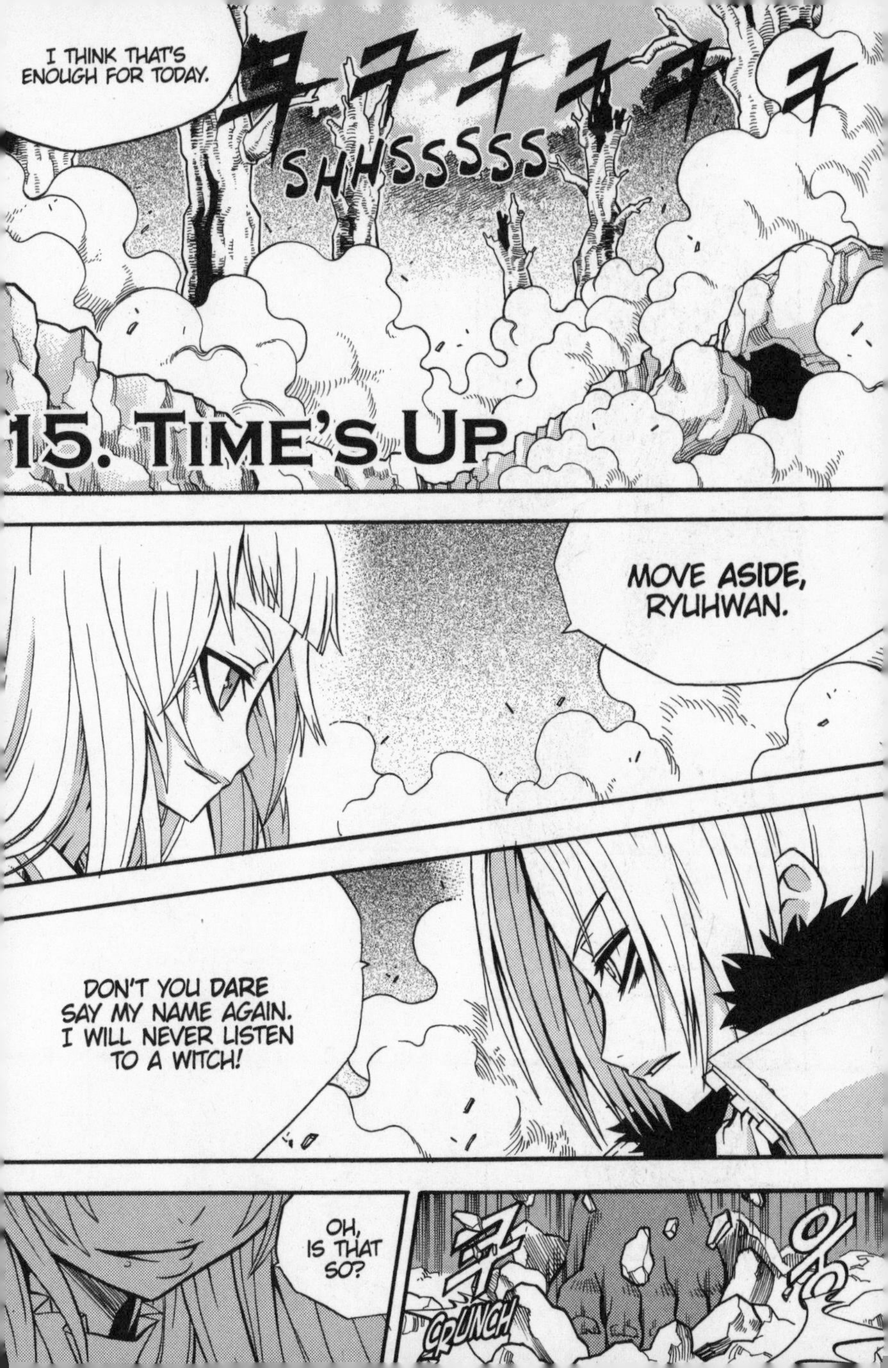
I THINK THAT'S ENOUGH FOR TODAY.
SHHSSSSS
15. TIME'S UP
MOVE ASIDE, RYUHWAN.
DON'T YOU DARE SAY MY NAME AGAIN. I WILL NEVER LISTEN TO A WITCH!
OH, IS THAT SO?
CRUNCH

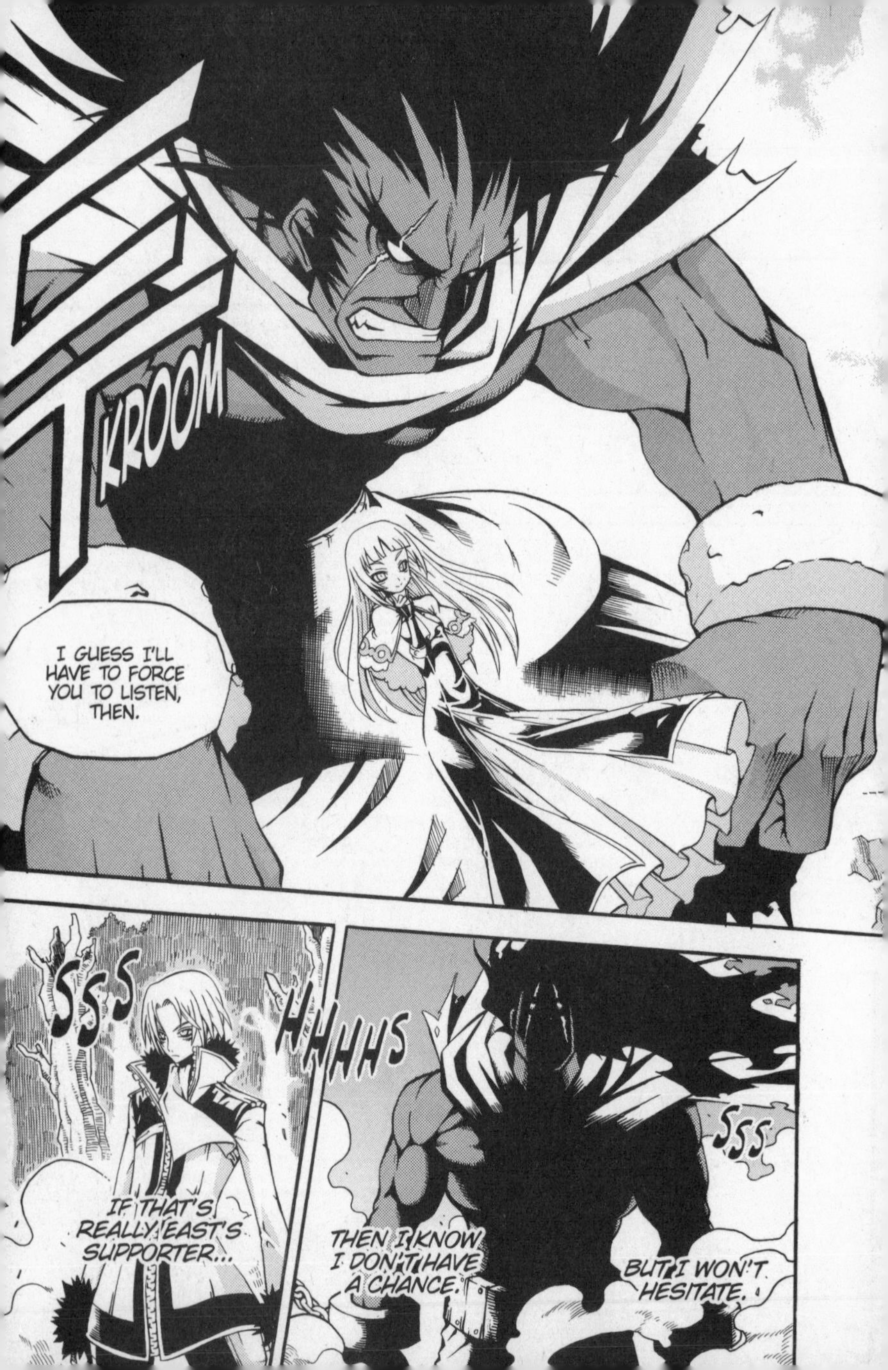

KROOM
I GUESS I'LL HAVE TO FORCE YOU TO LISTEN, THEN.
SSS
HHHHS
SSS
IF THAT'S REALLY EAST'S SUPPORTER...
THEN I KNOW I DON'T HAVE A CHANCE.
BUT I WON'T HESITATE.

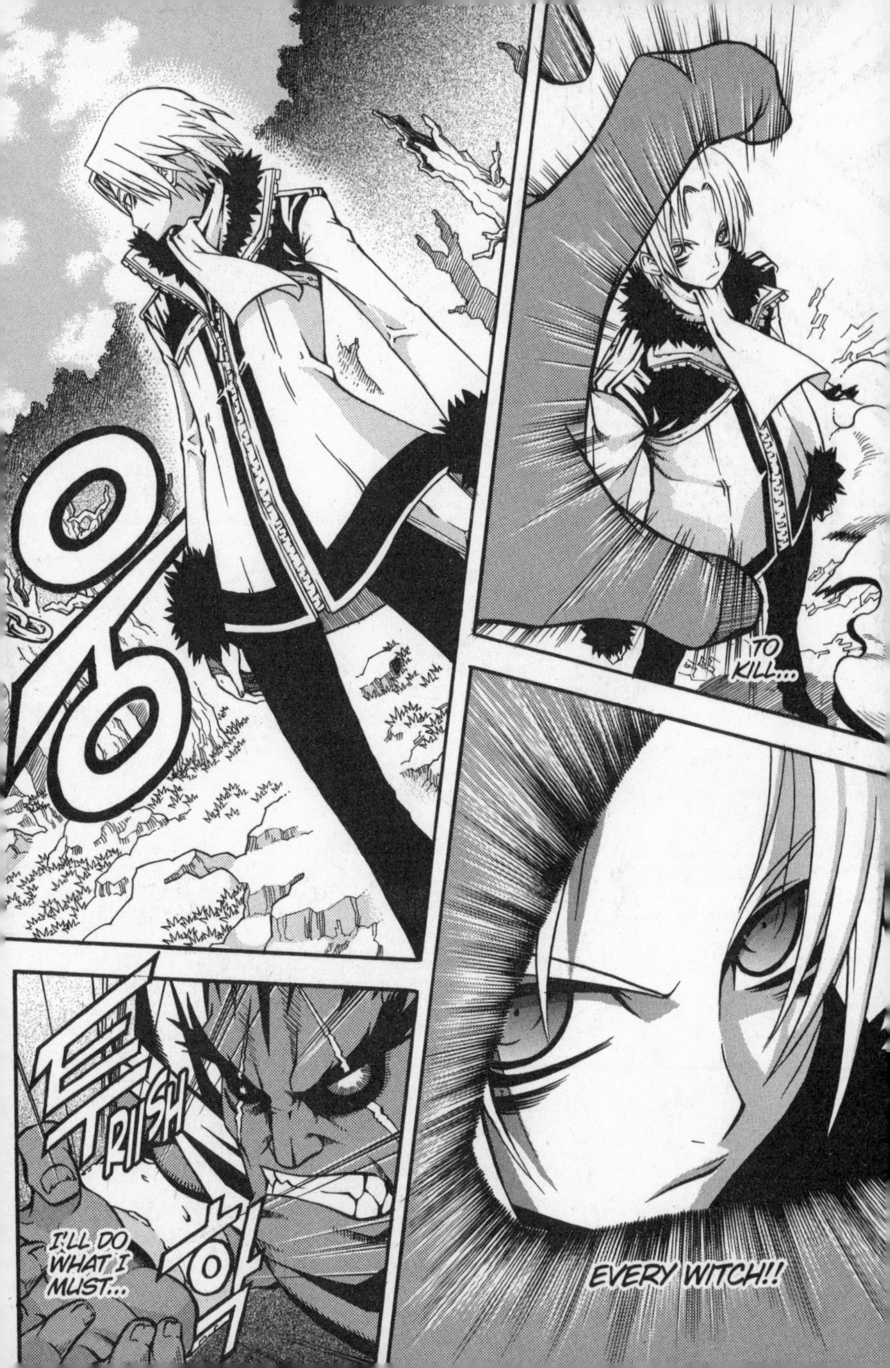
TO KILL...
EVERY WITCH!!
TRISH
I'LL DO WHAT I MUST...

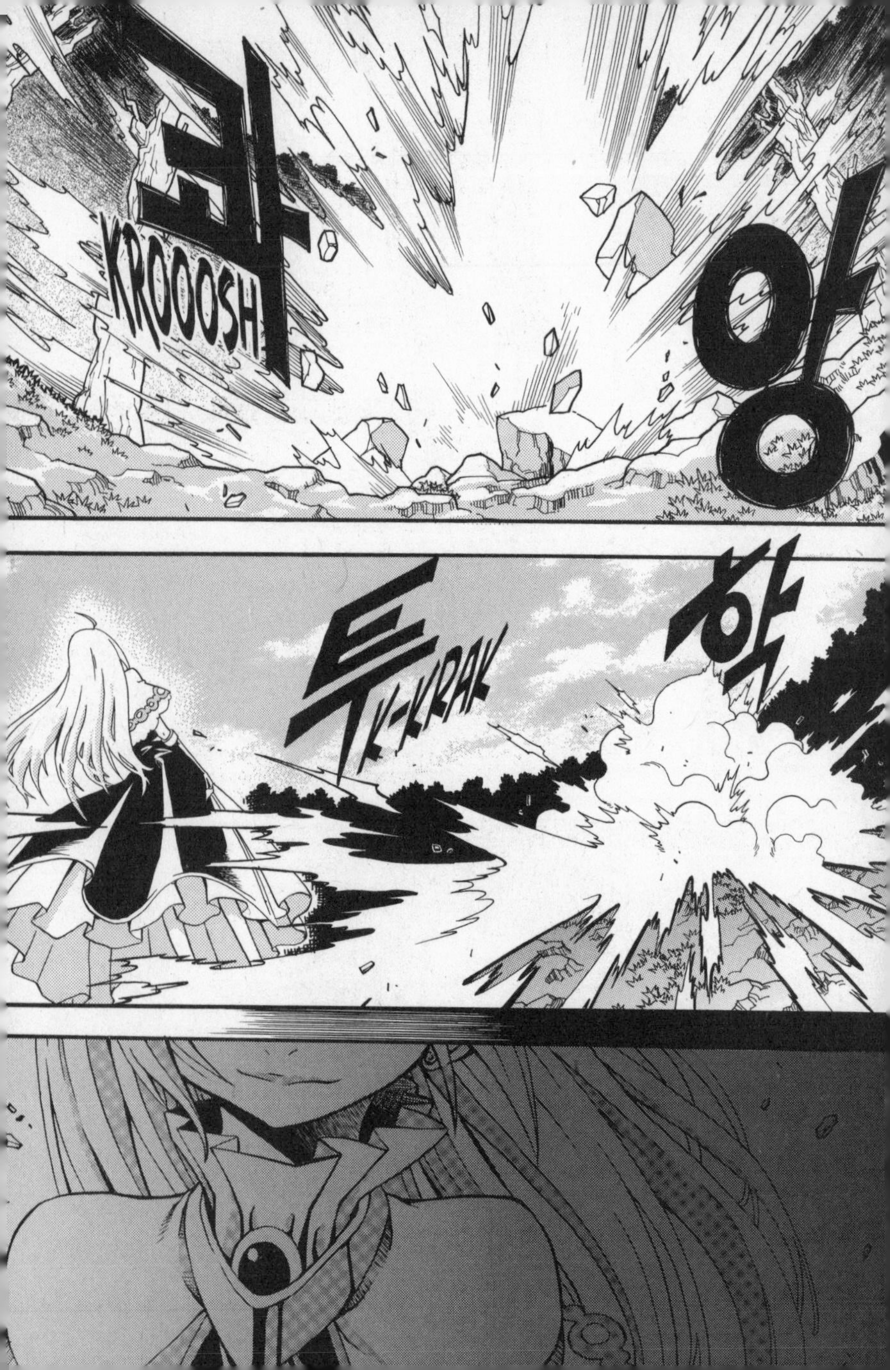
KROOSH
K-KRAK

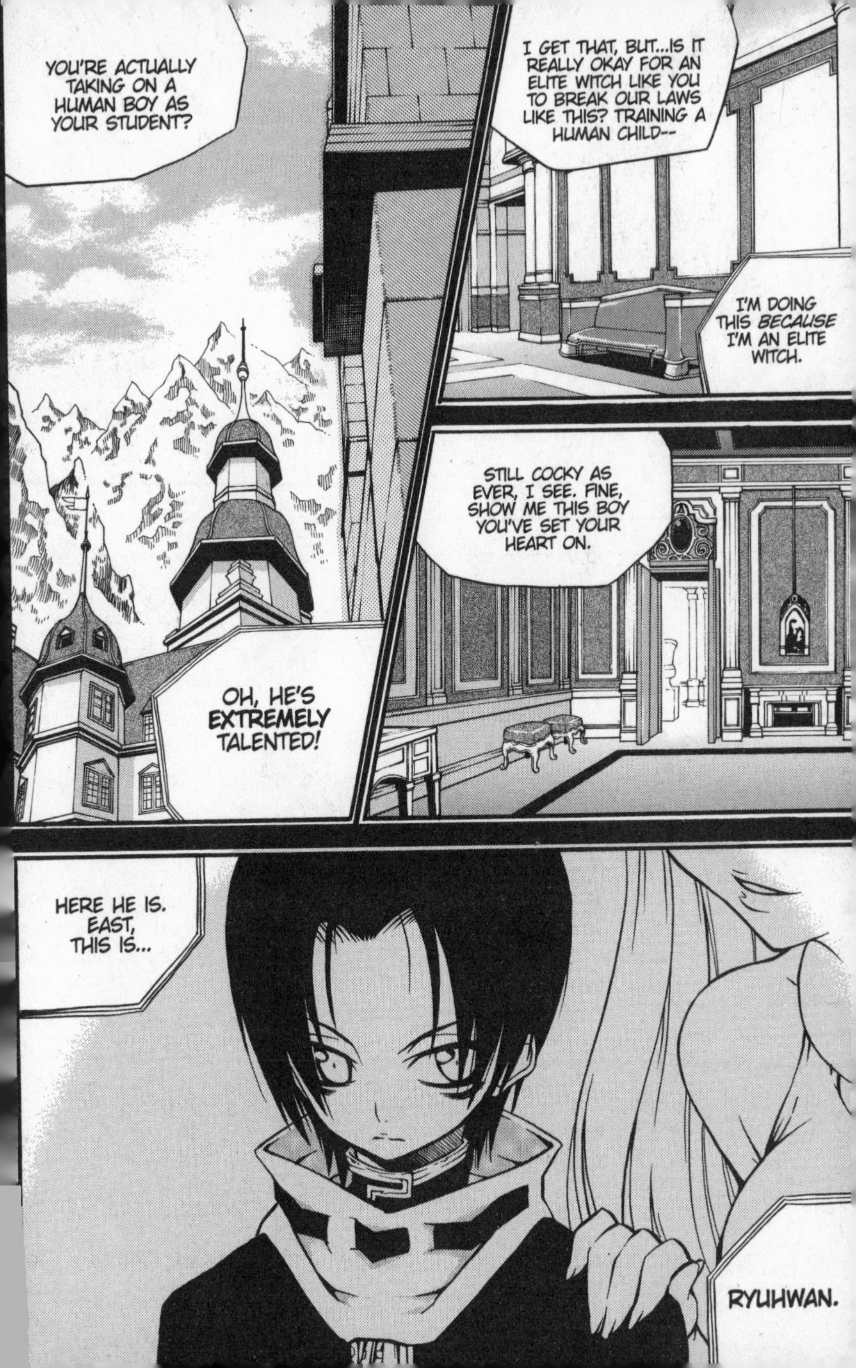
I GET THAT, BUT...IS IT REALLY OKAY FOR AN ELITE WITCH LIKE YOU TO BREAK OUR LAWS LIKE THIS? TRAINING A HUMAN CHILD--
YOU'RE ACTUALLY TAKING ON A HUMAN BOY AS YOUR STUDENT?
I'M DOING THIS *BECAUSE* I'M AN ELITE WITCH.
STILL COCKY AS EVER, I SEE. FINE, SHOW ME THIS BOY YOU'VE SET YOUR HEART ON.
OH, HE'S **EXTREMELY** TALENTED!
HERE HE IS. EAST, THIS IS...
RYUHWAN.

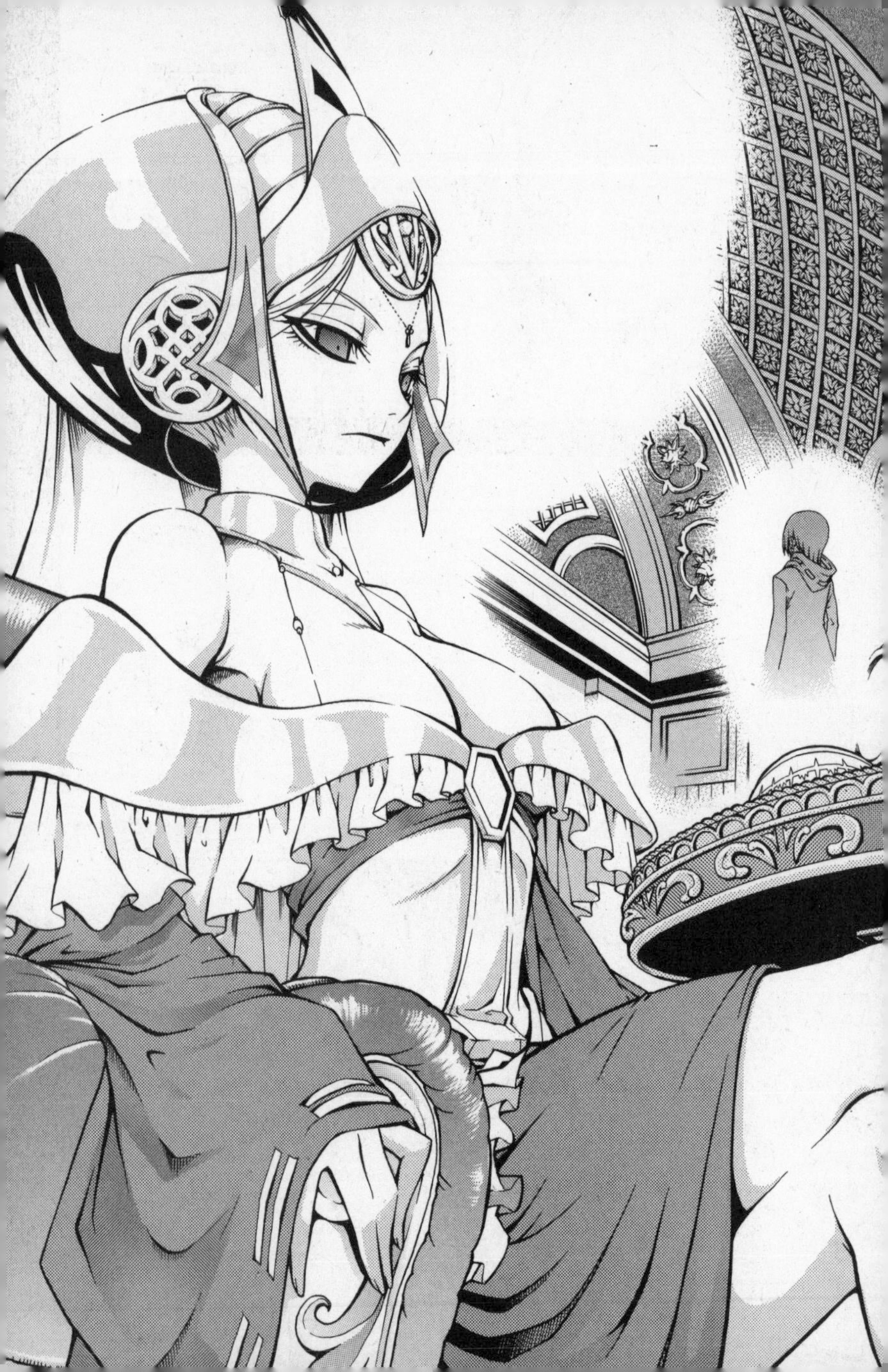

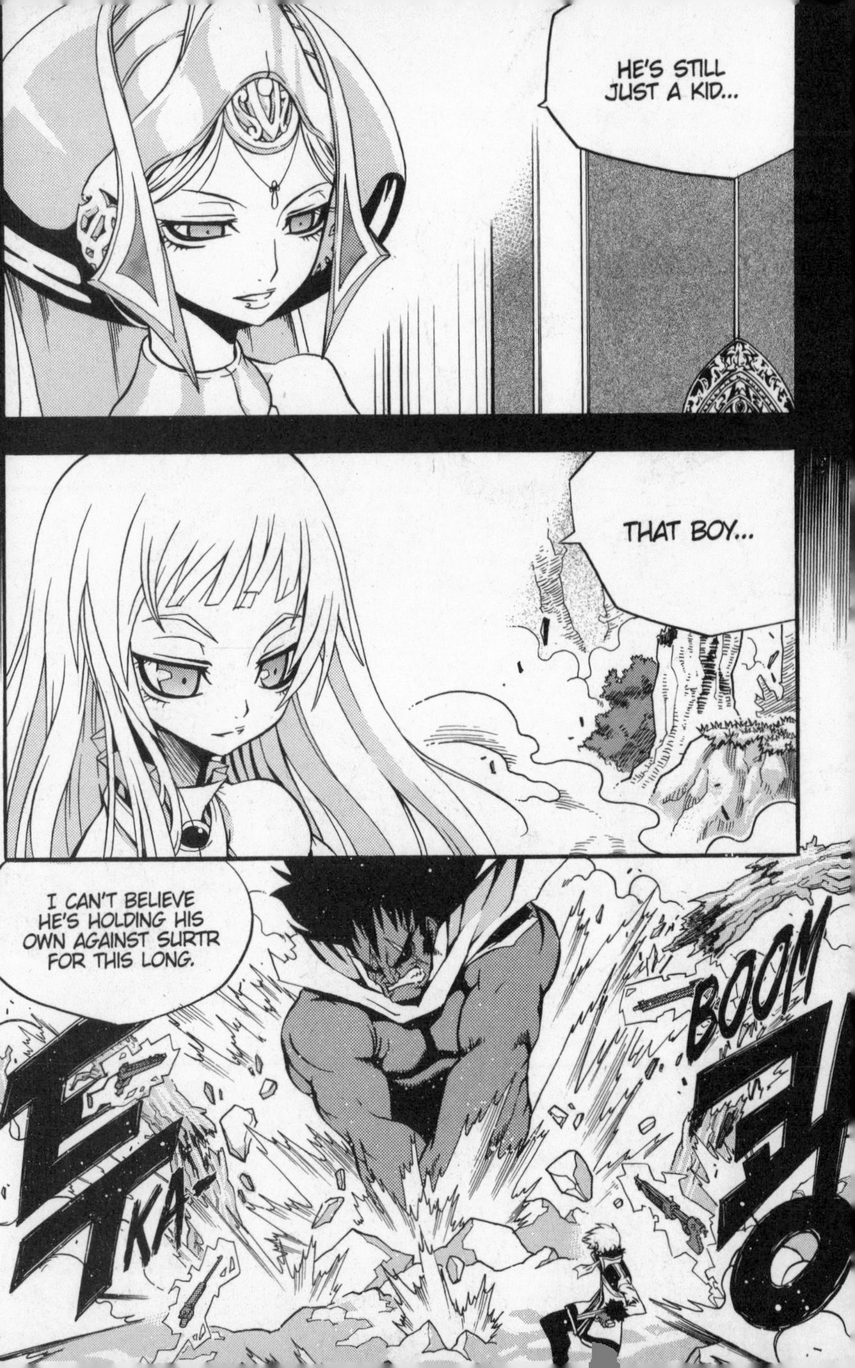
HE'S STILL JUST A KID...
THAT BOY...
I CAN'T BELIEVE HE'S HOLDING HIS OWN AGAINST SURTR FOR THIS LONG.
BOOM
KA

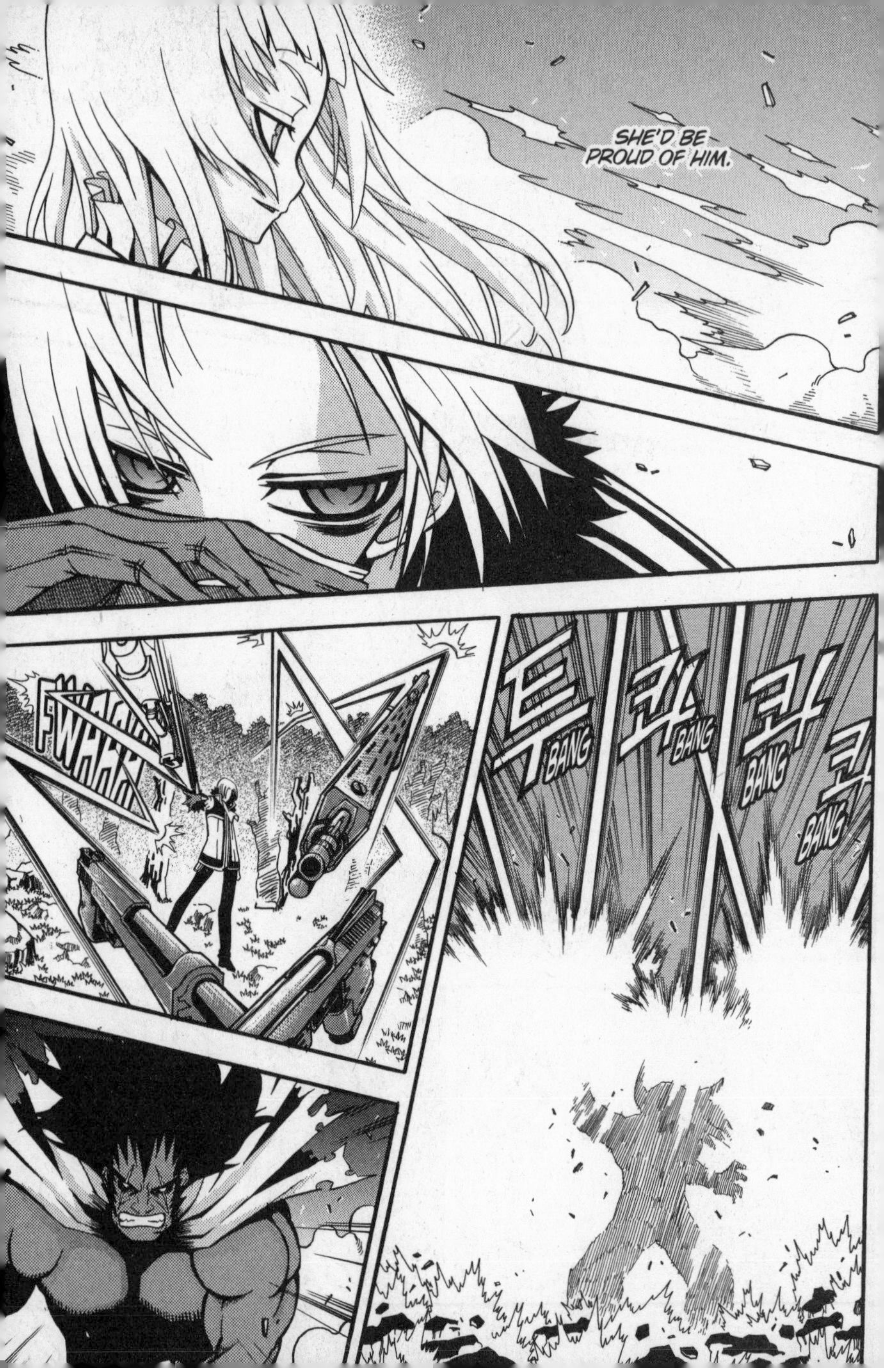

SHE'D BE PROUD OF HIM.
FWAAAH
BANG
BANG
BANG
BANG

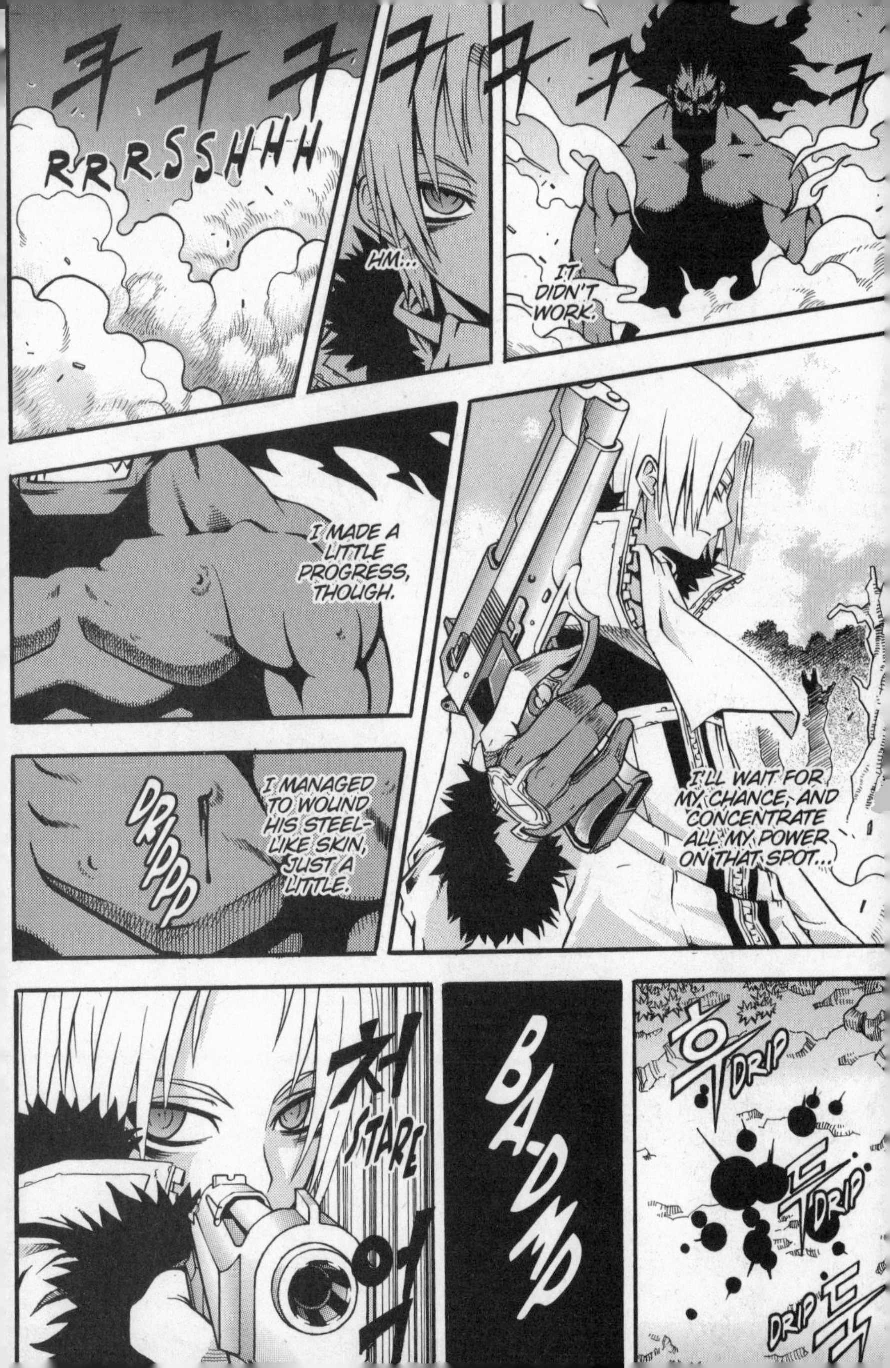
RRRSSHHH
HM...
IT DIDN'T WORK.
I MADE A LITTLE PROGRESS, THOUGH.
I'LL WAIT FOR MY CHANCE, AND CONCENTRATE ALL MY POWER ON THAT SPOT...
I MANAGED TO WOUND HIS STEEL-LIKE SKIN, JUST A LITTLE.
DRIPPP
DRIP
DRIP
DRIP
BA-DMP
STARE

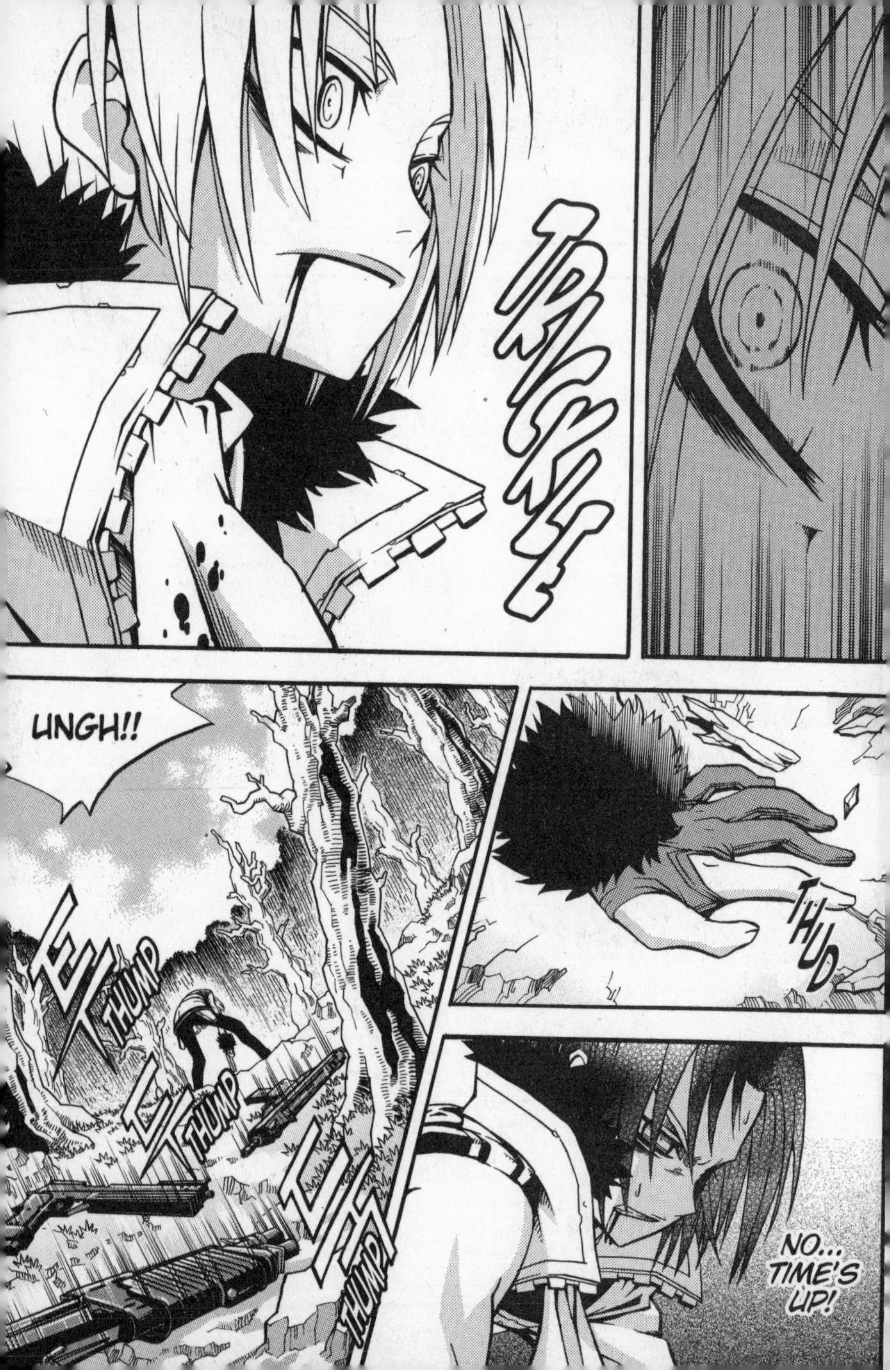

TRAAGHH
THUD
UNGH!!
THUMP
THUMP
THUMP!
NO... TIME'S UP!

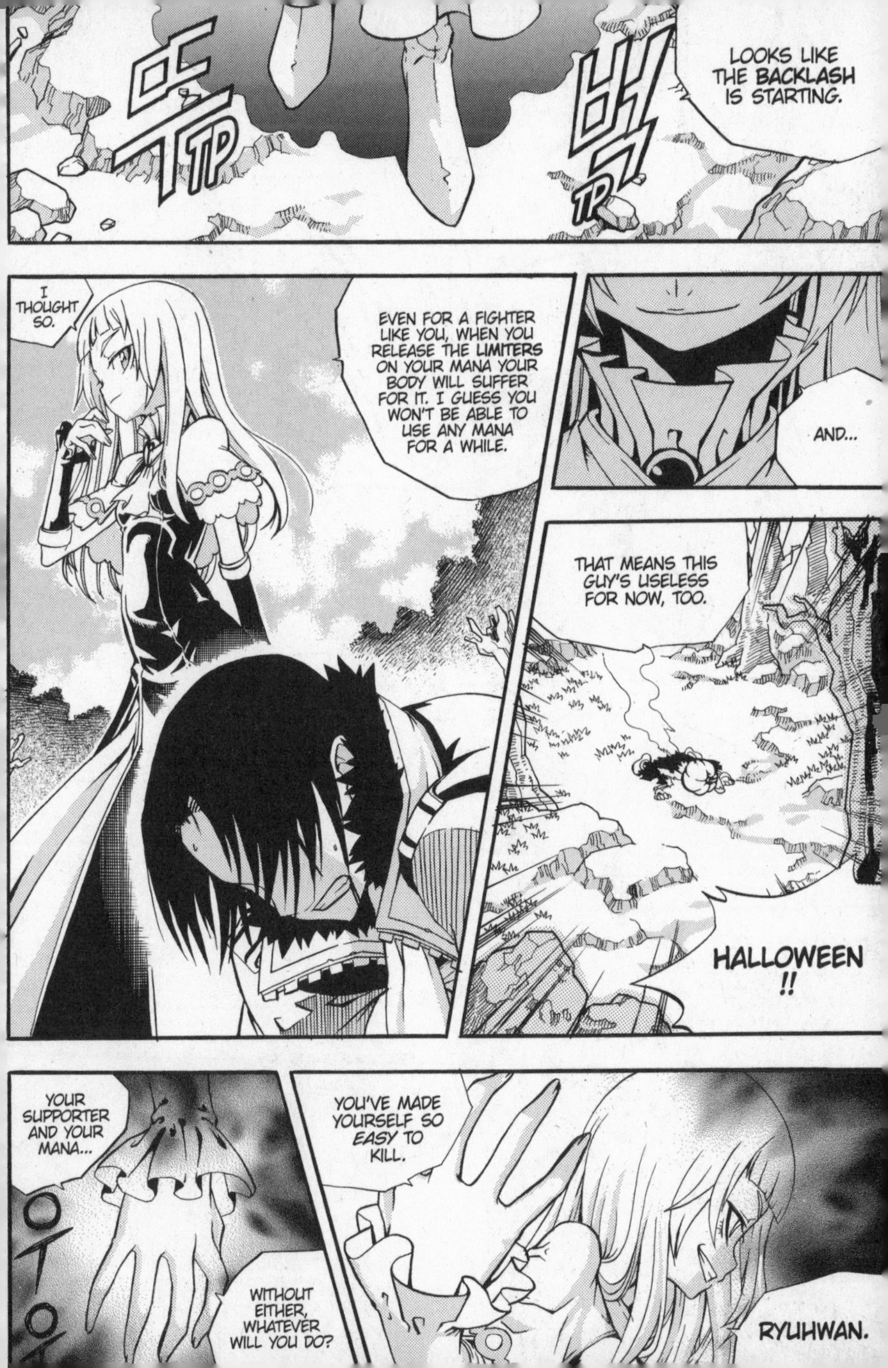
TP
TP
LOOKS LIKE THE BACKLASH IS STARTING.
I THOUGHT SO.
EVEN FOR A FIGHTER LIKE YOU, WHEN YOU RELEASE THE LIMITERS ON YOUR MANA YOUR BODY WILL SUFFER FOR IT. I GUESS YOU WON'T BE ABLE TO USE ANY MANA FOR A WHILE.
AND...
THAT MEANS THIS GUY'S USELESS FOR NOW, TOO.
HALLOWEEN!!
YOUR SUPPORTER AND YOUR MANA...
WITHOUT EITHER, WHATEVER WILL YOU DO?
YOU'VE MADE YOURSELF SO EASY TO KILL.
RYUHWAN.

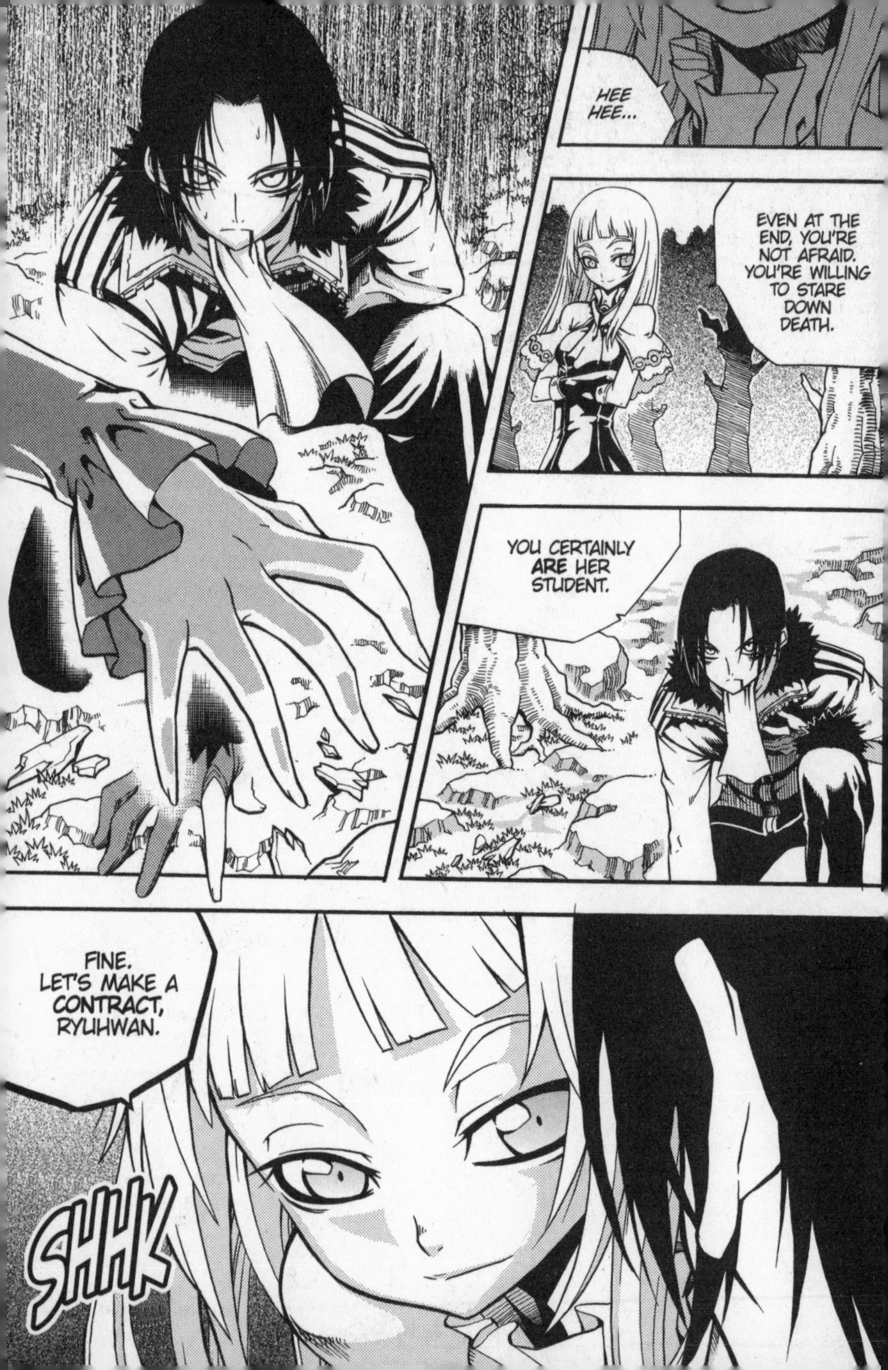
HEE HEE...
EVEN AT THE END, YOU'RE NOT AFRAID. YOU'RE WILLING TO STARE DOWN DEATH.
YOU CERTAINLY ARE HER STUDENT.
FINE. LET'S MAKE A CONTRACT, RYUHWAN.
SHHK

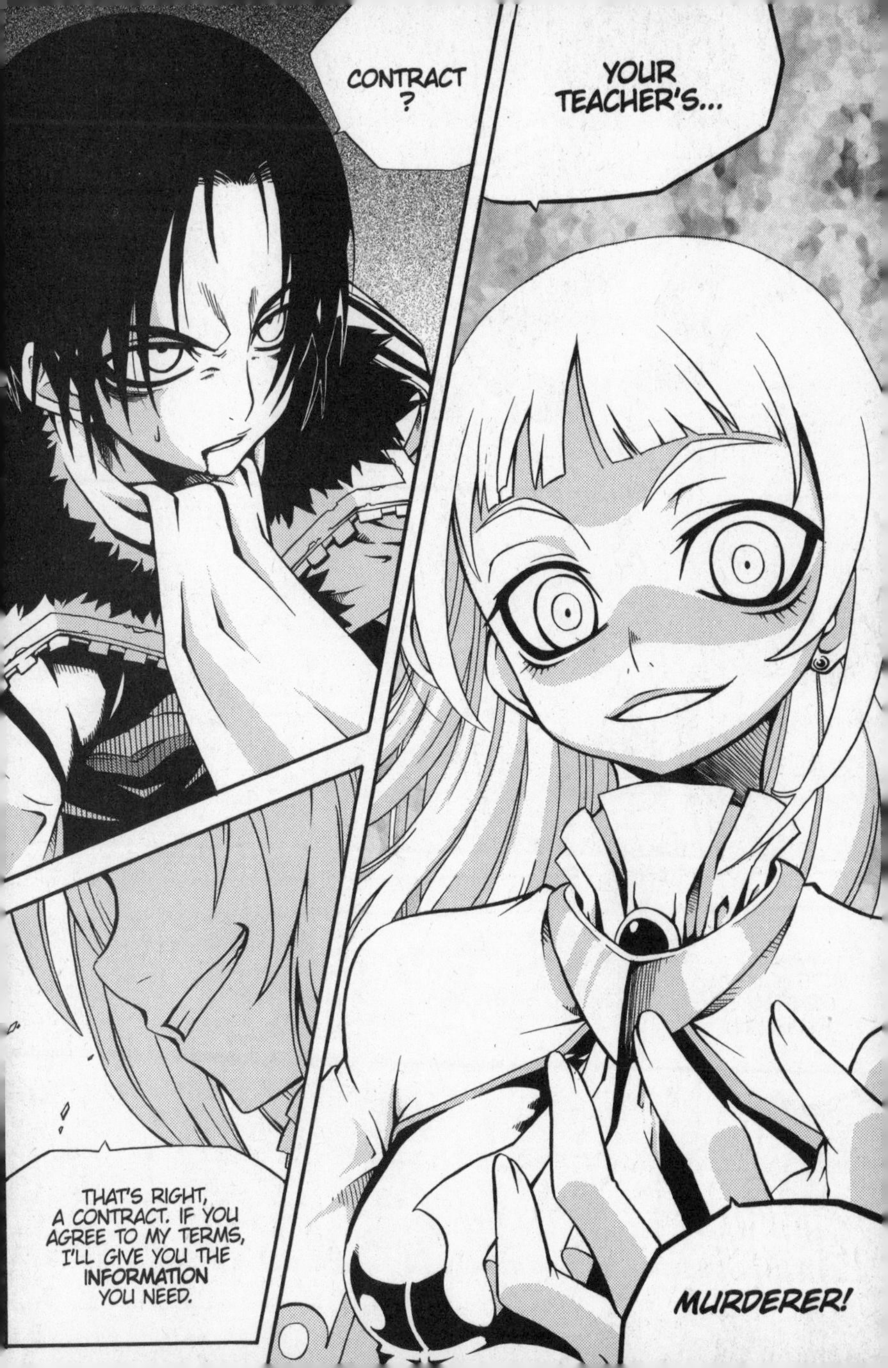
YOUR TEACHER'S...
CONTRACT ?
THAT'S RIGHT, A CONTRACT. IF YOU AGREE TO MY TERMS, I'LL GIVE YOU THE INFORMATION YOU NEED.
MURDERER!

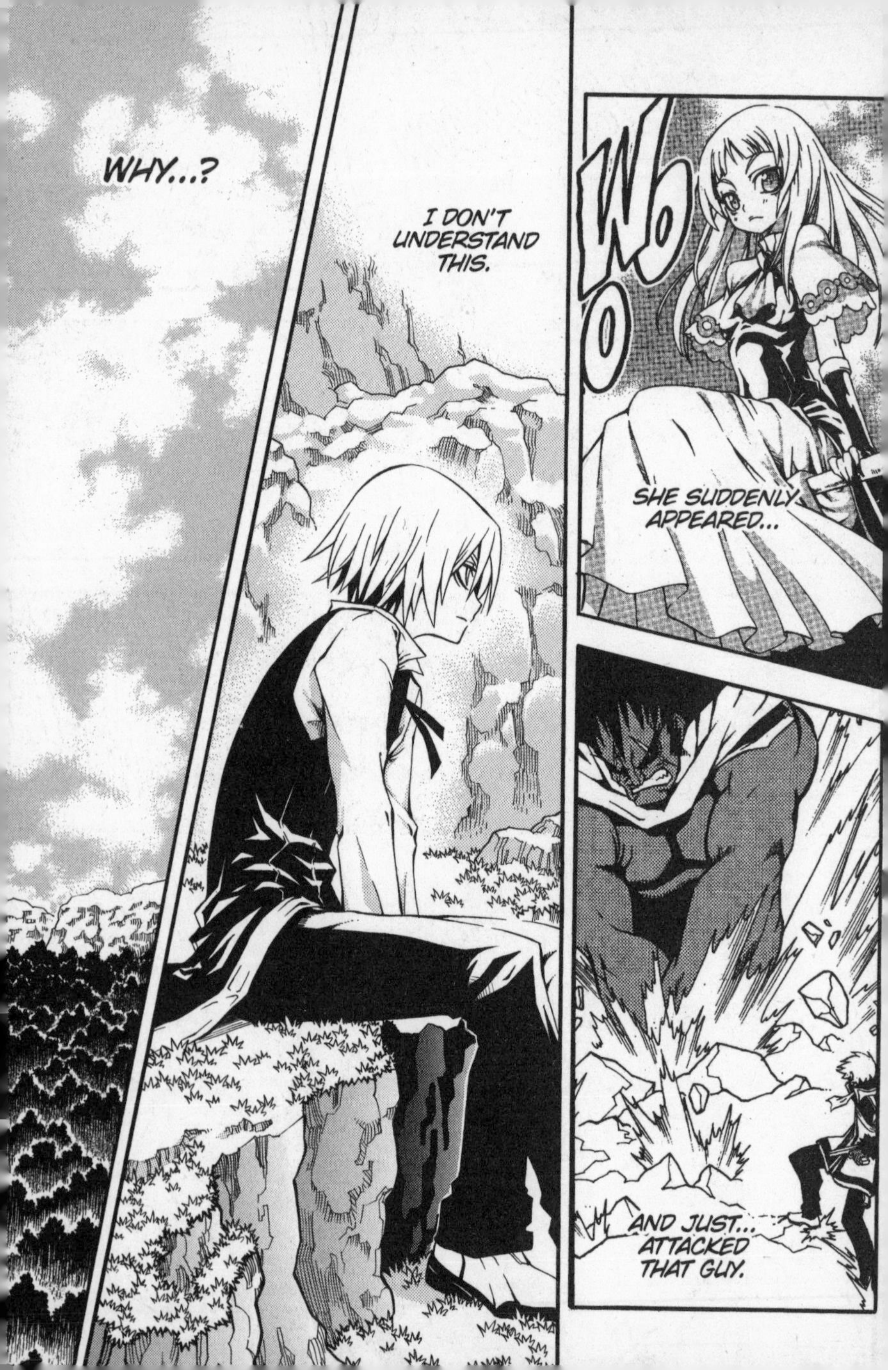
WOO
SHE SUDDENLY APPEARED...
AND JUST... ATTACKED THAT GUY.
WHY...?
I DON'T UNDERSTAND THIS.

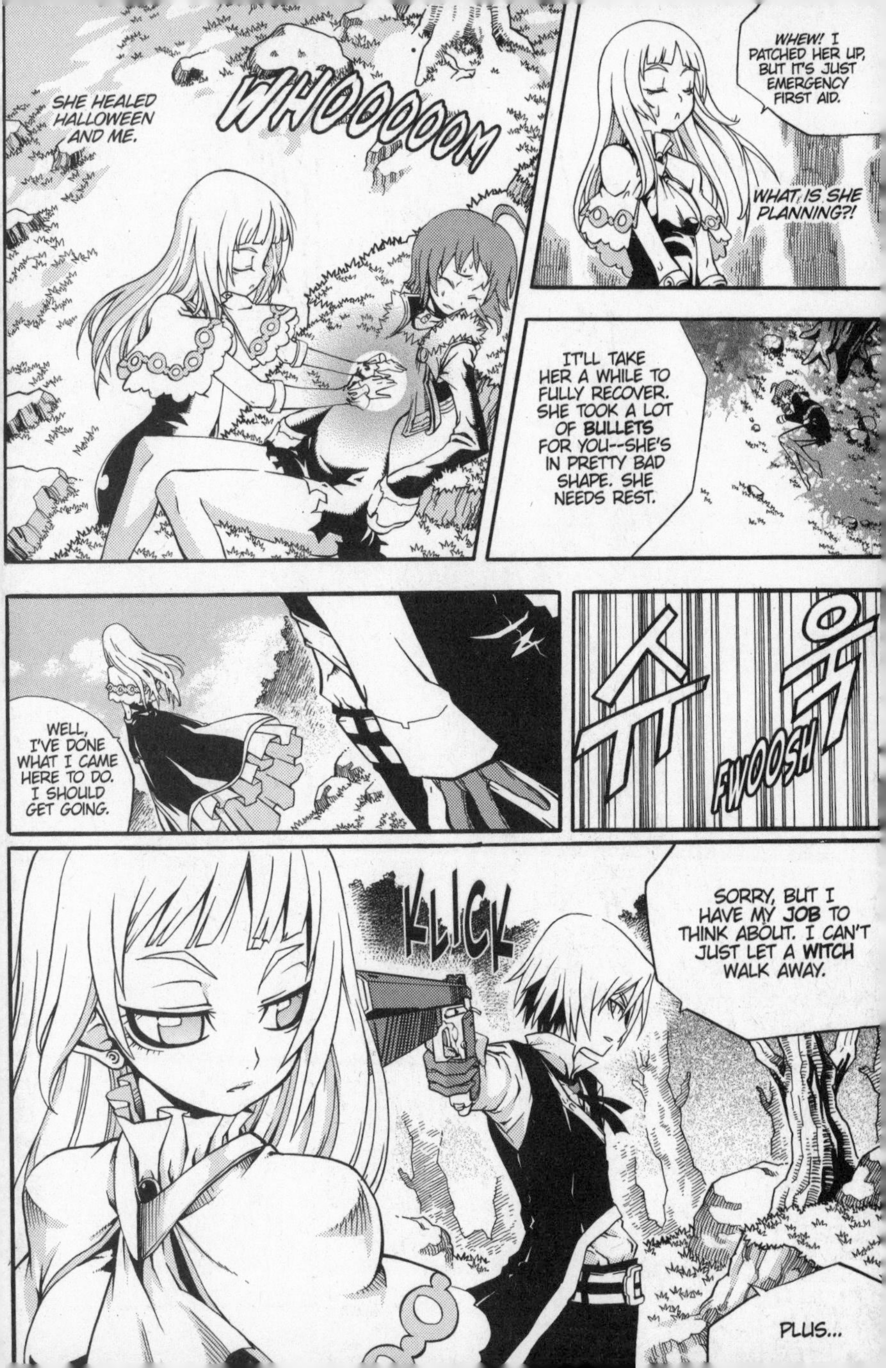
WHEW! I PATCHED HER UP, BUT IT'S JUST EMERGENCY FIRST AID.
WHAT IS SHE PLANNING?!
SHE HEALED HALLOWEEN AND ME.
WHOOOOOOM
IT'LL TAKE HER A WHILE TO FULLY RECOVER. SHE TOOK A LOT OF BULLETS FOR YOU--SHE'S IN PRETTY BAD SHAPE. SHE NEEDS REST.
FWOOSH
WELL, I'VE DONE WHAT I CAME HERE TO DO. I SHOULD GET GOING.
SORRY, BUT I HAVE MY JOB TO THINK ABOUT. I CAN'T JUST LET A WITCH WALK AWAY.
KLICK
PLUS...

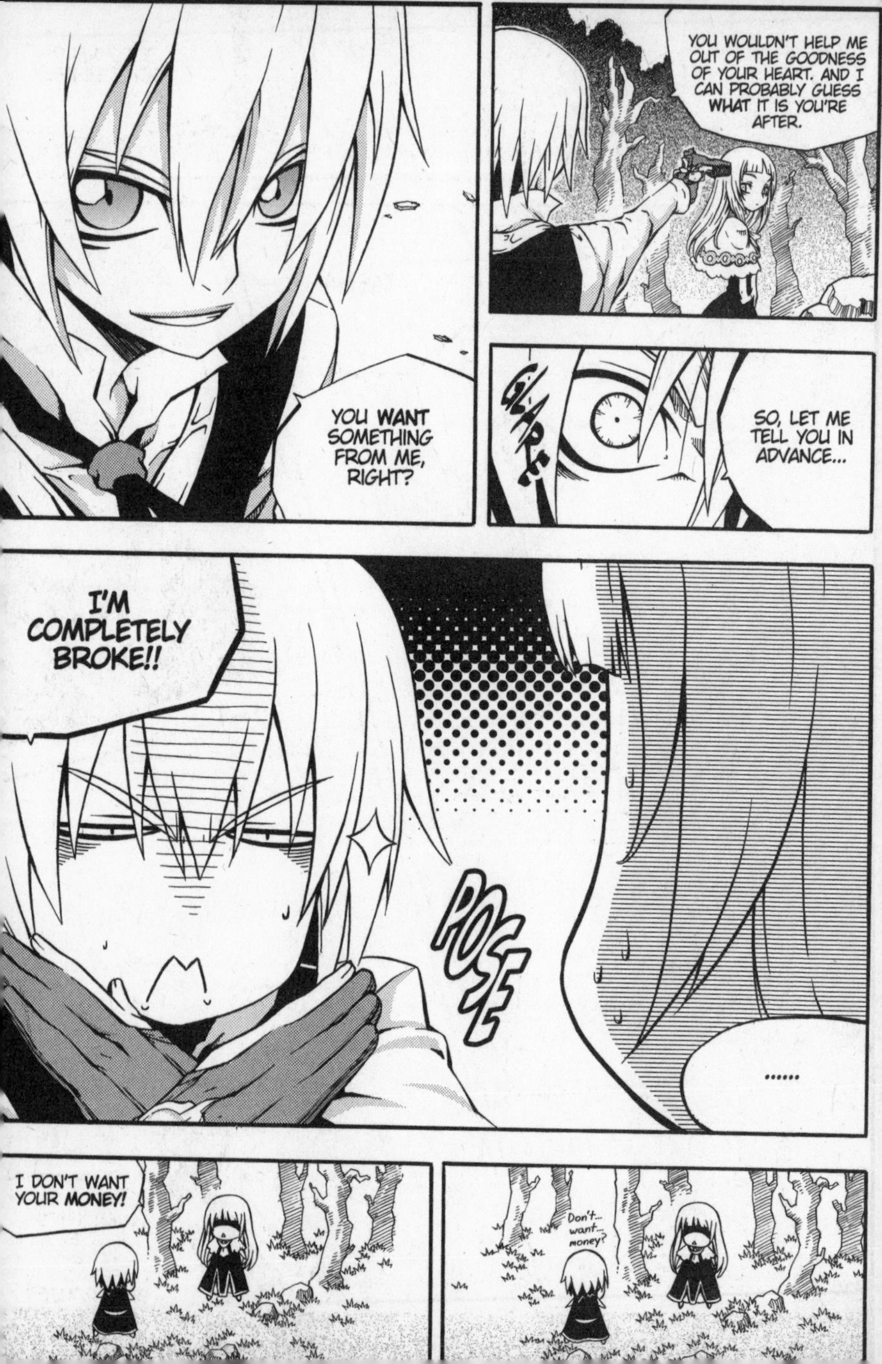
YOU WANT SOMETHING FROM ME, RIGHT?
YOU WOULDN'T HELP ME OUT OF THE GOODNESS OF YOUR HEART. AND I CAN PROBABLY GUESS WHAT IT IS YOU'RE AFTER.
GLARE
SO, LET ME TELL YOU IN ADVANCE...
I'M COMPLETELY BROKE!!
POSE
......
I DON'T WANT YOUR MONEY!
Don't... want... money?

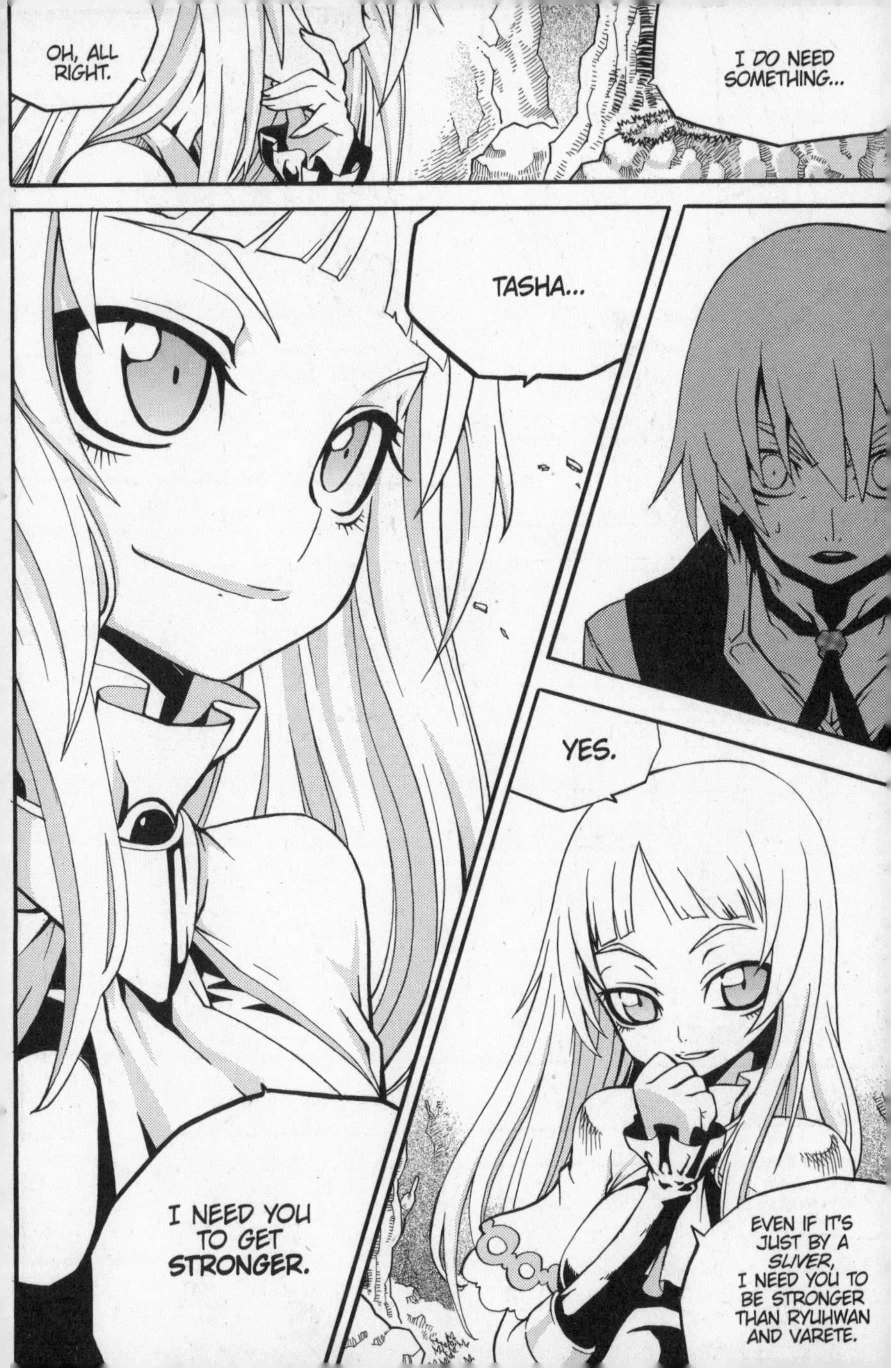
OH, ALL RIGHT.
I DO NEED SOMETHING...
TASHA...
YES.
I NEED YOU TO GET STRONGER.
EVEN IF IT'S JUST BY A *SLIVER*, I NEED YOU TO BE STRONGER THAN RYUHWAN AND VARETE.

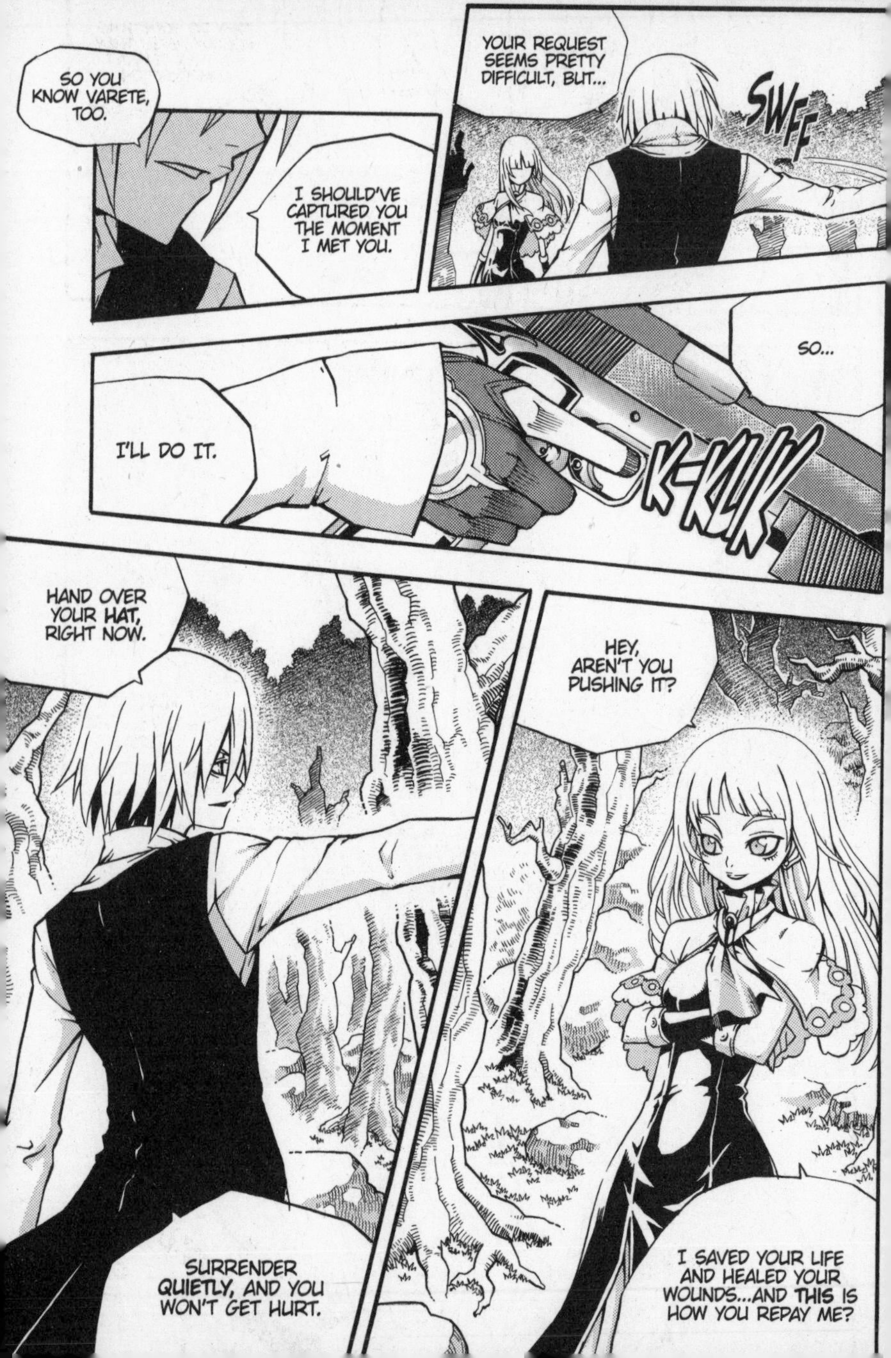
YOUR REQUEST SEEMS PRETTY DIFFICULT, BUT...
SWFF
SO YOU KNOW VARETE, TOO.
I SHOULD'VE CAPTURED YOU THE MOMENT I MET YOU.
SO...
I'LL DO IT.
K-KLIK
HEY, AREN'T YOU PUSHING IT?
HAND OVER YOUR HAT, RIGHT NOW.
I SAVED YOUR LIFE AND HEALED YOUR WOUNDS...AND THIS IS HOW YOU REPAY ME?
SURRENDER QUIETLY, AND YOU WON'T GET HURT.

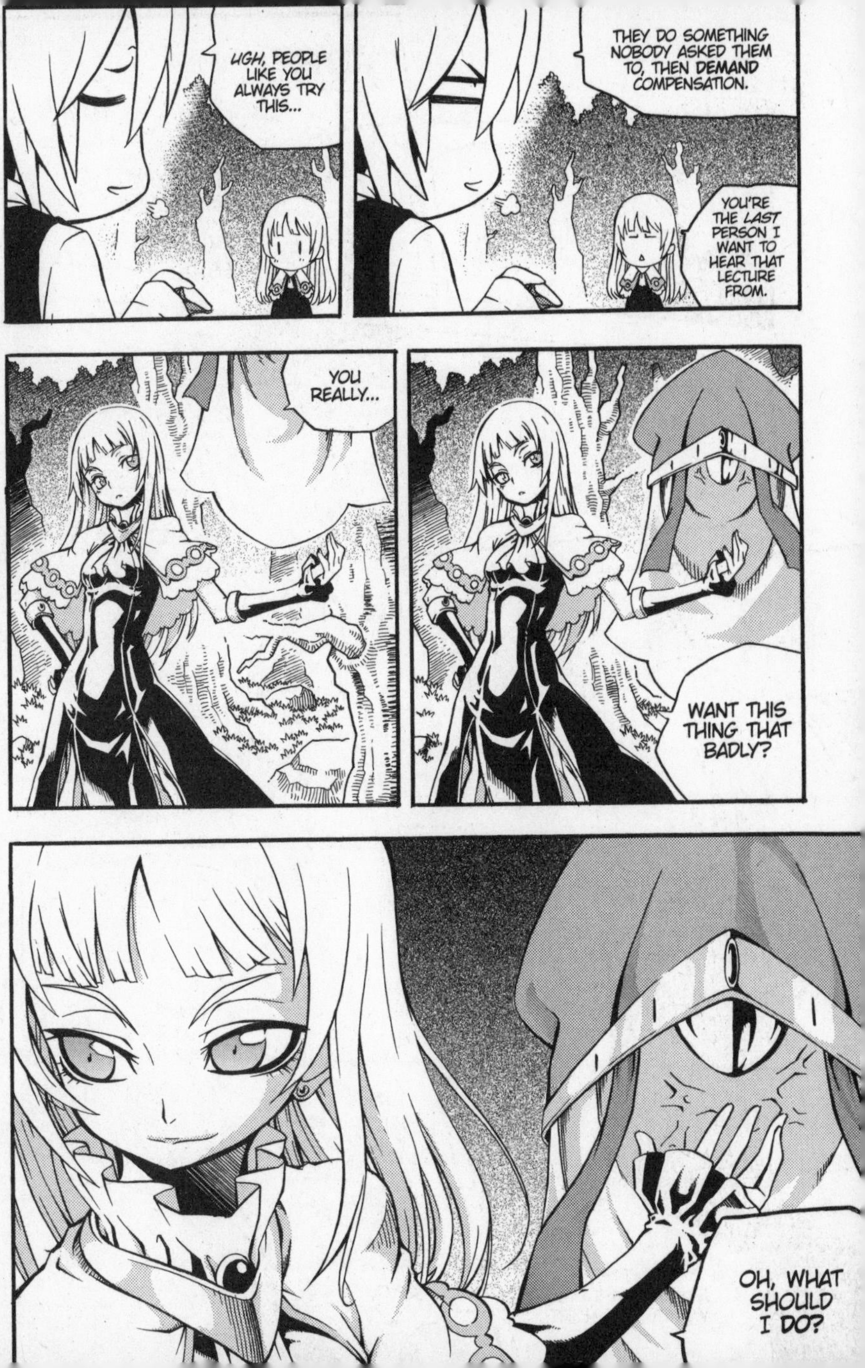
UGH, PEOPLE LIKE YOU ALWAYS TRY THIS...
THEY DO SOMETHING NOBODY ASKED THEM TO, THEN DEMAND COMPENSATION.
YOU'RE THE LAST PERSON I WANT TO HEAR THAT LECTURE FROM.
YOU REALLY...
WANT THIS THING THAT BADLY?
OH, WHAT SHOULD I DO?

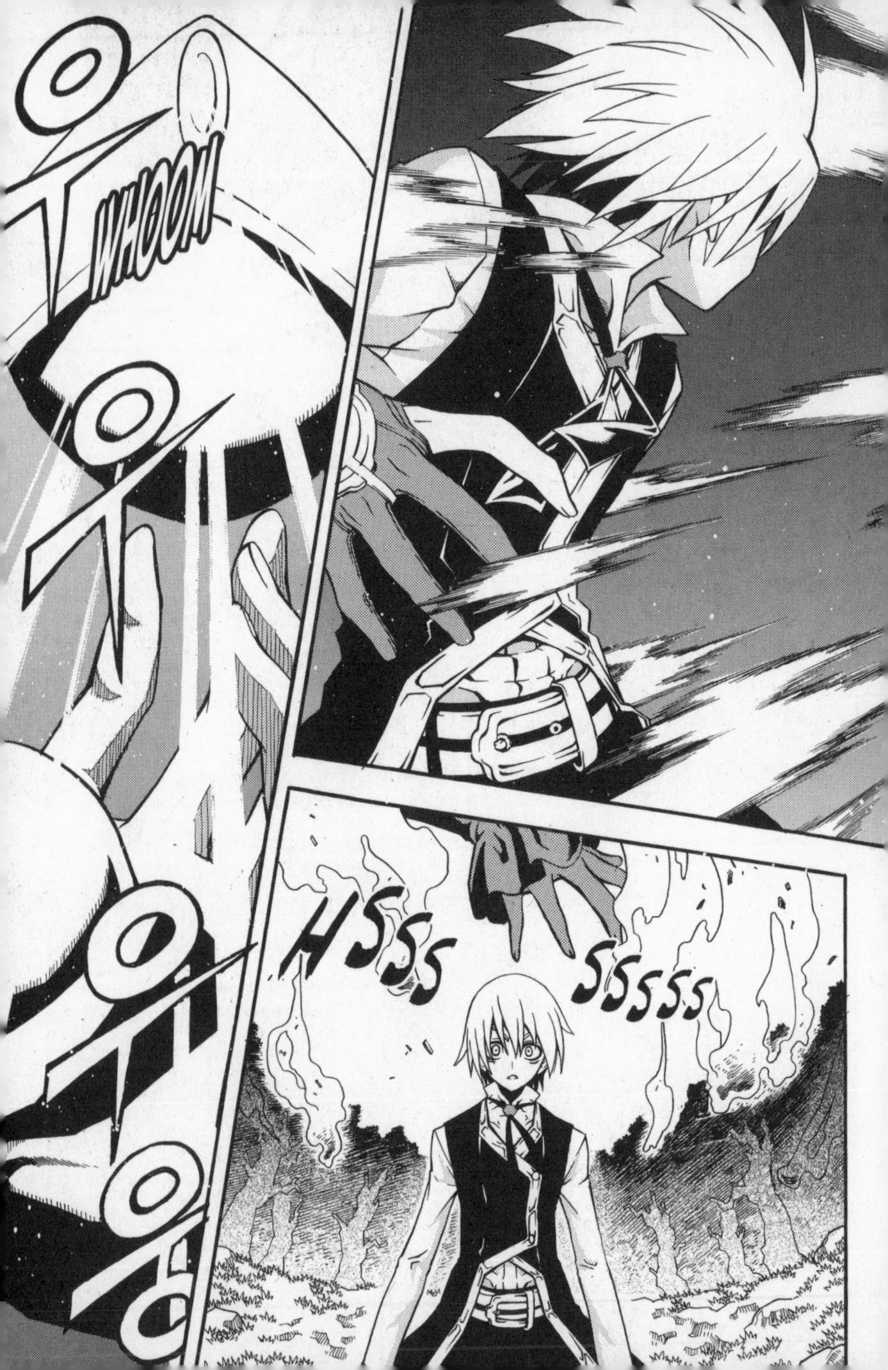

WHOOM
HSSS
SSSSS

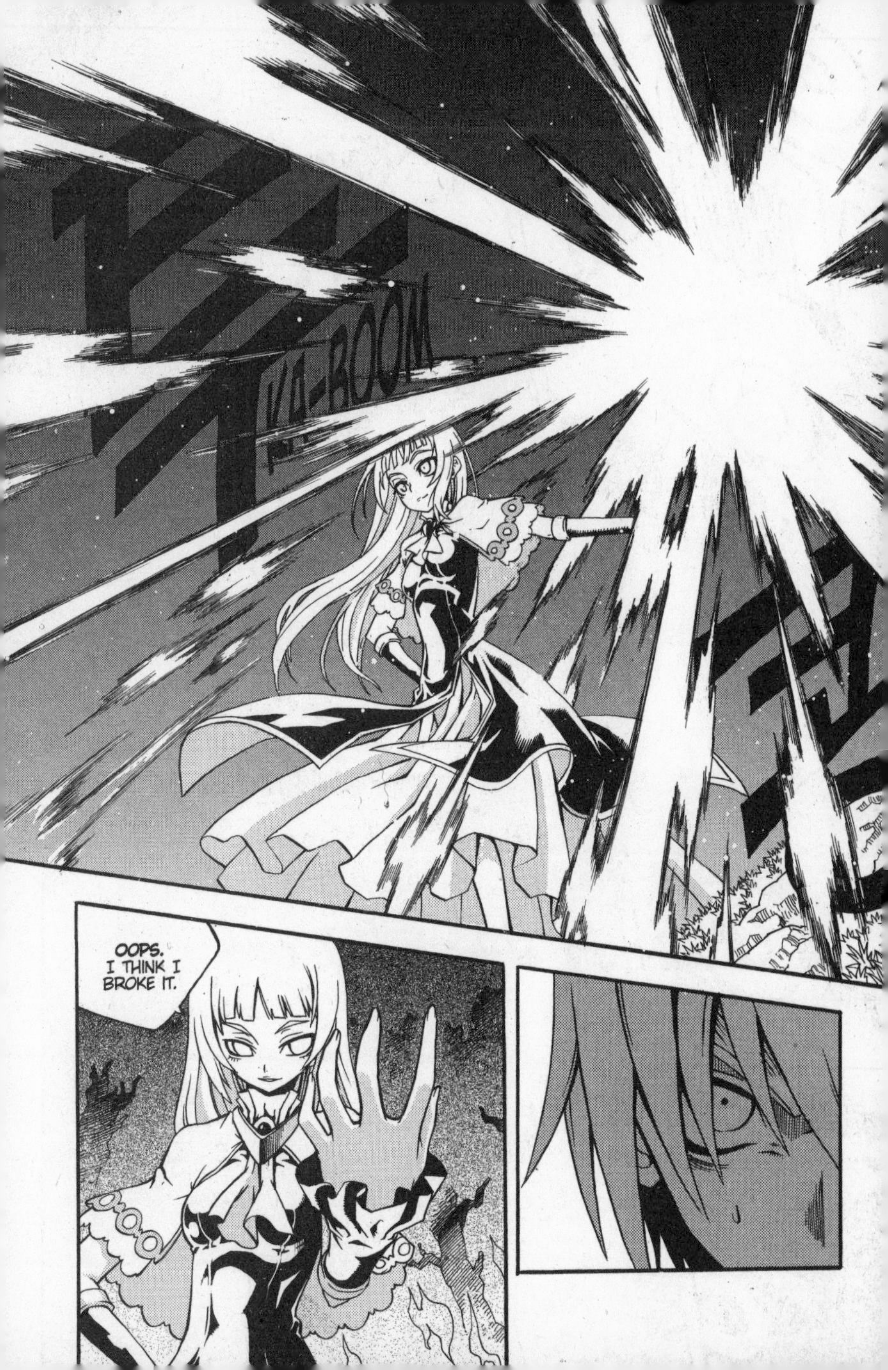
KA-BOOM
OOPS. I THINK I BROKE IT.

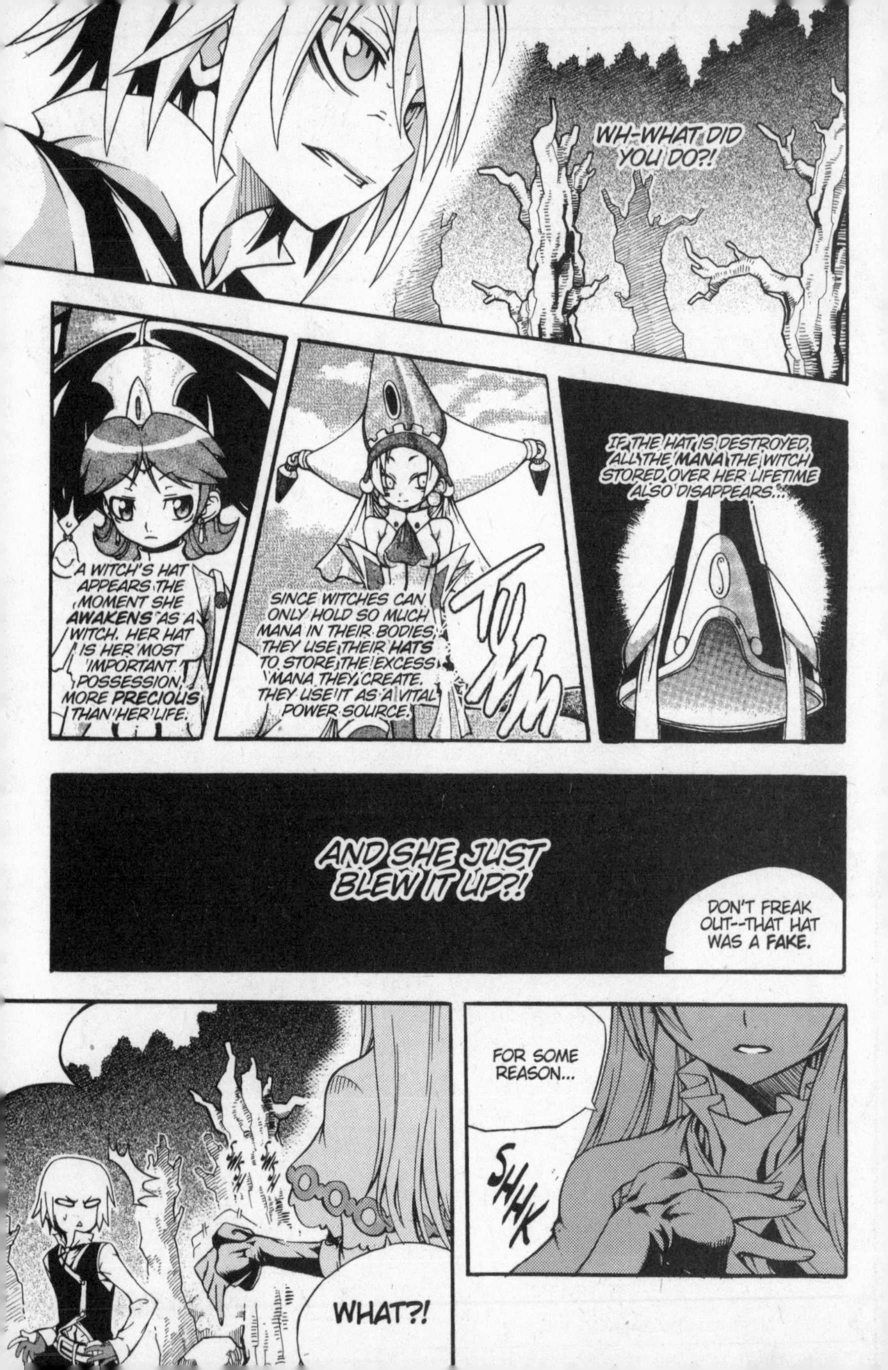
WH-WHAT DID YOU DO?!
IF THE HAT IS DESTROYED, ALL THE MANA THE WITCH STORED OVER HER LIFETIME ALSO DISAPPEARS...
SINCE WITCHES CAN ONLY HOLD SO MUCH MANA IN THEIR BODIES, THEY USE THEIR HATS TO STORE THE EXCESS MANA THEY CREATE. THEY USE IT AS A VITAL POWER SOURCE.
A WITCH'S HAT APPEARS THE MOMENT SHE AWAKENS AS A WITCH. HER HAT IS HER MOST IMPORTANT POSSESSION, MORE PRECIOUS THAN HER LIFE.
AND SHE JUST BLEW IT UP?!
DON'T FREAK OUT--THAT HAT WAS A FAKE.
FOR SOME REASON...
SHHK
WHAT?!

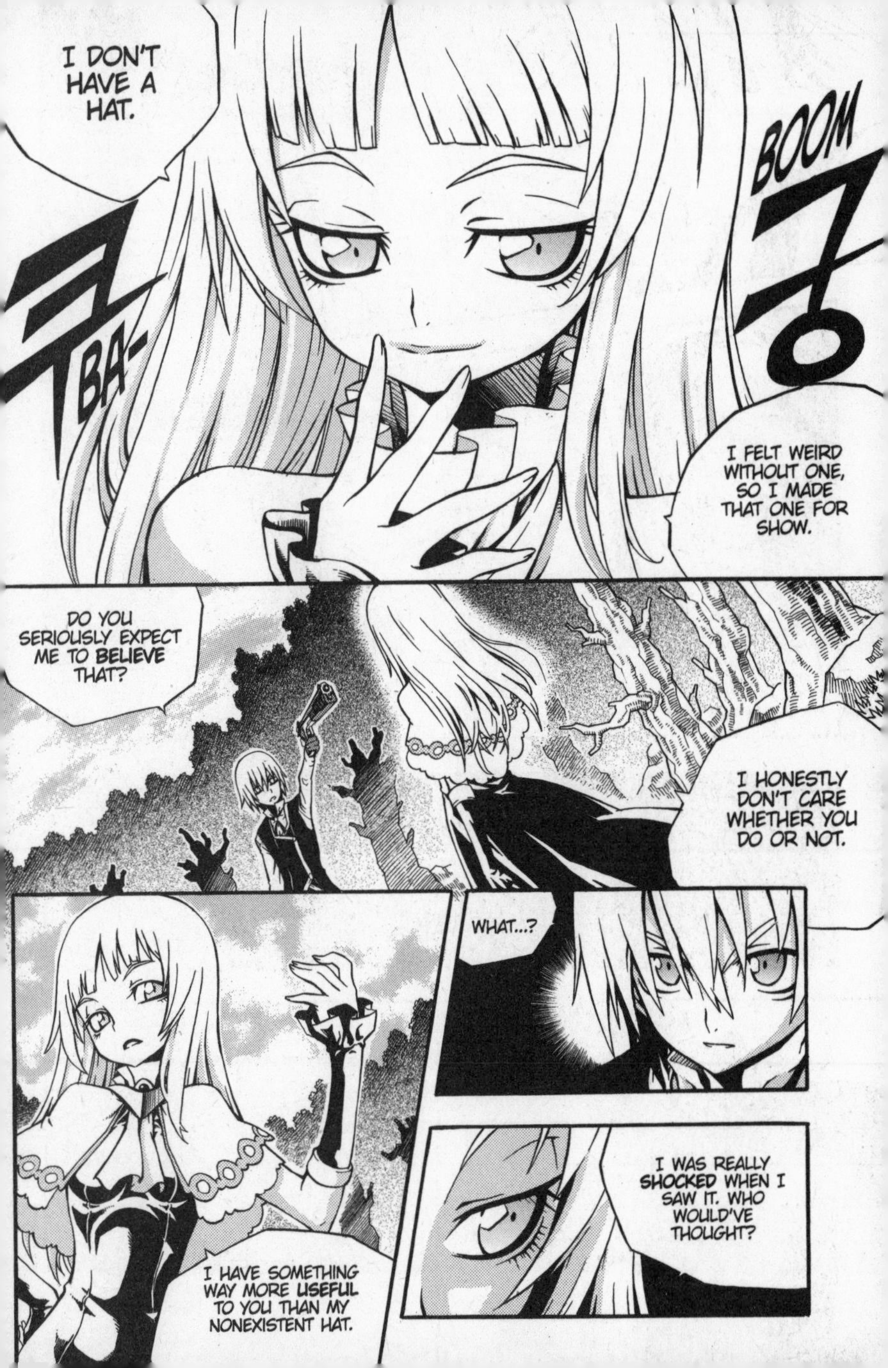
I DON'T HAVE A HAT.
BA-BOOM
I FELT WEIRD WITHOUT ONE, SO I MADE THAT ONE FOR SHOW.
DO YOU SERIOUSLY EXPECT ME TO **BELIEVE** THAT?
I HONESTLY DON'T CARE WHETHER YOU DO OR NOT.
WHAT...?
I WAS REALLY **SHOCKED** WHEN I SAW IT. WHO WOULD'VE THOUGHT?
I HAVE SOMETHING WAY MORE **USEFUL** TO YOU THAN MY NONEXISTENT HAT.

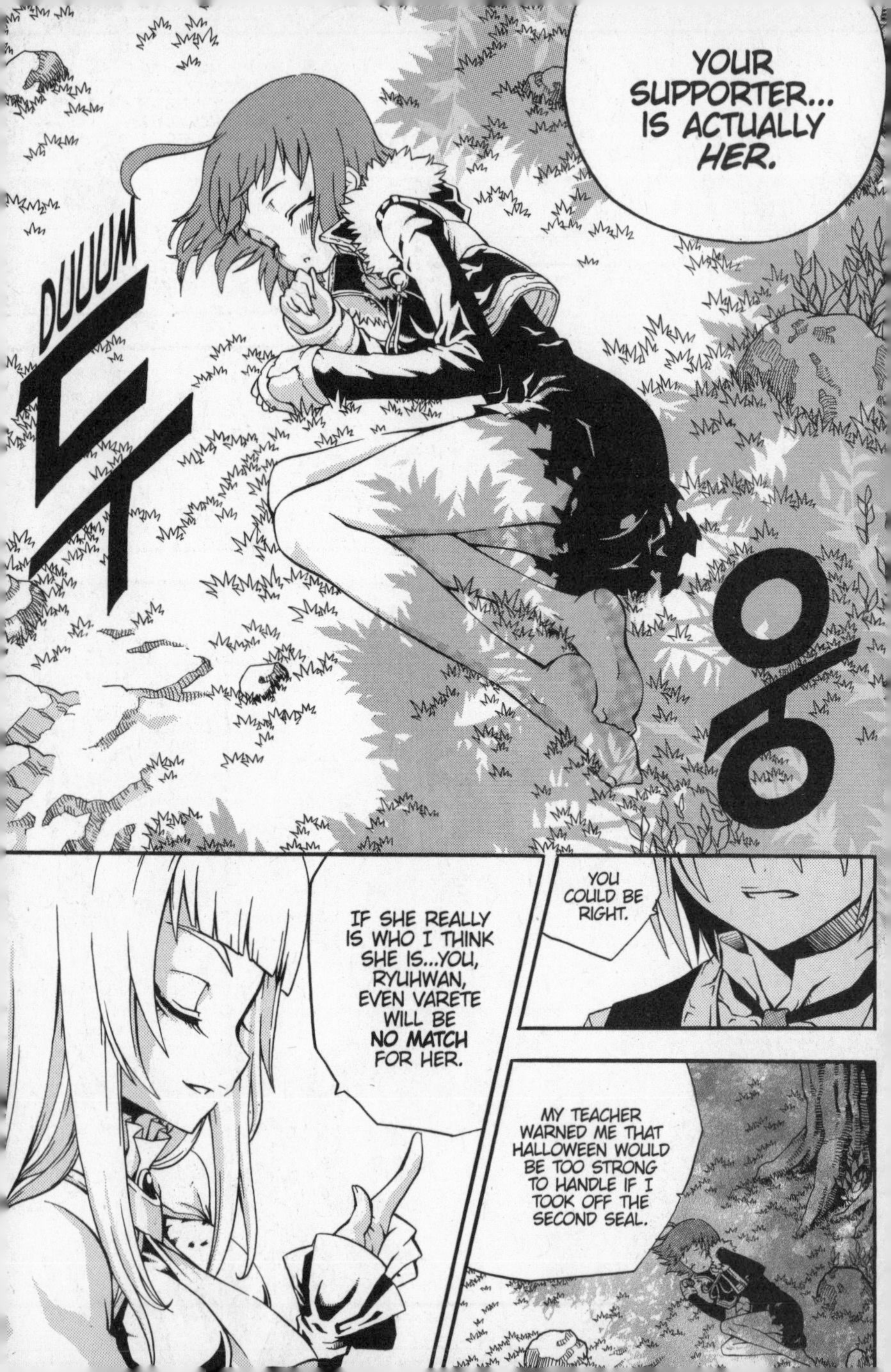
YOUR SUPPORTER... IS ACTUALLY HER.
DUUUM
IF SHE REALLY IS WHO I THINK SHE IS...YOU, RYUHWAN, EVEN VARETE WILL BE NO MATCH FOR HER.
YOU COULD BE RIGHT.
MY TEACHER WARNED ME THAT HALLOWEEN WOULD BE TOO STRONG TO HANDLE IF I TOOK OFF THE SECOND SEAL.

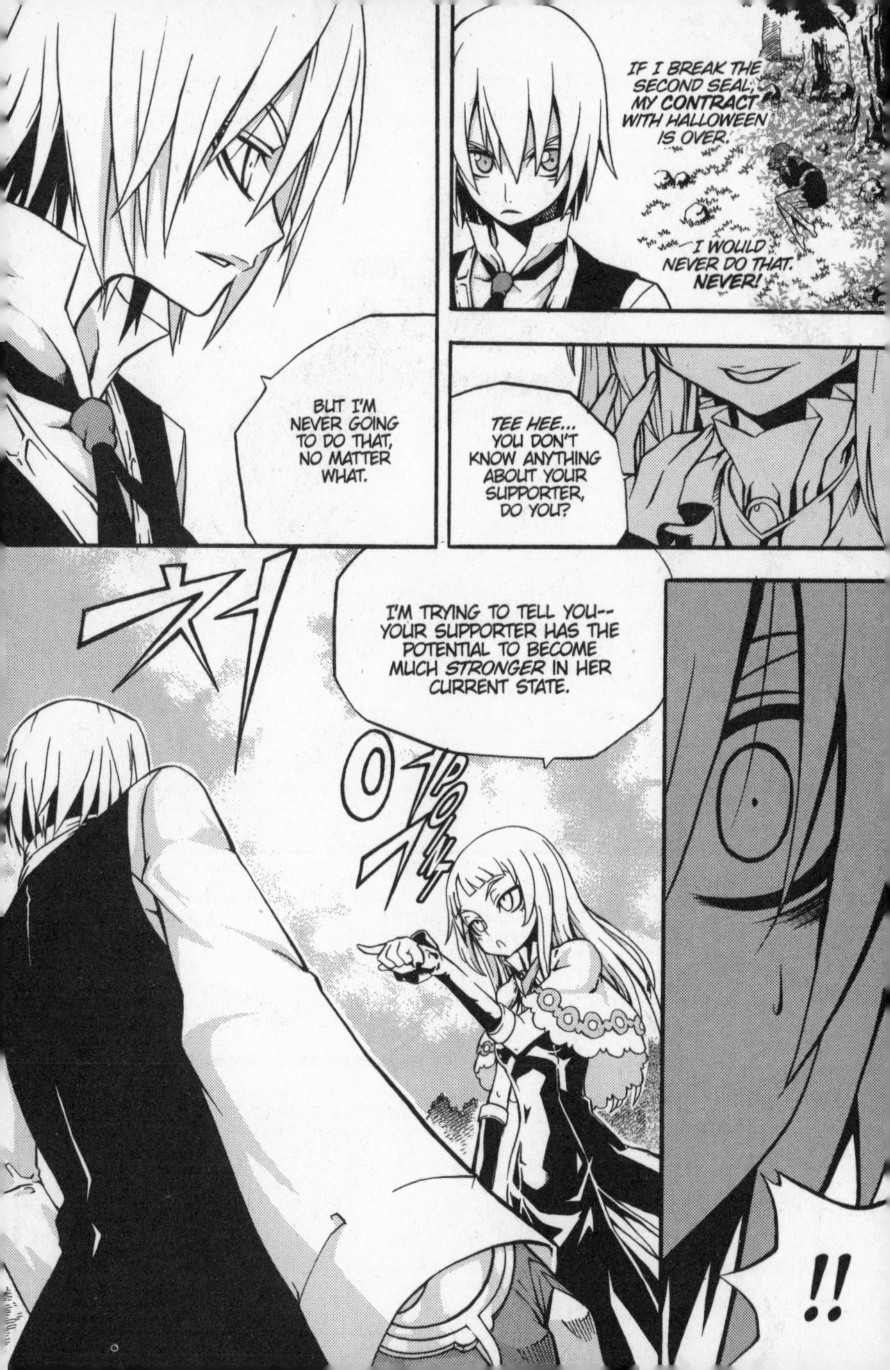
IF I BREAK THE SECOND SEAL, MY CONTRACT WITH HALLOWEEN IS OVER.
I WOULD NEVER DO THAT. NEVER!
BUT I'M NEVER GOING TO DO THAT, NO MATTER WHAT.
TEE HEE... YOU DON'T KNOW ANYTHING ABOUT YOUR SUPPORTER, DO YOU?
I'M TRYING TO TELL YOU-- YOUR SUPPORTER HAS THE POTENTIAL TO BECOME MUCH STRONGER IN HER CURRENT STATE.
!!

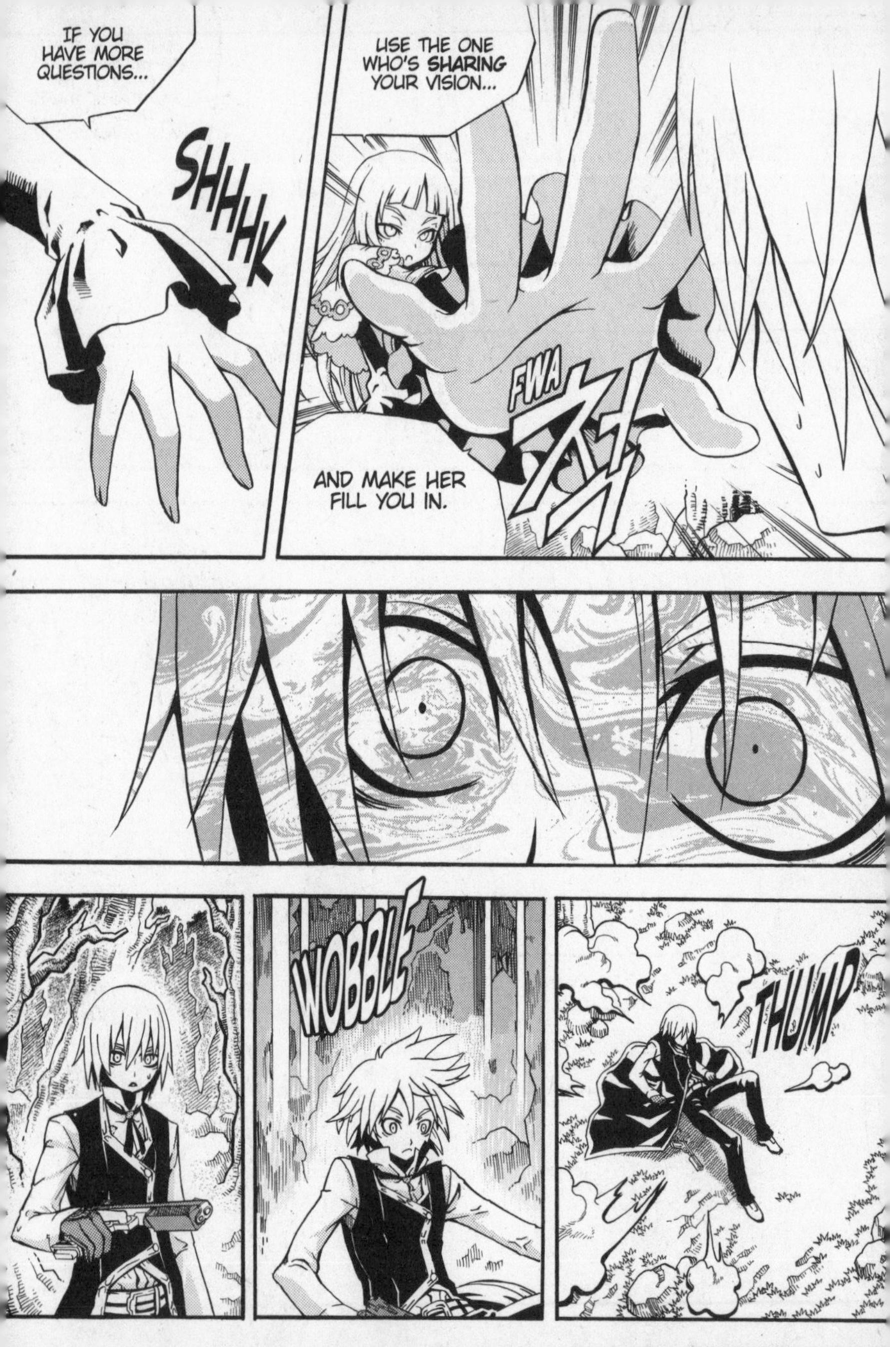
IF YOU HAVE MORE QUESTIONS...
SHHHK
USE THE ONE WHO'S SHARING YOUR VISION...
AND MAKE HER FILL YOU IN.
FWA
THUMP
WOBBLE

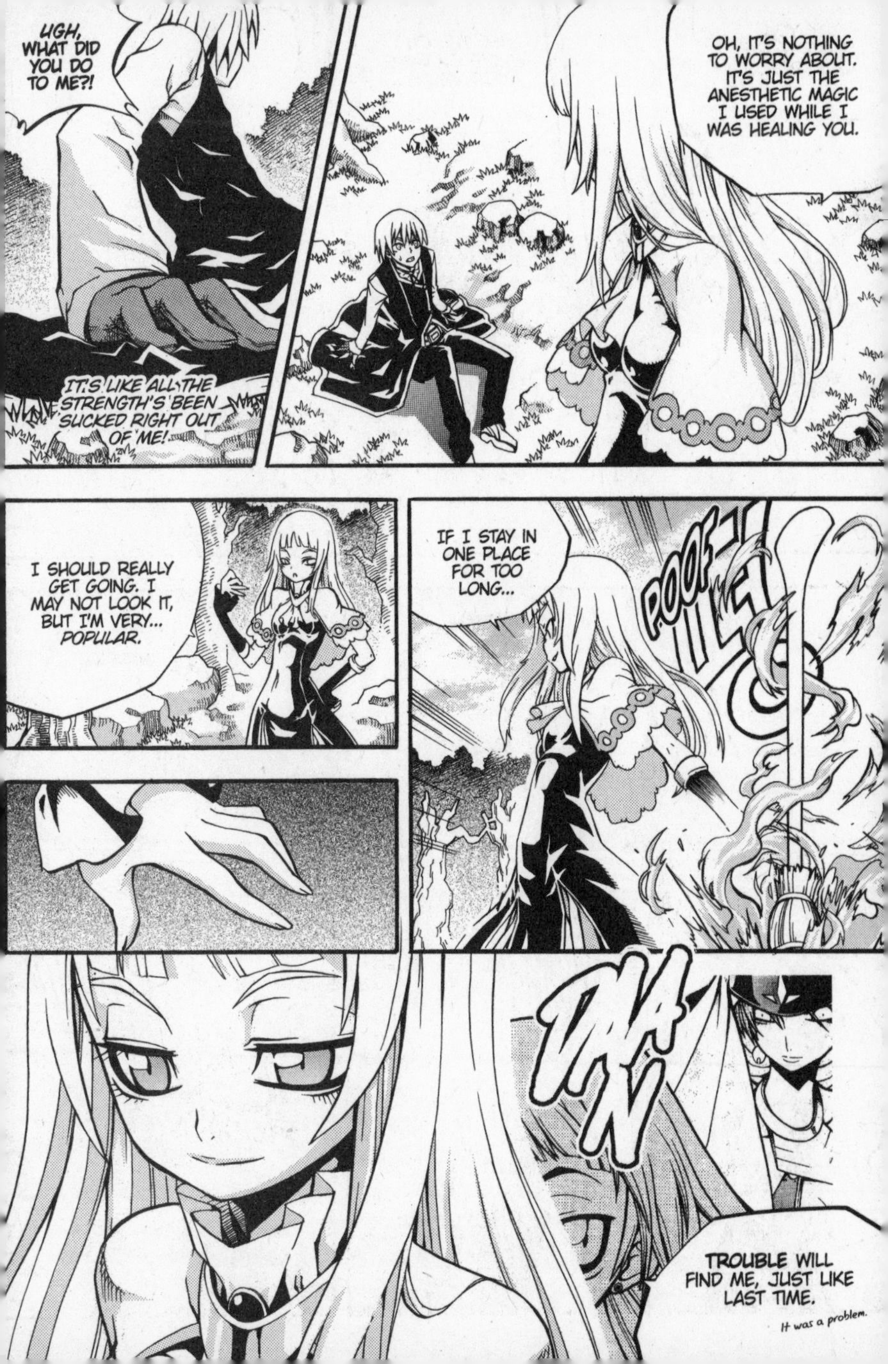
UGH, WHAT DID YOU DO TO ME?!
IT'S LIKE ALL THE STRENGTH'S BEEN SUCKED RIGHT OUT OF ME!
OH, IT'S NOTHING TO WORRY ABOUT. IT'S JUST THE ANESTHETIC MAGIC I USED WHILE I WAS HEALING YOU.
I SHOULD REALLY GET GOING. I MAY NOT LOOK IT, BUT I'M VERY... POPULAR.
IF I STAY IN ONE PLACE FOR TOO LONG...
POOF
TROUBLE WILL FIND ME, JUST LIKE LAST TIME.
It was a problem.

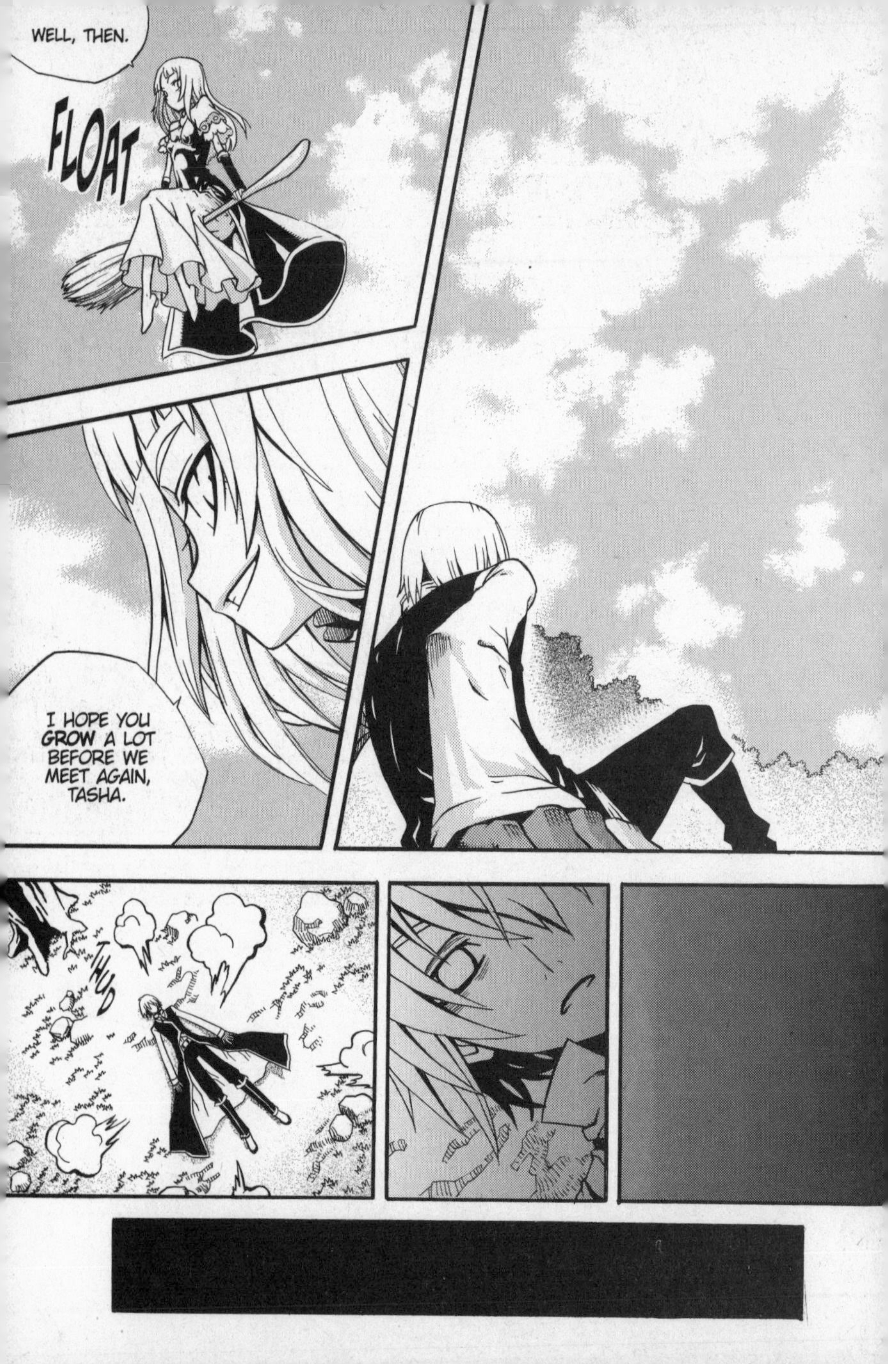

WELL, THEN.
FLOAT
I HOPE YOU GROW A LOT BEFORE WE MEET AGAIN, TASHA.
THUD

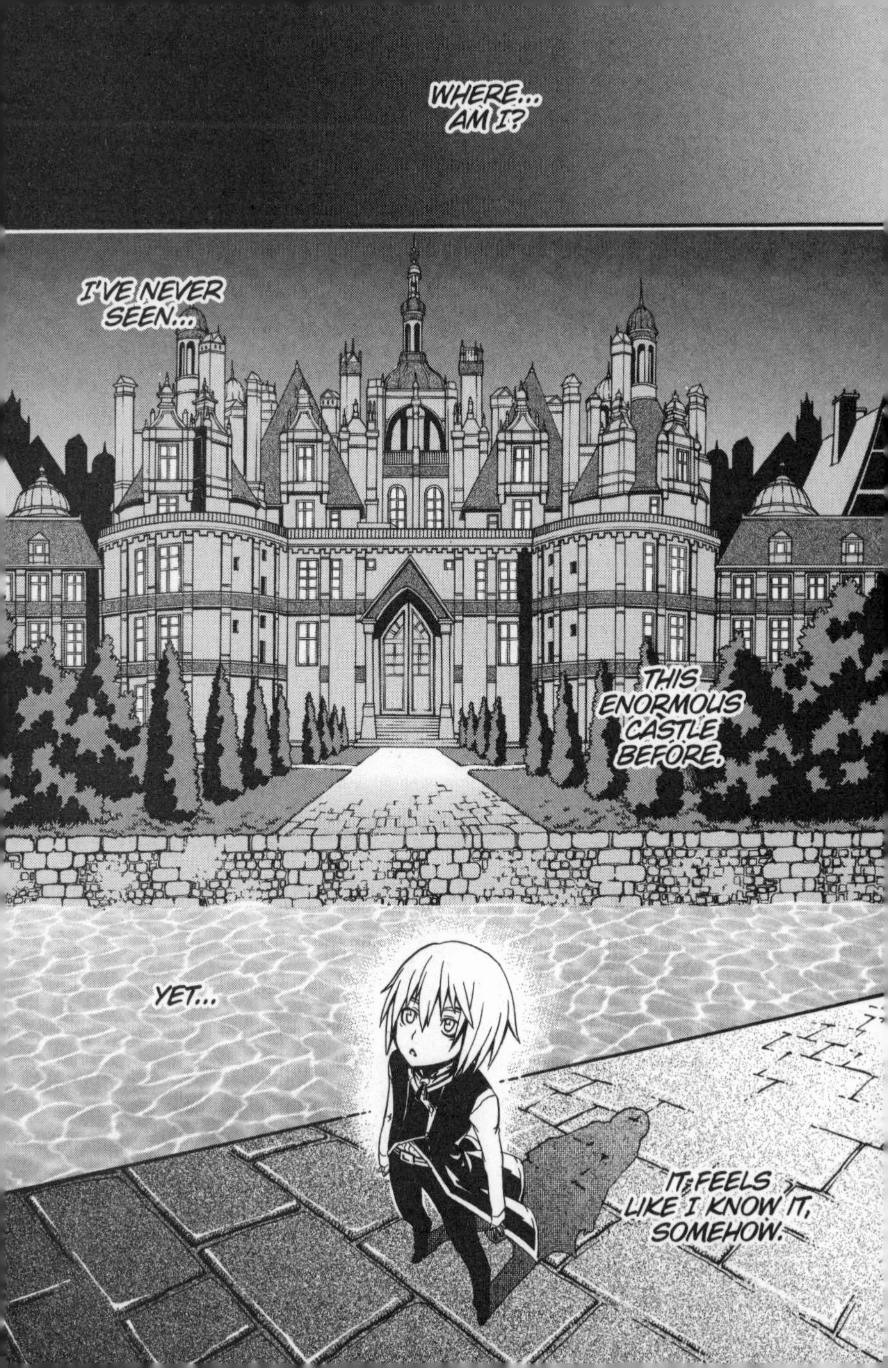
WHERE... AM I?
I'VE NEVER SEEN...
THIS ENORMOUS CASTLE BEFORE.
YET...
IT FEELS LIKE I KNOW IT, SOMEHOW.

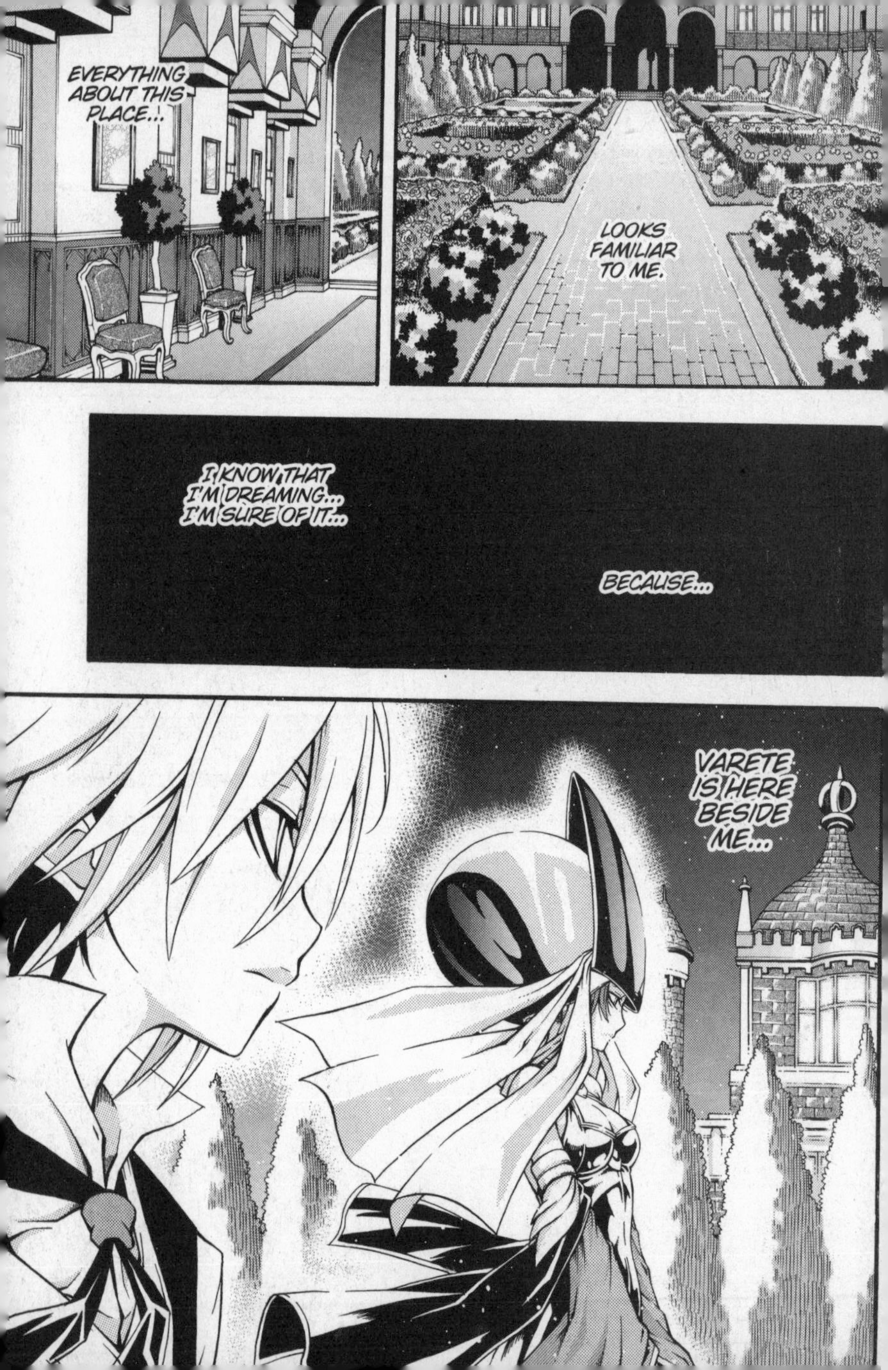
EVERYTHING ABOUT THIS PLACE...
LOOKS FAMILIAR TO ME.
I KNOW THAT I'M DREAMING... I'M SURE OF IT...
BECAUSE...
VARETE IS HERE BESIDE ME...

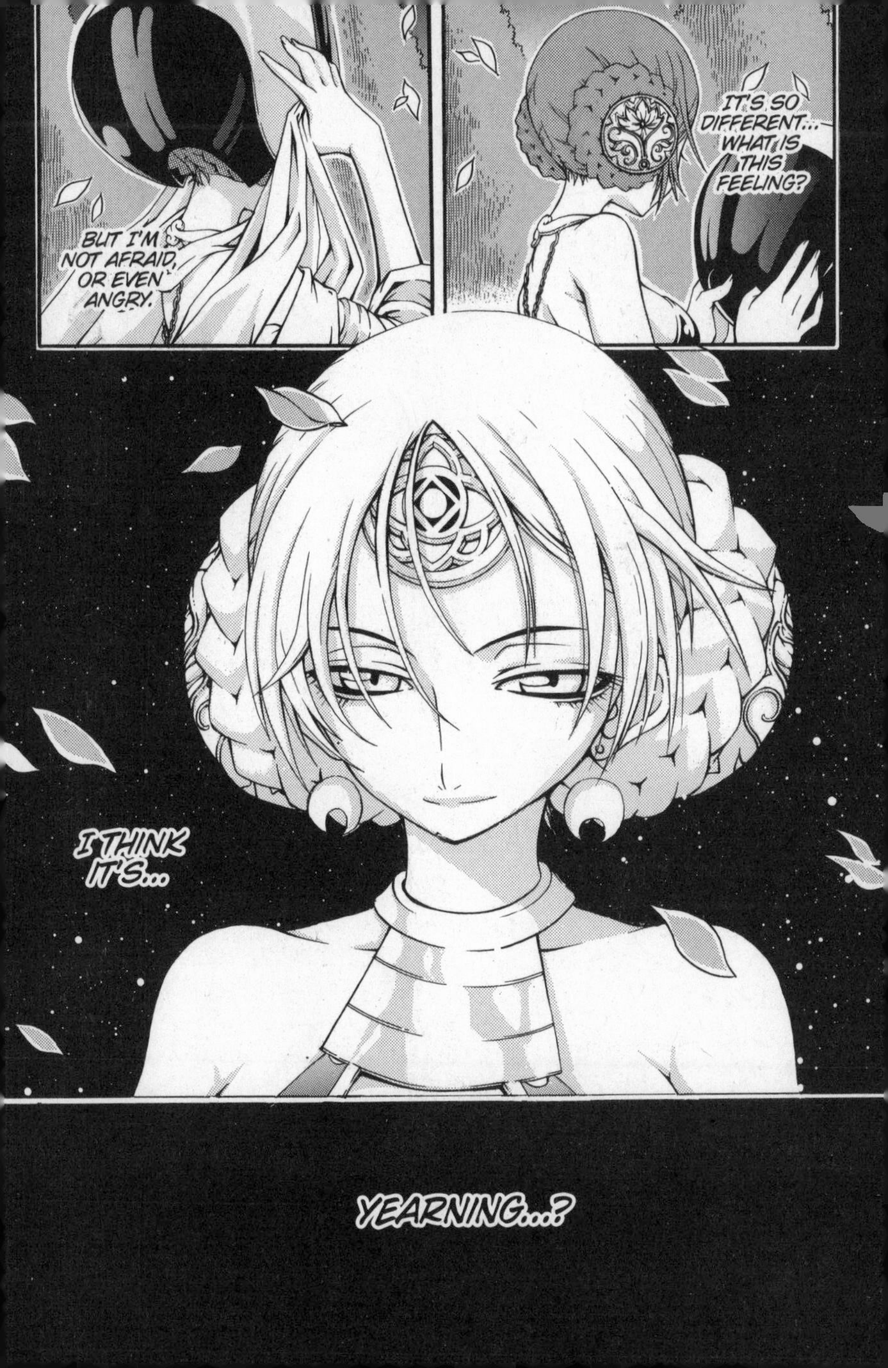
IT'S SO DIFFERENT... WHAT IS THIS FEELING?
BUT I'M NOT AFRAID, OR EVEN ANGRY.
I THINK IT'S...
YEARNING...?

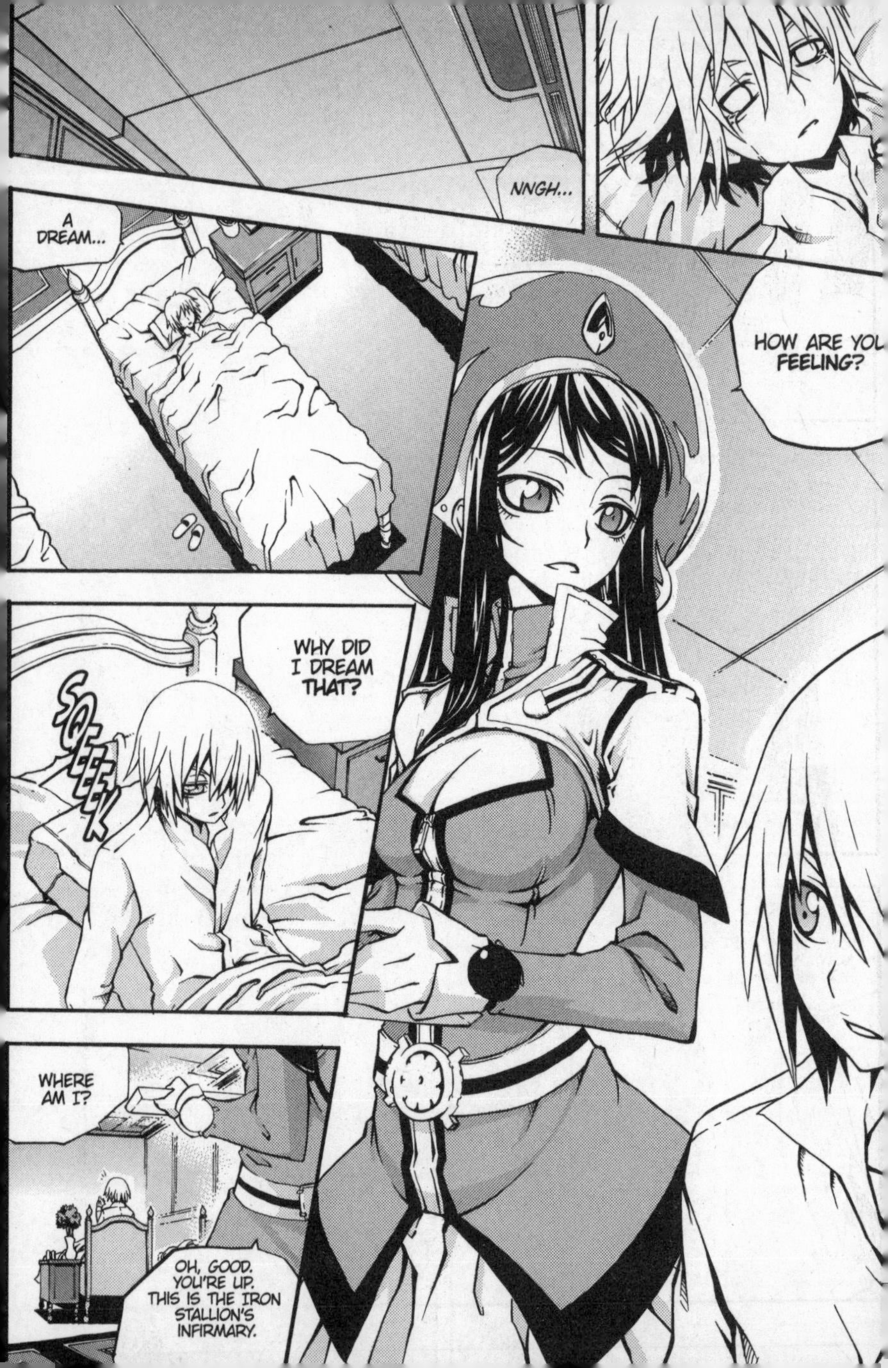
NNGH...
A DREAM...
WHY DID I DREAM THAT?
SQEEEK
WHERE AM I?
OH, GOOD. YOU'RE UP. THIS IS THE IRON STALLION'S INFIRMARY.
HOW ARE YOU FEELING?

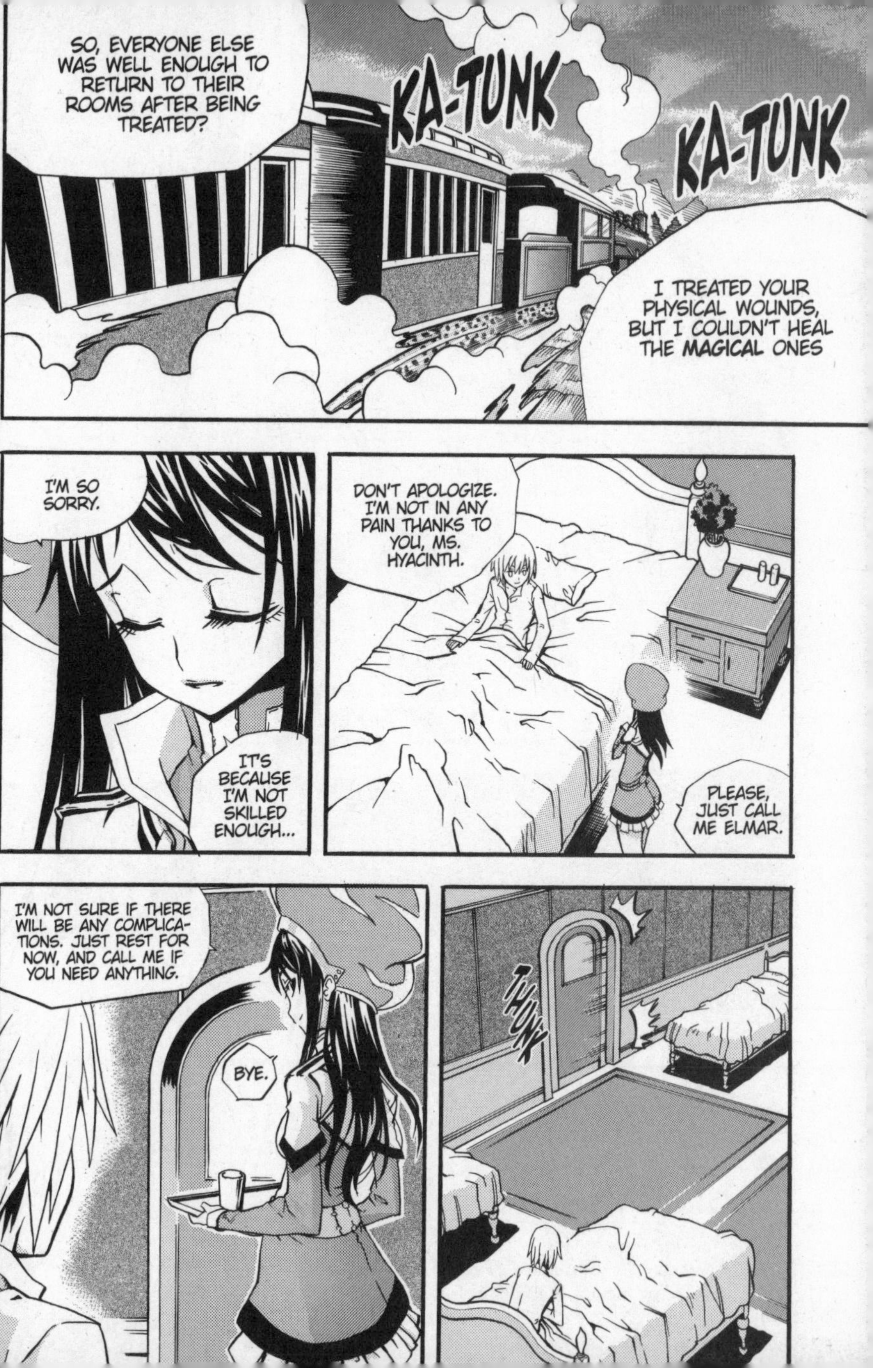
SO, EVERYONE ELSE WAS WELL ENOUGH TO RETURN TO THEIR ROOMS AFTER BEING TREATED?
KA-TUNK
KA-TUNK
I TREATED YOUR PHYSICAL WOUNDS, BUT I COULDN'T HEAL THE MAGICAL ONES
I'M SO SORRY.
IT'S BECAUSE I'M NOT SKILLED ENOUGH...
DON'T APOLOGIZE. I'M NOT IN ANY PAIN THANKS TO YOU, MS. HYACINTH.
PLEASE, JUST CALL ME ELMAR.
I'M NOT SURE IF THERE WILL BE ANY COMPLICATIONS. JUST REST FOR NOW, AND CALL ME IF YOU NEED ANYTHING.
BYE.
THUNK

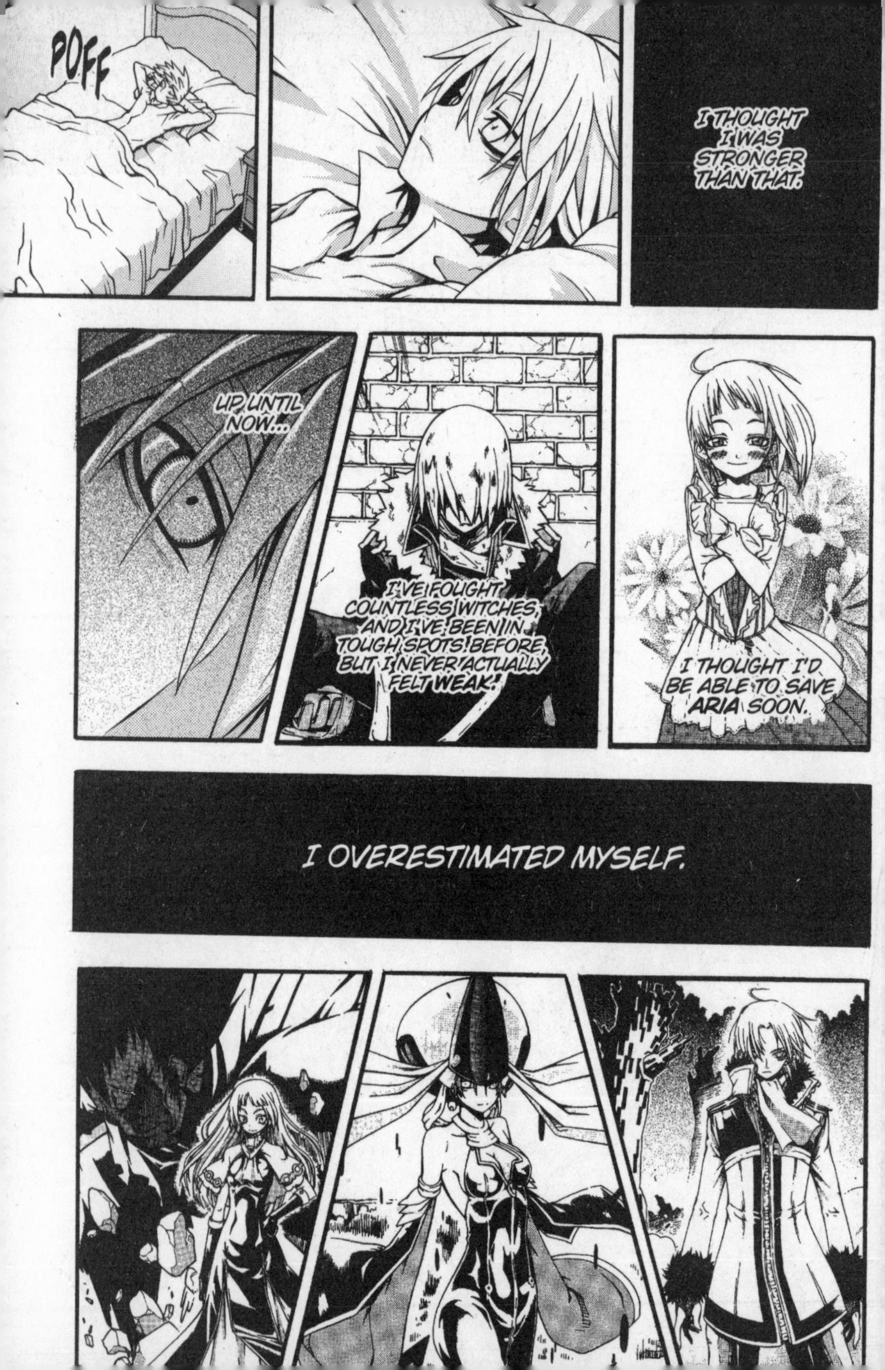
POFF
I THOUGHT I WAS STRONGER THAN THAT.
UP UNTIL NOW...
I'VE FOUGHT COUNTLESS WITCHES, AND I'VE BEEN IN TOUGH SPOTS BEFORE, BUT I NEVER ACTUALLY FELT WEAK!
I THOUGHT I'D BE ABLE TO SAVE ARIA SOON.
I OVERESTIMATED MYSELF.

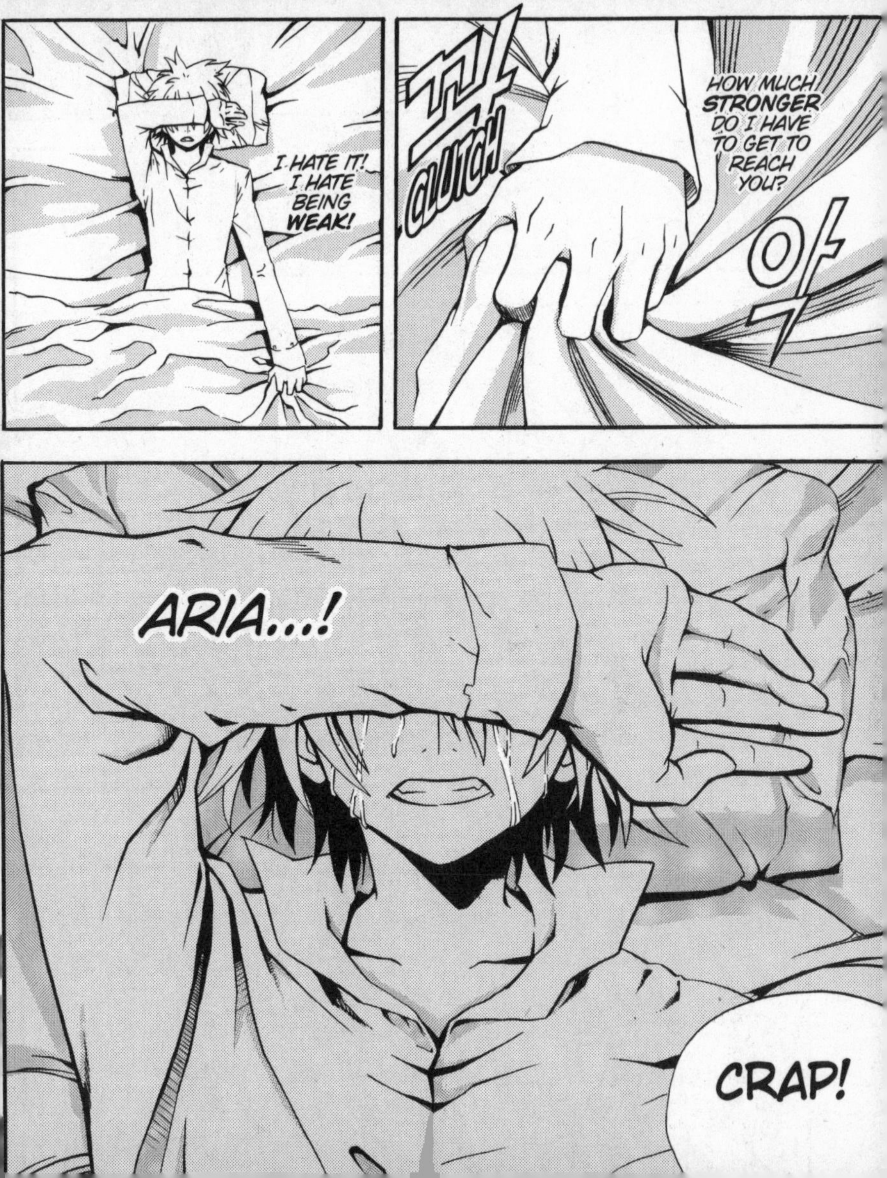
I HATE IT! I HATE BEING WEAK!
CLUTCH
HOW MUCH STRONGER DO I HAVE TO GET TO REACH YOU?
ARIA...!
CRAP!

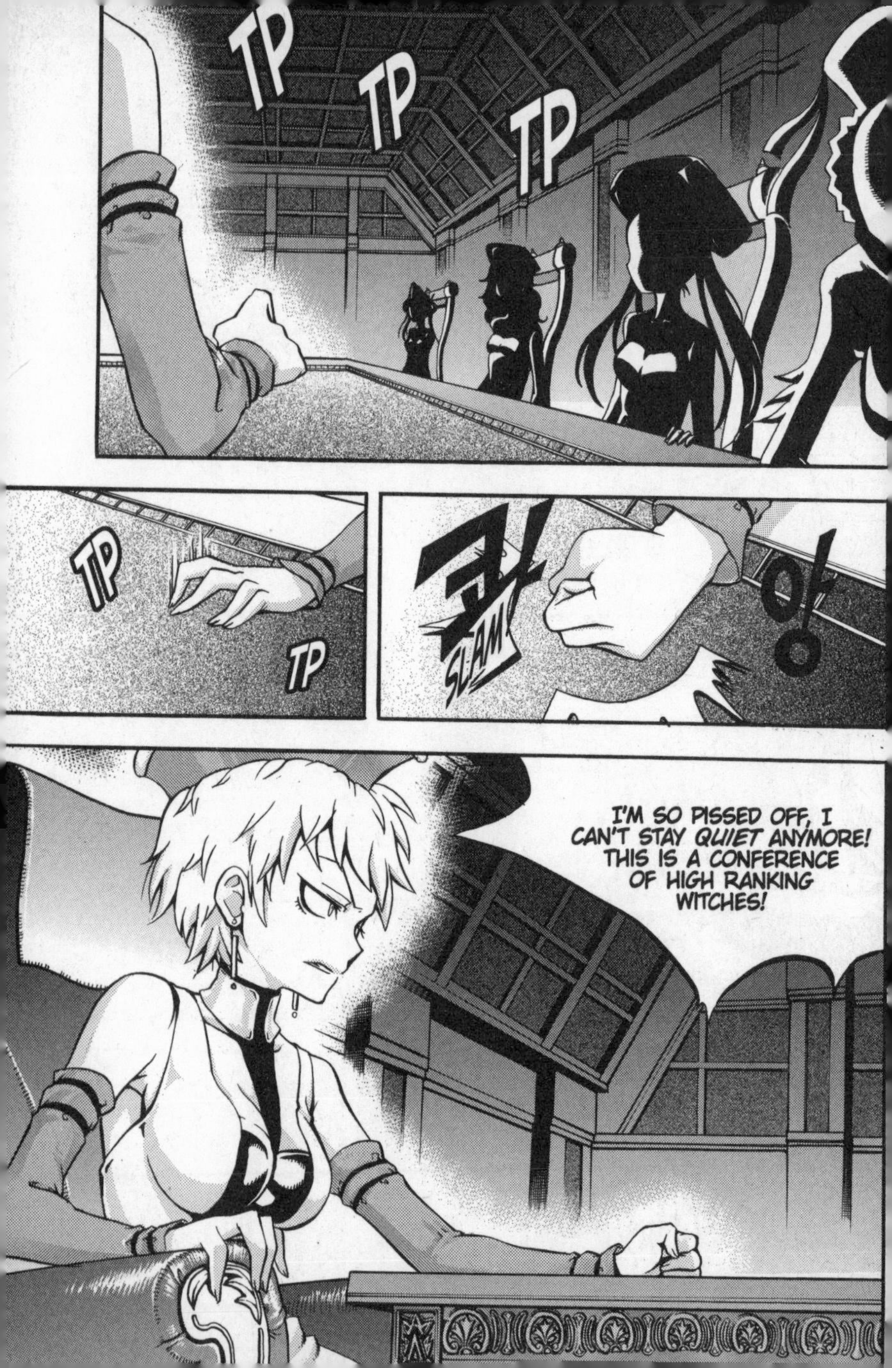
TP
TP
TP
TP
TP
SLAM
I'M SO PISSED OFF, I CAN'T STAY *QUIET* ANYMORE! THIS IS A CONFERENCE OF HIGH RANKING WITCHES!

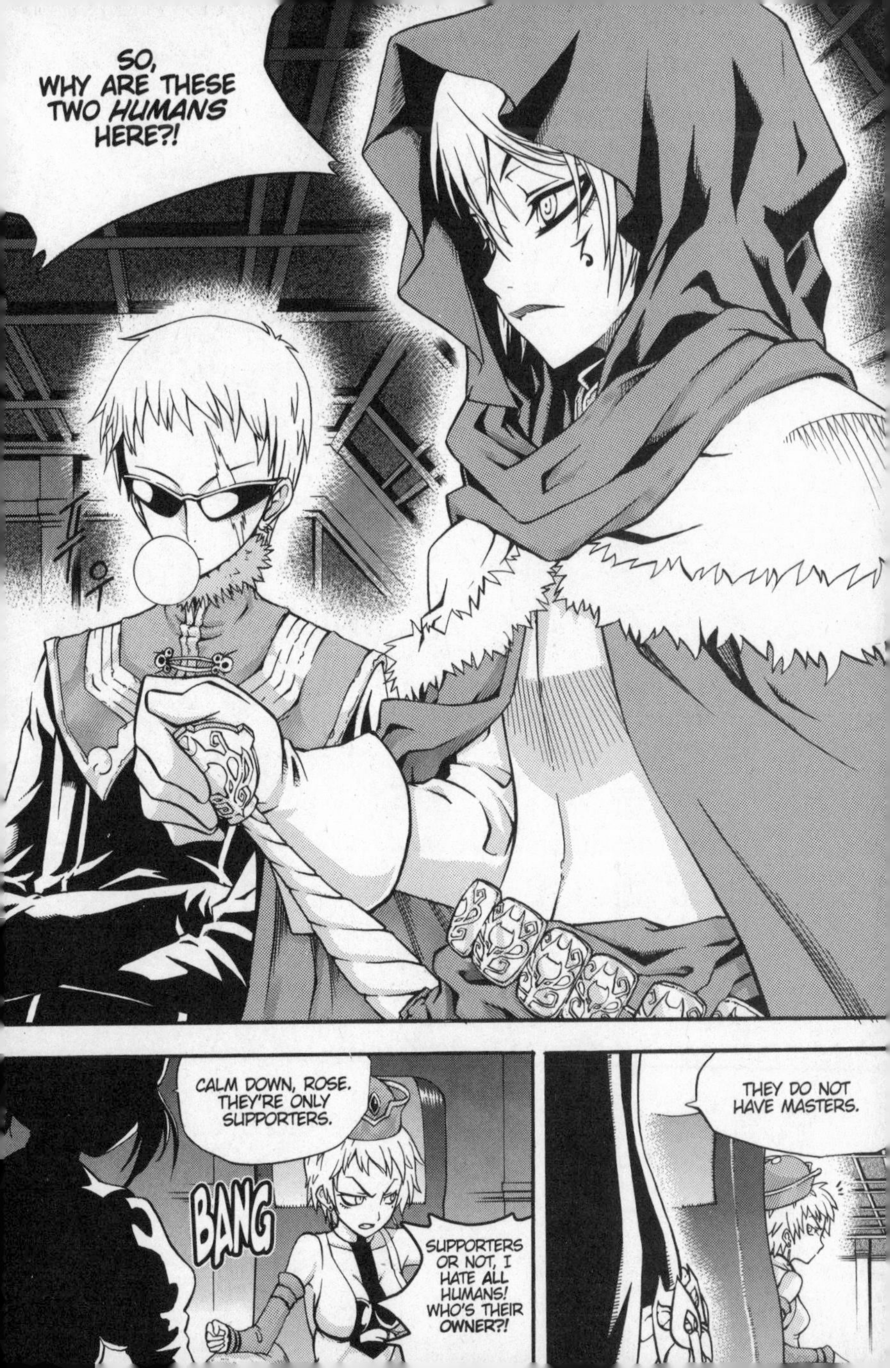
SO, WHY ARE THESE TWO HUMANS HERE?!
THEY DO NOT HAVE MASTERS.
CALM DOWN, ROSE. THEY'RE ONLY SUPPORTERS.
BANG
SUPPORTERS OR NOT, I HATE ALL HUMANS! WHO'S THEIR OWNER?!

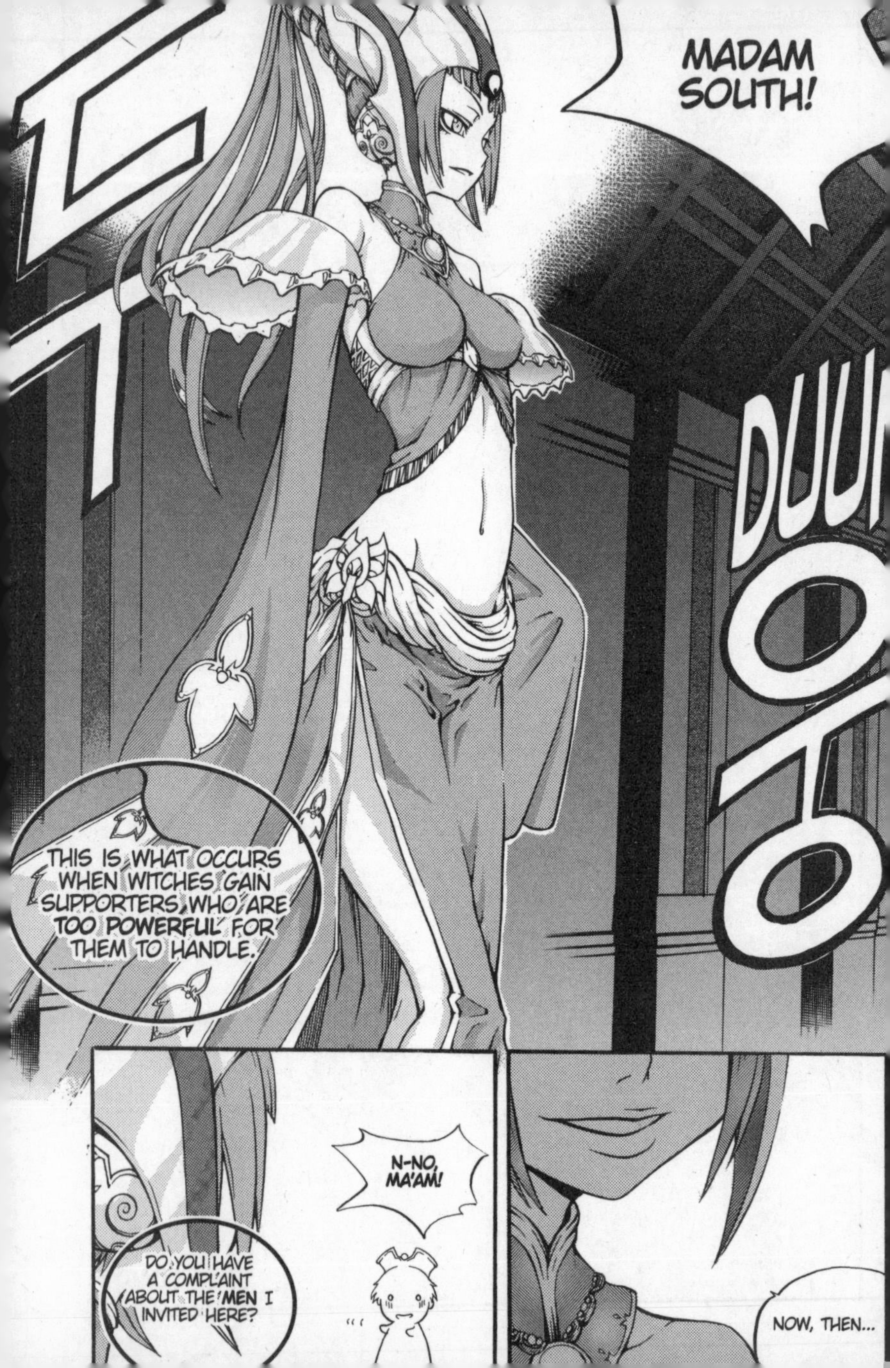
MADAM SOUTH!
DUUN
OHO
THIS IS WHAT OCCURS WHEN WITCHES GAIN SUPPORTERS WHO ARE TOO POWERFUL FOR THEM TO HANDLE.
NOW, THEN...
N-NO, MA'AM!
DO YOU HAVE A COMPLAINT ABOUT THE MEN I INVITED HERE?

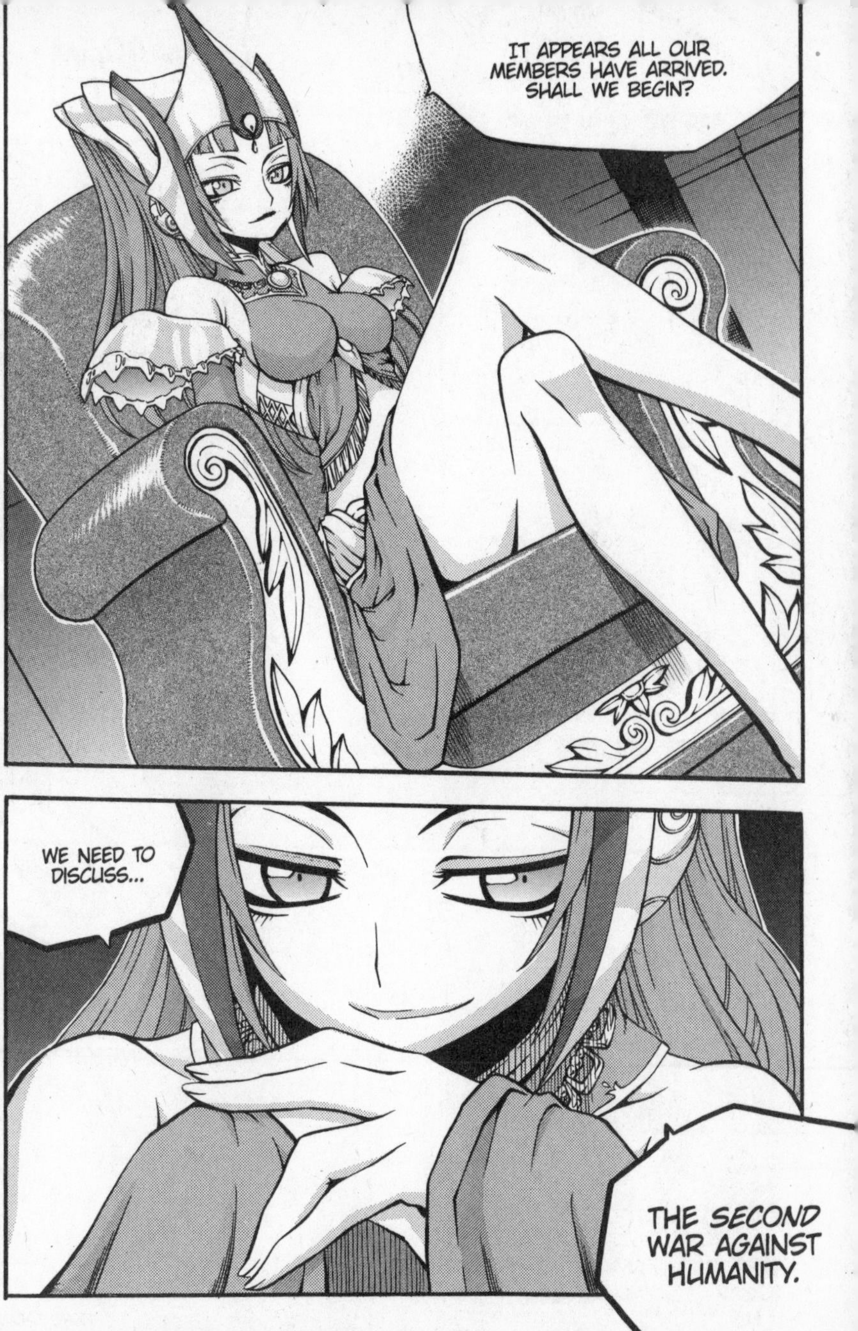
IT APPEARS ALL OUR MEMBERS HAVE ARRIVED. SHALL WE BEGIN?
WE NEED TO DISCUSS...
THE *SECOND* WAR AGAINST HUMANITY.

WHILE YOU WERE SLEEPING

FWAAA
SSSH
NEW SHEETS... DID SOMEBODY CHANGE THEM WHILE I WAS ASLEEP?

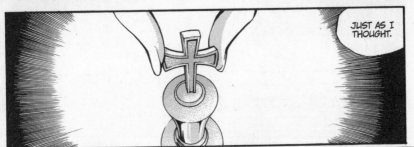

JUST AS I THOUGHT.

THE KING IS MOVING AS I PREDICTED.

WELL, IT'S SURPRISING THAT SOUTH HAS STAYED QUIET THIS LONG. THEY CALL HER THE "KING OF CONFLICT," AFTER ALL.

IT'S GOING TO GET NOISY VERY SOON.

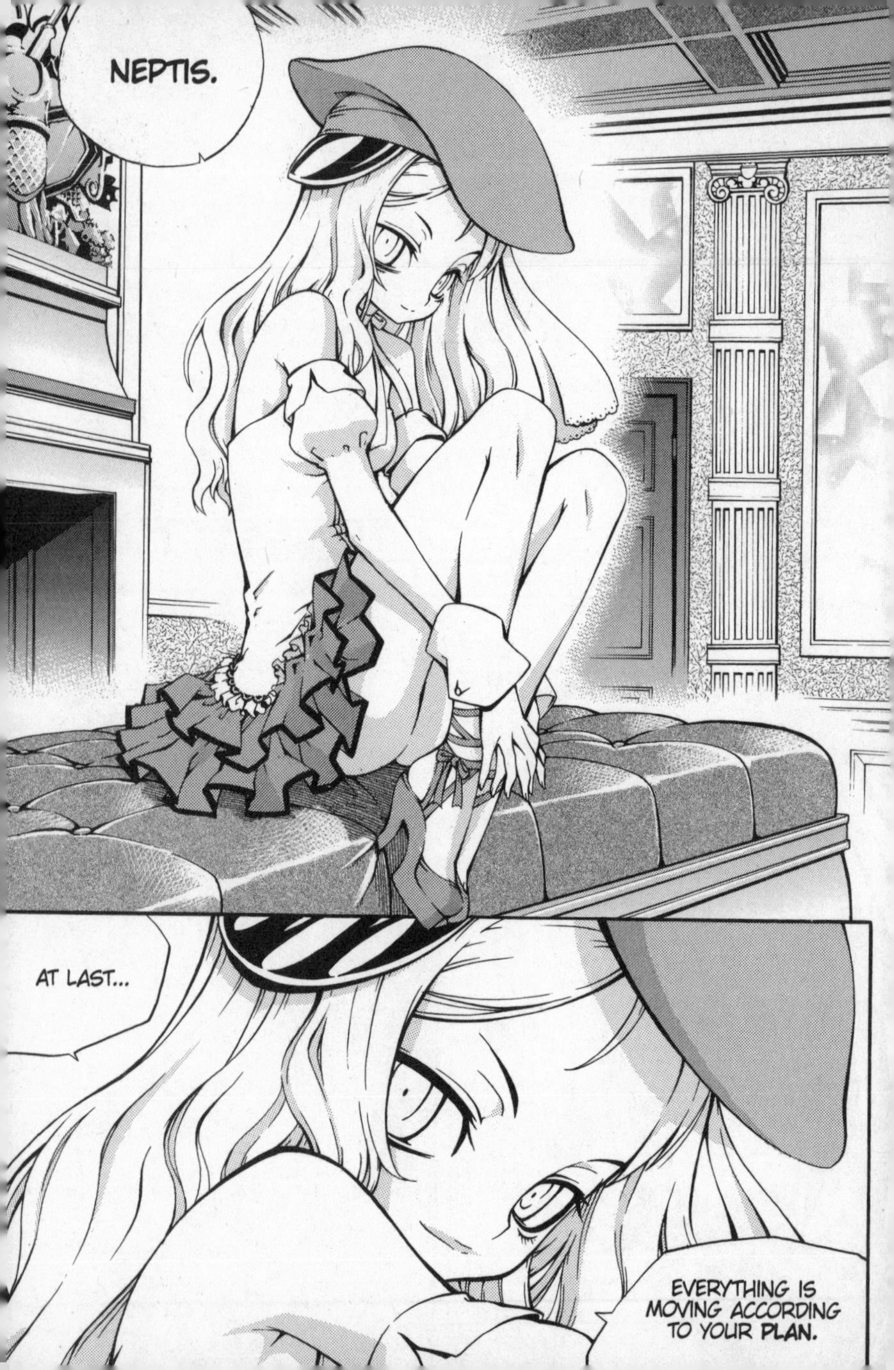
NEPTIS.
AT LAST...
EVERYTHING IS MOVING ACCORDING TO YOUR PLAN.

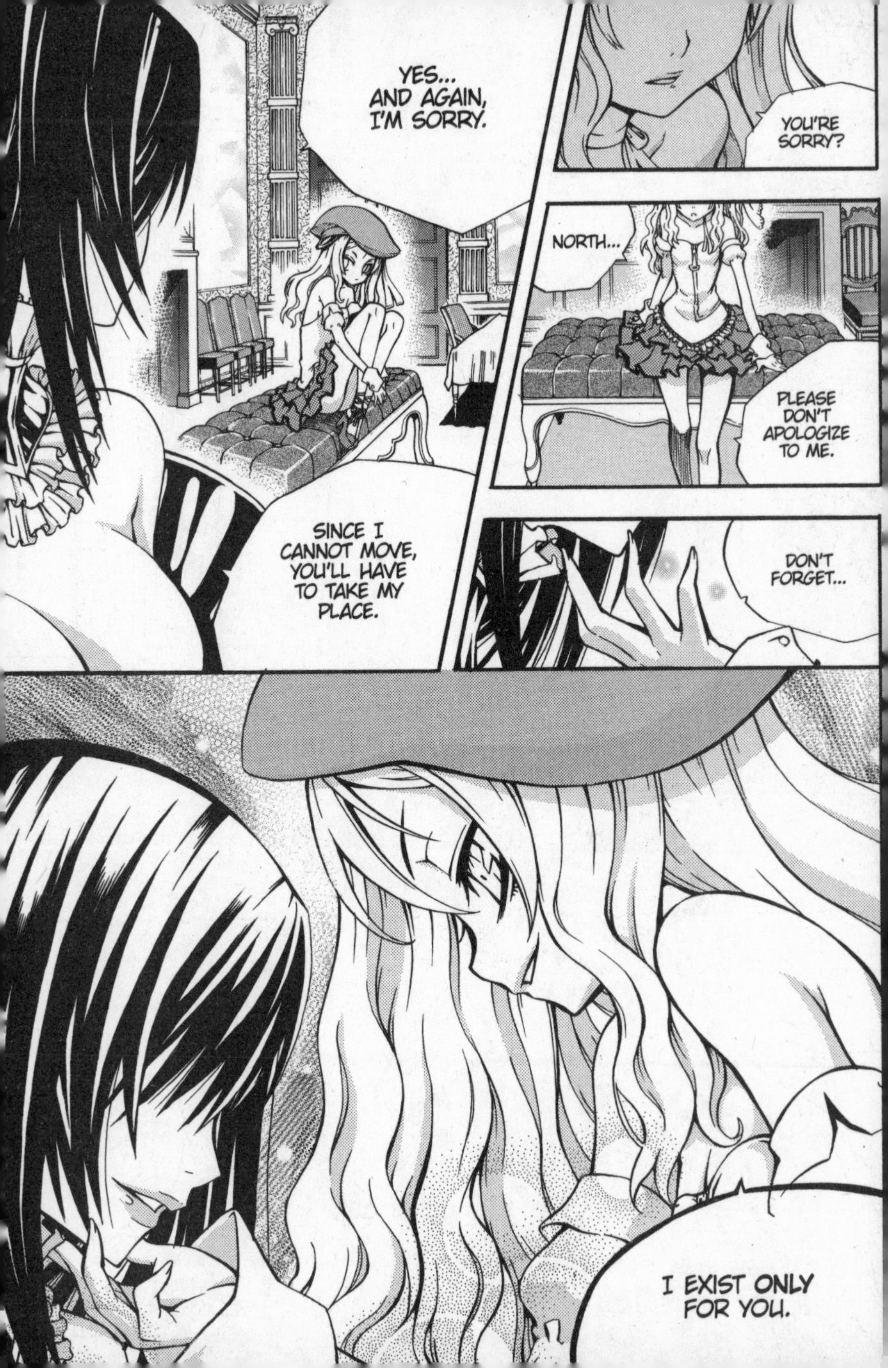
YES... AND AGAIN, I'M SORRY.
YOU'RE SORRY?
SINCE I CANNOT MOVE, YOU'LL HAVE TO TAKE MY PLACE.
NORTH...
PLEASE DON'T APOLOGIZE TO ME.
DON'T FORGET...
I EXIST ONLY FOR YOU.

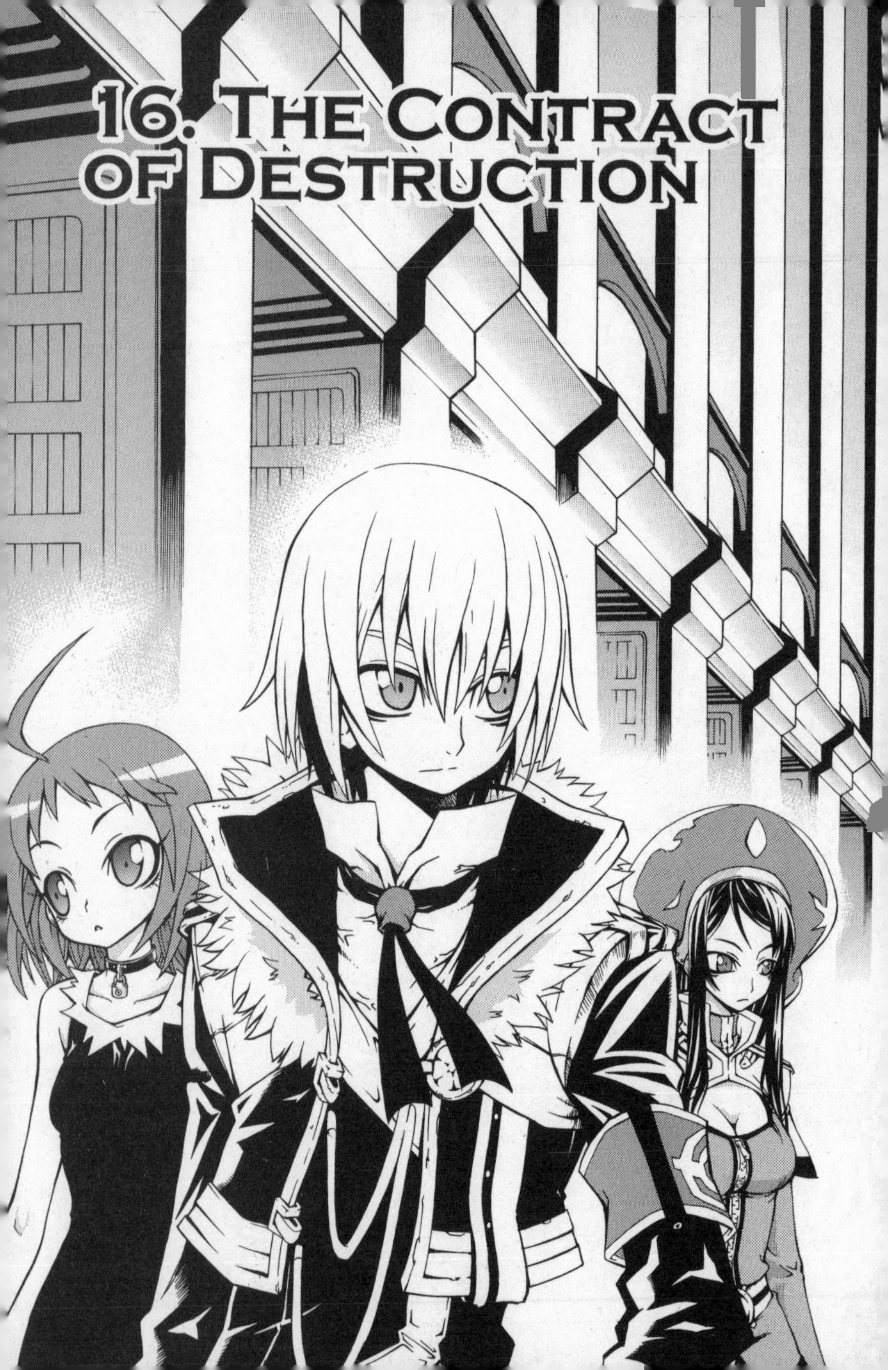
16. The Contract
of Destruction

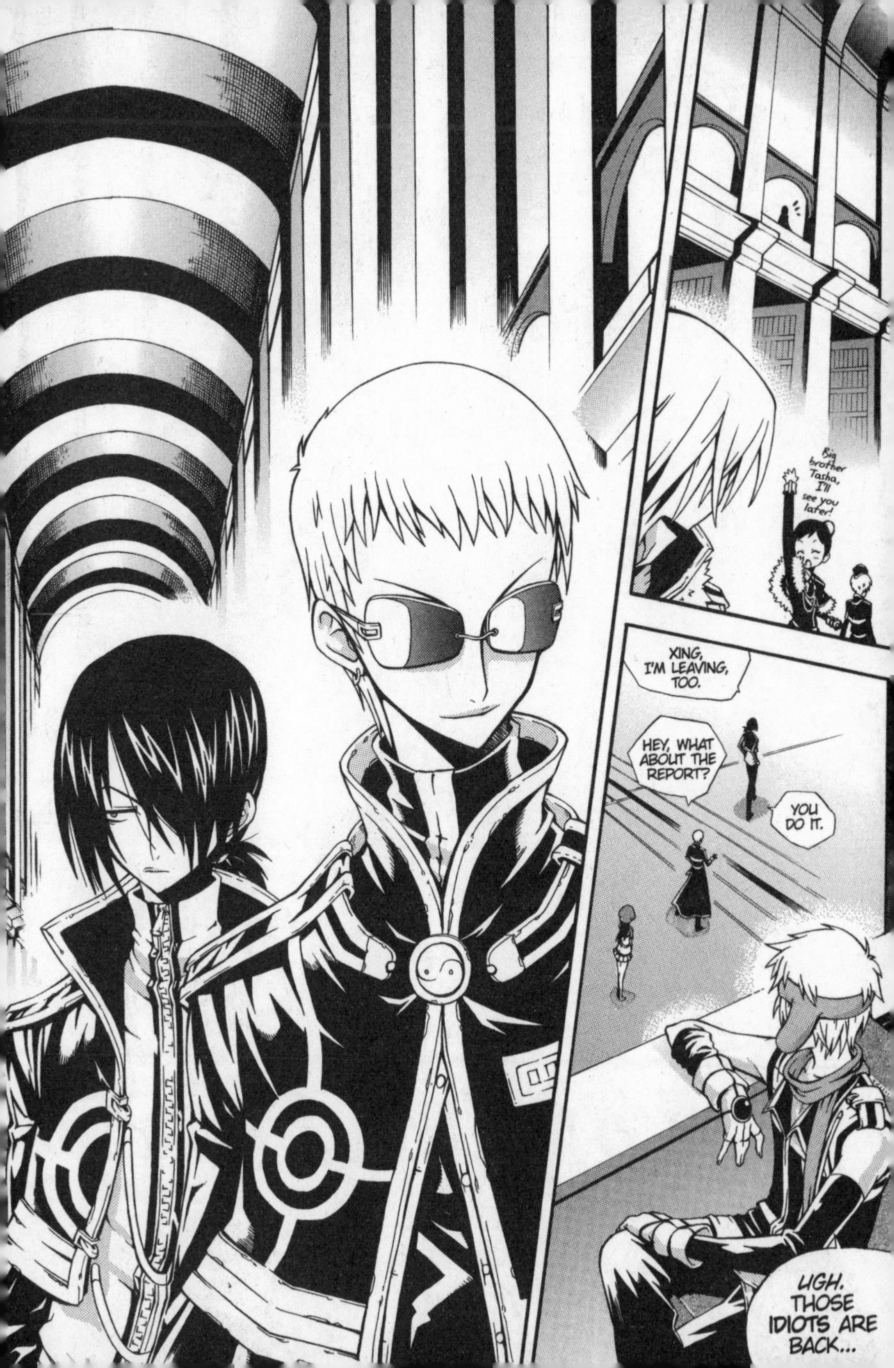
Big brother Tasha, I'll see you later!
XING, I'M LEAVING, TOO.
HEY, WHAT ABOUT THE REPORT?
YOU DO IT.
UGH. THOSE IDIOTS ARE BACK...

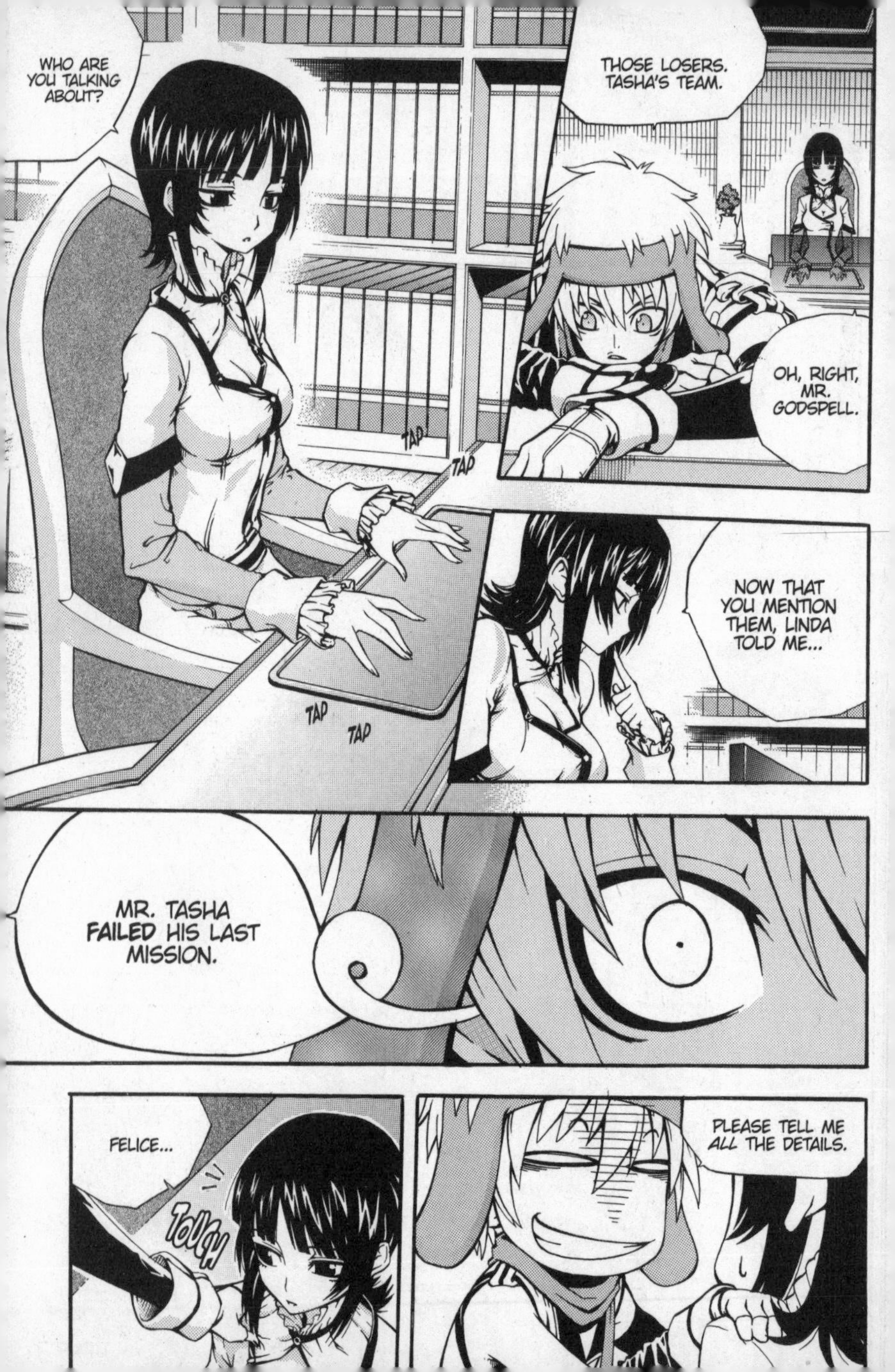

WHO ARE YOU TALKING ABOUT?
THOSE LOSERS. TASHA'S TEAM.
OH, RIGHT, MR. GODSPELL.
TAP
TAP
TAP
TAP
NOW THAT YOU MENTION THEM, LINDA TOLD ME...
MR. TASHA FAILED HIS LAST MISSION.
PLEASE TELL ME ALL THE DETAILS.
FELICE...
TOUCH

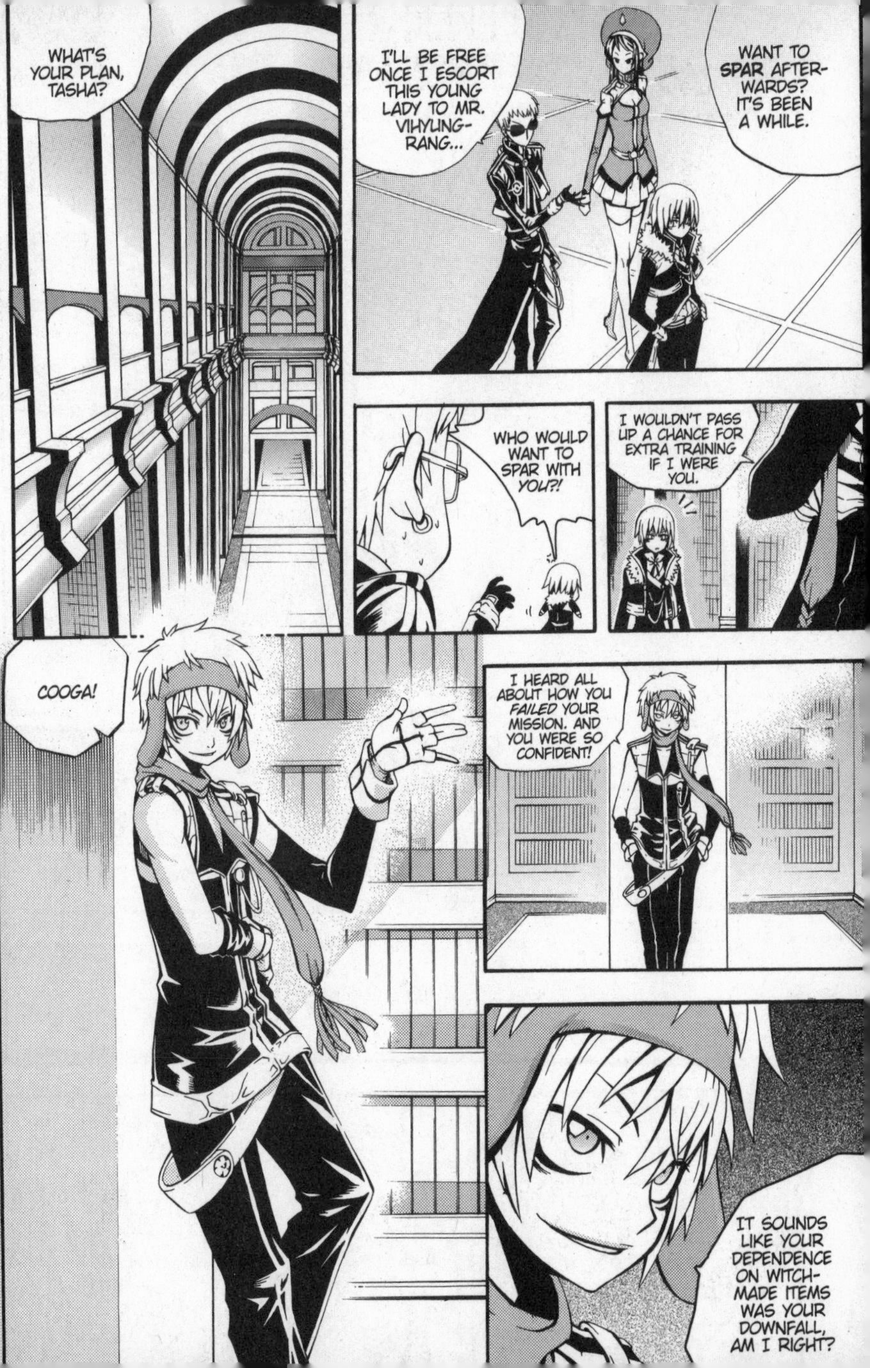
WHAT'S YOUR PLAN, TASHA?
I'LL BE FREE ONCE I ESCORT THIS YOUNG LADY TO MR. VIHYUNG-RANG...
WANT TO SPAR AFTER-WARDS? IT'S BEEN A WHILE.
WHO WOULD WANT TO SPAR WITH YOU?!
I WOULDN'T PASS UP A CHANCE FOR EXTRA TRAINING IF I WERE YOU.
COOGA!
I HEARD ALL ABOUT HOW YOU FAILED YOUR MISSION. AND YOU WERE SO CONFIDENT!
IT SOUNDS LIKE YOUR DEPENDENCE ON WITCH-MADE ITEMS WAS YOUR DOWNFALL, AM I RIGHT?

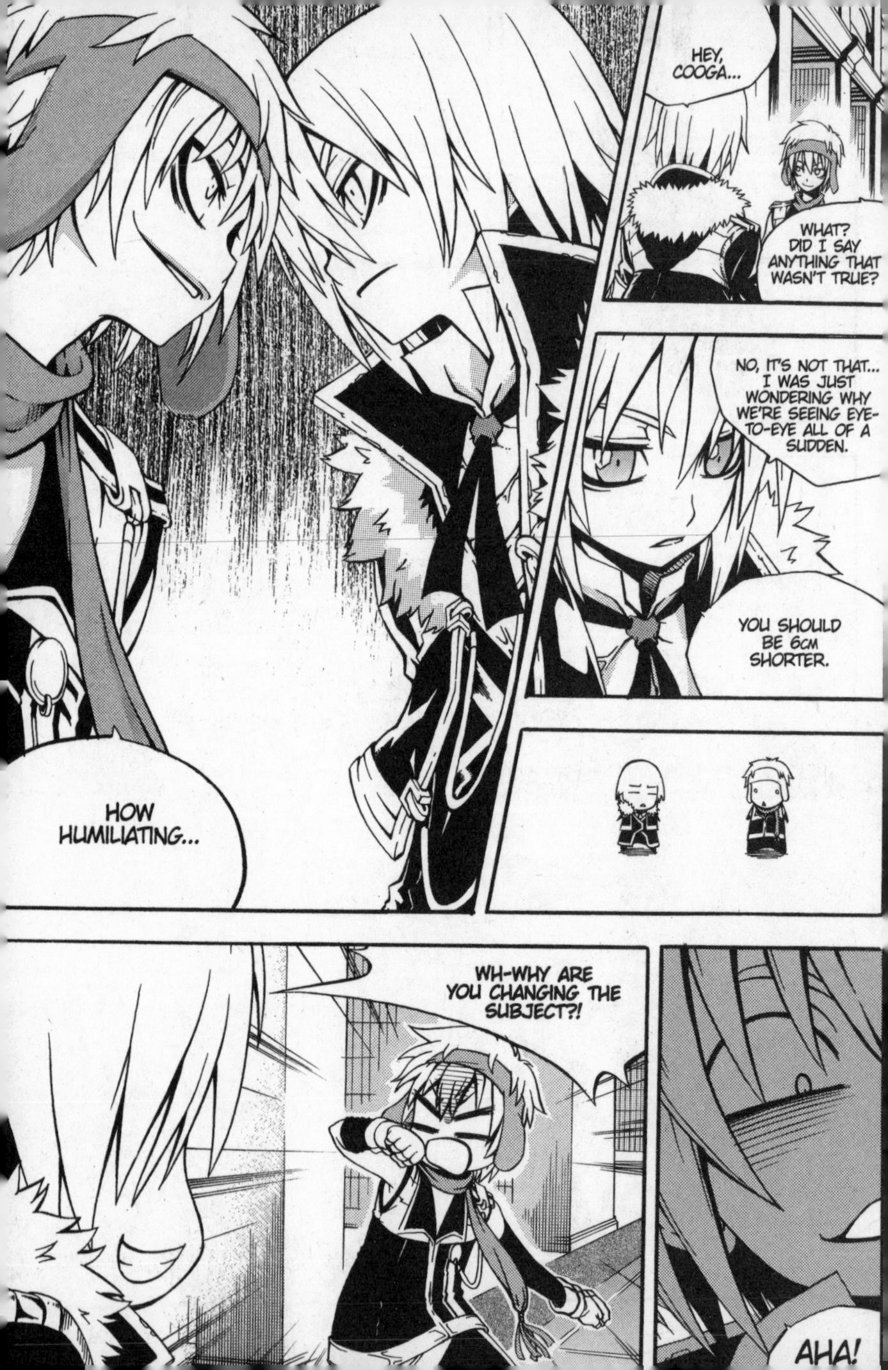
HEY, COOGA...
WHAT? DID I SAY ANYTHING THAT WASN'T TRUE?
NO, IT'S NOT THAT... I WAS JUST WONDERING WHY WE'RE SEEING EYE-TO-EYE ALL OF A SUDDEN.
YOU SHOULD BE 6CM SHORTER.
HOW HUMILIATING...
AHA!
WH-WHY ARE YOU CHANGING THE SUBJECT?!

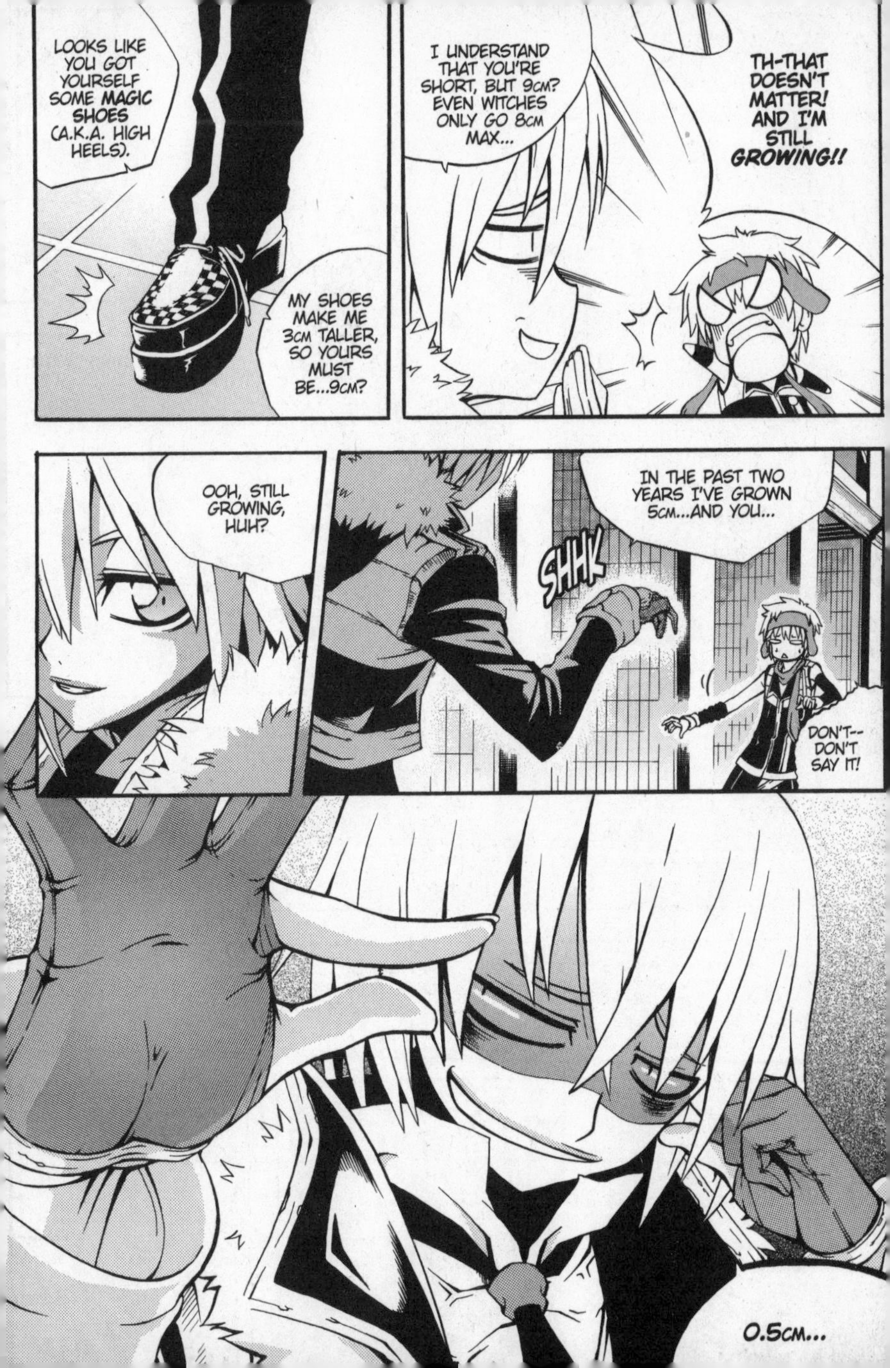
LOOKS LIKE YOU GOT YOURSELF SOME MAGIC SHOES (A.K.A. HIGH HEELS).
MY SHOES MAKE ME 3CM TALLER, SO YOURS MUST BE...9CM?
I UNDERSTAND THAT YOU'RE SHORT, BUT 9CM? EVEN WITCHES ONLY GO 8CM MAX...
TH-THAT DOESN'T MATTER! AND I'M STILL GROWING!!
OOH, STILL GROWING, HUH?
IN THE PAST TWO YEARS I'VE GROWN 5CM...AND YOU...
SHHK
DON'T-- DON'T SAY IT!
0.5CM...

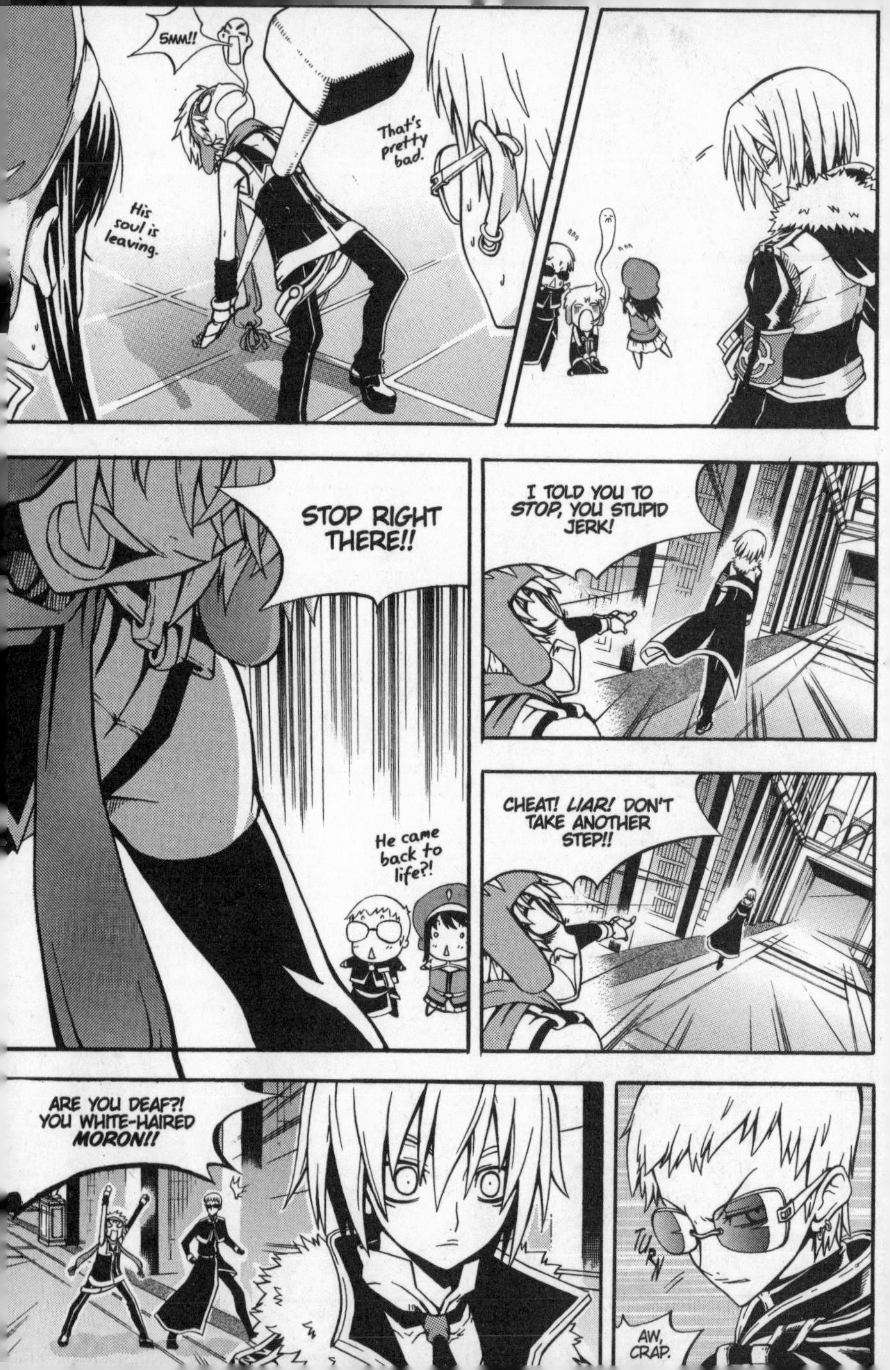
5MM!!
That's pretty bad.
His soul is leaving.
I TOLD YOU TO *STOP*, YOU STUPID JERK!
CHEAT! *LIAR!* DON'T TAKE ANOTHER STEP!!
STOP RIGHT THERE!!
He came back to life?!
TURN
AW, CRAP.
ARE YOU DEAF?! YOU WHITE-HAIRED ***MORON!!***

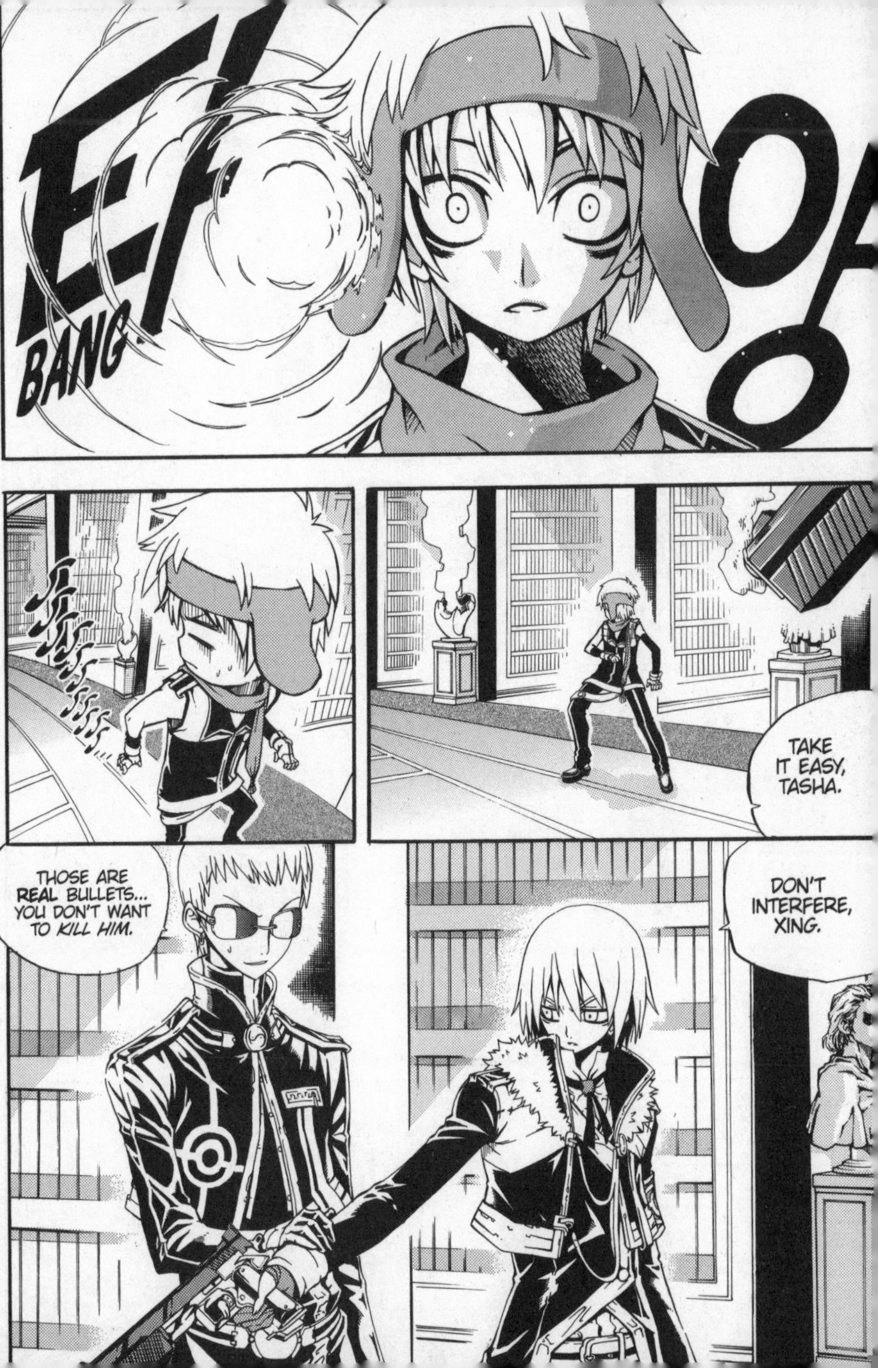
BANG
TAKE IT EASY, TASHA.
DON'T INTERFERE, XING.
THOSE ARE REAL BULLETS... YOU DON'T WANT TO *KILL HIM*.

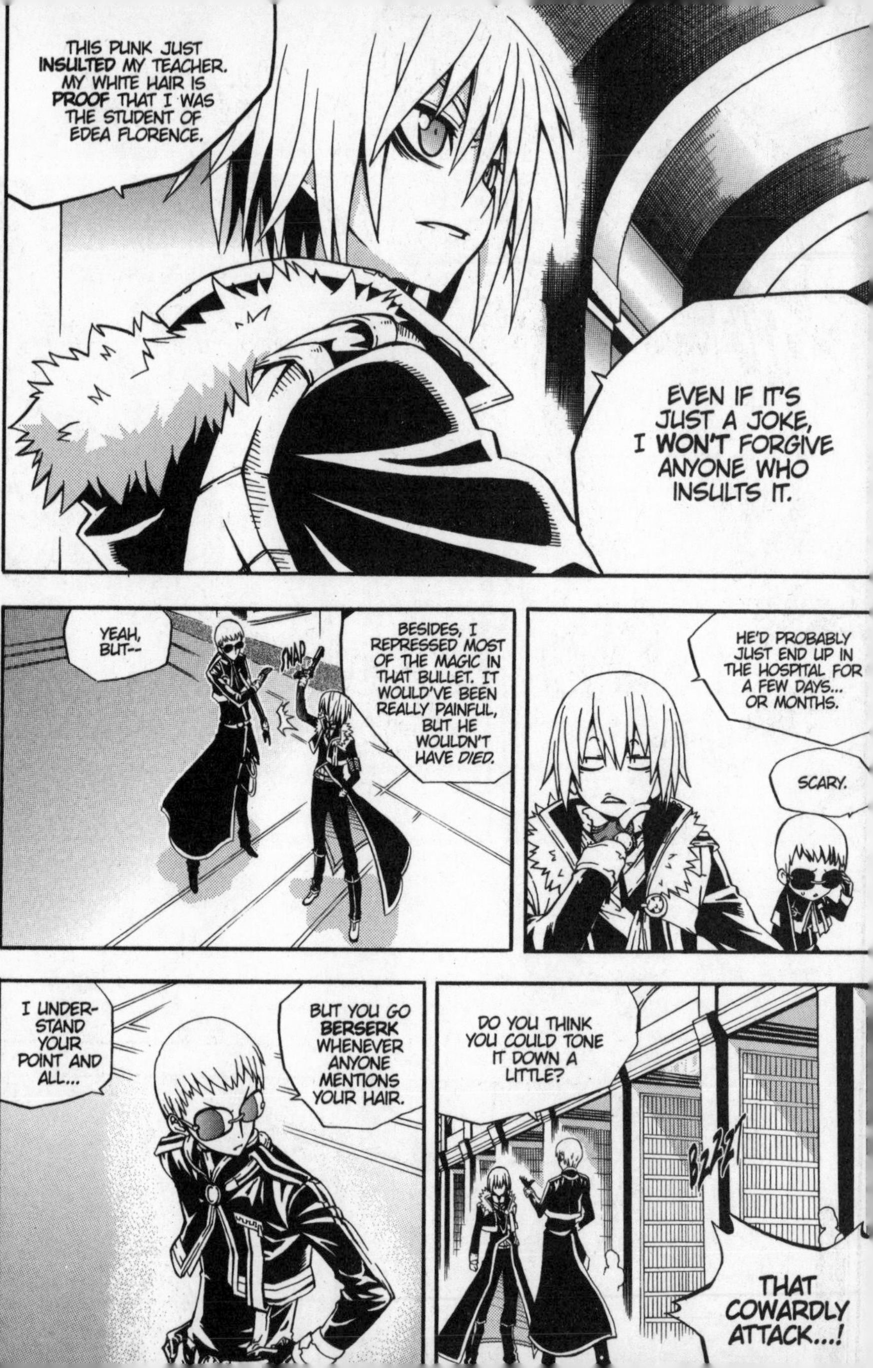

THIS PUNK JUST INSULTED MY TEACHER. MY WHITE HAIR IS PROOF THAT I WAS THE STUDENT OF EDEA FLORENCE.
EVEN IF IT'S JUST A JOKE, I WON'T FORGIVE ANYONE WHO INSULTS IT.
YEAH, BUT--
SNAP
BESIDES, I REPRESSED MOST OF THE MAGIC IN THAT BULLET. IT WOULD'VE BEEN REALLY PAINFUL, BUT HE WOULDN'T HAVE DIED.
HE'D PROBABLY JUST END UP IN THE HOSPITAL FOR A FEW DAYS... OR MONTHS.
SCARY.
I UNDER-STAND YOUR POINT AND ALL...
BUT YOU GO BERSERK WHENEVER ANYONE MENTIONS YOUR HAIR.
DO YOU THINK YOU COULD TONE IT DOWN A LITTLE?
BZZZT
THAT COWARDLY ATTACK...!

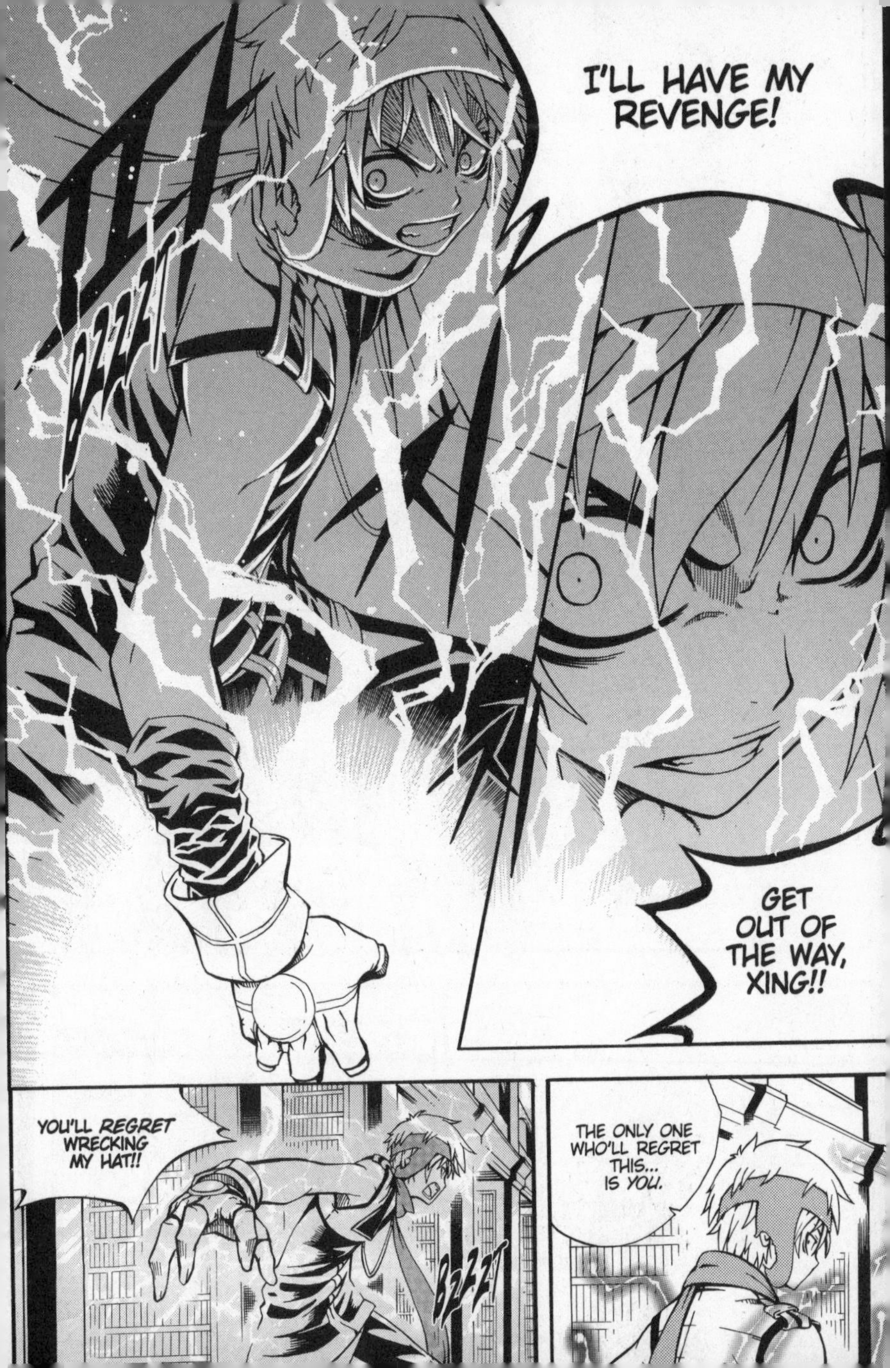
BZZZT
I'LL HAVE MY REVENGE!
GET OUT OF THE WAY, XING!!
YOU'LL *REGRET* WRECKING MY HAT!!
BZZZT
THE ONLY ONE WHO'LL REGRET THIS... IS *YOU*.

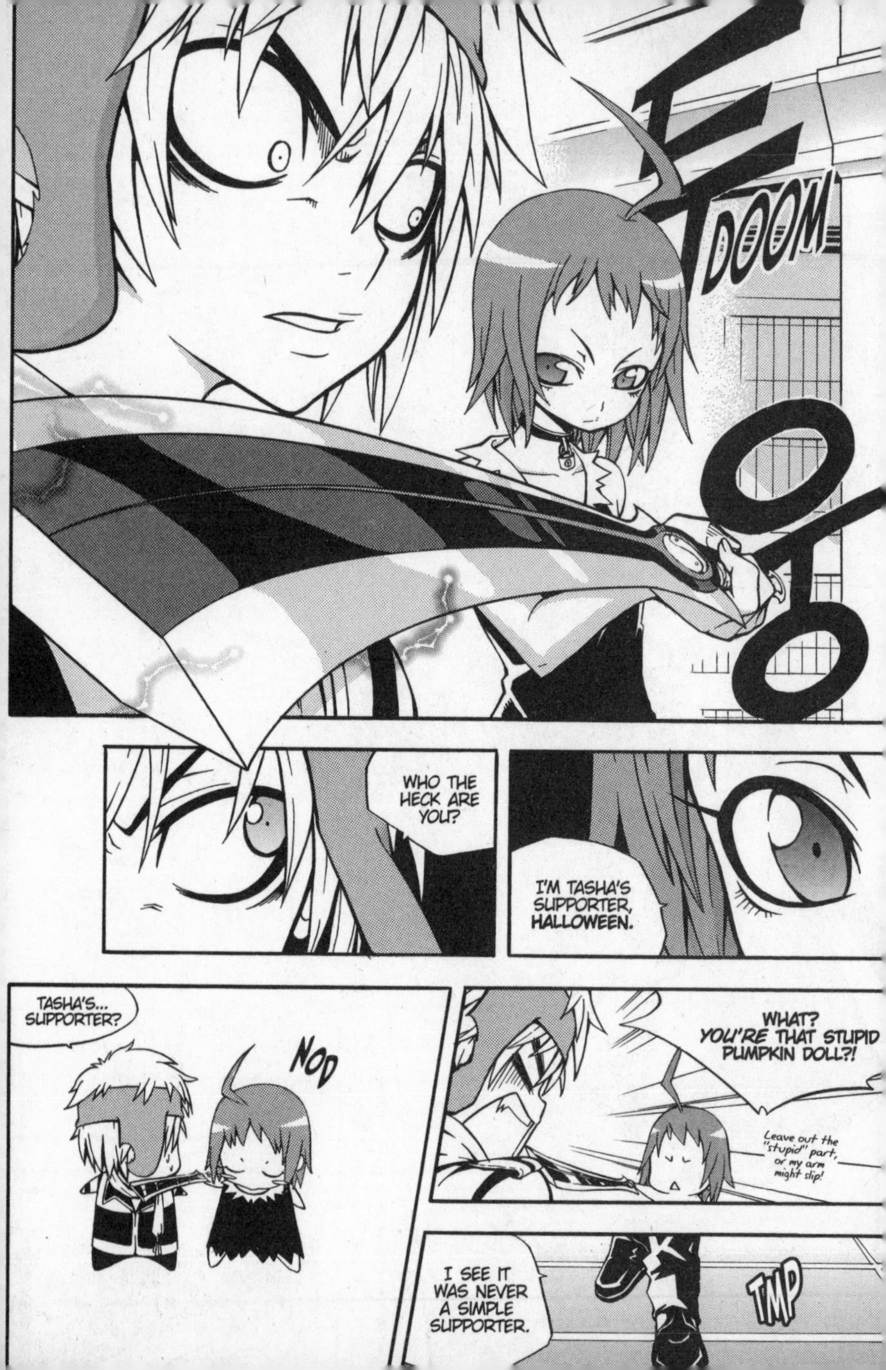
DOOM
WHO THE HECK ARE YOU?
I'M TASHA'S SUPPORTER, HALLOWEEN.
TASHA'S... SUPPORTER?
NOD
WHAT? *YOU'RE* THAT STUPID PUMPKIN DOLL?!
Leave out the "stupid" part, or my arm might slip!
I SEE IT WAS NEVER A SIMPLE SUPPORTER.
TMP

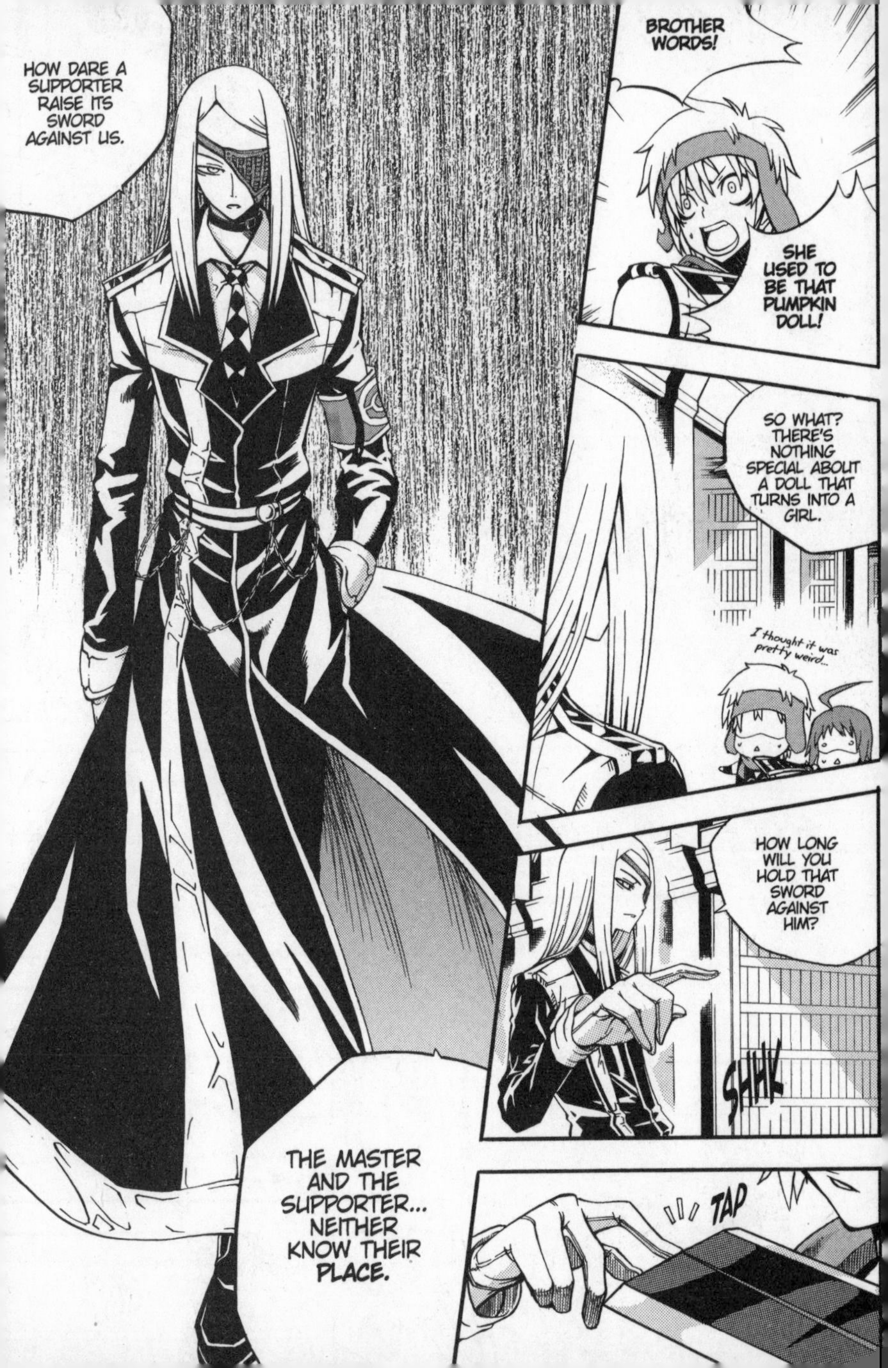
BROTHER WORDS!
SHE USED TO BE THAT PUMPKIN DOLL!
SO WHAT? THERE'S NOTHING SPECIAL ABOUT A DOLL THAT TURNS INTO A GIRL.
I thought it was pretty weird...
HOW LONG WILL YOU HOLD THAT SWORD AGAINST HIM?
SHHK
HOW DARE A SUPPORTER RAISE ITS SWORD AGAINST US.
THE MASTER AND THE SUPPORTER... NEITHER KNOW THEIR PLACE.
TAP

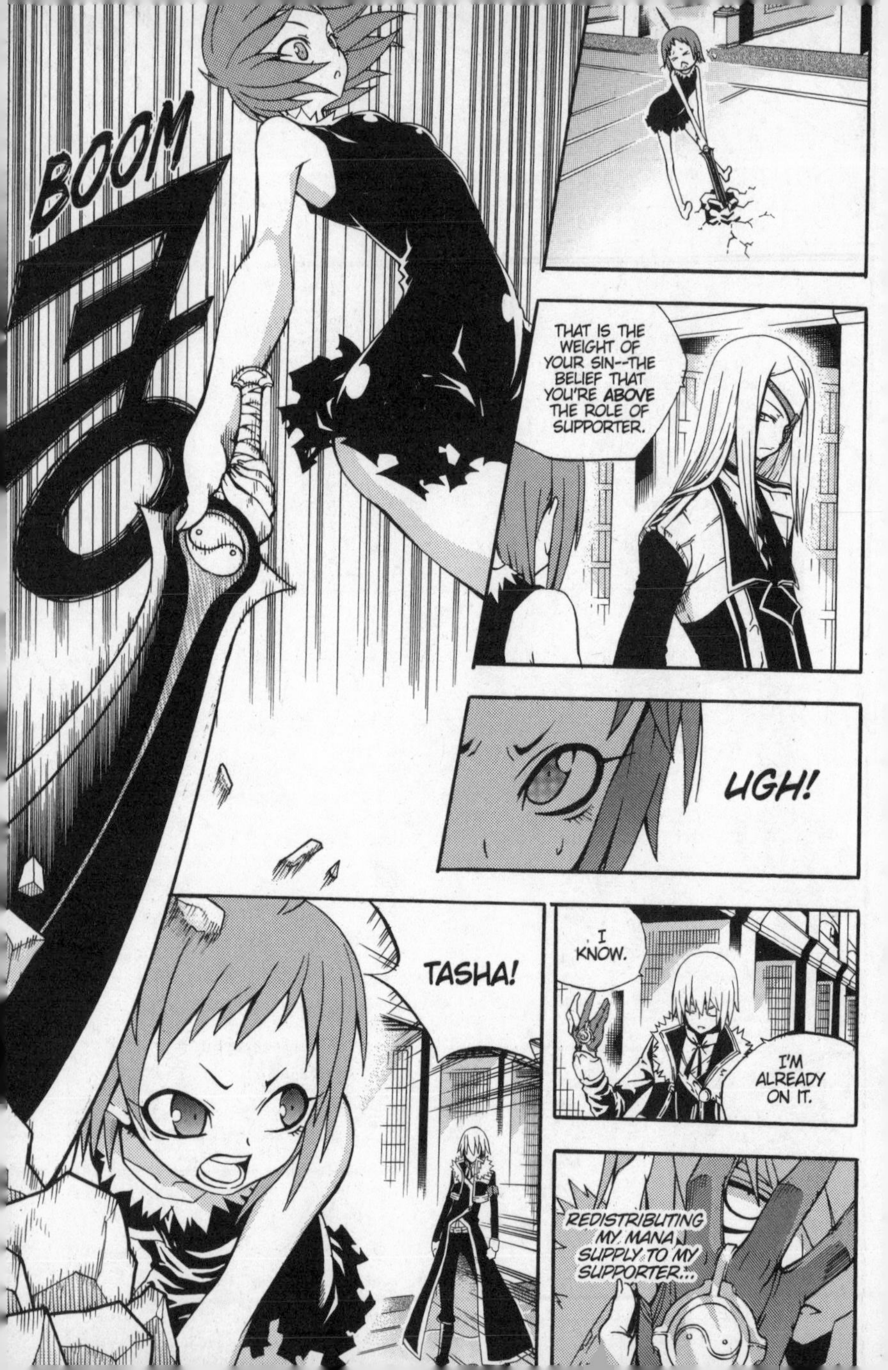
BOOM
THAT IS THE WEIGHT OF YOUR SIN--THE BELIEF THAT YOU'RE ABOVE THE ROLE OF SUPPORTER.
UGH!
I KNOW.
I'M ALREADY ON IT.
TASHA!
REDISTRIBUTING MY MANA SUPPLY TO MY SUPPORTER...

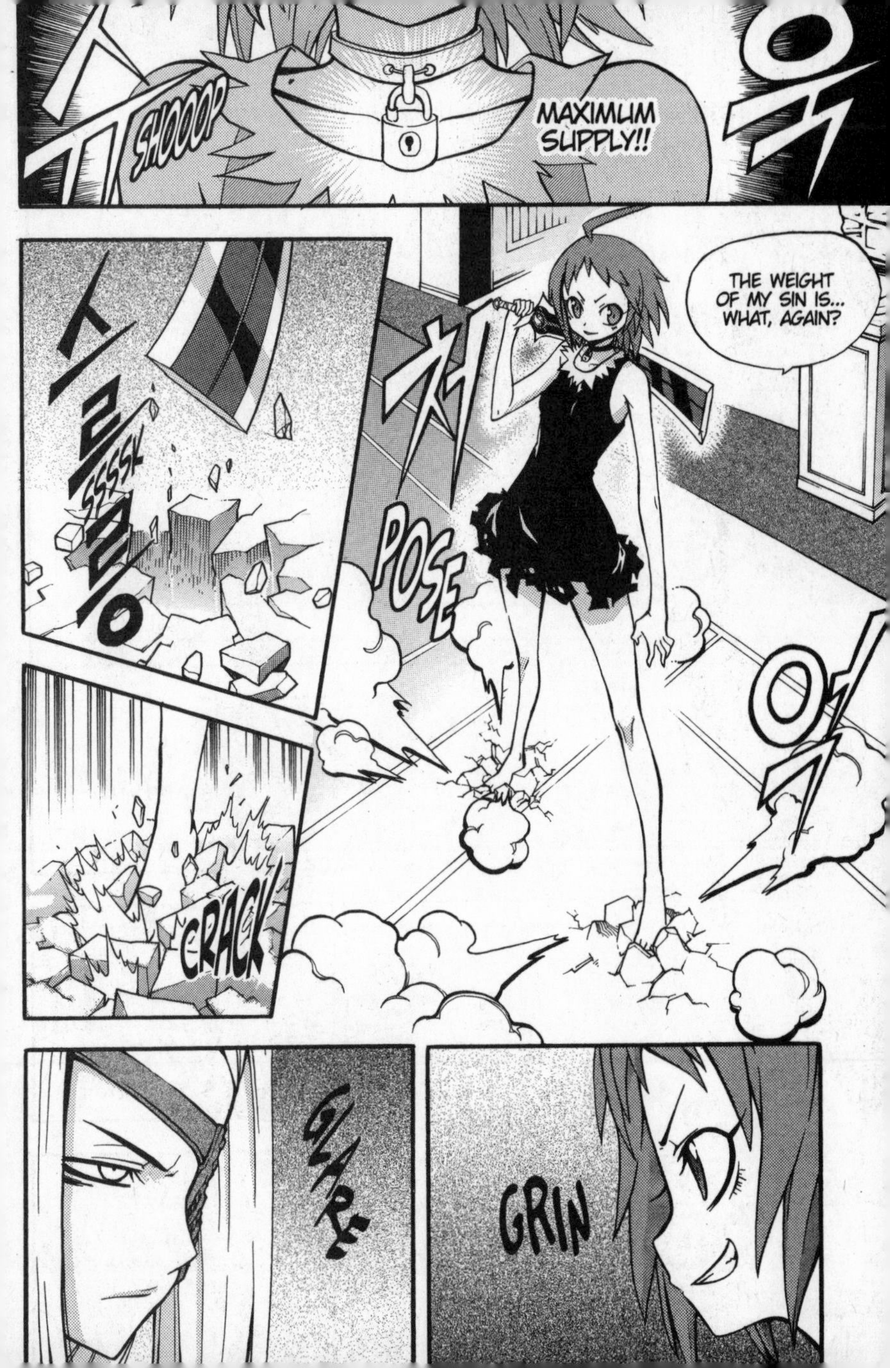
SHOOOP
MAXIMUM SUPPLY!!
THE WEIGHT OF MY SIN IS... WHAT, AGAIN?
SSSSK
POSE
CRACK
GLARE
GRIN

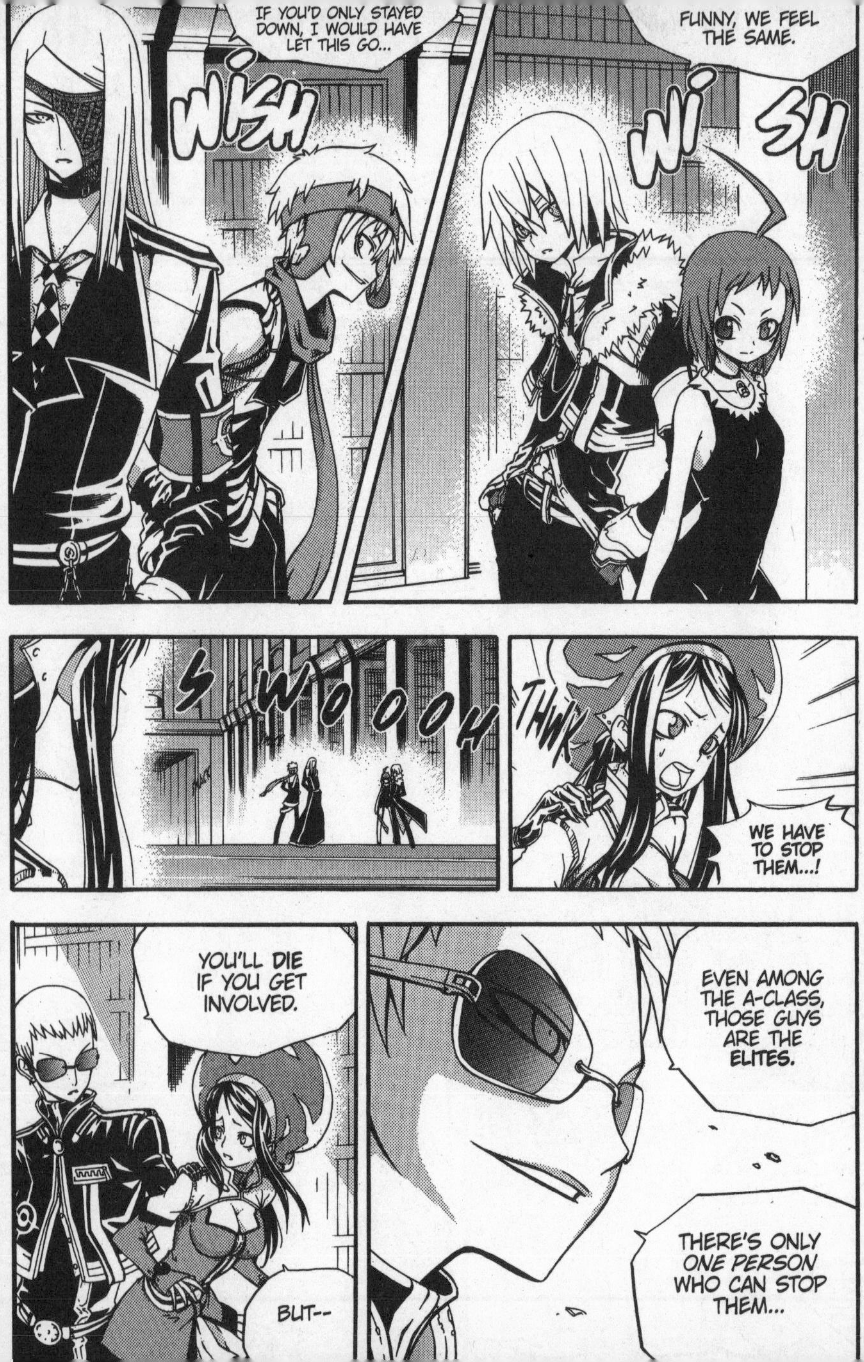

IF YOU'D ONLY STAYED DOWN, I WOULD HAVE LET THIS GO...
WISH
FUNNY, WE FEEL THE SAME.
WI SH
SWOOOOH
THWK
WE HAVE TO STOP THEM...!
YOU'LL DIE IF YOU GET INVOLVED.
BUT--
EVEN AMONG THE A-CLASS, THOSE GUYS ARE THE ELITES.
THERE'S ONLY ONE PERSON WHO CAN STOP THEM...

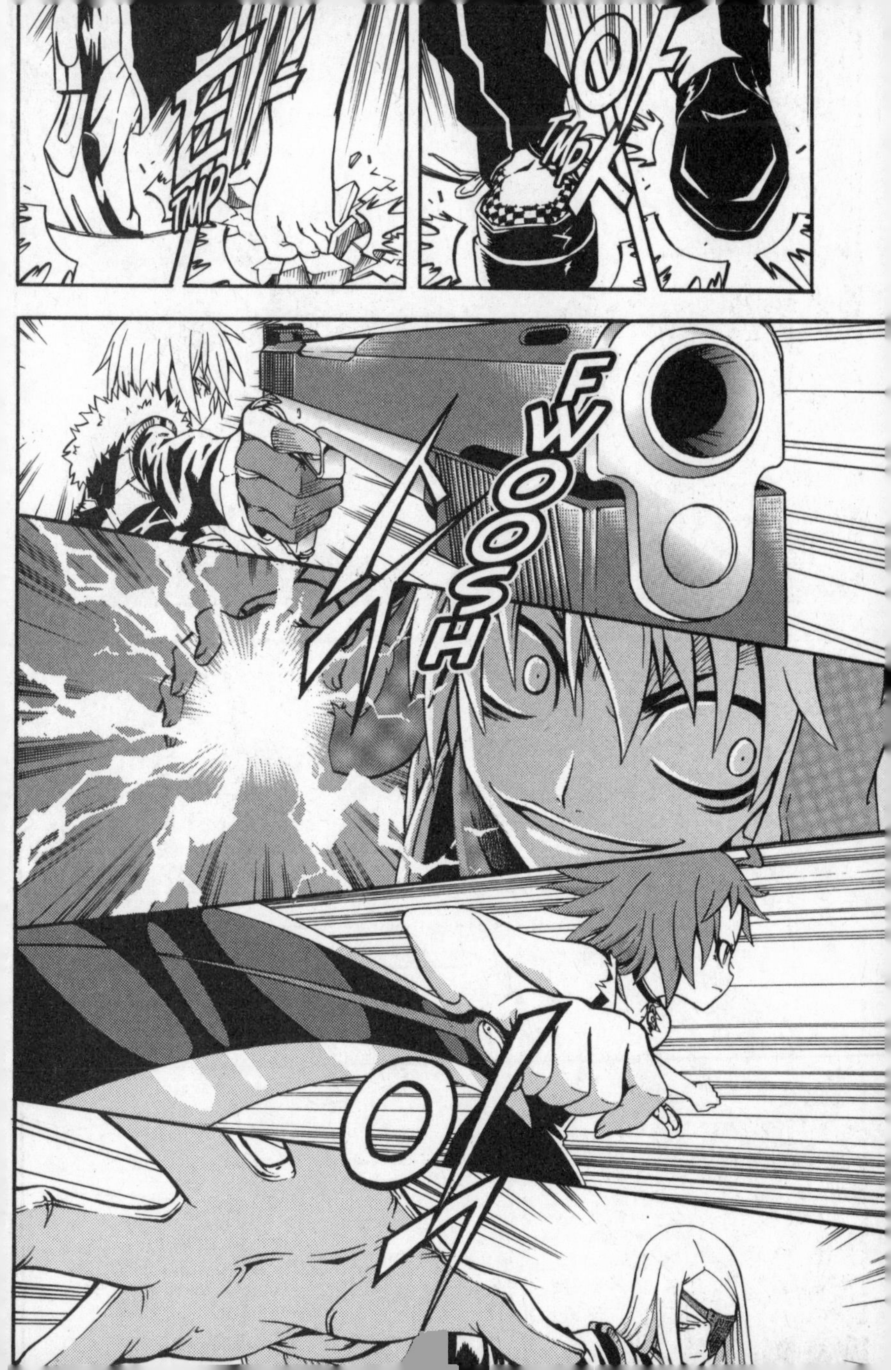
TMP
TMP
FWOOSH

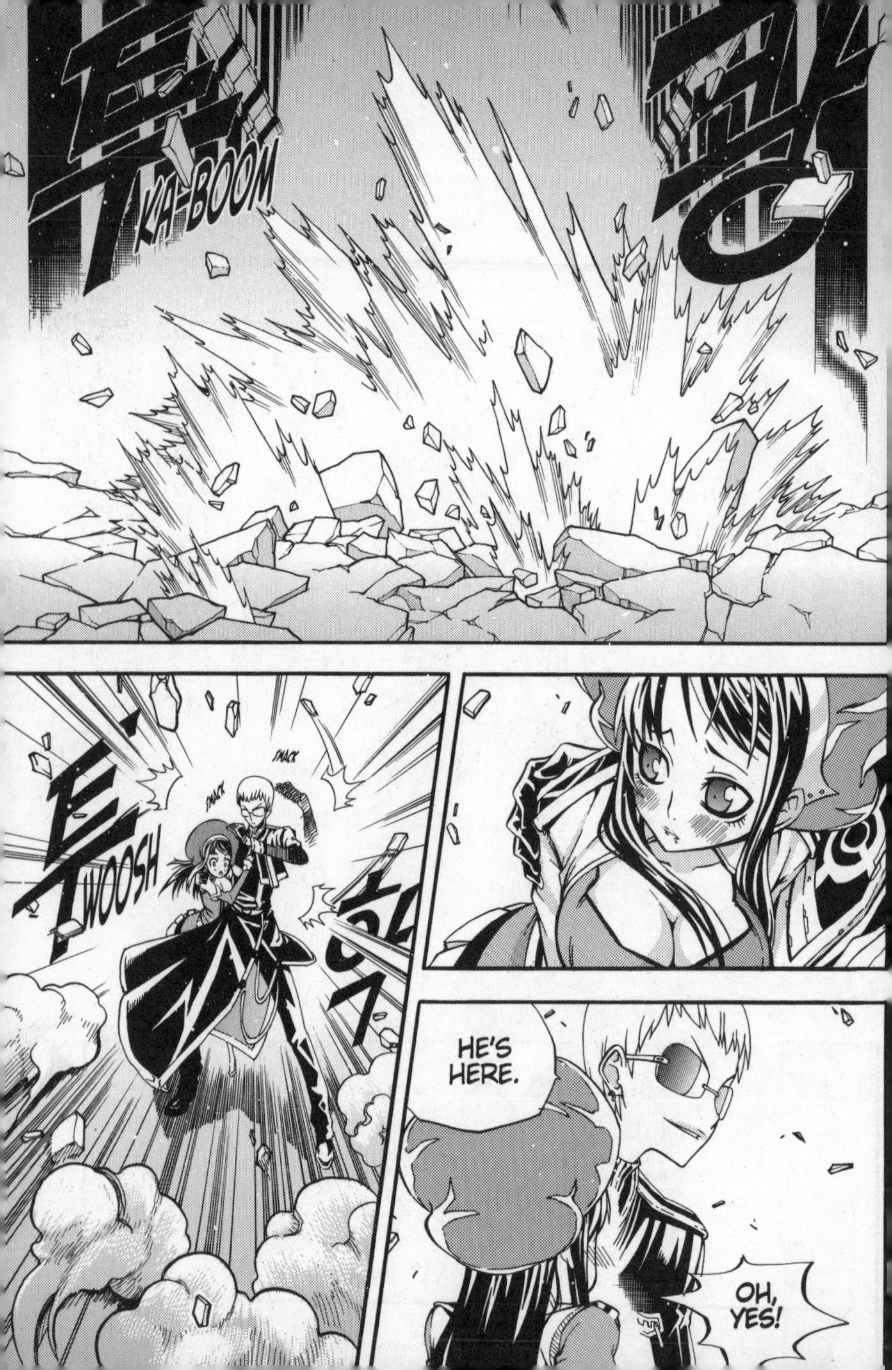
KA-BOOM
SMACK
SMACK
WOOSH
HE'S HERE.
OH, YES!

FRRRSSSS

TUMM

FFTHU

TUMM

INTERESTING.

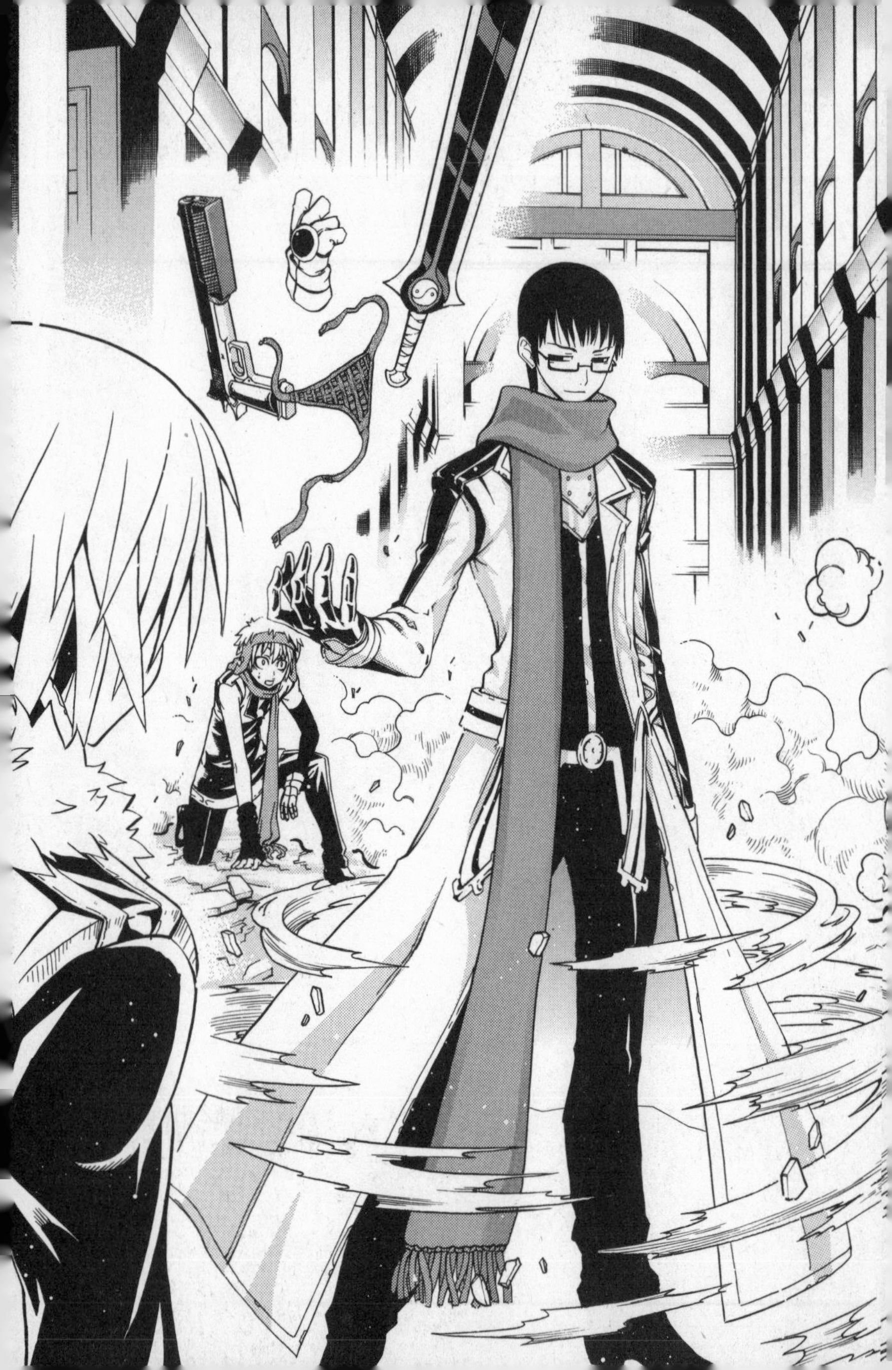

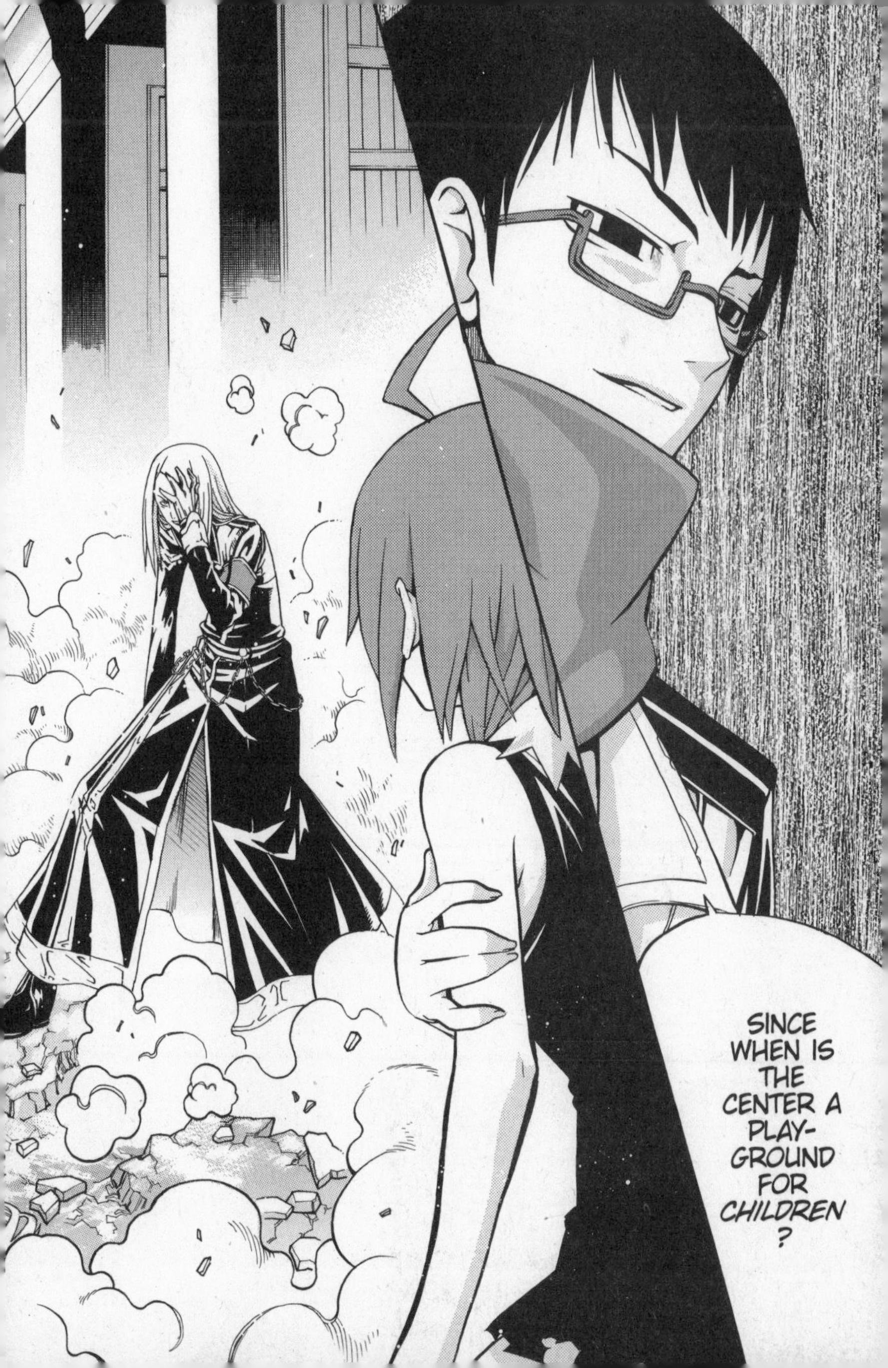
SINCE WHEN IS THE CENTER A PLAY-GROUND FOR CHILDREN?

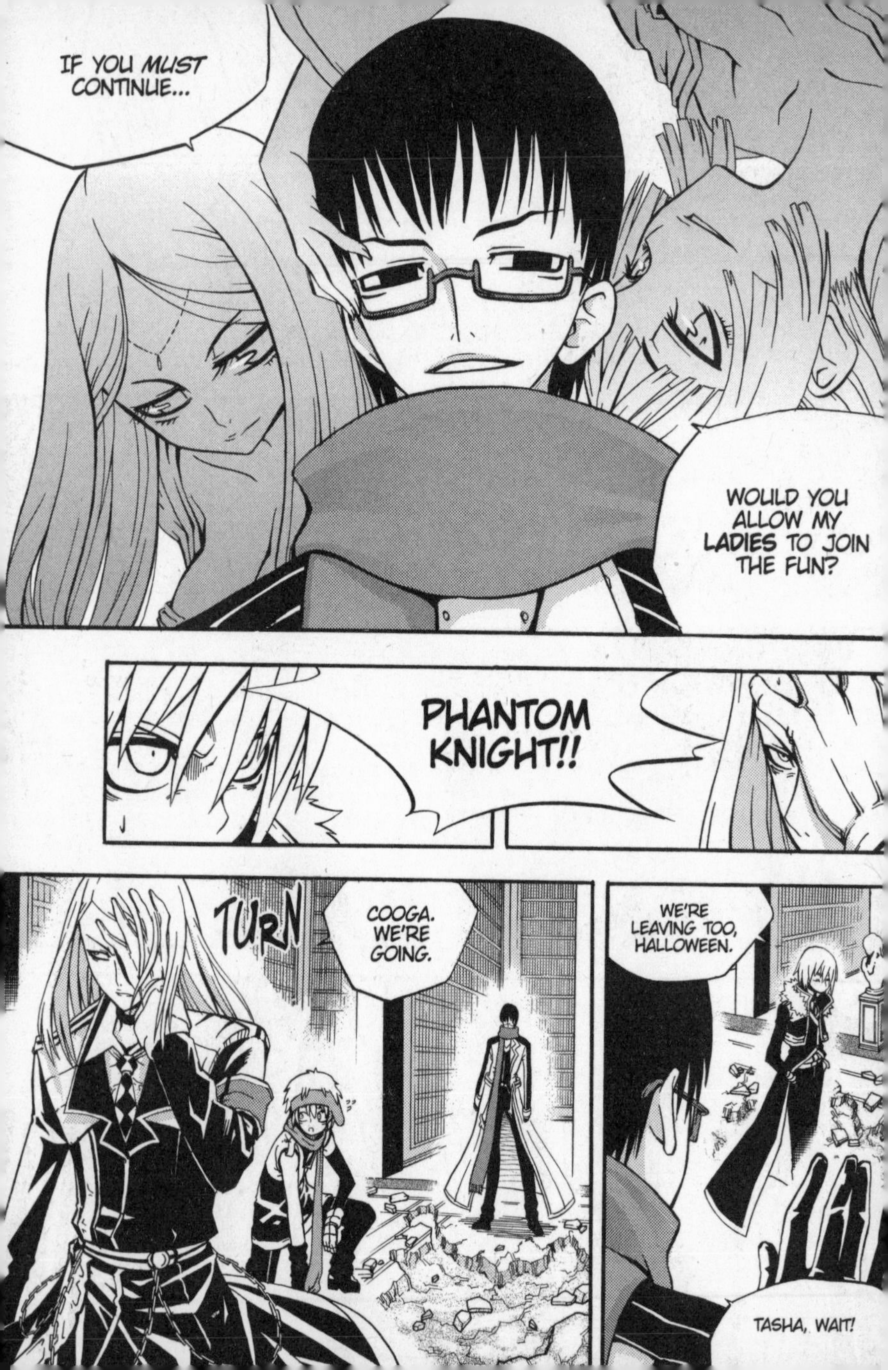
IF YOU MUST CONTINUE...
WOULD YOU ALLOW MY LADIES TO JOIN THE FUN?
PHANTOM KNIGHT!!
WE'RE LEAVING TOO, HALLOWEEN.
TASHA, WAIT!
COOGA. WE'RE GOING.
TURN

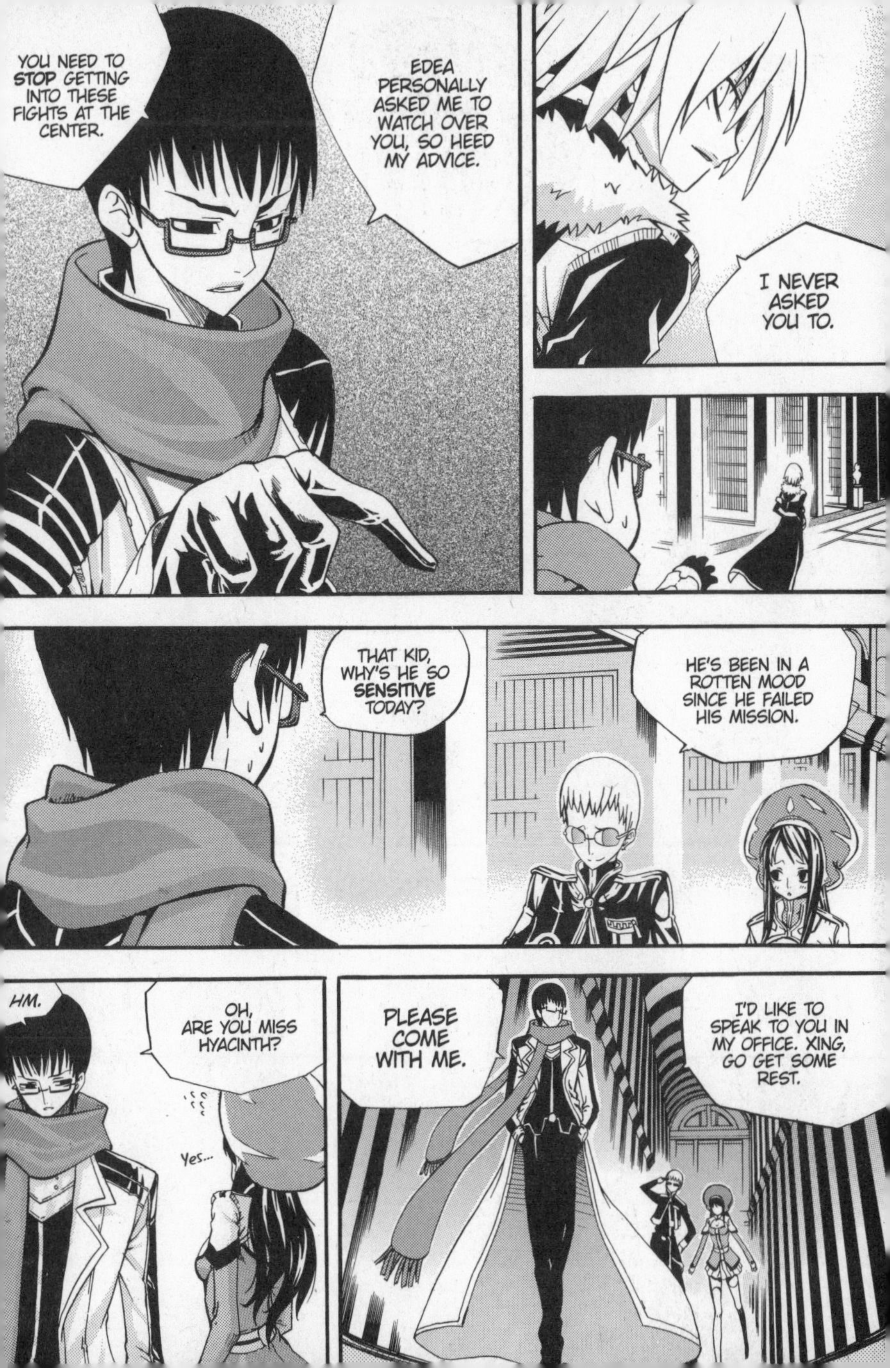
YOU NEED TO STOP GETTING INTO THESE FIGHTS AT THE CENTER.
EDEA PERSONALLY ASKED ME TO WATCH OVER YOU, SO HEED MY ADVICE.
I NEVER ASKED YOU TO.
THAT KID, WHY'S HE SO SENSITIVE TODAY?
HE'S BEEN IN A ROTTEN MOOD SINCE HE FAILED HIS MISSION.
HM.
OH, ARE YOU MISS HYACINTH?
Yes...
PLEASE COME WITH ME.
I'D LIKE TO SPEAK TO YOU IN MY OFFICE. XING, GO GET SOME REST.

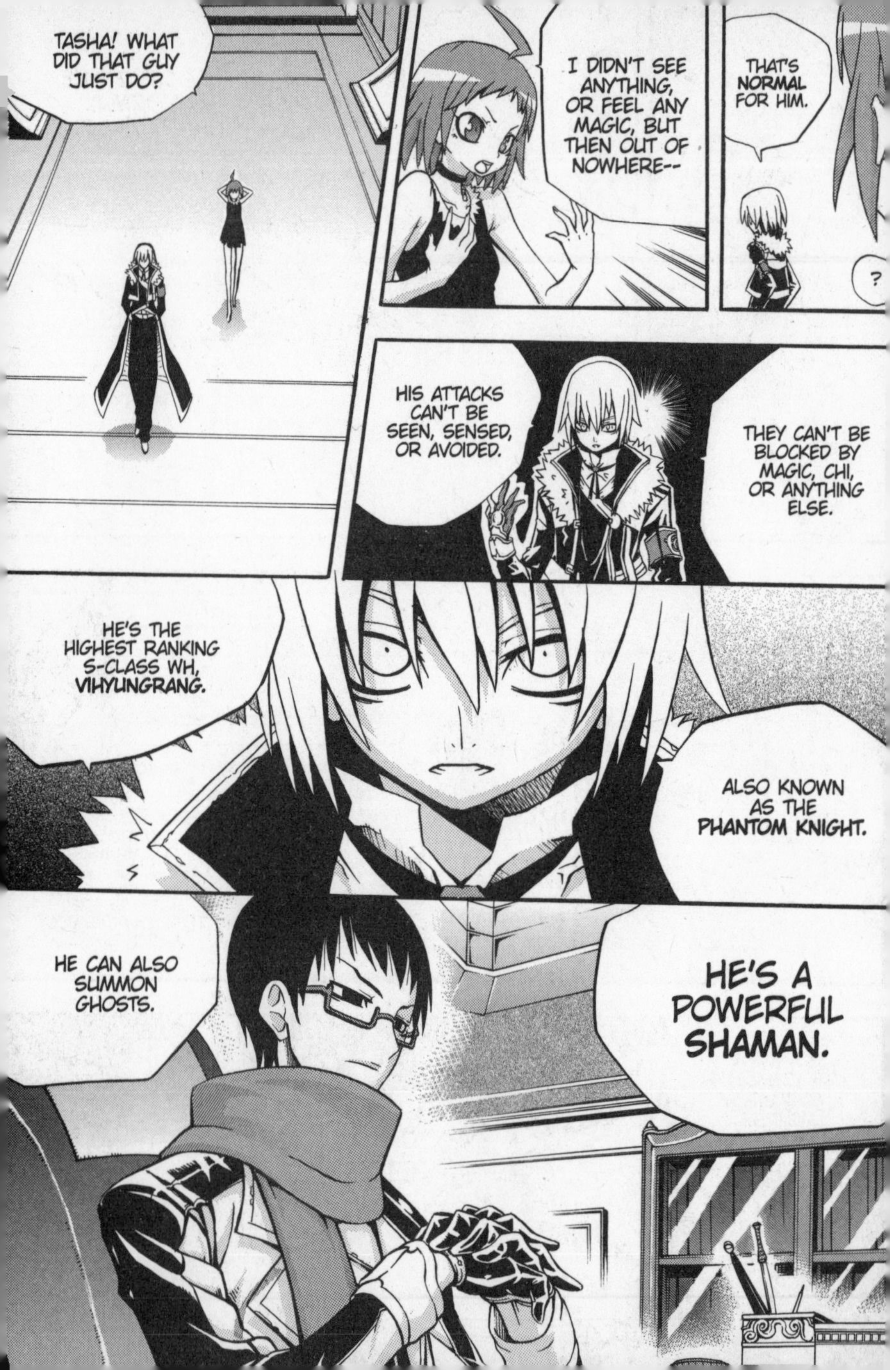
TASHA! WHAT DID THAT GUY JUST DO?
I DIDN'T SEE ANYTHING, OR FEEL ANY MAGIC, BUT THEN OUT OF NOWHERE--
THAT'S NORMAL FOR HIM.
?
HIS ATTACKS CAN'T BE SEEN, SENSED, OR AVOIDED.
THEY CAN'T BE BLOCKED BY MAGIC, CHI, OR ANYTHING ELSE.
HE'S THE HIGHEST RANKING S-CLASS WH, VIHYUNGRANG.
ALSO KNOWN AS THE PHANTOM KNIGHT.
HE CAN ALSO SUMMON GHOSTS.
HE'S A POWERFUL SHAMAN.

UM...

IT LOOKS LIKE A NORMAL SWORD HILT.

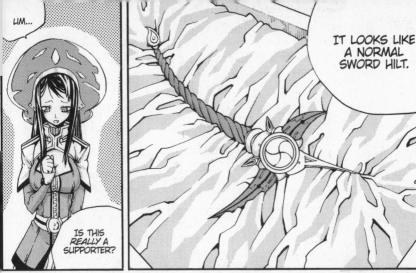

IS THIS REALLY A SUPPORTER?

THIS MAGIC SWORD HAS TAKEN COUNTLESS LIVES. DON'T BE FOOLED BY ITS APPEARANCE.

TO BE HONEST, I'M NOT SURE GIVING IT TO YOU IS THE RIGHT THING TO DO...

BUT WE DESPERATELY NEED MORE A-CLASS WHS RIGHT NOW, AND YOU ARE CURRENTLY THE **BEST** MATCH FOR IT.

HOWEVER, THE CHOICE IS ULTIMATELY YOURS...

MISS HYACINTH.

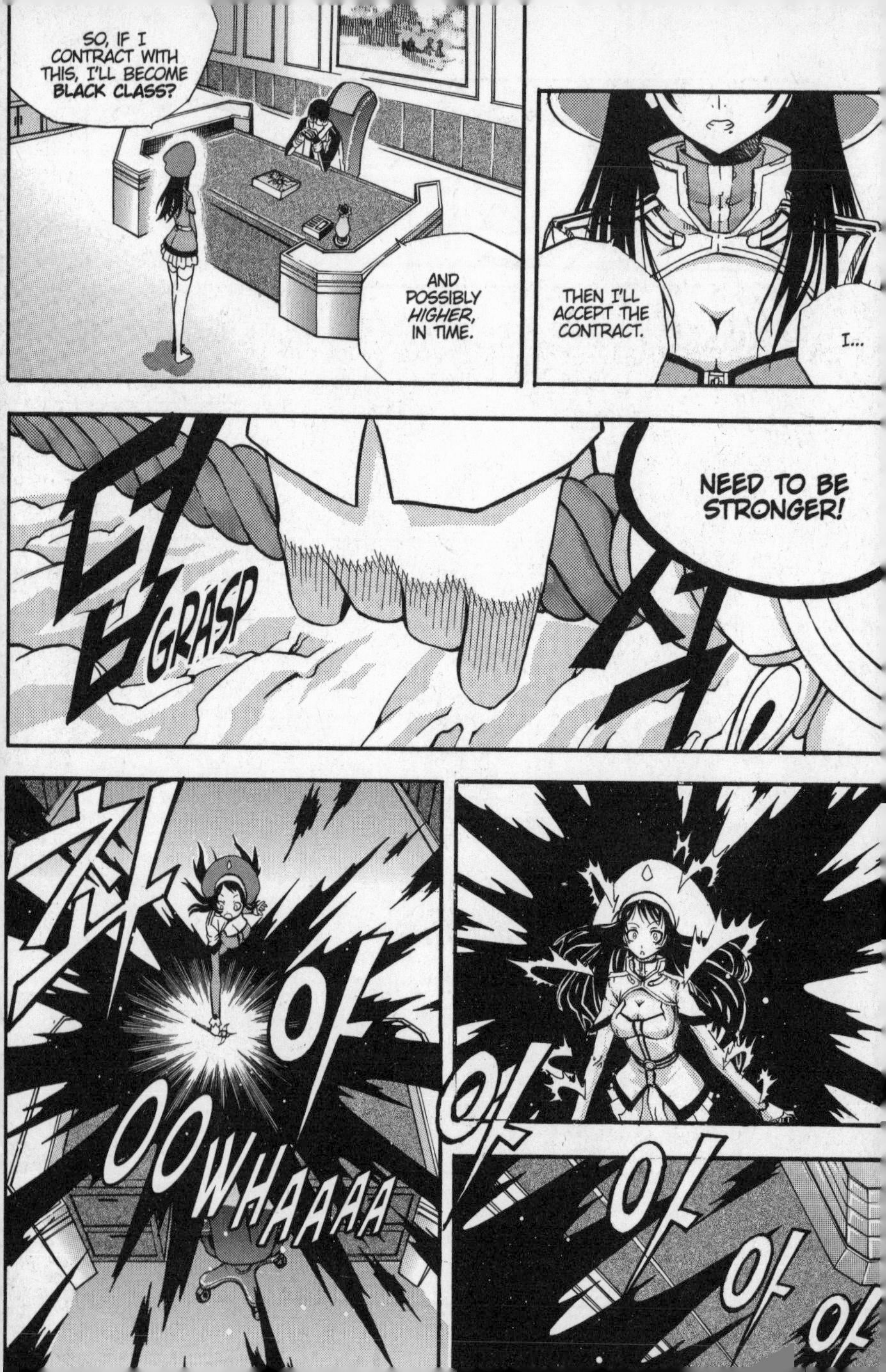
SO, IF I CONTRACT WITH THIS, I'LL BECOME BLACK CLASS?
AND POSSIBLY *HIGHER*, IN TIME.
THEN I'LL ACCEPT THE CONTRACT.
I...
NEED TO BE STRONGER!
GRASP
OOWHAAAA

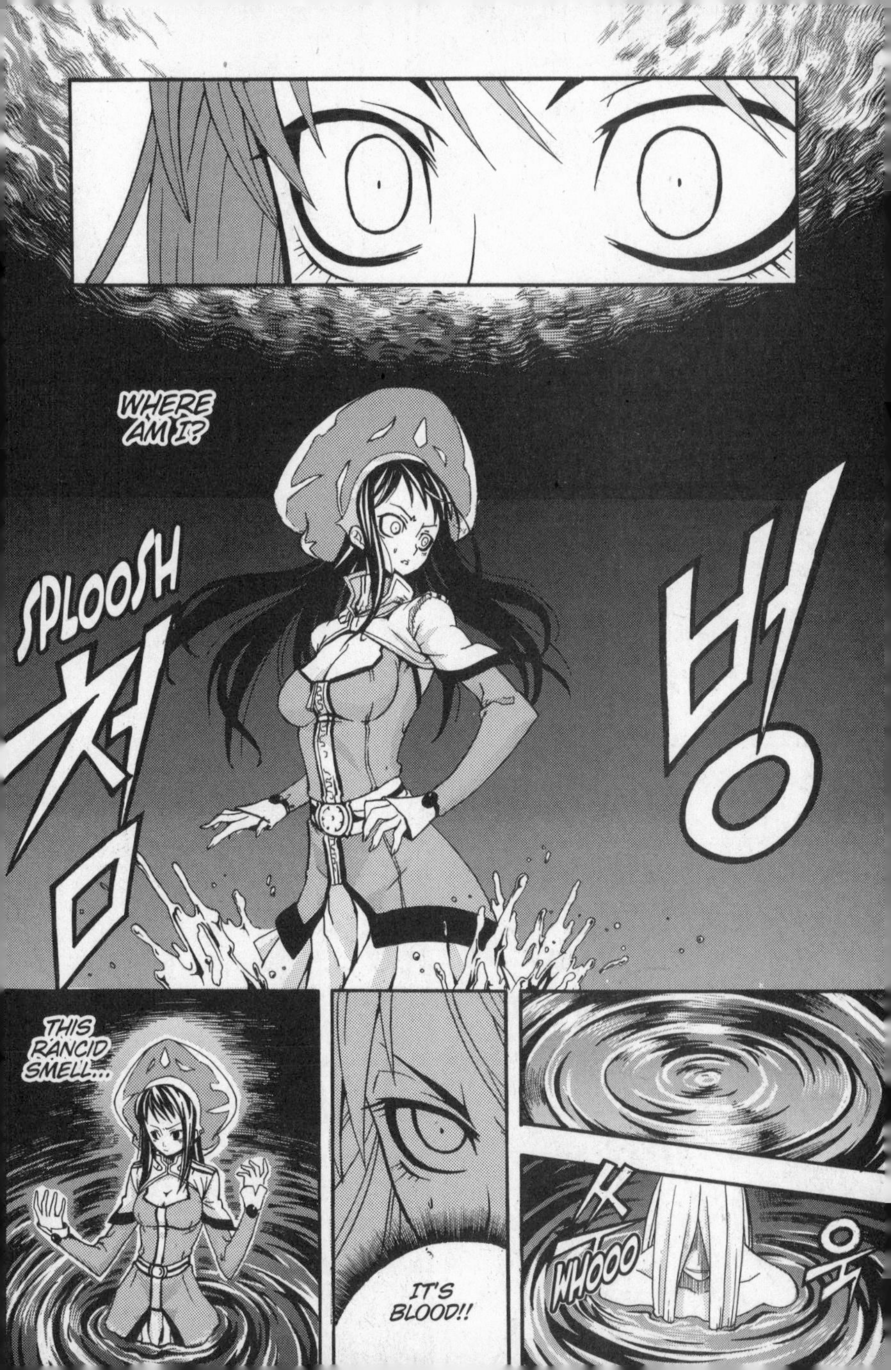
WHERE AM I?
SPLOOSH
첨
벙
THIS RANCID SMELL...
IT'S BLOOD!!
WHOOO
쏴
악

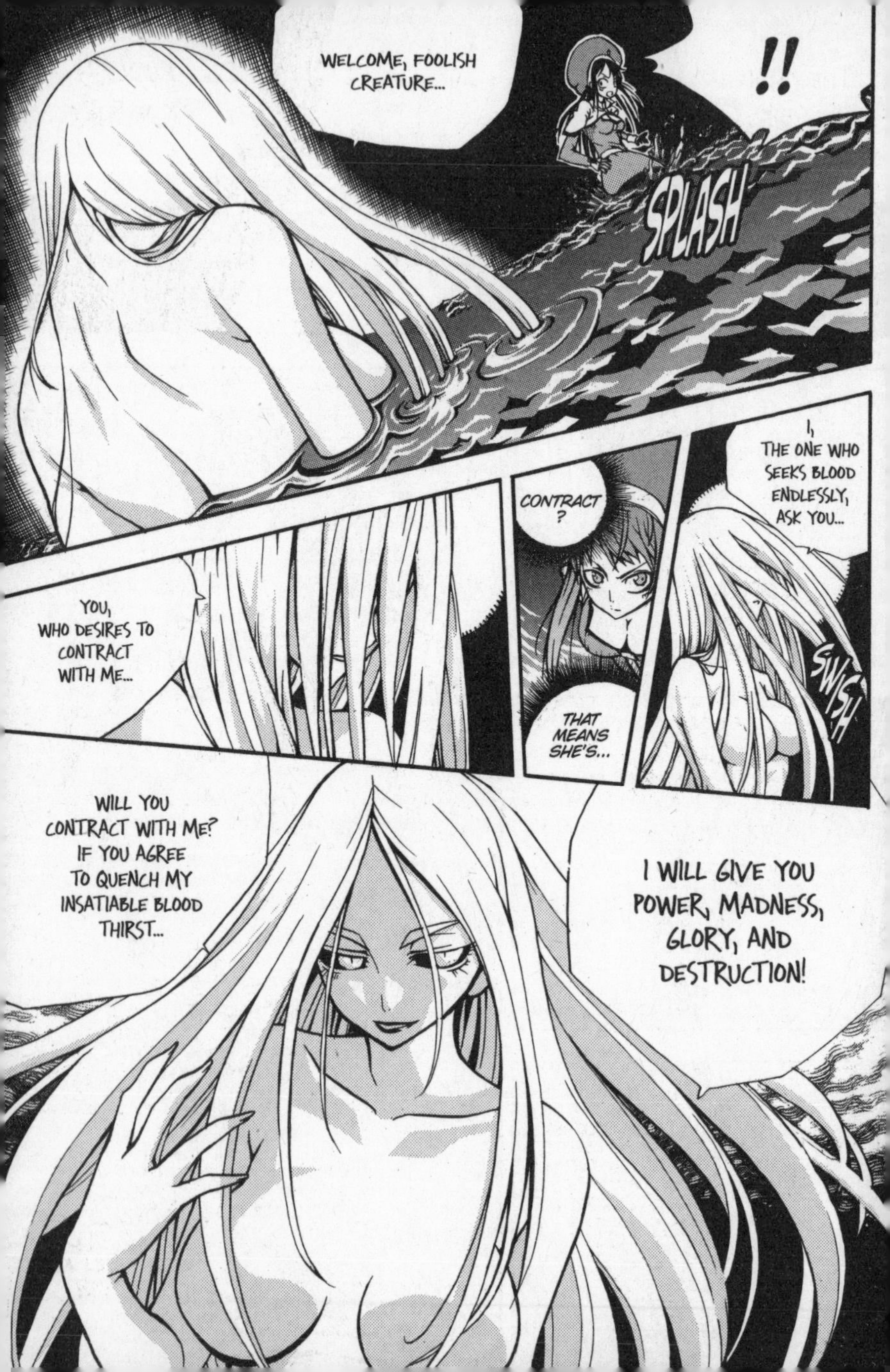
WELCOME, FOOLISH CREATURE...
!!
SPLASH
I, THE ONE WHO SEEKS BLOOD ENDLESSLY, ASK YOU...
SWISH
CONTRACT?
THAT MEANS SHE'S...
YOU, WHO DESIRES TO CONTRACT WITH ME...
WILL YOU CONTRACT WITH ME? IF YOU AGREE TO QUENCH MY INSATIABLE BLOOD THIRST...
I WILL GIVE YOU POWER, MADNESS, GLORY, AND DESTRUCTION!

THE CHOICE IS YOURS...

FOOLISH CREATURE.

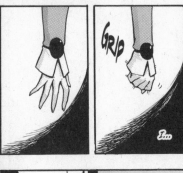

GRIP

I....

I KNOW WHAT IT'S LIKE TO BE WEAK.

I'VE STOOD BY, HELPLESS, AND WATCHED MY COMRADES DIE AROUND ME.

I WANT POWER!

GIVE ME YOUR STRENGTH, AND I'LL GIVE YOU MY BLOOD!

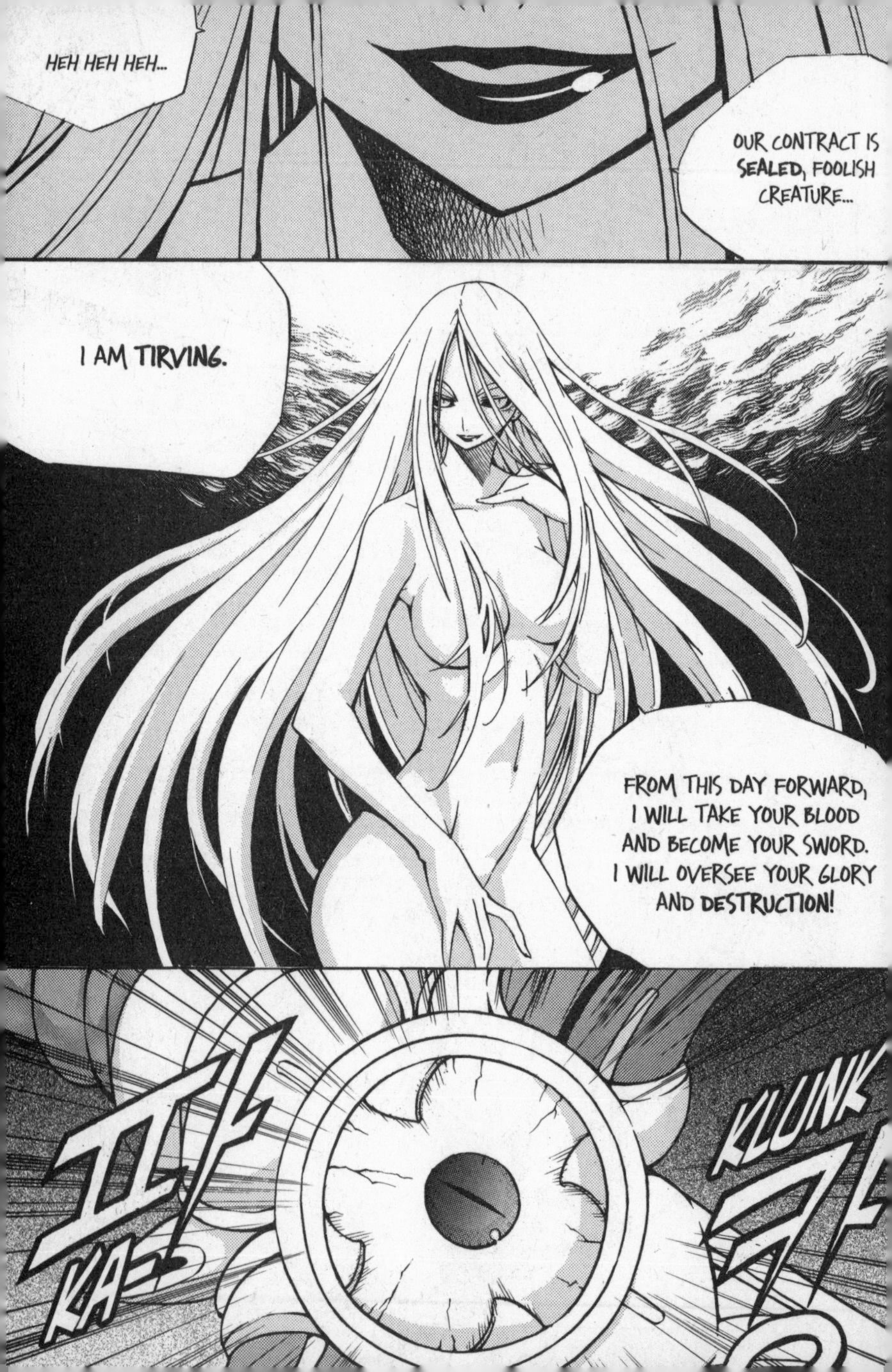

OUR CONTRACT IS SEALED, FOOLISH CREATURE...
HEH HEH HEH...
I AM TIRVING.
FROM THIS DAY FORWARD, I WILL TAKE YOUR BLOOD AND BECOME YOUR SWORD. I WILL OVERSEE YOUR GLORY AND DESTRUCTION!
KLUNK
KA-

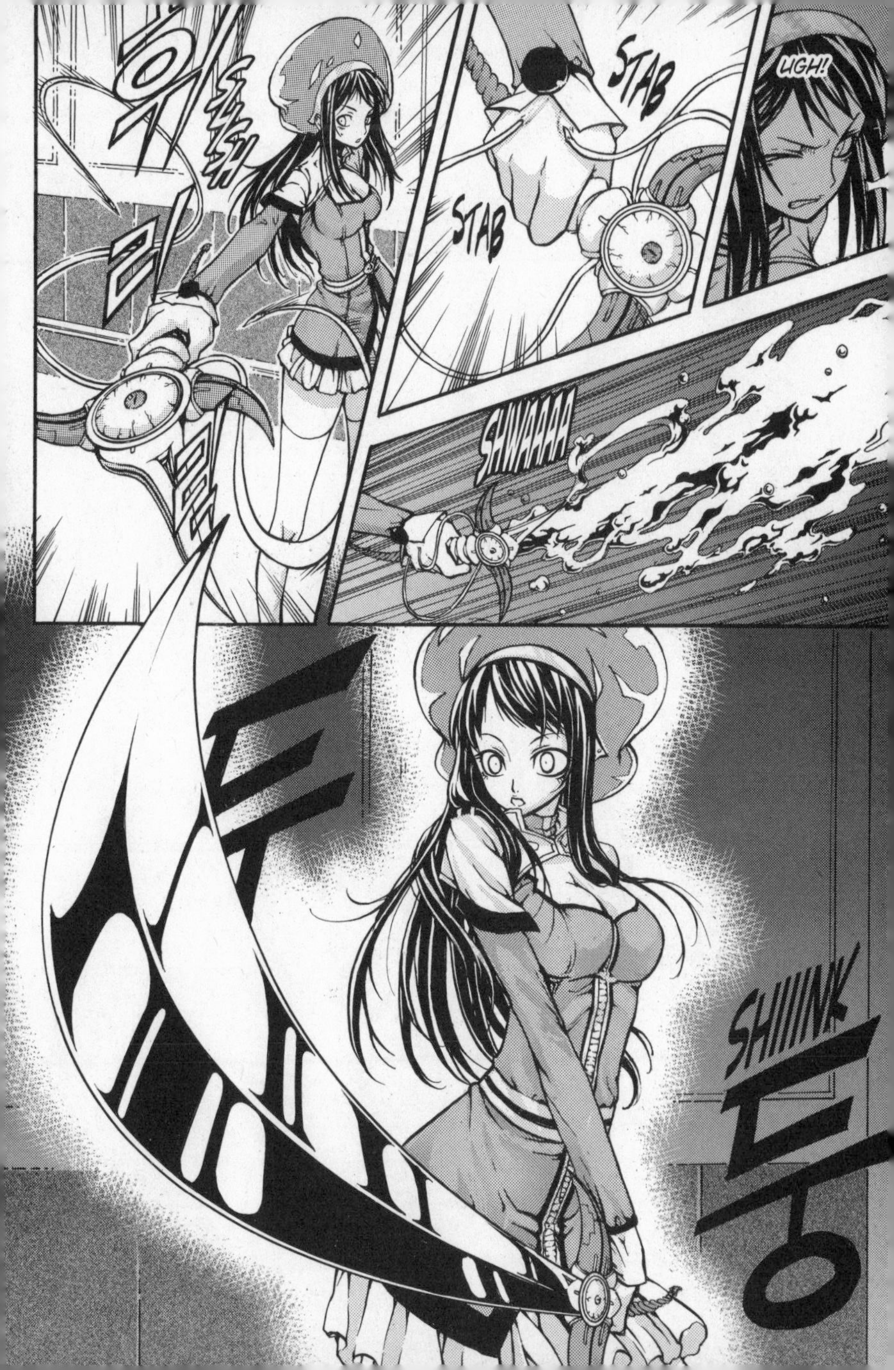
UGH!
STAB
STAB
SWISH
SHWAAAA
SHIIINK

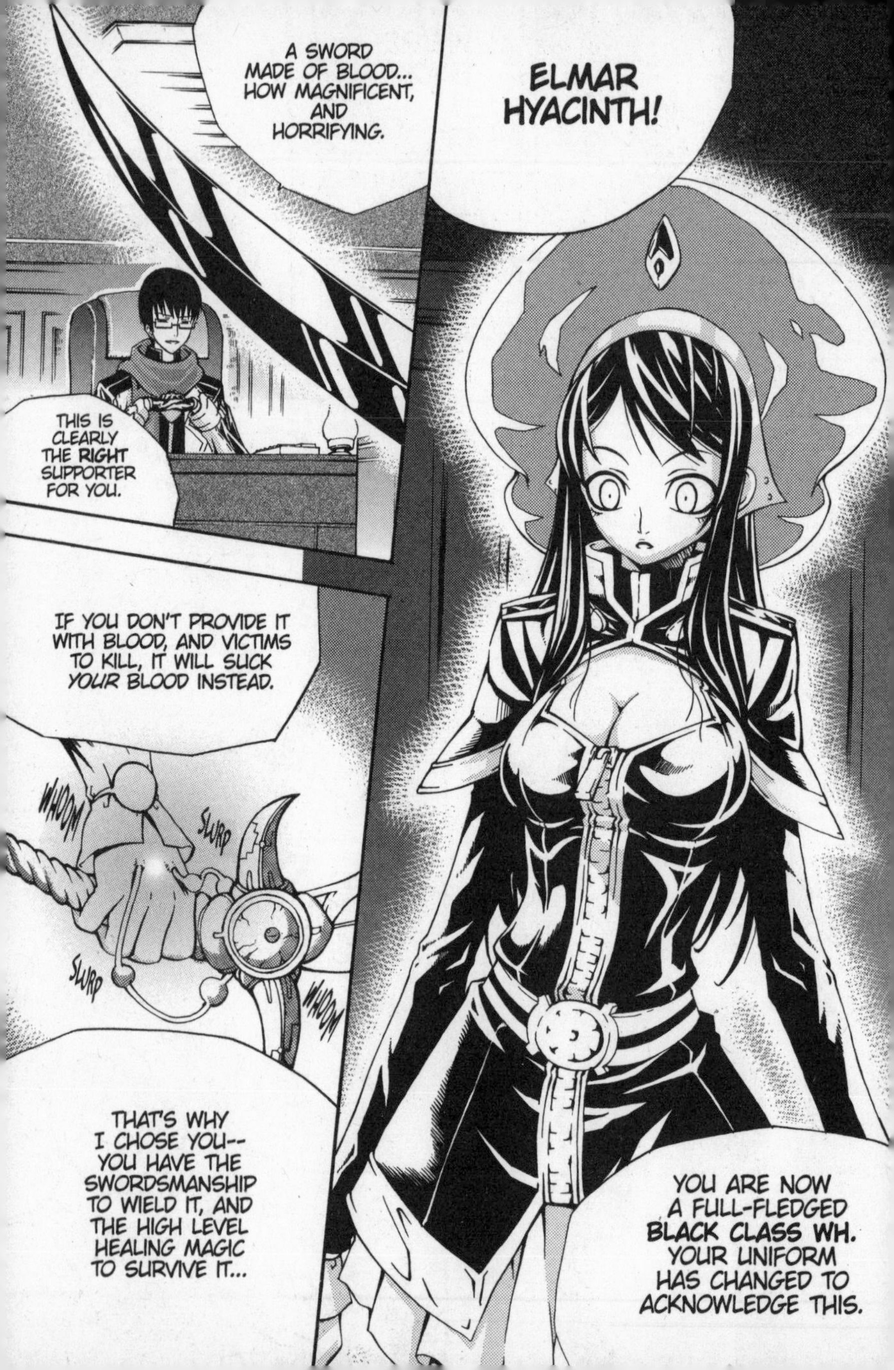
ELMAR HYACINTH!
YOU ARE NOW A FULL-FLEDGED BLACK CLASS WH. YOUR UNIFORM HAS CHANGED TO ACKNOWLEDGE THIS.
A SWORD MADE OF BLOOD... HOW MAGNIFICENT, AND HORRIFYING.
THIS IS CLEARLY THE RIGHT SUPPORTER FOR YOU.
IF YOU DON'T PROVIDE IT WITH BLOOD, AND VICTIMS TO KILL, IT WILL SUCK YOUR BLOOD INSTEAD.
WHOOM
SLURP
SLURP
WHOOM
THAT'S WHY I CHOSE YOU-- YOU HAVE THE SWORDSMANSHIP TO WIELD IT, AND THE HIGH LEVEL HEALING MAGIC TO SURVIVE IT...

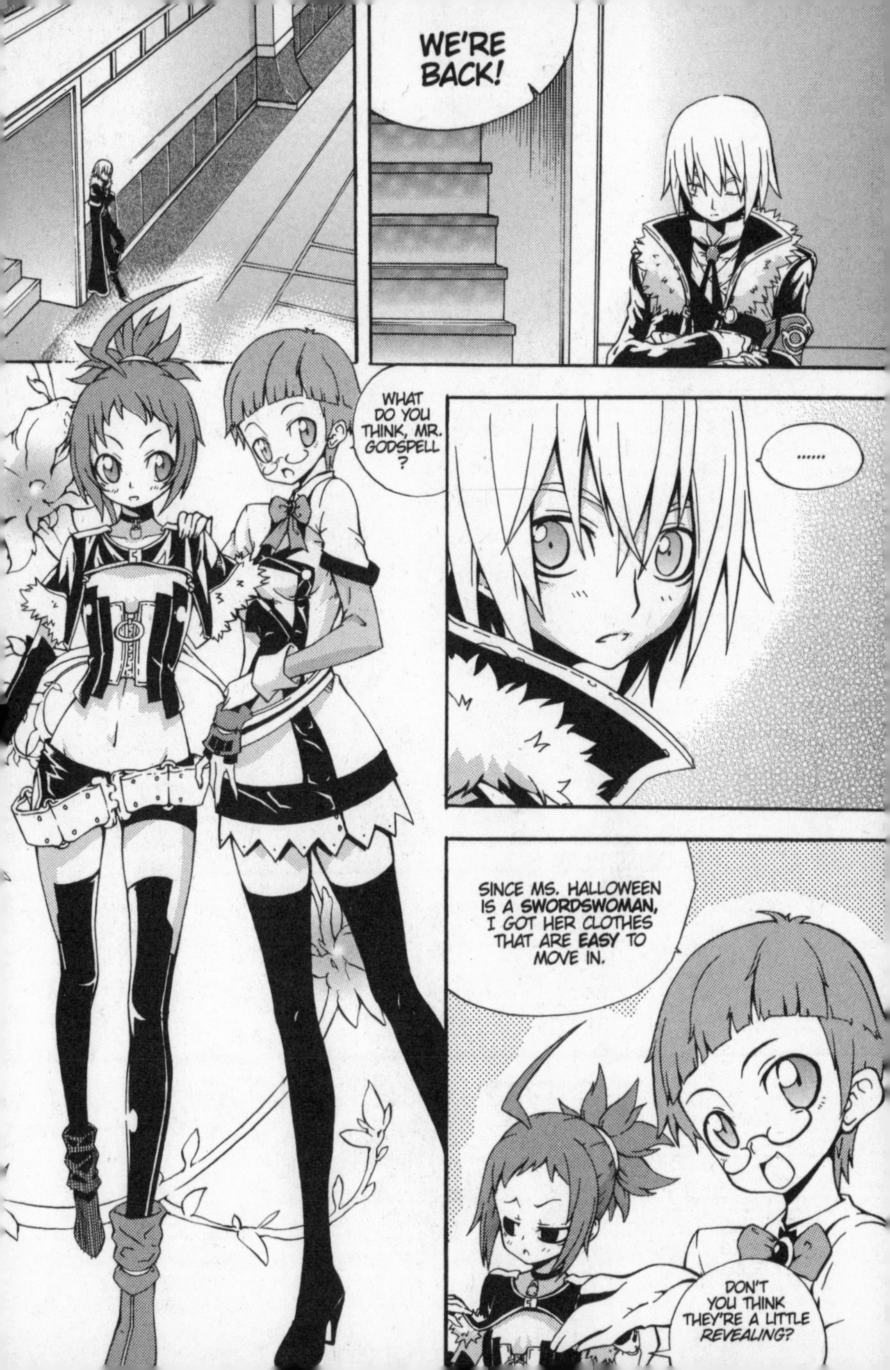
WE'RE BACK!
WHAT DO YOU THINK, MR. GODSPELL?
......
SINCE MS. HALLOWEEN IS A **SWORDSWOMAN,** I GOT HER CLOTHES THAT ARE **EASY** TO MOVE IN.
DON'T YOU THINK THEY'RE A LITTLE *REVEALING?*

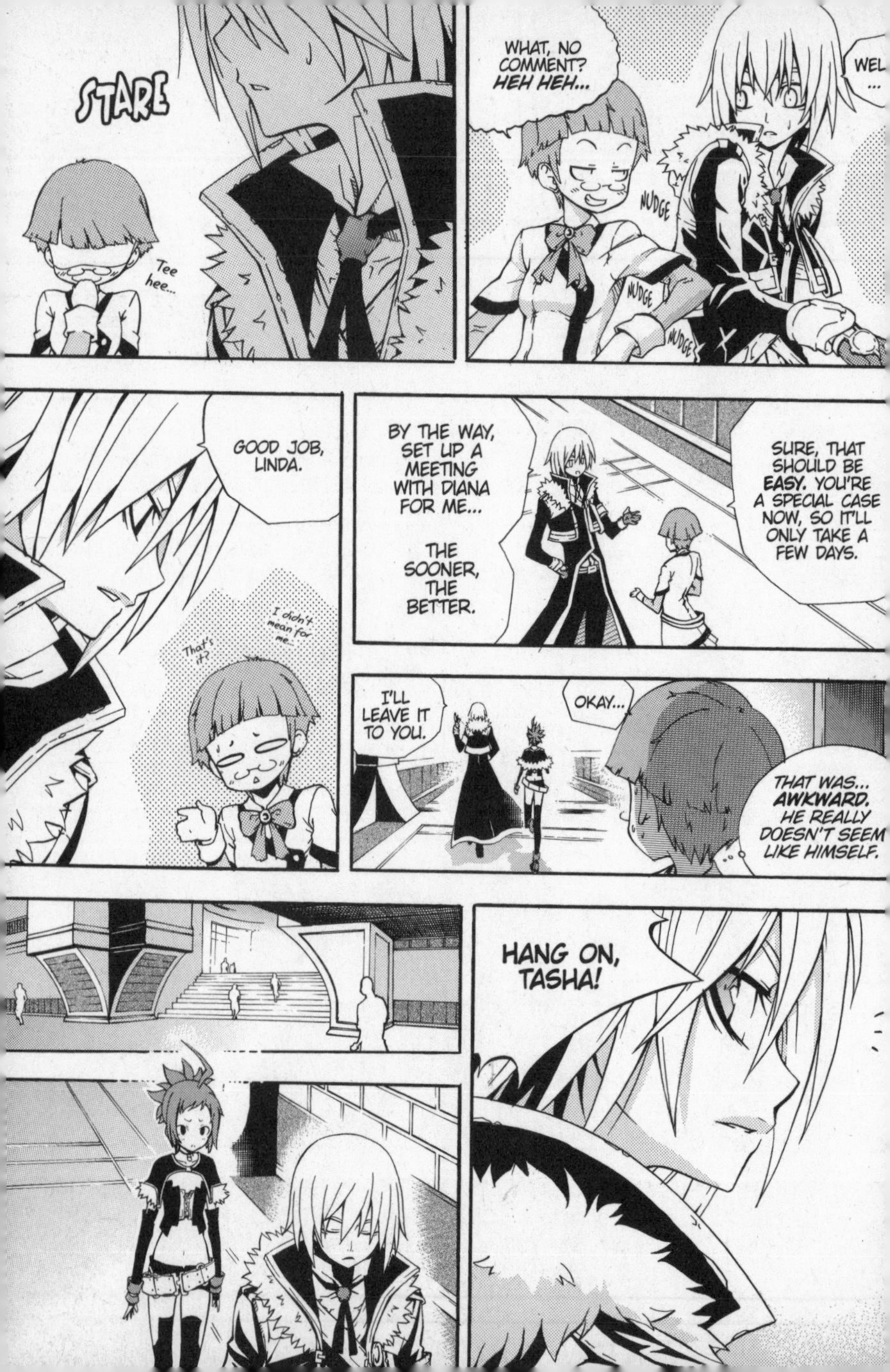
STARE
Tee hee...
WHAT, NO COMMENT? HEH HEH...
WEL...
NUDGE
NUDGE
NUDGE
GOOD JOB, LINDA.
That's it?
I didn't mean for me...
BY THE WAY, SET UP A MEETING WITH DIANA FOR ME...
THE SOONER, THE BETTER.
SURE, THAT SHOULD BE EASY. YOU'RE A SPECIAL CASE NOW, SO IT'LL ONLY TAKE A FEW DAYS.
I'LL LEAVE IT TO YOU.
OKAY...
THAT WAS... AWKWARD. HE REALLY DOESN'T SEEM LIKE HIMSELF.
HANG ON, TASHA!

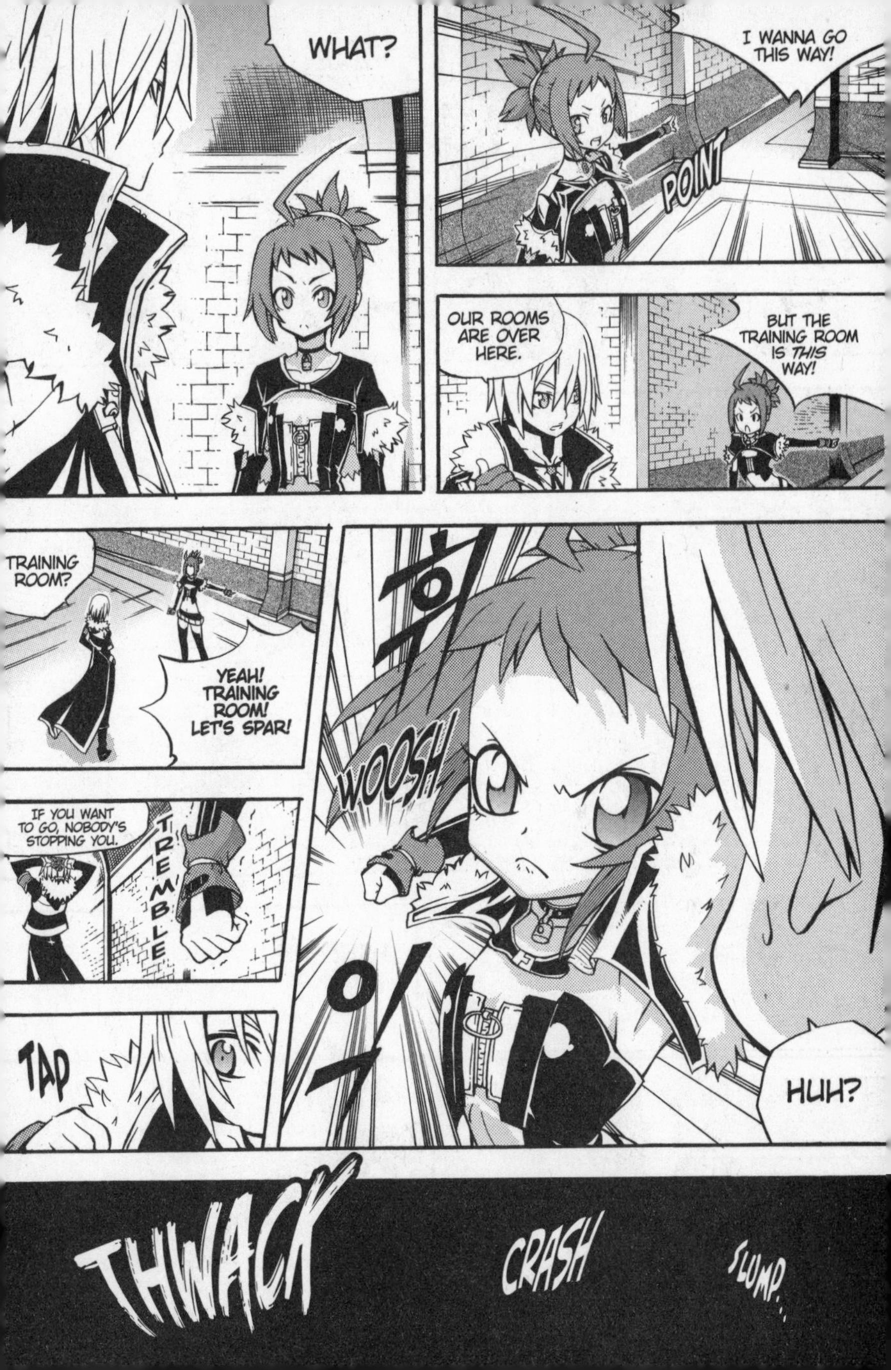
I WANNA GO THIS WAY!
POINT
OUR ROOMS ARE OVER HERE.
BUT THE TRAINING ROOM IS *THIS* WAY!
WHAT?
TRAINING ROOM?
YEAH! TRAINING ROOM! LET'S SPAR!
IF YOU WANT TO GO, NOBODY'S STOPPING YOU.
TREMBLE
TAP
HUH?
WOOSH
THWACK
CRASH
SLUMP...

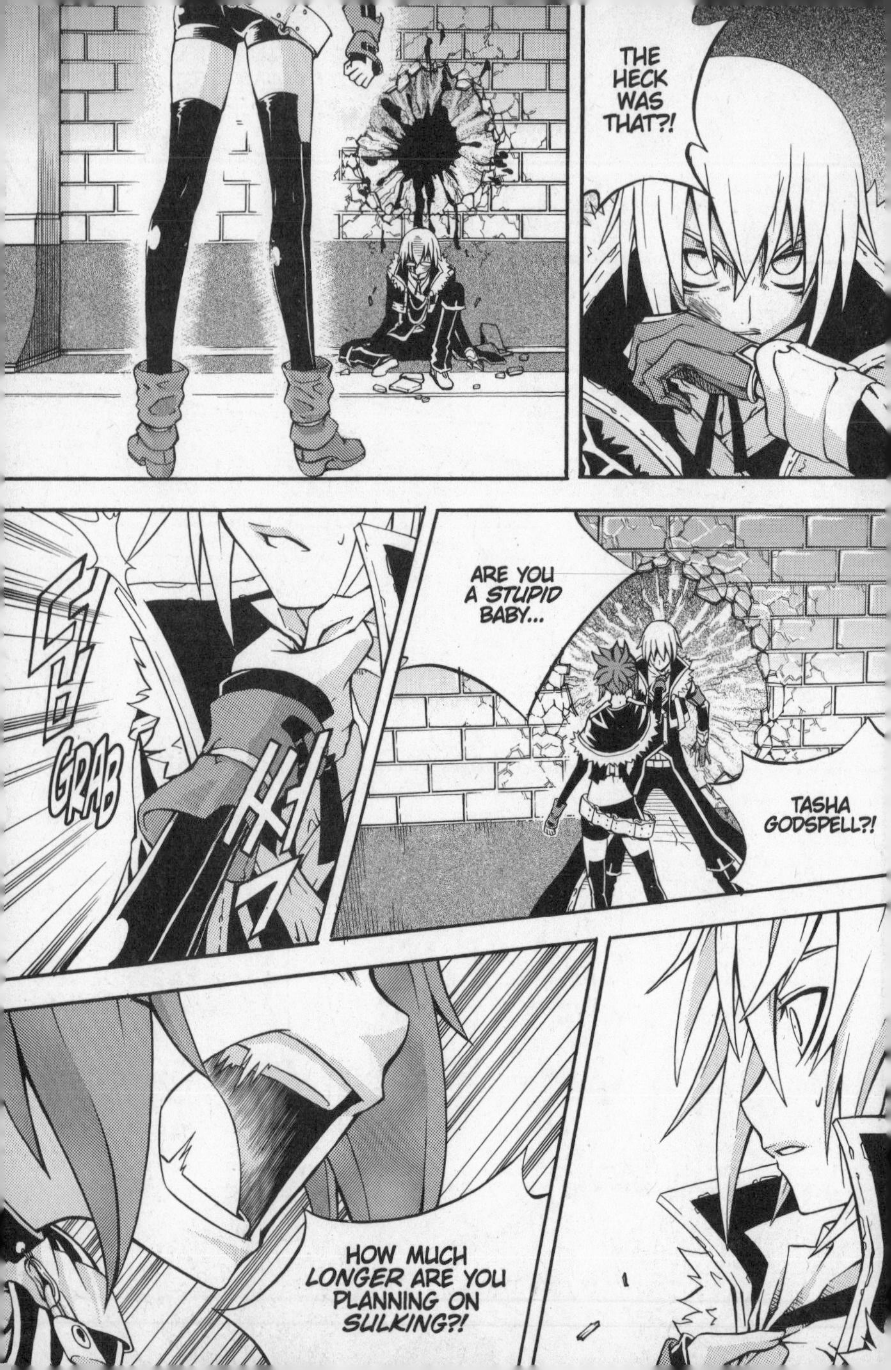

THE HECK WAS THAT?!
GRAB
ARE YOU A STUPID BABY...
TASHA GODSPELL?!
HOW MUCH LONGER ARE YOU PLANNING ON SULKING?!

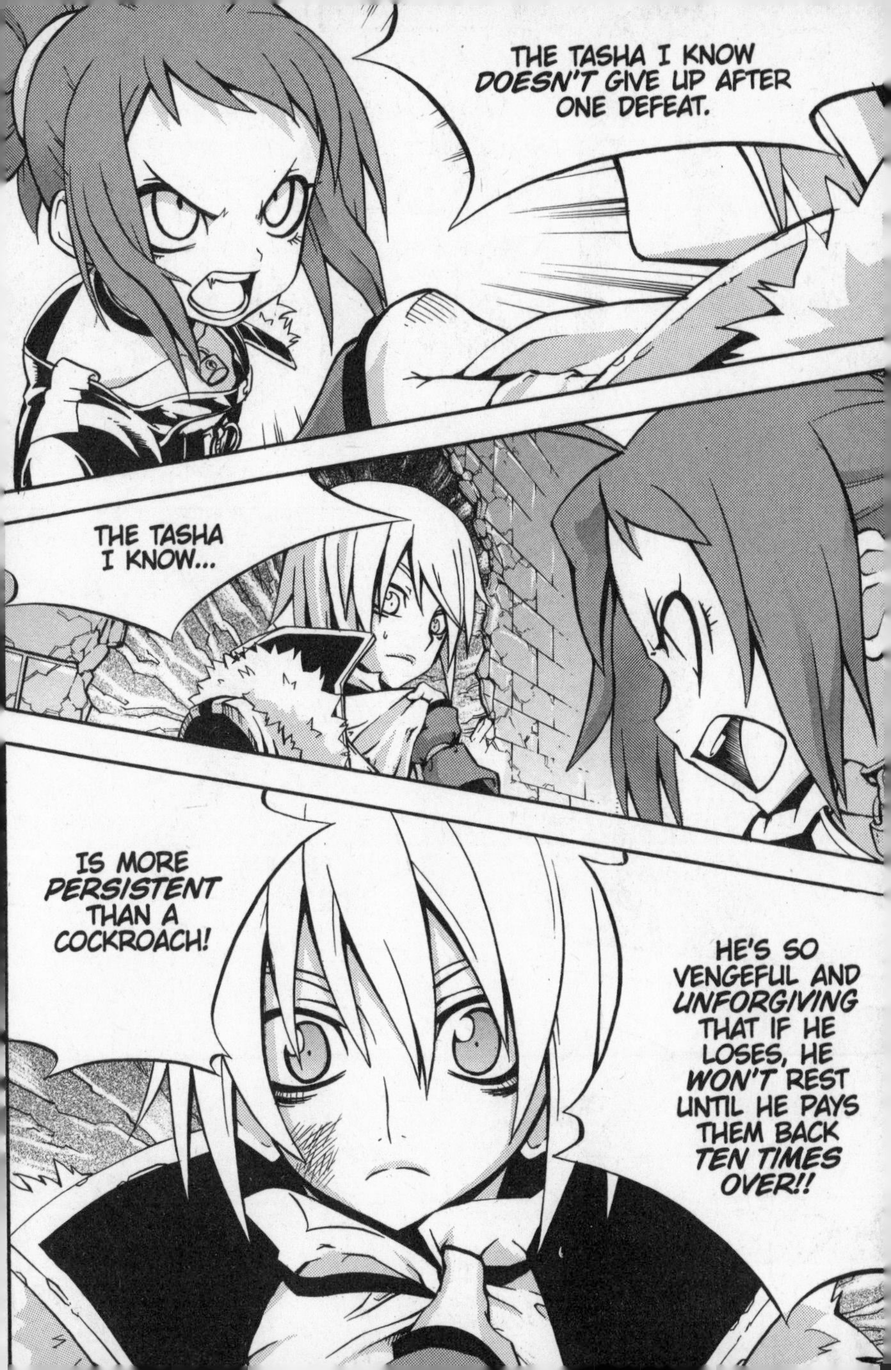
THE TASHA I KNOW DOESN'T GIVE UP AFTER ONE DEFEAT.
THE TASHA I KNOW...
IS MORE PERSISTENT THAN A COCKROACH!
HE'S SO VENGEFUL AND UNFORGIVING THAT IF HE LOSES, HE WON'T REST UNTIL HE PAYS THEM BACK TEN TIMES OVER!!

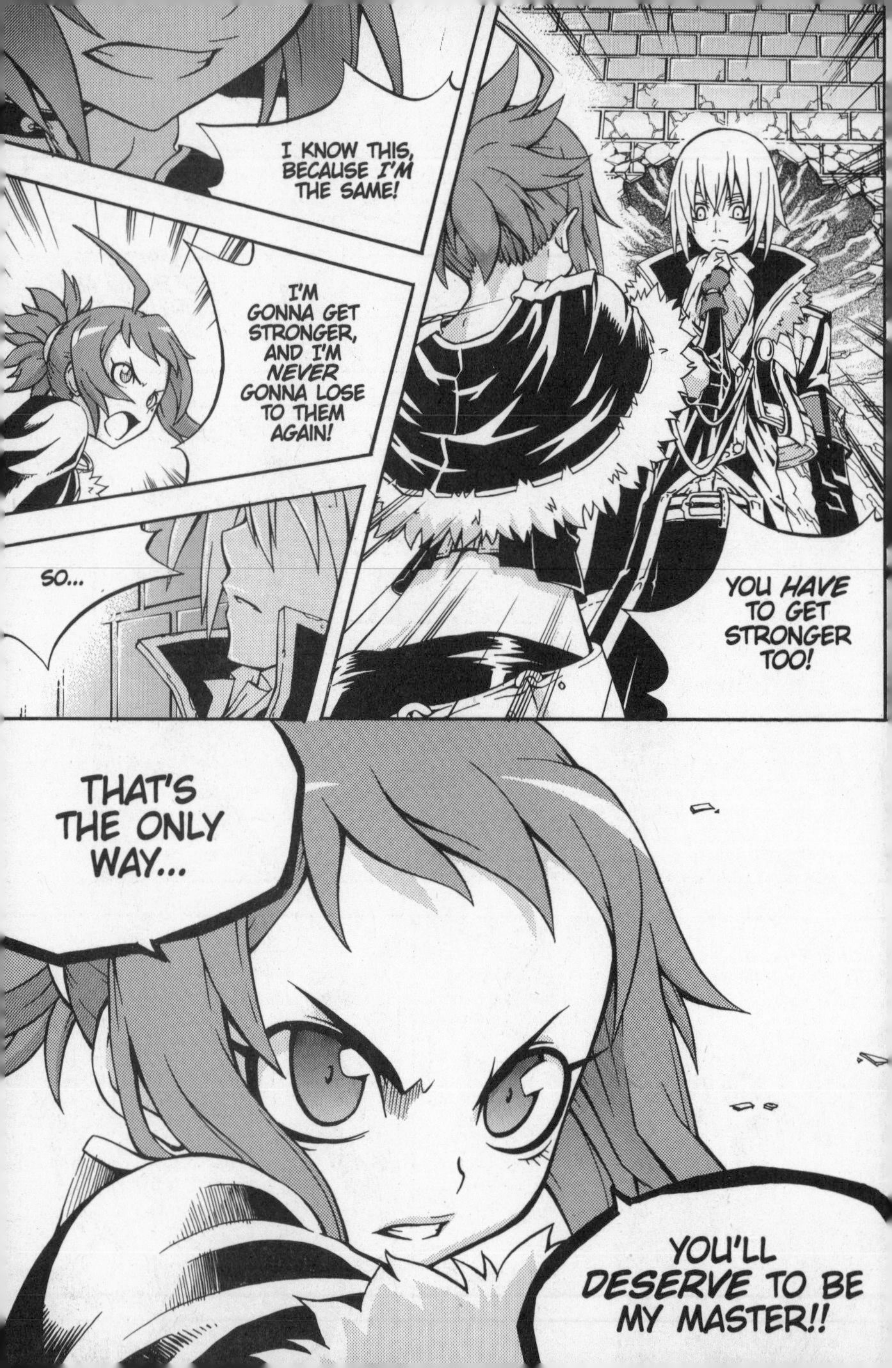

I KNOW THIS, BECAUSE *I'M* THE SAME!
I'M GONNA GET STRONGER, AND I'M *NEVER* GONNA LOSE TO THEM AGAIN!
SO...
YOU *HAVE* TO GET STRONGER TOO!
THAT'S THE ONLY WAY...
YOU'LL *DESERVE* TO BE MY MASTER!!

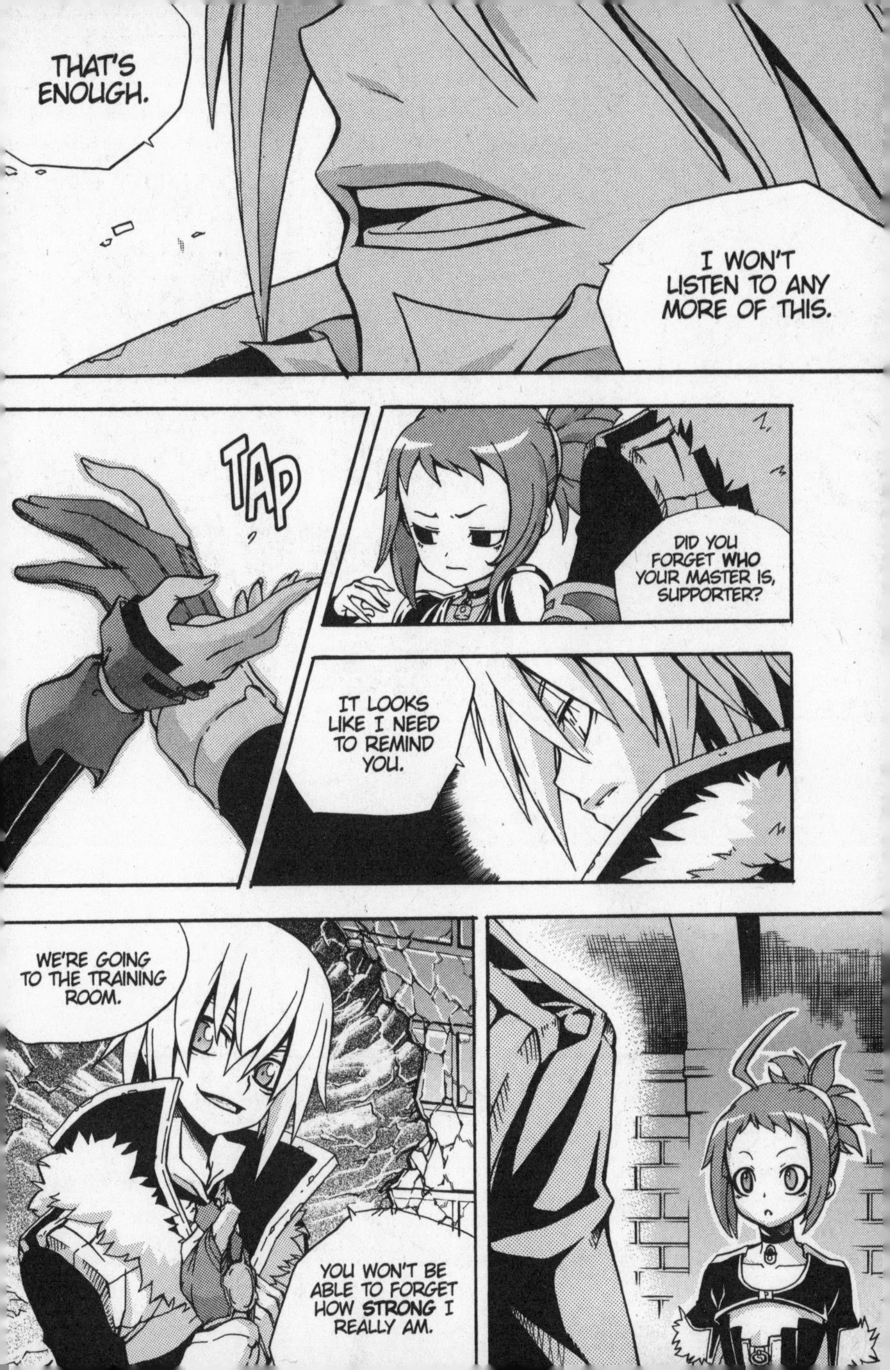
THAT'S ENOUGH.
I WON'T LISTEN TO ANY MORE OF THIS.
TAP
DID YOU FORGET WHO YOUR MASTER IS, SUPPORTER?
IT LOOKS LIKE I NEED TO REMIND YOU.
WE'RE GOING TO THE TRAINING ROOM.
YOU WON'T BE ABLE TO FORGET HOW STRONG I REALLY AM.

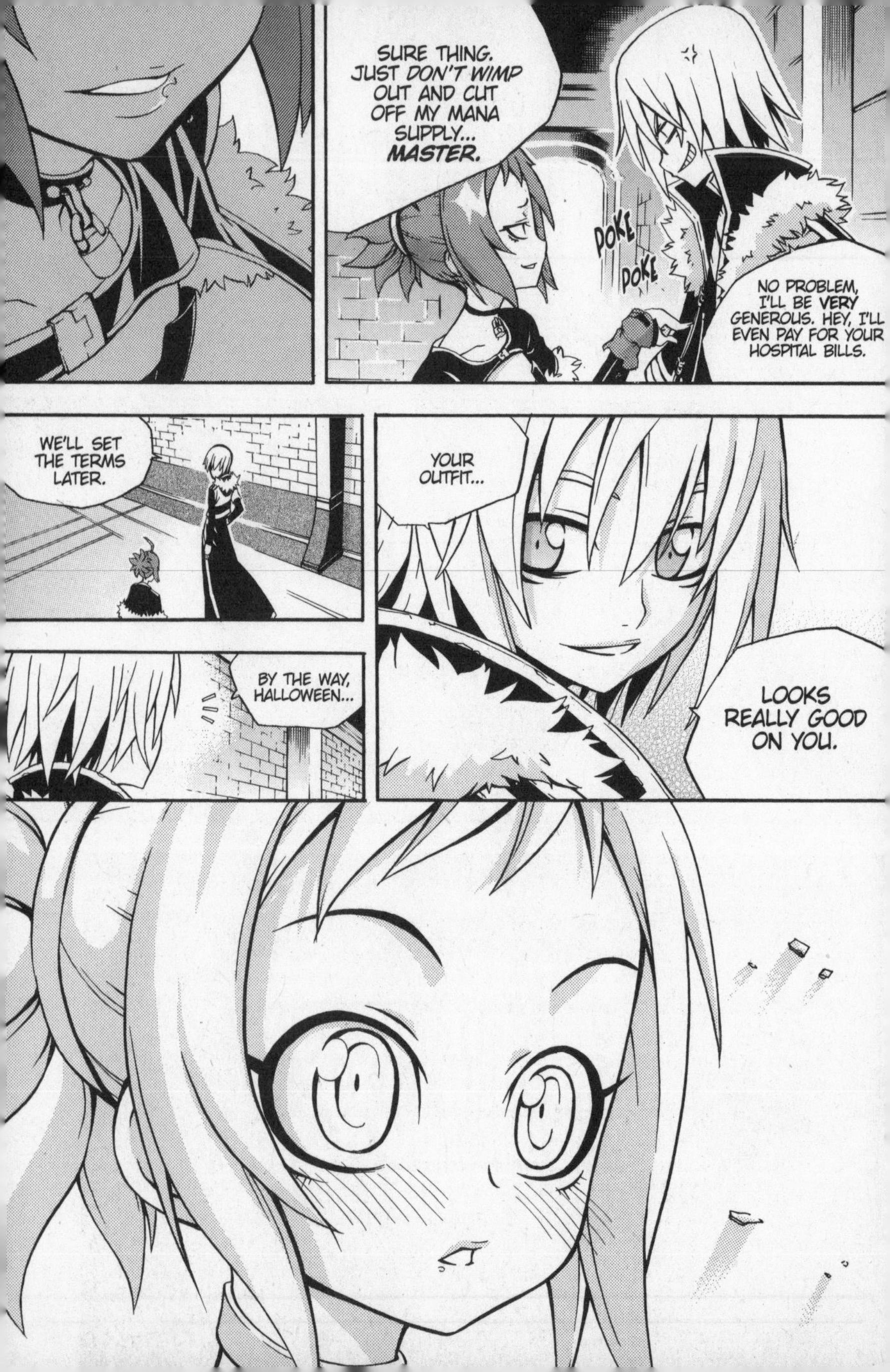
SURE THING. JUST *DON'T WIMP* OUT AND CUT OFF MY MANA SUPPLY... ***MASTER.***
POKE
POKE
NO PROBLEM, I'LL BE **VERY** GENEROUS. HEY, I'LL EVEN PAY FOR YOUR HOSPITAL BILLS.
WE'LL SET THE TERMS LATER.
BY THE WAY, HALLOWEEN...
YOUR OUTFIT...
LOOKS REALLY GOOD ON YOU.

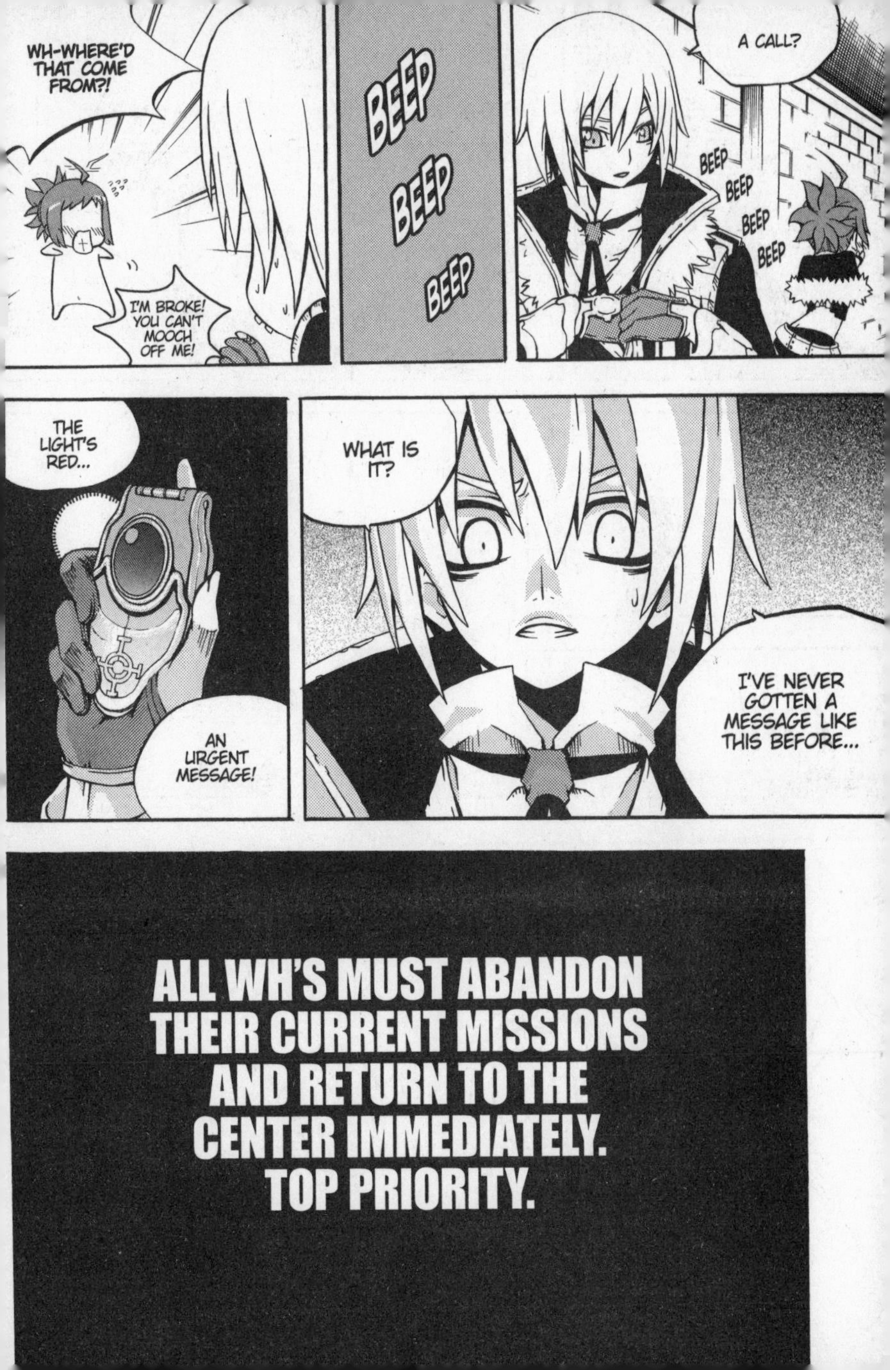
A CALL?
BEEP
BEEP
BEEP
BEEP
BEEP
BEEP
BEEP
WH-WHERE'D THAT COME FROM?!
I'M BROKE! YOU CAN'T MOOCH OFF ME!
WHAT IS IT?
I'VE NEVER GOTTEN A MESSAGE LIKE THIS BEFORE...
THE LIGHT'S RED...
AN URGENT MESSAGE!
ALL WH'S MUST ABANDON THEIR CURRENT MISSIONS AND RETURN TO THE CENTER IMMEDIATELY. TOP PRIORITY.

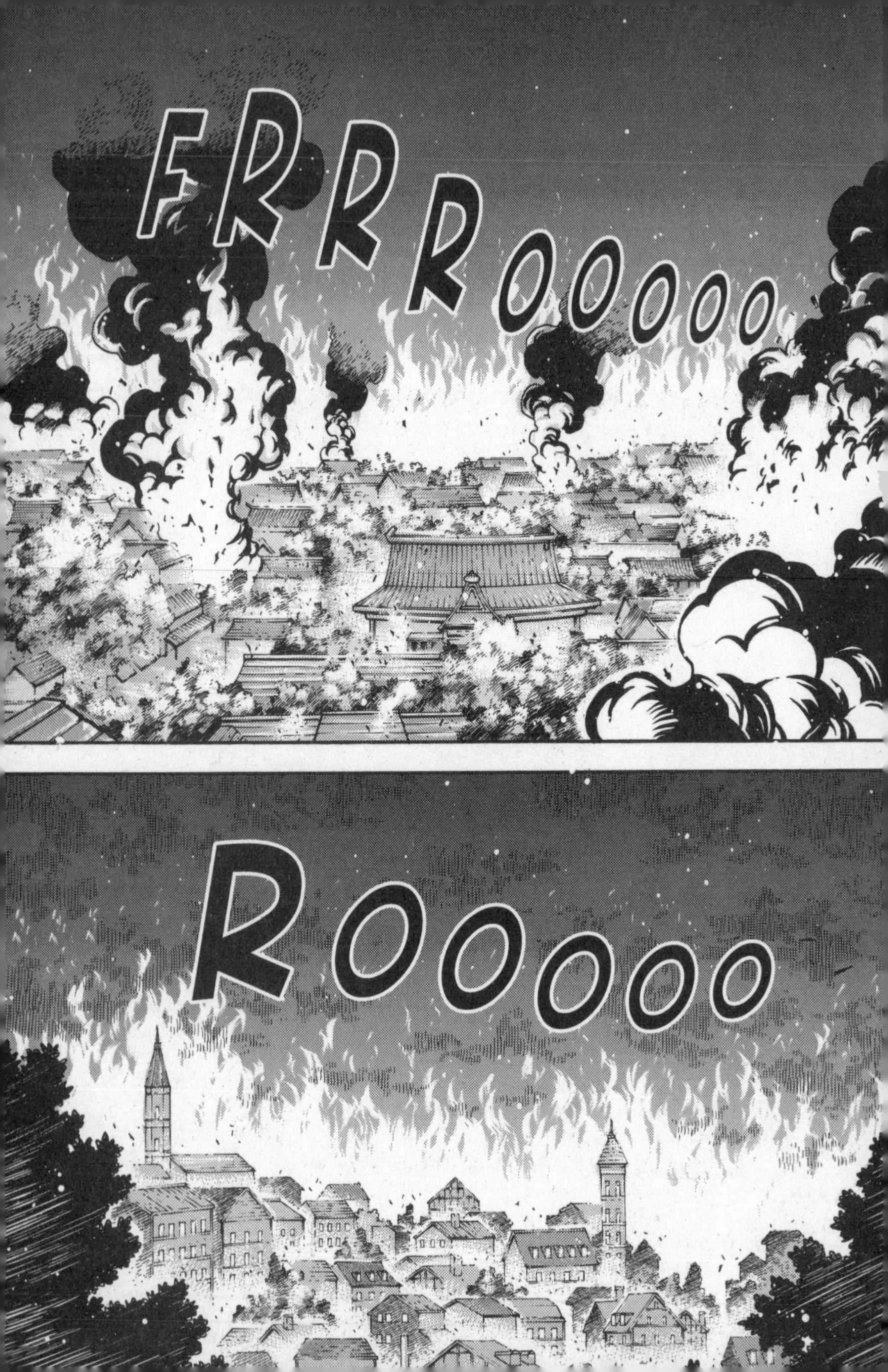
FRRROOOOO
ROOOOO

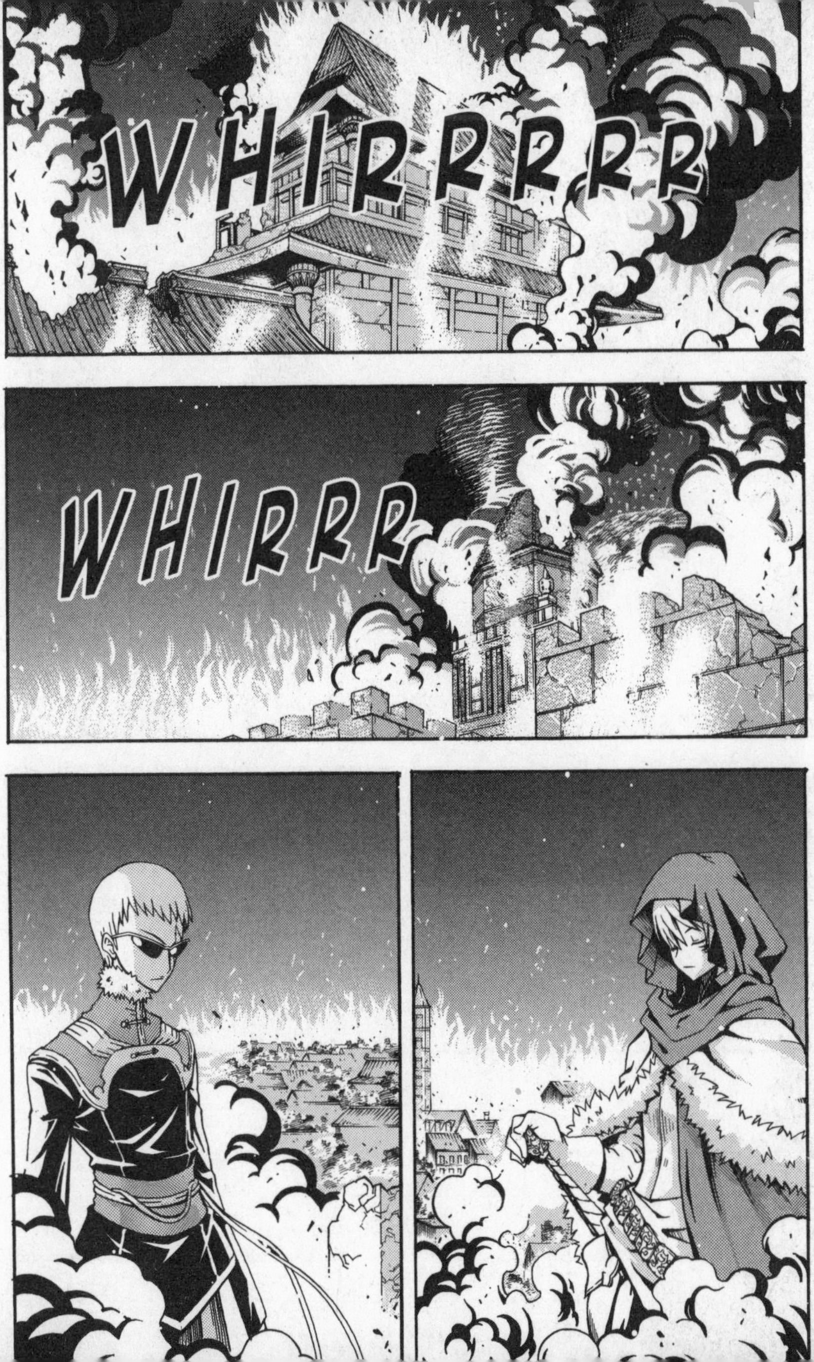
WHIRRRRRR
WHIRRR

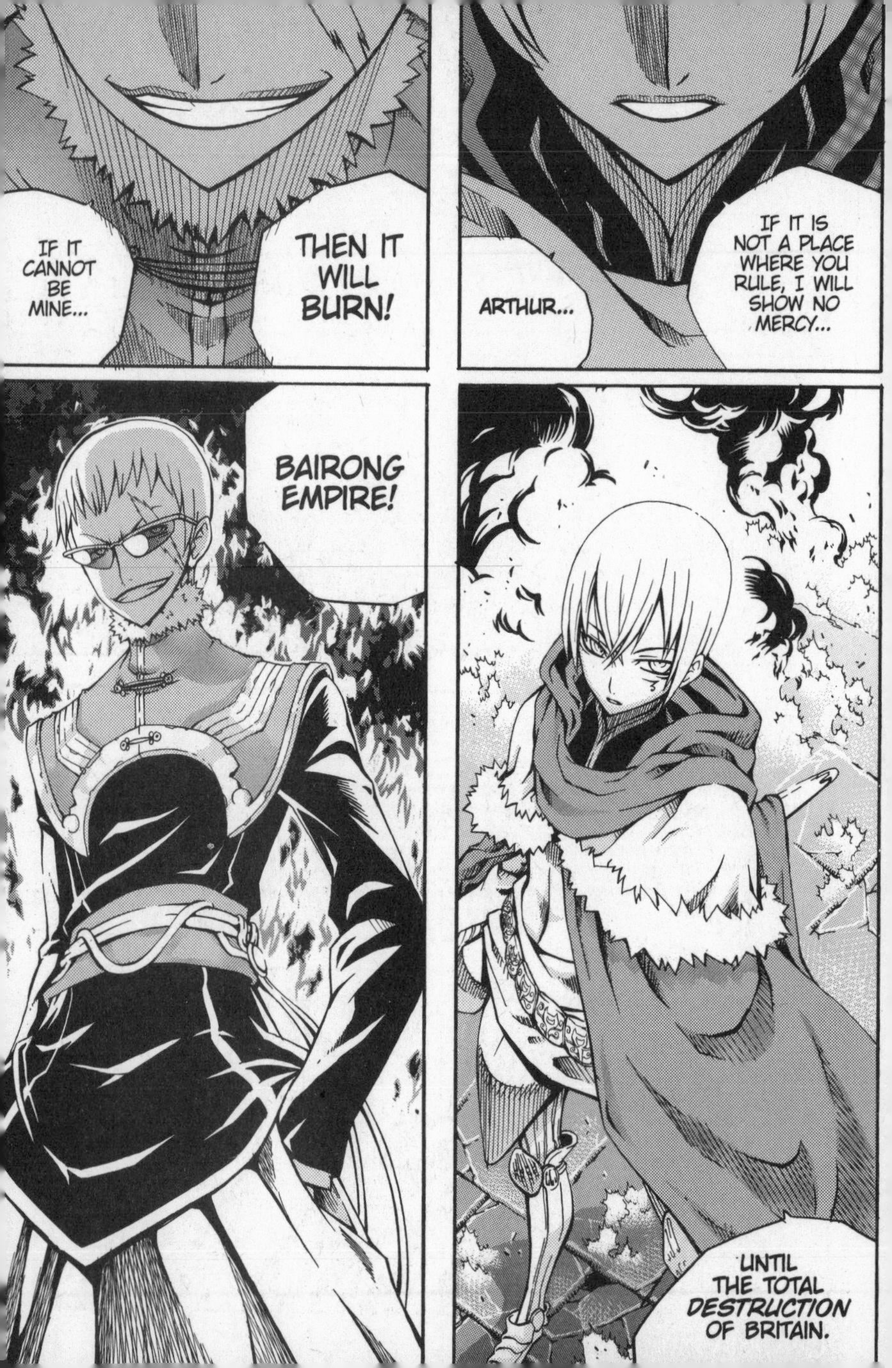
IF IT CANNOT BE MINE...
THEN IT WILL BURN!
ARTHUR...
IF IT IS NOT A PLACE WHERE YOU RULE, I WILL SHOW NO MERCY...
BAIRONG EMPIRE!
UNTIL THE TOTAL DESTRUCTION OF BRITAIN.

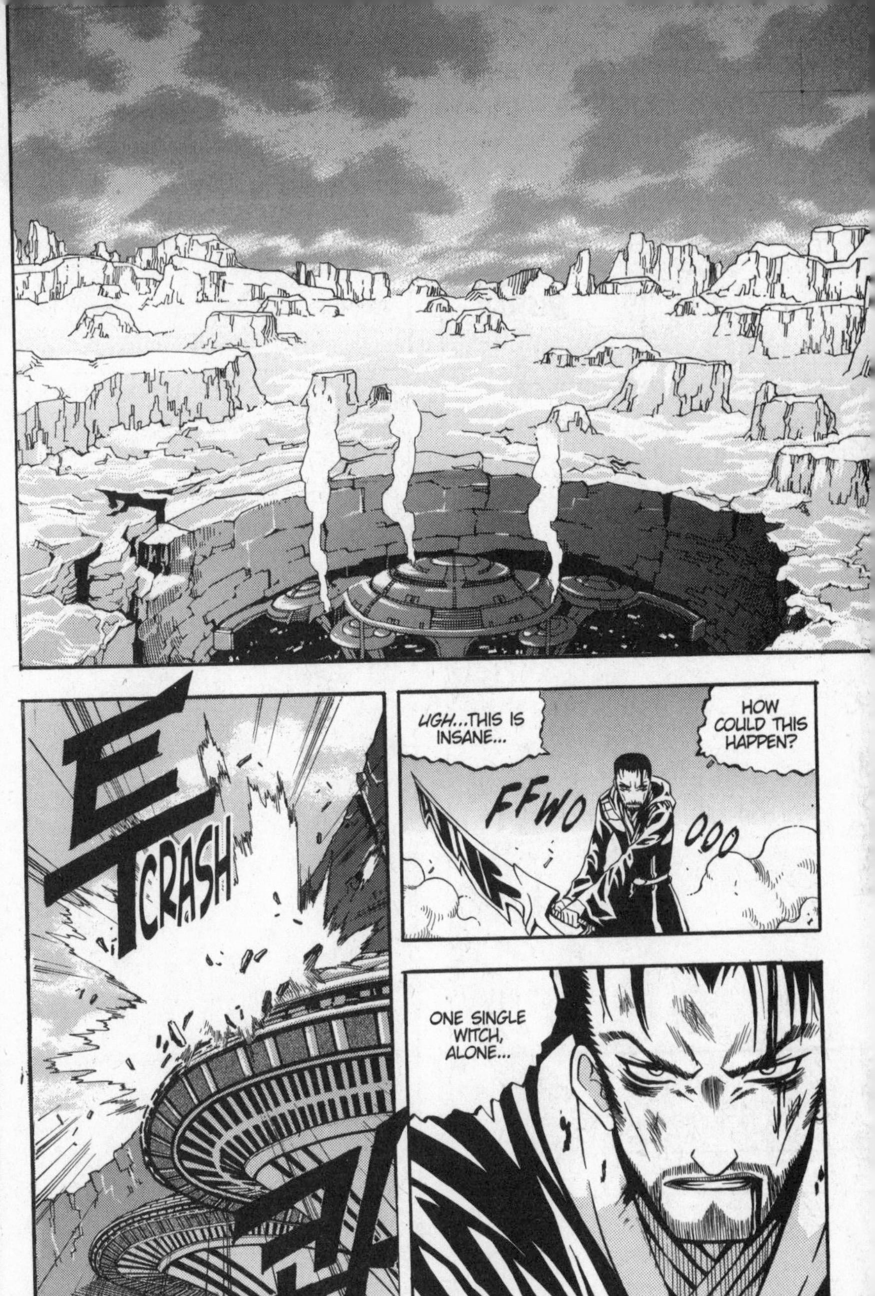
UGH...THIS IS INSANE...
HOW COULD THIS HAPPEN?
FFWOOOO
CRASH
ONE SINGLE WITCH, ALONE...

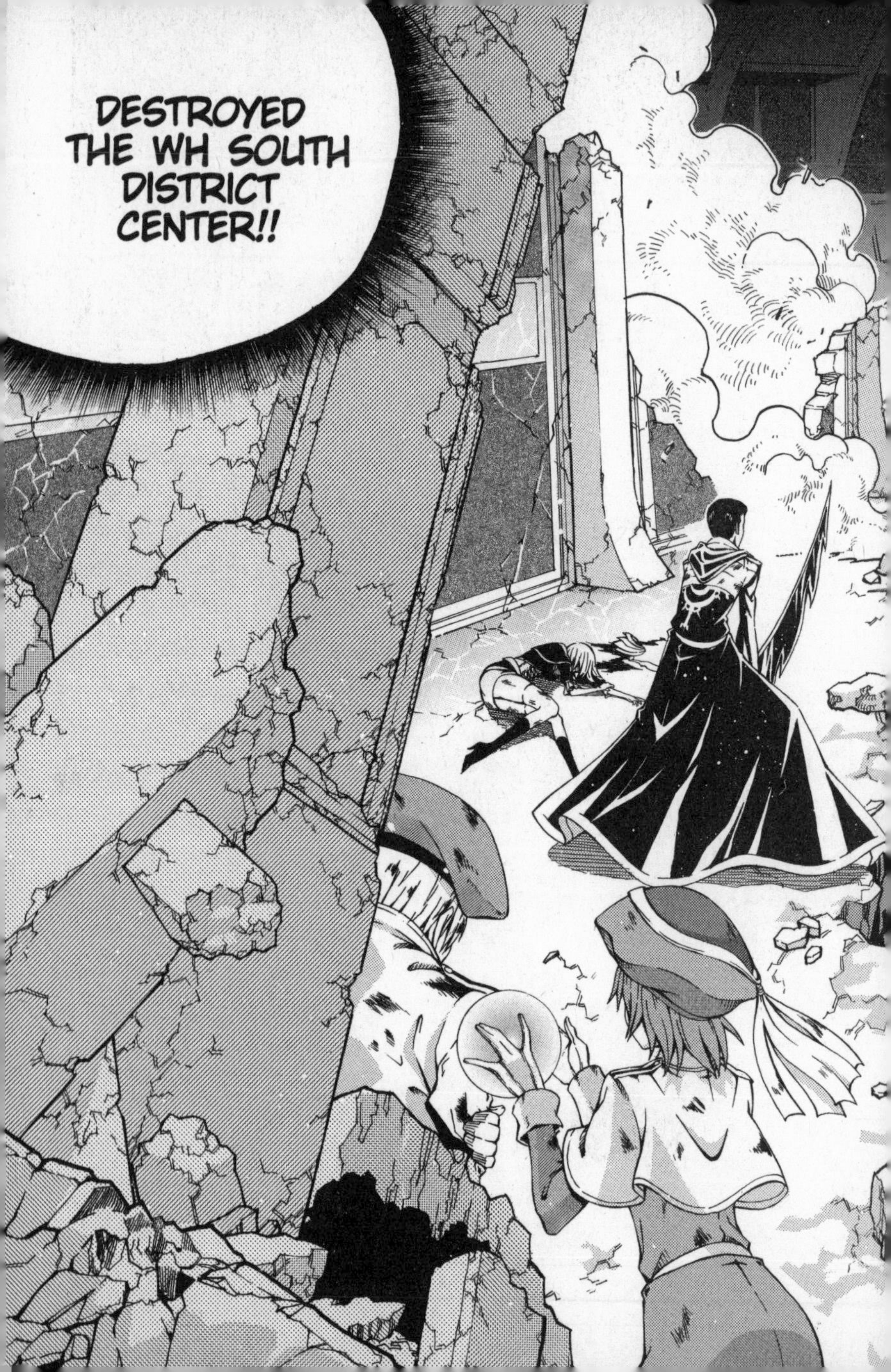
DESTROYED THE WH SOUTH DISTRICT CENTER!!

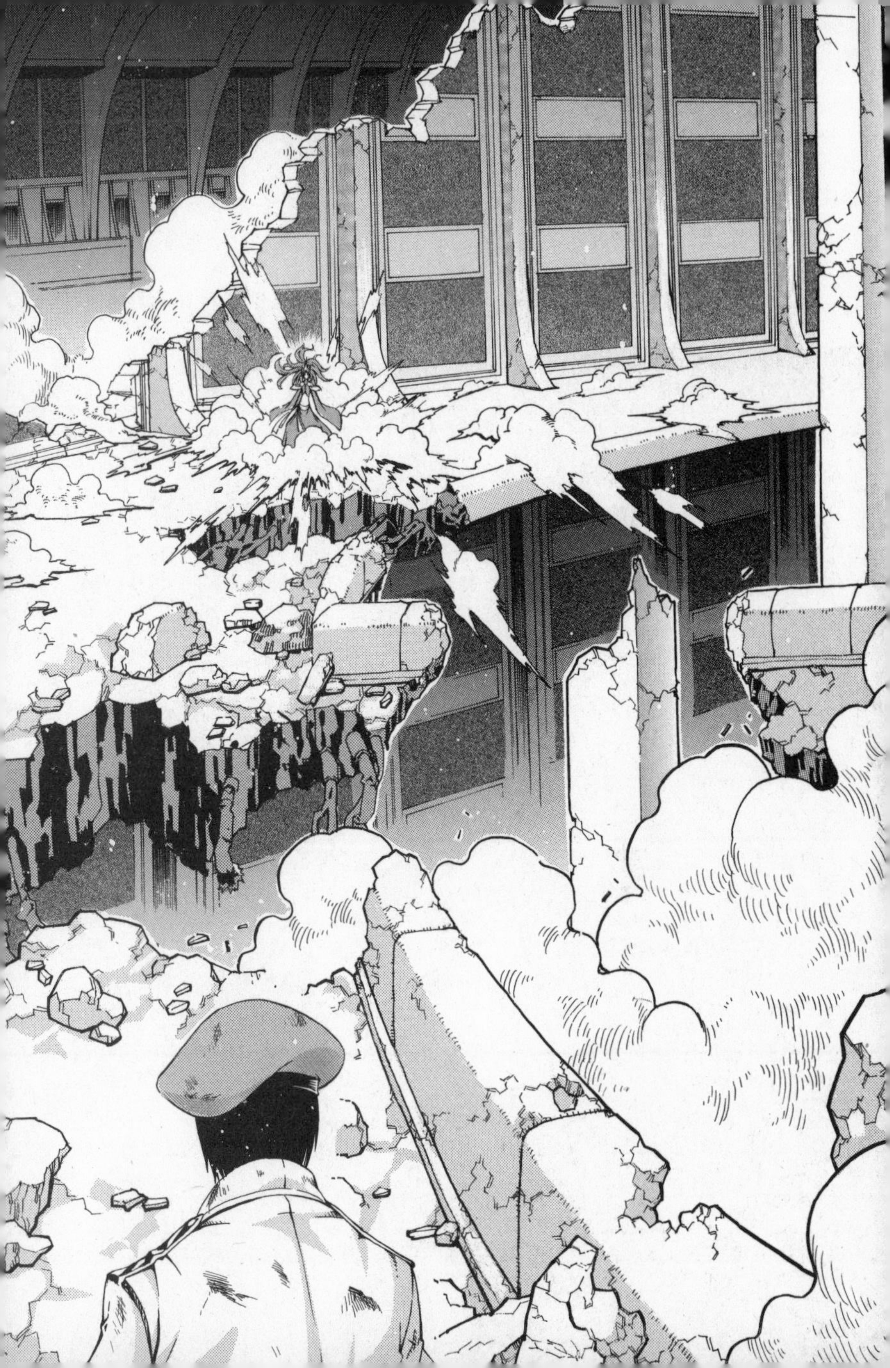

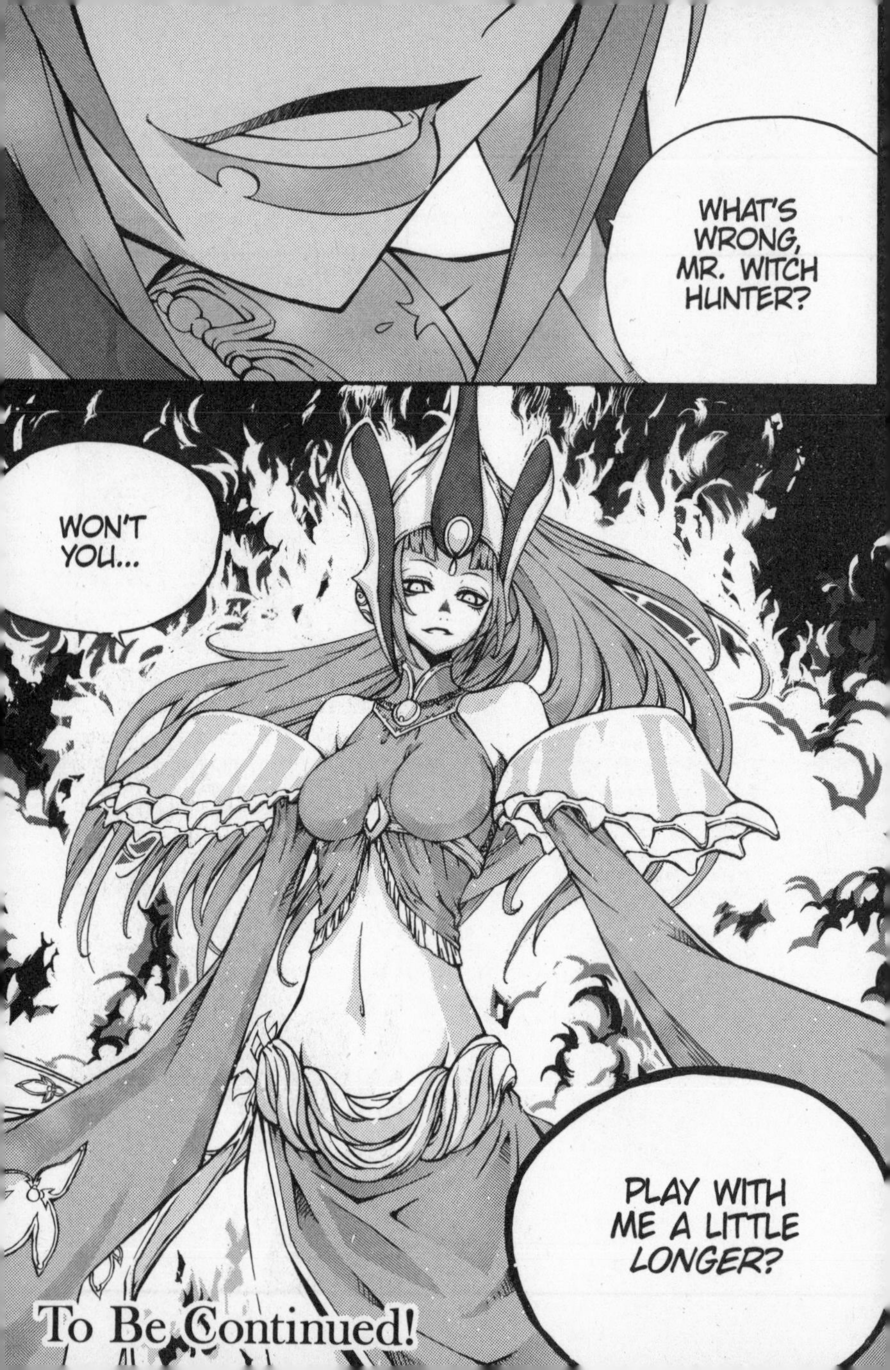
WHAT'S WRONG, MR. WITCH HUNTER?
WON'T YOU...
PLAY WITH ME A LITTLE LONGER?
To Be Continued!

RIVAL [2]

EVERYONE'S TALKING ABOUT HOW YOU AND MR. COOGA ARE RIVALS. WHAT DO YOU THINK?
What?!
I'M ABOVE ALL THAT! I WOULD NEVER BOTHER DECLARING A GUY LIKE THAT MY RIVAL!
HE'S THE ONE MAKING A BIG DEAL OUT OF IT!
IF YOU REALLY DON'T CARE... WHY DID YOU MEMORIZE HIS HEIGHT CHANGES FOR THE LAST TWO YEARS?

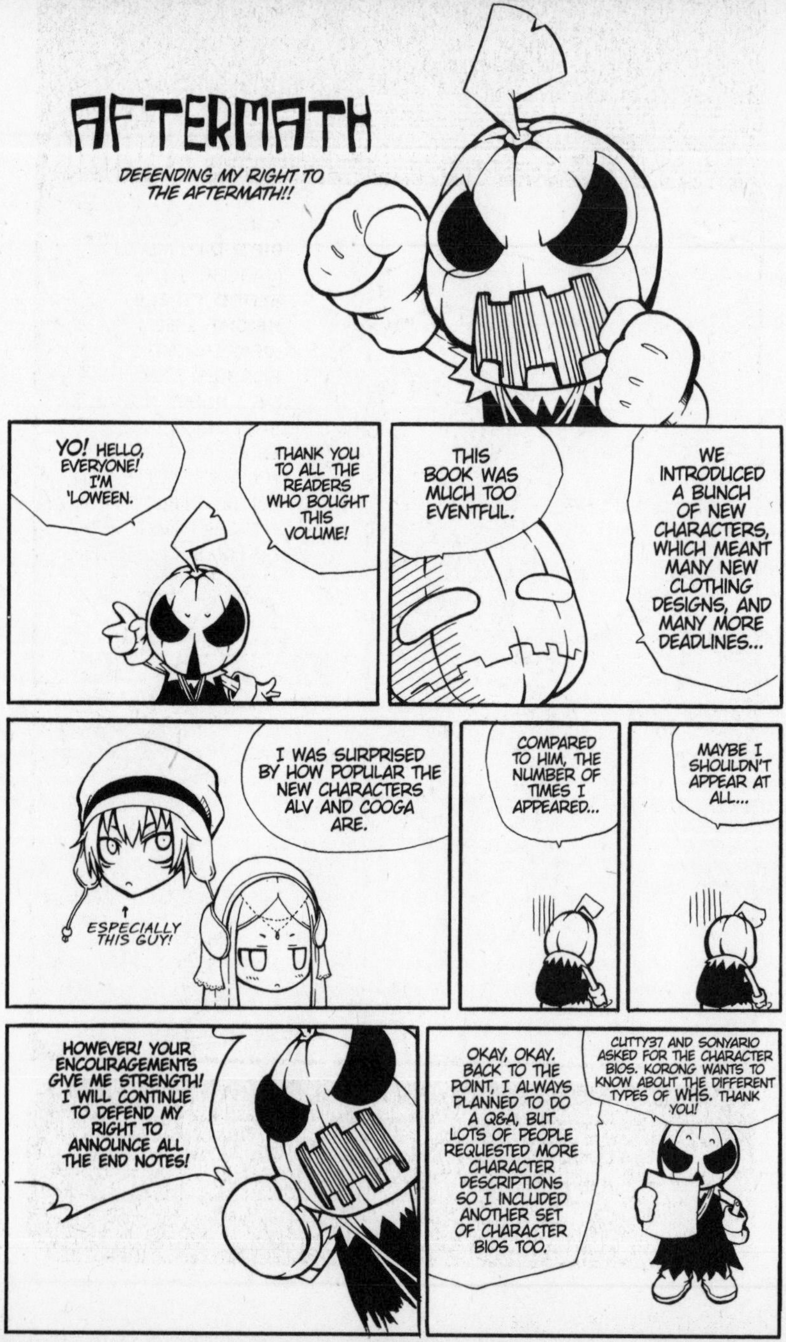
AFTERMATH
DEFENDING MY RIGHT TO THE AFTERMATH!!
YO! HELLO, EVERYONE! I'M 'LOWEEN.
THANK YOU TO ALL THE READERS WHO BOUGHT THIS VOLUME!
THIS BOOK WAS MUCH TOO EVENTFUL.
WE INTRODUCED A BUNCH OF NEW CHARACTERS, WHICH MEANT MANY NEW CLOTHING DESIGNS, AND MANY MORE DEADLINES...
I WAS SURPRISED BY HOW POPULAR THE NEW CHARACTERS ALV AND COOGA ARE.
ESPECIALLY THIS GUY!
COMPARED TO HIM, THE NUMBER OF TIMES I APPEARED...
MAYBE I SHOULDN'T APPEAR AT ALL...
HOWEVER! YOUR ENCOURAGEMENTS GIVE ME STRENGTH! I WILL CONTINUE TO DEFEND MY RIGHT TO ANNOUNCE ALL THE END NOTES!
OKAY, OKAY. BACK TO THE POINT, I ALWAYS PLANNED TO DO A Q&A, BUT LOTS OF PEOPLE REQUESTED MORE CHARACTER DESCRIPTIONS SO I INCLUDED ANOTHER SET OF CHARACTER BIOS TOO.
CUTTY37 AND SONYARIO ASKED FOR THE CHARACTER BIOS. KORONG WANTS TO KNOW ABOUT THE DIFFERENT TYPES OF WHS. THANK YOU!

MONICA

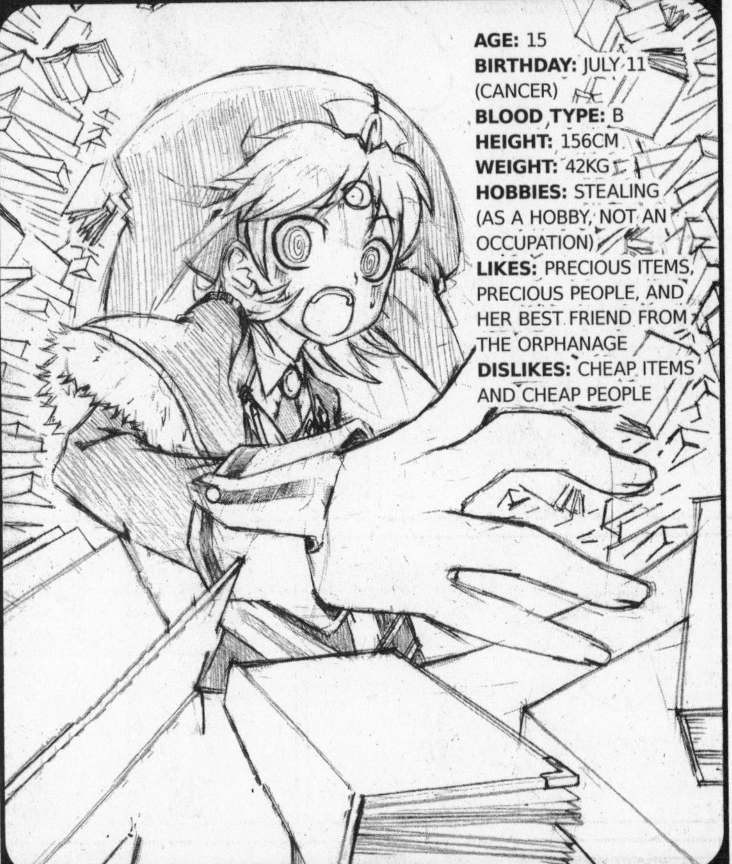

AGE: 15
BIRTHDAY: JULY 11 (CANCER)
BLOOD TYPE: B
HEIGHT: 156CM
WEIGHT: 42KG
HOBBIES: STEALING (AS A HOBBY, NOT AN OCCUPATION)
LIKES: PRECIOUS ITEMS, PRECIOUS PEOPLE, AND HER BEST FRIEND FROM THE ORPHANAGE
DISLIKES: CHEAP ITEMS AND CHEAP PEOPLE

THE MONICA PICTURED HERE IS IN CRISIS. POOR MONICA, WHO'S NEVER BEEN TO SCHOOL BEFORE... HAS TO LEARN 15 YEARS WORTH OF CLASSWORK ALL AT ONCE. ^^; SINCE MONICA'S AN ORPHAN, SHE DOESN'T HAVE A LAST NAME. HER BIRTHDAY IS ONE SHE MADE UP WITH HER BEST FRIEND. SHE WAS ONE OF THE MAIN CHARACTERS THROUGH VOLUMES TWO AND THREE, BUT SHE'LL HAVE A TOUGH TIME APPEARING FROM NOW ON (BECAUSE SHE HAS A LOT OF STUDYING TO DO). I MADE HER EXTREMELY COMPATIBLE WITH TASHA, BUT IT LOOKS LIKE SHE WON'T GET TO HANG OUT WITH HIM ANYTIME SOON. ^^; ANYWAY, YOU'LL SEE HER AGAIN AT SOME POINT, BUT UNTIL THEN, BYE BYE!

WORDS BLONDY VON WORTH

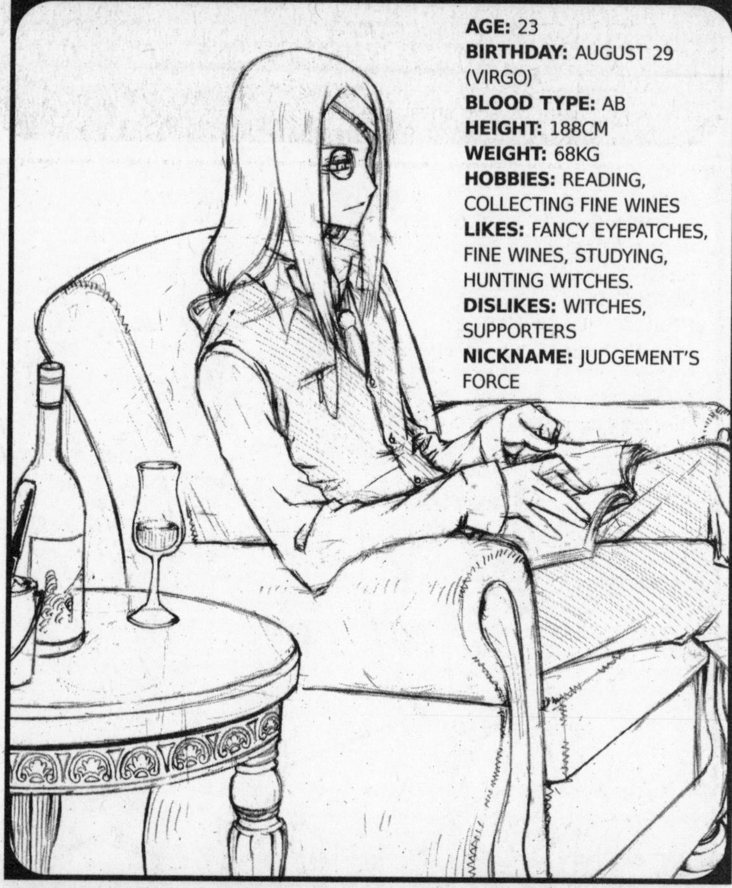

AGE: 23
BIRTHDAY: AUGUST 29 (VIRGO)
BLOOD TYPE: AB
HEIGHT: 188CM
WEIGHT: 68KG
HOBBIES: READING, COLLECTING FINE WINES
LIKES: FANCY EYEPATCHES, FINE WINES, STUDYING, HUNTING WITCHES.
DISLIKES: WITCHES, SUPPORTERS
NICKNAME: JUDGEMENT'S FORCE

NOBLE, FANCY, DIGNIFIED...HIS CHARACTER WAS CREATED WITH ALL THAT IN MIND. THIS IS HIS FIRST APPEARANCE (ORIGINALLY, TASHA WAS ALSO SUPPOSED TO BE OF NOBLE BLOOD, BUT HE WAS DEMOTED). STRANGELY, ALL THE WH MEMBERS SEEMED A BIT CHILDISH, SO I DECIDED I NEEDED SOMEONE MORE DIGNIFIED. THAT□S HOW I ENDED UP CREATING A MEMBER OF THE NOBILITY. PLUS, A CHARACTER WITH AN EYEPATCH IS AN ESSENTIAL PART OF EVERY COMIC (NOT TO MENTION SOMEBODY WITH GLASSES). ISN'T HE SEXY? ^^

THIS CHARACTER WAS MADE ALONGSIDE WORDS. HE'S THE COMPLETE OPPOSITE OF WORDS, BUT THEY GET ALONG VERY WELL (COOGA LOOKS UP TO HIM). HE STAYS WITH WORDS IN HIS LARGE, PRIVATE (EXPENSIVE) ROOM. ^^ THEY'RE ALSO TEAMMATES. TRUTH IS, COOGA AND WORDS WERE MADE TO DEMONSTRATE THAT THERE ARE WHs WHO HATE ALL WITCHES, EVEN THOSE WHO ARE SUPPOSED TO BE THEIR ALLIES.

AGE: 16
BIRTHDAY: AUGUST 2 (LEO)
BLOOD TYPE: B
HEIGHT: 164CM
WEIGHT: 55KG
HOBBIES: MAKING HATS (HE DESIGNS MOST OF HIS OWN HATS)
LIKES: STYLISH HATS, WORDS (RESPECTS HIM)
DISLIKES: WITCHES, TASHA
NICKNAME: SPEAR OF ODIN

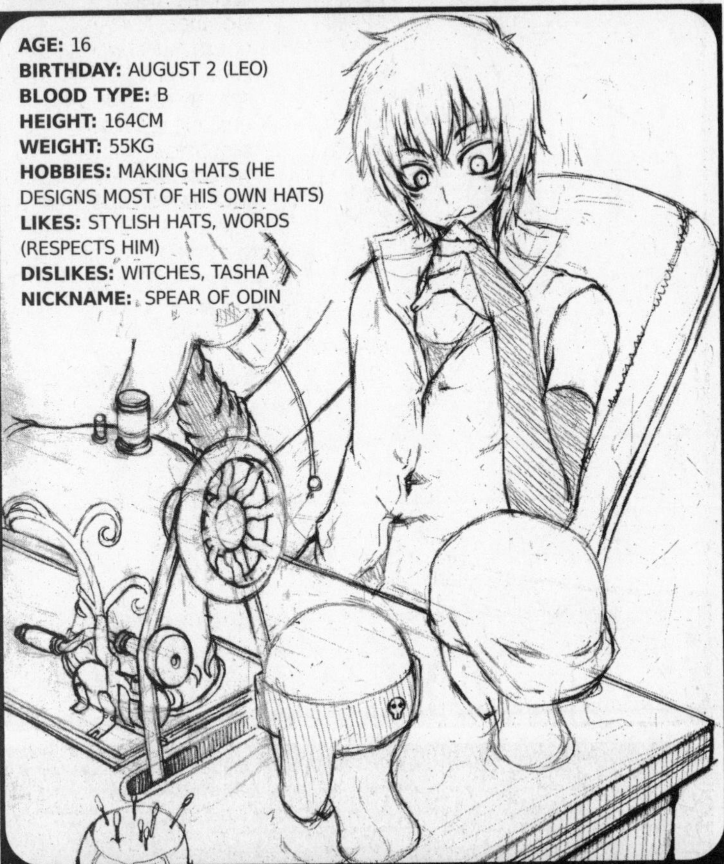

COOGA KUNEIN

ECLIPSE SHADENON

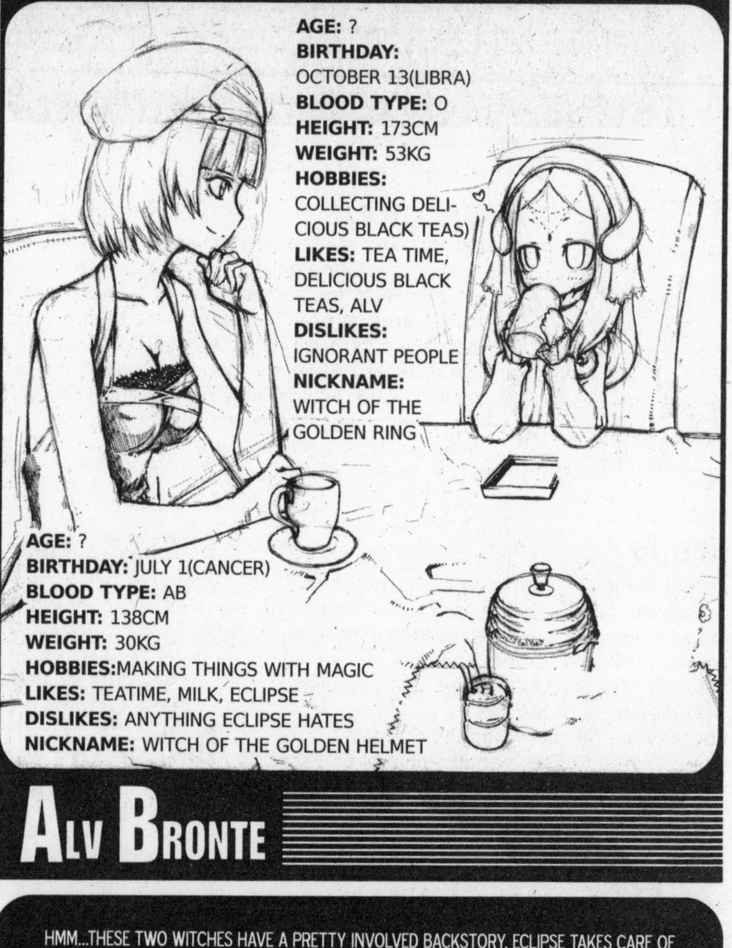

AGE: ?
BIRTHDAY:
OCTOBER 13(LIBRA)
BLOOD TYPE: O
HEIGHT: 173CM
WEIGHT: 53KG
HOBBIES:
COLLECTING DELI-
CIOUS BLACK TEAS)
LIKES: TEA TIME,
DELICIOUS BLACK
TEAS, ALV
DISLIKES:
IGNORANT PEOPLE
NICKNAME:
WITCH OF THE
GOLDEN RING

AGE: ?
BIRTHDAY: JULY 1(CANCER)
BLOOD TYPE: AB
HEIGHT: 138CM
WEIGHT: 30KG
HOBBIES:MAKING THINGS WITH MAGIC
LIKES: TEATIME, MILK, ECLIPSE
DISLIKES: ANYTHING ECLIPSE HATES
NICKNAME: WITCH OF THE GOLDEN HELMET

ALV BRONTE

HMM...THESE TWO WITCHES HAVE A PRETTY INVOLVED BACKSTORY. ECLIPSE TAKES CARE OF THE EMOTIONALLY UNSTABLE ALV (THERE'S A REASON FOR ALV'S INSTABILITY THAT I WON'T GO INTO HERE). I HOPE TO ONE DAY SHARE THE STORY OF HOW THEY MET. ^^ MANY TEAMS ARE SO CLOSE THAT THEY SHARE ROOMS; THESE TWO ARE ONE EXAMPLE. MORE OF THEIR STORY WILL BE REVEALED IN THE FUTURE, SO KEEP YOUR EYES PEELED!

THE DIFFERENT TYPES OF WITCH HUNTERS

KORONG ASKED IF DIFFERENT WITCH HUNTERS USE DIFFERENT TYPES OF MAGIC. I'LL USE THIS SPACE TO DESCRIBE ANOTHER SUBDIVISION OF WITCH HUNTERS. THEY CAN BE DIVIDED BOTH BY CLASS (OR LEVEL), AND ALSO BY THEIR TYPE OF MAGIC. THERE ARE FIVE DIFFERENT TYPES: NATURAL, ESPER, SHAMAN, WITCH, AND MUTANT.

Witch Hunter

NATURAL

Natural WHs are normal human beings, however, through rigorous training, they are able to perform feats far beyond those of mortal men. Xing is an example. There are more Natural WHs than any other type, but the majority of them are in B-class. They make up the smallest portion of the A-class, and in the highest White class, which only has eight members in the entire world, there is only one.

ESPER

Espers are male supernaturals. In the Witch Hunter world, all girls are born with innate magic power, but only a few develop into witches. Similarly, Espers are boys who develop powerful supernatural abilities that may even rival the power of witches--
but they are far rarer than their female counterparts. Cooga is an example of an Esper.

ARE YOU SURE YOUR FAILURE TO REPLICATE THE MANA GUN WASN'T JUST YOUR INCOMPETENCE?

SHAMAN

Shamans are people who don't have their own magic power, but instead borrow power from the world around them. Tarras is an example of a Shaman--he uses the element Earth. He is part of a family that passes this earth knowledge down from generation to generation. Tarras was recently appointed to learn the secrets of his family.

WITCH

These are witches who decided to side with humans. The WH witches gathered all the magic and information that the WHs use to fight, and the WH would never be able to defeat enemy witches without their help.

IT'S THE MANA GUN!

MUTANT

Within the WH, mutants hold the strongest grudge against witches. They are people whose bodies have been modified by witches—mostly as the forced test subjects of witches who tried to turn them into supporters.

Many mutants who manage to escape from their witch captors join the ranks of the WHs. Words is a mutant who killed the witch who modified his body (you can probably tell which of his body parts has been changed...) Strangely enough, Tasha is also technically a mutant because he received a modified weapon from a witch.

WITCH BUSTER

Q&A

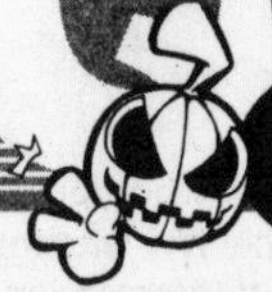

Q1: How did you come up with the clothing designs? (from mirinae)

A1: Many of my design ideas come from a Japanese manga I enjoy. I get some ideas from magazines that feature black and white fashion. I also keep up-to-date with the different styles of military uniforms around the world. A surprising number of my ideas come from military uniforms. ^^

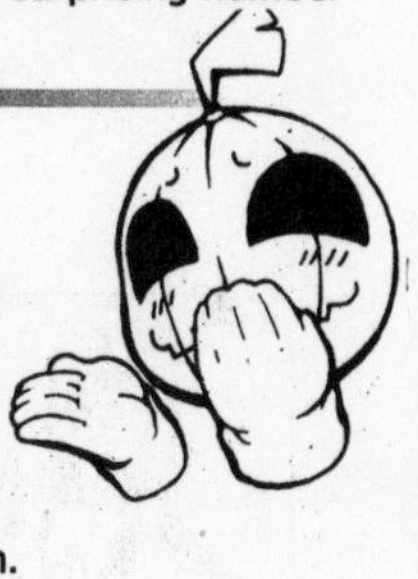

Q2: Are there any girl human WHs? (from ChungPoomMyungWhul)

A2: There are some, but only in Division 2's C-class and D-class, none in the Battle classes S, A, and B. All girls possess some innate magic, but normal human girls can't gather enough to become witches. They can train themselves to increase their mana, but any natural type female WH who is skilled enough to join the B-class has gathered enough mana to awaken as a witch. The same applies to female shamans and mutants.

Q3: In the first volume, Tasha contacts the Center to initiate HELP. How does one normally contact the Center? By cell phone? This world doesn't seem like it would have cell phones, though... (from Lucky)

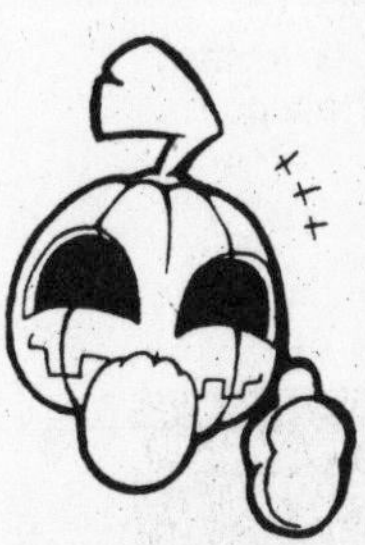

A3: Yes, he has a cell phone. Diana has created a network of cell phones that are connected through magic. In my manhwa, technology doesn't match up with the real world. That's because the people use witches' magic in place of science. ^^; The cell phones in this world don't have buttons; since they're magic, they respond to voices, or even will. They are made specifically for a single user and no one else can use them. If a non-WH finds a WH's cell phone, they won't even know what it is.

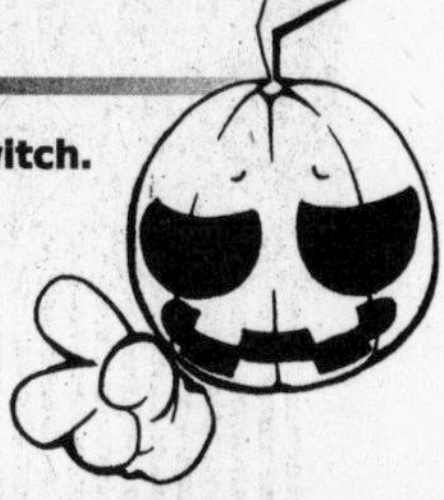

Q4: Please tell us the name of the mind-controlling witch. (from Lucky-D.S)

A4: That poor witch, there was never a chance to include her name. It was..."Vanice Grebake"!
It's Northern European... I chose such an extravagant name, and it never even saw the light of day...

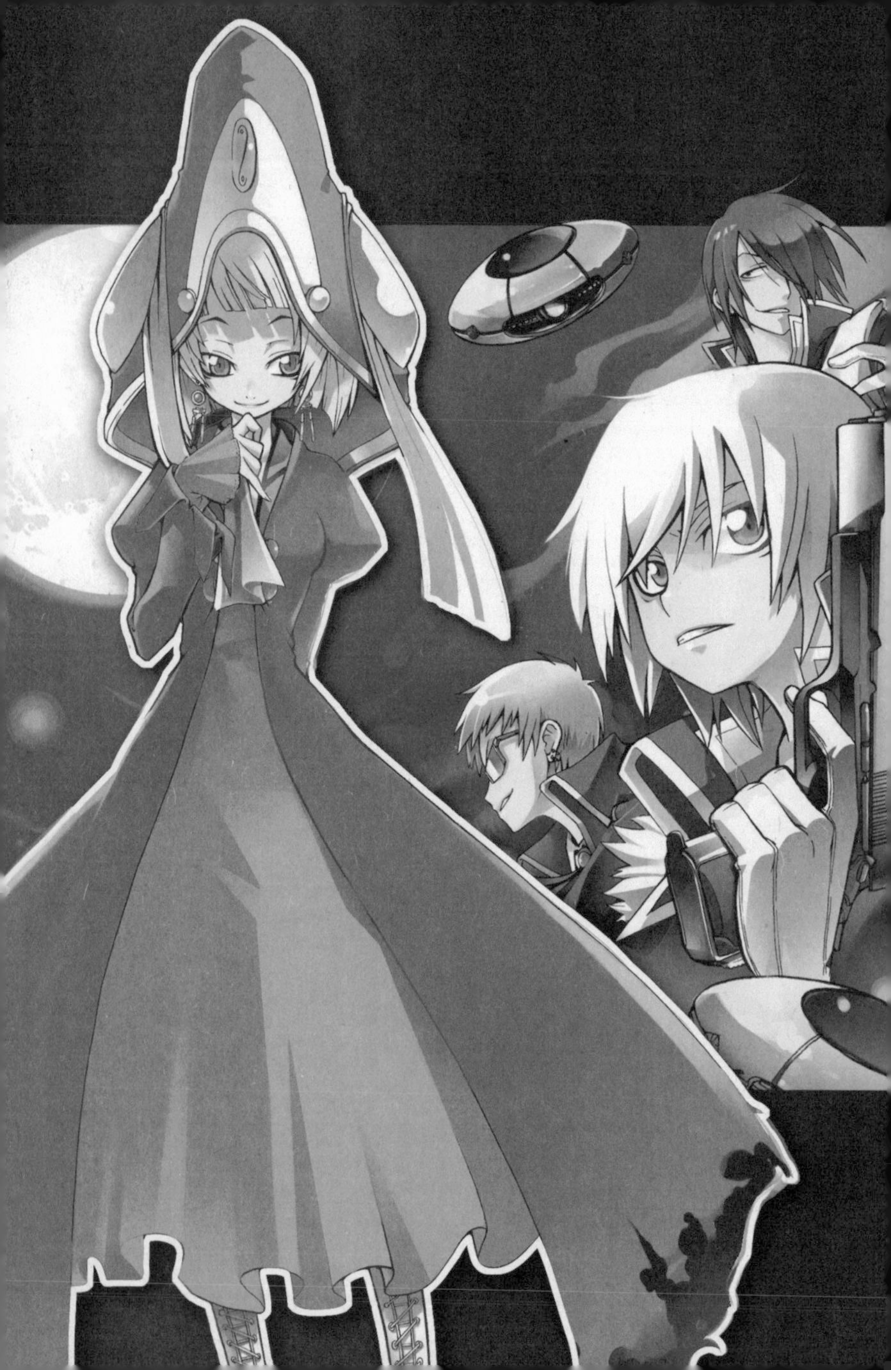

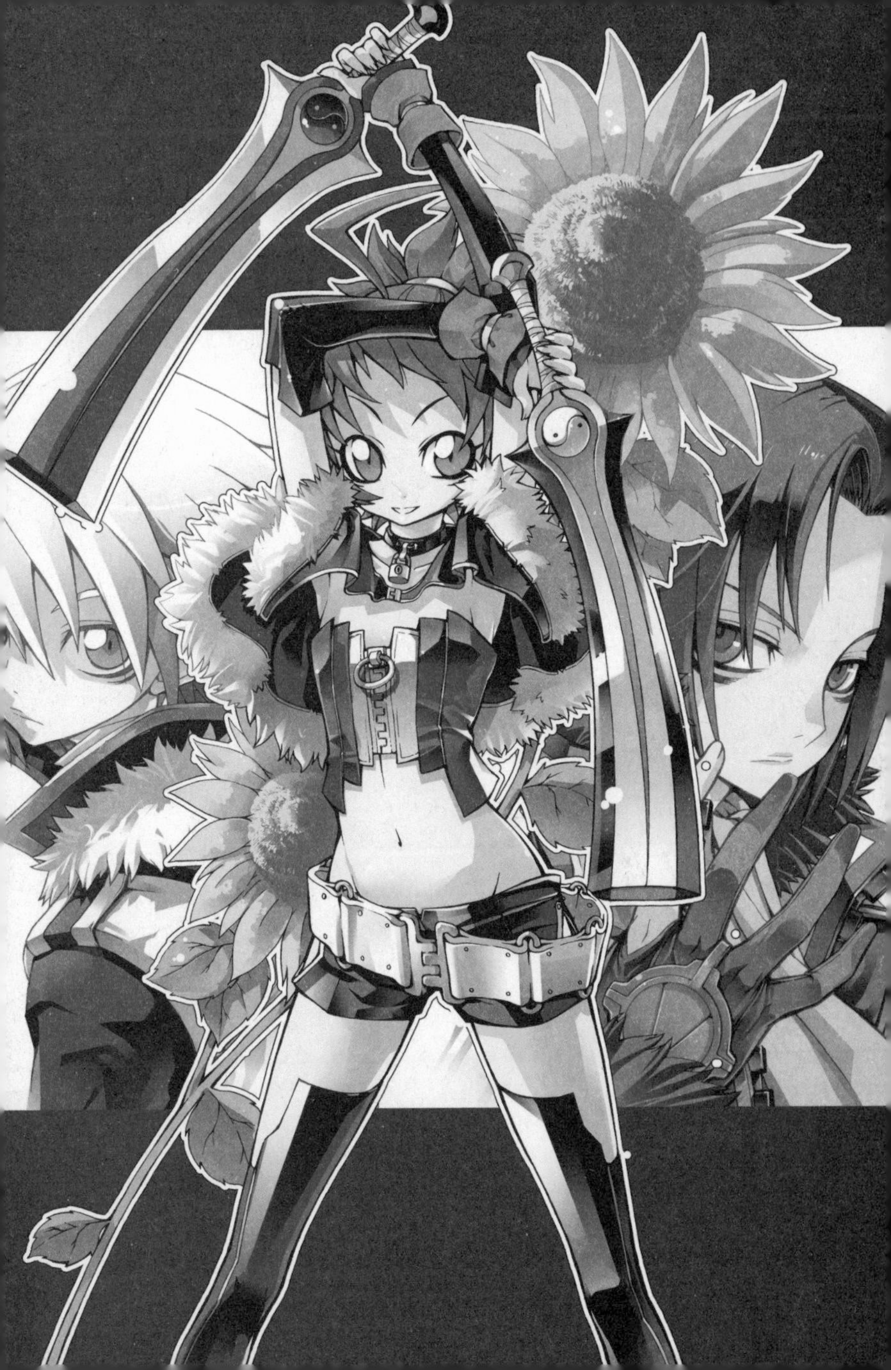

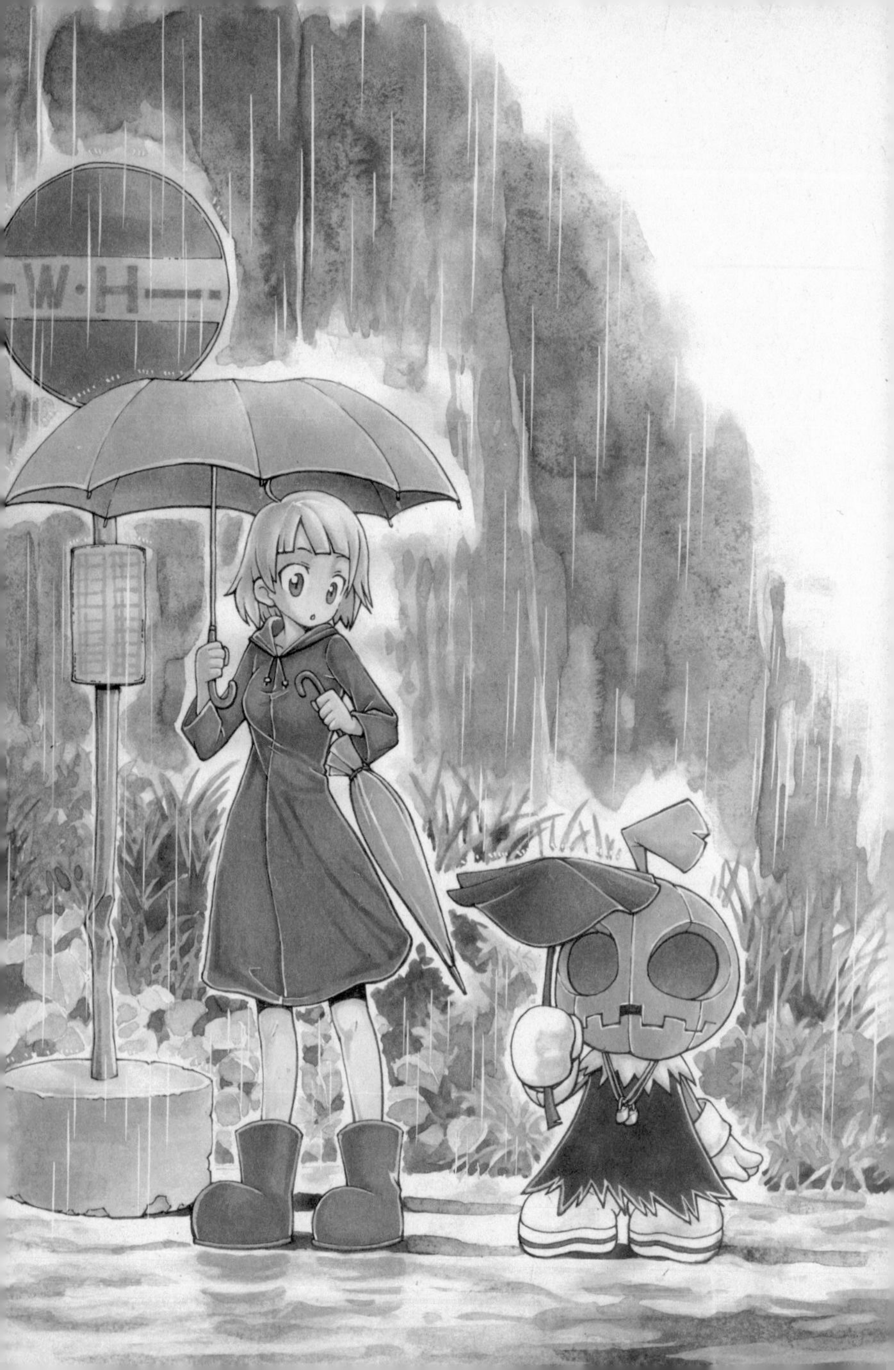
W·H

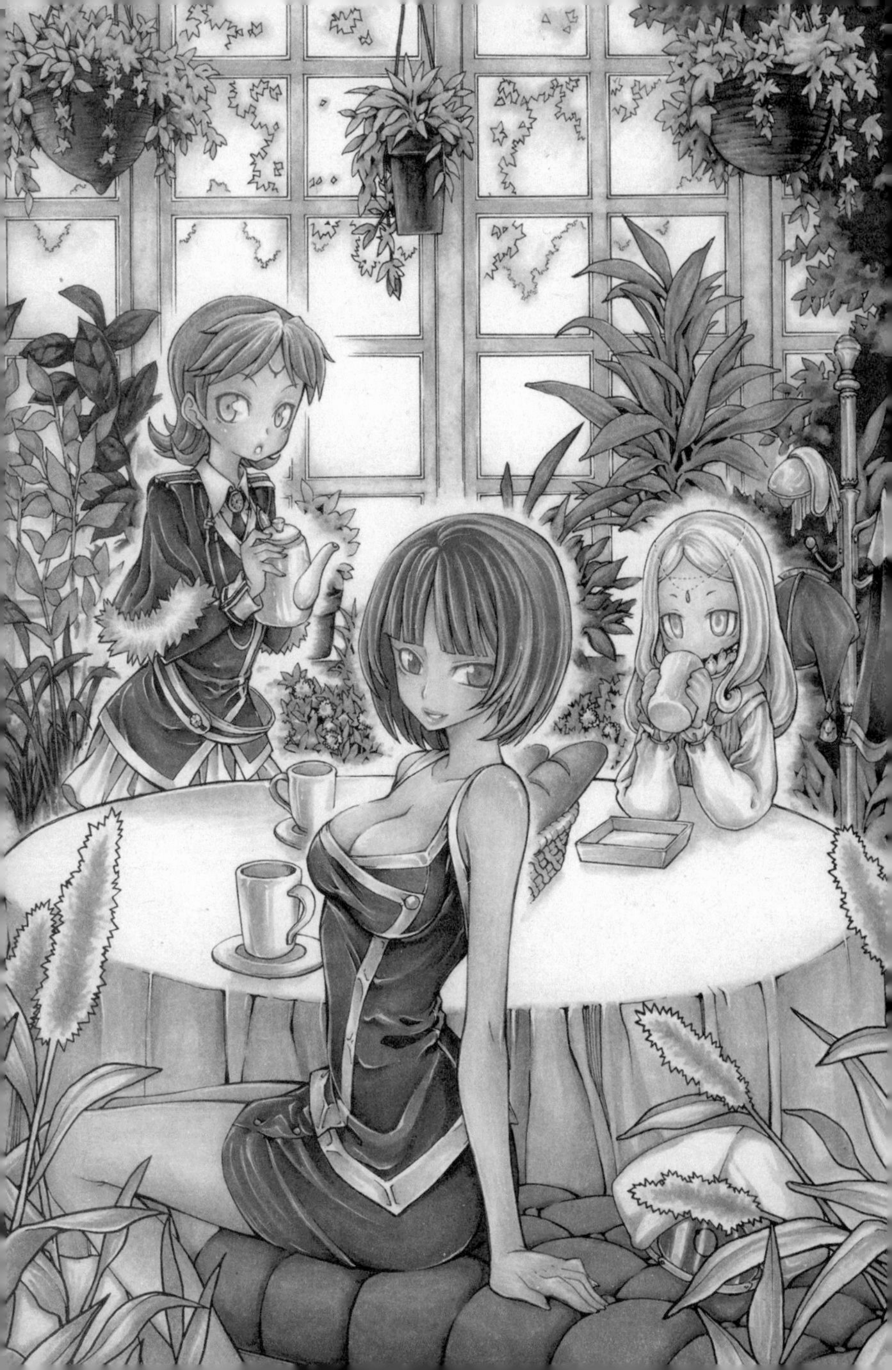

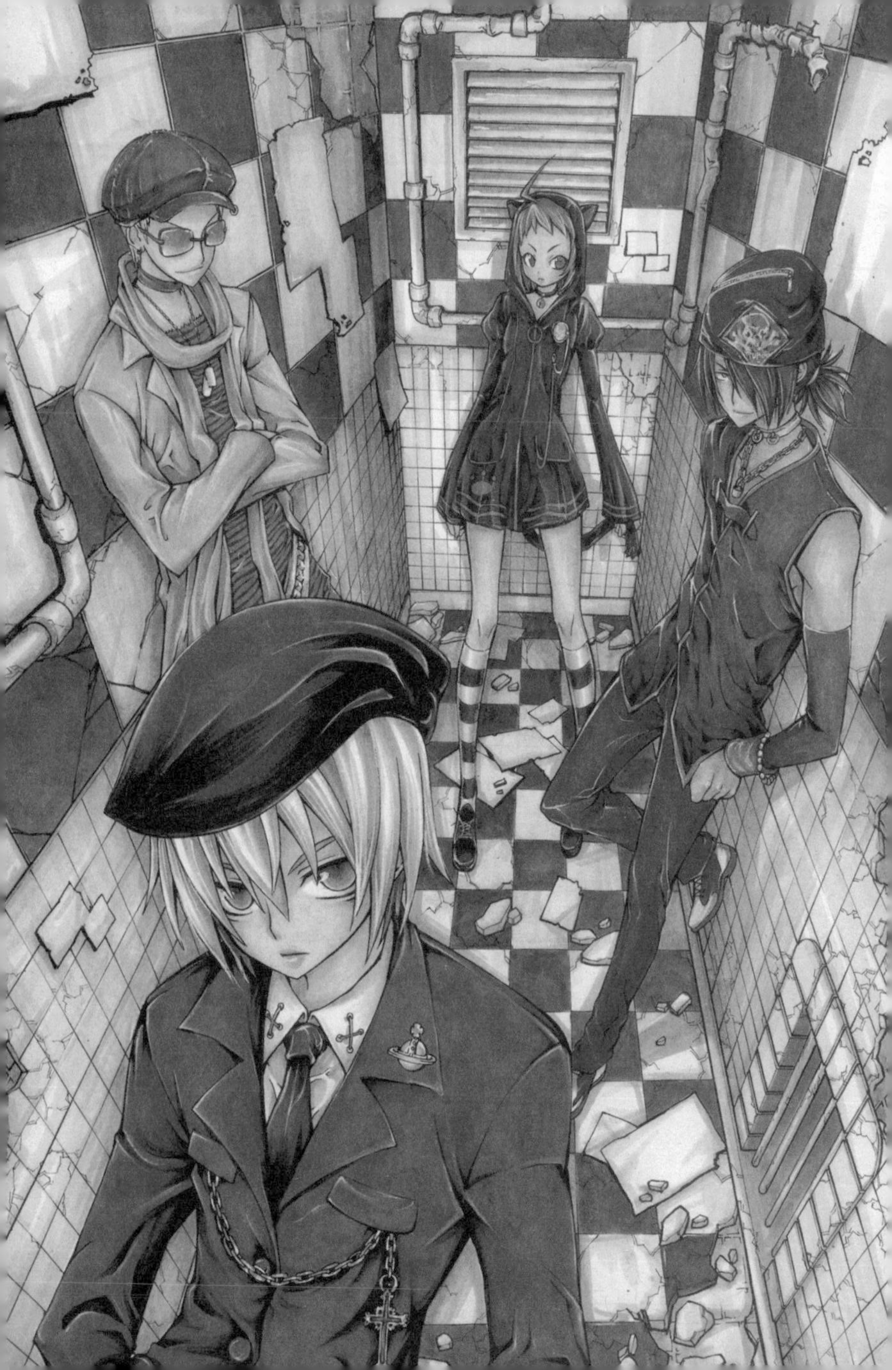

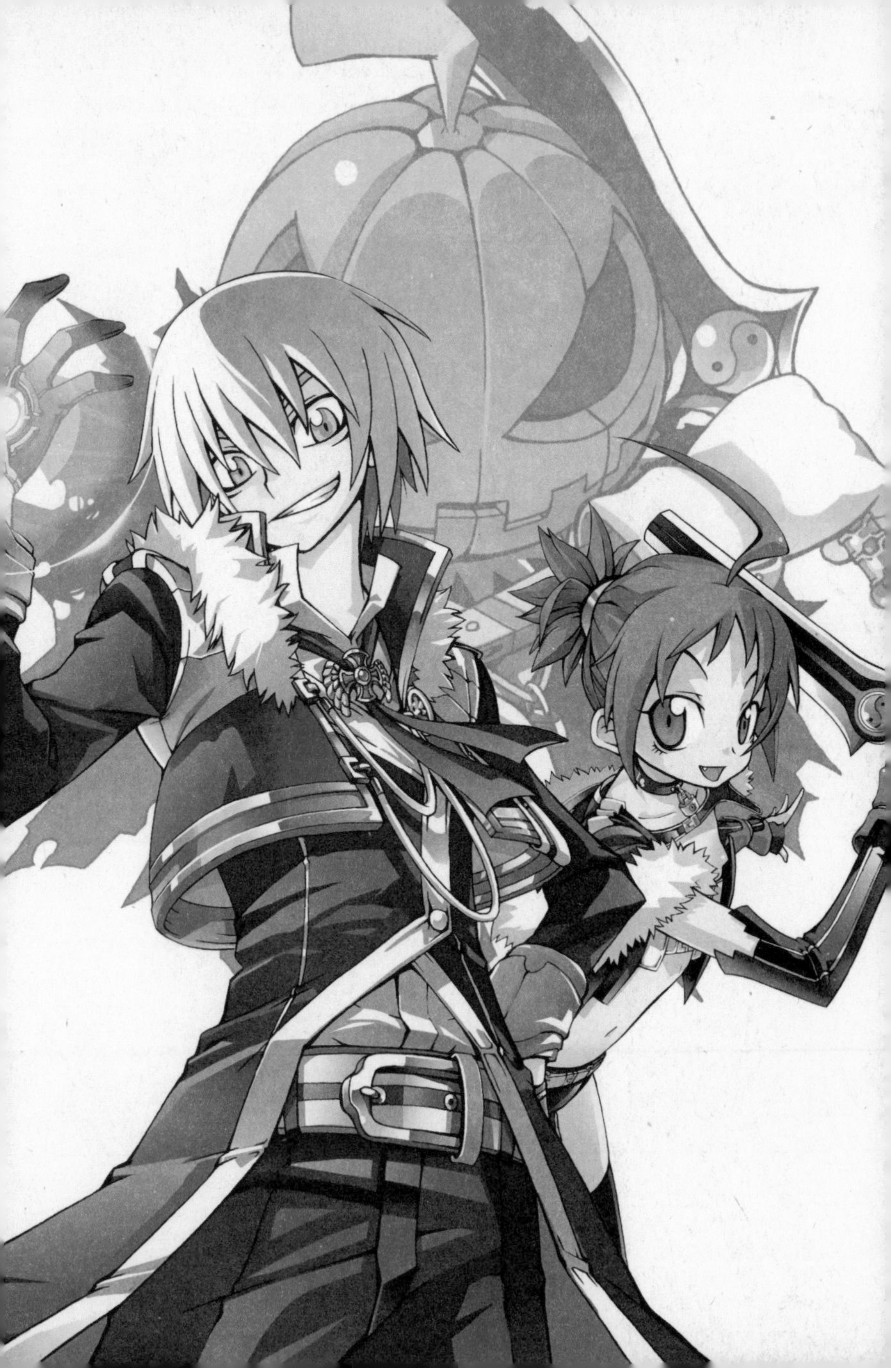

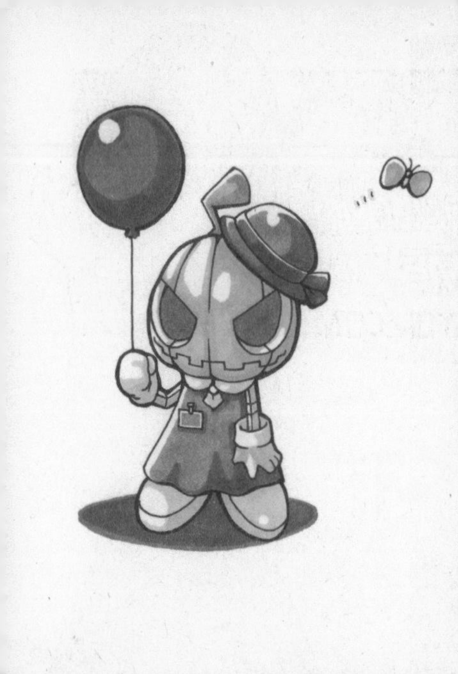

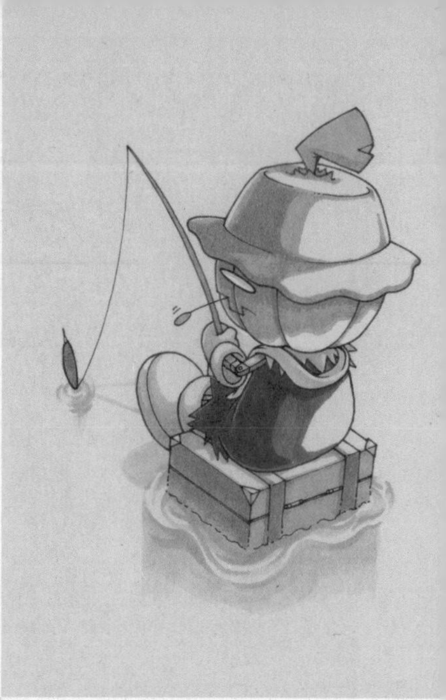

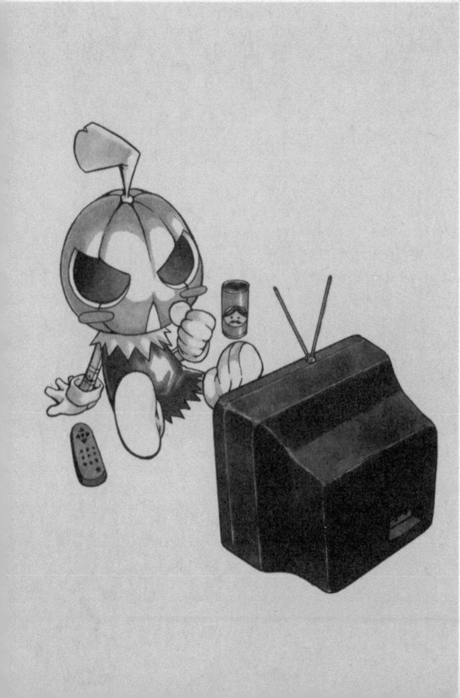

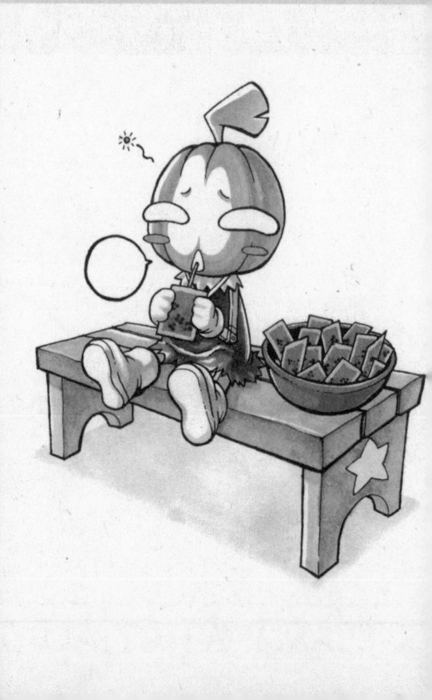

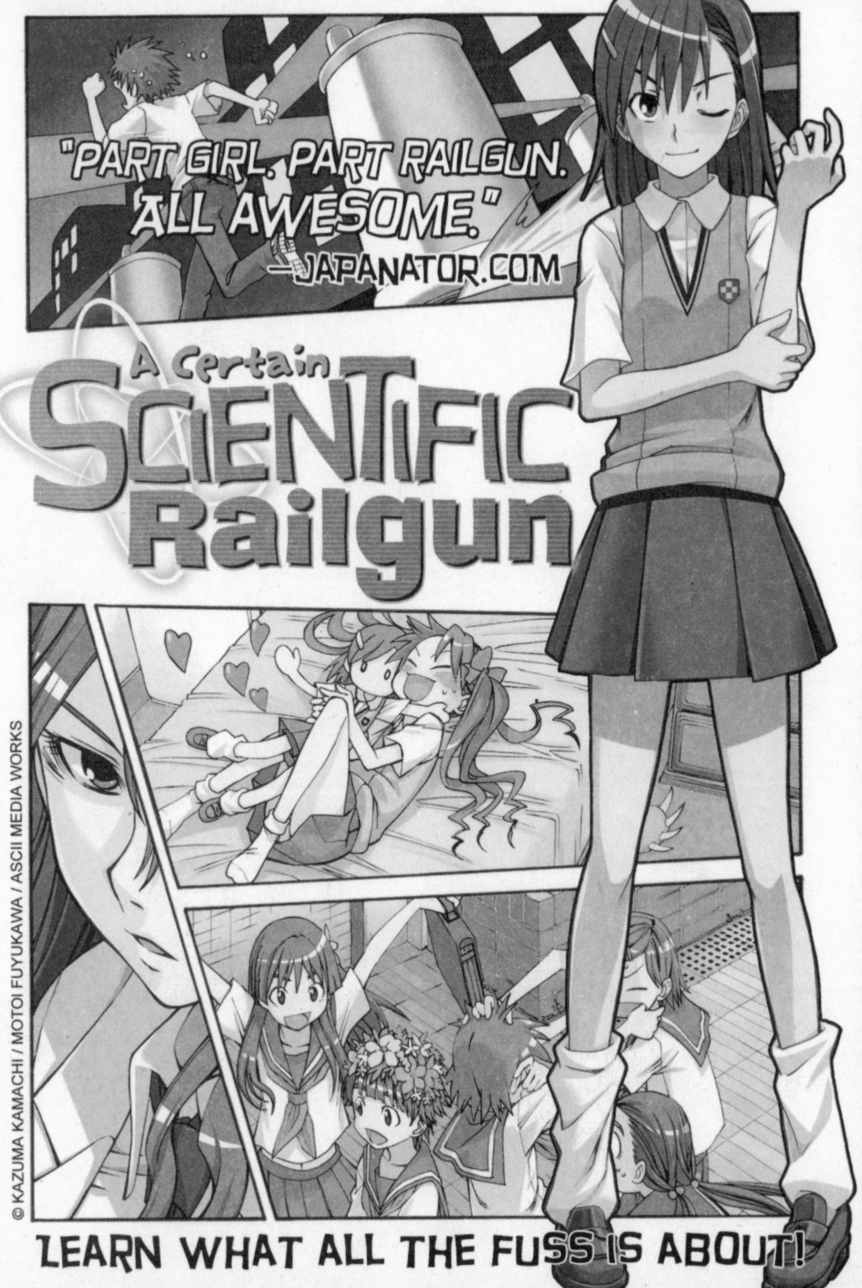

"PART GIRL. PART RAILGUN. ALL AWESOME."
—JAPANATOR.COM
A Certain SCIENTIFIC Railgun
© KAZUMA KAMACHI / MOTOI FUYUKAWA / ASCII MEDIA WORKS
LEARN WHAT ALL THE FUSS IS ABOUT!

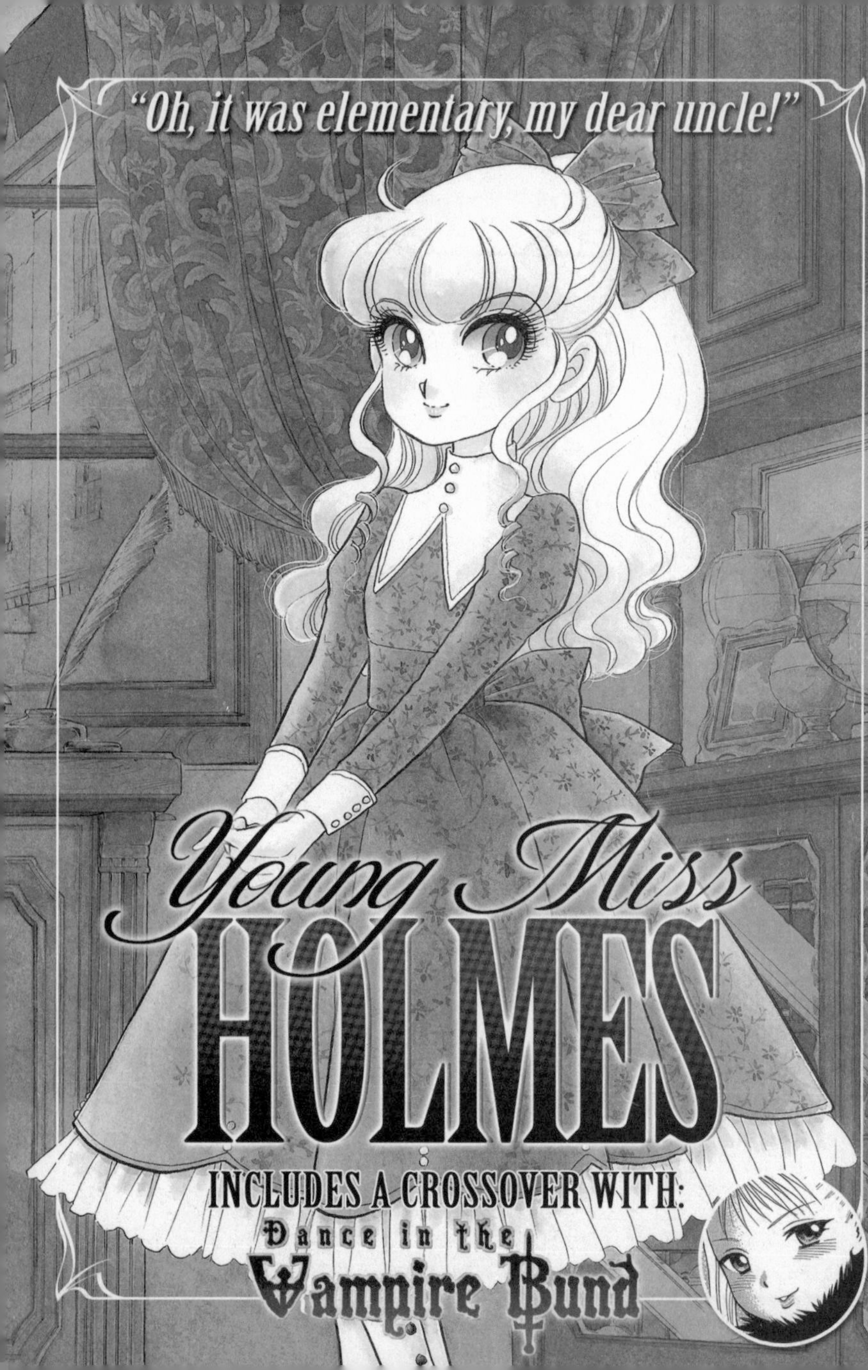
"Oh, it was elementary, my dear uncle!"
Young Miss
HOLMES
INCLUDES A CROSSOVER WITH:
Dance in the
Vampire Bund